BEGINNING SOLIDITY

BEGINNING

Solidity

BEGINNING

Solidity

LEARN TO PROGRAM SMART CONTRACTS WITH SOLIDITY

Alexandros Dolgov

Copyright © 2025 by John Wiley & Sons, Inc. All rights, including for text and data mining, AI training, and similar technologies, are reserved.

Published by John Wiley & Sons, Inc., Hoboken, New Jersey.
Published simultaneously in Canada and the United Kingdom.

ISBNs: 9781394290611 (Paperback), 9781394290635 (ePDF), 9781394290628 (ePub)

No part of this publication may be reproduced, stored in a retrieval system, or transmitted in any form or by any means, electronic, mechanical, photocopying, recording, scanning, or otherwise, except as permitted under Section 107 or 108 of the 1976 United States Copyright Act, without either the prior written permission of the Publisher, or authorization through payment of the appropriate per-copy fee to the Copyright Clearance Center, Inc., 222 Rosewood Drive, Danvers, MA 01923, (978) 750-8400, fax (978) 750-4470, or on the web at www.copyright.com. Requests to the Publisher for permission should be addressed to the Permissions Department, John Wiley & Sons, Inc., 111 River Street, Hoboken, NJ 07030, (201) 748-6011, fax (201) 748-6008, or online at www.wiley.com/go/permission.

The manufacturer's authorized representative according to the EU General Product Safety Regulation is Wiley-VCH GmbH, Boschstr. 12, 69469 Weinheim, Germany, e-mail: Product_Safety@wiley.com.

Trademarks: WILEY and the Wiley logo are trademarks or registered trademarks of John Wiley & Sons, Inc. and/or its affiliates, in the United States and other countries, and may not be used without written permission. Solidity is a trademark or registered trademark of Stiftung Ethereum (Foundation Ethereum). All other trademarks are the property of their respective owners. John Wiley & Sons, Inc. is not associated with any product or vendor mentioned in this book.

Limit of Liability/Disclaimer of Warranty: While the publisher and author have used their best efforts in preparing this book, they make no representations or warranties with respect to the accuracy or completeness of the contents of this book and specifically disclaim any implied warranties of merchantability or fitness for a particular purpose. No warranty may be created or extended by sales representatives or written sales materials. The advice and strategies contained herein may not be suitable for your situation. You should consult with a professional where appropriate. Further, readers should be aware that websites listed in this work may have changed or disappeared between when this work was written and when it is read. Neither the publisher nor author shall be liable for any loss of profit or any other commercial damages, including but not limited to special, incidental, consequential, or other damages.

For general information on our other products and services or for technical support, please contact our Customer Care Department within the United States at (800) 762-2974, outside the United States at (317) 572-3993 or fax (317) 572-4002. For product technical support, you can find answers to frequently asked questions or reach us via live chat at https://support.wiley.com.

If you believe you've found a mistake in this book, please bring it to our attention by emailing our reader support team at wileysupport@wiley.com with the subject line "Possible Book Errata Submission."

Wiley also publishes its books in a variety of electronic formats. Some content that appears in print may not be available in electronic formats. For more information about Wiley products, visit our web site at www.wiley.com.

Library of Congress Control Number: 2025930523

Cover image: © CSA-Printstock/Getty Images

Cover design: Wiley

SKY10100174_031525

To my parents for sacrificing a lot for me.

To Satoshi, whoever and wherever you are, for the most potent idea I have ever encountered.

To Hamid Rahimifar for lending me an ear when I most needed it.

To Gary Weimberg for the wonderful conversations and board game rounds.

To George Giaglis and the professors at the University of Nicosia for being the first university in the world to create an academic MSc in Blockchain and Digital Currency in 2014 and for teaching me.

To Vitalik, thank you for giving me something to write about.

Weirdly enough, to my life: to the Soviet Union, whose stories from my father about corruption and the economy made me realize the value of Bitcoin.

Finally, to Professor Philipp Sandner. Gone, but not forgotten.

ABOUT THE AUTHOR

Alexandros Dolgov from a young age, questioned why citizens were confined to using national currencies, wondering why they couldn't choose alternatives, whether foreign or self-created. Growing up amid Greece's financial turmoil and influenced by his father's stories of economic collapse in post-Soviet countries, Alexandros developed a deep skepticism of centralized systems and their susceptibility to corruption. His discovery of Bitcoin, DeFi, and DAOs solidified his vision of a fairer, decentralized world, and he saw Solidity as a key tool for building this future.

To deepen his expertise, Alexandros earned an MSc in Blockchain and Digital Currency from the University of Nicosia—the first university in the world to offer this degree—specializing in token economics, decentralized governance, and blockchain technology. He also holds the Chartered Blockchain Analyst Certification. Professionally, Alexandros has contributed to key areas of the blockchain ecosystem, including DeFi, decentralized identity, and token economics. As a guest lecturer at Karel de Grote, he shares his knowledge with future leaders, while his newsletter explores cryptocurrencies, Web3, and the fight against censorship and surveillance.

Motivated by a passion for education and advocacy, Alexandros now brings his expertise to this book on Solidity, helping readers unlock the potential of blockchain development to create innovative, decentralized solutions.

Alexandros can be found on LinkedIn at `https://www.linkedin.com/in/alexandros-ntolgkov` where he shares his expertise, on his LinkedIn newsletter where he writes new articles and shares news that have to do with blockchain and technology in general at `https://www.linkedin.com/newsletters/7006379762809978881`, and on X with the handle `@AlexDolgov93`.

ABOUT THE TECHNICAL EDITOR

Wim Van Renterghem is a key lecturer and researcher at Howest, where he plays a pivotal role in developing and teaching courses on blockchain and Web3 technologies. His dedication to continuous professional development is exemplified by his lifelong learning approach, including two microdegrees in blockchain and cybersecurity, and an MSc in Blockchain and Digital Currency from the University of Nicosia, demonstrating his commitment to staying at the forefront of technological advancements.

Wim Van Renterghem is deeply engaged in pioneering research at Howest, focusing on expanding the practical and theoretical boundaries of blockchain technology. His work in various research projects, including BLING and SecuWeb, showcases his innovative approach to integrating blockchain solutions into public services and enhancing web security. These initiatives underscore his ability to tackle complex challenges and drive forward the adoption and refinement of blockchain applications in both governmental and private sectors. Wim's contributions not only advance the technological landscape but also foster a deeper understanding and wider acceptance of blockchain capabilities in real-world scenarios.

ACKNOWLEDGMENTS

I am grateful to the University of Nicosia for its trail-blazing initiative to create an MSc in Blockchain and Digital Currency way back in 2013 when most people did not even know what a cryptocurrency was and most universities in the world laughed at UNIC for launching this degree. Constant year-over-year teaching of the program improved it. When I came along, it made me fall in love with blockchain technology even more than I was.

I am fortunate to have had wonderful teachers and professors at the University of Nicosia such as the one and only Professor George Giaglis, the legendary Andreas Antonopoulos, the UNIC CEO Andreas Polemitis, Lambis Dionysopoulos, Charis Savvides, Apostolos Kourtis, Soulla Louca, Elias Iosif, Marinos Themistocleous, Periklis Thivaios (even though he was the professor I overwhelmingly disagreed with), Christos Makridis, Ifigenia Georgiou, and last but not in any way least Klitos Christodolou. Additionally, I would like to thank Hazal Aripinar, Armantos Katsioloudes, and Andreas Michail.

I am moreover grateful to Wiley for giving me the opportunity to write the book and to the entire editorial team that worked hard to make this book come to life: Tom Dinse, Kenyon Brown, Navin Vijayakumar, Wim Van Renterghem, Kim Wimpsett, and Archana Pragash. I would like to give a warm thanks to Anne Jungers for introducing me to the Technical editor of this book, Wim.

I want to give special thanks to Alexandra Overgaag, CEO of Thrilld Labs, who provided emotional support to me, asked interesting thought-provoking questions, and answered some questions that I had from a reader's perspective during the process of writing this book.

I am lucky to live during a time when Bitcoin was released by Satoshi. Such events—a complete pseudonymous stranger releasing a technology and then disappearing for what seems to be forever without anyone knowing his true identity for sure, and a few years later, a gifted child like Vitalik showing up to come up with the idea of Ethereum—are scenarios that could easily have been in a fictional movie rather than events that happened in real life.

CONTENTS

INTRODUCTION

AT ITS CORE, THIS BOOK IS ABOUT LEARNING Solidity programming, specifically on the Ethereum blockchain, using the Foundry development framework. The goal is to create a resource for seasoned, aspiring, and beginning programmers to make their first steps in mastering the Solidity programming language. Foundry as a framework was selected over Hardhat and Truffle because Foundry is a straightforward framework when compared to those development frameworks. It is written in Rust, and it excels in speed, performance, and being lightweight. Additionally, when using Hardhat and Truffle, you need to be familiar with another programming language, JavaScript, to run tests and deployments. In Foundry, all this is done only through Solidity and cheat codes. The Foundry does not need any additional setup or plugins to work.

Foundry comes with its own native set of tools, such as Anvil, which is Foundry's own local Ethereum development node that helps simulate Ethereum's blockchain environment for testing and debugging. Another tool native to Foundry is Cast, which is a tool that uses the command line to interact with the Ethereum network and allows its command to interact with the different smart contracts that have been deployed on Ethereum's network. Additional interactions using Cast include sending transactions and retrieving blockchain data. The final component in Foundry's arsenal of tools is called the Forge. Forge is Foundry's smart contract development tool, which allows for smart contract compilation, testing, and deployment in Solidity without the need to use JavaScript or any other language.

WHAT THIS BOOK COVERS

When planning and writing this book, my aim was to go beyond simply teaching Solidity in isolation. I wanted to ensure you will gain an understanding of the broader context, including the implications, potential, and history of this technology. To do that, I begin the book by covering topics that, while not directly focused on Solidity, are crucial for building a well-rounded understanding of Ethereum and the underlying technology. Later chapters cover specific tools and techniques you need to know to begin to master Solidity programming.

The first chapter briefly discusses the history of money and how different forms of money have been perceived and used by the cultures that gave birth to each specific type of money. It provides brief overviews from barter and primitive money to today's cryptocurrencies while giving different use case examples of Ethereum's technology.

The second chapter goes briefly through Ethereum's architecture without doing a deep dive into it. It covers the basics of Ethereum's architecture, how it works, and why some decisions about its architecture were taken in the way they were taken. It also explores Ethereum's future developments to help you stay up-to-date with the state of Ethereum and with the planned future developments of the technology.

The third chapter is an introduction and tutorial on installing and using MetaMask, one of the most well-known wallets in the cryptocurrency industry. It covers using Ethereum faucets to get testnet ether—a fake version of Ethereum's cryptocurrency used for testing—and how to use block explorers to view and analyze transactions that happen on the Ethereum blockchain. This chapter also explains how developers can understand the smart contracts they interact with and interpret the information provided by block explorers. It also includes tips on avoiding being scammed by malicious parties and an overview of the different wallets currently in cryptocurrency. This chapter gives developers an understanding of the differences, advantages, and disadvantages of each type of wallet.

The fourth chapter of the book introduces Remix, a native online—and now available offline as well—Ethereum integrated development environment (IDE) that developers and aspiring developers can use to quickly test their smart contracts or take their first steps in Solidity programming. Within the fourth chapter, you will build your first simple smart contract.

In the fifth chapter, while still using and exploring new features the Remix IDE has to offer, you will start building more complex smart contracts, in this case, a zoo management contract that manages the animals of a small zoo as well as the number of visitors to the zoo.

The sixth chapter covers installing a professional IDE called Visual Studio Code (VS Code), which existing programmers know, but aspiring Solidity programmers might not. It also covers installing the Foundry framework to VS Code itself.

The seventh chapter of the book goes over the zoo management contract again, this time in a VS Code and Foundry environment. The main aim is to go through the Foundry framework and showcase its tools, how to use the Foundry tools, how to compile the contract within the framework, and how to deploy the contract both on Anvil's local integrated blockchain that comes with Foundry and on the Ethereum blockchain. It also covers how to manage your private keys when using Foundry and working on smart contracts.

The eighth chapter teaches you how to create a new smart contract. This time, instead of using Remix, you use VS Code and Foundry. The smart contract is a fundraising contract that allows someone to send money to the contract and for the owner of the contract to withdraw the money. The chapter also introduces blockchain oracles, a tool that allows blockchains to communicate data to and receive data from the real world, such as the prices of different currencies and assets.

The ninth chapter explains what an ERC-20 cryptocurrency is, its characteristics, and what ERC itself stands for. It also explains how proposals to change something in Ethereum are created, what they consist of, and, finally, how you can, step-by-step, create an ERC-20 cryptocurrency on your own.

The tenth chapter explains what stablecoins are, the types of stablecoins, how they work, and the mechanisms each uses to keep its price relatively stable. Finally, it explains how to create a stablecoin and a protocol step-by-step that allows the protocol user to borrow that stablecoin.

In the eleventh chapter, you will learn what nonfungible tokens (NFTs) are and how to create one. The chapter also introduces the Interplanetary File System database, a way of storing files worldwide in a decentralized manner to ensure censorship resistance for the NFT collection a developer might create.

The twelfth chapter explains upgradeable smart contracts—ways of upgrading and updating already developed and deployed smart contracts—and teaches you how to implement them.

The thirteenth chapter explains decentralized autonomous organizations (DAOs) in the context of blockchain and cryptocurrencies and teaches you how to create a DAO.

The fourteenth chapter discusses methods of keeping a smart contract secure, explains what a smart contract audit is, and details the process for conducting one.

USING AN AI TOOL

While reading the book, you can benefit from buying a subscription to an AI tool such as ChatGPT, Claude, or other tool to ask questions, request additional information, and enhance your learning. Questions and requests you might ask in AI prompts include but are not limited to asking the AI to break down complex concepts from ERC-20 to ERC-721 to DAOs, upgradable contracts, and others. In addition, you can ask the AI tool to provide analogies for complicated concepts to make it easier to understand something, which can be especially useful for complete beginners to programming, Solidity, and blockchain. Moreover, you can copy-paste into an LLM error messages and the code of a contract from this book and ask it to identify problems and how to fix them. Asking for clarification is crucial for learning and finding solutions.

Every book has limits in terms of scope, and this is no different. In addition, it is impossible to work through all the smart contracts imported and inherited through the different libraries you learn about in this book. A beyond-the-book exercise you can do is to ask the AI to explain snippets of code that are not examined in the book to enhance your understanding and deepen your knowledge and skill of not only writing code but also reading it and comprehending what a piece of code likely does.

Another way of using an AI companion is to ask it to create additional questions based on the book's material or something closely related to it and answer the questions to ensure a deep understanding of the material. Finally, the best way of using AI is not in the way that I am suggesting you use it—although this has its uses, too—but in how you come up with using it to enhance your learning. Think and be creative with how you use AI; try your ideas with prompts and see how effective they are.

To conclude this introduction, it is crucial to point out another limitation of books: they are usually slower to come up with new editions and updates than the industry and subject matter they delve into, making them a bit out-of-date after a couple of years. To minimize this as much as possible, it could be useful to go through the documentation of the tools and frameworks used in this book such as Foundry and Solidity itself to ensure that you stay up-to-date with any updates that might render some parts of the codebase in this book obsolete.

➤ **Foundry documentation link:** `https://book.getfoundry.sh`

➤ **Solidity documentation link:** `https://docs.soliditylang.org/en/latest`

Finally, on this book's website you'll find all the code available for download so you can work and experiment with the live code. The files are at:

`https://www.wiley.com/en-us/Beginning+Solidity%3A+Learn+to+Program+Smart+Contracts+with+Solidity-p-9781394290611`

1

What Is Money and a Brief History of It?

This chapter explores the fundamental concept of money and its evolution through human history, providing essential context for understanding blockchain-based financial systems and smart contract development. By examining how money functions as both a technology and a language for value exchange, you'll gain insight into why decentralized systems like Bitcoin and Ethereum represent the next evolution in monetary and contractual relationships.

The chapter addresses key questions: What makes something valuable enough to serve as money? How have societies historically solved the coordination problems of value exchange? How do cryptocurrencies and smart contracts build upon these historical patterns while introducing new capabilities?

Through detailed analysis of primitive money systems, modern banking, and emerging crypto networks, you'll learn how money's core properties—medium of exchange, store of value, and unit of account—manifest across different technological implementations. The chapter connects these concepts directly to smart contract development by examining real-world applications ranging from tokenized real estate to decentralized autonomous organizations (DAOs).

By working through historical examples and modern case studies, you'll develop a crucial foundation for understanding the problems that smart contracts aim to solve and the new possibilities they enable. These insights are essential for designing effective decentralized applications and financial protocols that align with fundamental economic principles while leveraging blockchain's unique capabilities.

WHAT IS MONEY?

This, first and foremost, is a Solidity book. However, money is integral to cryptocurrencies, to blockchains such as Ethereum, to Solidity, and to smart contracts. Thus, a short chapter on money in this book is essential for you to fully and deeply understand and appreciate the bigger picture of what it is that people are, in essence, building when they use Solidity to create smart contracts. In this chapter, we'll cover the history of money for a deeper understanding of Ethereum, Solidity, smart contracts, and cryptocurrencies in general.

Money has many meanings and definitions. Money has been called a medium of exchange. This commodity represents the time and energy given to an employer to build or do something. In exchange, we get money. Another way of defining money is as energy—spent in service of an employer or on creating a service or a product—that takes physical form as coins and paper notes that can then be used in exchange for someone else's energy, who was spending their energy building a car, organizing a vacation, working at a hotel we visit, preparing the meal we would eat, and so forth. These are just a few definitions of money throughout history.

Since this is a technology book, we will look at money not as a commodity but as a language and technology, seeing the current global economy—and those before it—as a protocol built on this language and technology. It is estimated that there are around 7,000 languages in the world that people use to communicate with each other every day. There are around 700 programming languages in the world. When it comes to computers, they fundamentally understand only binary sequences of 0s and 1s, with each separate sequence of 0s and 1s meaning something entirely different from the others. Money, on the other hand, no matter the currency, is a language humans use to communicate how much they value a product or a service. On the most basic level, money is saying, "Oh, you have a great kitchen knife for sale there. I value it at 50 amounts of money. Will you sell it to me?" (Replace "amounts of money" with dollars or euro or the currency of your country.) If the person selling the kitchen knife values the labor and time that went into creating the kitchen knife to 50 amounts of money, they will say "yes," and the kitchen knife will be sold. In this example, money acts as a language between two parties, conveying the value they assign to a specific item or service—in this case, a kitchen knife. Before finalizing the transaction, the parties use this shared "language" to communicate and agree upon the knife's value. Once agreed, the transaction proceeds: the buyer transfers the agreed-upon value to the seller, and the seller transfers ownership of the knife to the buyer.

Money as a form of technology—and the economic systems built upon it as protocols derived from this "language"—is a complex and expansive subject. It provides material spanning bachelor's, master's, and PhD programs, as well as countless books and even entire series of books, depending on the depth of exploration. In this chapter, however, we will take a condensed approach, focusing on the major milestones in the evolution of money as a technology. This will involve simplifying and omitting many details to provide a high-level overview.

Money as a Technology

Money as a technology is a contract in and of itself in two ways:

➤ A contract is an agreement among a community of people to use a specific type of money as a medium of exchange to transact with one another for goods and services. This agreement establishes their willingness to treat this form of money as the community's transactional tool.

➤ A contract between two parties that are not part of the same community needs a standard transactional tool to exchange goods and services. This ensures the transactional tool will be valuable to the party selling the goods and services. The following are two examples of that, one historical and one contemporary:

➤ **Historical:** Members of two different tribes engaging in commerce with one another—with each tribe using its type of money that may not be valuable to the other—agreeing to use another intermediary for commerce, such as coins, belts, animal skins, or anything else that may be of value to both tribes.

➤ **Contemporary:** Modern countries have agreed to use the US dollar (USD) as a medium of exchange for international business transactions. Before USD became the world's reserve currency, countries agreed to use the British Pound Sterling as a medium of exchange for international transactions. Before the pound, it was the Dutch guilder; before that, the Spanish Real; and before even that, the Italian Florin.

When it comes to using money as technology, money has three properties, each having a separate set of subproperties to fulfill for that property to be considered viable as use for money. Those three properties and their subproperties are discussed next.

Medium of Exchange

A *medium of exchange* is an intermediary technological tool between parties that can facilitate value communication in exchange for products and services. In turn, the party that exchanged their service or product for the medium of exchange can use that medium of exchange to buy the products and services that they need from someone else in an endless, circular way until the specific medium of exchange used, be it coins, paper money, or digital money, is destroyed by being taken out of circulation or is damaged irreparably to the point that no party would accept it as a medium of exchange. In the modern era, the currency issued by a country's central bank, also known as the national currency of a country, is the primary medium of exchange for participating in an economy and exchanging goods and services.

For a medium of exchange to be *reliable*, it must have certain subproperties:

➤ **Durability:** This is the extent to which a currency can be used without significantly being damaged or torn.

➤ **Transportability:** How easily can a currency be transferred from one place to another in terms of speed and weight?

➤ **Divisibility:** Can the money be divided into smaller chunks? Can a 100 USD bill be divided into smaller chunks of 50, 20, 10, 5, 2, and 1 USD and then into cents?

➤ **Fungibility:** Is money fungible? Following the earlier dollar example, is a 100 USD bill equal to another 100 USD bill?

➤ **Noncounterfeit ability:** How easily can the currency be counterfeited?

➤ **Scarcity:** Is the medium of exchange scarce enough in supply to ensure that there is value in it? In other words, is it rare enough to come by so that people want it? When a medium of exchange is available in abundant supply, it loses value. With a "reasonable" decrease in scarcity and consequent loss of value, people raise the price of their goods. When the surplus increases significantly, the money loses its value to the extent that it becomes useless, and nobody wants to use it anymore.

➤ **Acceptability:** The more acceptability a medium of exchange has, the more effective it becomes. Its acceptability can vary from one person to another or one store or merchant to another. The acceptability of a medium of exchange can be as narrow as only two parties agreeing to use something as a medium of exchange and transact with it. This would be extremely weak acceptability, but it is still nonetheless something that can be considered as acceptability of a medium of exchange. That said, when a medium of exchange is desired, its acceptability becomes much more potent and much more widely acceptable than just two parties, making it a more effective medium.

Store of Value

Another significant property of money is as a store of value. A *store of value* is a tool or property of money that allows for money's value to be saved and retrieved in the future with a degree of predictability about the value remaining, or at the very least, the same in the future. It is worth noting that a store of value is not a property of only money but also of assets, as there are different stores of value, such as gold, silver, diamonds, reserve currencies, government bonds, stocks, real estate, and other assets.

The property of being a good store of value is derived from the following:

➤ **Stability:** Current predictions of a stable or predictable demand for an asset, be it money or any previously mentioned assets.

➤ **Predictability:** An asset's stable or shrinking future supply. As all assets and currencies have a certain degree of unpredictability in value, today there is no perfect store of value.

➤ **Cultural and societal values:** The perceived cultural value of certain currencies or assets that may inflate their price beyond the apparent use in industrial or other uses.

➤ **Liquidity:** The ease with which a store of value can be converted into a medium of exchange without loss—or significant loss—in value. High liquidity means that an asset can be quickly sold or at least converted for cash (or its equivalents) when required, which enhances its utility as a store of value. For example, suppose you buy real estate and, after a few years or months, want to sell it. It could take months or possibly years to sell the real estate and convert it into money or cash. On the other hand, stocks can be sold much faster, increasing their liquidity and conversion into cash.

➤ **Portability and transferability:** Like the transportability of a medium of exchange mentioned earlier, how easy it is for someone to transfer the assets to someone else, from one party to another, or from one geographical location to another, without any compromise in value and reduced costs. This is, of course, much easier to do when a proof of ownership document—whether digital or physical—is available. In contrast, transporting 100 bars of gold poses numerous challenges, such as moving them from one US state to another or, even worse, from one continent to another. Such a scenario increases costs and exposes the stored value to risks including damage, theft, or other unforeseen issues.

Unit of Account

The final significant property of money is that of a *unit of account*. For a type of money to be considered a unit of account, prices must be communicated in terms of money and currency rather than other goods. For example, "I paid 10.000 USD for a trip to Europe" instead of "I paid four cows, or 66 shares of Alphabet (Google) stock for a trip to Europe." In money's language, prices in a unit of account properly communicate the value of goods and services, assets, liabilities, and other economic activity. In each country, the main currency tends to be the unit of account; certain exceptions apply, such as the European Union, a union of countries bound by a single currency, the euro.

For money to be considered a practical unit of account and used to communicate value for goods and services to others, it must be stable in price and not volatile. In the short term, national currencies such as the US dollar and the euro are much more stable than cryptocurrencies.

However, in the long term, the current structure of the global economy integrates inflation and the practice of printing money mainly due to money's endless supply as a natural aspect of annual economic operations. Inflation and the practice of money printing are seen as unavoidable in the current economy and desirable in activating the economy and stimulating spending by aiming for a 2 percent annual inflation. However, actual rates frequently exceed this target. Increasing the money supply through printing money and thus creating inflation impacts the currency's scarcity, decreasing its value over time.

The preceding discussions of money's properties explain why no form of money today can be considered perfect: none fulfills all the previously mentioned properties. When some of these properties are taken to the extreme, they tend to negate some of the other properties, which suggests that currently the ideal economic state is a balance between these properties while maintaining periodic adjustments toward higher or lower inflation based on the condition of the economy at a given time.

THE HISTORY AND EVOLUTION OF MONEY

Now that you have an understanding of what money is, let's pivot to gaining an understanding of its history and evolution.

Money is a fundamental part of human civilization, evolving alongside societies to meet the needs of trade, value storage, and wealth exchange. This chapter explores the history and evolution of money, from its earliest form—barter—to the development of primitive money, highlighting how humans transitioned from simple exchanges to complex economic systems.

Before currency was invented, people relied on barter within small, self-sufficient communities. Over time, the limitations of barter, such as the "double coincidence of wants," led to the creation of primitive forms of money, including shells, wampum belts, cattle, and even salt. These items were shaped by their cultural and environmental contexts, serving as both mediums of exchange and symbols of social value.

Through this exploration, we see that money is not just a tangible object but also a psychological and social construct. Its evolution reflects humanity's drive to create tools and systems that enable peaceful trade and cooperation, ultimately shaping the economic frameworks we rely on today.

Barter

Before any currency or form of money was invented, people lived in tiny, agrarian, self-sufficient communities where everyone practically knew each other and engaged in the communication of value, shaping of contracts, and trade of services and goods they found valuable through an activity called *barter*, which was simply trading goods and services directly and without having an intermediary tool representing money. Instead of paying to buy a cow with cash, people would trade six chickens for one cow or a few eggs from the chickens for milk from the cow. Since in many of those early communities everyone knew each other, there was no need for written contracts, and in any case contracts were mainly oral and based on honor until writing was invented. After that, people would transcribe their contracts on clay tablets. If someone from the community knew that Person X did not fulfill his part of the agreement with Person Y, their reputation would be at stake. People would refuse to enter into commerce contracts with them out of fear of them not reciprocating their part of the deal.

Barter can be an acceptable approach when an economy is tiny and based mainly on honor due to the people knowing one another. In those circumstances people could exchange the items they needed without the need for money as a technology serving as an intermediary of exchange. Such small economies were possible when humankind lived in caves or small communities. Another possibility could be when humans would start a new settlement or town. At the very beginning of the town's building, there would not be too many people living there, and hence, the villagers or townspeople could, in theory, implement a barter system instead of needing a currency or money to engage in trade of their services and products and satisfying their needs. Another historical example is when people are detained as prisoners for any reason. During World War II, Jewish people—and possibly other prisoners—used tobacco and cigarettes as currency for favors, products, services, bribes, and other economic activities, both ethical and unethical.

Barter as an economic system faces a major limitation known as the "double coincidence of wants." This occurs when two parties must each have something the other desires to make an exchange. For example, if one person trades 6 liters of milk for 12 eggs, both must agree on the value of this trade. However, problems arise if either party needs something else afterward. Suppose the person who now has milk and eggs wants to buy three fish for dinner. They must find a fish merchant willing to accept milk or eggs as payment. If the merchant agrees, they might, in turn, need a haircut. To get one, the merchant must find a barber willing to accept fish, milk, or eggs as payment. This chain of dependencies becomes increasingly impractical. Additionally, while goods like milk, eggs, or fish can be traded, intangible services like a haircut cannot be exchanged further as tradeable assets. This limitation reduces the efficiency of barter compared to monetary systems.

Moreover, there is no guarantee that the barber, fish merchant, or any other two people will want fish, eggs, or milk in exchange for the goods or services they provide. The more people entering the equation—or the more variables there are in a function—the more difficult it is to find someone who wants precisely the goods or services you specialized in to trade his goods and services with you. Furthermore, many products, including eggs, milk, and fish, are not suitable replacements for money or currency used as a medium of exchange or even a store of value since—among other drawbacks—they go bad quickly. They, hence, are not durable or feasible to transfer rapidly in large quantities and through considerable distances.

Finally, barter may be possible for an economy that is very local, small, and unsophisticated both economically and technologically and where people know each other enough to avoid the problem of double coincidence of wants. However, what about when an economy is technologically sophisticated? How many eggs, haircuts, fish, or milk would one need to spend to buy a flight from New York to Washington or Tokyo or Brussels? Even worse, how many goods would one company need to give to another to buy an airplane and provide flight services? Therefore, barter is suitable only for small, primitive economies. But once the economy is sophisticated enough and has enough people and technology, barter becomes outdated quickly, needing a type of intermediary of value to play the role of money—which everyone recognizes and would accept within a community and would use to exchange goods and services.

Barter survives today but in very few instances, such as gift exchanges between individuals during a holiday. Additionally, there are local barter markets that allow participants to swap one item for another. Until quite recently, specifically the 1990s, countries and businesses that wanted to do business with the Soviet Union had to use barter as a means of commerce. A well-known story is that of Pepsi getting a fleet of submarines in exchange for purchase orders of its soda drink which Pepsi then sold for US dollars to make a profit.

Primitive Money

As human societies evolved in sophistication and complexity from the primitive societies that used barter, people learned to cooperate in more significant numbers as a settlement community or tribe, and barter became outdated for the previously mentioned reasons. This brought forth the need for a new way of engaging in trade and commerce, paving the way for primitive money to be invented.

As mentioned in the "Store of Value" section earlier in the chapter, primitive money took various forms depending on the society's norms and culture. These were a few different forms of primitive money:

> **Shells:** Cowrie shells were primarily used in Africa, Asia, and the Pacific Islands in seafaring societies closer to the oceans. Besides monetary significance, shells also had a significant cultural importance, as they were used in various religious rituals and continued to be used as currency up to the nineteenth century in Western Africa. In Asia, besides being of spiritual and cultural use, shells were used for tiny transactions in the same way that we use cents and perhaps a few dollars. In the Pacific Islands, shells were used not only as currency but also as significant cultural value since they were used in ceremonies of marriage, various initiations, and peace negotiations. (Today, we see a pigeon as a symbol of peace.)
>
> Additionally, craftspeople created unique shells, which were used as ornaments and jewelry. Even today, in the Solomon Islands, shells are used in traditional exchanges and as a symbol of prestige and wealth. This demonstrates how the forms of money (shells) used by these communities were deeply ingrained in their culture. Additionally, for the technology of the time, these shells were durable, transportable, and fungible, although shells with ornaments were probably more expensive. The fungibility element would suffer noncounterfeitable scarcity through ornamentation. Additionally, these societies used whale teeth as an additional form of money. The conditions just described made it easy to predict a steady demand for shells as currency, money, and assets, while the work put into them made them resistant to supply shocks.

➤ **Wampum belts:** Wampum belts are belts made from quahog clam and were used by Native American tribes as money.

Wampum belts played a crucial role in formalizing agreements, treaties, alliances, and social contracts between different Native American tribes as they served as physical records of essential events very similar and in parallel to written documents and treaties that were used in the West. In addition to documenting events, wampum belts were used to record laws and lineages and preserve historical stories, such as tribal history, for younger generations, ensuring the preservation of cultural heritage and identity. Wampum belts were also profoundly woven into the religious and spiritual fabric of Native American tribes as they were used in religious rituals, and it was thought that they could convey messages and prayers to the spirit world. Wampum belts were durable due to the materials used in their construction and were relatively easy to transport. They were also resistant to counterfeiting, as their creation required significant labor, which contributed to their scarcity and value as a form of currency.

➤ **Cattle:** Cattle, as a form of money—although admittedly not entirely detached from barter—was used by many human societies, particularly the Maasai in East Africa, Ancient Romans, and Ancient Germanic Tribes. Cattle were used as money across many cultures because they represented wealth and status, offering essential resources such as milk, wool, and general food security. Cattle were used in various forms, such as for dowries, for trade, and as a unit of account.

➤ **Whale teeth:** Whale teeth were used in seafaring societies near open seas and islands where whales could be spotted, such as the Fiji Islands and other Pacific Islands. In addition to being used as money, whale teeth were used as adornments and symbols of status, signifying wealth and social rank. They were integral to defining social hierarchies and relationships bonds as they were exchanged during important life events such as births, marriages, and deaths among others. Whale teeth were also used in ceremonies that embodied themes of respect, honor, and societal cohesion. For the era and the technology available, whale's teeth provided the ideal balance between the properties of money. Durable, transportable, fungible, complex to counterfeit, scarce, and difficult enough to obtain to not over-inflate the supply and make people lose interest in that type of money. Using whale teeth as money solidified a shared cultural identity among Pacific Island societies. Whale teeth were a manifestation of a community's relationship with the sea and its creatures, as well as embodiments of bravery, skill, and spiritual and religious beliefs of the people using them.

➤ **Grain:** Grain was used as money on and off throughout human civilization. However, three standout places are Ancient Egypt, Ancient Sumer (modern-day Iraq), and Medieval Europe. Grain was used as money due to the human political and social structures of those fundamentally agrarian societies, just as whale teeth were the currency of seafaring societies such as the ones in the Fiji Islands. Like in Fiji, whales and other fish were used for their meat; among other uses, grain was a staple of the diet of agrarian societies, and workers in ancient Egypt were even paid in grain. Grain as a type of money was durable compared to eggs and other similar items that were used during the barter period of human history. Grain for the time's technology was easily transportable, fungible since more or less one grain is the same as another grain, noncounterfeitable, and scarce enough since automation or modern farming had not yet been invented.

Grain was also culturally crucial for the aforementioned societies of Egypt, Sumer, and Medieval Europe. It was central in Egyptian and Sumerian religious practices and ceremonies. It symbolized many of their gods, such as Ancient Greece's Demeter, the goddess of agriculture and grain—although Demeter is not a Medieval European Goddess but an Ancient one. In Medieval Europe, the church enhanced grain's cultural perception through Biblical stories by saying that bread is the body of Christ—while wine, his blood, symbolizes spiritual nourishment and community. In addition, the importance of grain, as described, predicted a stable demand for an asset that was used as money, and it was possible to predict the asset's stable long-term supply without any massive supply shocks that either expanded or minimized its supply—besides bad harvest years, which were an exception to the rule.

➤ **Tobacco:** Tobacco was used as primitive money in several situations, eras, and cultures. Tobacco's groundwork as an accepted medium of exchange was laid by Native American tribes, who used it for ceremonial purposes before European colonization as it was considered a gift from God. It was used in rituals and as an offering during peace and war negotiations. During the colonial American era, tobacco was used as a currency for internal trade and exports as tobacco leaves were standardized into units of account, allowing for transactions in a largely agrarian economy that had—at the time—no stable form of currency. Tobacco warehouses issued receipts, which could be used as money, just as banknotes and other paper money are used today. Tobacco as a currency was durable in dry environments and could be stored for long periods without going bad. It is easily transportable due to its lightweight. At the same time, governments tried to control scarcity through various mechanisms, such as trade and production regulation. Regarding fungibility, tobacco had challenges to overcome due to the significantly varied quality of tobacco. Still, it was standardized and used as units of account and medium of exchange known as hogsheads.

➤ **Salt:** Salt was used as money throughout different cultures, geographies, and times, but the most notable use came from Ancient Rome, where salt was used to pay soldiers, which is how and from where the word "salary" came to be. Besides its use in flavoring food, salt benefited from preserving food long-term before refrigeration was invented, increasing its value and demand as a currency. This property of maintaining and preserving food was powerful enough to elevate people in social status during times of hardship when salt could become very scarce, and people would not have a way to preserve their food long-term; hence, the food would go bad, and the people would starve. Salt, although not used in religious beliefs in the same way as the primitive types of money, was used to ward off evil and in hospitality customs, symbolizing protection, welcoming, and preservation. In terms of monetary properties, salt is durable and resistant to general corrosion, decay, and spoilage, which helped its status as a store of value and medium of exchange.

➤ **Tea bricks:** Tea bricks played significant roles in various societies in Asia. They were used as a medium of exchange and money in places where metal coins were scarce, such as remote areas, which led to tea bricks that were relatively transportable and durable so could be used as a currency for the exchange of goods and services. Tea bricks were used as items that provided medicinal and nutritional benefits while symbolizing status and wealth for those who owned rare or manufactured tea bricks in well-known regions. Like many other primitive money types, tea bricks were additionally part of the culture of ceremonies and rituals. More specifically, even today, tea ceremonies were of significant cultural value to those societies.

➤ **Feathers:** Feathers, just like the preceding items, were used by different communities and societies, such as Native American tribes, Pacific Islanders, and various African tribes and cultures, for different purposes. Among those purposes are money and a medium of exchange. The scarcity, value, and demand came from the difficulty of obtaining the feathers, and especially rare feathers were used as a currency. Due to rare feathers' scarcity, they were also used as a status symbol. They were worn as adornments to symbolize wealth and bravery, like how a whale's teeth were used. Like almost every primitive form of money mentioned earlier, feathers were used for ceremonial, cultural, spiritual, and religious events. The rarest were used to decorate ceremonial masks, honor, and please deities and ancestral spirits. Feathers, being more delicate than other forms of money, were not as durable but were transportable due to being extremely lightweight and could be transported easily in bulk if put in a sack.

➤ **Beads:** Beads were also used as a type of primitive money in Africa, the Americas, and Asia, and their value was determined by several factors such as the material, color, and even crafting difficulty. Beads were used in burial ceremonies as offerings of protection and spiritual power and as an adornment to identify tribe affiliation and cultural heritage. Regarding scarcity, the value of beads was determined by the shortage of the materials used to produce and use them in trade. Their small size and weight made them easy to transport—for the technology of the time.

Primitive Money: Conclusion

The previous examples may feel repetitive to someone. Still, they are so to illustrate several points in terms of money, humans, and human psychology. Money in itself, by default, is not a tangible object in the same sense as we would think a chair is a tangible object that we can take, move, and sit on.

Money is, first and foremost, an immaterial psychological and biological need and concept all humans need to remain peaceful and engage in trade, buy, and sell with one another items and services they deem valuable in a quiet way—the alternative is war and violence to take something one values from another. As mentioned, money as a psychological concept needs to have the three properties of a unit of account, store of value, and medium of exchange for a material object to be considered suitable to become a type of money. The basics remained the same, unlike chairs again, which differed in design from culture to culture. Primitive money was derived from one's surroundings. It was vastly different from culture to culture in material terms—from tobacco to tea bricks, feathers, and whale teeth—but the psychological and biological basics of what constitutes money in terms of subproperties of the three main properties of money remained the same cross-culturally and across time.

Modern Types of Money

Having learned about bartering and the different social and cultural dimensions each primitive money type had on the culture that used it, the next step is to look at modern types of money such as coins and banknotes.

In addition to modern types of money, it is crucial to briefly talk about precursors of modern institutions such as central banks and Bretton Woods, a major treaty that was the last major change to money before money transitioned to the type of money that it is today: fiat money.

Coins

As human societies evolved, advancing further in sophistication, technology, and complexity beyond barter-based economies—but still primitive by today's standards—they started to collaborate and cooperate in more significant numbers than simple tribes and started transitioning to kingdoms. This shift required a more standardized way of communicating and exchanging value: coins.

Modern coins, as we recognize them today, were invented in ancient Lydia (Ancient Greece and modern-day Turkey) in the seventh century BCE. Those coins were a mix of gold and silver. The invention of coins was a big step forward regarding money's properties of standardization, durability, divisibility, fungibility, and, in time, acceptability and liquidity. However, two things that took a hit in terms of properties when compared to the barter and primitive money were the noncounterfeit ability and scarcity.

It is difficult to impossible to counterfeit something like cattle, whale teeth, shells, tea bricks, feathers, beads, salt, tobacco, wampum belts, and grain. Convincing someone who knows what those are, what they look like, how they feel, and their cultural significance would be nearly impossible. On the other hand, coins—and, as we will see, paper money—are much easier to counterfeit and to manipulate their scarcity. You just need to have a process for creating coins and either use a different metal to create the coin or mix the actual coin metal with something much less valuable like copper, making someone believe it is made of gold or silver. The Roman Empire did this when they were debasing their currencies the Aureus (based on gold) and the Denarius (based on silver). This practice later led the Roman Empire into financial trouble.

The Roman Empire was not the only example of coin debasement, counterfeiting, or clipping. There are multiple historical examples of this.

Coins did not become the preferred way of paying until the eighteenth and nineteenth centuries when coins were issued privately in many combinations. Both the issuers of coins and the users were clipping the coins and scraping the excess metal to keep in order to profit, which in time led to people using debased money—since only debased money remained in circulation and used for the exchange of goods and services.

Paper Money

Paper money emerged for the first time in China in the tenth century AD. This happened through receipts and deposits of coin currency because the coins used then in China were in small denominations, thus making large transactions costly and problematic since many physical coins amplify the problem of transportability. A physical paper note was a certificate of ownership that allowed the owner of it to convert the certificate into the coins stored in a deposit store. This made trading, communicating, and transporting value for large transactions much more straightforward. Rather than transporting the coins needed for a large transaction, the owner of the paper certificate of ownership needed to trade only the certificate. The person who sold the goods and services could convert the certificate to coins if needed.

The problem with banknotes started in the twelfth century AD when the Chinese government recognized the usefulness and potential of paper and started issuing banknotes, which granted the government the monopoly in issuing banknotes. Even then, money remained regional and decentralized for a considerable time until the thirteenth century when the Song government decided to issue the first national currency in the world, eventually granting the whole area of money to the government as a monopoly.

In the Western world, depository receipts have existed for centuries. Still, the first genuinely public bank was not created until 1609 in Amsterdam, Netherlands. Its purpose was to bring efficiency to the circulation of coins in the city, which was one of the major commercial centers of that time. The bank accepted almost all kinds of coins including domestic, foreign, or even debased, and would weigh them in and evaluate them based on specific rules and common standards. Then they would exchange that money for its own bank money for which it would issue a physical certificate of receipt like China had done. This technological transformation of money helped with the standardization, communication, and use of funds between different parties as well as reduced the incentive to devalue or clip the common coins since now the confusion of other currencies was not as prevalent anymore. It was also the precursor for what would eventually become the central bank in the western world.

The Bank of Amsterdam initially operated only as an exchange, issuing a certificate of ownership. It was also a full-reserve depositing institution. Full reserve means that none of the money and valuables deposited by its customers were loaned out to other parties. This began to change when the Amsterdam bank started loaning its deposits to the Dutch East India Company on a short-term basis using other people's deposits. This is called *fractional-reserve banking* since the banks do not have all the money deposited by their customers—which is called *full-reserve banking*—available simultaneously and lending to them. This was one of the first steps toward the modern fiat-based financial system in which fractional-reserve banking activity is fully maintained and practiced today by our banks and financial institutions. It is one of the key aspects of how money is created and managed in today's economy.

One of the risks of such a system, as the Bank of Amsterdam eventually found out, is the potential for default by those it lends to. This happened when the Dutch East India Company ran into financial trouble and defaulted on its obligations to the bank, failing to pay its legal obligations. The bank ended up being saved by the city of Amsterdam. Still, it eventually went out of favor and was taken up by other banks in 1819.

Bretton Woods Conference

At the end of World War II in 1944, the major economies of the time held the Bretton Woods Conference. At the end of the conference, it was decided that the USD would be pegged to gold, and the other major currencies would be pegged to the USD. The USD would be redeemable for gold at 35 USD an ounce, but only by central banks, not citizens. The then newly formed International Monetary Fund would act as a bridge for payment imbalances among ratifying countries. The Bretton Woods agreement was abandoned by the United States in 1971. That was the end of metal-backed currencies as the world entered the era of fiat currencies, which still stands today.

Modern Types of Money: Conclusion

Between the time humans started using primitive types of money and the twenty-first century, many things have, obviously, changed technologically: humans managed to create sophisticated ships and tame the seas in ways seafaring cultures like the Vikings or Pacific Islanders would never have imagined; we managed to replace the horse and cart with a technological miracle called the car;

where our ancestors used myths such as Daedalus and Icarus, Pegasus, the ancient Greek mythical flying horse, the Norse Valkyries, and other similar creatures to imagine humans one day flying, we managed to create another technological miracle, the airplane, and can fly to wherever we want to go across the world, and, looking at SpaceX, we may soon—within our lifetimes—be able to travel in space for tourism. One thing, however, that did not change is human psychology and biology in terms of what we value as money and how it is tied to our cultures.

For example, primitive money was tied to tribal culture. If you transported an Asian who used tea bricks as currency to a Pacific Island, they would not immediately recognize whale teeth as a type of money used by the Pacific Islander culture. Similarly, if you took a Pacific Islander to an Asian tribe that used tea bricks as money, the Pacific Islander would not immediately recognize that this was a tool used as money by that culture.

Similarly, we are not that different from our ancestors; we may not use items that are used for money in religious or ceremonial events and rituals anymore as they used to do, yet, like their money, ours is emblazoned with our own cultures since our countries and nations decorate our money with our nation's heritage and achievements. For example, banknotes and coins were decorated both in old times and today with historical people, animals that symbolize the insignia of their kingdom or nation, or historical locations or buildings and landmarks of that nation, which serve as a tool for education and national pride in the nation's accomplishments and reinforces national unity and identity. The US dollar banknotes depict US presidents and the founding fathers of the nation.

However, there is a better example of this in the European Union, whose banknotes display the different architectural styles of Europe that were prominent throughout different epochs on the continent. On the other hand, the euro coins are meant to display and evoke national pride instead of continental one as the banknotes do, with each coin having different depictions in every country. For example, the German 2-euro coin depicts the Brandenburg Gate, France's 2-euro coin depicts the famous slogan "Liberty, Equality, Fraternity," in Italy's 1-euro coin one can see the depiction of the Vitruvian man by Leonardo Da Vinci, and the Greek 1-euro coin depicts Athena and her symbolic animal, the owl. Therefore, it is not far-fetched to conclude that modern countries are tribes or communities just like our ancestors when they used primitive money or barter to enter contracts with one another. The key difference is that our modern tribes are organized on a much larger scale and are much more complex in their workings and the contracts they use to cooperate than our ancestors.

CRYPTOCURRENCIES

After having seen the different forms modern money has taken and the type of money that we use today, it is time to transition to how money will likely look in the future, going completely digital. Moreover, it is crucial to briefly examine the properties of this new digital type of money using previously seen frameworks in this chapter.

Bitcoin

On October 31, 2008, a mysterious figure (or figures) known as Satoshi Nakamoto emailed several cryptographers saying "I've been working on a new electronic cash system that is fully peer-to-peer, with no trusted third party...." The paper proposed a decentralized system of money called bitcoin.

Bitcoin's Monetary Properties

Bitcoin and Ethereum have several properties:

➤ **Distributed:** The networks are spread across all their participants worldwide, and borders are not in a central place or one or two countries but anywhere with an Internet connection.

➤ **Secure:** They are secure as long as 50 percent of the miner nodes in Bitcoin are honest and 66 percent of the validator nodes in Ethereum are honest.

➤ **Reliable:** Transaction ledgers are replicated by all nodes (nodes is another word for the computer, but keep in mind that the term *node* encompasses all kinds of possible computers: laptops, desktops, phones, supercomputers, and those nodes are then further subdivided into types of nodes such as full nodes, lightweight nodes, etc.). However, adding the human element is crucial since humans set up all nodes and computers. Your iPhone might be, as it is called, a "lightweight, lightweight" node, but in the end, you control it; thus, it is an extension of a human.

➤ **Peer-to-peer:** Transactions can be made from one party to the other without a central authority.

➤ **Open:** Anyone can join or leave the network, validate transactions, and mine or stake coins.

➤ **Public:** All transactions recorded on the Bitcoin/Ethereum network are publicly verifiable and available to all the operators in the network.

➤ **Permissionless:** There is no need for credentials, IDs, or authorization to join the network.

➤ **Borderless:** The network operates freely across geographical boundaries and can be accessed practically anywhere.

➤ **Censorship-resistant:** No central authority or government can stop funds transfer from one peer to another.

➤ **Neutral:** The Bitcoin and Ethereum networks are agnostic about who, what, when, where, or why you send and receive bitcoin or Ether.

Bitcoin and the kind of currency type it falls into is a matter of debate. Fiat currencies, which are not backed by anything, rely on the trust and collective belief in the central issuer. Bitcoin may not have a central issuer, but if it is ever to work one way or another as a currency, it will be backed by individuals who believe that bitcoin has value and thus choose to enter contracts with the Bitcoin community and the broader world.

Thus, here we see again that bitcoin, ether, or any other cryptocurrency do not escape the fate of other currencies that came before them whose value is based on a biological and psychological need to transact and enter into contracts—smart contracts—with other parties and engage in trade peacefully even if both cryptocurrencies are not widely accepted as money at the time this book was written.

Bitcoin's "Monetary Policies"

If people see the decentralized issuance of bitcoin as a monetary policy, several interesting aspects can be observed. Bitcoin has a fixed and static supply with a deflationary issuance schedule:

➤ The protocol regulates the money supply, and only 21,000.000 bitcoin will exist. The last part of a bitcoin will be minted in 2140.

➤ They are currently being issued on a declining schedule. At the time of writing, they are 6.25 BTC approximately every 10 minutes, and by the time this book is published, there will be 3.125 BTC every 10 minutes.

➤ The inflation rate and the number of new bitcoin entering the economy's circulation halves every four years, and the next halving will be in April 2024.

Because the money supply is fixed and the halving takes place every four years, bitcoin's monetary policy is—unlike that of a central bank—predictable. From today to 2140, we know when the halvings will occur: every 210,000 blocks or every four years.

Moreover, since the blockchain and its code are public, the monetary policy of bitcoin is publicly viewable and verifiable. This can be done in a variety of ways:

➤ One way is to download the Bitcoin blockchain onto a computer. However, at the time of writing, the Bitcoin blockchain stores all bitcoin transactions from Satoshi's genesis block (the first Bitcoin block to be mined), and it is worth noting that each block of transactions adds to the overall size of the blockchain. At the time this sentence was written, the Bitcoin block-chain size is 560 GB.

➤ Another way is by using a block explorer such as blockstream.info, blockchain.com, or mempool.space. (Note that I am not endorsing any of these companies' products. They are being mentioned for educational purposes.)

➤ Also, you can go to GitHub and examine the code in the Bitcoin/Ethereum repository.

Finally, Bitcoin, Ethereum, and other open public blockchains are driven by consensus. This means anyone joining the network chooses to agree to the network rules.

Otherwise, they can join another *open public blockchain network besides Bitcoin and Ethereum.*

➤ They are free to propose changes to the network, which will be implemented if all the other participants agree.

➤ They can re-create the whole network with their own rules. Still, it will be independent from the original one and thus incompatible.

Key characteristics such as money supply cannot change unless most system participants vote to do so. Even then, the ones who disagree can re-create the network with the old rules and participate in that one, splitting the chain and creating two.

Now, let us examine bitcoin and ether according to the three main properties of money.

In terms of mediums of exchange, both bitcoin and ether are:

➤ **Durable:** Both blockchains run on thousands of computers worldwide, making them highly durable and almost impossible to break.

➤ **Portable:** Bitcoin and ether—Ethereum's native cryptocurrency—are highly portable. In addition, since there are no intermediaries, both networks are global. Bitcoin's confirmation takes about 10 minutes, and Ethereum's takes 12 seconds. The difference is due to different software architectures.

➤ **Fungible:** Both bitcoin and ether are highly fungible between themselves. One bitcoin equals another bitcoin. Similarly, one ether equals another ether. Although, of course, bitcoin and ether are not fungible among themselves.

➤ **Divisible:** One bitcoin can be divided into 100,000.000 smaller units called satoshis, whereas ether can be divided into 1.000.000.000.000.000.000 wei, the smallest unit of ether, making ether more divisible than bitcoin.

➤ **Resistant to counterfeiting:** Bitcoin and ether are assigned or sent to a specific address, and anyone in the network can verify the validity of this transaction.

➤ **Legal tender:** Bitcoin is legal tender in El Salvador, the first country to make the decentralized digital currency a recognized medium of exchange for the whole country. For now, ether is not a recognized national currency in any jurisdiction.

➤ **Subject to transaction fees:** One massive problem with Ethereum and ether is gas fees, which are the commissions taken by the network to process transactions. This is due to Ethereum's low transaction per second (TPS), which makes people worldwide compete in bidding each other out by paying a higher fee to the network to get their transaction processed first. This is something that people try to mitigate through Layer 2 solutions, which we will talk about in Chapter 2. Still, for the moment, it is a huge problem that even if either were to become the world's global reserve currency—theoretically speaking—it would dramatically hinder its adoption; the same goes for Bitcoin's transaction fees.

In terms of unit of account:

➤ Bitcoin cannot be considered a unit of account—at least for the moment—because even if someone pays in bitcoin for goods, services, or anything else, the price is quoted in a fiat currency, be that the USD, the Euro, or any other.

➤ A notable exception for Ether is nonfungible tokens (NFTs), whose prices are quoted in Ethereum's native token.

In terms of store of value:

➤ Bitcoin is highly volatile, which in the short term makes it a lousy store of value—and makes a significant fiat currency a better store of value in the short term, as mentioned earlier in the chapter. But in the long term, it tends to go up in price. Some of its properties, such as fixed supply and deflationary, have made people consider it digital gold. Thus, it is now considered a form of investment.

➤ Although ether has the same characteristics as bitcoin in that it is very volatile in the short term and its price tends to go upward in the long term, it has no limited supply.

ETHEREUM AND SMART CONTRACTS

After examining Bitcoin, which is seen as the first ever successful decentralized cryptocurrency, it is time to go through the next evolution, which came with Ethereum and smart contracts. Besides seeing what smart contracts are, it is vital to understand the different practical use cases of smart contracts, how they enable more complex cooperation between participants using the Ethereum blockchain, and how this more complex cooperation translates into social and cultural engagement. Finally, we'll reflect how and if smart contracts echo every type of money that has been discussed up to now in this chapter and what the implications of this might be in the decades to come.

What Are Smart Contracts?

Smart contracts are codified contracts made of code that can execute automatically without an intermediary when a function in the smart contract's code is triggered. In a nontechnical way, one could, in a way, see the function of the contract as a "term" in the contract.

Thus, a smart contract may be new and advanced as a technology in the sense that a contract can now be codified in code and stored on a blockchain where it gets all the properties of open public blockchains—if it were to be stored on a public blockchain that is—and executes when a function of the contract is called when terms or conditions are met. However, conceptually, a smart contract is as old as barter and primitive money since our ancestors used to enter contracts in terms of cooperating to transact goods and services with one another and cooperate in a community.

Bitcoin was the first successful crypto and digital currency or digital gold, depending on how one sees the technology and asset. Bitcoin also signaled a new form of contract but, at the same time, an ancient type of contract. As we saw earlier in the chapter, money is a contract of cooperation to trade between two parties who agree to use a specific currency or type of money to communicate, transact, and exchange value with one another. In the same way that our ancestors opted in when bartering to exchange eight chickens for one cow or six eggs for 1 liter of milk or different forms of primitive money, bitcoin can be seen as a new form of currency and contract that people can use. They can use this currency instead of any other currency to exchange and communicate value, goods, and services. This is true both on a human conceptual level and in code.

Bitcoin transactions can be seen as smart contracts, albeit weak, because Bitcoin is written in script. This simple programming language is not Turing complete. That is to say that bitcoin is naturally good in only one way: it sends value from one part of the world to another very quickly. However, you cannot use it on the protocol level for more complex contracts or cooperation unless you use protocols that are non-native to Bitcoin's protocol.

This was essentially Vitalik Buterin's—the founder of Ethereum—critique of Bitcoin before he invented Ethereum. Ethereum uses Solidity, among other languages that are Turing complete, allowing for much more sophisticated applications and cooperation between people across the globe without needing to meet each other in real life. Many applications are possible with smart contracts, and if I were to enumerate and name them here, I would need a whole new book just for that. Instead, I will give the big picture of what is possible.

Tokenization of Real-World Assets

The beginning of the chapter brought up the example of selling real estate. If one wants to sell a house, it can take months or even years because real estate is not as liquid as cash or its equivalents are. With smart contracts built on Ethereum, one can create cryptocurrencies on top of Ethereum that represent the house's value and make the asset liquid. For example, suppose a house is worth 100.000$, and one creates 100.000 cryptocurrency tokens to represent that house. In that case, they can have a value of 1 USD, and when someone buys that cryptocurrency for 1 USD, they own a small percent of the house. If they buy 1,000 tokens for 1,000 USD, they would own 1 percent of the house.

This could allow them to collect 1 percent of the monthly rent if someone in the house is renting it. Besides this, it globalizes the real estate market even further than it is now since someone in the United States could place the tokens in a smart contract to sell a house in a European country. Someone in India will go to this contract and buy the tokens. These tokens are called *fungible tokens* as they have equal value and are exchangeable with one another, just like 1 ether is fungible and can be exchanged for another ether.

Another form of tokenization is to represent the real estate as an NFT, go to an NFT marketplace, and list it for sale there, enabling people to buy the house in a global market rather than a localized one. Furthermore, the NFT can be tokenized into smaller pieces and become fungible if the owner of the NFT decides to do that in the future. In this case, it is an NFT, but can, through tokenization, transition into fungible tokens, the first form of tokenization.

SMART CONTRACT PRACTICAL APPLICATIONS

Example #1: Asset Tokenization

Propy is an American real estate tokenization platform. In 2022, a woman in Florida, United States, bought a tokenized physical home as an NFT for 653,000 USD through an online auction. The process entailed transferring the ownership of the house to a Limited Liability Company (LLC) and, from the LLC, transferring the ownership to the new owner. The old owner received the payment in a digital wallet.

This was one of the first use cases for selling a tokenized house. Since the legal system and people who still think in old ways are not yet prepared for such a change, an intermediary in the form of an LLC was necessary.

On the other hand, Red Swan CRE enables investors to have fractional ownership of real estate worldwide.

Example #2: Alcohol Tokenization

CryptoWine is an Austrian wine start-up that tokenizes bottles of Austrian and European wine as NFTs and stores them in the remote "private" cellar of the owner of the NFT. Therefore, whenever a buyer buys a wine on CryptoWine, they buy a digital representation and proof of ownership through the NFT of the wine, which they are free to keep for themselves, sell it to someone else, or gift it to a friend. When the owner of the wine clicks the digital NFT wine bottle and opens the bottle, the physical wine stored in the remote cellar is taken from the basement. It is shipped to the physical location of the owner of the NFT.

Example #3: Fundraising

Calladita by Miguel Faus is the first European movie funded entirely by smart contracts and NFTs. Buying NFTs raised money for the film through cryptocurrency for movie production. Depending on the NFTs to finance the movie, the investors can share profits from the movie, get access to the actors and stars of the film, or even decide on plot twists and how the story progresses in certain parts.

Such use cases will be especially valuable in the future when different book communities and fans will want to fund their favorite books and turn them into movies or fund fan-made, grassroots, low-budget short movies expanding their budget and allowing them to accomplish much more than they currently can accomplish with the low budget that they have.

Example #4: Digital Fashion

Mutani, a digital fashion start-up in Antwerp, Belgium, uses smart contracts and NFTs to create digital clothing for avatars and characters in video games and virtual reality. People can buy digital clothing, express themselves in fashion online, and let their avatars wear them. It is similar to skins in video games. Still, Antwerp is much more sophisticated in fashion as it is well known in Europe and worldwide for its fashion industry. In Mutani, some of the best fashion experts work on digital clothing.

Soon, when the Metaverse becomes more mainstream and usable, these clothes will be able to be used as assets and collateral for loans in cryptocurrencies and possibly even digital fiat currencies. Similarly, Louis Vuitton bags and clothing are considered assets, and their value may increase.

The same can be done with any in-game item, including fashion and clothing. If someone plays an RPG, they could use their digital weapons, armor, or other equipment as assets and sell them for cryptocurrency or as collateral for loans.

Example #5: Digital Books

Book.io is an online bookshop that sells e-books as NFTs. There are several differences between the e-books that Amazon sells and the books sold by Book.io. One of the differences is that the buyers of Book.io books truly own the books they buy. In contrast, people who buy e-books on Amazon buy a license to read the books. Still, at any moment, Amazon or any other seller of an e-book can revoke the access to the buyer of the book, be it because the book would not be available anymore from that particular seller or if the buyer has violated specific terms of the agreement they agree to at the beginning of when they sign up for their account. On Book.io, buying digital books is like purchasing a hardback or a paperback physical book that cannot be taken away from you. It is a digital book; hence, just like cryptocurrencies, they do not succumb to tear or wear.

Another interesting use case with book.io is that, unlike the licensed e-book versions of Amazon and other similar sellers of books, people can sell, lend, or donate their digital books to someone else. At the same time, authors and publishers can earn a percentage of the resale value to the secondary market, which they cannot do with hardback books if the owner decides to sell them to a thrift shop or someone else. Additionally, depending on how the publisher and the author manage the book, the value of the book when bought by the owner might increase instead of decrease since there are several things the author can do to increase the value of the book in the short term or long term such as giving a discount for his following books to the buyers of a specific limited edition of books or access to events or more content if they are educational books. Furthermore, the owners of a particular edition of books will have the opportunity to network with one another and earn the $Book token as they progress through the book's reading. At the same time, organizations and libraries can distribute digital books in bulk.

Example #6: Music

Violetta Zironi is an Italian singer, songwriter, and actor who sells her music directly to her fans through NFTs, allowing her to manage her community and fans directly without intermediaries. This allows her fans to manage her music as an asset. If a song or two of hers becomes popular or a hit, it will rise in value, and her fans can sell the digital NFT representing the song she created and profit from it. At the same time, she also gets a percent of the sale, transforming how she interacts with her fans, who can now be seen as investors in her music.

Additionally, in the future, she could seek the input of her community regarding songs or any other ventures she might pursue and allow her fans to benefit, too.

Example #7: Digital Art

One of the first NFT collections was the CryptoPunks, an experiment on NFTs of 10.000 pixelated people, which were given away for free as digital art. Depending on their rarity and features, they are now valued at millions of dollars. However, these pixelated digital people may not come close to the beauty of well-known physical and historical paintings. They are valued at such high prices due to the community value they provide and their historical significance since they were the first memorable NFT collection that worked out well and will always be considered one of the first digital art examples the world has ever seen. As NFT and digital art become more mainstream, we will see more sophisticated examples of digital art. Still, the CryptoPunks will remain in history due to their significance.

Example #8: Photography

I will not mention a specific use case for photography. Still, I will talk about potential use cases, such as having collections of photographs similar to having an exposé of art. Other use cases could be selling a photographer's photo of the year or giving access to additional content from the photographer who sells their photographs as NFTs.

Example #9: Customer Loyalty

Regarding customer loyalty, the hotel Le Bristol in France launched 11 NFT keys. The collection, called L'H3RITAGE CLUB, or in English, the Heritage Club, unlocks different experiences for its loyal customers and frequent travelers worldwide.

Holders of all 11 NFTs get:

➤ Access to the hotel's swimming pool for two people once a week

➤ Access to the secret dish at café Antonia by Chef Eric Frenchon that would be changed seasonally

➤ Access to a secret cocktail menu at the Bar du Bristol for four people

Additionally, each NFT has a unique perk depending on what the loyal customer may enjoy. Some of these perks include the following:

➤ A spa experience with a private swimming pool, aquatic massage, music, and champagne

➤ Chocolate masterclass

➤ Private vineyard tour

➤ Cooking masterclass in the three Michelin Star restaurant's kitchen

➤ Barbeque on the rooftop terrace of their Signature suite, "Suite Terrasse."

Example #10: Courses

In fall 2022, the University of Nicosia in Cyprus, Europe, organized the first course delivered on-chain and in the Metaverse on NFTs. Participants had to mint an NFT and hold it to access the course. Thereafter, the NFT becomes a digital item or artifact by which the university can engage the student community and holders—or ex-students—in diverse ways and maintain a relationship with them. They could even invite them to the university to network or give discounts on specific courses or other ways.

This is not only applicable to university courses but to any digital courses that can be given by a consultant or an expert on something. The NFT becomes the key by which the student or customer gets access to the course. Think of it as a digital badge that opens the door to the classroom of the digital course. Moreover, the students may use the NFT as an asset and trade it with or sell it to other potential and interested students, generating revenue for both the ex-student and the consultant/ teacher. The students of his classes or courses can get a discount on his consulting services, which adds a perpetual value to the NFT beyond the course and may incentivize either holding it or selling it to someone who may not only be interested in the course but also the consulting services of the consultant generating further revenue to the consultant.

Example #11: Decentralized Digital Identity

One of the problems we have in the digital age is that of data brokers and companies stealing their customers' data and selling it to third-party companies for profit, which kills the notion of privacy for those at least who value it. Smart contracts can be used to tokenize that data and put it on the blockchain and allow the owners of that data to manage the data as they see fit by allowing access to someone, be that a medical professional, for the reason they decide to do that instead of having companies bludgeoning the data without many times the known consent of the customer. Moreover, the customer may sell his data to a company or companies. Still, at least the customer will benefit economically and decide to do so in the first place through their agency.

Example #12: Membership NFTs

In December 2021, Flyfish Club Restaurant issued two collections of NFTs for their restaurant, which can be accessed only by people who own one NFT from either collection. One collection allows access to the restaurant's main room, while the second NFT provides access to another room. The customers are free to sell their NFTs, which enables the restaurant to benefit from loyalties.

This is a case of creating a restaurant membership through NFTs. Still, it can also be used for other businesses whose business models require memberships or are entirely based on membership, such as gyms.

DECENTRALIZED AUTONOMOUS ORGANIZATIONS

Decentralized autonomous organizations (DAOs) are organizations created through smart contracts. They have a decentralized type of governance powered by a predetermined codified smart contract(s), where the holders of the DAO's token can propose and vote on changes to the organization by calling functions that have been precoded. Chapter 13 discusses DAOs in depth.

The smart contracts of DAOs could be seen in a way as social contracts that we employ in our physical societies, such as laws, the constitution of a country, and how we govern ourselves with a representative democracy where we vote for our candidates. If our candidates gather enough votes, our ideas will have a place to be represented in our country's national parliament or senate. In principle, at least, we agreed to govern ourselves like that and are free to change what we do not like. Another social contract is the social structure of a business with its board of directors, CEO, and management. Fundamentally, these are societal (not smart yet) contracts we humans created and agreed upon mutually and collectively regarding how we will govern our society

DECENTRALIZED EXCHANGES

In the cryptocurrency industry, there are two types of exchanges: centralized exchanges (CEXs) such as Coinbase, Kraken, and Binance that are a bank's cryptocurrency equivalent; and decentralized exchanges. Decentralized exchanges (DEXs) don't have a centralized leader such as a CEO. Instead, the token holders spread across the world can propose changes and vote upon them. If a proposal gets enough votes (say 51 percent or more, although it can be coded to be depending on what people want to do), the change is implemented. A DEX is an automated market maker that allows one to exchange one type of token for another through algorithms and through using price feed oracles. (You can find more about oracles in Chapter 8.)

Several decentralized exchanges, including Uniswap, built on Ethereum, allow users to exchange their cryptocurrency for another cryptocurrency in a centralized exchange. However, it is worth noting that Uniswap is currently allowing only the swapping of ERC-20 tokens and ERC-721 NFTs—more on these technical terms in later chapters. This means only tokens built on Ethereum and not on any other blockchain can be swapped and traded. For example, Bitcoin cannot be exchanged for ether. Still, ether can be swapped for UNI, the governance token of Uniswap, and vice versa. It is also worth noting that this is not because Uniswap does not want to but because of current technological limitations. To bring in a previous example of tokenized real estate, be it in fungible fractionalized ownership form of 100,000 tokens or a single NFT representing a piece of real estate. In the future, it would be entirely possible to have the real estate NFTs and fungible fractionalized tokens be on Uniswap and people swapping one for the other or even 1 NFT for the real estate NFT if they want.

In addition to helping with cryptocurrency swaps, Uniswap gives grants in cryptocurrency to expand the Ethereum network and enhances Uniswap. This can include building something that is required by the network, organizing an event, educating people, and other things. Uniswap also hires people for the jobs that cannot be automated by a DAO or a smart contract, such as community management, business development, and so forth. It is worth noting that many of these roles are not necessarily decision-making roles for the organization as the token holders determine this, and the people being recruited for a job are seen more in a "caretaker" role. It is common for them to have job titles such as Community Steward or Ecosystem Steward.

Lending/Borrowing: Aave

Another DAO built on Ethereum is Aave. Aave works similarly to Uniswap, hiring people and giving grants. Still, the difference between Aave and Uniswap is that Aave is a peer-to-peer lending and borrowing protocol that creates a global borrowing and lending market. One person in the United States could deposit a cryptocurrency in Aave's smart contract. A person from India or anywhere else worldwide could borrow this deposited cryptocurrency as quickly as sending an email from Japan or South Africa to the United States or Brazil.

Travala

Another DAO built on the Binance smart chain and not Ethereum is Travala. Travala is a decentralized traveling agency that allows its customers and community to buy flight tickets and book hotels with cryptocurrency. The AVA token allows for the protocol's governance and discount bookings if paid with the AVA token. Additionally, Travala is using NFTs for customer loyalty with discounts, customer engagement, rewards, and gifts.

VitaDAO

VitaDAO is a decentralized autonomous organization that funds research on human longevity technology and tokenizes its intellectual property. Most of VitaDAO's community comprises of academics, medical doctors, and scientists worldwide in longevity-related fields—although anyone can join the DAO. Vita token holders decide on what research proposals to invest in and, in exchange, negotiate with the scientist a percentage of the intellectual property to be owned by the DAO. The DAO then uses that research to launch longevity start-ups.

BeerDAO

BeerDAO is a decentralized autonomous organization that has tokenized a beer brand. Whoever worldwide owns the NFT of the DAO owns part of the beer brand and is free to produce and sell this beer wherever they are.

CityDAO

CityDAO is a DAO that has bought a plot of land in Wyoming, United States, and is building a "city" on it. In essence, the DAO collectively manages the land through proposals and votes. Each NFT represents a "citizenship" to the DAO, and each citizen has one vote regarding managing the land/city. The citizens of CityDAO are also currently experimenting with what is known as the Harberger tax, a new property tax idea proposed by Arnold Harberger, an American economist.

CRYPTOCURRENCIES AND SMART CONTRACTS: CONCLUSION

There are many more DAOs and smart contract applications, enough that a whole book could be written about them. Additionally, there are the societal and economic implications of each smart contract use case. But this book is about Solidity and how to develop these smart contracts, so the previous examples serve to showcase and educate about the potential uses of smart contracts and cryptocurrencies. This should help you understand what it is you are building when you're developing smart contracts and cryptocurrencies. However, later in the book there will be a deeper dive into decentralized finance to give a better understanding of the technicalities behind smart contracts.

As promised at the beginning of the chapter, here is a definition of money based on this chapter and its content:

> Money is a complex technology and language humans use to communicate and facilitate the exchange of value governed by mutually agreed-upon protocols within or between different communities. It serves as a medium of exchange, a unit of account, and a store of value, representing the properties of durability, transportability, divisibility, fungibility, scarcity, and acceptability. Historically, money has gone through different evolutions, from barter to physical commodities to coins, paper, and digital forms of money. Cryptocurrencies and smart contracts reflect economic, social, political, and cultural dimensions. Money's purpose lies in its ability to represent and communicate the perceived value of goods and services between two or more parties, acting as a contract that organizes, stabilizes, and enables economic activities across different scales and eras.

Money further evolves from its traditional boundaries regarding cryptocurrencies and smart contracts. It now incorporates decentralization, transparency, and programmability principles, potentially reshaping economic, governance, and social contracts in the digital age.

In this chapter, we saw the history of money and contracts and their evolution throughout human history and various societies and how, through the evolution of money and contracts, humanity's political structures, as well as the structures that facilitate cooperation, changed, and how our economic system evolved to be what it is today and how cryptocurrencies hold the next evolution of money and potentially social and political structures. In a later chapter, we will see more examples of smart contracts and how they are being used in a specialized field of finance created by cryptocurrencies and smart contracts called decentralized finance. Chapter 2 will dive deeper into how Ethereum works under the hood before getting our hands dirty with Solidity.

CHAPTER 1 QUESTIONS

1. Explain bitcoin's fixed supply model and its halving schedule. How does this differ from traditional monetary policies?

2. Define smart contracts, and explain how they differ from traditional contracts. What are their key advantages?

3. What are the three main properties of money? For each property, explain how bitcoin and ether fulfill or fail to fulfill them.

4. Describe how asset tokenization works in real estate. What are the key benefits and challenges?

5. What is a DAO? Explain its governance structure and provide an example of a real-world DAO.

6. Compare and contrast centralized exchanges with decentralized exchanges. What are the key technological limitations of DEXs?

7. How do primitive forms of money like whale teeth and shells compare to modern cryptocurrencies in terms of the properties of money?

8. Explain how the Bretton Woods system worked and how its collapse led to the current fiat system.

9. What are the security features of the Bitcoin and Ethereum networks? How do they maintain network integrity?

10. Describe how fractional reserve banking emerged historically and its relationship to modern banking.

11. What role do NFTs play in digital identity and customer loyalty programs? Provide specific examples.

12. How does Aave's peer-to-peer lending system work, and how does it differ from traditional banking?

13. Explain the concept of fungibility in both traditional and crypto contexts. How do fungible and nonfungible tokens differ?

14. What were the limitations of the barter system, and how did they lead to the development of primitive money?

15. How have cultural and societal values historically influenced the acceptance and evolution of different forms of money? Provide examples from the text.

2

An Introduction to Ethereum's Architecture

This chapter explores the fundamental architecture of Ethereum, using the analogy of a distributed Excel spreadsheet to demystify blockchain concepts. You'll discover how Ethereum evolved beyond Bitcoin's limitations to become a "world computer" capable of running complex applications. Through practical examples, such as comparing a vending machine to smart contracts, you'll grasp how Ethereum's components work together to enable decentralized applications.

Imagine trying to build a global financial application that needs to be trustless, transparent, and accessible to everyone. How would you ensure that transactions are valid without relying on a central authority? How would you handle the competing demands of security, scalability, and decentralization? This chapter addresses these challenges by explaining Ethereum's architecture, from its consensus mechanism to its scaling solutions.

By understanding the concepts presented in this chapter, you will gain essential knowledge about Ethereum's infrastructure that will serve as a foundation for developing smart contracts and decentralized applications. You'll learn about real-world challenges such as gas fees and scalability, and you'll explore how solutions such as Layer 2 protocols and rollups are being developed to address these limitations. Whether you're building financial applications, voting systems, or digital identity solutions, understanding Ethereum's architecture is crucial for creating efficient and secure blockchain applications.

BASICS OF ETHEREUM

At its most basic, Ethereum and any other blockchain can be seen as a ledger, a digital ebook, or a file, with Excel sheets containing transactions of varying complexity, such as sending, lending, borrowing money, and other more complex transactions between different parties. These are the fund balances of each person who has executed one of these transactions as well as their

International Bank Account Number (IBAN) (their wallet or account address). Instead of being owned by one person, these Excel sheets are distributed among a number of people across the planet who have the sheets on their computers. Their computers communicate automatically through the Internet about the state of these Excel sheets (or the book with the transactions). Their communication aims to keep the transactions in the book or the sheets intact. If one of the computers—also called *nodes*—decides to change the state of the sheets by removing or changing a transaction, the rest of the computers in the network will communicate that action to each other. They will identify that the changed version of the Excel sheets is invalid and reject it. The Excel sheets of the malicious and fraudulent computer will then be out of sync with the other computers' version. The rest of the computers will continue operating as usual and continue communicating with one another about the state of the ledger or the Excel sheets.

Some of the computers mentioned can be special "validators." Every 12 seconds (approximately), they can take a number of the transactions in the Excel sheets, put them in a block together, and validate them, confirming that the transactions did take place. The block of transactions, in this case, can be seen as one of the Excel sheets or one page of the transactions in the book being validated by the computer. A computer signs a contract that commits a sum of money up front as a guarantee that it will not cheat. It then signals to other computers that it has taken a number of nonvalidated transactions from the mempool—a list of the newest and nonvalidated transactions—and validated a number of them by creating a block, stamping it as validated, and adding a hash, which is a unique identifier that also references the previous block (similar to a page in a ledger or Excel sheet) created by another computer 12 seconds earlier. This process links all the blocks together in a chain-like fashion. The other computers in the network communicate to verify that the validating computer followed the rules and did not cheat. If the validation is confirmed, the block of transactions is accepted as legitimate. The computer that performed the validation is rewarded: it receives a payment that includes a small fee from users whose transactions were validated (based on their complexity, also known as *gas fees*), a reward from the system itself (called the *block reward*), and the return of the money it initially put up as a guarantee.

This is what Vitalik Buterin in 2015 envisioned as a "world computer." These computers can be seen as one significant merged Ethereum.

Ethereum is a decentralized platform that enables the creation and execution of smart contracts—the complex transactions mentioned earlier—and the development of decentralized applications (dApps). dApps typically consist of multiple smart contracts bundled together, along with a user interface that allows people to interact with them. Ethereum relies on its blockchain—the Excel sheets described earlier—to secure its network. This involves a chain of blocks, a distributed network of computers (or nodes), and a validation system, as previously explained. Additionally, Ethereum ensures network state synchronization, meaning all computers in the network maintain an identical and accurate version of the blockchain (or Excel sheets).

Ethereum has its native cryptocurrency, Ether. Ether is used to pay fees to the validator computers that process and validate transactions. These fees are paid by the individuals initiating the transactions. Additionally, Ether is used as collateral by validator computers to ensure they remain honest in the validation process. This activity and process is also known as *staking*.

You can think of Ethereum as an Internet framework that operates without any centralized intermediaries or administrators. It is kept alive and running through many computers that connect to its network by downloading the Ethereum blockchain, performing smart contract calculations, and maintaining the network through synchronization. This method of running Internet applications directly on the blockchain is independent of private technology companies and service providers such as Google or Amazon.

As noted in Chapter 1, the founder of Ethereum, Vitalik Buterin, released a whitepaper in 2014 called the Ethereum white paper, where he criticized Bitcoin's limits regarding its scripting language. Bitcoin suffers from several issues:

➤ Bitcoin is not **Turing complete**: Bitcoin's language and script are suitable for basic transactions but are not good enough to create sophisticated applications and transactions, as the language cannot do all the calculations necessary to host dApps.

➤ Bitcoin suffers from **value blindness,** and its code comprises scripts that cannot evaluate transaction values. A Bitcoin script cannot compare transaction amounts. For example, a script cannot natively say "Only enable this transaction if it is less than 0.5 BTC," as the coding language is not that sophisticated. This prevents Bitcoin from natively creating dApps that make decisions based on transaction values.

➤ Bitcoin lacks **state**. This means Bitcoin lacks the means to track and store the state of complex applications. When Bitcoin processes a transaction, it does so independently without its system having a built-in way to "remember" previous transactions. This makes it especially difficult to create applications where one might need to track current balances, maintain user information, or handle even more complex processes.

➤ Bitcoin suffers from **blockchain blindness,** and its scripts cannot interact with or understand blockchain data beyond simple transactions. For example, Bitcoin's code cannot read block numbers (block heights), request historical blockchain information, or verify information about the state of its blockchain.

Ethereum was designed to overcome these limitations. Ethereum's initial vision was broad and all-encompassing in terms of the applications you can build using its technology—it is, however, worth noting that Ethereum is still a work in progress and will still be receiving updates until the project is considered complete. (More about that at the end of this chapter.)

Ethereum can be used to build the following:

➤ **Strict financial applications:** Ethereum's technology enables the creation of many financial services, from simple cryptocurrency transactions—like bitcoin's—to more sophisticated applications such as decentralized finance. These more sophisticated applications offer services such as creating your own cryptocurrency token and lending, borrowing, and managing general assets without the need for traditional financial intermediaries. Moreover, Ethereum allows for asset tokenization, which is a practice of creating or breaking an asset into digital tokens, either one whole token that cannot be broken—a nonfungible token (NFT)—or by creating a fungible token similar to bitcoin or ether and representing the value of the asset in percentages of the total supply of tokens. For example, if 100 fungible tokens were to be created representing a car, each fungible token would represent 1 percent of the car's value. Fungible tokens are helpful as they enable fractional ownership and improve liquidity—treating the tokens as cash or readily convertible to cash.

➤ **Nonfinancial applications**: Besides financial applications, Ethereum can facilitate nonfinancial applications related to data. One such use case is digital identity management, which puts the user in ownership and charge of their data while at the same time ensuring that the data cannot be changed and can be verified—with the user's consent—by institutions and sectors such as banks, hospitals, and the healthcare sector more broadly as well as government services among others. (Sending data, after all, can be seen as transactions.) Another crucial nonfinancial application is for online voting systems. Ethereum can enhance transparency, reduce voting fraud, and create entirely new decentralized governance models on the platform. These in turn can lead to more inclusive and democratic processes, facilitating collective decision-making within organizations and political systems as well. The digital identity use case and the voting and new governance use case can be unified such that one uses their digital identity to access a voting system on a specific topic and cast their vote.

Ethereum, just like Bitcoin, has the following properties as a blockchain:

➤ Ethereum is **permissionless** and **open-source**, enabling everyone to access, build, and participate in its network and services without permission. This allows for unparalleled innovation and collaboration without needing the approval or supervision of a central authority.

➤ Ethereum is **borderless**, which allows for global financial digital activities bypassing traditional banking systems and infrastructure while reducing complexities and costs—in theory, at least, it is a work in progress.

➤ Ethereum is **censorship-resistant**. Censorship resistance ensures freedom from external control or manipulation by a centralized entity that would otherwise control the transactions. This includes powerful parties such as governments and large corporations.

➤ Ethereum is **immutable**, as it is impossible to reverse or change transactions or their details once the network has executed and finalized them. In theory, it is possible, but the possibility of that happening is almost zero. The more blocks are added after one executed transaction, the more difficult it is to reverse. It is more profitable for someone to play by the rules and stake their coins and get a reward based on this than try to cheat and reverse a transaction. Even then, the capital you would need to do something like this would be vast, which would have to be spent constantly whenever someone would want to reverse a transaction, and there would be no return on investment to speak of for doing this, unlike from staking.

➤ Ethereum is **transparent**. One may hear that blockchain either builds trust or is trustless. Both expressions refer to the same phenomenon of blockchain being transparent and anyone being able to inspect transactions—the practicalities of that can be found in Chapter 3. By being able to examine the transactions, one does not need to trust a party as to whether an event took place on the blockchain. They simply need to ask for the transaction ID or hash of the transaction and can use a block explorer to check for themselves. Additionally, that helps with reducing fraud and having openly auditable transaction records.

➤ Ethereum is **global**. Its operations go beyond the reach of a specific national jurisdiction, creating an attractive international community of developers, users, and investors.

➤ Ethereum is **decentralized**. It is maintained by a distributed network of computers known as nodes, which eliminates centralized control or the need for a "supercomputer" that gives access to other computers to manage or maintain the network. The more nodes in the network, the more secure, resilient, and trustless the Ethereum network becomes.

THE BLOCKCHAIN TRILEMMA

One of the main limitations blockchains have is what Vitalik Buterin coined the "blockchain trilemma" theory. The blockchain trilemma states that any blockchain—Ethereum included—can, with the technology available today, excel in only two out of the following three functions:

➤ **Scalability:** The ability to process tens of thousands or hundreds of thousands of transactions per second (TPS)

➤ **Security:** Having the blockchain's network be secure and free of malicious attacks

➤ **Decentralization:** The ability to have no central entity or a small number of entities control the blockchain network

A blockchain can be scalable and secure but not decentralized, decentralized and secure but not scalable (which is Ethereum's case at the moment), or decentralized and scalable but not secure and thus very open to attacks.

SMART CONTRACTS

The main component differentiating Ethereum from Bitcoin is the smart contracts Ethereum can support natively. But what are smart contracts?

Smart contracts are self-executing contracts where the terms of an agreement between a set of parties are written and embedded into code instead of a standard legal document. They are immutable and deterministic—predetermined or preprogrammed to execute in a certain way—computer programs. Smart contracts operate within the Ethereum Virtual Machine (EVM), which allows them to run in a decentralized infrastructure, often referred to as the world computer mentioned in the "Basics of Ethereum" section.

A physical analog to a smart contract would be the vending machine. When someone inserts a coin, they can choose the drink or other item they like, and the machine will dispense it. The machine has been preprogrammed to do this repeatedly until it runs out of items, after which someone replenishes the supply. A smart contract is similar: it is programmed to execute the same functions repeatedly without end, but it does not need to be replenished.

From the vending machine's perspective, it could be characterized as a "smart" contract with a bearer. That is, the contract has been programmed to execute with anyone who holds a coin of monetary value.

In essence, smart contracts have four properties that one should always keep in mind:

➤ A smart contract is a computer program that represents a digital self-executable contract.

➤ Once a smart contract has been deployed on the blockchain, its code becomes immutable. Any desired changes to the smart contract require deploying an entirely new contract, which distinguishes it from traditional software.

➤ Smart contracts are deterministic, meaning they will consistently execute similarly for all users. Unless a new contract is deployed, they have been preprogrammed, and no changes are possible.

➤ Smart contracts are executed within the EVM. Consequently, their context is quite limited: a smart contract can access its internal state, the details of the transactions that triggered a function within the contract, and blockchain data, but other than that, it operates in an isolated environment.

Smart contracts have several pros and cons, as well as challenges, as shown in Table 2.1.

TABLE 2.1: Pros and cons of smart contracts

PROS	CONS
Practical: Through their automation, smart contracts reduce the need for human intervention in their operations.	**Lack of expertise:** Smart contracts are still quite a new technology, and hence, it is difficult to find good technical experts with deep knowledge of the subject.
No or reduced intermediaries: Through their automation, smart contracts either eliminate or, in some cases, reduce the dependency on traditional intermediaries—depending on the use case—which saves costs and streamlines processes.	**Dependence on inputs:** Smart contracts may rely on external data sources such as oracles (see Chapter 8), which may introduce potential failures if these external data sources are centralized.
Transparent: Transactions are recorded on a public blockchain, providing a transparent history that anyone can see and audit.	**Lack of privacy:** On the other end of transparency is the lack of privacy. Since every transaction, asset, amount, and address is visible to the public, there is a severe concern about privacy. Thankfully, some solutions are being worked on to solve this challenge. They will be mentioned later in the chapter.
Trustless transactions: Smart contracts allow parties that do not trust or necessarily know one another to transact as the code and the blockchain enforce the execution.	**Scalability:** Scalability issues may arise, especially in Ethereum's case, as it falls in the decentralization and security part of the blockchain trilemma. However, solutions have been worked on regarding this challenge as well. They will be mentioned later in this chapter.

PROS	CONS
Immutability: Once deployed, the code of a smart contract cannot change unless a whole new version is deployed.	**Immutability:** Code immutability is a two-sided coin. It can also mean rectifying bugs and problems that might be detected only after the contract is deployed, which is difficult to do.
Security: Smart contracts, among other things, use cryptography and blockchain properties to construct a secure environment.	**Security:** The contract code is public and thus can be read by malicious actors, and it is difficult to rectify deployed contract bugs and mistakes. As a result, security vulnerabilities surface that hackers and malicious individuals can exploit.
Programmability: A smart contract before deployment can be flexible and programmable, allowing for complex executable functions.	
Speed: Smart contracts usually settle transactions faster than traditional systems, especially cross-border payments or operations.	
Accessible globally: A smart contract is accessible to anyone, regardless of where they are or travel. A local bank in the United States might not be available if one person moves to Europe. Still, a smart contract is globally accessible to everyone.	

In addition to the pros and cons, these additional challenges exist:

➤ **Emerging technologies:** New technological advancements in the Web3 and blockchain industry and other sectors, such as quantum computing and artificial intelligence (AI), may lead to advancements that necessitate updates to smart contracts already deployed and smart contract standards themselves. There will be more on smart contract standards later in the book.

➤ **The complexity of debugging:** Debugging smart contracts can be seen as more difficult due to the immutable nature of the blockchain, which does not forgive if a bug has not been identified or fixed beforehand. This adds pressure to find all bugs before deployment, whereas in traditional software, fixing bugs is much easier due to the technology's mutability.

➤ **Limited legal precedent:** Smart contracts are a new technology not legally recognized in many jurisdictions.

Decentralized applications run on a peer-to-peer network—a network with no intermediaries—called a *blockchain*. This means no single person or entity has control of the network or the application.

If they do, it should not be considered peer-to-peer. For something to be considered a dApp, the following must be true:

➤ It must be open-source and operate independently without any single party controlling it.

➤ Its record and data must be public.

➤ It must use a token to keep the network secure.

Mobile games, financial applications, and others can be examples of dApps. When people talk about "decentralized finance," they speak—whether they realize it or not—just about a specific subset of these apps.

As will be seen in the discussion of decentralized autonomous organizations in Chapter 13, "Decentralized Autonomous Organization," the community—the collection of users of a dApp—can be given the governance of the dApp's future behavior through so-called governance tokens. Essentially, those bestow voting rights.

THE ETHEREUM VIRTUAL MACHINE

Ethereum has two types of wallets: externally owned accounts (EOAs) and contract accounts. The EOAs are opened, used, and operated by everyday users. In contrast, the smart contract and its code operate the contract accounts executed by the EVM.

At the beginning of the chapter, Ethereum was mentioned as a world computer that has no central authority running it but instead has a vast number of computers that connect to its network by downloading the Ethereum blockchain and running smart contracts, and the whole Ethereum system by performing smart contract calculations and maintaining the network through synchronization. This, as a whole, in the way Ethereum works is the EVM.

THE ETHER COIN

The native coin of the Ethereum blockchain is called ether. Ether uses the ticker ETH and is referred to with the Greek letter Ξ, which, while in Greek is pronounced as ksee, in blockchain speak, it is pronounced as an E.

Ether, like bitcoin, can be subdivided into smaller units, with the smallest unit being called a *wei*. An Ether is made out of 1 quintillion wei, or, more importantly, to remember for later in the book, 18 zeros after a 1, in other words, 1,000,000,000,000,000,000. Ether powers all applications that run on the Ethereum blockchain, from simple transactions to complex decentralized applications, and it is the currency with which one pays gas fees—the unit of measurement by which computational energy on the Ethereum blockchain is used to process and validate transactions.

All ether's units include the following:

➤ An ether (ETH) is equal to 1,000,000,000,000,000,000 (18 zeros) wei—the smallest unit of Ether.

➤ A milliether is equal to 1,000,000,000,000,000 (15 zeros) wei.

➤ A microether is equal to 1,000,000,000,000 (12 zeros) wei. (This is also called a Szabo—a reference to Nick Szabo, a computer scientist and legal scholar who created the first smart contracts.)

➤ A gwei is equal to 1,000,000,000 (9 zeros) wei. (This is also called a Shannon—a reference to Claude Shannon, an American mathematician and cryptographer known as the father of information theory, which was the ancestor of what is today known as computer science and cryptography.)

➤ A mwei equals 1,000,000 (6 zeros) wei. (This is also called Lovelace—a reference to Ada Lovelace, considered the first computer programmer.)

➤ A kwei is equal to 1,000 (3 zeros) wei. (This is also called a Babbage—a reference to Charles Babbage, known as the father of the computer)

➤ A wei is equal to 1 wei.

THE BYZANTINE GENERAL'S PROBLEM AND ETHEREUM'S CONSENSUS MECHANISM

One of the fundamental problems in computer science is the Byzantine General's problem, which reflects the problem of trust in a distributed system with no central authority to enforce rules, such as, in this case, a blockchain. The participants in the distributed system struggle to agree about what is true due to a lack of trust, technical failures, and misinformation.

Satoshi Nakamoto was the first to solve this problem by reaching a consensus through bitcoin's proof-of-work (PoW) mechanism. Proof of stake (PoS) is an alternative consensus mechanism that solves the same problem but in a different way than PoW. Validating in PoS is the process by which new blocks are added to the blockchain, and new units of Ether are minted into the economy.

Proof of stake as a consensus mechanism requires that a validator—the node/computer/person behind the computer who adds a block to the blockchain—lock some of their money into a smart contract as a guarantee that they will be truthful, be selected randomly by several validators that did the same thing, and then add the block of transactions to continue the chain of blocks. When a validator wants to add a block to the chain, the block is first broadcast to the other Ethereum network nodes and simply runs the blockchain to maintain the network. A new block is added approximately every 12 seconds.

The nodes then initiate a process called *gossiping* (communication between nodes). This involves automatically exchanging information with one another within seconds, across the globe. The goal is to synchronize and verify whether the validator is being truthful by adding the block to the chain without attempting to cheat. Once the nodes agree on the one actual state of the blockchain, the validator adds the block to the chain and gets his reward, which consists of fees and a block reward. If the validator lies, the money he put into the smart contract as a guarantee gets slashed or forfeited.

To stake, one requires 32 ETH, although there are currently conversations about reducing it to 1 ETH. People who do not have 32 Ξ create what are known as staking pools. That is, they pool their ETH together to get to 32 Ξ and then share the rewards proportionally to their staked amount.

When a validator adds a block to the blockchain, it usually takes about 12 minutes to reach finality. *Finality* means that a block and its transactions are considered irreversible and permanent.

Ethereum has two major types of nodes or computers:

➤ **Full nodes:** These nodes store the history of the Ethereum blockchain by downloading it on their computer. They verify all the transactions and blocks being validated onto the blockchain and maintain the most decentralization out of all the nodes in the network. The downside of someone being a full node is that they would require a substantial hard drive memory capacity to become one, as currently the Ethereum blockchain is more than 1 TB. With each new added and finalized block, the 1 TB grows. Full nodes are desktop computers and laptops with large memory or an external drive that allows them to run the blockchain and store the whole history of the Ethereum blockchain. There are two types of full nodes:

➤ **Archive nodes:** Archive nodes have the entire transaction history of the Ethereum blockchain from the genesis block—the very first block created—up to the most recent one and validate each block, block by block. The whole version of the Ethereum network these nodes store is terabytes big and not attractive for the everyday user to download as it requires a substantial hard drive capacity to download them.

➤ **Standard full nodes:** Standard full nodes validate downloading a much smaller version of the blockchain, usually the most recent 128 blocks, and allow the rest to be deleted to save space but still validate block to block, just like archive nodes. If standard full nodes need older data, they can still retrieve it by re-downloading it.

GAS FEES

Gas in Ethereum refers to a unit measuring the computational resources required to execute specific operations. Since computers perform computational work to manage transactions and smart contracts, these resources must be paid for to prevent Ethereum from receiving spam transactions and overwhelming the network. The payments are measured and made in a gas fee(s).

The gas fee is the amount of gas one uses to execute operations multiplied by the cost per unit of gas. Gas fees are paid in Ether, Ethereum's native currency, and the prices are quoted in gwei, one of the lower denominations of Ether. A gwei is equal to a billionth of an ether. This helps, as instead of saying that your transaction's cost was 0.000000001 ether, one can say it was instead one gwei.

The total gas a user pays is divided into the *base fee* and the *priority fee*. Imagine a person going to a restaurant and ordering food. The base fee is the fee the person pays for the price of the food on the menu. In contrast, the priority fee is the tip given to the waiter/validator to choose to include your transaction in the block first or to serve your food first. This is an automated process; hence, the tip does not go to a person in the traditional sense as giving a fee to a human but rather to the protocol as it has been preprogrammed to act in such a way.

When a user sends a transaction, they can choose the amount of gas they are willing to pay for a transaction they want to be appended to the blockchain as part of a block. This can be seen in Figure 2.1, which shows the MetaMask wallet—installing the wallet and explaining how to use it will take place in Chapter 3.

FIGURE 2.1: Gas fees demonstration

In the left-hand image, one is trying to send a 0.001 ETH to another address and can see the fee. The MetaMask wallet automatically estimates the transaction to be accepted, and it will take approximately 60 seconds for the transaction to be processed. If you click the pen across the "Estimated Fee," you are transported to the middle image. There, you can see at the very bottom that the base fee is five gwei and, a priority fee would take between 0 to 2 gwei and that the gas fees at the time of taking the picture were extremely high, probably due to the high usage of the network.

On the top of the center image, you can choose three predefined priority fees. One on the Aggressive end, meaning that the fee will be the highest of the three and will be executed in approximately 15 seconds, another paying the market rate, which would take 60 seconds to be executed, and finally, low, which will take more than 60 seconds to be processed. Clicking the "Advanced" cog wheel will transfer you to the right-hand image.

There, you can manually choose how much gwei you will pay. You can see a max base fee of 7.8+ gwei, while the base fee in the center image is 5 gwei. The 2.8+ gwei difference in the fee is a range. The base fee changes every 12 seconds as a new block is appended onto the blockchain. A new base fee is calculated—automatically not by a person but by the protocol a person is using—and the difference makes up for any potential increases in gwei when the transaction is sent to the validator to be processed and appended. Thus, although the base fee might be 5, by the time the transaction is sent, it might be 6 or 7. In that case, it is still within the 7.8+ range. However, the transaction would not have been sent if it had been more than that.

Additionally, you can see the priority fee below the max base fee and manually change it. If the priority fee is 0, then there is very little chance that the transaction will be appended as part of a block on the blockchain, and it will simply fail. The same applies to the max base fee. The transaction will fail if the base fee exceeds the market rate. If the demand to use the Ethereum blockchain is high, then the base and priority fees will be equally higher than those shown earlier. If the market to use it is lower, then the fees drop.

The equation for the calculation of the Gwei fee is as follows:

$$\text{units of gas used} * (\text{base fee} + \text{priority fee})$$

Thus, if the units of gas used were 20,000, the base fee was 5, and the priority fee was 3—remember, in equations, brackets with the addition are calculated first and then the multiplication:

$$20,000 * (10 + 2) = 240,000 \text{gwei}$$

In short, 240,000 would be 0,0024 ETH or, at the time of writing, 58 cents in USD terms.

The size of each block has a capacity of 15 million gas. However, the size of the block will increase to 30 million gas if the market's demand is required to use the Ethereum blockchain. At 15 million gas, the block achieves an equilibrium in size. If the block size of gas is higher than 15 million, the base fee will increase, whereas if it is lower than 15 million, it will decrease. The proportion of decreases and increases in terms of adjustment depends on how far the current block being appended onto the blockchain is from the 15 million equilibrium.

Gas fees are crucial for smart contract development. The more complex and heavy a smart contract is designed, written, and deployed, the more gas fees users will pay to have their transaction processed.

THE SCALING PROBLEM OF ETHEREUM

Two of the problems mentioned earlier in Table 2.1 were privacy and scalability. If we are to recall Buterin's trilemma triangle, Ethereum falls into the decentralized and secure blockchains.

Although Ethereum is decentralized and secure, it is not scalable. Its Layer 1 infrastructure—everything described in this chapter about how Ethereum works is called Layer 1—supports only up to 20 TPS. Compared to companies such as Mastercard, which can handle up to 38,000 TPS, and Visa, which can manage 65,000 TPS, Ethereum lacks competitiveness.

Ethereum has only 20 TPS, which has consequences for its gas fees (see Figure 2.2). When there is a high demand to use the Ethereum blockchain, the transactions become more expensive, as the equilibrium of the 15 million gas is exceeded near to or to its limit of 30 million gas. In addition to this, many people enter into a bidding war by offering an ever-increasing amount as the priority fee to the validator to include their transaction in the block to be appended.

Consider an example in which the priority fee is 1.5 gwei, with 100 people entering into a bidding war. The first bidder bids one gwei more than the 1.5 starting point. Then each person after that bids one gwei more than the previous person. The priority fee has already risen 100 times in price to get the transaction included in the next block. This situation becomes even worse if the number of people is 1,000 or 10,000 as the price grows exponentially. In Figure 2.2, we see specific peaks during high usage time. The biggest peak was an average price of 939 gwei. The highest price one paid to have their transaction processed that day was 36.267,774+ gwei, which translates into 0.036+ ether.

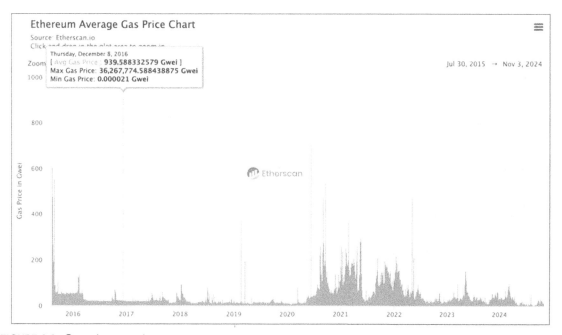

FIGURE 2.2: Gas price over time

If you translate 0.036+ ether to USD, that would be almost 90 USD at the time of this writing—you can search for online converters of gwei to ether and from ether to USD if you want to do similar conversions. This example shows that on that day, someone paid nearly 90 USD to send money from one wallet to another. This is the equivalent of going to the supermarket to buy tomatoes, which would cost around 6 USD per kilo in total, but having to pay 90 USD on top for your payment to be processed, ending up spending 96 USD for a kilo of tomatoes.

This is not sustainable in the long term. If people have to pay anything near or even far from 90 USD—even 5 or 10 USD—then they would no longer be using the Ethereum blockchain. As a consequence, a number of different solutions are currently being worked on Ethereum and other blockchains to scale them. As this book is about Solidity and Ethereum specifically, the solutions discussed are for the Ethereum blockchain. That does not mean the exact solutions are not being worked on in other blockchains. Many other blockchains use the same or a similar strategy to Ethereum to scale their blockchains. However, it does mean that solutions unique to other blockchains will not be mentioned as they are not in the plans currently to be implemented on Ethereum. Although Layer 2 solutions are the main scaling solutions topic discussed, Ethereum might explore and scale its Layer 1 base chain in the future as well, but there are no immediate plans for scaling its Layer 1 currently.

LAYER 2 SOLUTIONS

Layer 2 refers to solutions and frameworks that offer different transaction execution environments for Ethereum transactions that are currently being developed to address Ethereum's scalability problem. They are called Layer 2 as they are operating on top of Ethereum. Each Layer 2 solution—or most of them—uses different techniques and strategies to take the transactions of Ethereum and process them outside the main chain to take off some of the burdens of the main chain, increasing TPS and reducing gas fees when it comes to using the blockchain for different operations overall while not compromising security.

The different techniques used vary, and they can incorporate side-chains and rollups. The connection between Layer 1 and Layer 2 solutions is made through smart contracts that serve as "bridges." This happens because users deposit assets into a contract whose purpose is to act as a bridge from Layer 1. The contract locks the assets deposited, and an equivalent contract on Layer 2 mints cryptocurrencies that represent the locked assets on Layer 1.

Several different Layer 2 solutions are currently being built; they are discussed in the following sections.

Rollups

Rollups execute transactions outside the main blockchain—what is also called *off-chain*—and then combine all these transactions into a batch. While the transaction data is processed and stored off the main chain, the results of those transactions are published on the main blockchain. This method significantly reduces pressure on the main chain. It allows for more transactions to be processed in a shorter time.

There are two different types of rollups, each with its own method of processing transactions as well as advantages and disadvantages:

➤ **Optimistic rollups:** Assume transactions are valid by default and run calculations only in the event of a dispute.

   ➤ Optimistic rollups use the Optimistic Virtual Machine (OVM), which is compatible with the EVM; as a consequence, they can work together. The OVM processes transactions off-chain, reducing the costs of calculating them as the OVM assumes they are valid.

   ➤ After the transactions are processed off-chain, the OVM calculates a state root—a complex number—that represents the updated state of the ledger.

   ➤ Advanced cryptographic techniques such as SNARKs and STARKs produce proofs that validate the correctness of the off-chain calculations.

   ➤ The state root and the cryptographic proofs from the SNARKs and STARKs are submitted to the Ethereum chain, which verifies the off-chain calculations without executing the transactions on-chain. This technique significantly reduces the burden of transactions on Ethereum. Some well-known protocols using Optimistic Rollups include the following:

- ➤ Optimism

- ➤ Arbitrum

- ➤ Base

- ➤ Metis

- ➤ Boba Network

- ➤ As transactions are automatically assumed to be valid, validators and other nodes monitor the rollup in case an incorrect submission takes place to ensure that the network maintains its integrity. These nodes can generate fraud proofs against suspected inaccurate state roots being submitted.

- ➤ Transactions that may be considered fraudulent have a time window for objections and disputes to be corrected. The proofs provided can be examined, and if true, they are included in the transactions again. The rollup has a system to punish or reward validators to ensure their truthfulness.

➤ **Zero-knowledge rollups (ZK-rollups):** ZK-rollups improve scalability by reducing calculation demands from Ethereum's main chain. By processing transactions off-chain, they create a cryptographic proof called zero-knowledge proof (Zkp) for each batch of transactions they process.

- ➤ Zero-knowledge proofs enable one person, called the *prover*, to prove to another person, called the *verifier*, that a statement is true without revealing any information beyond the validity of the statement itself. For example, someone could prove they are 18 years old, and thus an adult, without disclosing other information. Regarding Ethereum's transactions, this cryptographic proof is used to confirm a whole batch of processed transactions and that they have followed Ethereum's rules without giving away any other data.

  - ➤ In Table 2.1, besides scalability, another challenge was the lack of privacy due to the blockchains and data being public knowledge. Zero-knowledge proofs are one solution being worked on to address the lack of privacy on a public blockchain.

  - ➤ The key difference between optimistic rollups and zero-knowledge rollups is that zero-knowledge rollups are being validated on Ethereum, while optimistic rollups are assumed to be valid by default.

- ➤ Well known protocols that use zero-knowledge proofs include the following:

  - ➤ ZkSync

  - ➤ Polygon zkEVM

  - ➤ StarkNet by StarkWare—a company

  - ➤ Scroll

  - ➤ Loopring

  - ➤ Aztec

  - ➤ Polygon ID

Validiums

Validiums are another Layer 2 scaling solution that uses off-chain calculations, data storage, and only on-chain verification. Validiums process transactions off the main Ethereum chain and generate validity proofs verified on Ethereum. As with the previous solutions, validiums reduce the burden on the main Ethereum chain through off-chain processing and storage. Validiums excel in privacy and confidentiality.

The way validiums are integrated with Ethereum is through several smart contracts:

➤ **A verifier contract:** The verifier contract ensures that the proofs provided are accurate and by Ethereum's rules.

➤ **A central contract:** The primary contract manages the state of the validium chain on Ethereum, managing user interactions such as deposits and withdrawals.

➤ **Ethereum:** Ethereum acts as the final check before the transaction is settled.

In validiums, the transaction process is a bit different than the previous ones you've seen:

➤ Users send their transactions to the validium operator—a software system.

➤ Transaction in validiums are aggreged. Transactions are bundled together and proved true, and a validity proof is generated.

➤ The validium operator then sends the state root and proofs to Ethereum's main contract, which verifies and updates them.

➤ Users deposit assets into Ethereum's smart contract and then credit them to the validium chain.

➤ When users want to withdraw their funds, they send a request on the validium chain, which, after a proof verification on Ethereum, allows them to withdraw the user's funds.

Validium proofs are unique as they can employ recursive proofs and validate multiple blocks by consolidating all the proofs together. This increases the number of transactions that can be verified each time the process described is repeated, dramatically improving Ethereum's scalability.

These are two protocols using validiums on Ethereum:

➤ dYdX

➤ zkPorter

Side-Chains

Side-chains are secondary blockchains that run in parallel with Ethereum. Side-chains have their own consensus mechanism and rules. Still, they are connected to Ethereum and allow assets to be transferred from one blockchain to the other using a smart contract on each chain to lock assets and mint new tokens on the other chain. As users transfer their assets to these side-chains and these side-chains process transactions independently, a particular burden that would otherwise have been processed on Ethereum's main chain is lifted. In addition, side-chains are helpful as they allow for experimentation with new parameters, rules, and everything else that the community might introduce to the main chain.

Side-chains on Ethereum include the following:

➤ Polygon

➤ Ronin

➤ Gnosis Chain

➤ Metis Andromeda

Sharding

Sharding is a method of designing or architecting databases in which a large dataset is split across multiple database servers, with each piece called a *shard*. Each shard contains a complete subset of the whole database but only a portion of the actual data, as shown in Figure 2.3.

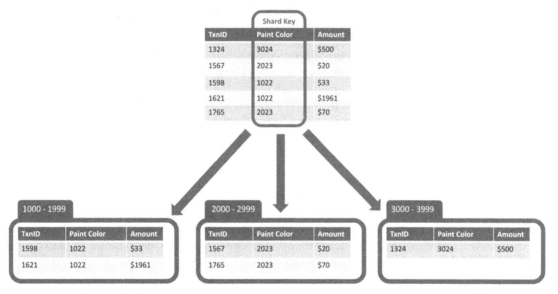

FIGURE 2.3: Sharding example

Let's take the Excel sheet example from the beginning of this chapter. Sharding takes an Excel table and breaks the table and its data into different parts so that all parts together form the whole table. Still, each part has only part of the data. In blockchain, sharding splits a blockchain into smaller chains that work in parallel and communicate with each other through a process called *cross-shard communication*. The chains are called *shards*, which process transactions simultaneously. Each shard processes its transactions and has its validators, but all shards together form the whole original blockchain.

Each shard reaches consensus independently, and a beacon chain—the main chain—coordinates between the different shards. Sharding on blockchains increases scalability and the number of TPS, which is possible since the blockchain is broken into smaller blockchains that process their transactions.

Danksharding

Danksharding is an advanced sharding technique proposed to scale Ethereum's Layer 1. Like the sharding already mentioned, it involves splitting Ethereum's Layer 1 into smaller parts to distribute transaction processing. However, danksharding introduces data blobs. Data blobs allow large data pieces to be attached to the blocks produced by Ethereum. They are helpful for more efficient data storage and retrieval across shards. Unlike traditional data storage on Ethereum, the data in these blobs is not accessible to the EVM and is set to be automatically deleted after a predetermined period of approximately two weeks.

Danksharding does not focus on scaling transactions but instead focuses on scaling data; it changes Ethereum's strategy to focus on rollups optimizing for data space in blobs. This allows Layer 2 protocols, such as rollups, to function with higher throughput and lower costs. A proposal to improve Ethereum called EIP-4844—more on Ethereum Improvement proposals in Chapter 10—smooths the way for this sharding mechanism by introducing components and methodologies crucial for the successful deployment of the whole mechanism of danksharding. However, the entire mechanism of danksharding requires additional tweaks to the consensus layer.

Ethereum's strategy is to achieve a synergy between the different Layer 2s mentioned previously and danksharding. With this strategy, Layer 2s can handle more transactions due to the increased data efficiency that danksharding provides on the main chain for all the rollups and other data communicated through Layer 2s to Layer 1. Both components aim to—in the long term—reduce gas fees and increase transaction processing times, making Ethereum much more accessible to the average user by making it cheaper to use, improving user experience, and eventually achieving widespread adoption.

LAYER 3 SOLUTIONS

Layer 3 networks are a layer on top of Layer 2 solutions. They focus on specific applications and efficient environments for these purposes. Specialized use cases of Layer 3s include specialized and complex finance applications for gaming networks, decentralized social media networks, and decentralized artificial intelligence.

An example of a Layer 3 network is Arbitrum's Orbit L3 development framework. Orbit's feature is its customization capability, which allows it to adapt and be customized to the unique requirements of the various specialized use cases mentioned.

ETHEREUM: TOWARD FINALIZATION

Ethereum is still under development; thus, the developer community plans to upgrade or update it before it is seen as a completed project. As a Solidity developer, it is helpful to know what Ethereum will encounter down the road.

➤ **The Merge:** The Merge was completed on September 15, 2022, and the main change was Ethereum's transition from a PoW consensus mechanism to a PoS consensus mechanism.

➤ **The Surge:** The Surge aims to increase Ethereum's scalability to 100,000 TPS through the protodanksharding mentioned earlier. Protodanksharding will switch Ethereum's focus from scaling TPS to scaling the data layer so that Layer 2s can flourish. This involves breaking the transaction data into smaller shards, each managing its subset of transactions. The first mini-upgrade for the Surge to be completed occurred on March 13, 2024, with the Dencun upgrade.

➤ **The Scourge:** The Scourge aims to solve censorship resistance and any decentralization concerns that Ethereum has yet to address by solving Miner Extractable Value (MEV) and front-running. This involves tweaking the consensus mechanisms and smart contract execution to eradicate incentives to practice MEV and, through decentralized oracle networks, minimize the dependence on centralized components—more on oracles in Chapter 8.

➤ **The Verge:** The Verge aims to further increase Ethereum's scalability and efficiency by improving how data is organized and accessed.

➤ **The Purge:** The Purge will improve Ethereum's network by reducing unnecessary burdens when nodes calculate transactions. One fundamental change will be that nodes will not need to store the complete data of all blocks, making it easier and cheaper to run Ethereum nodes and increasing decentralization.

➤ **The Splurge:** Finally, the Splurge is an update that introduces account abstraction that minimizes the differences between EOAs—accounts used by users and contract accounts to the point that there is no difference between them. The Splurge will also improve efficiency by differentiating roles into block builders and block validators instead of having only block validators.

You can follow the roadmap and its progress on `https://ethroadmap.com`.

CHAPTER 2 QUESTIONS

1. Explain how Ethereum's proof-of-stake consensus mechanism works and what role validators play in block creation.

2. What is the blockchain trilemma, and how does it currently affect Ethereum?

3. Compare and contrast optimistic rollups versus zero-knowledge rollups as Layer 2 scaling solutions.

4. Describe how gas fees are calculated in Ethereum. What components make up the total gas fee?

5. What key limitations of Bitcoin did Ethereum aim to address according to Vitalik Buterin's whitepaper?

6. Explain the concept of smart contracts and their four key properties.

7. What is danksharding, and how does it differ from traditional sharding?

8. Describe the different types of Ethereum nodes and their roles in the network.

9. How do validiums work as a Layer 2 scaling solution, and what are their main advantages?

10. Explain the remaining stages in Ethereum's development roadmap (Surge, Scourge, Verge, Purge, Splurge).

11. What is the relationship between wei and Ether? Name three denominations of Ether and their values.

12. How does Ethereum achieve finality in its block confirmation process?

13. What are the essential characteristics that define a dApp?

14. Explain how side-chains work with Ethereum, and provide two examples.

15. What roles do the base fee and priority fee play in transaction processing on Ethereum?

3

Wallets, MetaMask, and Block Explorers

This chapter provides a comprehensive guide to the tools and practices essential for interacting with blockchain networks, focusing on cryptocurrency wallets, the MetaMask browser wallet, and block explorers. These foundational topics are critical for developers and users navigating decentralized systems, enabling safe and effective management of funds, deploying smart contracts, and engaging with decentralized applications (DApps).

Through detailed discussions, you'll explore the various types of cryptocurrency wallets—hosted, browser-based, hardware, mobile, and multisignature—and their respective strengths, weaknesses, and best-use scenarios. You'll gain an understanding of how private and public key cryptography underpin wallet functionality, the security trade-offs of different wallet types, and best practices for safeguarding digital assets against scams, phishing attacks, and hardware vulnerabilities.

The chapter also introduces MetaMask, a popular browser-based wallet used for accessing Ethereum test networks and interacting with DApps. Step-by-step tutorials guide you through installing, setting up, and using MetaMask, including creating new wallets, importing existing ones, and configuring test networks like Sepolia. Practical exercises, such as claiming test Ether from faucets and performing your first transaction, reinforce these concepts.

Block explorers like Etherscan are another focal point, illustrating their role as a transparent window into blockchain activity. You'll learn to inspect wallet addresses, analyze transaction details, and understand block data, equipping you with the tools to audit and verify on-chain activities. The chapter also explores advanced topics like proxy contracts, multisignature setups, and hierarchical deterministic (HD) wallets, connecting these tools to real-world applications and security strategies.

By the end of this chapter, you'll have the skills to confidently manage wallets, secure your digital assets, and engage with decentralized systems. These insights will serve as a practical foundation for deploying smart contracts, interacting with blockchain applications, and understanding the broader implications of blockchain technology in real-world scenarios.

UNDERSTANDING WALLETS

Although in the physical world there is essentially one type of wallet to hold your money, with variations and add-ons as well as material from which the wallet is created, in the cryptocurrency and blockchain space, there are various types of wallets one can use to access their cryptocurrency, and every kind of wallet has different levels of security. It is suitable for different needs and uses. Before looking at the various types of wallets, why there are other types of wallets, their strengths and weaknesses, and how to use them best, it is imperative to talk about how the different types of wallets work.

The various types of wallets include the following:

➤ Hosted

➤ Browser

➤ Desktop (full node and lightweight)

➤ Mobile

➤ Cold storage/hardware

➤ Multisignature

➤ Hierarchical deterministic (HD)

Each of these is discussed in this chapter. Let's begin with hosted wallets.

Hosted Wallets

Hosted wallets are wallets whose private key does not belong to you, and a third party manages the money. Such wallets are operated by cryptocurrency exchanges that typically create a public address for you to deposit your money and then manage it for you through the private key. The cryptocurrency space, characterized by its ethos of decentralization using crypto exchanges and not managing your own money, is considered controversial. That being said, if you want to participate in the cryptocurrency economy, you do not necessarily have to go along with what a group of people thinks—even if they may be right most of the time in this case—but should look to fulfill your own needs and use the wallets and methods you may be comfortable with since, after all, we are talking about money here.

Advantages, Disadvantages, Best Practices, and Case Studies

There are advantages and disadvantages to using hosted wallets or cryptocurrency exchanges.

Advantages

➤ You are giving your cryptocurrencies to a third party to be managed by someone else, which absolves you from managing the funds yourself.

➤ There are no extra costs to buy a hardware wallet.

➤ You do not need to learn about different wallet options, their pluses and minuses, and when it is best to use each wallet; you also do not need to experiment with them, saving you time.

Disadvantages

- You re-create the old system of a bank—a crypto exchange—managing your funds for you, which kills the ethos of cryptocurrencies and decentralization.

- Suppose the third-party exchange you are using for a hosted wallet goes bankrupt due to mismanagement of funds. In that case, your money is most likely gone forever.

- If the third-party exchange you use for a hosted wallet is not a reliable third party to whom you can entrust your money and is run by criminals or to-be criminals, your money will be gone.

- Suppose an authoritarian government that may have been a bit more lenient to crypto in the past decides one day to ban cryptocurrencies or confiscate the cryptocurrencies of its citizens from the exchanges. In that case, it can very well do so. However, with hardware wallets and proper management, it becomes much more difficult since the governments needs a list of who owns a hardware wallet and then go door by door to confiscate them.

Best Practice 1

If you decide to use a hosted wallet either permanently—not advised at all—or temporarily but for a prolonged period, it is best practice to open multiple accounts on different reputable crypto exchanges and diversify your holdings by dividing your funds by the number of exchanges you will use.

In this way, if one of the cryptocurrency exchanges turns out to be a scam or goes bankrupt, you will not lose all of your money, but just part of it.

Best Practice 2

To ensure that you access the correct website, one best practice is to bookmark the websites you visit frequently. That way, you do not need to trust a link, be it an ad or a malicious link sent by a malicious party. If you want to access the decentralized exchange Uniswap.org, bookmark the legitimate website, add the bookmark to a folder with other decentralized applications, and access it consistently through the bookmarks.

Best Practice 3

When verifying the legitimacy of an Airdrop or prize on a Discord or Telegram server, ensure that any reply you get comes from a team member who has a verified badge identifying them as an official team member. Scammers sometimes join a Discord or Telegram server using the name and profile picture of a legitimate team member to deceive users. When they see someone asking about the Airdrop, the malicious person on purpose confirms that it is legitimate, and the victim may connect the wallet to the malicious website and lose their cryptocurrencies.

By double-checking that the person from the team who answers has a team badge signifying their membership in the team, the user ensures that it is indeed the legitimate team member answering, as a scammer would not be able to mimic the badge.

CASE STUDIES

Mount Gox

Mount Gox was a crypto exchange launched in the early days of cryptocurrency in 2010 and rose to prominence very quickly. As of 2014, it handled more than 70% of all bitcoin buys, sells, and sends in circulation.

The exchange reported multiple times the theft of Bitcoin by hackers, and even their database of clients leaked, which worsened the problem of theft and hacking.

Finally, to top it all off, in 2014, Mount Gox—an acronym for Magic The Gathering Online Exchange—suspended all trading, conversions, and activity on its website and filed for bankruptcy and bankruptcy protection from creditors and customers.

As of October 2023, 9 (almost 10) years after filing for bankruptcy, Mount Gox clients are still trying to reclaim at least part of the money that they lost.

For reference purposes, the price of Bitcoin when Mount Gox filed for bankruptcy was 600–650 USD per coin. In October 2023, the price was 30,000 USD, more or less.

QuadrigaCX

QuadrigaCX was a crypto exchange founded in Canada in 2013 by Gerald Cotten. It quickly became the biggest or at least one of the biggest crypto exchanges in Canada, with thousands of customers. In 2018 Cotton traveled to India, where he mysteriously "died," and the cryptocurrency exchange ceased operations soon thereafter while owing almost 200,000,000 USD to its customers.

There are several theories as to what happened to Cotton, such as him faking his death; changing his appearance, name, and anything else he could change; and now living a life of luxury somewhere in the middle of nowhere. This is mainly due to Cotton's history of scamming people online before starting the crypto exchange. Others believe he is genuinely dead, but no one knows for sure. The people who lost money were not made whole.

There is a Netflix movie on QuadrigaCX called *Trust No One: The Hunt for the Crypto King*, which you can watch for entertainment rather than historical accuracy.

FTX

FTX was a crypto exchange founded in 2019 by Sam Bankman-Fried and Gary Wang and, in time, managed to accumulate a significant number of users. It became one of the biggest crypto exchanges in the world, such as Binance, Kraken, and Coinbase. FTX was so popular as a crypto exchange that the exchange even renamed the American Airlines Arena in Miami, Florida, to FTX arena, and Bankman-Fried organized events with well-known past leaders such as Tony Blair and Bill Clinton, among others, in an FTX event in the Bahamas. Moreover, FTX worked with famous actors such as Larry David to release a Super Bowl commercial and had collaborations with and the endorsements of other celebrities such as Kevin O'Leary, Naomi Osaka, and more.

However, in November 2022, FTX suddenly filed for bankruptcy within a few days, and its customers lost the money they had deposited and kept on the exchange without transferring the money to a hardware or any other wallet for self-management. Bankman-Fried was convicted of fraud and was sentenced to 25 years in prison. FTX—now bankrupt—is trying to make a comeback as a crypto exchange by making as many customers as possible whole. This process is still pending at the time this book was written.

Lessons Learned

The situations mentioned here illustrate that even the most trusted exchanges, even those endorsed by high-profile individuals such as former prime ministers and presidents of countries as well as actors or sports teams, do not constitute proof of trustworthiness. In blockchain, the only thing one can truly trust is something that occurred on-chain and there is a proof of it: a transaction hash, a hash of a block, or the address of a wallet or a smart contract account that can be verified. In blockchain there is a mantra that goes "do not trust, verify" to denote that one should only trust that which they can verify on-chain. Chain trust will be discussed in the "Block Explorers" section later in this chapter where we will see on-chain verifiable transactions. If you are unable to use a wallet to manage your funds, it is best to diversify the exchanges you use rather than keeping all your funds in one place. This way, if an issue arises with one exchange, your entire investment is not at risk.

Browser Wallets

As their name suggests, these wallets are integrated upon downloading into your web browser.

Advantages, Disadvantages, and Case Studies

As with hosted wallets, browser wallets have their advantages and disadvantages.

Advantages

➤ Browser wallets are easy to use for day-to-day transactions of small value, ensuring that the user does not lose a lot of money if the wallet gets compromised.

➤ Quick and straightforward access is available as you connect and browse the Internet through your browser.

Disadvantages

➤ Vulnerable to phishing and other attacks, the victim is redirected to a malicious website that asks the user to connect their wallet. Once they do, they lose control of their wallet, and the money is gone.

CASE STUDIES

Malicious Websites

Do you see a difference between `binance.com` and `binαnce.com`? The second `binαnce.com` uses the Greek version of the letter α instead of the Latin or English version, which is a. When a user clicks a link via an app such as Telegram or even a phishing email and inputs sensitive information, the malicious party will get that information.

Another similar example is `acala.network` and `acaIa.network`. Although the difference between a small L and capital I is much more apparent in the book; it is not so on a browser. The small L and the capital I look identical on the surface, which can deceive users into thinking that the website they are accessing is the legitimate one when, in fact, it is not.

Job Search Scams

Another sophisticated reverse engineering scam involving browser wallets occurs when someone is looking for a job in the industry and encounters people posing as recruiters asking for the public address of the user/job applicant to ensure that the person has made transactions with the wallet and is an experienced Web3 user. What they may want is to see what the balance in your wallet is.

The scam continues as a typical job interview where the person is examined over a week or two for the hypothetical job position. The "interviewee" may go through various classic job interview hoops such as a couple of interviews or exercises. In the last interview, the "interviewer" may ask the interviewee to access the team's website and connect their wallet to test a new feature and give feedback. As the unsuspecting victim, whose trust has been won, clicks the link and connects their wallet to use the feature, the scammers end the interview, get a control of the user's wallet, and drain it.

Desktop Wallet (Full Nodes)

Desktop wallets that operate as full nodes mean someone takes the whole Blockchain and downloads the software onto their computer. Blockchain software comes pre-installed with a wallet that can be used to manage funds.

Advantages and Disadvantages

Several advantages and disadvantages come with downloading your cryptocurrency's blockchain to your desktop.

Advantages

➤ You are contributing to the maintenance of the blockchain's network.

➤ You have complete control and protection, especially if private keys are encrypted with strong passphrases and regularly backed up.

➤ It is more challenging, and there is less incentive for an attacker to compromise each person's computer and attack an individual than to target a centralized exchange, which serves as a honeypot and where the funds of many users reside.

Disadvantages

➤ Hosting the whole blockchain on a computer requires tremendous amounts of hardware space; depending on someone's Internet connection, it may take days or weeks.

➤ Although attackers are, in principle, disincentivized from attacking one computer at a time, this is not impossible, and computers are vulnerable to malware and other computer viruses that may compromise the full node wallet.

➤ Downloading the whole blockchain and using its wallet, interface, and functionalities might confuse a beginner.

Desktop Wallet (Lightweight)

On the other hand, lightweight wallets do not download the whole Blockchain on their device. Instead, they rely on the nodes closest to them to relay information, verify, and receive transactions, but only those relevant to the specific wallet used and not all the transactions on the Blockchain.

Advantages and Disadvantages

As with the wallets described earlier in this chapter, lightweight desktop wallets have their advantages and disadvantages.

Advantages

➤ Like with full nodes, lightweight wallets provide full control and protection, especially if private keys are encrypted with strong passphrases and regularly backed up.

➤ Just like with full nodes, it is more challenging, and there is less incentive for an attacker to compromise each person's computer and attack an individual than to target a centralized exchange where the funds of many users reside. Those centralized exchanges serve as a honeypot.

➤ Lightweight wallets require less hard disk space and less bandwidth compared to a full node.

➤ Private keys are stored on the computer itself. Thus, the wallet owner has complete control without relying on third parties for the private keys.

Disadvantages

➤ As you rely on other full nodes to relay information, verify transactions, and receive and send transactions, you rely on a third party. If they are malicious, such a party may be spying on your transactions for one reason or another. In the future, as the blockchain and Web3 spaces become more mainstream and more people use cryptocurrencies, these third parties may be somehow working with marketing agencies and businesses to notify them about the transactions and the information this may bring to the businesses.

➤ Like full nodes, computers are prone to malware attacks that may attract thieves and hackers. Again, though, it is much more discouraging to attack one computer at a time than focusing on a centralized exchange, which is home to the cryptocurrencies of hundreds, thousands, or even millions of cryptocurrency users and can act as a honeypot.

Mobile Wallets

As their name suggests, mobile wallets are downloaded and used on the mobile phones of the wallet users. Some of these wallets may be a version of a browser wallet or even a lightweight desktop wallet with a mobile version.

Advantages, Disadvantages, and Case Studies

There are advantages and disadvantages of mobile wallets too.

Advantages

➤ They are portable, easy, and comfortable—the smartphone's camera scans the QR codes of merchants.

➤ They are good for daily transactions.

➤ If your mobile device is stolen or lost, the funds are not gone if you have made a proper backup. However, most mobile wallets are stolen.

Disadvantages

➤ If used in the presence of others or cameras, the PIN or other sensitive wallet information may be visible if the owner does not take proper care of it, which may result in stolen funds.

➤ SIM swap attacks are common and can be a catalyst as to how someone may lose their cryptocurrencies.

➤ Mobile devices are also vulnerable to malware and viruses, which can lead to the loss of cryptocurrencies. This can happen if a user downloads a malicious file from the Internet via a browser or unknowingly installs malicious software from a trusted app platform, such as Google Play or Apple's App Store. For example, someone might believe they are downloading a legitimate wallet application but instead install malware designed to steal their seed phrase. A *seed phrase* is a crucial set of 12 or 24 words (depending on the wallet type) that grants access to your funds when imported into wallet software. If a malicious app gains access to this phrase, it can use it to take control of your funds. We'll discuss seed phrases in more detail later in this chapter.

CASE STUDY

Sim Swap Attacks

If you ever fall victim to a sim swap attack or any other hack despite doing your best not to be attacked or hacked, do not feel bad about being tricked. Vitalik Buterin, the founder of Ethereum, fell prey to a SIM swap attack. The attacker got control of his Twitter (X) account and posted a malicious link, which caused users and his followers to lose 700,000 USD collectively.

The attack happened after someone managed to socially engineer not Vitalik Buterin but T-Mobile, Vitalik's phone service provider, into performing a SIM swap and swapping Vitalik's information from his SIM card to another. This enabled the attacker to access Vitalik's Twitter account, causing people to lose money.

Cold Storage/Hardware Wallet

One of the safest and simplest ways to protect your private keys is to store them offline so they are never exposed online. That way, no one can access them even if your computer is compromised. The keys are offline in the real, analog world, which safeguards your cryptocurrencies from digital threats and attacks. There are several ways that cold storage can be implemented:

➤ **Hardware wallet:** A hardware wallet is a device that stores a wallet's private key offline in a physical device. This is done for security purposes and to keep the private key safe. When the private key is stored in a nonhardware format, it is highly vulnerable to hacks and malware. Out of all the wallets allowing users to keep custody of their cryptocurrencies without trusting a cryptocurrency exchange, a hardware wallet is considered the safest option.

➤ **Air-gapped hardware wallets:** These are hardware wallets whose keys are entirely generated offline. They sign transactions offline and are not connected to the Internet or any other method that may transmit or leak the device's private key.

Hardware wallets include Trezor, NGRAVE ZERO, Keystone, Tangem, and others.

Advantages, Disadvantages, and Best Practices

Although hardware wallets are considered one of the safest options to store one's cryptocurrencies, just like all the wallets discussed in this chapter, they come with trade-offs, advantages, and disadvantages.

Advantages

➤ It uses offline isolation to secure the user's funds. Thus, it is much less prone to attacks—unless the user selects to connect the wallet to a browser wallet, when its security falls dramatically.

➤ Private keys are generated and kept offline and thus controlled by the owner—although, depending on the owner, this might be an advantage or a disadvantage.

➤ It is protected by additional PIN encryption from someone who may steal the wallet and want to access it, giving the owner time to react and use the private keys to move the funds in case of such an incident.

➤ Backups provided in the form of metal or paper—that come with the wallet's package—enabling the owner to note down and back up the seed phrase immediately upon turning on the device for the first time. When you write the seed phrase on a piece of paper, the paper becomes a "paper wallet." That means that the seed phrase, which gives you access to your funds, serves as the wallet, which has been transcribed on a piece of paper.

Disadvantages

➤ Whereas most wallet options described in this chapter are free to use, hardware wallets come with a price tag that, at the time this chapter was written, may range from 60 to 80 USD up to 500 to 600 USD, depending on any extra security features you might want on the wallet, such as 2FA, biometric recognition, hidden wallets, choosing your seed phrase, water resistance, etc.

➤ Hardware wallets are not as convenient as mobile, browser, lightweight desktop wallets for day-to-day transactions.

➤ It may be vulnerable to supply chain attacks, where the attacker intercepts the hardware wallet during transportation from the seller to the buyer. They may open the package and the device to access the seed phrase and then repack everything carefully so it appears untouched. Once the money is deposited into the address, the attacker may use the seed phrase to whisk away the funds. A reputable and respectable hardware wallet provider should have strategies to mitigate this. Remember this when buying a hardware wallet and ask via email or on the company's Discord server. If you are not satisfied with the security provided, you may choose not to buy the device.

➤ Never buy from third-party resellers as similar dangers to supply chain attacks may loom. The reseller or a previous customer could have carefully opened and resealed the package. They might have appropriated the seed phrase, giving them access to the private key. Once the wallet buyer moves their funds to the wallet's address, the malicious party can use the seed phrase to access the funds.

Best Practice

If the wallet of your choice does not provide a metal backup to secure the seed phrase (which gives access to the private keys) and provides only paper to record it, consider ordering a metal backup separately online, Relying on paper transforms your wallet in a paper wallet susceptible to damage from water or a fire or loss of the paper and consequently of your funds. A metal backup is more resistant and secure and makes noise when it falls, attracting your attention.

Although hardware wallets usually cost money, there are ways to minimize these costs to almost 0$ such as converting a USB drive you may have or can buy for a low price into a hardware wallet. You can do this by downloading and installing open-source encryption software for the USB drive, such as Veracrypt, and then downloading and installing a software wallet, such as Coinomi. You can find information about these online. To avoid scams, Veracrypt can be downloaded on `veracrypt.fr`, and Coinomi can be downloaded on `Coinomi.com`.

Another way to create a hardware wallet at zero cost is to convert an old smartphone or iPhone into a hardware wallet. The steps for converting the old smartphone into a hardware wallet is outlined next. However, it is imperative to know that this method also has its trade-offs and is not bulletproof or the perfect solution. Hence, be extra careful with how you manage hardware wallets of any type.

Advantages

➤ You can save costs by using a USB drive you already own or by buying one, which is much cheaper than buying a hardware wallet.

➤ Private keys are kept offline on the USB.

➤ This is a homemade cryptocurrency hardware wallet, so it is not vulnerable to supply chain attacks like ordinary hardware wallets.

➤ There is no need for third-party resellers, as this is a homemade solution.

➤ It is even more permissionless and privacy-oriented than hardware wallets since it is a homemade wallet. In practice, no one would know that you ordered it. With hardware wallets from a seller, you need to give your address or the address of someone nearby so you can pick it up later in the day.

Disadvantages

➤ Depending on how you use a USB stick, it may be prone to being infected with malware or other viruses. These may compromise the wallet and give a malicious party control of the wallet, the seed phrase, or both.

➤ The device is a USB, and it has been designed to work as a USB and not as a hardware wallet. Therefore, security measures that may be present in regular hardware wallets may not be present in a USB. However, the USB is kept offline and does not encounter a computer contaminated with malware or other viruses, so it should not pose too many problems.

Convert Your Old Phone into a Hardware Wallet

If you want to practice with a hardware wallet but do not have a budget to spend on it, but you have an old iPhone or Android lying around, you can use that instead to make it into a hardware wallet. I will outline the steps to take as well as the pros and cons of this approach.

To start with this approach, follow these steps:

1. Remove all SIM and SD cards on your old mobile device. Reset the phone to its factory settings. All data not originally shipped with the phone will be gone.

2. Turn the device off and on.

3. Connect it to Wi-Fi and download the latest phone updates.

4. Enable a lock screen and encryption if your device supports them for extra security.

5. Go to Airgap. Install the appropriate Airgap Vault application on your device, depending on your operating system.

6. After downloading the Airgap Vault application, disconnect your phone from the Internet and enable airplane mode forever on this device. Also, never turn on Bluetooth. Never connect this device to Bluetooth or the Internet ever again!

7. Start the Airgap Vault application.

8. When asked for the installation type, choose Offline.

9. You can now import your existing seed phrase or create a new one and use the wallet as an air-gapped cold storage/hardware wallet.

10. Now, download the Airgap wallet on your everyday mobile wallet device. (Important, the Airgap wallet is a different app; this is not Airgap Vault!)

11. You must sync the wallet created on your old phone to your new one. Open the Airgap Vault application on your old phone, click Account, and the device will show a QR code.

12. On your everyday phone, open the wallet app, click Scan QR Codes, and scan the QR code shown in your old wallet. This will sync the wallet to your everyday phone without transferring the private key.

13. You can use your daily phone to check your balance, scan QR codes, and sign transactions, or use your old phone to do both.

Advantages

➤ You do not need to spend money on a hardware wallet as long as you have an old phone that semi-works.

➤ This method supports a circular economy (reuse, repair, refurbish to minimize waste and pollution).

➤ Since you have used your old phone a lot of times, you would not have a learning curve.

➤ It is portable since it is a mobile phone.

➤ It is private key extraction resistant.

➤ It supports major chains such as Bitcoin, ETH, Polkadot, Tezos, Cosmos, Kusama, and others.

➤ Airgap, the application, is open-source and transparent.

Disadvantages

➤ It is not fire, water, or extreme weather conditions resistant.

➤ There is no NFT support—at least at the time of writing this.

➤ A phone is designed to be a phone, not a hardware wallet. Thus, it does not have the same security levels as a hardware wallet, designed from the start to be a hardware wallet. That said, it should be safe if you do not connect your old phone, which has now turned into a hardware wallet, to the Internet or via Bluetooth. However, I recommend upgrading to a hardware wallet once you have the budget.

➤ You always need your old phone or hardware wallet to sign transactions somewhere outside. This makes it prone to theft, breaking, loss, and every other phone peril.

Multisignature Wallets

In cryptocurrency, multisignature wallets allow for and require more than one signature or confirmation from a person to spend money. Multisignature wallets can be helpful for both businesses and individuals. These types of wallets work straightforwardly.

An N of M method is applied to release the funds in a multisignature wallet. N is the number of signatures required from the addresses registered in the multisignature wallet M. For example, suppose a multisignature wallet registers four signatures from four different addresses. In that case, three out of the four total signatures are required for the funds to be released (or four out of four, or two out of four). It depends on how many people the organization entrusts with the multisignature scheme. The strategy for this must, however, be carefully crafted since if enough malicious signatories approve the spending of funds, they may be able to send it to their wallet, leaving the organization without funds, at least in that specific multisignature address. Such an action may be mitigated if the organization has funds to pursue legal action. Still, depending on the organization's structure, it may not yet be recognized legally in the jurisdiction where its team members performed the scam and stole the money. An example of such an incident could be a just-starting DAO with very few initial members.

For individuals, multisignature wallets may be an additional security measure to protect their funds. Suppose a person has a significant amount of funds somewhere. In that case, it may be beneficial to create a multisignature wallet requiring two signatures out of three, or three out of five. This ensures that if one or two of the wallets or addresses get compromised by someone or something, the person compromising the address cannot access the funds unless they have more wallets and addresses in their control, depending on the scheme employed in the multisignature structure. A multisignature scheme that can integrate hardware wallets is the most secure security strategy to secure someone's funds. However, the big drawback of this is complexity. Where one may need to manage one private key usually, now they need to do so with multiple keys for a multisignature wallet, which can add to the complexity of the security solution, and a not-so-sophisticated user may lose enough of the keys never to recover their money.

One example of a multisignature wallet is Gnosis Safe.

However, one way of mitigating the complexity of multisignature wallets for an individual could be Hierarchical Deterministic (HD) wallets.

Hierarchical Deterministic Wallets

HD wallets generate a master private key. Other child private keys for addresses can be created and derived from that master private key, simplifying the complexity of multisignature wallets requiring different addresses to manage the multisignature wallet.

The problem is that generating one master private key can create different child private keys and addresses. If someone holds the master private key, they can access all addresses. The good thing about using something like Gnosis Safe, however, is that even if someone gets access to one's master private key, as long as they are not aware that the addresses are connected to a multisignature wallet, then they would not have access to the funds, giving the owner of the funds precious time to use the master private key to recover the funds before they are gone forever.

INSTALLING METAMASK

For this book, MetaMask will be used as a browser wallet to access testnets and faucets and deploy test contracts to test them. It is essential to say that MetaMask is not directly affiliated with any of the stakeholders involved in publishing this book, including the author. However, an effortless way of testing, deploying, and getting test Ether is necessary, and we do not need to spend real money from our pocket; thus, MetaMask is the choice for this book.

To download MetaMask, the following steps must be performed:

1. Open your browser of choice.

2. Go to www.metamask.io. Examine your address bar to ensure that it has the correct URL.

3. On the website, click Download at the top-right corner, or if you see the choice of Download For [*your browser's name*], click that. Either way works.

4. If you are using Google Chrome or a Chromium-based browser, the Download link will redirect you to the Chrome Web Store for extensions, themes, and MetaMask's extension page. Click Add To Chrome or the name of your browser. If you use Firefox, you must go to the Firefox add-ons store to install MetaMask. For the Opera browser, you must go to the Opera add-ons store. Other browsers are currently not supported.

5. Once you do this, the extension will be added to your browser, and a window will pop up asking you to agree to MetaMask's terms of use. Click Create New Wallet.

6. A request will ask you if you agree to MetaMask collecting your data. You can choose to agree or not, depending on your personal preference.

7. Next, MetaMask will ask you to input your MetaMask wallet password, which you must input every time you click your installed browser wallet. It also serves as a defense mechanism if someone else sits on your computer. This is *not* your private seed phrase. Additionally, a checkbox will pop up to acknowledge that MetaMask cannot help you recover your password.

> **WARNING** *If you forget the password you input in an already imported wallet for protection from prying eyes and malicious parties, it is not the end of the world. You can uninstall and reinstall the software, import the private key, and choose a new password.*
>
> *However, if you lose the seed phrase, there is nothing anyone can do, and you will lose your money forever.*

8. A video will pop up briefly explaining private key management. I recommend you watch it, even if you know. It serves as a good reminder.

9. The next step will be revealing your seed phrase. Click the words to be revealed.

Figure 3.1 shows the generated seed phrase I created by going through the process described to create a throwaway wallet for demonstration purposes. If you use this seed phrase the next time to import a wallet, you will get access to the throwaway wallet that I created. Take your seed phrase, write it, or inscribe it somewhere—preferably on something sturdier than a piece of paper; otherwise, you are making a paper wallet. *Do not show it to anyone* and store it somewhere safe, with a couple of backups stored elsewhere.

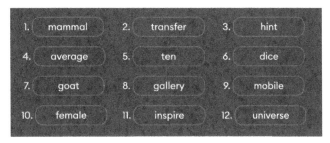

FIGURE 3.1: Creating your own seed phrase

After the previous steps, MetaMask may or may not ask you to confirm parts of your seed phrase to ensure you have noted them somewhere.

After a few more steps, during which you should click Next, the installation should be successful.

When you click your browser's MetaMask logo, you should get something that looks like Figure 3.2.

FIGURE 3.2: MetaMask browser extension's front end

LOGGING IN AGAIN WITH THE SEED PHRASE

After having installed MetaMask correctly, it is time to uninstall it and install it again to showcase how one can import a pre-existing wallet instead of creating a new one.

As was demonstrated, instead of creating a new wallet, it is time to import the one just made to learn how to import those seed phrases and, secondly, get used to installing a MetaMask wallet.

1. To uninstall MetaMask from the browser, right-click the fox icon shown in Figure 3.3.

FIGURE 3.3: MetaMask's logo

2. Then, click Remove from Chrome, Brave, or any other Chromium-based browser (see Figure 3.4).

FIGURE 3.4: Uninstalling MetaMask's browser extension

3. A window will pop up asking you for feedback on why you uninstalled MetaMask; choose whatever option you would if you use Firefox. Clicking the jigsaw puzzle piece at the top right of the browser, clicking the cog next to MetaMask in the pop-up, and selecting Remove Extension should do the trick.

   After that, repeating some steps from the Installing MetaMask section are the next steps that need to be taken.

4. Go to www.metamask.io, and verify that it is the correct URL.

5. On the website, click Download at the top-right corner; of if you see the choice of Download For [*your browser's name*], click that. Either way works.

6. If you are using Google Chrome or a Chromium-based browser, the download link will redirect you to the Chrome Web Store for extensions, themes, and MetaMask's extension page. Click Add to Chrome or the name of your browser.

7. Once you do this, the extension will be added to your browser, and a window will pop up asking you to agree to MetaMask's terms of service. This time, do *not* click Create New Wallet. Click Import An Existing Wallet instead.

8. Then agree or not to the data collection notification and request.

9. In this step, you have to input your seed phrase to import your wallet and get access to it, as shown in Figure 3.5, although keep in mind that the figure has the phrase hidden (in your case it might not be hidden unless you click the eye icon beside every word).

FIGURE 3.5: MetaMask importing seed phrase

10. Click Confirm Secret Recovery Phrase, which will prompt you to the next step: using a password for the browser wallet.

11. MetaMask will ask you to input your MetaMask wallet's password, which you must input every time you click your installed browser wallet. This password is a defense mechanism if someone else sits on your computer. This is *not* your private seed phrase.

12. After this is done, you should be able to access your imported MetaMask wallet, as shown in Figure 3.6.

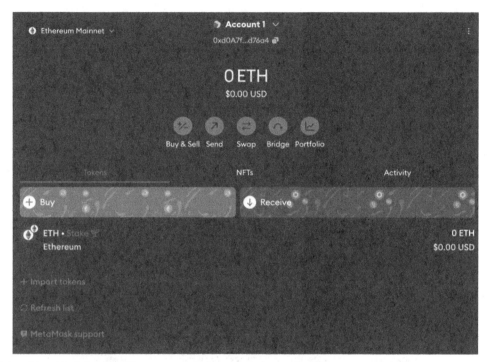

FIGURE 3.6: MetaMask front-end browser window

CHANGING NETWORKS

In blockchain, there are two main types of networks:

➤ The leading network, or *mainnet*, is where all the actual actions, transactions, contract deployment, swapping, voting, and everything else occur.

➤ The test networks, also known as *testnets*, are used mainly to test different functions, contracts, and anything someone wants to test with their wallet without spending real money or real ether but testnet ether instead.

Test networks are convenient for developers, especially since deploying a contract that has been coded costs money through gas fees. Thus, test networks are ideal for deploying test contracts and testing how they work before deploying them to the actual network for users to use. Test networks are also handy because of the free deployment using test net, meaning that someone can deploy multiple contracts when testing without the actual cost of mainnet ether.

MetaMask itself is handy because it already has these test net networks integrated. There is not much of a hassle when setting up and connecting to these test net networks, which we will use in upcoming chapters to deploy our smart contracts. In this book, we will be using the test network that is called ETH Sepolia, and to do so, the following steps have to be taken to connect to the network:

1. Open the browser which has MetaMask installed.

2. Then click the red fox logo of MetaMask.

3. MetaMask's wallet should pop up, as shown in Figure 3.7.

FIGURE 3.7: MetaMask's front end

4. Click the top-left logo of the Ethereum logo beside the Account 1, as shown in Figure 3.7.

5. Toggle the Show Test Networks button, as shown in Figure 3.8.

6. Then click Sepolia (see Figure 3.9). You will see the SepoliaETH testnet, as shown in Figure 3.10.

Please keep in mind that the testnet ether has zero real-world value. As mentioned earlier in this chapter, it is used only to test different things a person may want to do, be that a network, a smart contract, a test sending money to someone else via a test network, or anything else.

ENGAGING WITH FAUCETS

Faucets in Ethereum are applications and websites that send a minimal amount of ether to the public address specified by the user for testing purposes. This allows new users to practice using ether transactions to learn how to do so step-by-step. Faucets also help developers by sending them test network ether to deploy decentralized applications and smart contracts first to a test network and later to the leading Ethereum network.

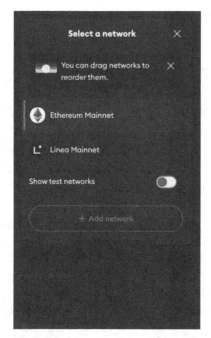

FIGURE 3.8: Changing networks using MetaMask

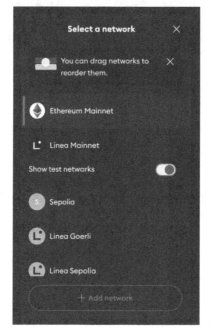

FIGURE 3.9: Showing MetaMask's test networks

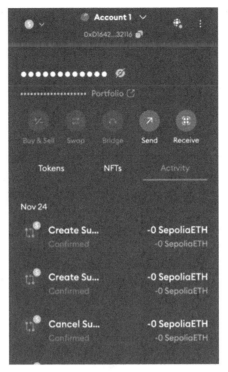

FIGURE 3.10: MetaMask's SepoliaETH testnet

To engage with a faucet and to receive test network Ethereum, follow these steps:

1. Change networks from the leading Ethereum network to a test network Ethereum as outlined in Figures 3.8, 3.9, and 3.10.

2. Go to a reputable faucet website—beware, as scam websites will attempt to steal your private keys or get control of your wallet. Make sure to use a reputable website for your faucet. Two reputable websites are:

    ➤ The Alchemy Faucets at www.alchemy.com/faucets. Choose the faucet you want to use. For this book, we will use Ethereum Sepolia. Ethereum has a number of different testnets, and each testnet has its own main purpose:

        ➤ Sepolia was created to be efficient and light to download and run as a blockchain. Developers mainly use it to deploy and test their smart contracts.

        ➤ Goerli primarily aims to test staking and different validator node operations.

        ➤ Holesky is the newest of the three blockchains. It has been designed for the same purpose as Goerli and will eventually replace it. Holesky is a more advanced test net, allowing for larger-scale tests, more validator nodes, and blockchain upgrades.

    ➤ The Infura faucet at www.infura.io/faucet/sepolia.

Infura and Alchemy require a minimum balance of 0.0001 ETH to send the address SepoliaETH. This limitation discourages spammers from collecting all the SepoliaETH.

If a user wants to, they can load up their wallet or send a very minimum amount to their wallet by opening an account on a cryptocurrency exchange such as Kraken, Coinbase, or Binance or by buying some cryptocurrency. Cryptocurrency can also be purchased on MetaMask itself through switching to the leading network and topping up the wallet.

Otherwise, if the user has ether in another wallet, they can send a small amount to the wallet they are using to be able to use the previously mentioned faucets.

➤ Another avenue of collecting testnet ether is the chainlink faucets website at `faucets .chain.link`—although it requires the mainnet wallet to hold 1 LINK token, which can be procured by buying it and sending it through an exchange, sending it from a preexisting wallet, or swapping a LINK token on a decentralized exchange (DEX) such as Uniswap.

3. If topping up the wallet one way or another or sending ether to it is impossible, you can try `sepolia-faucet.pk910.de`, which gives testnet SepoliaETH for free (see Figure 3.11). Enter your ETH address in the Please Enter ETH Address Or ENS Name text box. The window shown as outlined in Figure 3.12 will display.

FIGURE 3.11: Ethereum faucet at `sepolia-faucet.pk910.de`

4. After copying and pasting the address. clicking the I'm Not A Robot CAPTCHA, and attempting to start to mine, a message should pop up asking to use the Gitcoin passport, as shown in Figure 3.13. This means that one has to register with a Gitcoin passport and complete a number of verification tasks to be able to mine.

Some of the tasks are shown in Figure 3.14 include logging in with your Google, LinkedIn, GitHub, and Discord accounts to gather points.

FIGURE 3.12: MetaMask's wallet address

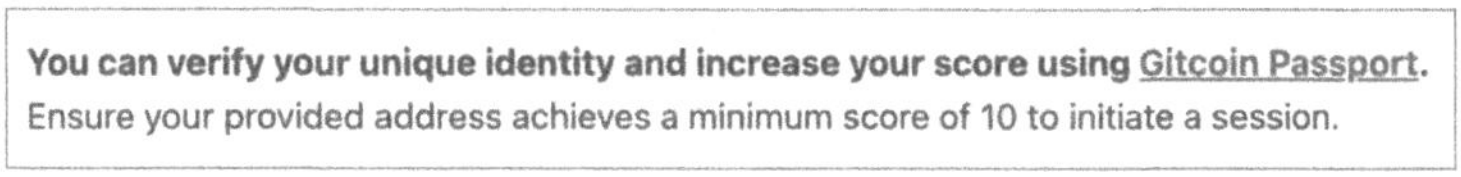

You can verify your unique identity and increase your score using <u>Gitcoin Passport</u>.
Ensure your provided address achieves a minimum score of 10 to initiate a session.

FIGURE 3.13: Gitcoin passport message

FIGURE 3.14: Social and professional platform Gitcoin passport confirmation

5. To mine ETH on the Sepolia testnet, you need a number slightly higher than 2 (2.056). You can decide what tasks you would like to complete, but logging in for confirmation with a number of accounts is the simplest way to mine SepoliaETH without needing any funds in your mainnet wallet.

6. After having successfully gathered more than 2 points, Figure 3.15 should appear when you try to start the mining process again.

   After you see the screen in Figure 3.15, wait for your testnet ETH to be mined. Get a drink from the fridge, make a coffee, or have breakfast, brunch, lunch, or dinner. When you return, the zero SepoliaETH should have been raised to a number that will allow you to withdraw ETH.

> **NOTE** *Even though the short wait I suggest should be sufficient to get enough ETH to begin, I highly recommend you wait for 20–30 minutes. If you want to ensure that you have enough ETH for the book and do not want to use the faucet again when you reach almost 0, wait a couple of hours.*
>
> *I also recommend you come back to practice this whole process repeatedly. That way you'll know how to claim testnet ETH without relying on something or someone else. This testnet ETH will come in handy in the following chapters.*

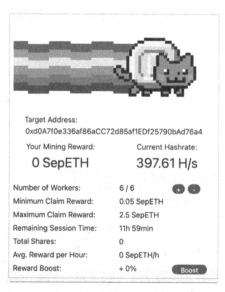

FIGURE 3.15: Ethereum faucet loading screen while mining SepoliaETH

7. To claim testnet ETH, you have to click Stop Mining or an equivalent option. Then you must select Claim Rewards or a similar option. Otherwise, the mining will keep continue indefinitely.

SENDING YOUR FIRST TRANSACTION

Now that the MetaMask address has testnet ether, it is time to execute your first transaction and send (fake) money to someone. To do that, perform the following steps:

1. Click the MetaMask red fox logo on our browser, and your MetaMask wallet appears.

2. Click the Send button to send ether to someone, which should bring up the address to which you want to send the ether (see Figure 3.16).

FIGURE 3.16: Sending transactions with MetaMask

3. Enter the Ethereum address you want to send the money to (see Figure 3.17).

   Figure 3.18 shows the address I want to send your money to; the current balance of my account, which is 0.62+ ether; and the amount of ether I want to send (with the option to send the whole balance).

   Finally, you will see the estimated gas fee for this transaction and two buttons. You can cancel the transaction or click Next to confirm that you want to send ether to this address.

4. Click the Next button.

   Figure 3.19 shows the result. Everything is the same apart from the decision to send 0.01 SepoliaETH to the 0x2Bf07b33566ea5a259d574E97CEe1E7336C4f88f address.

   You can send testnet ETH to the same address and use a block explorer to see the balance before and after sending it. Block explorers are discussed later in this chapter.

FIGURE 3.17: Address to which to send the transaction on MetaMask

FIGURE 3.18: Sending SepoliaETH on MetaMask

FIGURE 3.19: Confirmation on MetaMask on sending SepoliaETH

5. Click Next to display the screen shown in Figure 3.20, which displays the final details of the transaction, including the amount to be sent and the gas fees to be spent.

FIGURE 3.20: Transaction summary and last confirmation of the transaction on MetaMask

6. Click Confirm to see that the transaction has been sent and the confirmation is pending (see Figure 3.21). It should read "Confirmed" if all goes well, and in a few seconds you will see the screen shown in Figure 3.22.

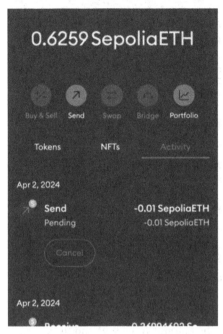

FIGURE 3.21: Transaction is pending the network's confirmation in MetaMask

Congratulations—you have sent your first cryptocurrency transaction!

BLOCK EXPLORERS

Previous chapters referenced Bitcoin and Ethereum as public blockchains, but what does that mean in practice? It means that all transactions made on either blockchain are publicly verifiable by anyone. Bitcoin's transactions and Ethereum's transactions work slightly differently. In this book, we will go through only Ethereum's transactions.

One way to inspect Ethereum transactions is to become a full node and download the whole blockchain to your computer. It is, in theory, doable but takes a lot of time due to its vast size, which keeps growing every minute or, actually, every 12 seconds.

An alternative approach is to use services called *block explorers*, enabling people to inspect specific transactions they are interested in. Let's take the previous example of our first transaction.

If you click the transaction on April 2, 2024, with the status of Send, Confirmed, as shown in Figure 3.23, you get more detailed information about the transaction, as shown in Figure 3.24. Near the top of that screen, click View On Block Explorer.

FIGURE 3.22: Transaction is confirmed by the network on MetaMask

FIGURE 3.23: Transactions in MetaMask

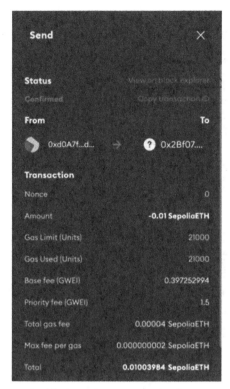

FIGURE 3.24: Viewing transactions on the block explorer in MetaMask

You are transported to the test network of the Sepolia version of Etherscan, one of the block explorers mentioned earlier in this chapter. Etherscan can also be accessed separately from the MetaMask wallet—or any wallet, for that matter—by going to Etherscan.io. There, you can see all the transactions on the Ethereum blockchain, including individual, unique, and whole blocks of transactions.

ETHERSCAN ALTERNATIVES

Since the blockchain space is still emerging and its infancy, Etherscan.io may (or may not) fail, and if it does, its block explorer website would not be available to the public. Just to be on the safe side, there are alternatives to Etherscan.io:

➤ Ethplorer.io

➤ `Blockchain.com`

   (This is not, in any way, an endorsement of these products by me or my publisher.) The block explorer encompasses blockchains such as Bitcoin, Ethereum, and Bitcoin Cash.

➤ `Blockscout.com` and, more specifically, `eth.blockscout.com` for Ethereum's block explorer.

Test Network (Testnet) Block Explorer

In Figure 3.25, you see the information about the transaction of 0.01 SepoliaETH sent to the address that was shown earlier in Figure 3.19.

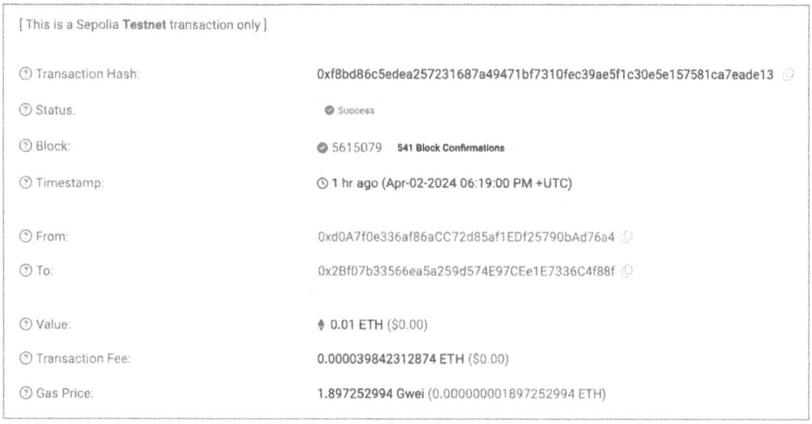

FIGURE 3.25: MetaMask's transaction viewed on block explorer

The information is broken out as follows:

➤ **Transaction hash:** The transaction's hash, which uniquely identifies the transaction on the blockchain.

➤ **Status:** The status of the transaction and whether the transaction was completed.

➤ **Block:** The number of blocks in Sepolia Ethereum's blockchain. Within the testnet's blockchain, there were at least 5,615,979 blocks, and the specific transaction was added to block 5,615,979. We can also see how many blocks of transactions have been confirmed after block 5,615,979 was confirmed. In this context, *confirmed* means that the network of nodes has confirmed the block of transactions after having been appended to the blockchain by a validator node.

➤ **Timestamp:** Shows the day and time of the transaction in the UTC time zone.

➤ **From:** The cryptocurrency address that sent the cryptocurrency.

➤ **To:** The cryptocurrency address that received the cryptocurrency.

➤ **Value:** The value is in ether and USD. Since SepoliaETH was sent, which is a test network, not the leading one, the USD value is shown as 0.

➤ **Transaction fee:** The transaction fee taken by the validators in exchange for processing the transaction and for the computational energy used to validate the transaction.

➤ **Gas Price:** The sender will pay an additional Ether per gas unit. Each transaction consumes gas to execute, and the sender sets the gas price based on the demand and use of the Ethereum network at the time. If many transactions are being processed, the gas fee will be higher to process some transactions earlier than others. To calculate the gas fee, you must multiply the gas price by the total amount of gas used.

Block Explorer: Transaction Anatomy

The next transaction, shown in Figure 3.26, is from Ethereum's main network—which, as you can see, has the same attributes as those shown in Figure 3.25. The only difference is that the Transaction Action is an additional parameter that describes what the specific transaction does, which is sending money from Beaverbuild to the MEV builder.

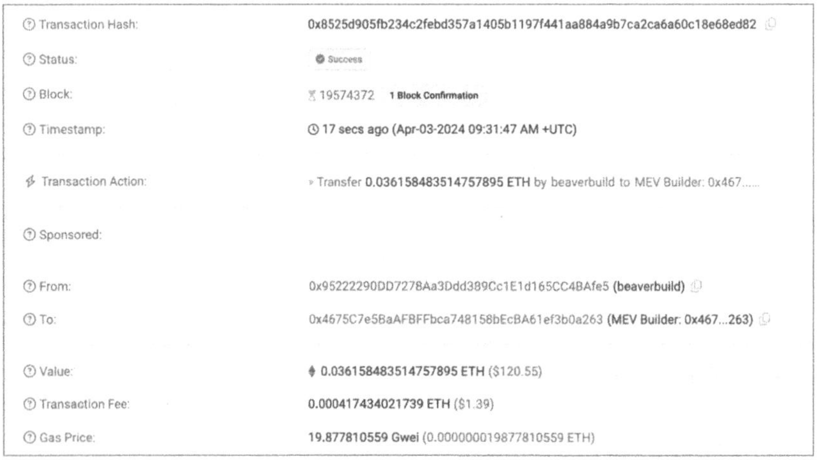

⊙ Transaction Hash:	0x8525d905fb234c2febd357a1405b1197f441aa884a9b7ca2ca6a60c18e68ed82
⊙ Status:	✔ Success
⊙ Block:	🗒 19574372 **1 Block Confirmation**
⊙ Timestamp:	⊙ 17 secs ago (Apr-03-2024 09:31:47 AM +UTC)
⚡ Transaction Action:	▸ Transfer **0.036158483514757895 ETH** by beaverbuild to MEV Builder: 0x467.....
⊙ Sponsored:	
⊙ From:	0x95222290DD7278Aa3Ddd389Cc1E1d165CC4BAfe5 (beaverbuild)
⊙ To:	0x4675C7e5BaAFBFFbca748158bEcBA61ef3b0a263 (MEV Builder: 0x467...263)
⊙ Value:	◆ 0.036158483514757895 ETH ($120.55)
⊙ Transaction Fee:	0.000417434021739 ETH ($1.39)
⊙ Gas Price:	19.877810559 Gwei (0.000000019877810559 ETH)

FIGURE 3.26: Transaction on Ethereum's main network

Beaverbuild and MEV builder represent addresses just like From and To; however, in Ethereum, you can buy what is called an Ethereum Name Service, which is a tag that converts your Ethereum address into a human-readable address of your choice and hence the names. Think of them as pseudonyms or names you insert for characters when playing video games. The Ethereum Name Service is buying the equivalent of the video game character name.

Block Explorer: Block Anatomy

Figure 3.27 shows information not of one transaction as with the previous two examples, but of a whole block of transactions instead.

The information displayed is as follows:

➤ **Block Height:** Block height is the block number dating back to the genesis block—or the first block mined or validated, depending on the consensus mechanism one may use. Block height is a structure that grows without an end regarding blocks to be added onto the chain. Hence, it is more accurate to see it as a building whose floors keep expanding, with the Genesis block being the foundation; the first is the first floor, and the second is the second floor, and so on. Hence, if you ask how high a building is, one may say 200 meters, or they may say it is 15 floors or stories high. Similarly, a block is measured by its height instead of the number by asking essentially, how high is the blockchain?

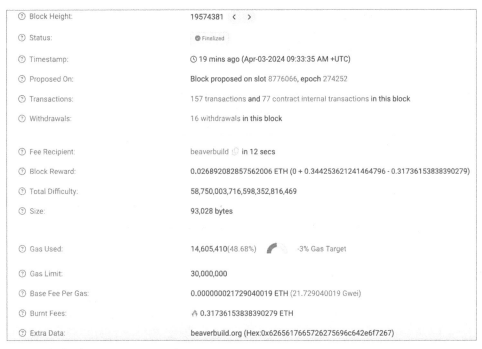

? Block Height:	19574381 ‹ ›
? Status:	● Finalized
? Timestamp:	⏱ 19 mins ago (Apr-03-2024 09:33:35 AM +UTC)
? Proposed On:	Block proposed on slot 8776066, epoch 274252
? Transactions:	157 transactions and 77 contract internal transactions in this block
? Withdrawals:	16 withdrawals in this block
? Fee Recipient:	beaverbuild 🛈 in 12 secs
? Block Reward:	0.026892082857562006 ETH (0 + 0.344253621241464796 - 0.31736153838390279)
? Total Difficulty:	58,750,003,716,598,352,816,469
? Size:	93,028 bytes
? Gas Used:	14,605,410(48.68%) -3% Gas Target
? Gas Limit:	30,000,000
? Base Fee Per Gas:	0.000000021729040019 ETH (21.729040019 Gwei)
? Burnt Fees:	🔥 0.31736153838390279 ETH
? Extra Data:	beaverbuild.org (Hex:0x6265617665726275696c642e6f7267)

FIGURE 3.27: A block of transactions on Ethereum's mainnet

➤ **Status:** Like with a single transaction as shown previously, the status shows whether a block has been successfully added to the blockchain.

➤ **Timestamp:** This is when the block was confirmed, which in the picture is 19 minutes ago, or more precisely, April 3, 2024, at 9:33 a.m. UTC.

➤ **Proposed on:** Proposed On indicates that the block was proposed during slot number 8,776,066 and epoch 274,252.

As this may be somewhat cryptic to someone who encounters this for the first time, let's look at what slot number and epoch number mean:

➤ **Epoch** is the Greek word for "era" in English. As such, it represents a particular division of time or blocks of time. These are figurative blocks, not the ones on the blockchain. Epochs themselves are composed of several fixed slots, which, in turn, are a period during which the validator can propose a new—actual, not figurative—block. After the rest of the network nodes gossip through the information and agree on the one actual state of the blockchain, the block can be validated onto the blockchain by the validator proposing it.

➤ Think of an epoch as a day at the university or school; the **slots** are like the courses one may take during the university day. A day at the university can be compared to an epoch on the Ethereum blockchain; both represent a particular division of time or a cycle. Just as a year consists of 365 cycles (days), an epoch consists of slots, analogous to the courses taken during the day. In this analogy, the students represent the nodes in the network, attending classes (slots) to engage with and learn the material. Students can ask questions and contribute to the discussion, just as nodes participate in the network and gossip. The professor acts as the validator, proposing or teaching new course material during each class.

The key difference between an epoch and a slot on the Ethereum blockchain, as opposed to a day and a university class, is the duration of each cycle. On the blockchain, a slot—the time a validator has to propose a new block on the blockchain—is 12 seconds, whereas an epoch consists of 32 slots. Thus:

➤ 12 (seconds in one slot) * 32 (slots in an epoch) = 384 (seconds in all slots within one epoch).

➤ 384 (seconds in all slots within an epoch) / 60 (seconds within a minute) = 6.4.

One way of calculating the number of slots within one epoch is as follows:

8,776,066 (slot number) / 274,252 (Epoch Number) = 32 slots or one epoch.

The time slots and epochs are split this way to ensure security within the blockchain.

➤ **Transactions:** The number of unique transactions included in the block with height 19574381. The 77 internal transactions refer to transactions that have been called from one contract to another (see Figure 3.28). This is something you'll see in the following chapters. However, one of the powerful features of smart contracts is that one smart contract on the blockchain can import and inherit the properties of another unrelated smart contract and call its transactions.

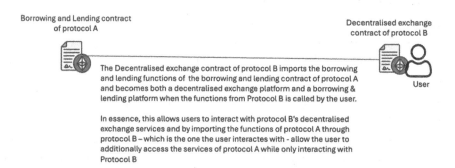

FIGURE 3.28: Contract composability example

For simplicity, imagine it like Amazon maintaining a constant stock of 500 Bosch washing machines. Every time a customer clicks Buy and purchases a washing machine, an algorithm connected to Bosch's ordering system automatically triggers a new order to replenish the stock. This ensures that the total number of available washing machines always remains at 500.

➤ **Withdrawals**: As mentioned in Chapter 2, where we discussed Ethereum's architecture, withdrawals in Ethereum 2.0e, refer to staking, which can be either:

 ➤ Removing staked Ether from a contract and putting it back into a wallet

 ➤ Removing it from the Beacon Chain after the Ether has been unlocked

➤ **Fee Recipient**: Fee recipient refers to the node that proposed and validated the block and receives transaction fees for that specific block. In this case, it is Beaverbuild.

➤ **Block Reward**: This is the reward received by the block validator after successfully validating a block onto the blockchain, and it is 0.0268+ ETH. The original reward was 0.34+ ETH, but 0.31+ ETH gets burned due to the burning mechanism mentioned in Chapter 2.

➤ **Total Difficulty**: This is the cumulative difficulty miners and validators use to add a block to the blockchain if the blockchain is running on PoW, which is the case for Ethereum Sepolia. The difficulty starts from the genesis block—the very first block—up to the block height of 19574381.

➤ **Size**: The size of the block, which in this case is 93,028 bytes. This size adds cumulatively to the Ethereum Blockchain with each block, increasing the size of the blockchain constantly. As of April 6, 2024, it is more than two terabytes in size if using the lighter version of the blockchain or 12 TB if using the full version of the blockchain, and thus, the size of the blockchain increases every single time.

➤ **Gas Used**: The gas used refers to all the gas spent by all transactions added to the block. In this case, it is 14,605,410 gas units, which is 48.68% of the gas limit in this block. The gas limit has been set to 30,000,000 gas units maximum to ensure that block stability, processing, production, and communication between the nodes remain stable at 12 seconds per block.

➤ **Gas Limit**: As explained, the gas limit is the total gas allowed within one block to ensure the stability of the Ethereum blockchain in terms of mathematics when it comes to block production, communication, and processing.

➤ **Base Fee per Gas**: The base fee per gas refers to the smallest unit of weight (the smallest Ethereum denominations, such as cents in dollars) that must be paid per unit of gas for a transaction to be processed. This means that even if no one used the Ethereum blockchain for a whole day other than one random person who executed one transaction within 24 hours, they would still pay that small amount.

 Another way of looking at it is the base fee per gas, the starting bid for a transaction to be included and processed first.

➤ **Burnt Fees**: This is the amount of ETH that was burned, or, in other words, removed from circulation—from the base fee per gas. This specific block, as mentioned, burned 0.31+ ETH.

➤ **Extra Data**: In the extra data field, block validators can include additional data that they want to have per block proposed and validated, such as the validator's name, which is Beaverbuild.

ENS DOMAINS

As you may have noticed, the block validator has his pseudonym instead of Beaverbuild having their ETH address. This is due to a service called Ethereum Name Service (ENS), which can replace—on the surface at least—the number of the address of someone with a humanly readable name, such as, in this case, beaverbuild, and when someone looks up this address on Etherscan, they can type beaverbuild instead.

This adds convenience into the mix since instead of having to use an ETH address to send your money to your friend, you can use the name or pseudonym it makes, which makes, however, at the same time, several people add their ENS domain on their profile on the social media X or any other that may make them a target of scammers and people with malicious intent as they can quickly go on Etherscan and see how much money the person has in that wallet and try to scam them through social engineering or by other means.

Connecting to DApps

One way to interact with a smart contract or decentralized application is to visit its website, such as uniswap.org. However, ensure you use the correct link, as scammers can often redirect you to an identical website through phishing links. If you connect your wallet to the application, the malicious actor will drain the money.

1.   After arriving on the website, click Launch App at the top right, as shown in Figure 3.29.

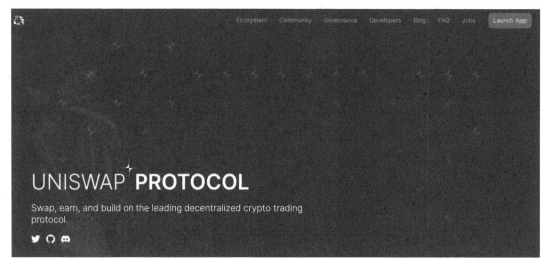

FIGURE 3.29: Uniswap protocol landing page

The application's interface opens (see Figure 3.30), where you can swap tokens, in this case ETH, for another token that has not been selected yet.

FIGURE 3.30: Uniswap protocol landing page of decentralized application

2. Before doing the swap, however, you have to connect your wallet. Click Connect, shown at the top right in Figure 3.30.

3. After clicking Connect, a list of wallets will pop up, as shown in Figure 3.31. Choose the wallet you have installed—in this case, MetaMask.

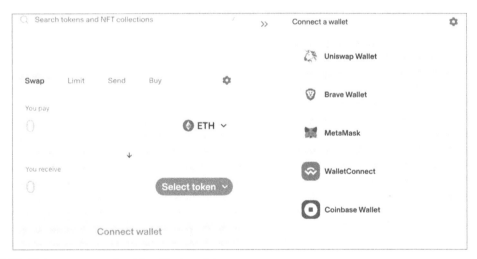

FIGURE 3.31: Uniswap connecting MetaMask wallet

4. After connecting, you can see your balance. (In this example, it's 0.616 ETH.) Click Select Token (see Figure 3.32) to select the token to swap.

FIGURE 3.32: Uniswap wallet connected and balance shown

After clicking Select Token, a menu pops up where you can select the token you want to swap. In this case, within the testnet, Wrapped Ether (WETH) and Uniswap (UNI) are available to swap, as shown in Figure 3.33. Additionally, you may enter the contract of a specific token, import it into the contract, and start swapping your Ether for that token.

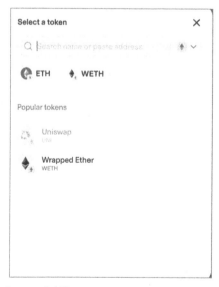

FIGURE 3.33: Uniswap swapping token availability screen

For example, you can find the contract address of the Aave Token or the DAI stablecoin on Google, import it into Uniswap, and swap it. The top right of Figure 3.33 shows the ETH logo with a downward arrow beside it.

5. Click this arrow, to see the blockchains Uniswap is integrated with, as shown in Figure 3.34: Arbitrum, Optimism, Polygon, Base, BNB Chain, Avalanche, Celo, and Blast. When you click one of those blockchains, your wallet will be transitioned to that blockchain. It will no longer be on the Ethereum blockchain.

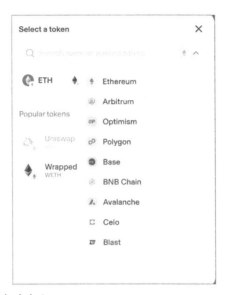

FIGURE 3.34: Uniswap changing blockchain screen

Figure 3.35 shows that after choosing Uniswap (UNI) and trading all my testnet ETH for UNI, in this testnet version my 0.6 ETH would be worth 0.15+ UNI. However, in this example I decided to swap only 0.1 ETH to show the next steps.

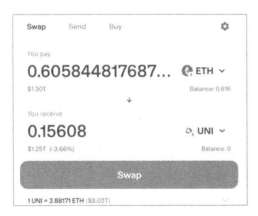

FIGURE 3.35: Uniswap value swap overview

As shown in Figure 3.36, after choosing 0.1 ETH to be swapped, I will receive 0.02+ UNI. You can also see the rate: 1 UNI = 3.87 ETH, which is equal to 8+ trillion dollars (on a fake network, not in real life). Also, the fee is 0 USD (also in a fake network, not in real life, as you always pay a fee).

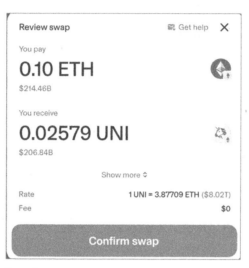

FIGURE 3.36: Uniswap swap confirmation

6. Confirm the swap. You will see a loading screen asking you to Proceed in your wallet, as shown in Figure 3.37.

FIGURE 3.37: Confirm swap loading screen

On MetaMask, you see the transaction details and, for the curious, the same information in a hexadecimal format. Also note that the network was busy during the swap, and gas prices were high. Estimates of gas prices are less accurate—this is not something to be worried about in a test; as Figure 3.38 shows, no one pays real money for the transaction swap in a fake network, as everything being paid is paid in Testnet ETH and not real ETH. The estimated fee is 0.0002958 ETH, and the total cost will be 0.1 (the amount that I want to swap) + 0.0002958 ETH (the transaction fee), which, when added, gives 0.10002958 ETH.

FIGURE 3.38: Uniswap swap overview on MetaMask

7. After confirming the transaction in the MetaMask wallet, you can see in Figure 3.39 that the swap has been submitted to the network, and a confirmation is pending. You can also see a View On Explorer option, which we will discuss later in this chapter.

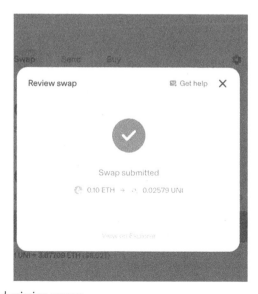

FIGURE 3.39: Uniswap swap submission screen

After 12 seconds you can see that 0.1 ETH has been successfully swapped for 0.026 UNI, as shown in Figure 3.40.

FIGURE 3.40: Uniswap swap confirmation

8. As the last step in this example, swap the UNI back into ETH (since we will be doing a lot of coding in the next chapters).

    Follow the same process you did when swapping ETH to UNI, except this time clicking the arrow in the center between the UNI token and the ETH token (see Figure 3.41). Specify how much you want to swap, the ETH currency, and the 0.1 ETH you want to get back.

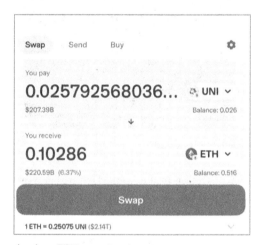

FIGURE 3.41: Uniswap UNI swap back to ETH overview

Click Swap, and the same process should occur.

> **NOTE** *If something is different when you try this, that's okay—do not hesitate to make mistakes since this is a test network.*
>
> *But you do not want to make mistakes in a real network since you lose real money, whether cryptocurrency or fiat, that you consider real cash or both.*

Block Explorer: Anatomy of a Wallet

Another significant and essential feature of block explorers is their ability to provide detailed information about wallet addresses. This information includes balances, transactions, NFT holdings, internal transactions, token transfers, produced blocks, and other analytics for all types of wallets, whether hosted, browser-based, hardware, desktop, mobile, multisignature, or hierarchical deterministic. All this data can be accessed, verified, and viewed through a block explorer (see Figure 3.42).

In Figure 3.42, we can see the address:

```
0x8186b214A917fb4922Eb984fb80CFAfA30EE8810
```

FIGURE 3.42: ETH address block explorer

We can see the ETH balance of the address, which is 1.269+ ETH, which was equal to 4,230.24 USD. We can also see, besides the whole value, the ratio value of dollars to 1 ETH where the 3,333.08 USD equaled 1 ETH. Moreover, in the section beside the balance, we can find any private name tags one may want to add to the address and also the information about when was the last transaction from this wallet sent (12 seconds ago) as well as the very first transaction that was sent—150 days ago. Additionally, looking at the ETH value, we can see the token holdings that the address has (see Figure 3.43).

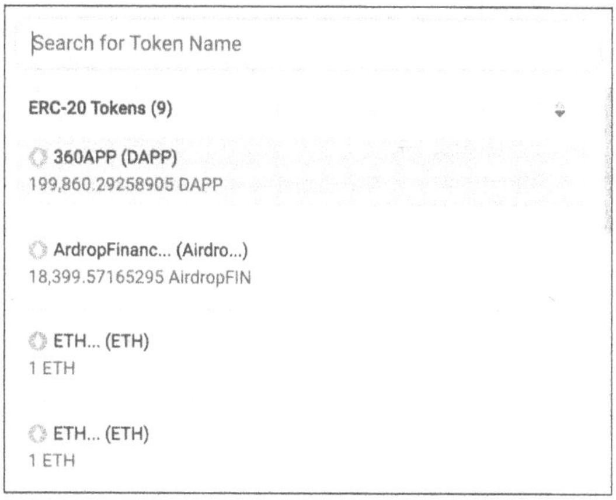

FIGURE 3.43: ETH ERC-20 tokens

Nine tokens are of the ERC-20 type, as shown in Figures 3.43 and 3.44. They are fungible tokens similar to how ether is fungible—each ether coin (or fraction of a coin) is equivalent in value to any other ether coin. (ERC-20 tokens are discussed in more detail in Chapter 9.) However, the fact that the tokens shown in Figure 3.43 do not have a USD value means that they are all at 0$ and are most likely scams that were sent to the wallet of the owner, or maybe the tokens are not linked to an Oracle that relays real-world information and pricing. (Chapter 8 gives more information about oracles.)

⚫ Strong (STRONG)	$1,922.08
394.6776 STRONG	@4.87
▰ DerivaDAO (DDX)	$576.28
8,164.64733013 DDX	@0.0706
⬥ Tether USD (USDT)	$209.36
209.355461 USDT	@1.00
⬤ Refereum (RFR)	$13.54
132,371.4289 RFR	@0.0001
⬡ SONM (SNM)	$2.33

FIGURE 3.44: ETH ERC-20 tokens part 2

Looking at another wallet non-scam tokens and tokens with an Oracle connected to relay the price information of the token, such as in the examples shown in Figure 3.44, we can see a real-time USD value that reflects the value of the tokens.

Going back to the original 0x8186b214A917fb4922Eb984fb80CFAfA30EE8810 wallet introduced in Figure 3.42, we can click token holdings to see that the holder has several NFTs such as the NameWrapper from the ENS (see Figure 3.45) which is the first result in the "NFT Tokens" result and the liquidETH.org NFT token being the second after the NameWrapper that the owner received through Airdrop (see Figure 3.45). Finally, we also see ERC-1155 Tokens, a standard that combines fungible and nonfungible tokens but with the tag of [Suspicious], alluding to the possibility that these tokens are most likely scams that were sent to the owner to somehow engineer the owner to interact with them and possibly corrupt their wallet in one way or another. Hence, it is helpful to use block explorers to ensure that one's wallet does not carry such scam tokens. If it does, never import or interact with these tokens.

Looking at the details for the 0x8186b214A917fb4922Eb984fb80CFAfA30EE8810 wallet, one can also see the transactions the wallet has been doing since its inception in chronological order from the most recent to the oldest (see Figure 3.46).

The information includes the following:

➤ **Transaction hash:** The transaction hash is a unique identifier for each transaction. Upon clicking it, we can inspect the transaction as we did with the transaction anatomy in Figure 3.25 and the text that follows it.

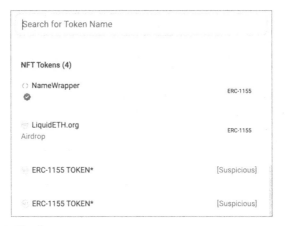

FIGURE 3.45: Block explorer NFT tokens

➤ **Method:** The types of transfers or methods in the pictured list are all money transfers.

➤ **Block:** This is the number of the Ethereum block in which the specific transaction is located.

➤ **Age:** This is the age of the transactions, again from the newest to the oldest.

➤ **From:** This is the transaction's sender; in all the pictured cases, it is the wallet owner.

➤ **Out:** This signifies that the amount of money is going *out* of the wallet of Loki Builder.

➤ **To:** This is the destination of the money sent from Loki Builder's wallet.

➤ **Value:** This is the value of the transaction being sent.

➤ **Transaction fee:** The transaction fee is taken for the specific transaction that was executed.

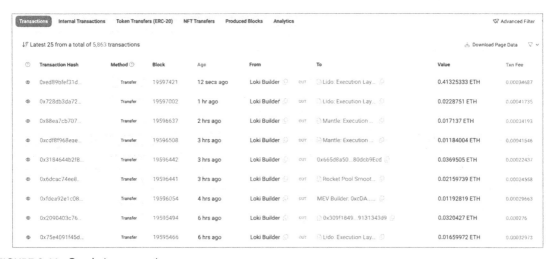

FIGURE 3.46: On-chain transactions

Figure 3.47 shows the list of internal transactions that took place while using the wallet we've been looking at. The information is almost identical between the previous transactions and the internal transactions; the only difference is that the transaction hash is the parent transaction hash this time. Parent transaction hashes refer to the transactions associated with the original transaction triggered by a contract that has imported functions from another contract, making those functions callable. For example, if Uniswap (mentioned earlier in this chapter) was to import the lending and borrowing functions of Aave (also mentioned in Chapter 1), and then a Uniswap user—in this case Loki Builder—were to trigger Aave's contract through Uniswap, that would be referred to as internal transaction and would have a parent transaction hash related to the two contracts of Aave and Uniswap.

Parent Txn Hash	Block	Age	From		To	Value
0x16c2bb2b3af...	19597421	12 secs ago	MEV Bot: 0x74b...f1d	→	Loki Builder	0.16967994 ETH
0x3defc07d957...	19596442	3 hrs ago	MEV Bot: 0x5dd...35f	→	Loki Builder	0.001 ETH
0xbf189122559...	19596441	3 hrs ago	MEV Bot: 0x74b...f1d	→	Loki Builder	0.00806314 ETH
0xe640e4c5a8...	19595331	7 hrs ago	MEV Bot: 0x74b...f1d	→	Loki Builder	0.0066067 ETH
0xfc7925269ff...	19594921	8 hrs ago	MEV Bot: 0x74b...f1d	→	Loki Builder	0.01147388 ETH
0xbf9fa43d50e...	19594636	9 hrs ago	MEV Bot: 0x74b...f1d	→	Loki Builder	0.00585766 ETH
0x6bc0e0a07a...	19594331	10 hrs ago	MEV Bot: 0x74b...f1d	→	Loki Builder	0.00551228 ETH
0xf5e164ad5b2...	19594082	11 hrs ago	MEV Bot: 0x5f9...efd	→	Loki Builder	0.00272036 ETH
0xcf5d9995048...	19594082	11 hrs ago	MEV Bot: 0x74b...f1d	→	Loki Builder	0.00307883 ETH
0x1e9036e691...	19593150	14 hrs ago	MEV Bot: 0x8d7...ff5	→	Loki Builder	0.0001 ETH

FIGURE 3.47: Internal transactions

In Figure 3.48 you can see the transfers, specifically the transactions evolving only fungible ERC-20 tokens. The information per transaction is similar to that in Figure 3.47. The only significant difference is the address Null: 0x0000…0000. This address is used to send burnable tokens that someone no longer needs, either to remove them from their wallet or to take them out of circulation within a specific token's economy. Additionally, the null address serves as a destination for minting tokens, which is the process being demonstrated in this example.

Figure 3.49 shows the NFT transfers from the wallet. In this case, the information shown includes the transaction hash of the transaction transferring the NFT(s), the method of transfer (which in the examples above are Airdrop and Register), the block height, the age of the transaction, from and to, and the type of the token (in this case, ERC-1155, a token standard beyond the scope of this book). Still, it combines NFT tokens with fungible tokens, and the item transfers itself.

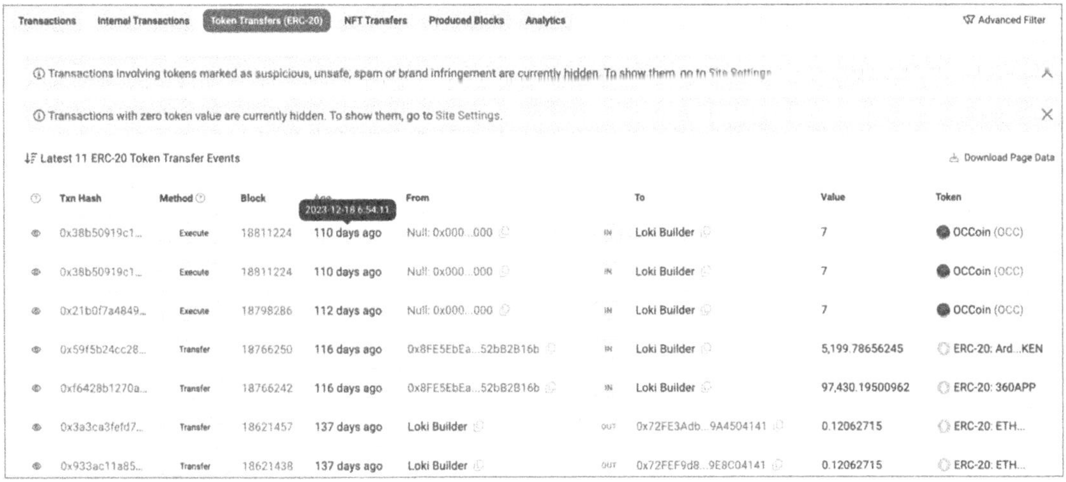

FIGURE 3.48: Token transfers

FIGURE 3.49: NFT Transfers

> **NOTE** *Airdrops occur when a cryptocurrency project rewards users by sending tokens to their wallets, either for performing a specific action requested or sometimes without any action. For example, a project may offer an Airdrop to early adopters who engage with its testnet multiple times. Alternatively, a project might reward users with an Airdrop as a token of appreciation for contributing to the project in a meaningful way.*

In Figure 3.50 you can see the blocks produced or validated by the specific address, and the validated block's height, the block's age, the transaction, the difficulty, the gas used, and the reward for the block that was validated.

In Figure 3.51, we see the address of a smart contract, not a hash of a transaction or a wallet address. Nothing differs from what we have learned except the tabs Contract and Events. The events in this contract are empty, and we will see and explain them in later chapters, including Chapter 9. However, we will focus for the remainder of this chapter on the Contract tab.

Transactions	Internal Transactions	Token Transfers (ERC-20)	NFT Transfers	Produced Blocks	Analytics

↓F Latest 25 blocks (From a total of 5,772 blocks with 262.90 Ether produced)

Block	Age	Transaction	Difficulty	Gas Used	Reward
19597421	12 secs ago	177	0.00 TH	16,196,821 (53.99%)	0.243920265536572479 ETH
19597002	1 hr ago	188	0.00 TH	14,857,958 (49.53%)	0.02162681440819373 ETH
19596637	2 hrs ago	143	0.00 TH	11,927,732 (39.76%)	0.015468677042351536 ETH
19596508	3 hrs ago	142	0.00 TH	8,396,988 (27.99%)	0.010192543985259941 ETH
19596442	3 hrs ago	338	0.00 TH	29,050,345 (96.83%)	0.034348645193073366 ETH
19596441	3 hrs ago	62	0.00 TH	4,921,948 (16.41%)	0.017146988028370924 ETH
19596054	4 hrs ago	64	0.00 TH	2,621,280 (8.74%)	0.115313003901031309 ETH
19595494	6 hrs ago	55	0.00 TH	4,337,336 (14.46%)	0.030321405172565316 ETH
19595466	6 hrs ago	124	0.00 TH	11,052,704 (36.84%)	0.037043837170993391 ETH
19595331	7 hrs ago	211	0.00 TH	21,531,930 (71.77%)	0.007221943861213423 ETH

FIGURE 3.50: Produced blocks

Contract 0x68b3465833fb72A70ecDF485E0e4C7bD8665Fc45

Transactions	Internal Transactions	Token Transfers (ERC-20)	NFT Transfers	Contract	Events	Analytics	Multichain Portfolio

↓F Latest 25 from a total of 18,476,446 transactions
(More than 25 Pending Txns)   ⬇ Down

Transaction Hash	Method	Block	Age	From		To	Value
0xa8d77f34416...	Exact Input Si...	(pending)	1 min ago	0xb1b2d032...5216E8404	IN	Uniswap V3: Router 2	0 ETH
0xe57c7b1228...	Multicall	(pending)	3 mins ago	0xddA53701...34cF13B8E	IN	Uniswap V3: Router 2	0.001 ETH
0x436e0edd2d...	Multicall	(pending)	11 mins ago	0xc43D65a4...9aCa66BBB	IN	Uniswap V3: Router 2	0.001 ETH
0xe701e5f8c35...	Multicall	(pending)	13 mins ago	0x27eFd067...B0B0eF9be	IN	Uniswap V3: Router 2	0.004 ETH
0x442ace5f2a6...	Multicall	(pending)	13 mins ago	0x67D43783...907C21952	IN	Uniswap V3: Router 2	0.0002 ETH
0xd7d870aa71...	Multicall	(pending)	15 mins ago	0x92529653...8434c6688	IN	Uniswap V3: Router 2	0.002 ETH

FIGURE 3.51: Smart contract address

By clicking the Contract tab, users can view and inspect the smart contract's code, as shown in Figures 3.52 and 3.53, along with any related contracts, directly within the interface—without needing to consult GitHub. However, this is possible only if the contract deployer has verified the contract on Etherscan. Verification involves uploading and publishing the smart contract code on Etherscan, making it accessible to the public.

FIGURE 3.52: Smart contract code

```
1  // SPDX-License-Identifier: GPL-2.0-or-later
2  pragma solidity =0.7.6;
3  pragma abicoder v2;
4
5  import '@uniswap/v3-periphery/contracts/base/SelfPermit.sol';
6  import '@uniswap/v3-periphery/contracts/base/PeripheryImmutableState.sol';
7
8  import './interfaces/ISwapRouter02.sol';
9  import './V2SwapRouter.sol';
10 import './V3SwapRouter.sol';
11 import './base/ApproveAndCall.sol';
12 import './base/MulticallExtended.sol';
13
14 /// @title Uniswap V2 and V3 Swap Router
15 contract SwapRouter02 is ISwapRouter02, V2SwapRouter, V3SwapRouter, ApproveAndCall, MulticallExtended, SelfPermit {
16     constructor(
17         address _factoryV2,
18         address factoryV3,
19         address _positionManager,
20         address _WETH9
21     ) ImmutableState(_factoryV2, _positionManager) PeripheryImmutableState(factoryV3, _WETH9) {}
22 }
```

ile 3 of 63 : SelfPermit.sol

```
1  // SPDX-License-Identifier: GPL-2.0-or-later
2  pragma solidity >=0.5.0;
3
4  import '@openzeppelin/contracts/token/ERC20/IERC20.sol';
5  import '@openzeppelin/contracts/drafts/IERC20Permit.sol';
6
7  import '../interfaces/ISelfPermit.sol';
8  import '../interfaces/external/IERC20PermitAllowed.sol';
9
10 /// @title Self Permit
11 /// @notice Functionality to call permit on any EIP-2612-compliant token for use in the route
12 /// @dev These functions are expected to be embedded in multicalls to allow EOAs to approve a contract and call a function
13 /// that requires an approval in a single transaction.
14 abstract contract SelfPermit is ISelfPermit {
15     /// @inheritdoc ISelfPermit
16     function selfPermit(
```

FIGURE 3.53: Smart contract code #2

When someone clicks the Read Contract subtab and connects their wallet (as shown in Figure 3.54), they can see information about the contract without making any changes to the state of the Ethereum blockchain. The Read Contract functionality retrieves and displays data from the blockchain, such as the balance, token supply, and other read-only data. This process does not change the balances of any smart contract or wallet and does not change the state of the blockchain.

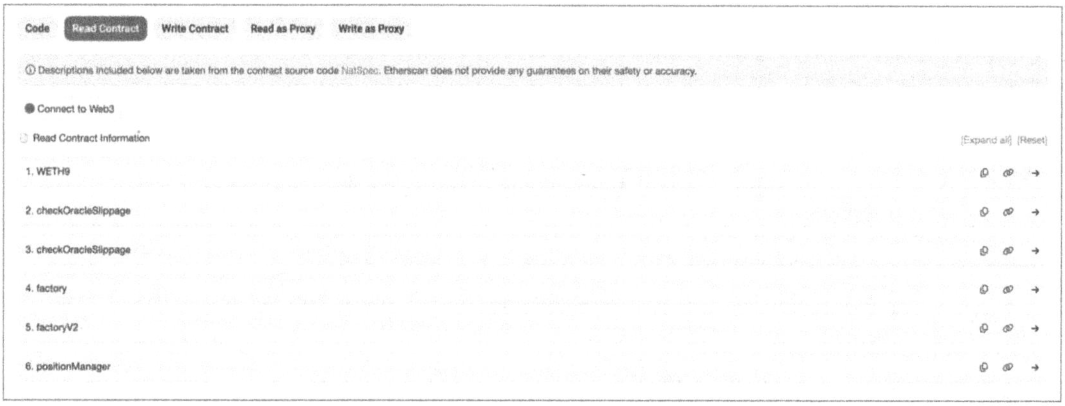

FIGURE 3.54: Read contract

On the other hand, connecting a wallet and using the functions in the Write Contract subsection (see Figure 3.55) can call and use contract functions from Etherscan, which can be seen as a Web3 interface to smart contracts.

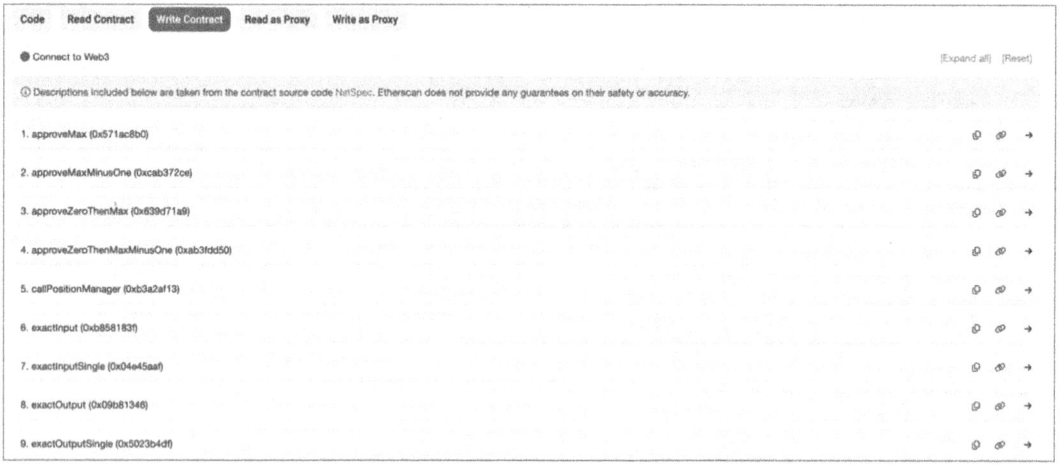

FIGURE 3.55: Write contract

Finally, there is the option—although not always available—of reading or writing a contract as a proxy (see Figure 3.56). Chapter 12 discusses proxy and upgradable contracts.

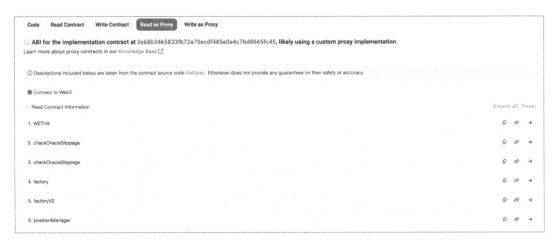

FIGURE 3.56: Read As Proxy

As we will see in Chapter 12, although smart contracts may be immutable for the most part, there are a couple of ways of working around this immutability, such as introducing proxy contracts that separate a contract's logic from its data storage. These contracts allow the logic to be upgraded, allowing for new features or correcting mistakes by deploying a new contract that the proxy points towards.

In the case of Etherscan, Read As Proxy means that the contract functions through the proxy contract instead of directly. Thus, the data stored by the proxy contract will be read and managed by the proxy contract. This is because even if a new contract is implemented behind the proxy, the way you access the data in this contract remains the same.

Finally, we can also see Write As Proxy (see Figure 3.57). Like Read As Proxy, the contract writes and executes code through the proxy contract.

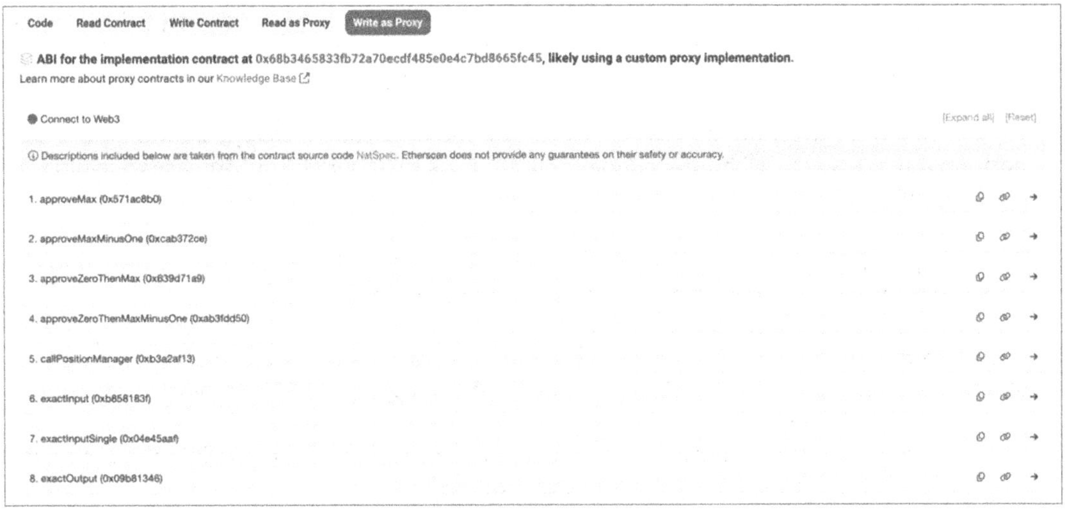

FIGURE 3.57: Write As Proxy

CHAPTER 3 QUESTIONS

1. Explain the key differences between hosted wallets, browser wallets, and hardware wallets, including their respective advantages and disadvantages.

2. What are the risks associated with hosted wallets, and how can users mitigate these risks effectively?

3. Describe how to set up and use a homemade hardware wallet using an old smartphone. What are the trade-offs compared to commercially available hardware wallets?

4. How can malicious websites exploit users by mimicking legitimate URLs? Provide examples and strategies for mitigating this risk.

5. Describe a sophisticated job search scam involving browser wallets. What steps can individuals take to avoid falling victim to such schemes?

6. Explain the concept of SIM swap attacks and provide an example of how even high-profile individuals, such as Vitalik Buterin, have been affected. What steps can users take to protect themselves?

7. What is a multisignature wallet, and how does it enhance security? Provide an example of its use in both individual and organizational contexts.

8. What are HD wallets, and how do they simplify managing multisignature setups? What is a potential vulnerability associated with HD wallets?

9. Describe the process of installing MetaMask, creating a new wallet, and importing an existing wallet using a seed phrase. What security precautions should users take during these steps?

10. What are Ethereum testnets, and why are they essential for developers? Provide examples of testnets and their primary use cases.

11. Explain how to connect MetaMask to a decentralized application (DApp) like Uniswap and perform a token swap. What precautions should users take during this process to avoid phishing attacks?

12. What are proxy contracts, and how do they allow for upgradability in smart contract logic? How can users interact with proxy contracts using Etherscan?

13. What information can be obtained from block explorers like Etherscan? Explain the anatomy of a transaction, wallet, and block using specific attributes provided by a block explorer.

14. How can block explorers be used to identify scam tokens or NFTs in a wallet? What should users do if they find suspicious tokens in their wallets?

15. Vitalik Buterin, the founder of Ethereum, burned or removed from circulation 6 billion USD in Shiba Inu tokens, half of the supply of the meme token sent to his wallet for free by the founders of the meme token project. Vitalik used a null address to burn the tokens.

Go to one of the block explorers and take a look at the address to which Vitalik sent the burned tokens. The burned tokens are still—of course—there since no one uses the address or has the keys to it:

Address: 0xdEAD000000000000000042069420694206942069

Based on what you learned, use your new skills to detect how many Shiba Inu Tokens the address has. What else, if anything, can you see the address containing it?

This is the transaction hash of Vitalik's transaction to burn the Shiba Inu Tokens:

0x125714bb4db48757007fff2671b37637bbfd6d47b3a4757ebbd0c5222984f905

Go on a block explorer and take a look at it. What is the block height within which the transaction is? How many block confirmations have occurred since the transaction and block were confirmed? How many Shiba Inu tokens did Vitalik send to the zero address? What is the difference in numbers between the current Shiba Inu Tokens in the address and the amount Vitalik sent?

Since block confirmations happen approximately every 12 seconds and are updated in real time on a block explorer, how long ago was the burning of half of the Shiba Inu token supplied by Vitalik? Use the number of block confirmations you observed when you first accessed the transaction to calculate your hours, days, weeks, months, and years.

Finally, this is the transaction hash of another of Vitalik's transactions:

0x7a69f558bdc4aaf1e6bab9473c84cb2fddbd1e419c44d5c22eb88bedeb09657c

Remix, Data Types, Visibility, and HelloWorld

This chapter introduces you to the Remix integrated development environment (IDE). You will write your first smart contract, the classic `HelloWorld`, and will start exploring the most crucial concepts in programming. Additionally, the chapter will state under which license a contract is being released as well as the Solidity version the contract uses.

Moreover, we will explore fundamental Solidity-specific concepts such as data types, function visibility, and function modifiers.

WHAT IS PROGRAMMING?

Programming is often viewed as a cornerstone of modern digital technology. While this might seem intimidating to beginners, it can be reassuring to realize that programming is simply a language you learn to communicate with computers—just as learning Spanish allows you to communicate with Spanish speakers.

Much like human languages, programming languages have unique structures, rules, and expressions. For example, to fully appreciate Spanish culture or Russian literature, you must learn the respective languages. Similarly, understanding programming fields like data analysis or game development requires learning specific languages such as Python for its versatility in data science, C++ for game development, or Solidity for creating smart contracts.

Human languages evolve over time, incorporating new words and discarding outdated ones—consider *selfie* or *lol*, which have become part of global lexicons. Programming languages evolve similarly, with new versions introducing features and improvements while phasing out older syntax. Each programming language also has its own "culture" or ethos: Python emphasizes simplicity, while Solidity reflects blockchain principles like transparency, security, and decentralization.

The primary difference between human and programming languages lies in their purpose: the former facilitates human communication, while the latter enables communication with computers. Additionally, programming languages are translated into binary code (0s and 1s) by a *compiler*, serving as a bridge between human-written code and computer understanding—much like a translator for human languages.

If you're new to programming, think of it as learning a new language to communicate with computers. With time, effort, and practice, anyone can master it, just as they can learn any human language.

STARTING WITH SOLIDITY, REMIX, AND HELLOWORLD

Solidity is a high-level programming language. Compared to low-level programming languages, which are usually difficult for humans to read, high-level programming languages are easier to read and understand because they more closely resemble human language. That allows programmers to focus on building applications and, in Solidity's case, decentralized applications. However, high-level languages tend to suffer in efficiency, which is where low-level languages excel.

> **NOTE** *Generally speaking, low-level languages (for example, C++) are used to build operating systems such as Windows, macOS, and Android. High-level programming languages are used to build applications like Shopify, Spotify, and Netflix, or to perform data analysis. These applications run "on top of" Windows, macOS, and Android. For example, when you buy a MacBook, macOS is pre-installed, and any application you download and install runs on macOS. Even web browsers (often developed with high-level languages), operate within the framework of macOS or Windows, which are themselves developed with high-level languages.*

To get started with Solidity, it's important to know that Solidity is a case-sensitive programming language. This means that it matters whether something is written with uppercase or lowercase letters. For example, if you write `pragma`, Solidity would recognize it as valid; however, writing `Pragma` will result in an error because Solidity does not recognize the uppercase P. In other words, for Solidity, *p* and *P* are as different as *a* and *b*.

> **NOTE** `pragma` *is used to specify compiler directives. A compiler translates code to machine code, a type of code that the computer can understand, process, and execute. Compiler directives in Solidity are special instructions that provide metadata or configuration settings to the Solidity compiler.*

Second, you need to use an IDE. In this book, we are going to use two IDEs: Remix and Visual Studio Code. We'll start in this chapter with Remix and later expand to a more classic development environment: Microsoft Visual Studio Code.

Creating the HelloWorld.sol File in Remix

In this section, you will use Remix to create a new file named `HelloWorld`

1. Go to the `https://remix.ethereum.org` website where you will see the interface shown in Figure 4.1.

FIGURE 4.1 Remix interface

In the workspaces shown to the left in Figure 4.1, you can see several folders and files: `contracts`, `scripts`, `tests`, a `.json` file, and a `readme.txt` file. You are going to delete them all and add your own first file called `HelloWorld.sol`.

2. To delete the files, either right-click each folder and file and click Delete, or hold the Shift key and click each individual folder and file and then right-click Delete All, as shown in Figure 4.2.

3. After having deleted the folders and files, it is time to right-click anywhere in the File Explorer pane and click New File, as shown in Figure 4.3.

    A new file will pop up without a name, as shown in Figure 4.4.

4. Name the file `HelloWorld.sol`, as shown in Figure 4.5.

`HelloWorld` is the name of the file, while `.sol` indicates that the file contains Solidity code that the compiler can translate to 0s and 1s.

Figure 4.6 shows the screen where you can start typing your first piece of "code."

FIGURE 4.2 Remix interface deleting files

FIGURE 4.3 Remix interface creating a new file

FIGURE 4.4 Remix interface naming a new file

FIGURE 4.5 Remix workspaces with a newly created file

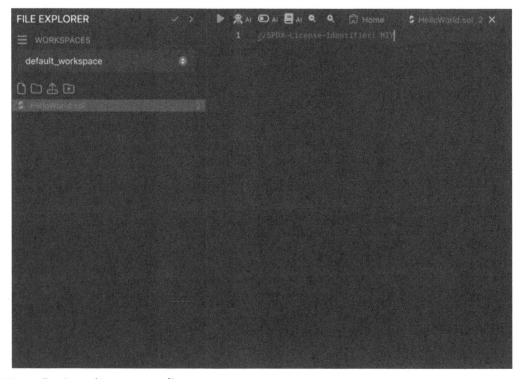

FIGURE 4.6 Remix working on a new file

SPDX-LICENSE-IDENTIFIER

In Solidity, using two forward slashes (//) creates a comment. Anything written on the same line after // is ignored by the compiler and is not treated as code so is not considered when compiling the contract.

Here's an example to illustrate how comments work in Solidity. You don't need to understand the code itself yet; we'll cover it later in this chapter. For now, just focus on the last comment:

```
//SPDX-License-Identifier: MIT
Pragma solidity 0.8.25;
Contract HelloWorld {
uint public number = 25;
// Hello, my name is Alexandros, nice to meet you.
}
```

In this code, everything from //SPDX-License-Identifier: MIT up to the declaration of the number 25 will be seen by the compiler as normal code to be processed and translated into 0s and 1s, while the // Hello, my name is Alexandros, nice to meet you will be ignored.

Comments can be useful in multiple ways:

- All the developers in your team will have different codebases and ways of writing code. Using the two forward slashes and adding comments can be a useful way to leave a remark to one of your colleagues so they can better understand the nuances of your code.

  - Comments can be essential for documentation within the codebase. New team members will integrate much faster if they review code with comments than without.

  - Comments can also assist with other tasks such as debugging, updating the codebase, documenting why it was updated, and generally facilitating a better collaboration experience between team members. That can help the development process be smoother and save time over the course of the project.

  - Since everything on open public blockchains is open-source, adding comments can help people who inspect the code see what it does. They not only allow developers to look professional but also explain their development choices. Without comments, there's a risk that code inspectors will think that the project may have malicious intent. Such misunderstandings could force the project to engage in damage control, public relations efforts, and spend funds on other similar measures.

- You can add comments for yourself. When building a smart contract, adding comments and a list of what kind of functionality you want to add makes you think a bit clearer and gives you a clearer understanding of how to proceed.

- If you are working on a task that requires you to focus on two or three different things, commenting on the lines of code you need to revisit can work as a reminder for you. This is especially helpful if you stop working for the day and must continue the next day.

While comments starting with // will be ignored by the compiler, there is one exception to this rule. The SPDX-License-Identifier line should start every Solidity file. Despite it starting with the comment characters, it does not get ignored by the compiler. If this line is not present, the compiler will show a warning. Think of it as greeting someone with "Hi" or "Hello" when you first see them. SPDX-License-Identifier is the "Hello" of Solidity. More specifically, SPDX-License-Identifier specifies the license under which your smart contract will be available for use and interaction. SPDX stands for "Software Package Data Exchange," which is a format to communicate the license and copyrights associated with a software package.

```
//SPDX-License-Identifier: [Insert Name of License]
```

For example:

```
//SPDX-License-Identifier: MIT
```

Here is the human language translation: "The //SPDX-License-Identifier MIT signifies that the code in this Solidity file is licensed under the MIT license."

SOLIDITY VERSIONS AND THE PRAGMA LINE

Earlier in this chapter, human languages and programming languages were compared, noting how both evolve over time. Human languages incorporate new expressions, idioms, and words, often updated officially through dictionaries. Similarly, programming languages, including Solidity, evolve and undergo updates and changes. For Solidity, every update or function or any other change can be accessed on Solidity's documentation website, which can be thought of as "Solidity's dictionary" where you can study deeply the language and its possibilities.

You can access the website at `https://docs.soliditylang.org/en/v0.8.25`. If the link has changed by the time you read this book, simply use a search engine and type "Solidity documentation" to find the correct site. Just as Solidity evolves with updates documented in its official repository, smart contract applications built with Solidity also evolve—sometimes through trial and error. The first decentralized autonomous organization (DAO) was created in 2016 and was quickly hacked, and the people who invested money into the DAO lost it. This is a pivotal moment in Ethereum's history because there was an argument and a split in opinion as to what to do about it.

In Chapters 1 and 2, I mentioned that if someone wants to create their own version of Bitcoin or Ethereum, they are free to do so through a *hard fork*—a separate chain from the original. Those who agree with that version of the chain can join as nodes in that chain, while the original one is supported by people who agree with the old rules. The DAO hack caused an argument over whether the Ethereum blockchain should implement a hard fork to a rollback on the chain to return the lost money to the owners. Approximately 85% of the Ethereum community agreed to do the hard fork, and when it was implemented, that 85% switched to the new chain, while 15% of people who disagreed remain in the old chain, which is now known as "Ethereum Classic."

This hard fork was proposed as EIP-779. Another pivotal Ethereum Improvement Proposal (EIP) was EIP-3675, which proposed and specified the switch of Ethereum from proof of work to proof of stake as a consensus mechanism. But the most important EIPs that developers should be aware of are the Ethereum request for comment (ERC) standards. ERCs have created standards that are used every day. Examples include ERC-20 tokens, which are for fungible tokens; ERC-721, which is for nonfungible tokens (NFTs); and ERC-1155, which supports both fungible and nonfungible tokens. In a similar way, the Ethereum community can propose changes and updates to the Solidity language. These updates are similar to how human language evolves through community use, with a centralized entity that controls the dictionary updating it when it deems necessary.

The result of all this is that the second line after `//SPDX-License-Identifier` is the Solidity version that the contract will be written in:

```
//SPDX-License-Identifier: MIT
pragma solidity [insert version of solidity to work with]
```

For example:

```
//SPDX-License-Identifier: MIT
pragma solidity 0.8.25;
```

Here is the human language translation: "The //SPDX-License-Identifier MIT signifies that the code in this Solidity file is licensed under the MIT license. The `pragma solidity 0.8.25` signifies that the smart contract will be using the 0.8.25 Solidity compiler version to compile without errors."

Now, let's break down pragma solidity 0.8.25; in its entirety:

➤ **pragma.** pragma is used to communicate with the compiler specifically. In Solidity, pragma is used to let the compiler know what version of Solidity you would like to work with. Think of it a bit like talking to a person through a translator and letting the translator know exactly how to translate one very important part in the conversation to the other person rather than simply talking to the person—in our case the computer—and letting the translator translate like always.

➤ **Solidity:** Solidity lets the compiler/translator know that the statement we want to translate to the computer/person is in the Solidity language.

➤ **0.8.25:** This lets the compiler/translator know to communicate the version of Solidity we want to use to the computer/person going forward when developing our smart contract.

> ➤ **0:** The first number in Solidity's version statement is the "major version number" and tracks the major changes that were implemented within the language. As the time of writing this book, the major version number was 0. Thus, no major changes had/have been implemented yet. These major changes can include changes in the syntax of the language or how to write functions and other major components of the language. In a human language, think of it as changing or updating an idiom or the grammar. Greeks going from Ancient Greek to Modern Greek, for example, would be seen, in Solidity terms, like going from 0 to 1. Another similar example would be going from Old English to modern English.

> ➤ **8:** The second number in Solidity's version statement is the minor version number, which tracks the small changes that were implemented within the language. At the time of writing this book, the minor changes within the language were 8. Think of the minor version number as adding a new word to a human language such as *selfie* or a new word from another language.

> ➤ **25:** The third number in the Solidity version statement is the patch version number, which indicates bug fixes or minor updates that address issues in the previous minor version. In a human language, think of patch fixes such as the words *color* and *colour*. Both mean the same thing; in this scenario, say they are both used interchangeably in a country, but then the country's main dictionary decides that one of them is the official spelling. If you speak another language, think of any word in your mother tongue that may be written in two different ways and the dictionary deciding that one is the official way of writing a word. That would be a minor patch fix.

> ➤ **;:** In Solidity a semicolon is always added at the end of each statement (unless it is a comment). Think of each statement in Solidity such as pragma solidity 0.8.25 as a human sentence like "Today I am going to the beach." Just like in human sentences, we would add a period at the end of each sentence; in Solidity we add a semicolon instead. Thus, when you add a semicolon, think of it as if you are adding a period at the end of each Solidity statement or sentence.

Figure 4.7 shows what this looks like in Remix.

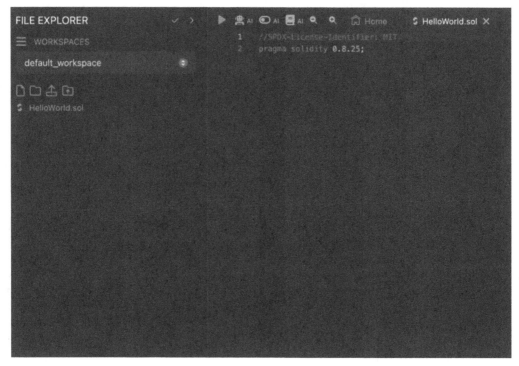

FIGURE 4.7 `pragma solidity` *version*

CONTRACT HELLOWORLD {}

A third and last thing that each smart contract should have immediately before starting to code anything is the smart contract itself:

```
//SPDX-License-Identifier: MIT
pragma solidity 0.8.25;
contract HelloWorld {}
```

Here is the human language translation: The //SPDX-License-Identifier MIT signifies that the code in this Solidity file is licensed under the MIT license. The `pragma solidity 0.8.25` in its turn signifies that the smart contract will be using the 0.8.25 Solidity compiler version to compile without errors. The `contract HelloWorld {}` creates a smart contract with the name HelloWorld in the Solidity file."

This specifies the name of the contract we are creating. In this case, our contract's name will be `HelloWorld`, while the two brackets, {}, signify what is going to be within the contract itself. The opening bracket, {, is the beginning of the contract, and the closing brace, }, signals its end. The integrated developing environments that we are going to use automatically generate the braces as soon as you type the opening one. Then you can just go in between them to start writing code.

Figure 4.8 shows how the `HelloWorld` contract looks in Remix with the opening and closing backets.

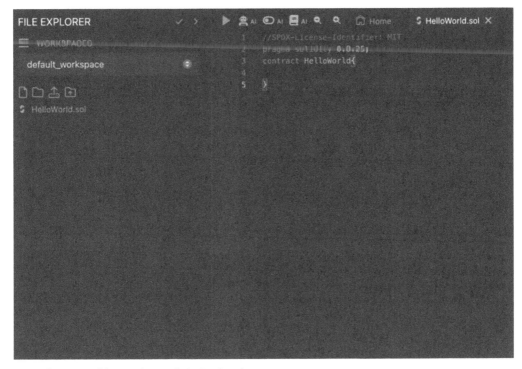

FIGURE 4.8 Contract with opening and closing brackets

DATA TYPES AND VARIABLES IN SOLIDITY

In human language, we convey information (data) through words, phrases, or letters. For example:

➤ "Today I went to the supermarket" communicates specific information.

➤ "Today I went" conveys less detail but still implies action.

➤ Even a single word (*Today*) or letter (*T*) can be data depending on the context.

Similarly, Solidity communicates with computers through *data types*. These define the kind of data the program will handle. There are six basic data types in Solidity. For context, remember that each syntax example (based on the `HelloWorld` example in this chapter) would appear after the following lines:

```
//SPDX-License-Identifier: MIT
pragma solidity 0.8.25;
contract HelloWorld {
```

int

The `int` data type is an abbreviation of the word *integer* and represents whole numbers, which can be positive or negative (e.g., 3, –3).

Here is the syntax to declare an integer:

```
int number = -5;
```

Here is the explanation:

➤   `int`: Specifies the integer data type

➤   `number`: Variable name

➤   `=`: Assigns a value

➤   `-5`: Value assigned to the integer

uint

The `uint` data type is an abbreviation of "unsigned integer" and represents whole, positive numbers (e.g., 35).

Here is the syntax to declare an unsigned integer:

```
uint number2 = 35;
```

Here is the explanation:

➤   `uint`: Specifies the unsigned integer data type

➤   `number2`: Variable name

➤   `=`: Assigns a value

➤   `35`: Value assigned to the unsigned integer

string

The `string` data type represents a sequence of letters or characters (e.g., Alexandros).

Here is the syntax to declare a string:

```
string name = "Alexandros";
string letter = "A";
```

Here is the explanation:

➤   `string`: Specifies the string data type

➤   `name`/`letter`: Variable names

➤   `=`: Assigns values

➤   `"Alexandros"`, `"A"`: Values assigned to the string variables

address

The address data type represents an Ethereum address used for transactions. Figure 4.9 shows where to find the Ethereum address in MetaMask.

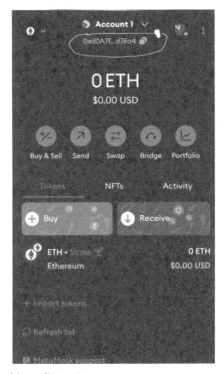

FIGURE 4.9 MetaMask Ethereum address illustration

Here is the syntax to declare an address:

```
address MyETHaddress = 0xd0A7f0e336af86aCC72d85af1EDf25790bAd76a4;
```

Here is the explanation:

➤ address: Specifies the address data type

➤ MyETHaddress: Variable name

➤ =: Assigns the Ethereum address

bool

The bool data type represents a true/false value.

Here is the syntax to declare a Boolean:

```
bool isTrue = true;
bool isFalse = false;
```

Here is the explanation:

➤   `bool`: Specifies the Boolean data type

➤   `isTrue/isFalse`: Variable names

➤   `=`: Assigns a truth value (true or false)

bytes

The `bytes` data type represents a sequence of byte data.

➤   A byte consists of 8 bits. (A bit is the smallest unit of data in computer science, representing either a 1 or 0.)

Here is an example:

```
bytes1 smallByte = 0x01; // Fixed size
bytes dynamicBytes = "Hello"; // Dynamic size
```

Bytes are useful for reducing gas fees by minimizing computational effort when handling string data.

Here is an example smart contract with variables initialized:

```
// SPDX-License-Identifier: MIT
pragma solidity 0.8.25;
contract HelloWorld {
    int number = -5;
    uint number2 = 35;
    string name = "Alexandros";
    string letter = "A";
    address MyETHaddress = 0xd0A7f0e336af86aCC72d85af1EDf25790bAd76a4;
    bool isTrue = true;
    bool isFalse = false;
}
```

Here is the explanation:

➤   `SPDX-License-Identifier` ensures compliance with the MIT license.

➤   `pragma solidity` specifies the Solidity compiler version.

➤   `contract HelloWorld` defines a smart contract named HelloWorld.

➤   Variables (`int`, `uint`, `string`, `address`, `bool`) are declared and initialized.

At first glance, `string` and `bytes` seem to store the same value: Alexandros. However, they function differently under the hood. While the `string` data type holds the text *Alexandros* as its value, `bytes` has converted the Alexandros value to bytes. This conversion happens behind the scenes and is not apparent in the contract code.

In a deeper demonstration where we deploy the contract on a fake environment to experiment with it, we get the two buttons, as shown in Figure 4.10.

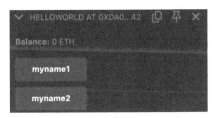

FIGURE 4.10 Showcasing `myname1` as string and `myname2` as bytes

`myname1` and `myname2` are the variables declared in the preceding code. When we click `myname1`, we get the result shown in Figure 4.11.

FIGURE 4.11 Showcasing `myname1`

Alexandros as a value, exactly what we declared with the line `string public = "Alexandros";`.

However, when we click `myname2`, we get the result shown in Figure 4.12.

FIGURE 4.12 Showcasing `myname2`

The value `0x416c6578616e64726f73` is the byte value of Alexandros. This conversion helps the network perform fewer calculations, and thus the user pays fewer units of gas, making the Ethereum network cheaper to use.

> **NOTE** It is a useful fact that when someone writes `string myname1 = "Alexandros"`, the `"Alexandros"` part is normally referred to as Unicode Transformation Format 8-bit (UTF-8). This is a widely used method of representing text in computers generally and has been created to include characters (including symbols) from all human writing systems around the world. UTF-8 is also the standard way of encoding in web pages and text files on the Internet.

FUNCTION VISIBILITY LEVELS

Solidity—and most other programming languages—have pieces of code called *functions* that are set to execute a certain programmed task. Think of functions as orders that you give the computer to execute a program.

FUNCTION ANATOMY

In Solidity, a function has a standard way of being declared and has a number of modifiers that affect its visibility, mutability, and the value that the function will return:

```
function helloWorld() public view returns (string) {}
```

This is an example of a function declaration. The following explains the syntax:

➤ `function`: This declares to the computer that what follows is a function.

➤ `helloWorld`: This is the name of the function being declared.

➤ Braces (): Within the braces you can declare parameters that later can be manipulated or changed (more on that in Chapter 5).

➤ `public`: This is the visibility of the function—who can "call" or use the function. When a function is `public`, anyone can call it be it internally or externally.

➤ `view`: The function is not going to execute a task that would change the state of the blockchain. For example, it won't send or receive money, which would change the addresses involved in the transaction. A `view` function simply retrieves information from the blockchain and shows it to the function's caller. For example, it could return the ETH balance of an address rather than sending money to it.

➤ `returns (string)`: `returns` means that the function, after it is done executing, will return a certain data type. In this case, it is a `string`, but the `return` function can declare any of the data types discussed earlier in this chapter.

➤ {}: The code of the function to be executed is written within the braces.

VISIBILITY LEVELS

Solidity has several visibility levels that allow or restrict who can call a specific function:

➤ **Public:** As mentioned earlier, a public function can be called by anyone, both internally and externally. This can be a user calling the function, the owner of the contract, a contract that inherits the function from this contract, or even unrelated third parties. For example, a platform like Uniswap could call the function if they integrated the contract into their decentralized exchange.

➤ **Private:** When a function is defined as private, it can be called only within that contract. No inherited or any other contracts can call it as they can with a public function. Not even users can call this function.

➤ **External:** When a function is defined as external, it can be called only by outside contracts and parties, including inherited contracts. It cannot be called internally within the same contract unless specialized commands are used to convert the internal call into an external call.

➤ **Internal:** When a function is declared as internal, only the contract itself and contracts that inherit from it can call the function. No external parties including contracts and individuals can call an internal function.

For product managers or designers, understanding the visibility levels of functions is crucial when designing a smart contract. It helps them clarify who can call certain functions, optimizing usability and avoiding any miscalculations or events where an unwanted external party could call a specific function. For smart contract developers, reviewing the visibility levels of a contract's functions is useful in determining what other functions there might be in the contract that you as a user will not be able to call.

VIEW AND PURE KEYWORDS

Solidity has two basic keywords: `view` and `pure`. Each of them can be used for different reasons:

➤ **View:** A function with the `view` keyword does not—as mentioned earlier—change the state of the blockchain; it just retrieves and shows data from the blockchain, which does not require gas. However, if a function marked with the `view` keyword is called within another function that costs gas, that call will contribute to the gas cost.

➤ **Pure:** The `pure` keyword ensures that a function does not read or modify the blockchain at all, making the function dependent on the parameters defined within the function itself. This can improve gas efficiency when needed. It also improves safety by proactively helping to avoid bugs or other unforeseen issues.

HELLOWORLD CONTRACT

Now that you have learned the basics of Solidity programming, in this section you will use that knowledge to create your first contract, a `HelloWorld` contract. This is the simplest contract you can create, and it's a classic starting point when learning any new programming language.

The first thing to do whenever you begin a new contract is to define the license under which the contract will be released:

```
//SPDX-License-Identifier: MIT
```

As a reminder, SPDX is an abbreviation of Software Package Data Exchange, `License-Identifier` identifies the license, and MIT is the license under which the `HelloWorld` contract would be released once finished and deployed on the blockchain.

```
pragma solidity 0.8.25;
```

`pragma` tells the compiler that the version of Solidity that will be used in this contract follows. Solidity is, of course, the language we are using in this book, and `0.8.25;` is the language version we are going to be using in this contract. What 0.8.25 means was explained in the "Solidity Versions and the pragma Line" earlier in this chapter.

The following states the name of the contract and signals the beginning of the contract through the braces, `{}`:

```
contract HelloWorld {}
```

The above following is the simplest way to return the "Hello World" message in Solidity:

```
contract HelloWorld {
    string public helloWorld = "Hello World";
}
```

In Remix, after you have written the contract, you have to click Deploy & Run Transactions and then on the Deploy button shown in Figure 4.13 in order to deploy the contract.

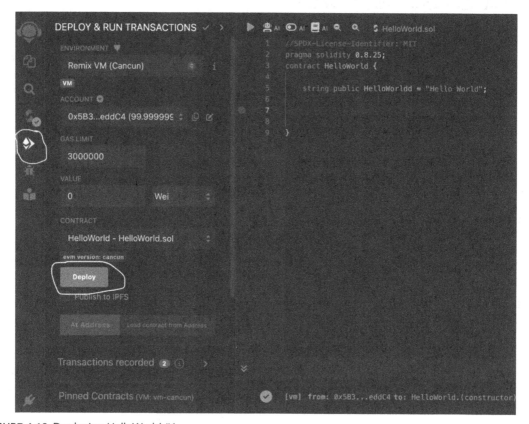

FIGURE 4.13 Deploying HelloWorld #1

After deploying the contract, click the HelloWorld button (see Figure 4.14) to see the deployed `HelloWorld` contract, as shown in Figure 4.15.

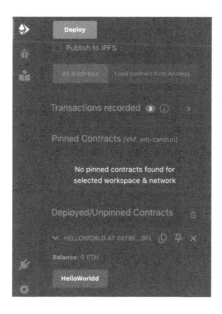

FIGURE 4.14 Contract deployed

FIGURE 4.15 `HelloWorld` #1 reflected

A second way to write a smart contract to return "Hello World" is as follows:

```
//SPDX-License-Identifier: MIT
pragma solidity 0.8.25
contract HelloWorld {
    string helloWorld = "Hello World";
    function returnHelloWorld() public view returns(string memory) {
        return helloWorld;
    }
}
```

This method creates a variable of data type string named helloWorld, and a public function that is view. The function reads information from the blockchain (in this case, the value of the string helloWorld) and returns a string. The function has only one command, which returns the value of the helloWorld variable. It closes the declaration with a ;.

The function returnHelloWorld has a memory keyword, which will be explained promptly in the next chapter.

CHAPTER 4 QUESTIONS

1. How does learning Solidity compare to learning a human language in terms of syntax, vocabulary, and grammar? Provide examples to illustrate these similarities and differences.

2. Explain the role of the Remix IDE in developing, testing, and deploying Solidity contracts. How do its features support smart contract development?

3. What is the purpose of the SPDX-License-Identifier, and why must every Solidity file begin with it?

4. What does the pragma directive communicate to the compiler, and how does specifying a Solidity version enhance compatibility and security?

5. Describe the difference between signed (int) and unsigned (uint) integers in Solidity. How would you declare and initialize each?

6. How are string and address data types declared in Solidity? Provide examples of their use in smart contracts.

7. What are Booleans and bytes in Solidity, and how are they declared? Discuss how bytes can optimize gas usage.

8. What are the key components of declaring a variable in Solidity, and why is proper initialization critical?

9. Discuss the four function visibility levels in Solidity: public, private, external, and internal. When would you use each?

10. Differentiate between `view` and `pure` functions in Solidity. Provide examples of when each might be used and their impact on gas usage.

11. Explain the structure of the `HelloWorld` contract as described in the text. How does it demonstrate the basics of Solidity?

12. Why is gas optimization important in Solidity, and how do smaller data types like `uint8` and bytes contribute to efficiency?

13. How does case sensitivity in Solidity help prevent errors? Provide examples where incorrect capitalization might lead to a compiler error.

14. Outline the steps to deploy a Solidity contract in Remix IDE and interact with it. What common mistakes might occur during deployment?

15. If a Solidity contract fails due to a type mismatch or incorrect visibility, how would you identify and resolve the issue using Remix IDE tools?

5

ZooManagement

This chapter delves into Solidity programming concepts using a ZooManagement contract as a guiding example. You'll reinforce fundamental Solidity skills while learning to effectively use structs, mappings, and arrays to manage complex datasets. Additionally, you'll explore inheritance, contract importation, and best practices for efficiency and security in Solidity development. By the chapter's end, you'll have developed a sophisticated contract capable of tracking zoo visitors, managing animal data, and implementing reusable, secure code components.

Imagine managing a zoo's operations, from counting visitors to cataloging animals with their species, names, and ages. For instance, how would you efficiently update visitor counts while simultaneously keeping detailed records of animals in the zoo? This chapter resolves such challenges through a structured approach to contract design and implementation, providing a hands-on example with the ZooManagement contract.

By working through this chapter, you will gain practical skills that translate into real-world blockchain applications, enabling them to handle similar data-driven use cases in decentralized environments.

SETTING UP THE ZooManagement CONTRACT

We will be using Remix, as we did in the previous chapter. You can access the Remix website at https://remix.ethereum.org. As shown in the previous chapter, be sure to delete any folders and files at the left of your Remix workspace.

You have created three contracts in this book so far; this next one will be called ZooManagement. It will involve creating information about specific animals in our zoo and collecting the number of visitors, the species of the animals that inhabit the zoo, and the visitors' and animals' names and ages.

To begin, define the open-source license under which our contract will be available:

```
//SPDX-License-Identifier: MIT
```

The next step is defining the Solidity version that we will use for the ZooManagement contract:

```
pragma solidity 0.8.26;
```

By the time you read this book, there might be a newer Solidity version of the compiler. Remix might refuse to compile your contract if it lacks the newest version.

You will likely see squiggly lines with the preceding statement if a newer version is available. However, when you hover the cursor over the red squiggly lines, you get an error.

```
ParserError: Source file requires different Solidity version (current compiler
is 0
.8.26+commit.8a97fa7a.Emscripten.clang) - note that nightly builds are
considered
to be strictly less than the released version --> ZooManagement.sol:2:1:
| 2 |
 pragma solidity 0.8.25; |
 ^^^^^^^^^^^^^^^^^^^^^^^^
PragmaDirective
ZooManagement.sol 1:0
```

In this error, look for the following:

```
ParserError: Source file requires a different Solidity version (current
compiler is
 0.8.26+commit.8a97fa7a.Emscripten.clang).
```

The part of the error that mentions "Source file requires different Solidity version (current compiler is 0.8.26...)" reveals the Solidity version needed to get the contract accepted by the compiler.

An alternative way to see the latest Solidity version is to click the Solidity compiler icon, shown in Figure 5.1.

FIGURE 5.1: Solidity compiler icon

In place of workspaces, the Solidity version information will pop up, enabling you to see the current latest version of Solidity, as shown in Figure 5.2.

FIGURE 5.2: Solidity version error

In Figure 5.2, we can see that the Solidity version used in the contract itself is `0.8.25;`, while the compiler information on the left shows that the latest release of the compiler is `0.8.26;`. Thus, for the contract to work, and for the squiggly lines to disappear, you need to change the Solidity version from `0.8.25;` to `0.8.26;`, as shown in Figure 5.3.

FIGURE 5.3: Solidity version error solved

However, there can be times when you work on a smart contract and the Solidity version used is an older one. In that case, you will click the compiler's version and choose from the list to specifically use an older version, as shown in Figure 5.4.

Click the Solidity version to see past versions of Solidity. Scroll through the list of Solidity versions, and you'll see plenty of them, as shown in Figure 5.5.

You can choose the Solidity version you need to work with by clicking it.

In this case, version 0.8.9 has been selected. As shown in Figure 5.6, on the sheet beside the Solidity compiler, the Solidity version has also been changed to 0.8.9 to fit the versions.

FIGURE 5.4: Solidity version

FIGURE 5.5: Solidity version list #1

FIGURE 5.6: Previous Solidity version 0.8.9 chosen

The question is, why would a developer decide to work on an older compiler version and release a smart contract with older compiler versions instead of using the latest version?

There are several possible reasons to use older compiler versions for their code:

➤ **Stability and security:** Older compiler versions have been in use for longer, minimizing the risk of bugs found as there is a more significant probability that older versions have been identified and fixed. In comparison, newer versions might introduce new bugs that are not yet known or that have not yet been identified, especially because newer versions introduce experimental features that might not have been tested enough by developers and auditors. Addressing bugs in Solidity is paramount, as a minor bug can cost millions or billions of dollars locked in the smart contract.

➤ **Compatibility:** Smart contracts may depend on libraries that developers created with older compiler versions. (You learn more about libraries later in the book.) Suppose you were to update the compiler version. That might affect the code by producing incompatibilities—similar to the compiler version examples discussed earlier in this chapter but with more sophisticated incompatibilities—and thus may require significant code changes and time. Additionally, as we will see later in this chapter, developers can import smart contracts and make the smart contracts inherit properties from one another. Using different compiler versions in the inherited contracts may introduce unnecessary problems.

➤ **Audited code:** In blockchain, smart contracts are audited either by in-house competent contract auditors or by external third-party security firms that employ smart contract auditors. The auditing is done to minimize the possibility of a vulnerability in the smart contract. Smart contracts that use older compiler versions have been audited many times, thus minimizing the probability of a vulnerability being discovered. If someone were to change the older compiler version used by a smart contract to a newer one, this may cancel out some of the audit findings.

➤ **Gas optimizations:** Older versions of Solidity have been around for longer, so they may implement specific gas optimizations. As explained in Chapter 2, gas costs are the unit used to measure computation costs the different computers incur to process code and transactions on the Ethereum blockchain. The less complex the code, the fewer the gas costs—that the newer versions do not have or do not support. Using older Solidity versions, in turn, makes the smart contract transactions cheaper for users once a developer has deployed the smart contract onto the Ethereum blockchain.

➤ **Developer familiarity:** Developers might be familiar with an older version that they have used extensively and know how it behaves and functions, and thus, they prefer to use that version instead of newer ones. However, the downside to this method is that newer compiler versions introduce new features unavailable in the older versions. Thus, if the developer continues to use a specific old version of Solidity, they may stay behind if enough time passes.

➤ **Better documentation:** Because of their extensive use in the past, older compiler versions tend to have better usage documentation and more significant community support. These resources help developers produce code more efficiently than by working with newer versions where less information may be available.

➤ **Regulatory compliance:** Although smart contracts are a new technology and there is not yet much regulation regarding them, in the future, as regulation continues to expand throughout different jurisdictions, regulators may regulate and dictate that older versions be used by users and developed by developers in certain jurisdictions.

➤ **Conservative managers and governance:** A company's management or governance structure may be conservative and resistant to change. This resistance leads to restricted upgrades for smart contracts, especially if the smart contract is considered critical infrastructure.

➤ **Community norms:** In some communities, the developer community may agree to use an older compiler version for consistency, especially if the smart contracts are interdependent.

After having typed the license under which the developer will release the ZooManagement contract as well as the Solidity version, it is time to define the name of the contract:

```
contract ZooManagement {}
```

Next it is time to write the contract contents by starting with an unsigned integer variable signifying the number of total visitors to the zoo:

```
uint256 public totalVisitors;
```

This unsigned integer variable is public, meaning users can call it internally and externally.

Next comes the function for updating the visitor count of the zoo:

```
function updateVisitorCount(uint256 _newVisitorCount) public {
    totalVisitors = _newVisitorCount;
}
```

This function is named updateVisitorCount. It has one local variable, an unsigned integer uint256 named _newVisitorCount. The function has a public visibility level, meaning anyone can call it internally or externally.

Inside the function, the value of _newVisitorCount is assigned to totalVisitors. The assignment updates the total number of visitors to the new number provided when the smart contract is deployed. It is important to remember that each time a user uses the deployed contract to update the number of visitors, the state of the blockchain changes.

Next, after adding or updating the total number of zoo visitors, a function is required to return that number for everyone to see instead of simply updating it so no one can see it. To add the new function, type the following:

```
function getTotalVisitors() public view returns (uint256) {
return totalVisitors;
}
```

The getTotalVisitors function shown earlier, unlike updateVisitorCount, has no local parameters. The function is public, which means that anyone can call it externally or internally. The function is also a view function, meaning that it does not alter the state of the blockchain when called; it retrieves information only from the blockchain and, hence, is a gasless function. In other words, it does not cost any gas to use. The function also returns an uint256, which is an unsigned integer.

Within the function, we can see the return keyword, a command to return a specific value. In this case, the function will return totalVisitors. If you follow this to the letter, you should see the following result reflected on your Remix:

```solidity
//SPDX-License-Identifier: MIT
pragma solidity 0.8.26;
contract ZooManagement {
    uint256 public totalVisitors;
    function updateVisitorCount(uint256 _newVisitorCount) public {
        totalVisitors = _newVisitorCount;
    }

    function getTotalVisitors() public view returns(uint256) {
        return totalVisitors;
    }
}
```

When deploying the contract, go to the Deploy & Run Transactions tab or the Ethereum logo—the fourth sign from the top left. After clicking the Deploy button and scrolling to the bottom of the Deploy & Run Transactions tab, you should see three functions, as shown in Figure 5.7.

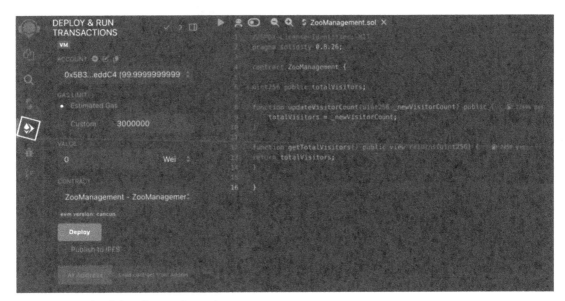

FIGURE 5.7: Deploy & Run Transactions tab

The functions are updateVisitorCount, getTotalVisitors, and totalVisitors. When you click getTotalVisitors and totalVisitors without adding anything to the typing space of update VisitorCount, the result is 0, as no visitors have been registered or entered. (see Figure 5.8.)

FIGURE 5.8: ZooManagement contract result

However, if you enter the value "10" into the updateVisitorCount function and then click that function, then click either or both getTotalVisitors or totalVisitors, the value returned will be "10" as in 10 visitors. (see Figure 5.9.)

FIGURE 5.9: ZooManagement contract, update visitors

STRUCTS

After adding a number to update and returning the number of visitors, it is time to add the zoo's animals. The first step is to define a struct at the beginning of the contract below the uint256 public totalVisitors.

First, understanding a struct is helpful before defining a struct in Solidity.

In Solidity, a *struct* is a data structure that allows you to create a group called X and combine different Y and Z data types inside that group.

For example, imagine you want to create a list of your friends. You want to remember each friend's name, age, and favorite food. A struct would help you create a group or container called Friends. You would define different data types within that group to store your friends' information, as shown in Figure 5.10.

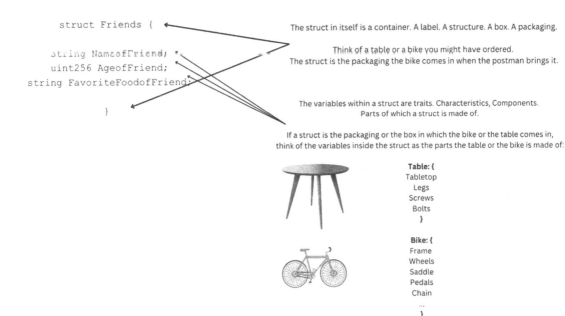

FIGURE 5.10: Visual explanation of a struct
Source: Pro Hi-Res/Adobe Stock Photos

In Solidity, to create this struct, you have to type this:

```
struct Friends {
    string nameofFriend;
    uint256 ageofFriend;
    string favoriteFoodofFriend;
}
```

This code tells the compiler, "I want to create a group called Friends with a name in letters, an age in numbers, and a favorite food in letters."

After you have created this struct, you can store information. To do that, type this:

```
Friends public alex = Friends("Alex", 30, "Spaghetti");

Friends public laila = Friends ("Laila", 45, "Shoarma");
```

This code creates a new friend, Alex, who is 30 and likes spaghetti as her favorite food. Then, another friend is added, Laila, who is 45 years old and likes shoarma as her favorite food. Structs are helpful as they help keep information together and organized instead of having separate variables for different types of data such as age, food, name, or anything else one may be working with.

Returning to our ZooManagement contract, a struct has to be added to define the zoo's type of animals. Therefore, the struct would look like this:

```
struct Animal {+
    string species;
```

```
        string name;
        uint256 age;
    }
```

The struct would be placed above or below the `uint256 public totalVisitors;` variable.

After defining the `Animal` struct, the next step is to start defining different species of animals that are in the zoo:

```
Animal public tiger = Animal("Tiger", "Peanut", 3);

Animal public bear = Animal ("Bear", "Honey", 4);

Animal public lion = Animal ("Animal", "Simba", 8);
```

The contract should now look like this:

```
//SPDX-License-Identifier: MIT
pragma solidity 0.8.26;
contract ZooManagement {

    uint256 public totalVisitors;
    struct Animal {
          string species;
          string name;
          uint256 age;
    }

    Animal public tiger = Animal("Tiger", "Peanut", 3);
    Animal public bear = Animal ("Bear", "Honey", 4);
    Animal public lion = Animal ("Animal", "Simba", 8);

    function updateVisitorCount(uint256 _newVisitorCount) public {
    totalVisitors = _newVisitorCount;
    }

    function getTotalVisitors() public view returns(uint256) {
     return totalVisitors;
        }
    }
```

When the contract is deployed, you will see the result shown in Figure 5.11.

When you click on the bear, lion, and tiger buttons, you see the result shown in Figure 5.12.

ARRAYS

Listing the variables of tiger, bear, and lion, as pictured in the previous section, is fine when there are only a few variables to define. However, when we have more variables (and in smart contracts, that can be hundreds of thousands or even millions in the long term) including all these variables manually, as we did in the previous example, presents a problem of efficiency.

FIGURE 5.11: ZooManagement contract result #2

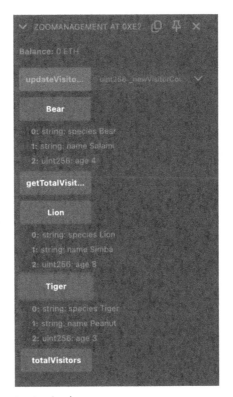

FIGURE 5.12: ZooManagement contract animals

To improve efficiency, you have to use another data structure called an *array* that a developer can combine with a struct. Before using the array in our ZooManagement contract, we are going to define what arrays are in Solidity.

Arrays in Solidity can be considered lists that store data types of the same type. In our case of the ZooManagement contract, those would be data types of the type Animal and include two strings and a uint256 as species, name, and age.

➤ **Dynamic arrays:** Dynamic arrays are lists with no fixed number defined by the developer that can store a custom number of data types. Although less gas efficient than fixed-size arrays, dynamic arrays have the advantage of storing many data types. Storing many data types is especially useful when storing the addresses that interact with the smart contract one deploys.

➤ **Fixed-size arrays:** Fixed-size arrays have a fixed number of data types that a developer can store in their list. The developer defines this fixed number as anything they'd like (3, 5, 10, etc.). The good thing about fixed-size arrays is that they are more gas efficient as the number of data types the developer stores is fixed as opposed to dynamic arrays that have no fixed number of data types to be stored.

DYNAMIC ARRAYS

In Solidity, a developer can create a dynamic array in the following way:

```
Animal[] public listofAnimals;
```

This line of code creates a variable of type Animal, taken by the struct. Next, the [] means that it will be a list of variables of the Animal type and then names this array listofAnimals.

To add an Animal type to the array, you use the push function to add the Animal and its local parameters into the array. That requires the developer to create a separate function, as shown in the following instance:

```
function addAnimal(string memory _species, string memory _name, uint256 _age)
 public {
listofAnimals.push(Animal(_species, _name, _age));
}
```

Here's a breakdown of what we just typed:

1. The function addAnimal declares a new function with the name addAnimal.

2. The (string memory _species, string memory _name, uint256 _age) defines local parameters that are similar to the variables of the Animal struct.

3. public is the function's visibility level, indicating that the function can be called externally and internally.

   Inside the function there is the action of listofAnimals.push(Animal(_species, _name, _age));.

   ➤ The listofAnimals references the listofAnimals array that we created.

➤ The .push() signifies that the data to follow after .push() will be added to the list of animals.

➤ The data type Animal(_species, _name, _age) creates a new Animal instance using the parameters passed to the function. In combination with the .push previously, it adds the new Animal struct instance to the listofAnimals array.

The code looks like this at the moment:

```
//SPDX-License-Identifier: MIT
pragma solidity 0.8.26;
contract ZooManagement {

    uint256 public totalVisitors;

    struct Animal{
         string species;
         string name;
         uint256 age;
    }

    Animal [] public listofAnimals;

    // Animal public tiger = Animal("Tiger", "Peanut", 3);
    // Animal public bear = Animal("Bear", "Honey", 4);
    // Animal public lion = Animal("Lion", "Simba", 8);

    function updateVisitorCount(uint256 _newVisitorCount) public {
         totalVisitors = _newVisitorCount;
    }

    function getTotalVisitors() public view returns(uint256) {
         return totalVisitors;
    }

    function addAnimal(string memory _species, string memory _name, uint256
 _age)
 public {
         listofAnimals.push(Animal(_species, _name, _age));
    }
}
```

FIXED-SIZE ARRAYS

In the previous section, we implemented a fixed-size array with no fixed amount of data that a developer can store in its list. In this section, we implement a fixed-size array instead with the same code base.

In the previous example, before the creation of the dynamic array, three types of animals were stated as variables:

```
Animal public tiger = Animal("Tiger", "Peanut", 3);
```

```
Animal public bear = Animal("Bear", "Honey", 4);

Animal public lion = Animal("Lion", "Simba", 8);f
```

Suppose that in the zoo, we have only these three animals (a tiger, a bear, and a lion) and we do not expect to add any new animals to the zoo. Instead of creating a dynamic array, the developer can create a fixed-size array. Again, the first thing in the contract would be to create a struct to define the animals:

```
struct Animal{
    string species;
    string name;
    uint256 age;
}
```

After the struct, a fixed-size array has to be defined, as shown in the following example:

```
Animal[3] public listofAnimals;
```

In this example, we create a fixed-size array in the same way we made the dynamic struct.

The only difference is that within the square brackets of the fixed-size array, an arithmetic value represents the number of values the struct will hold.

The code for a fixed-size array is going to be different. Here are the familiar parts of the code that will stay the same (bar the fixed-size array):

```
//SPDX-License-Identifier: MIT
pragma solidity 0.8.26;

contract ZooManagement {
        uint256 public totalVisitors;

    struct Animal {
        string species;
        string name;
        uint256 age;
    }

    Animal[3] public listofAnimals;
    uint256 public animalCount;

    function updateVisitorCount(uint256 _newVisitorCount) public {
        totalVisitors = _newVisitorCount;
    }

    function getTotalVisitors() public view returns(uint256) {
        return totalVisitors;
    }
}
```

addAnimal

With fixed-sized arrays, you need to add two functions. The first is addAnimal (the next is getAnimal, described in the next section):

```
function addAnimal(string memory _species, string memory _name, uint256 _age)
 public {
     require(animalCount < 3, "Zoo is full");

     listofAnimals[animalCount] = Animal(_species, _name, _age);

     animalCount++;
}
```

This declares a function addAnimal and local parameters of _species, _name, and _age. It is a public function, much like the previous addAnimal function. Where it diverges from the last function is in the first line of the function:

```
require(animalCount < 3, "Zoo is full");
```

This line has the require keyword whose syntax and anatomy are like this when declared:

```
require(condition, "error message");
```

The require keyword is crucial in Solidity; it requires that a statement be necessarily true before the rest of the function is executed.

If the condition the require keyword checks is not true, the function will not execute further. In the preceding example, we use the require keyword and then add a condition so the require keyword will check if it is true.

If the condition is false, we can add a comma. Then, in double quotation marks, we add the error message we want to display to the person who calls the function.

In our addAnimal function, we can see that the require keyword requires that animalCount, the global uint256 variable that we declared, does not exceed 3 due to the limitation of the fixed-size array, which has a limit of three data types to store. Suppose a person tries to add a new animal and exceeds the number limitation imposed by the fixed-size array. In that case, a message will pop up saying "Zoo is full."

When using require statements, one should remember to add the statement at the beginning of a function because a function executes from top to bottom. If the require statement is somewhere in the middle of a function, whatever came before it within that function will spend gas that is not refundable. Thus, the person who calls that function will lose money.

This is the next line in the function addAnimal:

```
listofAnimals[animalCount] = Animal(_species, _name, _age);
```

This line creates a new Animal struct and assigns it to the listofAnimals array. The assignment happens because when one types listofAnimals[animalCount], it also adds the =, which means the listofAnimals[animalCount] will be set; that is, it will not be equal to a new instance of the Animal statement whatever that Animal statement is. (The *equal to* in Solidity is declared by using another sign, which will be discussed later in the book.)

As we have declared the Animal statement a struct, it will inherit the properties of the Animal struct and be set to it.

The [animalCount] in the listofAnimals [animalCount] signifies that the user will add the new Animal to the index or number specified by the animalCount variable. Since the animalCount variable has no value set, it will automatically represent zero.

Thus, the first Animal added through this function to the index of animalCount will be in index 0, the second Animal added will be in index 1, and the third Animal added will be in index 2, thus completing the requirement that the three animals be added to the fixed-size array that we have initially declared.

The (_species, _name, _age); part of the = Animal(_species, _name, _age) code means that the Animal data type to be added to the listofAnimals and the index of animalCount will have the properties and variables _species, _name, and _age that the developer has defined locally at the beginning of the function.

Finally, the final line of the function:

```
animalCount++;
```

communicates that every time the addAnimal function is called and successfully executed until the end, add a +1 to the animalCount or increment it by 1. Incrementing the addAnimal function ensures that the next time a user calls the addAnimal function and adds a new animal into the fixed array, the user will add it in the correct position of the array.

The user adds a new Animal to the index specified by animalCount.

The Animal struct is created using the function parameters _species, _name, and _age. These were specified at the beginning of the function as local parameters, as demonstrated here:

```
function addAnimal(string memory _species, string memory _name, uint256 _age)
    public {}
```

getAnimal

The second function that is added for the static array, getAnimal, is called and is written like this:

```
function getAnimal(uint256 _index) public view returns (string memory, string
    memory, uint256) {

        require(_index < animalCount, "Animal does not exist");

        Animal memory animal = listofAnimals[_index];

        return (animal.species, animal.name, animal.age);
}
```

The function declares a function of getAnimal with an uint256 _index as a parameter. The function is public, meaning a user can call it internally and externally. It is a view function, which means that it does not alter the state of the blockchain by initiating a transaction but instead retrieves information from the blockchain. Finally, the function returns three variables: two strings and an uint256.

Within the function's first line, we have a require keyword to ensure a statement is true before the rest of the function is executed.

```
require(_index < animalCount, "Animal does not exist");
```

Specifically, the keyword checks if the provided local variable uint256 _index is less than the animalCount. Suppose this condition is proven to be false. In that case, the function will stop executing and revert, displaying the typed error "Animal does not exist.".

This example's require keyword prevents accessing an animal not added to the array.

The second line of the code is as follows:

```
Animal memory animal = listofAnimals[_index];
```

This line of code creates a new Animal struct named animal because Solidity is case-sensitive.

Case-sensitive means that case matters: a declared value with a capital *A* letter differs from a value written similarly but with a small *a* instead of a capital *A*.

The new animal struct is assigned the values of the listofAnimals array.

Finally, the last line of the function:

```
return (animal.species, animal.name, animal.age);
```

returns three values: the animal's species, name, and age, which have now been assigned the values of the listofAnimals;.

The return of the values allows information about a specific animal in the zoo to be retrieved through its _index.

Returning to dynamic arrays, what happens when the number of added animals is significant, such as more than 100? 1,000? 10,000? A person would have to go animal by animal every time to find the animal they are looking for.

Is there an easier way in Solidity to retrieve information from different data types without going through each individually and spending much of our precious and finite time? There is, and this way is called a *mapping*.

MAPPINGS

Mappings in Solidity are an incredibly powerful data structure that allows developers to store key-value pairs. Each pair is associated with a specific value, and a user can use the key to look up the particular value the key is associated with.

The easiest way to understand mappings is to think of the following:

➤ **Books:** Each book one buys has a unique ISBN to identify it. In this case, the ISBN is the key paired with a value. The ISBN (key) can be paired with the book (value) when one types the ISBN of the book to find to what book the specific ISBN corresponds to.

➤ **Phones:** Each mobile phone (with a SIM card) has a specific phone number (key), which one then gives away to companies, family, friends, acquaintances, and other people who associate the phone number with the phone (value) and can "look up" the owner of the phone and call or send them a message.

➤ **Identity cards:** Every identity card has a unique register number (key) of the citizen (value) that owns that identity card. Every time someone goes to the town hall of their city or in other countries, it can even be the pharmacy or other services; people associate the person with the register number (data type) of their identity card and can look up this person and their information and history if required.

➤ **Products in the supermarket:** Every product has a unique barcode, and that barcode has a unique number (key). This number is used to identify and associate the number with the product in the supermarket (value). One can look up details and additional information about the product by filling in the barcode of the supermarket product into the supermarket's computer—or even online for some of the information that everyone can access.

➤ **Websites:** Each website that people visit, be it Facebook, Instagram, TikTok, LinkedIn, ChatGPT, or the Remix IDE used by aspiring developers of this book and others, has its own website, such as, for example, `https://remix.ethereum.com`. This unique key, when entered into a browser, allows the browser to identify the website and retrieve associated data from the server hosting it. The browser then displays the website's landing page content to the user.

Mappings are similar to the preceding examples, as they define a data type. By specifying that data type, we can look at another data type without having to search for that data type for minutes or hours between a lot of data. They are also more gas-efficient than arrays when looking up functions.

Creating a Mapping

In this section, you add a mapping to the following Solidity code we wrote to create the dynamic array earlier in this chapter:

```
//SPDX-License-Identifier: MIT
pragma solidity 0.8.26;
contract ZooManagement {

    uint256 public totalVisitors;

    struct Animal{
        string species;
        string name;
        uint256 age;
    }

    Animal [] public listofAnimals;
```

```
    // Animal public tiger = Animal("Tiger", "Peanut", 3);
    // Animal public bear = Animal("Bear", "Honey", 4);
    // Animal public lion = Animal("Lion", "Simba", 8);

    function updateVisitorCount(uint256 _newVisitorCount) public {
        totalVisitors = _newVisitorCount;
    }

    function getTotalVisitors() public view returns(uint256) {
        return totalVisitors;
    }

    function addAnimal(string memory _species, string memory _name, uint256
 _age)
 public {
        listofAnimals.push(Animal(_species, _name, _age));
    }
```

You can create a mapping in Solidity in the following way:

```
mapping (string => uint256) public nameToAge;
```

The word mapping declares a mapping where the key is the string, which signifies a word and, in this case, a name of the animal species in our zoo. The => symbol indicates that the string data type corresponds to the uint256 data type. By adding this word/name into the mapping, one can find the value, which is an uint256 and signifies the age of our animal in the zoo. The mapping is public, meaning anyone can call it externally or internally, and it is called nameToAge.

To retrieve a value from a mapping (in the earlier example that would be an uint256 and the age of the animal), when running the contract, one types the name of the animal that has been added. In the case of the lion, that would be Simba; in the case of the bear, it would be Honey; and the tiger would be Peanut.

```
nameToAge[_name] = _age;
```

The almost-finished final result of the contract looks like this:

```
//SPDX-License-Identifier: MIT
pragma solidity 0.8.26;
contract ZooManagement {

    uint256 public totalVisitors;

    struct Animal{
        string species;
        string name;
        uint256 age;
    }

    Animal [] public listofAnimals;

    mapping (string => uint256) public nameToAge;
```

```
    // Animal public tiger = Animal("Tiger", "Peanut", 3);
    // Animal public bear = Animal("Bear", "Honey", 4);
    // Animal public lion = Animal("Lion", "Simba", 8);

    function updateVisitorCount(uint256 _newVisitorCount) public {
        totalVisitors = _newVisitorCount;
    }

    function getTotalVisitors() public view returns(uint256) {
        return totalVisitors;
    }

    function addAnimal(string memory _species, string memory _name, uint256
_age)
 public {
        listofAnimals.push(Animal(_species, _name, _age));
        nameToAge[_name] = _age;
    }
}
```

We get the result shown in Figure 5.13 when navigating to the Deploy & Run Transactions tab and deploying the preceding contract.

FIGURE 5.13: ZooManagement contract result #3

When we use the red AddAnimal function, we need to give it three values separated by commas. In Figure 5.14, they are species, name, and age.

Lion is the species, Simba is the name of the lion, and Simba is 8 years old. After typing these values, click the AddAnimal function to add the animal. (see Figure 5.15.)

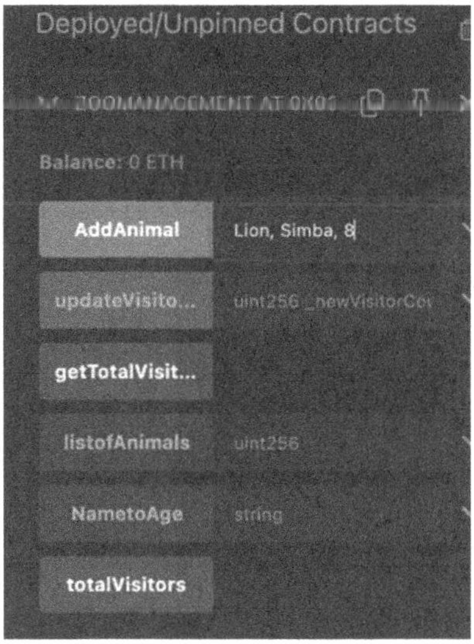

FIGURE 5.14: `ZooManagement AddAnimal`

FIGURE 5.15: `ZooManagement listofAnimals`

After adding Simba to the list of animals, you can also add the value 0. In computer science, counting often starts from 0 rather than 1. Refer to Figure 5.15, which shows the dynamic array we mentioned earlier. Once you've made these additions, click on the button. This will display the result: the species name, the lion's name, and the lion's age.

Then, type **Simba** on the `nameToAge` mapping that we just added to get 8, which is the age of the lion. In this chapter, we have added only three animals. But in real life, hundreds of thousands of users will interact with our protocols. Suppose we want to keep track of which addresses interact with our protocol. Creating a mapping where we can quickly find a specific address or how much they transacted with it saves time compared to simply using arrays. With arrays, we would need to go through all the transactions and addresses one by one by typing 0, 1, 2, 3, and so on until we find the transaction or address we want. Moreover, since the contract is live 24/7, while we search for that one address or transaction, more addresses would interact with our contract, thus piling up even more transactions in the array that we would have to go through.

We can add additional mappings with key pairs based on the struct we have created. Here, we can see all the possible mapping combinations with the three variables _species, _name, and _age that we have made:

```
mapping (string => uint256) public nameToAge;
mapping (string => string) public speciesToName;
mapping (uint256 => string) public ageToName;
mapping (uint256 => string) public ageToSpecies;
mapping (string => string) public nameToSpecies;
mapping (string => uint256) public speciesToAge;
```

Additionally, the following code implements all these mappings in the addAnimal function:

```
function addAnimal(string memory _species, string memory _name, uint256 _age)
  public {
      listofAnimals.push(Animal(_species, _name, _age));
      nameToAge[_name] = _age;
      speciesToName[_species] = _name;
      ageToName[_age] = _name;
      ageToSpecies[_age] = _species;
      nameToSpecies[_name] = _species;
      speciesToAge[_species] = _age;
}
```

When we deploy and run the contract, we see what is shown in Figure 5.16.

We can see different values as we add the age, name, or species beside each corresponding function. Adding the variables beside each corresponding function illustrates that multiple mappings, not just one mapping, can manipulate and retrieve the data in the same contract. However, as discussed later in the book, the more mappings you add, the more gas-heavy the contract will be, so think carefully about what to include.

CONTRACT IMPORTING

One of Solidity's essential tools and properties is smart contract importing: the ability to load or import already premade smart contracts. Importing of contracts helps split contracts and code into different files and maintain organized code, and importing allows you to reuse premade existing code instead of writing repetitive code all over again all the time. Additionally, audited contracts are imported. In that case, importing also ensures security by reducing potential errors in code and increasing trust in the code.

FIGURE 5.16: ZooManagement mappings

To import one contract to a current contract you are working on, you need to have two contracts to begin with. Hence, a new contract has to be created in the Remix workspace. For the following example, the contract is named ContractInheritance.sol (see Figure 5.17).

FIGURE 5.17: ContractInheritance.sol creation

Next, as always, begin with defining the license under which the contract will be available:

```
//SPDX-License-Identifier: MIT
```

and then defining the Solidity version:

```
pragma solidity 0.8.26;
```

For any contract where you plan to import other contracts in the future, the next step after defining the Solidity version is to import the required contracts. This is achieved using the following code:

```
import {ZooManagement} from "ZooManagement.sol";
```

The `import` keyword communicates that we are importing a contract. `{ZooManagement}` specifies the contract name we want to import. In this example, our file `ZooManagement.sol` has a contract named `ZooManagement`, as shown in Figure 5.18.

FIGURE 5.18: `ZooManagement` name demonstration

`from` points to the file path. In this case, `ContractInheritance.sol` is "in the same folder"—no folders—as `ZooManagement.sol`. Thus, the path will be in double quotation marks, simply `"ZooManagement.sol"`. Hence, `"ZooManagement.sol"` signifies the path to the contract's Solidity file.

If we create a sample folder in the Remix workspace and put the `ZooManagement.sol` inside the folder, as shown in Figure 5.19, we see that the `ContractInheritance.sol` file has an error.

FIGURE 5.19: `SampleFolder` with `ZooManagement.sol` added

This is because, opposite the filename, we can see 1. If the numbers were 2 or 3, there would also be the respective number of errors.

The error we get is caused by the contract's inability to find the `ZooManagement.sol` file, as shown in Figure 5.20. In contrast, just a few moments ago, it had no problems locating it. The inability occurred because we relocated the `ZooManagement.sol` file by creating the `SampleFolder` and putting it inside the folder. This action changed the path of the `ZooManagement.sol` file from being in the same folder as `ContractInheritance.sol` to being in the `SampleFolder`.

To fix this error, you have to change the path of the importation code from this:

```
import {ZooManagement} from "ZooManagement.sol";
```

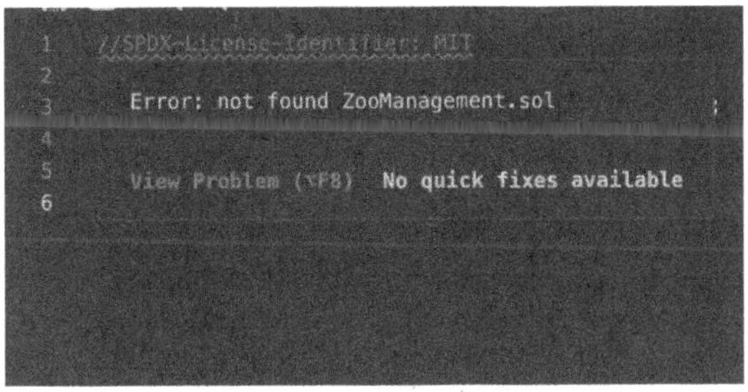

FIGURE 5.20: Error on `ContractInheritance`

to the following:

```
import {ZooManagement} from "SampleFolder/ZooManagement.sol";
```

As shown in Figure 5.21, the error has disappeared.

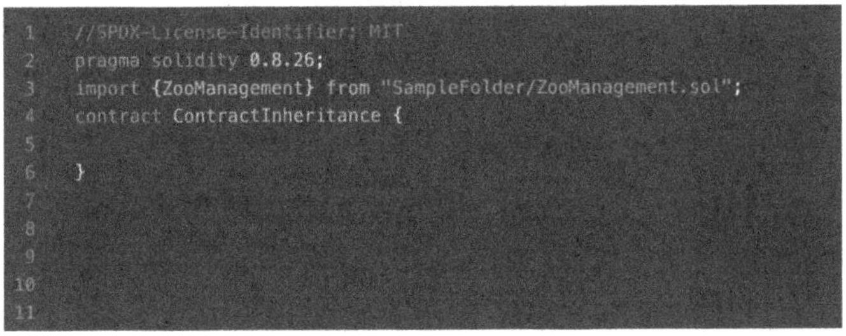

FIGURE 5.21: `ContractInheritance.sol` importation

The error disappeared because the path now correctly specifies where to find the `ZooManagement` contract. When importing `ZooManagement`, the path indicates that you should first go to the `SampleFolder` and then locate the `ZooManagement.sol` file, which contains the `ZooManagement` contract that needs to be imported.

Hence, the error has been resolved since the file that hosts the contract has been found by giving the right path.

If we were to change the location of the contracts, placing `ContractInheritance.sol` in the `SampleFolder` and the `ZooManagement.sol` contract outside of the `SampleFolder`, then the path of importing the `ZooManagement` contract would change again. (see Figure 5.22.)

Figure 5.23 shows that the `ContractInheritance.sol` has an error again.

Although the error message is not identical to the previous message when we added the `ZooManagement.sol` contract to the `SampleFolder`, it is similar. This time, it needs help locating the `ZooManagement.sol` contract again. Still, it is not found in `SampleFolder` this time since the developer moved the file outside the folder. Inside, we added the `ContractInheritance.sol` contract instead.

FIGURE 5.22: Changing the contract path

FIGURE 5.23: `ContractInheritance.sol` incorrect path error

To fix this error, we again have to change the path of the import code from this:

```
import {ZooManagement} from "SampleFolder/ZooManagement.sol";
```

to the following:

```
import {ZooManagement} from "../ZooManagement.sol";
```

As shown in Figure 5.24, the developer fixed the error. The ".." in import {ZooManagement} from "../ZooManagement.sol"; means "going up a folder" or leaving our current folder. In this case, SampleFolder where the ContractInheritance.sol contract currently resides and then adding "ZooManagement.sol" means since we are now outside our folder and in the folder where ZooManagement.sol resides, we can mention it to import it.

FIGURE 5.24: `ContractInheritance.sol` new path importation

If `ContractInheritance.sol` were located in two folders instead of one, the path would be as follows:

```
import {ZooManagement} from "../../ZooManagement.sol";
```

if three folders, then it would be as follows:

```
import {ZooManagement} from "../../../ZooManagement.sol";
```

One final import path to know about is when two contracts are in different folders, as shown in Figure 5.25. In this case, I created `SampleFolder2` and added `ZooManagement.sol` inside it while `ContractInheritance.sol` stays in the original `SampleFolder`.

FIGURE 5.25: `ContractInheritance.sol` changing paths

To fix the error and correct the path of this:

```
import {ZooManagement} from "../ZooManagement.sol";
```

you have to add the following path so that the code recognizes it:

```
import {ZooManagement} from "../SampleFolder2/ZooManagement.sol";
```

Adding this path fixes the error. In this path, we leave our folder, `SampleFolder`, and then enter `ZooManagement.sol`'s folder, `SampleFolder2`, where the `ZooManagement.sol` file is located, and then we specify that we want to import that contract by naming it.

INHERITANCE

Inheritance in Solidity works analogously to biological inheritance: children inherit characteristics from their parents. This means that, in Solidity, one contract can inherit the properties and functions of another contract and create a parent/child relationship. Similarly, most of the time, the original contract that a newer contract inherits from is called the *parent* contract, and the newer contract that inherits from the parent contract is called a *child* contract. Another term for the parent contract is the *base* contract, and the contract inherited from it is called the child contract.

The types of inheritance in Solidity are discussed in the following sections.

Single Inheritance

When a (child) contract inherits from one single parent—or base—contract, it is called a *single inheritance* contract. Single inheritance enables code reuse and the creation of more specialized contracts that inherit from a general contract.

A code snippet example looks like this:

```
//SPDX-License-Identifier: MIT
pragma solidity 0.8.26;
contract CreateNumber {
    uint256 number;
    function addNumber(uint256 _number) public {
    number = _number;
    }
}
```

The CreateNumber contract states the license under which it is released, the version of Solidity used, and the name of the contract. It then creates an uint256 variable called number. Finally, it states a function addNumber with a parameter uint256 _number.

Inside the function, the global variable number is set to the value of _number;.

The setting of the _number variable means that when this contract is run and deployed, the person who calls the function (the caller) for it to execute will be able to enter the number they want for number.

As shown in Figure 5.26, the caller adds the number 12 to the value of the number through the addNumber function.

```
//SPDX-License-Identifier: MIT
pragma solidity 0.8.26;
import {CreateNumber} from "CreateNumber.sol";
contract AddSubtractiontoAdditionContract is CreateNumber{

    function addNumber(uint256 _newnumber) public override {
        number = _newnumber - 5;
    }

    function returnNumber() public view returns(uint256) {
        return number;
    }
}
```

In the preceding AddMultiplicationtoAdditionContract contract, the developer states the license of the contract and the version of Solidity, imports the previous CreateNumber contract from the CreateNumber.sol file, and then states the name of the contract. Through a new keyword—is—the contract inherits all the functions and variables of the CreateNumber contract.

Then, the contract proceeds by using the addNumber function from the previous contract and adding a new local uint256 local variable named _newnumber. The function is public and can be overridden through the override keyword.

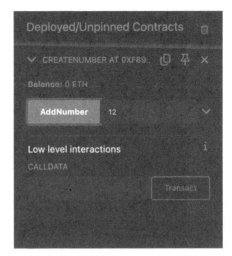

FIGURE 5.26: CreateNumber addNumber

The `override` keyword is always in a function used in a derived or child contract to indicate that the same function in the base or parent contract will be overridden or ignored. The child contract's version of that function will do something else. However, for the `override` function to work, the child contract has to have specific parameters as the original parent or base contract from which it inherits:

➤ **Name:** In this example, that would be `addNumber`.

➤ **Local parameters stated within the function:** In this example, that would be (`uint256 _number`).

➤ **Keyword types:** In this example, that would be `public`. If the function had such a keyword, that would be `returns`. Whatever the function would return in the `returns` keyword would be `uint256`, a `string`, or any other variable defined in the original function of the parent or base contract.

➤ **Global number variable:** Within the `addNumber` function, the global number variable is set to the local variable `_newnumber – 5`. That would mean that, unlike the original `addNumber` function, this function would take the set number and would remove 5 from the original number in case there was a reason a person who created this contract needed to subtract 5 every single time a user adds a number.

Finally, a public `returnNumber()` function is created, meaning that anyone can call the function internally and externally. It is a view function, meaning it reads data only from the blockchain and does not alter its state by, for example, sending money from one address to another. It returns a `uint256` value.

Within the function, it is stated that the function has to return the number variable.

In Figure 5.27, we can see that the function's caller adds 12 as a value. Still, due to the - 5 in the `addNumber` function, it ultimately returns 7 since 12 – 5 = 7.

FIGURE 5.27: `AddSubtractionToAddition AddNumber`

For the `addNumber` function of the `AddMultiplicationtoAdditionContract` contract to be called and executed and for the child contract `AddSubtractiontoAdditionContract` not to return an error, an additional keyword has to be added to the `CreateNumber` function besides its own `AddNumber` function:

```
//SPDX-License-Identifier: MIT
pragma solidity 0.8.26;
contract CreateNumber {

    uint256 number;

    function addNumber(uint256 _number) public virtual {
        number = _number;
    }
}
```

The `virtual` keyword is added in the `CreateNumber` contract to the function `addNumber`. This indicates to the compiler that the `addNumber` function of this specific contract can be overridden in the `AddSubtractiontoAdditionContract`. When using the `is` keyword to allow a child contract to inherit the functions and properties of a parent (or base) contract, you must add the `override` keyword to any function in the child contract that you want to modify. Additionally, you need to mark the same function in the parent contract with the `virtual` keyword. This ensures that the function changes in the child contract work correctly without causing errors.

Multilevel Inheritance

When a parent contract inherits from one grandparent—or base—contract and then a child contract inherits from the parent contract, it creates even more complex and specialized contracts.

Here is a code example:

```
//SPDX-License-Identifier: MIT
pragma solidity 0.8.26;
contract CreateNumber {

    uint256 number;
```

```
function addNumber(uint256 _number) public virtual {
    number = _number;
}
}
```

The developer also used the original CreateNumber contract in the earlier single inheritance example. In this example, the only difference is that it has become the grandparent contract from which the parent contract inherits functions and parameters.

```
//SPDX-License-Identifier: MIT
pragma solidity 0.8.26;
import {CreateNumber} from "CreateNumber.sol";
contract SubtractionContract is CreateNumber{

    function addNumber(uint256 _newnumber) public override virtual {
        number = _newnumber - 5;
    }

    function returnNumber() public view returns(uint256) {
        return number;
    }

}
```

The preceding is the SubtractionContract child contract used in the previous example for the single inheritance. However, things are different in this case as the child contract has now become the parent contract, inheriting from the grandparent contract of CreateNumber.

Since the SubtractionContract is going to be inherited by a child contract this time, besides the override keyword that was added in the previous example, the SubtractionContract has, just like the CreateNumber contract, an additional keyword: virtual. The virtual keyword indicates that a child contract can override this function.

```
//SPDX-License-Identifier: MIT
pragma solidity 0.8.26;
import {SubtractionContract} from "SubtractionContract.sol";
contract AdditionContract is SubtractionContract {

    function addNumber(uint256 _newnewnumber) public override {
        number = _newnewnumber + 5;
    }
}
```

We can see that the preceding contract has imported and inherited the SubtractionContract. It uses the function addNumber, which is the original function of the addNumber contract. The SubtractionContract is being used now in the AdditionContract, which then inherited and utilized it. The function gets the number variable, sets it to _newnewnumber, and adds 5. Unlike the SubtractContract, which subtracts 5, this contract adds 5 instead.

When you deploy and run this contract on Remix, you'll see that despite declaring a function, the contract has two functions when it is running instead of one that has been defined in the

`AdditionContract`. This is because the contract inherits the functions of the parent contract and there is no need to define the functions again in the `AdditionContract`.

As shown in Figure 5.28, in the `addNumber` function the user adds 12, and when clicking the `ReturnNumber` function, the user gets 17.

FIGURE 5.28: `AdditionContract AddNumber`

Multiple Inheritance

Multiple inheritance is when one child contract inherits from two or more parent contracts.

See Contract 1 for a code example.

CONTRACT 1

```
//SPDX-License-Identifier: MIT
pragma solidity 0.8.26;
contract Contract1 {

    uint256 numberofVisitors;

    function defineNumberofVisitors(uint256 _numberofVisitors) public {
        numberofVisitors = _numberofVisitors;
    }
    function showNumberofVisitors()public view returns(uint256) {
        return numberofVisitors;
    }
}
```

In Contract 1, the function `defineNumberofVisitors` sets the global variable `numberofVisitors` to the local variable `_numberofVisitors`. This will allow the caller of the function once the contract is deployed to define the number of visitors.

Additionally, the `showNumbeofVisitors` function returns the `numbeofVisitors`.

Contract 2 does the same thing as Contract 1 but for the number of refunded tickets.

CONTRACT 2

```
//SPDX-License-Identifier: MIT
pragma solidity 0.8.26;
contract Contract2 {

    uint256 numberofRefundedTickets;

    function defineNumberofRefundedTickets(uint256 _numberofRefundedTickets)
 public {
          numberofRefundedTickets = _numberofRefundedTickets;
    }

    function showNumberofRefundedTickets() public view returns(uint256){
        return numberofRefundedTickets;
    }
}
```

Contract 3 imports Contract 1 and Contract 2 and inherits both contracts but has no function of its own. However, when the contract is deployed and is running, you can see in Figure 5.29 that the available functions of Contracts 1 and 2 have been inherited.

CONTRACT 3

```
//SPDX-License-Identifier: MIT
pragma solidity 0.8.26;
import {Contract1} from "Contract1.sol";
import {Contract2} from "Contract2.sol";
contract Contract3 is Contract1, Contract2{
}
```

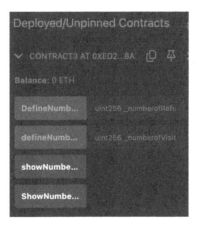

FIGURE 5.29: Contract3 defineNumber and showNumber

Hierarchical Inheritance

Hierarchical inheritance is when multiple child contracts inherit from the same base or parent contract. See Contract 4.

CONTRACT 4

```
//SPDX-License-Identifier: MIT
pragma solidity 0.8.26;
contract Contract1 {

    uint256 numberofVisitors;

    function defineNumberofVisitors(uint256 _numberofVisitors) public {
        numberofVisitors = _numberofVisitors;
    }
    function showNumberofVisitors()public view returns(uint256) {
    return numberofVisitors;
    }
}
```

Contract 4 defines the license under which it will be available, the Solidity version, and the name of the contract; then, it states a variable `uint256` that represents the number of visitors. Moreover, it creates a function called `showNumberofVisitors` and states a local parameter of type `uint256` with the name `_numberofVisitors`. The function is public, meaning that the function can be called both internally and externally, and inside the function, it sets the global variable `numberofVisitors` to the local parameter `_numberofVisitors`, which allows the caller of the function to set a number of visitors to the zoo.

The second function of the contract, `showNumberofVisitors`, has no local parameters and is public, meaning it can be called both internally and externally. `view` means that it does not alter the state of the blockchain and only reads data from it. `returns(uint256)` returns the data read by view and returns a uint256 type. Inside the function it states that the function should return the value of the `numberofVisitors` variable, which is an `uint256` variant as stated in the `returns(uint256)`.

Contract 5 states the license under which it will be released, and the Solidity version it is using. It imports `Contract1`; states the name of the contract, which is `Contract2`; and then inherits the properties of Contract 4. Contract 5 has no functions, but when running, it will use the functions of Contract 4, which it inherited the functions of.

CONTRACT 5

```
//SPDX-License-Identifier: MIT
pragma solidity 0.8.26;
import {Contract1} from "Contract1.sol";
contract Contract2 is Contract1{
}
```

Contract 6, similarly, states the license under which it will be released and the Solidity version it is using. It imports Contract 4; states the name of the contract, which is Contract 6; and then inherits the properties of Contract 4. Contract 6 has no functions, but when it runs, it will use the functions of Contract 4, which it inherited.

CONTRACT 6

```
//SPDX-License-Identifier: MIT
pragma solidity 0.8.26;
import {Contract1} from "Contract1.sol";
contract Contract3 is Contract1{
}
```

Thus, inheritance, as a mechanism in Solidity, is similar to biological inheritance, allowing contracts to inherit variables and functions just as children inherit the different biological traits of their parents, such as hair color, eye color, skin color, etc. Inheritance enables developers to create more powerful and specialized smart contracts by building on the characteristics of pre-existing contracts. Inheritance allows developers to maintain code better if required by breaking a large contract into smaller parts.

Figure 5.30 illustrates the four types of inheritance discussed in this section.

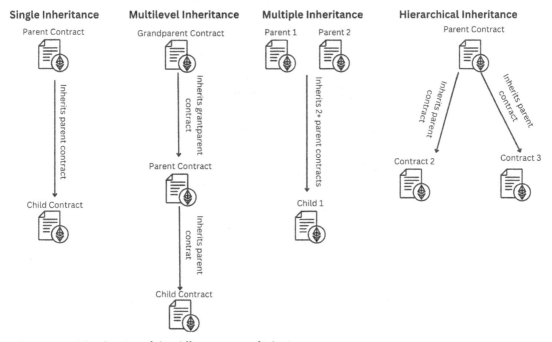

FIGURE 5.30: Visualization of the different types of Inheritance contracts

DEPLOYING AND RUNNING A CONTRACT FROM ANOTHER CONTRACT

Another possibility of interacting with contracts is deploying one contract from another. This has several advantages depending on the use case and the situation. For example, deploying a contract from another contract may help reduce errors in the code if you were to deploy a contract multiple times. It helps keep track of each contract deployed if it is defined to do so.

To demonstrate, since we are familiar with its functions, we will deploy our previous ZooManagement contract from another contract we will create.

To do so, on Remix, we need to create a new file called ZooManagementFactory, as shown in Figure 5.31.

FIGURE 5.31: ZooManagementFactory

Then, when opening the file, the first thing to do, as always, is to define the license under which the smart contract will be released:

```
//SPDX-License-Identifier: MIT
```

The next step is to state the version of Solidity you will use with this contract:

```
pragma solidity 0.8.26;
```

Next, you import the ZooManagement contract. Since the contract is not in any additional folder but in the same place as the ZooManagementFactory, there is no need to use .. in the importation process:

```
import {ZooManagement} from "ZooManagement.sol";
```

The final thing a contract has to have before writing in the contract itself is a name:

```
Contract ZooManagementFactory {}
```

Within the contract, this is the first thing you can do:

```
ZooManagement public zooManagement;
```

This code declares a new public variable, zooManagement, of type ZooManagement, meaning that zooManagement can reference a ZooManagement contract.

> **NOTE** As mentioned earlier in this chapter, Solidity is case-sensitive, meaning that a hypothetical variable called Apple is different from a variable called apple. That is, Solidity interprets these as two completely different variables.
>
> Hence, the ZooManagement type is entirely different from zooManagement because the former uses a capital Z and the latter a small z.

This is because in Solidity when one declares a contract variable such as zooManagement of type ZooManagement, which is the actual contract, the zooManagement does not store the ZooManagement contract but creates a reference or a pointer that points to or shows another contract, which in this case will be a ZooManagement contract that will be deployed in the next part of this section.

An easy way of thinking about this for beginners is to imagine a construction company that is planning to construct a new building; in this case, the building is a ZooManagement "building," while the zooManagement variable can be thought of as the address where this building will be built and exist. In other words, currently the following:

```
ZooManagement public zooManagement;
```

is better thought of as "At the zooManagement address a skyscraper named ZooManagement will be built, but the address is currently empty since construction has not begun yet. Once the skyscraper is built on the address zooManagement, people going to this address will be able to interact with the ZooManagement skyscraper by going inside of it, going to the floor they want, and visiting any friends who may be living there."

The next step is to construct this "building" by deploying the new ZooManagement contract by typing this:

```
function deployZooManagement() public {zooManagement = new ZooManagement(); }
```

This code declares a public function, `deployZooManagement`, that uses the `zooManagement` variable to deploy a new `ZooManagement` contract.

The `new` keyword in Solidity is used to deploy new contracts.

The `=` operator assigns a newly deployed `ZooManagement` contract to the `zooManagement` variable. Think of this like recording the address of a newly constructed building. When we deploy the contract, we create a new instance of `ZooManagement`, similar to constructing a new building from blueprints. The `zooManagement` variable stores the contract's address, just like how a building has a specific street address where people can find it. Once deployed, users can interact with the contract by calling its functions, similar to how people can visit different floors of the building to access different services.

If you deploy this contract, it should now look like this on Remix:

```
//SPDX-License-Identifier: MIT
pragma solidity 0.8.26;
import {ZooManagement} from "ZooManagement.sol";
contract ZooManagementFactory{

    ZooManagement public zooManagement;

    function deployZooManagement() public {
        zooManagement = new ZooManagement();
    }
}
```

Figure 5.32 shows the result.

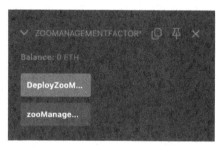

FIGURE 5.32: `ZooManagementFactory DeployZooManagement`

Upon clicking the deployZooManagement button, a new `ZooManagement` contract is deployed.

After deployment, if you call the `zooManagement` variable, you will see the address of the newly deployed `ZooManagement` contract, as shown in Figure 5.33.

If you click the deployZooManagement button again, a new `ZooManagement` contract will be deployed.

If once a new `ZooManagement` contract is deployed the caller again calls the `zooManagement` contract, a new address will appear, as shown in Figure 5.34.

FIGURE 5.33: `ZooManagementFactory zooManagement #1`

FIGURE 5.34: `ZooManagementFactory zooManagement #2`

Then again, if you deploy yet another `ZooManagement` contract and then call the `zooManagement` variable, a new address would appear. The problem with this is that although the contracts deployed live always on the blockchain and do not disappear, one "loses" them in the contract you develop at the time since you do not keep track of the contracts and, hence, cannot interact with them in any way. To solve this, you have to expand the initial contract:

```
//SPDX-License-Identifier: MIT
pragma solidity 0.8.26;
import {ZooManagement} from "ZooManagement.sol";
contract ZooManagementFactory{

    ZooManagement public zooManagement;

    function deployZooManagement() public {
        zooManagement = new ZooManagement();
    }
}
```

To solve this and to be able to track all deployed contracts, you have to create an array:

```
ZooManagement[] public listOfZooManagementContracts;
```

This creates a public array called `listOfZooManagementContracts` that stores data types of type `ZooManagement` and can be placed below this line in the `ZooManagementFactory` contract:

```
ZooManagement public zooManagement;
```

The function `DeployZooManagement` needs to be slightly changed as well:

```
function deployZooManagement() public {
    ZooManagement newZooManagement = new ZooManagement();
}
```

This modifies the `DeployZooManagement` function, which is public, meaning that it can be called both internally and externally. A new variable, `newZooManagement`, of type `ZooManagement`, is created within the function.

The new `ZooManagement()` part deploys a new instance of the `ZooManagement` contract on the blockchain. The = part assigns the newly deployed `ZooManagement` contract address to `newZooManagement`.

This allows for `NewZooManagement` to become a reference point that can be used to interact with the newly created `ZooManagement` contract on the blockchain upon deployment.

The parentheses, `()`, will be explained later in the book as they refer to the contract's constructor.

Additionally, to track each new `ZooManagement` contract deployed with the new keyword, you have to push it into the following array:

```
ZooManagement[] public listOfZooManagementContracts;
```

by typing this:

```
function deployZooManagement() public {
    ZooManagement newZooManagement = new ZooManagement();
    listOfZooManagementContracts.push(newZooManagement);
}
```

This function is the same as the previous one, with the only difference being the addition of the following:

```
listOfZooManagementContracts.push(newZooManagement);
```

part of the code that takes the `newZooManagement` instance, which points to the newly deployed `ZooManagement` contract and pushes it into the `listOfZooManagementContracts` array.

The code so far has to look like this:

```
//SPDX-License-Identifier: MIT
pragma solidity 0.8.26;
import {ZooManagement} from "ZooManagement.sol";
contract ZooManagementFactory{

    ZooManagement public zooManagement;
    ZooManagement[] public listOfZooManagementContracts;
```

```
function deployZooManagement() public {
    ZooManagement newZooManagement = new ZooManagement();
    listOfZooManagementContracts.push(newZooManagement);
}
}
```

When deploying the `ZooManagementFactory` contract, you should see what is in Figure 5.35.

FIGURE 5.35: `ZooManagementFactory` **array #1**

If you click DeployZooManagement button and type 0 on the listOfZooManagementContracts button, you should get the address of the newly deployed `ZooManagement` contract, as shown in Figure 5.36.

FIGURE 5.36: ZooManagementFactory array #2

If you click the deployZooManagement button again to deploy another `ZooManagement` contract and type 1 on the listOfZooManagementContracts button, you'll get what you see in Figure 5.37.

You will see the newly deployed contract appear. If you type 0 again on the listOfZooManagement-Contracts button, you'll see what is shown in Figure 5.38.

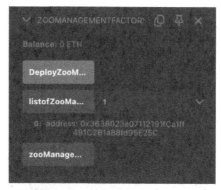

FIGURE 5.37: ZooManagementFactory array #3

FIGURE 5.38: ZooManagementFactory array #4

The older contract appears. If you deploy another new ZooManagement contract and type "2" on the listOfZooManagementContracts button, a new address is reflected, that of the most newly deployed contract. This allows for tracking each new ZooManagement contract deployed.

The final functions that need to be added are the ones that allow for interacting with the newly deployed contract:

```
function fUpdateVisitorCount(uint256 _zooManagementContractIndex, uint256
 _myNewVisitorCount) public {
     ZooManagement myNewZooManagement = listOfZooManagementContracts
[_zooManagement
ContractIndex];
     myNewZooManagement.updateVisitorCount(_mynewVisitorCount);
}
```

This defines a function named fUpdateVisitorCount. The f stands for factory, and it has two local parameters of type uint256: _zooManagementContractIndex and _mynewVisitorCount. The function is public, meaning it can be called externally and internally from the contract.

Then, it declares a new variable, myNewZooManagement, which refers to the ZooManagament contract. It then assigns the myNewZooManagement variable to the listOfZooManagementContracts[_zooManagementContractIndex].

The _ zooManagementContractIndex parameter is the index—or number—of a specific ZooManagement contract in the listOfZooManagementContracts array—the one pushed in the preceding function. The function caller needs to specify the parameter, which is thus used to access a previously deployed ZooManagement contract—the one deployed in the deployZooManagement function.

In the next part of the code, the new myNewZooManagement contract instance is used by adding the . next to the myNewZooManagement variable, which is a reference to the previously deployed and now accessed ZooManagement contract and is used to call the updateVisitorCount function of that contract. The _myNewVisitorCount parameter is the new _newVisitorCount of the update VisitorCount function that the caller will use upon deployment to type the number of visitors to the zoo.

The contract should now look like this:

```
//SPDX-License-Identifier: MIT
pragma solidity 0.8.26;
import {ZooManagement} from "ZooManagement.sol";
contract ZooManagementFactory {

    ZooManagement public zooManagement;
    ZooManagement[] public listOfZooManagementContracts;

    function deployZooManagement() public {
        ZooManagement newZooManagement = new ZooManagement();
        listOfZooManagementContracts.push(newZooManagement);
    }

    function fUpdateVisitorCount(uint256 _zooManagementContractIndex, uint256
_myNewVisitorCount) public {
        ZooManagement myNewZooManagement = listOfZooManagementContracts
[_zooManagementContractIndex];
        myNewZooManagement.updateVisitorCount(_mynewVisitorCount);
    }
}
```

When the contract is deployed on the Remix Virtual Machine, the result is as shown in Figure 5.39.

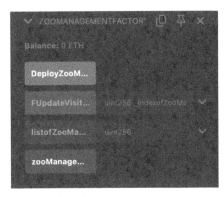

FIGURE 5.39: ZooManagementFactory final deployment

You can add a number to be stored in the `fUpdateVisitorCount` function, just like in the `ZooManagement` contract. Still, since there is no equivalent to the `getTotalVisitors` function, the number of visitors cannot be displayed yet.

Therefore, the next step is to create a function that will call the function of the deployed contract to enable the caller to get the number of visitors reflected:

```
function fGetTotalVisitors(uint256 _zooManagementContractIndex) public
view returns
(uint256){
    ZooManagement myNewZooManagement = listOfZooManagementContracts
[_zooManagement
ContractIndex];
    return myNewZooManagement.getTotalVisitors();
}
```

This code defines a function named `fGetTotalVisitors`, with a local parameter being an `uint256` `_zooManagementContractIndex`, just like in the `fUpdateVisitorCount`. A `uint256 _ myNew VisitorCount` is unnecessary since this function will read and return a number from the blockchain, just like the `getTotalVisitors` function from the original `ZooManagement` contract.

The function is public, like the `getTotalVisitors` function from the `ZooManagement` contract, allowing it to be called internally and externally. It is also `view`, which means that it does not alter the state of the blockchain but reads data from it and returns (`uint256`). By the end of the function, it will return a variable of type `uint256`.

Then, just like in the `fUpdateVisitorCount` function, the function declares a new variable, `myNewZooManagement`, referencing the `ZooManagement` contract. It then assigns the `myNewZoo Management` variable to the `listOfZooManagementContracts [_zooManagementContractIndex]`.

Just like in the `fUpdateVisitorCount` function, the `_zooManagementContractIndex` parameter is used to access a previously deployed `ZooManagement` contract—again, the one that was deployed in the `deployZooManagement` function at the beginning of the contract.

Finally, the function states that it will return the `getTotalVisitors` function from the deployed `ZooManagement` contract by interacting with the `myNewZooManagement` variable that references the `ZooManagement` contract, adding a ., and calling the `getTotalVisitors` function of the contract.

CHAPTER 5 QUESTIONS

1. What is the main difference between dynamic arrays and fixed-size arrays in Solidity, and how does this affect gas efficiency?

2. When implementing a `require` statement in a Solidity function, why is it important to place it at the beginning of the function?

3. How does the `mapping` data structure in Solidity differ from arrays, and what advantage does it offer when looking up values?

4. Explain the relationship between the `virtual` and `override` keywords in Solidity inheritance. When are they required?

5. In Solidity, what is the purpose of `memory` keyword when working with string parameters in functions?

6. How do you properly import a contract that is located two folders above the current contract's location in Solidity?

7. What happens when you try to add more elements than specified to a fixed-size array in Solidity?

8. What are the key differences between single inheritance and multilevel inheritance in Solidity?

9. When creating a `struct` in Solidity, what types of data can be stored within it, and how is it typically used?

10. What is the significance of case sensitivity in Solidity, particularly when working with contract names and variables?

11. How does the `new` keyword function in Solidity when deploying contracts, and what does it return?

12. Why might a developer choose to use an older version of the Solidity compiler instead of the latest version?

13. In the context of the `ZooManagement` contract, how does the `push()` function work with dynamic arrays?

14. What is the purpose of a factory contract in Solidity, and what advantages does it offer?

15. How are mappings used to track multiple variables in a contract? (Use the `ZooManagement` example's animal tracking system.)

6

Installing Microsoft Visual Studio Code and Foundry

This chapter provides a practical introduction to setting up a professional Solidity integrated development environment (IDE) using Visual Studio (VS) Code and Foundry. Rather than relying on web-based tools such as Remix, you'll learn how to configure a robust local development setup that scales with your needs.

By following the setup instructions in this chapter, you'll establish a professional-grade development environment that serves as the foundation for building sophisticated smart contracts. You'll learn how to leverage VS Code's powerful features such as multifile editing, terminal integration, and essential extensions to streamline your development process. Whether you're building simple contracts or complex protocols, having a properly configured development environment is crucial for writing secure and maintainable smart contracts.

The chapter introduces IDE concepts step-by-step, starting from basic editor usage and moving to advanced features such as split terminals and integrated debugging. Throughout the setup process, you'll gain hands-on experience with command-line tools and package management—essential skills for any blockchain developer.

WHAT IS MICROSOFT VS CODE?

In the previous two chapters, Remix was used as an IDE. Remix is helpful when taking your first steps in Solidity programming as its interface is simple and intuitive. It is web-based, and thus, there is no requirement for installation, making it beginner-friendly. It is also useful when you need to test code quickly. Regarding professional development, Remix is essential for various reasons.

However, Remix supports only Solidity and not any other programming languages. Thus, as a developer, if you plan to learn another language, Remix is not an ideal tool. Moreover, Remix has limited performance in projects more lengthy and complex than a simple `ZooManagement` contract. Because it's web-based, you need an Internet connection 24/7. In other words, if something happens where you need to work on code, it would not be possible without an Internet connection. To mitigate that and use Remix offline without an Internet connection, you can download the Remix desktop application by going to `https://remix-project.org`. Scroll down to the Remix Desktop IDE area and click Get Our Desktop App button to download the version appropriate for your operating system.

There are many integrated development environments and code editors you can download and use, which vary according to user-friendliness, with some requiring more technical knowledge. In contrast, others, such as Remix, are much more intuitive and user-friendly in terms of interface. If you are interested in exploring other IDEs and code editors, you can research, install, and use one from the following list. Although we will install and use Microsoft Visual Studio Code in this book, it is good to have at least an awareness of other major IDEs and code editors.

➤ Atom

➤ Eclipse

➤ Sublime Text

➤ JetBrains IntelliJ IDEA

➤ WebStorm

➤ Notepad++

➤ Brackets

➤ Remix Desktop

VS Code is one of the leading text editors many professional developers use to build projects in Solidity and other programming languages, such as JavaScript, PHP, Python, C#, Java, and other languages. VS Code is lightweight, which means it is small in size compared to comparable programs—in theory at least—and when you launch it, it starts up quickly, so you don't have to wait a long time. VS Code is cross-platform: it runs on Mac, Windows, and Linux.

To download VS Code, go to `https://code.visualstudio.com` or do an Internet search for "download Visual Studio Code."

This will lead to the VS Code website, as shown in Figure 6.1 (which may change depending on when you are reading this book).

The landing page automatically detects what operating system a visitor is using. In this example, it displays a Download For macOS button.

There are two versions of VS Code:

➤ **The stable edition:** This is the standard latest version of VS Code.

➤ **The Insiders edition:** The beta version has the latest updates and new features. However, since the new features are still being tested and have yet to reach the final, stable edition, they may not always work and can present problems.

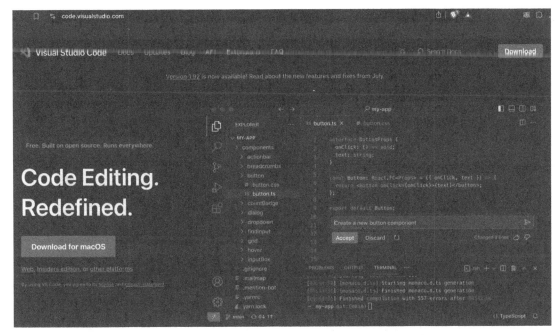

FIGURE 6.1: VS Code website

To download the Insiders edition, click the Insiders Edition link below the Download For button, as shown in Figure 6.2.

FIGURE 6.2: The VS Code Insiders Edition link

It is possible to install both the standard version of VS Code and the Insiders version simultaneously and use both depending on your needs.

MICROSOFT VISUAL STUDIO CODE LAYOUT

Installing VS Code differs slightly depending on your operating system, such as macOS, Windows, and Linux. It is standard procedure to also install VS Code.

Upon running VS Code for the first time, the Welcome page shown in Figure 6.3 will pop up asking you to modify VS Code to your liking. You can change the theme color, set up the programming language extensions, modify settings, sync settings across devices in case you are using VS Code with different laptops, open the command palette, open your code file, and watch tutorial videos.

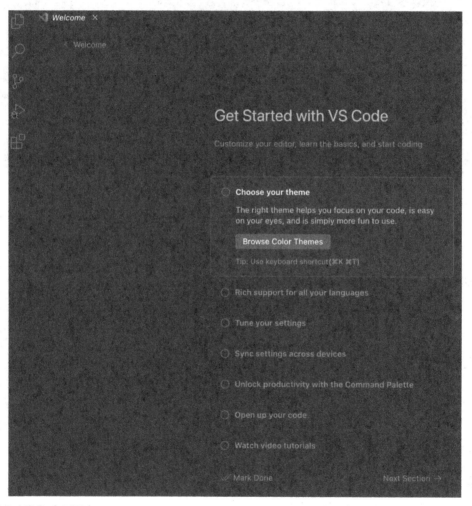

FIGURE 6.3: VS Code's Welcome page

Explorer Pane

The icon on the top left of the VS Code opens the Explorer pane, as shown in Figure 6.4, where developers open and manage the projects they are working on. The pane in this image is empty since I don't have any projects active yet.

There are two options shown in Figure 6.4:

▶ **Open Folder:** This option prompts you to open a folder on your computer with a project written in a specific programming language. You can continue working on the project or, if it is in its very early stages, start working on it.

At the end of this chapter, you create a Solidity project so you will see how that is done.

▶ **Clone Repository:** You can re-create an external project found online on websites such as GitHub. (You see this later in this book.) Other programmers work on these projects, and if someone wants to work on the project, modify it, or create an entirely new project based wholly or partially on the code available, they are free to do so—as long as the license under which the code is released allows for that.

FIGURE 6.4: Explorer pane

When you click the three dots icon on the top right of the pane, you can edit the look of the pane, as shown in Figure 6.5.

Feel free to select the options Open Editors, No Folder Opened, Outline, and Timeline to see what each one does and how it changes the looks of the pane.

> **NOTE** *Later in this chapter, after you add a Solidity project, you can return to this pane to compare what it looks like with and without a project loaded.*

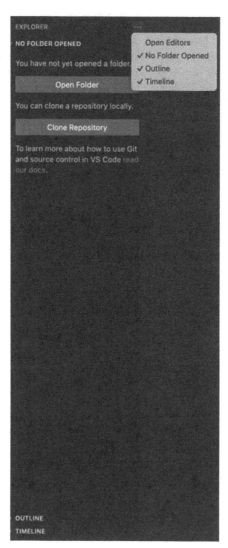

FIGURE 6.5: Exploring the Explorer pane

Search Pane

The icon for the Search pane is just below the Explorer icon, and clicking the icon will open the pane. (see Figure 6.6.)

FIGURE 6.6: Magnifying glass icon and Search pane

The Search pane is similar to the one that opens when pressing Command+F on a Mac or Ctrl+F on Windows. You can search for a specific letter, symbol, word, or phrase in a file or on a website by typing that letter, symbol, word, or phrase and pressing the Enter button. The only difference with the search pane on VS Code is that instead of searching one file, the pane searches all the files in the Explorer pane.

There is also a Replace option, which allows you to replace certain letters, symbols, words, or phrases with others within the Explorer pane. To restrict the search to specific files within the Explorer pane, click the three dots at the bottom right of the Replace text box.

This allows you to include specific files from the Explorer pane in the Files To Include and Files To Exclude text spaces, making the general search more focused and specific, as shown in Figure 6.7.

FIGURE 6.7: Including and excluding certain files

Extensions

Extensions in VS Code are additional programs developed by individuals and companies that developers can use to enhance their coding experience, sometimes adding new functionality or making it easier to code and develop projects. Extensions allow you to customize VS Code, such as by adding new programming languages, highlighting code that may be wrong, changing the background color and theme of VS Code, using artificial intelligence (AI) to help with code generation, creating reusable code templates, and more.

These extensions can be enabled and disabled. It is additionally important to keep in mind that the extensions are not checked by Microsoft, the company that produced VS Code. As a consequence, avoid installing any extensions that you think might not be safe, especially in the context of crypto-currencies, wallets, and private keys that could be easily stolen.

Night Owl

This section walks you through installing the Night Owl theme.

Type the name of theme, as shown in Figure 6.8.

FIGURE 6.8: Searching for the Night Owl theme

The first result for Night Owl shows that it has 2.7 million downloads and a rating of 5. When you click the Night Owl extension, the window shown in Figure 6.9 opens.

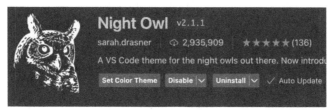

FIGURE 6.9: Night Owl extension window

The extension's description describes what it is and why it was created. Scroll down to find the steps to install the extension (not shown in Figure 6.9).

Click the Features link near the top of the window (below the owl picture) to see its features. Upon clicking Changelog, you will see the different versions of the extension and how they have changed over time, such as what new features were added or removed.

To install the extension, click the blue Install button beside the owl picture shown in Figure 6.9.

After installing the theme, the background color of VS Code changes to the color of the Night Owl theme. You can click any other options the extension offers to change the color to Night Owl Light, Dark Modern, and others, as shown in Figure 6.10.

FIGURE 6.10: Installed Night Owl theme

Night Owl is not the only theme available in VS Code. Themes include Winter is Coming, Shades of Purple, Palenight, Atom One Light, Noctis, Nord, Panda, Omni, Dracula at Night, gruvbox, and many more. Search for "VS Code themes" to see a vast list of themes.

You can also go to `https://vscodethemes.com` to find VS Code themes. Another way of looking for themes is to ask ChatGPT or a similar tool about it through a prompt. Here are some hints for constructing the prompt:

➤   Describe your favorite colors to ChatGPT and ask it to propose themes based on these colors.

➤   Describe your mood when working or coding and ask ChatGPT to propose themes based on your mood.

➤   Describe your personality and ask ChatGPT to propose themes based on that.

➤ Describe your values to ChatGPT and ask it to propose themes based on your values.

➤ If you value productivity at work, ask ChatGPT what colors are associated with more productivity. Then, ask It to propose themes based on that

Installing those themes can be done in the same way as installing Night Owl. Type the theme name in the search bar, for example, Dracula at Night theme, and it should appear as the first or among the first results. Clicking Install will install the theme and show it automatically in your installed version of VS Code.

Polacode

Polacode is an extension for VS Code that can help you take a nice screenshot of part of your code that you might want to share with someone.

To download Polacode, go to the extensions pane of VS Code, search for Polacode, and install it. You read how to use Polacode and take screenshots with it in the extension's details, shown in Figure 6.11.

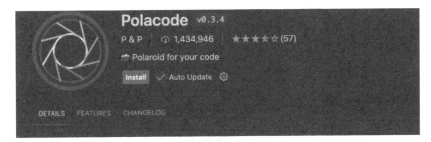

FIGURE 6.11: Polacode

Bookmarks

Another helpful extension you can use, download, and install is Bookmarks. Bookmarks, shown in Figure 6.12, is helpful when you have files with many lines of code, as the extension allows you to bookmark parts of code and make them easily accessible when you need to refer to a specific part of the code frequently.

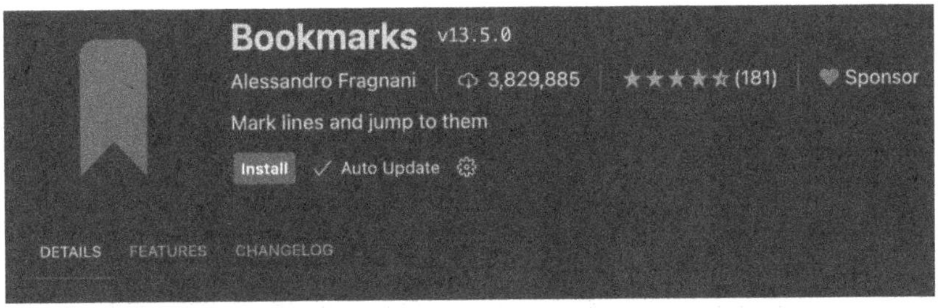

FIGURE 6.12: Bookmarks

Cloak

Cloak (see Figure 6.13) can be helpful for developers who work in crowded environments such as co-working spaces or who stream their code online. It can hide vulnerable parts of your code to prevent people with malicious intent from damaging the code, infrastructure, or anything else on the project you are working on.

FIGURE 6.13: Cloak

Solidity Juan Blanco

When it comes to Solidity-specific extensions, Solidity by Juan Blanco (see Figure 6.14) is one of the crucial extensions to add. It helps in various ways, such as highlighting syntax, giving you information on your code whenever you hover over a specific part of it, and more.

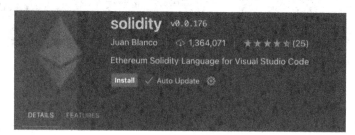

FIGURE 6.14: Solidity

Even Better TOML

Even Better TOML (see Figure 6.15) adds syntax highlighting to parts of your code that Solidity by Juan Blanco does not.

FIGURE 6.15: Even Better TOML

GitHub Copilot

GitHub Copilot (see Figure 6.16) is a handy extension, especially when you start coding professionally, as it autocompletes code, which can save a lot of time. However, if you are learning Solidity, I don't recommend installing GitHub Copilot, as the repetition of code snippets can help you better understand parts of code you may struggle with. Just keep it in mind and install it after learning Solidity and feeling confident.

FIGURE 6.16: GitHub Copilot

It is also worth noting that GitHub Copilot is a paid extension available through a monthly subscription.

VS CODE KEYBOARD SHORTCUTS

To display all the shortcuts you can use with VS Code, click the cogwheel on the bottom left of the VS Code window and then click Keyboard Shortcuts to open the window shown in Figure 6.17. You do not necessarily need to memorize all the shortcuts, but it is good to know the ones you use multiple times a day. You can change the shortcuts or use the buttons already assigned to them to save time when coding.

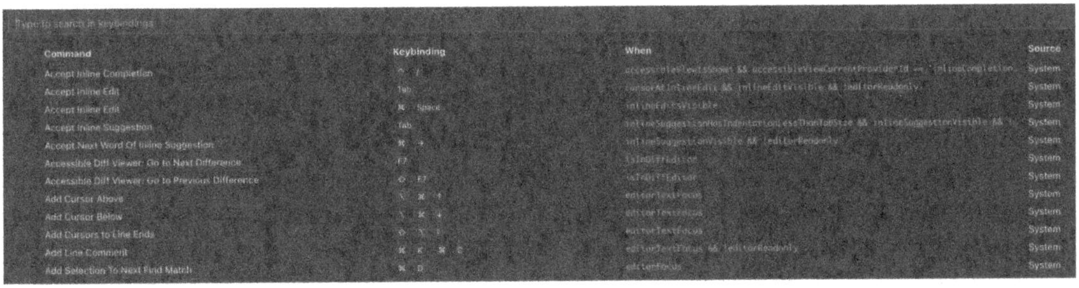

FIGURE 6.17: VS Code shortcuts

For example, developers use Command+S on macOS and Ctrl+S on Windows to save a file quickly, which they do constantly to ensure that the code they wrote has been saved. You can continue using Command+S or Ctrl+S, or you can change these to different keys you want to use.

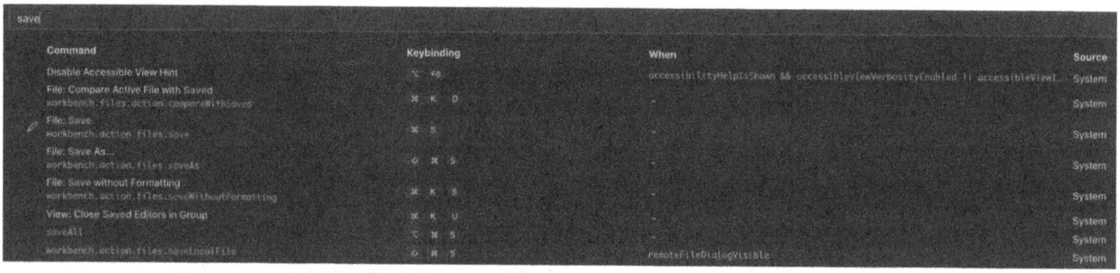

FIGURE 6.18: VS Code File: Save shortcut

Double-click the File: Save shortcut to determine what keyboard shortcut you want to use for this command (see Figure 6.18).

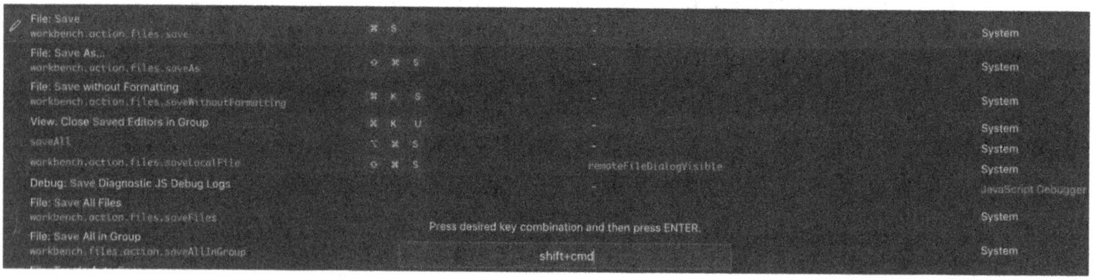

FIGURE 6.19: VS Code changing the File: Save shortcut

Pressing Shift+Command or any other combination on macOS and Windows can change the shortcut to your liking.

There are various commonly used shortcuts that you can use to save time. You have likely used them if you have experience with tools such as Microsoft Word, Microsoft Excel, or even web browsers. Table 6.1 lists the shortcuts that are transferrable to coding in VS Code.

TABLE 6.1 VS Code shortcuts

WHAT THE SHORTCUT DOES	MACOS SHORTCUT	WINDOWS SHORTCUT
Saves file	Command+S	Ctrl+S
Copies a part of the text/code	Command+C	Ctrl+C
Pastes a part of the text/code	Command+V	Ctrl+V
Cuts a part of the text/code	Command+X	Ctrl+X
Undoes a previous action	Command+Z	Ctrl+Z
Redoes a specific action	Command+Shift+Z	Ctrl+Shift+Z

WHAT THE SHORTCUT DOES	MACOS SHORTCUT	WINDOWS SHORTCUT
Finds something in a file	Command+F	Ctrl+F
Finds and replaces something in a file	Command+Option+F	Ctrl+H
Selects everything in a file	Command+A	Ctrl+A
Opens a file you click	Command+0	Ctrl+0
Close a file you are working on	Command+W	Ctrl+W
Create a new file	Command+N	Ctrl+N
Add a comment line in the file	Command+/	Ctrl+/
Open Sidebar	Command+B	Ctrl+B
Open Terminal	Command+J	Ctrl+J
Clean Terminal	Command+K or typing clear in the terminal	Ctrl+K or typing clear in the terminal
Duplicate lines of code	Highlight code and press Shift+Option+Down Arrow	Highlight code and press Shift+Alt+Down Arrow
Add full screen	Ctrl+Command+F	F11
Go to the Explorer pane	Command+Shift+E	Ctrl+Shift+E
Going to the Search pane	Command+Shift+F	Ctrl+Shift+F
Going to the Source Control pane	Ctrl+Shift+G	Ctrl+Shift+G
Going to the Debugging pane	Ctrl+Shift+D	Ctrl+Shift+D
Changing from file to file in case multiple files are open at the same time	Ctrl+Tab	Ctrl+Tab

[1] Add the file's name when saving the file with the Command/Ctrl+S shortcut. The file extension must be appropriate to the language you are working on. For Solidity, this is .sol.

For example, if you create an Alexandros, add .sol as in Alexandros.sol. This tells the compiler that the file it opens uses Solidity.

WORKING ON DIFFERENT FILES AT THE SAME TIME

VS Code has the capability to work on multiple files simultaneously, even if you do not have a second screen on your computer. For example, Figure 6.20 shows two files, Example1.sol and Example2 .sol, open at the same time. You know this because there are two tabs at the top of the screen.

FIGURE 6.20: Two files, Example1.sol and Example2.sol, open at the same time

If you click and drag Example2.sol into Example1.sol, you will see both files, one below the other, as shown in Figure 6.21.

FIGURE 6.21: Dragging Example2.sol into Example1.sol

Now Example2.sol is at the very top of the window, and Example1.sol is at the bottom, as shown in Figure 6.22.

If you drag Example2.sol to the right of Example1.sol instead of on top of it, then Example2 .sol would be beside Example1.sol instead of being at the top, allowing you to work on both files simultaneously or work on one file while having access to the second file at the same time. See Figure 6.23.

In Figure 6.24, Example3.sol was created and dragged to the side of Example2.sol. Three files are now open simultaneously and can be worked on.

You could also take Example3.sol and drag it below Example1.sol when it is side-by-side with Example2.sol. In that case, Example1.sol and Example2.sol are still side-by-side, while Example3 .sol is below Example1.sol and side-by-side with Example2.sol as well, as shown in Figure 6.25.

Finally, as shown in Figure 6.26, I created Example4.sol, which I dragged below Example2.sol. The screen has been split into four files: Example 1.sol, Example2.sol, Example3.sol, and Example4.sol. With this arrangement, you can work on or have access to all four files simultaneously.

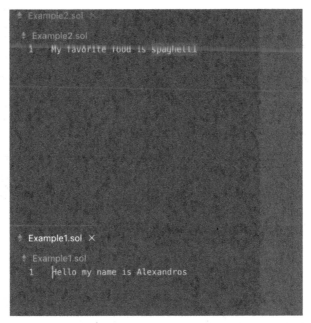

FIGURE 6.22: Split screen with `Example2.sol` at the top and `Example1.sol` at the bottom

FIGURE 6.23: Split screen with `Example1.sol` and `Example2.sol` beside each other

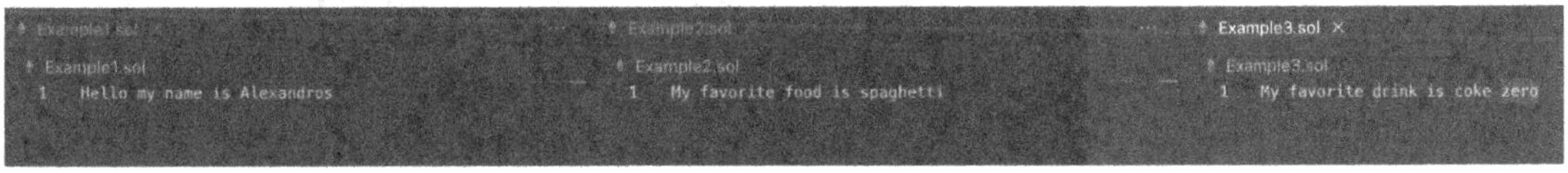

FIGURE 6.24: Split screen with `Example1.sol`, `Example2.sol`, and `Example3.sol` side-by-side

There is no maximum number of files that can be displayed on a single screen. However, depending on your screen size, the fewer files that are open, the more you can see and focus. The bigger the screen, the more files that can be opened simultaneously and still be legible.

FIGURE 6.25: Split screen with `Example1.sol` atop `Example3.sol` and both side-by-side with `Example2.sol`

FIGURE 6.26: Split screen with `Example1.sol`, `Example2.sol`, `Example3.sol`, and `Example4.sol`

MIRROR/MINI-MAP

The file shown in Figure 6.27 contains 285,696 lines of text. Scrolling up through this line by line would take a lot of time. However, to make navigating through the file easier, to the right of the file, there is what is called a *mini-map*, which has a small map of the whole document the developer is currently working on. It first appears when a file is long enough to be scrolled; thus, more than 10 lines of code will make the mini-map appear.

FIGURE 6.27: Mini-map

> **NOTE** *You will see a lighter background at the bottom of the mini-map. If you click and hold that light background while scrolling, you will quickly travel through the lengthy document.*

ZEN MODE

Using the shortcut Shift+Command+P on macOS or Shift+Ctrl+P on Windows, you open the Command palette, where you can access many commands by simply typing them.

After bringing up the Command palette, if you type **Toggle Zen Mode,** as shown in Figure 6.28, everything extra on the screen will disappear. Only the contract the person is working on at that time would be available, as you can see in Figure 6.29.

Zen Mode is useful for eliminating distractions when you want to focus intensely on work without distractions. To exit Zen Mode, press Shift+Command+P again and click Toggle Zen Mode.

VS CODE TERMINAL

There are two main ways you can use or communicate with a computer:

➤ **Using the graphical user interface (GUI):** Using this method, you click with a mouse or touchpad on files or computer programs, opening and using them. You can click a file and copy it, paste it, edit it, and do anything else you want or can do with a file.

➤ **Using the command-line interface (CLI):** With this method, you communicate with the computer via text by giving the computer commands. This method can be much more precise than using the GUI. In the early days of computers (in the 1950s, 60s, 70s, and even the beginning of the 80s), for some computers, the CLI was the only way to communicate and interact with a computer. Now the CLI is used mainly by programmers and other computer specialists. You need to activate or open a terminal window when using the CLI.

FIGURE 6.28: Command palette

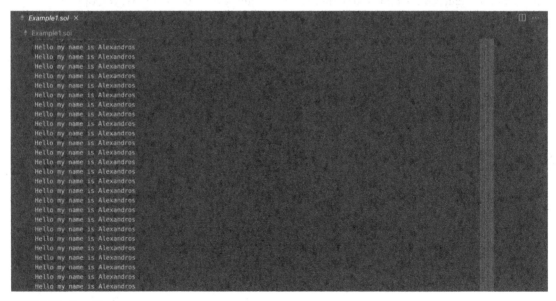

FIGURE 6.29: Zen Mode on

VS Code has a built-in terminal (see Figure 6.30) which can be used to communicate with the computer, organize files, install programs, and do other tasks. To open the terminal in VS Code, press Command+J on a Mac, or press Ctrl+J on Windows. Starting in this chapter and for the rest of the book, the terminal will be used frequently.

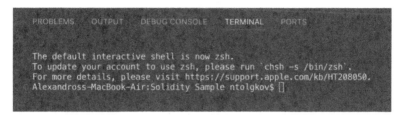

FIGURE 6.30: VS Code terminal

VS Code allows you to have multiple instances of a terminal running. Thus, if you click the Split Terminal button at the top right of the screen (see Figure 6.31), a new terminal appears and splits the part of the screen in which the terminal appears, in a similar way as when splitting the screen while working with different files, as discussed in the previous section.

FIGURE 6.31: Split Terminal button

This split can be increased to three, four, or as many different terminals you need (see Figure 6.31). However, just such as with the split screen when working on different VS Code files, the more screens you have open, the more difficult it is to keep track of the work itself.

FIGURE 6.32: Two split terminals

To close a split screen, hover over the Zsh option at the top right of the terminal and click the recycling bin icon, as shown in Figure 6.33. That terminal instance will close.

FIGURE 6.33: Closing the split screen

Another button that can be useful when using the terminal is the Maximize Panel Size button, shown in Figure 6.34.

FIGURE 6.34: Maximize Panel Size button

After clicking it, the window will become full screen inside the VS Code application, as shown in Figure 6.35.

FIGURE 6.35: Maximized panel demonstration

There are several types of terminals you can use depending on personal preference and operating system:

> **Bash:** Bash is a terminal type used on Linux and macOS. It helps create, arrange, and delete files; run programs; and automate specific tasks through the available commands.

➤ **Z shell (Zsh):** Zsh is like Bash but has certain additional features, such as guessing what you are trying to type—also known as autocompletion. Zsh is more user-friendly and makes programming more accessible.

➤ **JavaScript Debug Terminal:** This is mainly used when programming in JavaScript, not Solidity. JavaScript is a programming language used primarily in web development.

➤ **PowerShell:** PowerShell can be thought of as the Bash of Windows due to it being the primary way developers interact and communicate with Windows computers.

➤ **Cmd:** cmd is used on Windows and is like PowerShell but is much less powerful. It is the primary type of terminal that comes by default on Windows computers.

INSTALLING FOUNDRY

There are two ways to install Foundry:

➤ Go to `https://getfoundry.sh`, as shown in Figure 6.36.

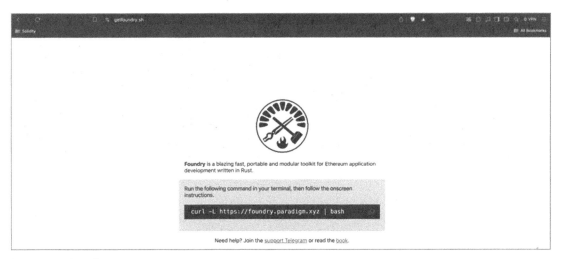

FIGURE 6.36: Landing page `getfoundry.sh`

➤ Copy the copy the command from the landing page, as shown in Figure 6.37.

```
ntolgkov@Alexandross-MacBook-Air ~ % -L https://foundry.paradigm.xyz | bash
```

FIGURE 6.37: Script copy pasted into the terminal

➤ Press Enter.

> **TIP** As each computer's and terminal's state might differ, if the installation in this section does not work, do not hesitate to use ChatGPT or another AI tool to help you install Foundry and—if required—the components mentioned in this section.
>
> Usually, the best prompt is something like the following:
>
> "I am trying to install Foundry, the smart contract programming framework, on VS Code. I have already done steps X and Y, but whenever I do step Z, I get this error: [Copy and paste the error message]. How can I fix this or proceed step by step?"
>
> If a new error arises, feed it as a prompt to the AI tool saying something like this:
>
> "My previous problem was solved, but now I get this error when I try to install Foundry: [error here]. How can I fix that?"

Depending on the situation of the files on your computer, once Foundry starts loading, the terminal might show the message in Figure 6.38.

```
Alexandross-MacBook-Air:~ ntolgkov$ curl -L https://foundry.paradigm.xyz | bash
  % Total    % Received % Xferd  Average Speed   Time    Time     Time  Current
                                 Dload  Upload   Total   Spent    Left  Speed
100   167  100   167    0     0     68      0  0:00:02  0:00:02 --:--:--    68
100  2196  100  2196    0     0    495      0  0:00:04  0:00:04 --:--:--  1437
Installing foundryup...

warning: libusb not found. You may need to install it manually on MacOS via Homebrew (brew install libusb).

Detected your preferred shell is zsh and added foundryup to PATH.
Run 'source /Users/ntolgkov/.zshenv' or start a new terminal session to use foundryup.
Then, simply run 'foundryup' to install Foundry.
```

FIGURE 6.38: libusb missing

The message shown in Figure 6.38 means that a library—or more libraries later—is missing and needs to be installed. To do so, you have to install Homebrew. Homebrew is a package manager that is used only for macOS and Linux that helps developers install a wide range of applications, software, and libraries they may need.

Installing libusb and Homebrew

If you get the error message shown in Figure 6.38 when trying to install Foundry, you must first install libusb and then Homebrew.

To install Homebrew, follow these steps:

1.   Go to the website `https://brew.sh`. You should see the page shown in Figure 6.39.

2.   Copy the command shown on the website and paste it into the terminal, as shown in Figure 6.40.

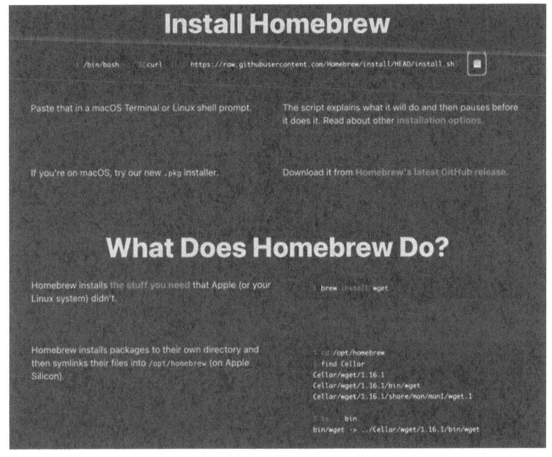

FIGURE 6.39: Homebrew landing page

```
Alexandross-MacBook-Air:~ ntolgkov$ curl -L https://foundry.paradigm.xyz | bash
  % Total    % Received % Xferd  Average Speed   Time    Time     Time  Current
                                 Dload  Upload   Total   Spent    Left  Speed
100   167  100   167    0     0     93      0  0:00:01  0:00:01 --:--:--    93
100  2196  100  2196    0     0    858      0  0:00:02  0:00:02 --:--:--  3383
Installing foundryup...

warning: libusb not found. You may need to install it manually on MacOS via Homebrew (brew install libusb).

Detected your preferred shell is zsh and added foundryup to PATH.
Run 'source /Users/ntolgkov/.zshenv' or start a new terminal session to use foundryup.
Then, simply run 'foundryup' to install Foundry.
```

FIGURE 6.40: Homebrew link pasted into terminal

3. Press Enter. After a few seconds, the terminal should ask you for a password (see Figure 6.41).

This password is the first thing you use to log into your macOS profile when rebooting or turning on your laptop or computer.

```
Alexandross-MacBook-Air:~ ntolgkov$ curl -L https://foundry.paradigm.xyz | bash
  % Total    % Received % Xferd  Average Speed   Time    Time     Time  Current
                                 Dload  Upload   Total   Spent    Left  Speed
100   167  100   167    0     0    202      0 --:--:-- --:--:-- --:--:--   202
100  2189  100  2189    0     0   1212      0  0:00:01  0:00:01 --:--:-- 11832
Installing foundryup...

warning: libusb not found. You may need to install it manually on MacOS via Homebrew (brew install libusb).

Detected your preferred shell is zsh and added foundryup to PATH.
Run 'source /Users/ntolgkov/.zshenv' or start a new terminal session to use foundryup.
Then, simply run 'foundryup' to install Foundry.
Alexandross-MacBook-Air:~ ntolgkov$ /bin/bash -c "$(curl -fsSL https://raw.githubusercontent.com/Homebrew/install/HEAD/install.sh)"
==> Checking for `sudo` access (which may request your password)...
Password:
```

FIGURE 6.41: Terminal asking for password

After adding your password and pressing Enter, the terminal should display the files to be installed and the new directories/folders to be created, as shown in Figure 6.42.

```
==> This script will install:
/opt/homebrew/bin/brew
/opt/homebrew/share/doc/homebrew
/opt/homebrew/share/man/man1/brew.1
/opt/homebrew/share/zsh/site-functions/_brew
/opt/homebrew/etc/bash_completion.d/brew
/opt/homebrew
==> The following new directories will be created:
/opt/homebrew/bin
/opt/homebrew/include
/opt/homebrew/lib
/opt/homebrew/sbin
/opt/homebrew/opt
/opt/homebrew/var/homebrew/linked
/opt/homebrew/Cellar
```

FIGURE 6.42: Terminal showcasing the installation and new directories/folders

4. Press Enter.

The installation should begin. You have to wait from a few seconds to a few minutes depending on your Internet speed and the speed of the device being used, among other factors. (see Figure 6.43.)

```
==> /usr/bin/sudo /bin/chmod ug=rwx /opt/homebrew/bin /opt/homebrew/include /opt/homeb
room /opt/homebrew/Frameworks
==> /usr/bin/sudo /usr/sbin/chown ntolgkov /opt/homebrew/bin /opt/homebrew/include /op
ew/Caskroom /opt/homebrew/Frameworks
==> /usr/bin/sudo /usr/bin/chgrp admin /opt/homebrew/bin /opt/homebrew/include /opt/ho
askroom /opt/homebrew/Frameworks
==> /usr/bin/sudo /usr/sbin/chown -R ntolgkov:admin /opt/homebrew
==> /usr/bin/sudo /bin/mkdir -p /Users/ntolgkov/Library/Caches/Homebrew
==> /usr/bin/sudo /bin/chmod g+rwx /Users/ntolgkov/Library/Caches/Homebrew
==> /usr/bin/sudo /usr/sbin/chown -R ntolgkov /Users/ntolgkov/Library/Caches/Homebrew
==> Downloading and installing Homebrew...
remote: Enumerating objects: 281079, done.
remote: Counting objects: 100% (23651/23651), done.
remote: Compressing objects: 100% (772/772), done.
Receiving objects:   3% (9661/281079), 4.64 MiB | 1.66 MiB/s
```

FIGURE 6.43: Homebrew downloading

Depending on your situation, the next step might be to add Homebrew to the path in the terminal, as shown in Figure 6.44.

```
These scripts need to be run to add Homebrew to the path;
(echo; echo 'eval "$(/opt/homebrew/bin/brew shellenv)"') >>
 /Users/ntolgkov/.zprofile
and
```

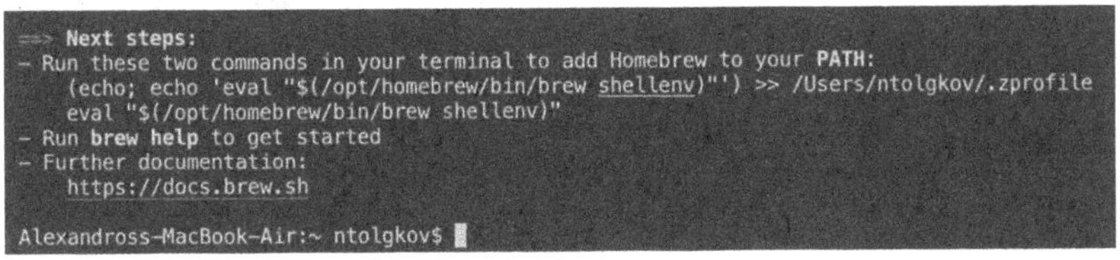

FIGURE 6.44: Running scripts to add Homebrew to path

```
eval "$(/opt/homebrew/bin/brew shellenv)"
```

5. To finish installing Foundry, close the terminals that are currently open by clicking the recycling bin and then re-open the terminal and type **foundryup**. If done correctly, you should see what is shown in Figure 6.45.

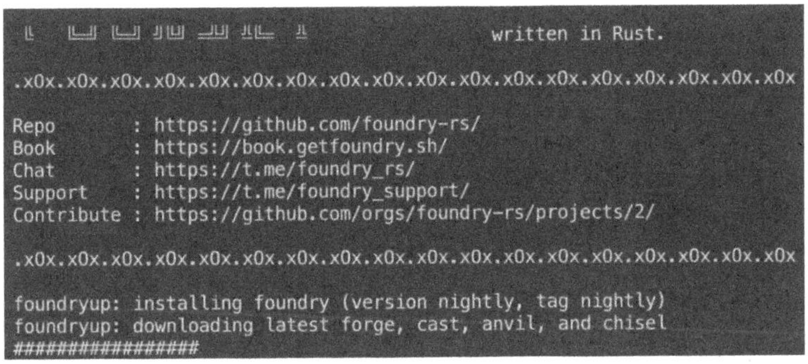

FIGURE 6.45: Foundry being downloaded in the terminal

Foundry should start downloading, and depending on your computer's operating system and your Internet connection, it should take anywhere from a few seconds to a few minutes to complete. See Figure 6.46.

Once completed, the message foundryup: done! will be displayed.

To ensure that Foundry has been installed, you can type the following in the terminal, as shown in Figure 6.47:

```
forge -version
```

FIGURE 6.46: Installing Foundry

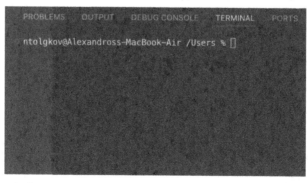

FIGURE 6.47: `forge --version` command

In this case, the answer the terminal gives us is Forge 0.2.0. This is the version that Foundry's Forge was using when this book was written. The version might be different when you read it, but what is crucial is that it shows a version of Forge.

STARTING A FOUNDRY PROJECT

To create a new Foundry project, follow the steps in this section:

1. Open the terminal by pressing Command+J on macOS or Ctrl+J on Windows. See Figure 6.48.

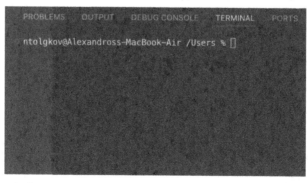

FIGURE 6.48: VS Code terminal

2. Type **ls** in the terminal (ls stands for "list") and then press the Enter key. See Figure 6.49.

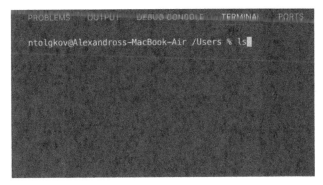

FIGURE 6.49: Typing ls in the terminal

This will enable you to see where in your computer's files you are located and what folders are there, as shown in Figure 6.50.

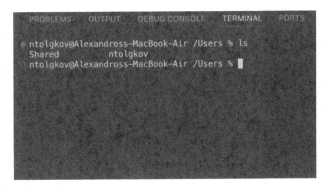

FIGURE 6.50: File locations

As we can see, my environment has two folders: Shared and Ntolgkov.

3. Create a folder for the *Beginning Solidity* book by typing mkdir beginning-solidity (which stands for "make directory") and the directory's name and then press Enter.

You might get an error message saying you need permission to do this. In that case, you should run this command and enter the password you use to log in to your computer when it asks you, and it should be resolved.

```
sudo mkdir beginning-solidity
```

If not, copy the error message you see, go to ChatGPT, and explain what you are doing: "I am trying to create a new directory beginning-solidity with my terminal, but I get this error: [*paste error*]. How can I fix it step-by-step? Then, follow what the AI tells you.

4. Now type **ls** again to be sure the folder exists in the list, as shown in Figure 6.51.

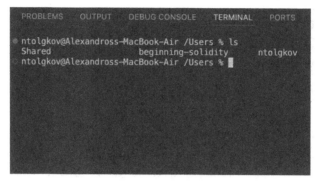

FIGURE 6.51: The beginning-solidity folder has been created.

5. Now that you have confirmed that the beginning-solidity folder exists, go into that folder by typing in the terminal **cd beginning-solidity** (cd stands for change directory), as shown in Figure 6.52.

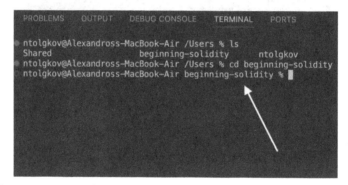

FIGURE 6.52: Using the cd command to enter the beginning-solidity folder

You can now see that you are located in the beginning-solidity folder.

6. Here, create one more folder called ZooManagement-Foundry by typing **mkdir ZooManagement-Foundry**. Then, type **ls** to see if the folder is indeed there. If it is, type **cd ZooManagement-Foundry** to get inside the folder.

7. Now it is time to open the folder by going to the top left of VS Code and clicking File to open the File menu, as shown in Figure 6.53.

8. Click the Open Folder option from the drop-down menu, as shown in Figure 6.54.

9. Click the beginning-solidity folder you created previously with the mkdir command, as shown in Figure 6.55.

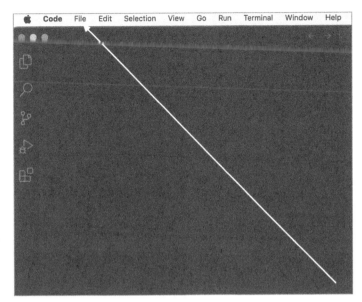

FIGURE 6.53: Opening the File menu

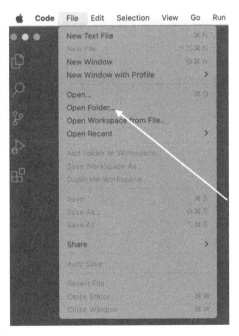

FIGURE 6.54: Clicking Open Folder

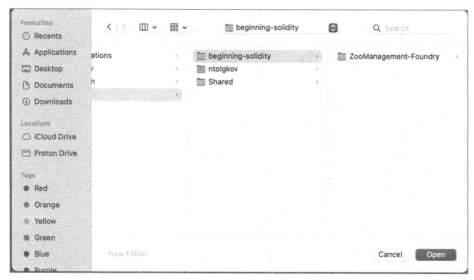

FIGURE 6.55: Clicking the `beginning-solidity` folder

10.   Click the `ZooManagement-Foundry` folder inside the `beginning-solidity` folder created through the `mkdir` and click the blue Open button to display the window shown in Figure 6.56.

FIGURE 6.56: Clicking the `ZooManagement-Foundry` folder and the blue Open button

11.   After doing this, a new instance of VS code will pop up with the window shown in Figure 6.57 asking if you trust the authors of the folder being opened. Since you are the author, aka creator, of this folder, click Yes, I Trust The Authors.

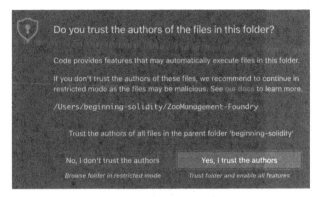

FIGURE 6.57: "Do you trust the authors?" window

12. Now, since the folder has been opened, create a new Solidity project by opening the terminal in the latest VS Code instance and typing **forge init:**, as shown in Figure 6.58.

FIGURE 6.58: `forge init:` example

After this is done, you should see a message saying `Initialized forge project` at the end, as shown in Figure 6.59.

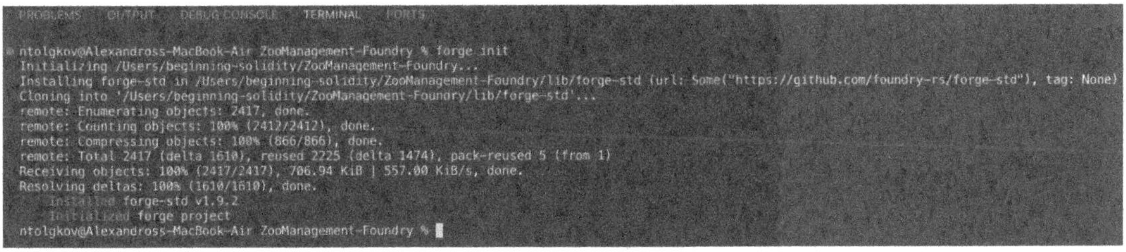

FIGURE 6.59: Foundry project created

If you get a message saying there is an error and that the directory is not empty, you should try to use `forge init --force` instead.

Another possible error might be that the action is denied due to your permissions being denied. In such a case, you might not have permission to change or create folders. If that happens, use ChatGPT multiple times until you solve the problem, which can occur for several reasons. Depending on the structure of your files on your computer, you might need to use slightly different commands to fix it.

Additionally, in the pane on the left, you should see several folders and files within the `ZooManagement-Foundry` folder, as shown in Figure 6.60.

FIGURE 6.60: ZooManagement-Foundry folder after forge init installation

CHAPTER 6 QUESTIONS

1. What are three key advantages of VS Code over the Remix IDE for professional Solidity development?

2. Describe the process of configuring multiple synchronized terminals in VS Code and explain why this might be useful during blockchain development.

3. Compare and contrast the five terminal types available in VS Code (Bash, Zsh, JavaScript Debug Terminal, PowerShell, cmd). When would you use each?

4. Walk through the complete process of installing Foundry, including handling potential dependency issues with libusb. What troubleshooting steps would you take if installation fails?

5. How would you utilize VS Code's split screen functionality to effectively monitor smart contract tests, deployment scripts, and contract code simultaneously?

6. Explain how you would configure essential Solidity extensions in VS Code, specifically Juan Blanco's Solidity extension and Even Better TOML. What functionality do they provide?

7. What security considerations should be taken when installing VS Code extensions, particularly for blockchain development?

8. Outline the step-by-step process of initializing a new Foundry project and handling common permission-related errors.

9. How would you use VS Code's search functionality to find specific function definitions across multiple smart contract files?

10. Describe how to effectively use VS Code's mini-map feature when navigating large smart contract codebases.

11. What's the difference between VS Code's stable and Insider editions? When would you recommend using each for blockchain development?

12. Explain how to configure the Cloak extension to protect sensitive contract deployment information when coding in public spaces.

13. Detail the process of syncing VS Code settings across multiple development machines for consistent blockchain development environments.

14. How would you utilize keyboard shortcuts to optimize your smart contract development workflow in VS Code?

15. Describe how to effectively use VS Code's Explorer pane for managing multiple smart contract projects and their dependencies.

7

Foundry ZooManagement

This chapter provides a practical guide to developing, deploying, and interacting with Solidity smart contracts using Foundry, with a focus on the ZooManagement project. You'll explore the structure of a Foundry project, including key files like foundry.toml and README.md, while learning about Anvil, Foundry's built-in testing environment. Step-by-step exercises guide you through compiling contracts, deploying them locally and on the Ethereum Sepolia test network, and securely managing private keys.

Key tools like Alchemy and Foundry's cast utility are introduced, enabling seamless contract deployment, interaction, and verification. You'll perform tasks such as configuring MetaMask for Anvil, deploying the ZooManagement contract, and analyzing transaction data on Etherscan. The chapter emphasizes secure practices, ensuring you can avoid vulnerabilities like private key exposure.

By the end, you'll have the skills to confidently manage Foundry workflows, deploy smart contracts to test networks, and interact with blockchain systems, providing a strong foundation for Solidity development.

THE FOUNDRY PROJECT FILES

After downloading and installing Microsoft VS Code and Foundry in the previous chapter and creating a project called ZooManagement-Foundry, in this chapter you review some of the main features Foundry offers. Figure 7.1 shows the starting point you should see when picking up where the previous chapter left off.

The figure shows the following:

> **GitHub/workflows:** This folder stores GitHub's workflow files. These files automate specific tasks, perform certain tests automatically, and notify the developer to inform the developer of any issues with their code. (You find out more about GitHub at the end of this chapter.)

> > **test.yml:** This file performs the tests mentioned.

FIGURE 7.1: ZooManagement-Foundry **project overview**

➤ **lib/forge-std:** This is the folder of the Forge standard library (std). It contains various contracts and tools inherited or integrated with smart contracts.

  ➤ A *library* is a pre-tested and pre-made collection of smart contracts with functions that all developers can readily use. Libraries help developers avoid re-creating repetitive use cases and functions from scratch by standardizing reusable contracts. Thus, they help save time and prevent human-made errors since other developers have reviewed and reused these contracts "countless" times.

➤ **.gitattributes:** This file defines how Git should manage specific files.

  ➤ Git is a version control system: a mechanism that helps developers track changes in their files, facilitates collaboration with other developers, allows retrieval and reversion to previous file versions if required, and provides different features when something goes wrong.

➤ **.gitignore:** Developers add the name of the files that Git should ignore and not track. These can be files containing sensitive data. In the blockchain world, that could be private keys, public addresses if one wants to remain pseudonymous, and other sensitive information.

➤ **CONTRIBUTING.md:** This file provides potential project contributors with a short guide on how they can help with your project.

➤ **foundry.toml:** This file allows a developer to customize how various tools within forge-std behave when you test, deploy, and develop smart contracts.

- ➤ **LICENSE-APACHE:** This file states that the project is released under an Apache license.

- ➤ **LICENSE-MIT:** This file states that the project is also released under an MIT license.

- ➤ **package.json:** This file lists all the dependencies `forge-std` has to run. Dependencies are anything a project is dependent upon to run successfully. In a smart contract scenario involving two contracts, Contract A and Contract B, where Contract B imports and inherits Contract A, Contract B relies on Contract A to function correctly. Similarly, every piece of software has its dependencies, either in prominent examples, such as the one with the contracts, or in software that "sits" in the background.

- ➤ **README.md:** This file includes documentation and information about the `forge-std` project. It usually lists any software that needs to be installed before running, instructions on how to run it, what the software is about, and similar information.

- ➤ **Script:** The `Script` folder is used to store the smart contracts intended for deployment and the associated deployment scripts.

  - ➤ **Counter.s.sol:** `Counter.s.sol` is a standard smart contract that comes pre-installed with every new Foundry project initiated. The `.s` in the name indicates that this script contract is intended to run deployment scripts. The `.s` inclusion is a convention for every smart contract in the `Script` folder. Thus, you have to always add the `.s` in the name of a contract that you intend to include in the Script folder.

- ➤ **Src:** This stands for source or source code. This is where your actual smart contract(s) is placed and located.

  - ➤ **Counter.sol:** `Counter.sol` is the standard contract pre-installed with every new Foundry project.

- ➤ **Test:** Contracts are added to the test folder to test scripts and ensure the smart contracts work as intended.

  - ➤ **Counter.t.sol:** The `Counter.t.sol` contract is the standard test contract that comes pre-installed with every Foundry project. The `.t` in the name is a naming convention for every test contract located in the test folder. Thus, one must always add the `.t` when adding a contract to the test folder.

- ➤ **.gitignore:** Developers add the name of the files that `git.ignore` should not track. These can be files containing sensitive data—in the blockchain world, that could be private keys, public addresses if one wants to remain pseudonymous, and other sensitive information. The previous file was specifically for `forge-std`, while this one is for everything outside of `forge-std`.

- ➤ **.gitmodules:** This references any Git submodules the current project might depend on.

- ➤ **foundry.toml:** This file allows a developer to customize how various tools within `forge` behave when testing, deploying, and developing smart contracts.

- ➤ **README.md:** This file includes documentation and information about the Forge project. Usually, this includes any software that needs to be pre-installed before running the software, instructions on how to run it, what the software is about, and similar information.

COMPILING A CONTRACT

Figure 7.2 shows the `Counter.sol` contract in the `src` folder.

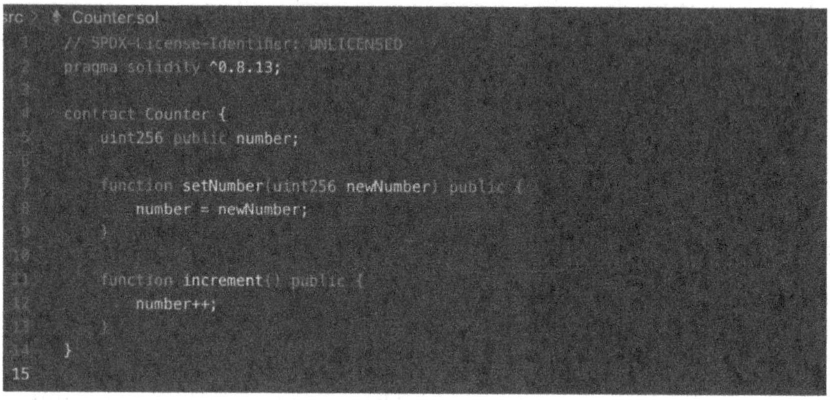

FIGURE 7.2: `Counter.sol` contract

The `Counter.sol` contract is a straightforward contract:

➤ It defines the license (in this case unlicensed).

➤ It defines the version of the contract.

➤ It defines the name.

➤ It defines an `uint256` that is public called `number`.

➤ It creates a function that adds a local parameter of `uint256 newNumber`.

➤ It is public and sets the global variable of number to the local parameter `newNumber`.

The following function, `increment`, which is public, gets the number variable and adds a + 1.

Normally, if you want to add a + 1 to the global variable number, you would type this:

```
number = number + 1
```

This means setting the variable number to the variable number—the same variable and hence the same result—and adding 1. However, to save time and be more efficient, when adding 1 to a variable, you can type `number++`, which has the same meaning as this:

```
number = number + 1.
```

To compile this contract, you have to open the terminal with Command+J or Ctrl+J and type **forge build** or **forge compile**, as shown in Figures 7.3 and 7.4.

Press the Enter key to get a message that the project is compiling and then a message that the compiling process was successful, as shown in Figure 7.5.

FIGURE 7.3: `forge build`

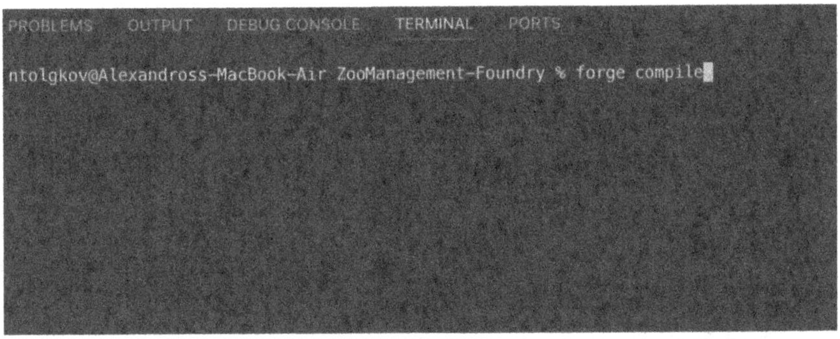

FIGURE 7.4: `forge compile`

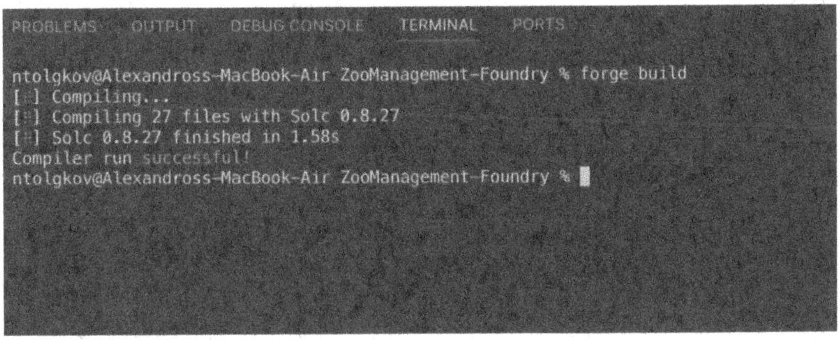

FIGURE 7.5: Compiler run successful!

Compilation is helpful as it transforms the human-readable code into bytecode. In the context of Foundry, it can often be used to ensure the code has no errors. If a code has errors, then the terminal will show it. For example, Figure 7.6 shows the closing curly brace of the `Counter.sol` contract is missing.

If you save the document by pressing Command+S or Ctrl+S and then compile the smart contract by typing **forge build** or **forge compile**, you will see the error shown in Figure 7.7.

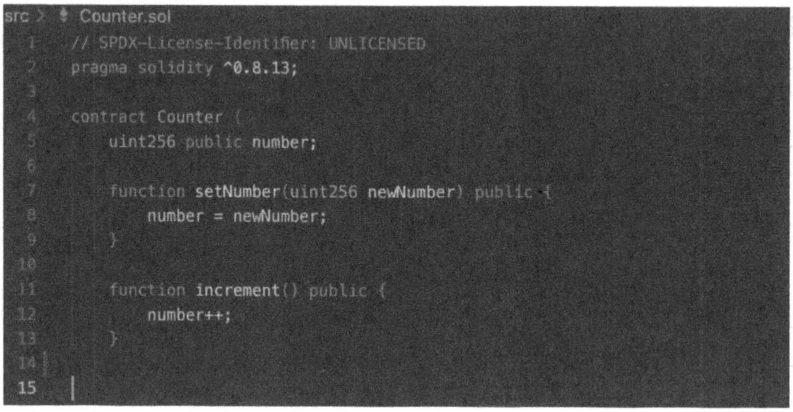

```
src >  Counter.sol
  1    // SPDX-License-Identifier: UNLICENSED
  2    pragma solidity ^0.8.13;
  3
  4    contract Counter {
  5        uint256 public number;
  6
  7        function setNumber(uint256 newNumber) public {
  8            number = newNumber;
  9        }
 10
 11        function increment() public {
 12            number++;
 13        }
 14  }
 15    |
```

FIGURE 7.6: `Counter.sol` without closing curly brace

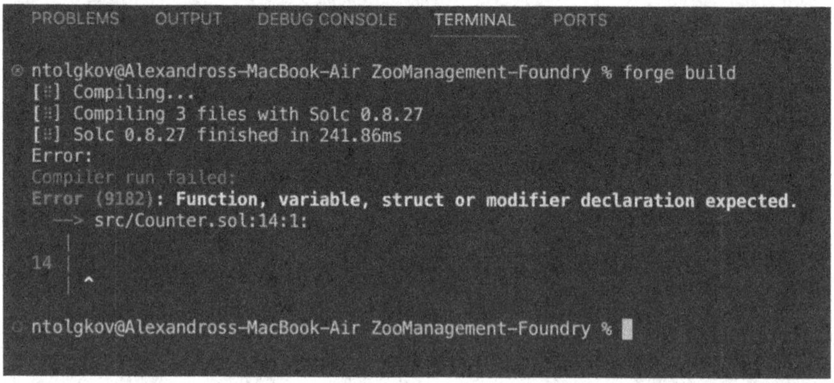

```
PROBLEMS    OUTPUT    DEBUG CONSOLE    TERMINAL    PORTS

ntolgkov@Alexandross-MacBook-Air ZooManagement-Foundry % forge build
[⠿] Compiling...
[⠿] Compiling 3 files with Solc 0.8.27
[⠿] Solc 0.8.27 finished in 241.86ms
Error:
Compiler run failed:
Error (9182): Function, variable, struct or modifier declaration expected.
  --> src/Counter.sol:14:1:
    |
 14 |
    | ^

ntolgkov@Alexandross-MacBook-Air ZooManagement-Foundry % █
```

FIGURE 7.7: Compilation failed

However, if the curly brace is restored, you save the document saved with Command+S or Ctrl+S, and you compile the contract again, you will be informed that the compiler run was successful (see Figure 7.8).

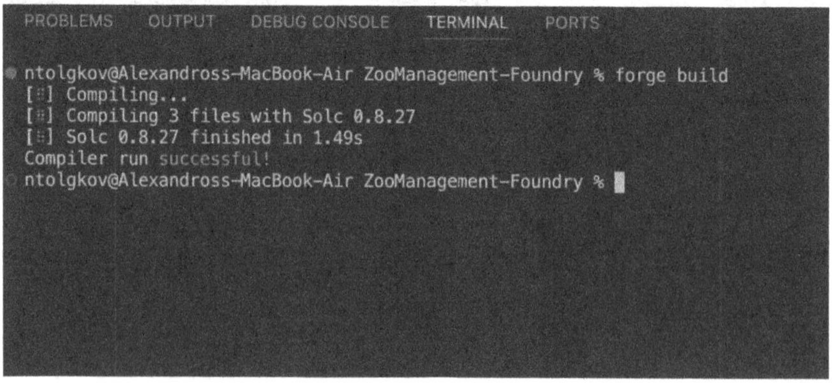

```
PROBLEMS    OUTPUT    DEBUG CONSOLE    TERMINAL    PORTS

ntolgkov@Alexandross-MacBook-Air ZooManagement-Foundry % forge build
[⠿] Compiling...
[⠿] Compiling 3 files with Solc 0.8.27
[⠿] Solc 0.8.27 finished in 1.49s
Compiler run successful!
ntolgkov@Alexandross-MacBook-Air ZooManagement-Foundry % █
```

FIGURE 7.8: Compilation is successful again

INTRODUCTION TO ANVIL

Foundry has a built-in environment called Anvil to test the deployment of smart contracts. To use an Anvil, follow these steps:

1. Type **anvil** in the terminal, as shown in Figure 7.9, and press Enter.

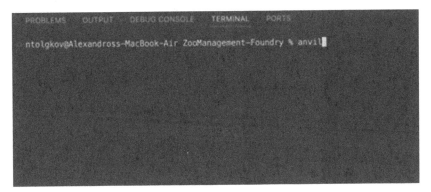

FIGURE 7.9: Anvil terminal

Anvil will run, and you will get the result shown in Figure 7.10.

```
Available Accounts
==================

(0) 0xf39Fd6e51aad88F6F4ce6aB8827279cffFb92266 (10000.000000000000000000 ETH)
(1) 0x70997970C51812dc3A010C7d01b50e0d17dc79C8 (10000.000000000000000000 ETH)
(2) 0x3C44CdDdB6a900fa2b585dd299e03d12FA4293BC (10000.000000000000000000 ETH)
(3) 0x90F79bf6EB2c4f870365E785982E1f101E93b906 (10000.000000000000000000 ETH)
(4) 0x15d34AAf542670B7D7c367839AAf71A00a2C6A65 (10000.000000000000000000 ETH)
(5) 0x9965507D1a55bcC2695C58ba16FB37d819B0A4dc (10000.000000000000000000 ETH)
(6) 0x976EA74026E726554dB657fA54763abd0C3a0aa9 (10000.000000000000000000 ETH)
(7) 0x14dC79964da2C08b23698B3D3cc7Ca32193d9955 (10000.000000000000000000 ETH)
(8) 0x23618e81E3f5cdF7f54C3d65f7FBc0aBf5B21E8f (10000.000000000000000000 ETH)
(9) 0xa0Ee7A142d267C1f36714E4a8F75612F20a79720 (10000.000000000000000000 ETH)

Private Keys
==================

(0) 0xac0974bec39a17e36ba4a6b4d238ff944bacb478cbed5efcae784d7bf4f2ff80
(1) 0x59c6995e998f97a5a0044966f0945389dc9e86dae88c7a8412f4603b6b78690d
(2) 0x5de4111afa1a4b94908f83103eb1f1706367c2e68ca870fc3fb9a804cdab365a
(3) 0x7c852118294e51e653712a81e05800f419141751be58f605c371e15141b007a6
(4) 0x47e179ec197488593b187f80a00eb0da91f1b9d0b13f8733639f19c30a34926a
(5) 0x8b3a350cf5c34c9194ca85829a2df0ec3153be0318b5e2d3348e872092edffba
(6) 0x92db14e403b83dfe3df233f83dfa3a0d7096f21ca9b0d6d6b8d88b2b4ec1564e
(7) 0x4bbbf85ce3377467afe5d46f804f221813b2bb87f24d81f60f1fcdbf7cbf4356
(8) 0xdbda1821b80551c9d65939329250298aa3472ba22feea921c0cf5d620ea67b97
(9) 0x2a871d0798f97d79848a013d4936a73bf4cc922c825d33c1cf7073dff6d409c6

Wallet
==================
Mnemonic:          test test test test test test test test test test test junk
Derivation path:   m/44'/60'/0'/0/

Chain ID
==================

31337

Base Fee
==================

1000000000

Gas Limit
==================

30000000
```

FIGURE 7.10: Anvil running

The following are the sections shown in Figure 7.10:

➤ **Available accounts:** These are 10 (from 0 to 9) test pre-funded accounts that come with 10,000 ETH to be able to test contracts.

➤ **Private keys:** As shown in Chapter 3, MetaMask has a private key consisting of 12 different words. Anvil has 10 private keys, they are a private key. The difference between a private key and a mnemonic phrase is that a mnemonic phrase is more human-readable, more accessible to remember, and can generate several different accounts. On the other hand, a private key, like the ones shown in Figure 7.10 below the available accounts, is a hexadecimal number with 64 characters only associated with one account.

➤ **Wallet:**

➤ **Mnemonic:** The mnemonic phrase "test test test test test test test test test test test test junk" is a 12-word phrase just like MetaMask, as shown in Chapter 3. Still, it gives access to all 10 available Foundry accounts at once.

➤ **Derivation path:** A wallet's derivation path is like giving information to access a safe. In the case of Anvil, the derivation path is m/44 /60/ 0/ 0.

➤ m stands for master seed key.

➤ 44 refers to Bitcoin Improvement Proposal (BIP) number 44—more on Improvement Proposals later in the book—a standard wallet for organizing different cryptocurrency addresses. Bitcoin pioneered it, and it was then adopted as a standard for other cryptocurrencies.

➤ 60 refers to the coin type, and the coin type with the number 60 is an Ethereum token.

➤ The first 0 refers to the account number. In computer science, counting starts from 0; hence, the 0 would signify the first account.

➤ The second 0, like the first, signifies the first of something. In this case, it is the first address index.

Hence, the standard in "human" language would say something like this: "By using the 44th standard for tokens, go to the coin type with the number 60, which refers to an Ethereum coin type, and go to the first (0) account and then to the first (0) address of the account." Hence, you can see them as instructions to a safe that you need to open, but in computer science terms.

➤ **Chain ID:** Every blockchain has a chain ID, even networks such as the Ethereum test networks, Anvil, and the test networks of every other blockchain. This helps identify them when you want to work with them in any capacity. The Chain ID for the Anvil is 31337.

➤ **Base fee:** This is the base fee to pay a (fake) validator when using Anvil for transactions—these fees are paid from the available accounts mentioned previously, not through real ETH.

➤ **Gas Limit:** The maximum gas limit one can spend when using Anvil's test chain. These fees are paid from the available accounts mentioned previously, not through real ETH.

➤ **Genesis timestamp:** The Genesis timestamp is the number during which a blockchain started.

➤ **127.0.0.1:8545:** This is the address to which the smart contract will connect after deployment to interact.

2. Add Anvil to your MetaMask, installed in Chapter 3. To do that, go to your browser and open MetaMask by clicking the fox icon. MetaMask can also be in the extensions button, which can take different forms depending on the browser you use. Still, usually, it looks like a puzzle piece, as shown in Figure 7.11.

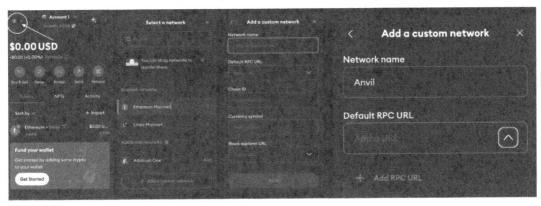

FIGURE 7.11: First part of the process of adding Anvil to MetaMask

3. After opening MetaMask, click the Ethereum logo on the top left of MetaMask (see the white arrow in Figure 7.11). Once this has been done, a list of networks will appear.

4. Click Add A Custom Network." After that, different spaces will appear where you have to add other information:

➤ **Network Name:** This is the network name to which you will connect. It can be called Local Network, Anvil, or any other name.

➤ **Default RPC url:** This is the URL or link the network will connect to. Anvil's RPC URL is as follows:

➤ `http://127.0.0.1:8545`—you have to add `http://` before the number.

➤ When adding the RPC URL, you have to click Default RPC URL, which will direct you to add an RPC URL. The RPC URL of `http://127.0.0.1:8545` will have to be added, as will the RPC Name (Optional). This can be left blank or added a name such as "Anvil."

➤ **Chain ID:** This is the Chain ID of the network you will connect to. Anvil's chain ID can also be found in the terminal. It is 31337.

➤ **The currency symbol:** That could be AnvilETH or anything else one might want to name the currency.

➤ **Block Explorer URL:** Normally, a block explorer URL is also added to track transactions, but in this case, this is not needed.

After adding everything, the form with the spaces filled should look more or less like the screen in Figure 7.12, in addition to the custom network names and the currency symbol if you want to add a different currency symbol. However, following the steps in the chapter is highly recommended to ensure minimal differences in case of an error.

FIGURE 7.12: Second part of the process of adding Anvil to MetaMask

5.   After completing the form, click Save. After clicking Save, you are taken back to the initial page of MetaMask and have to click the Ethereum logo again to go to the list with the available networks. The Anvil network should be available. Click it to connect to it.

6.   After adding the Anvil network on MetaMask, the next step is to add one of the previously mentioned accounts from the terminal. To do so, open the MetaMask extension again and click Account 1 (see the arrow in Figure 7.13).

7.   Next click "Add Account Or Hardware Wallet" and you will see three options. Click Import Account. You will then be asked to add the private string to a blank space.

8.   Return to the terminal and use one of the private keys to the available accounts shown in Figure 7.14. Choose one of the keys, copy it, paste it into the space shown, and then click Import. Upon doing this, either the USD of the imported fake amount or the ETH amount will be displayed. A second or third key should work if one private key does not work. Otherwise, feel free to ask an AI assistant what might be going wrong by describing the process, any errors in messages or anything else one might encounter, and how to solve the error.

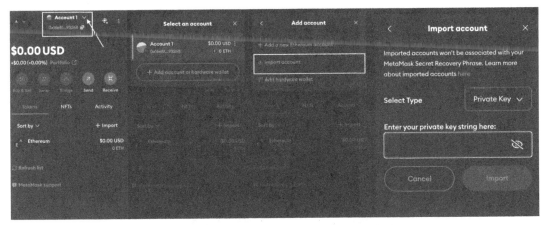

FIGURE 7.13: First part of the process of adding a private key of an Anvil account

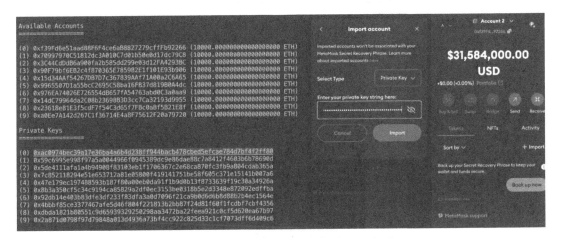

FIGURE 7.14: Second part of the process of adding a private key to an Anvil account

LOCAL SMART CONTRACT DEPLOYMENT

To locally deploy a smart contract, create a second type of terminal to run alongside Anvil. Follow these steps:

1. Click the plus button displayed above the terminal, as shown in Figure 7.15.

   You will see two terminals listed on the right side, as shown in Figure 7.16.

   The contract is deployed on the `zsh` terminal or any other terminal version, and the script for contract deployment is written while Anvil is still running in the background.

2. Type a script in the terminal to deploy a contract:

```
forge create *name of the contract* --rpc-url *the url of the rpc*
--interactive
```

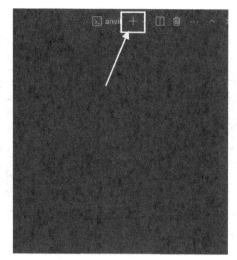

FIGURE 7.15: Adding a new terminal

FIGURE 7.16: The two terminals

In other words, if you were to use the `Counter.sol` smart contract as a blueprint (see Figure 7.17), you would type the following in the terminal and press Enter:

```
forge create Counter --rpc-url http://127.0.0.1:8545 --interactive
```

You will be asked to enter a private key, as shown in Figure 7.18.

3. In this case, you have to go back to Anvil, get one of the private keys, and copy it (see Figure 7.19).

4. Then go back to the `forge create` script shown in Figure 7.18 and paste it in the Enter Private Key field. The private key is not visible when pasting it, and you need to press Enter to see that the contract has been deployed, as shown in Figure 7.20.

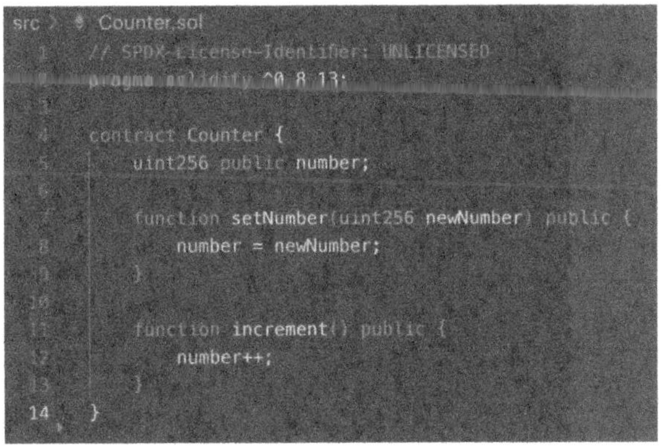

FIGURE 7.17: `Counter.sol`

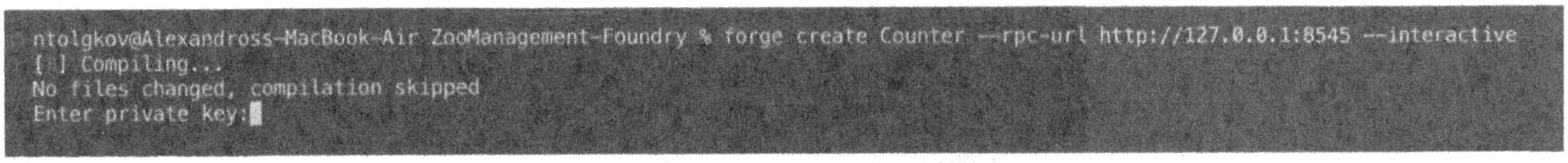

FIGURE 7.18: Entering private key

FIGURE 7.19: Private keys and accounts

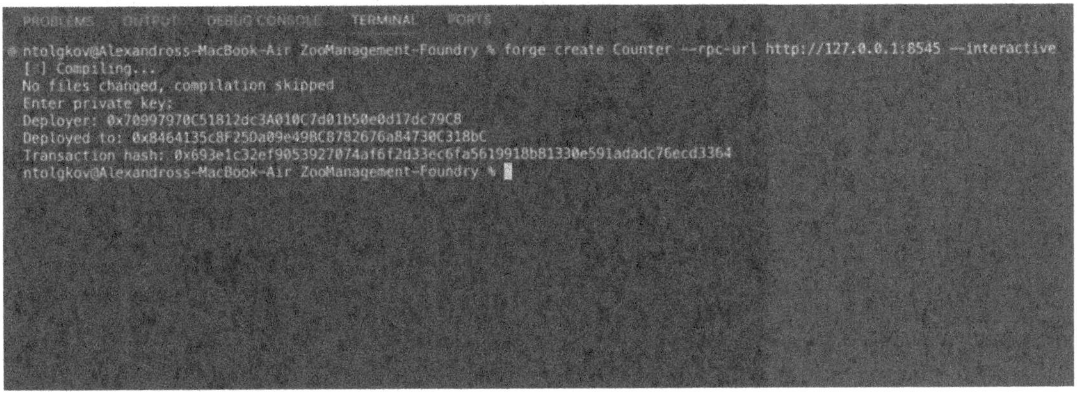

FIGURE 7.20: Contract deployed

The following information is provided:

➤ **Deployer:** The address that deployed the contract

➤ **Deployed to:** The address of the contract that was deployed

➤ **Transaction hash:** When the Deployer address deployed the contract to the Deployed address

USING SCRIPTING TO DEPLOY A CONTRACT

Rather than using the `Counter.sol` contract as demonstrated in this chapter, in this section you create a new file named `ZooManagement.sol` in the `src` folder.

1. Copy the code previously used in Remix to set up the simple `ZooManagement` contract (see Figure 7.21). Meanwhile, delete all instances of the Counter contracts from all folders. Follow the steps in this section to accomplish this.

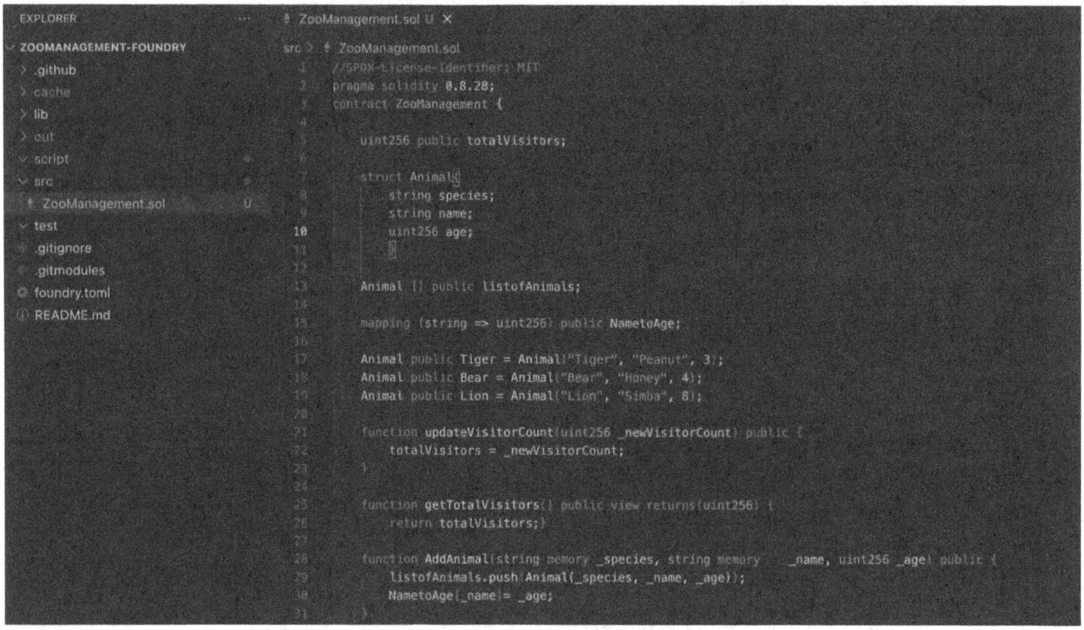

FIGURE 7.21: `ZooManagement` contract

2. Start by developing a new contract called `ZooManagement.s.sol` in the script folder, as shown in Figure 7.22.

3. Within the `ZooManagement.s.sol` contract, create the following contract:

   //SPDX-License-Identifier: MIT

FIGURE 7.22: `ZooManagement.s.sol`

This defines the license under which the contract will be released.

`pragma solidity 0.8.28;`

This defines the Solidity version to be used for the contract.

`import {Script} from "forge-std/Script.sol";`

This line imports the Script contract from the `forge-std` folder and the `Script.sol` file.

The `Script` contract helps by adding functionality to the contract.

`import {ZooManagement} from "../src/ZooManagement.sol";`

The `ZooManagement` contract is imported from the `src` folder and the `ZooManagement.sol` file.

`contract DeployZooManagement is Script {`

This defines the name of the contract and inherits the `Script` contract.

`    function run() external returns(ZooManagement) {`

The `run` function is external, meaning it can be called outside the contract and returns a `ZooManagement` contract.

Regarding contracts in the `Script` folder, they all start with the `run` function as a standard.

`        vm.startBroadcast();`

The `vm.startBroadcast` is a cheat code in Solidity. It is a keyword that adds functionality to the contract through the script contract.

After `vm.startBroadcast()`, the next lines of code will be broadcasted to the blockchain as a transaction.

`        ZooManagement zooManagement = new ZooManagement();`

This creates a new version of the `ZooManagement` contract. It utilizes the `new` keyword to deploy it on the blockchain. The new contract version is stored in `ZooManagement`.

`        vm.stopBroadcast();`

This stops broadcasting transactions to the blockchain.

```
return zooManagement;
```

This returns the newly deployed ZooManagement instance stored in zooManagement.

```
    }
}
```

At its most basic, the contract deploys a version of the ZooManagement contract more professionally.

4. Now, to deploy the contract, you have to use the terminal and type this:

```
forge script script/ZooManagement.s.sol
```

Then press Enter.

Figure 7.23 shows that the forge script was run successfully; the gas was used to deploy the ZooManagement contract and the contract address of ZooManagement.

FIGURE 7.23: Deployed contract with script

When forge does not have an Anvil blockchain running in the background through the terminal, it temporarily spawns its Anvil blockchain to deploy the contract.

The last message mentions that, if one wants to simulate on-chain transactions, an RPC-URL is needed. In such a case, a new terminal message must be typed:

```
forge script script/ZooManagement.s.sol --rpc-url http://127.0.0.1:8545
--broadcast
  --private-key
0x59c6995e998f97a5a0044966f0945389dc9e86dae88c7a8412f4603b6b78690d
```

The result is shown in Figure 7.24.

The contract has been deployed on Anvil. Thus, for deployment on Anvil, the formula is as follows:

1. `forge script`

2. `script/*nameofthefile*`

3. Two dashes: `--rpc-url: http:// 127.0.0.1:8545`

4. Two dashes `--broadcast`

5. Two dashes `--private-key`
   `0x59c6995e998f97a5a0044966f0945389dc9e86dae88c7a8412f4603b6b78690d`

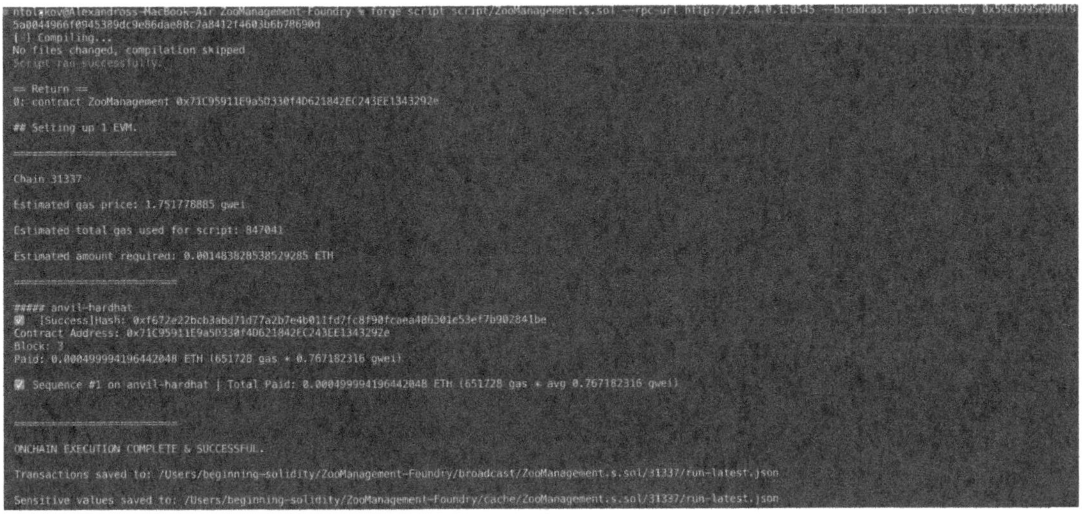

FIGURE 7.24: Contract deployed

> **WARNING** *When using the preceding method to deploy smart contracts, there is a huge red flag: the exposure of a private key. In this case, this happens with dummy private keys that Anvil offers for testing and learning material. However, when a developer works in a natural environment, with real private keys and actual sums of money, exposing the private key in such a way would only ensure that the funds in the address will be gone. Therefore, never use it as, in the best case, you expose your private keys; in the worst, the private keys you expose could be those of a friend, colleague, organization, or decentralized autonomous organization. Depending on the specific case, you will have varying degrees of responsibility for the harm caused as well as sums of money lost.*
>
> *The reason the wrong way of deploying the contract is shown is to ensure that you recognize the pattern, know the risks involved, and do not adopt it in the future. It is hoped that, by knowing this, you won't mistakenly view it as a simpler or faster alternative when you see others using it, instead of following the recommended deployment process described next.*

Deploying a smart contract requires a slightly different process to prevent the exposure of private keys.

1. Open the terminal of your device:

MacOS:

➤ Click the launchpad.

➤ In the search pane on the top, type **terminal**.

➤ Click the Terminal icon that pops up.

Windows:

➤ Click the Start button or press the Windows key.

➤ Type **cmd** in the search pane.

➤ Click Command Prompt in the results.

2. After opening the terminal, go to Anvil and copy one of the private keys; then go back to the terminal and type this:

```
cast wallet import wallet1 --interactive
```

In this example, `wallet1` is the name of the private key to be stored. You do not need to use `wallet1` as a name. You can use whatever name is required for different private keys you may want to store. `wallet1` is simply a demonstrable example (see Figure 7.25).

```
Last login: Tue Nov 12 22:49:20 on ttys008
ntolgkov@Alexandross-MacBook-Air ~ % cast wallet import wallet1 --interactive
```

FIGURE 7.25: `cast wallet import wallet1 --interactive` in terminal

3. Press Enter to see the terminal asking for a private key to be entered, as shown in Figure 7.26.

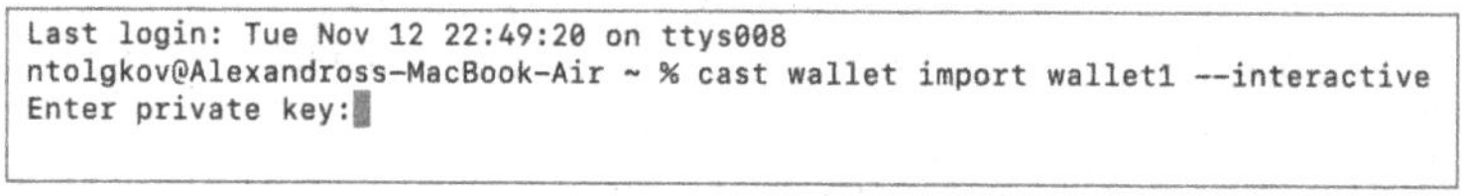

```
Last login: Tue Nov 12 22:49:20 on ttys008
ntolgkov@Alexandross-MacBook-Air ~ % cast wallet import wallet1 --interactive
Enter private key:
```

FIGURE 7.26: Enter private key

4. Paste the private key previously copied from Anvil. After pasting it, you won't see any visual changes or results (see Figure 7.27).

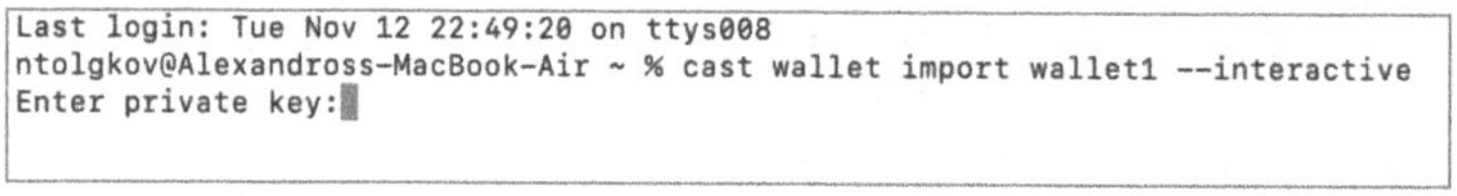

```
Last login: Tue Nov 12 22:49:20 on ttys008
ntolgkov@Alexandross-MacBook-Air ~ % cast wallet import wallet1 --interactive
Enter private key:
```

FIGURE 7.27: Having pasted the private key

5. Press Enter.

6. After pasting the private key and pressing Enter, the terminal will display a message asking you to enter a password, as shown in Figure 7.28. This password will be helpful whenever you want to use this private key. Hence, an easy-to-remember password would be the best fit.

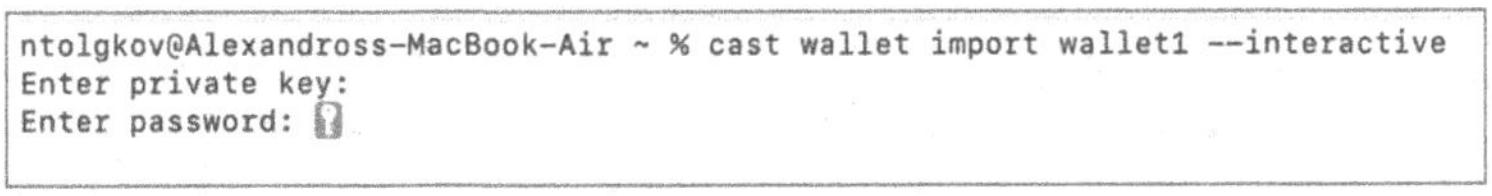

```
ntolgkov@Alexandross-MacBook-Air ~ % cast wallet import wallet1 --interactive
Enter private key:
Enter password:
```

FIGURE 7.28: Entering password

7. After adding the password, the terminal will display that the `wallet1` private key has been saved successfully and will display the address of the keystore (as shown in Figure 7.29), which one should copy and save somewhere easy to access. That somewhere easy to access could be a text file, Word document, or something similar, but generally, it is somewhere you can easily access the address of the keystore, as it will be highly reusable when working with the stored private key.

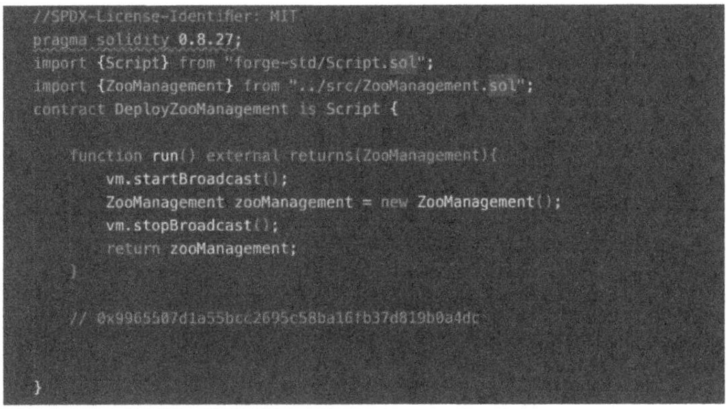

```
//SPDX-License-Identifier: MIT
pragma solidity 0.8.27;
import {Script} from "forge-std/Script.sol";
import {ZooManagement} from "../src/ZooManagement.sol";
contract DeployZooManagement is Script {

    function run() external returns(ZooManagement){
        vm.startBroadcast();
        ZooManagement zooManagement = new ZooManagement();
        vm.stopBroadcast();
        return zooManagement;

    }

    // 0x9965507d1a55bcc2695c58ba16fb37d819b0a4dc

}
```

FIGURE 7.29: Do not store the keystore address in a comment in the contract to be deployed due to security risks. This illustration is for demonstration purposes

8. Close the custom-made terminal and go to the VS Code terminal. The reason the VS Code terminal was not used is security-related. If there is a bug or anything else in the latest version of the VS Code, the private key might be leaked to someone, and another party will have access to the funds. By using the terminal that comes with your computer device, an extra layer of security is added to the whole process.

In the terminal of the VS Code, type this:

```
forge script script/ZooManagement.s.sol:DeployZooManagement --rpc-url
http://127.0.0.1:8545 --account wallet1 --broadcast
```

You should add the keystore password and press Enter. After that, the result is shown in Figure 7.30.

The contract has been successfully deployed.

FIGURE 7.30: Deployed contract address

CONTRACT INTERACTION WITH FOUNDRY

Now that you have deployed the contract in several ways, knowing how to interact with it through Foundry is crucial. To do so, follow these steps.

1. Type the following:

```
cast send *address of deployed contract* *name of the function to call and
the type
of variable it takes* the input --rpc-url and the account.
```

> **NOTE** *Cast is another Foundry tool employed to interact with deployed smart contracts and the blockchain more generally. Hence, when you want to interact with a function of a deployed contract, you need to use Cast.*
>
> *Cast has several commands that it can use. One of those commands is* send, *used to sign and publish a specific transaction.*
>
> *Therefore, when you want to interact with a deployed contract, type the following:*
>
> ➤ **cast:** To let the compiler know that one wants to interact with a deployed smart contract
>
> ➤ **send—or anything else:** To let the compiler know what kind of interaction it will be
>
> ➤ **The address of the deployed contract:** To let the compiler know the "location" of the smart contract one wants to interact with
>
> ➤ **The name of the function to call:** To let the compiler know which function one wants to interact with after having found the location of the contract one wants to interact with

➤ **The input:** The value to be inserted into the interaction itself

➤ **The --rpc-url:** To know what node to query for the interaction

➤ **The account:** The private key that should be used to sign the transaction

In the case of the deployed `DeployZooManagement` contract, the contract address is `0x31A65C6d4EB07ad51E7afc890aC3b7bE84dF2Ead`, as shown in Figure 7.31.

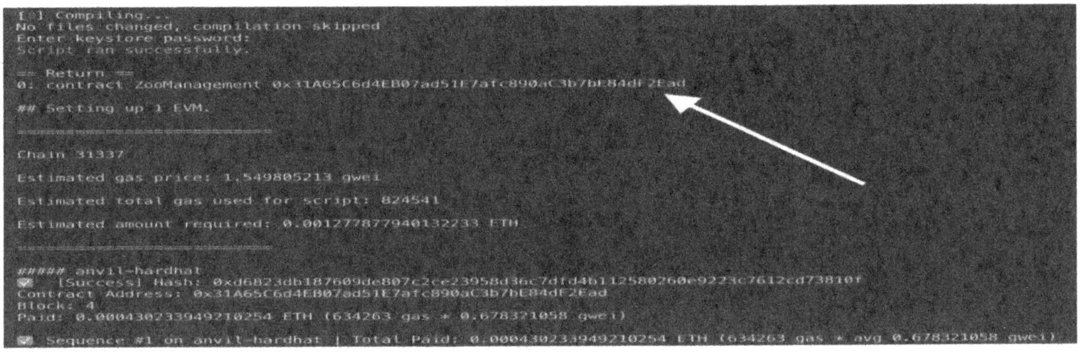

FIGURE 7.31: Contract address

The name of the function that will be called is `updateVisitorCount`, which takes an `uint256` parameter/variable (see Figure 7.32).

FIGURE 7.32: `updateVisitorCount` function

Anvil's rpc-url is still the same, `http://127.0.0.1:8545`, and the account is `wallet1`.

Hence, the command that this results in is as follows; remember the 21 stands for the input number. In this case, updating the visitor count:

```
cast send  0x31A65C6d4EB07ad51E7afc890aC3b7bE84dF2Ead
"updateVisitorCount(uint256)" 21 --rpc-url http://127.0.0.1:8545
 --account wallet1
```

2. Run this command in the terminal to produce the screen shown in Figure 7.33.

3. The terminal asks for the keystore password that was assigned previously. Once the keystore password has been added successfully, you can see that the transaction has been executed successfully, as shown in Figure 7.34.

Another command that can be used with cast is the `call` command.

```
☑ Sequence #1 on anvil-hardhat | Total Paid: 0.000430233949210254 ETH (634263 gas * avg 0.678321058 gwei)

=======================
ONCHAIN EXECUTION COMPLETE & SUCCESSFUL.

Transactions saved to: /Users/beginning-solidity/ZooManagement-Foundry/broadcast/ZooManagement.s.sol/31337/run-latest.json

Sensitive values saved to: /Users/beginning-solidity/ZooManagement-Foundry/cache/ZooManagement.s.sol/31337/run-latest.json

Alexandross-MacBook-Air:ZooManagement-Foundry ntolgkov$ cast send 0x31A65C6d4EB07ad51E7afc890aC3b7bE84dF2Ead "updateVisitorCount(uint256)" 21 --rpc-url http://127.0.0.1:8545
--account wallet1
Enter keystore password:
```

FIGURE 7.33: Keystore password

```
blockHash              0x1d841dc090f77786e34eda652e1df23272a22a20d5d3961c6a87fbeb2044a734
blockNumber            5
contractAddress
cumulativeGasUsed      43558
effectiveGasPrice      597116209
from                   0x9965507D1a55bcC2695C58ba16FB37d819B0A4dc
gasUsed                43558
logs                   []
logsBloom              0x00000000000000000000000000000000000000000000000000000000000000000000000000000000000000000000000000000000000000000000000000000000000000000000000000000000000000000000000000000000000000000000000000000000000000000000000000000000000000000000000000000000000000000000000000000000
root
status                 1 (success)
transactionHash        0x4eca86145d0f55416b0804d91d7e9f3eafe45ac6910d38882a355c21236ebc7b
transactionIndex       0
type                   2
blobGasPrice           1
blobGasUsed
authorizationList
to                     0x31A65C6d4EB07ad51E7afc890aC3b7bE84dF2Ead
Alexandross-MacBook-Air:ZooManagement-Foundry ntolgkov$
```

FIGURE 7.34: Transaction executed

Use `Cast send` when you want to interact and add an input. In Remix, those were the functions with the red buttons that add inputs, as shown in Figure 7.35.

FIGURE 7.35: `updateVisitorCount` on Remix

The `cast call` command is used to interact with the blue buttons that are used to retrieve the data inputs, as shown in Figure 7.36.

FIGURE 7.36: `getTotalVisitors` on Remix

To interact with the value 21 that was added in Foundry and VS Code as an input with `cast send`, you have to use `cast call` and precisely the following sequence:

```
cast call 0x31A65C6d4EB07ad51E7afc890aC3b7bE84dF2Ead 'getTotalVisitors()'
```

When you type the previous command, you get the result shown in Figure 7.37.

```
Alexandross-MacBook-Air:ZooManagement-Foundry ntolgkov$ cast call  0x31A65C6d4EB07ad51E7afc890aC3b7bE84dF2Ead 'getTotalVisitors()'
0x0000000000000000000000000000000000000000000000000000000000000015
```

FIGURE 7.37: TotalVisitors HexNumber

This is the 787 number, but in a hexadecimal format. To get the original decimal number, type this:

```
cast --to-dec 0x00000000000000000000000000000000000000000000000000000000
000000000015
```

Once the command is typed and Enter is pressed, the hexadecimal number is converted to a decimal: 787.

DEPLOYING A SMART CONTRACT TO A TEST NETWORK THROUGH FOUNDRY

After having deployed a smart contract to the built-in Anvil test network, the next step is to deploy the smart contract to an actual test network of Ethereum. For that, you need to use a service called Alchemy. Alchemy is one of the leading Web3 infrastructure providers providing different types of blockchain infrastructure. In this section of the chapter, Alchemy will be used as a node-as-a-service provider. It will serve as a node that will communicate with the other nodes on the blockchain during the deployment of the ZooManagement smart contract.

> **NOTE** Alchemy can be accessed at www.alchemy.com. If you need an Alchemy account, the first step is to create one by signing up and logging in. This book will not go through registering for an account, which is generally considered a basic process. However, if you have trouble creating an account, ask an AI assistant such as ChatGPT for step-by-step instructions on registering an account.

After creating an account and signing in, you should see the signed-in landing page shown in Figure 7.38 (or a similar one if the design has changed when you read this book).

To create a new app, follow these steps:

1. Click Create New App at the top right of the sign-in landing page, as shown in Figure 7.38.

2. You will be presented with a form that needs to be filled in, shown in Figure 7.39.

    The form asks for a name, an optional description, a use case, and a name for the Other project type if the use case differs. Once filled in, click Next.

3. After that, you will be confronted with several different blockchains, as shown in Figure 7.40. You can either click Ethereum in the Most Popular section or go to the search pane and type **Ethereum** for the Ethereum option to show up. Click it.

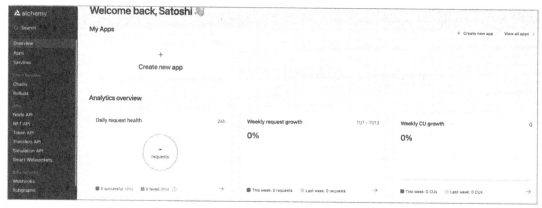

FIGURE 7.38: Alchemy sign-in landing page

FIGURE 7.39: Alchemy: create new app

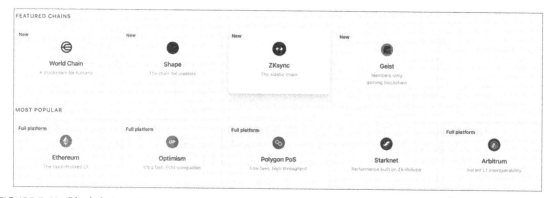

FIGURE 7.40: Blockchain options

4. Next, you will be confronted with the service activation section shown in Figure 7.41, where you should click Next to move to the next section unless a service needs to be included. In that case, click the service you need and then click Next. Alchemy already has the Token, NFT, and Webhooks API preselected. You may also want to click the Node API whenever you create a new project, as it is one of the most common use cases.

FIGURE 7.41: Service selection

5. After creating the application, you are confronted with its landing page, where you can choose the chain, the network, the method, the language, and the software development kit (SDK), as shown in Figure 7.42. Click the Networks button below the application name.

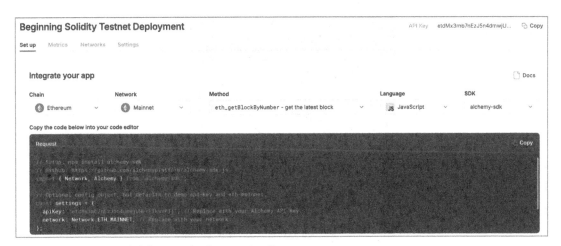

FIGURE 7.42: Beginning Solidity test deployment landing page

6. The Networks tab (shown in Figure 7.43) shows the networks available and their RPC URL. Click the Mainnet ETH and choose Sepolia from the options available. After choosing Sepolia, copy the link and store it in a document that is easily accessible.

7. After storing the ETH Sepolia's RPC URL, go to you MetaMask browser extension and change it to the Sepolia testnet, a Sepolia testnet network with testnet ETH. If that is not available to you, go to a faucet to get Testnet ETH, as shown in Chapter 3.

FIGURE 7.43: Blockchain networks

8. After opening MetaMask, click the three dots at the top right of the application, as shown in Figure 7.44, and click Account Details.

FIGURE 7.44: Sepolia Testnet ETH

9. As shown in Figure 7.45, you will see a QR code with an address and a Show Private Key button on account details. Click the button and add the password of your MetaMask browser.

10. You will see the Hold To Reveal Private Key message shown in Figure 7.46. Hold the button to reveal the key, as shown in Figure 7.47.

FIGURE 7.45: Account Details QR code

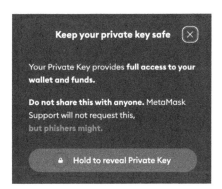

FIGURE 7.46: Hold to reveal the key button.

11. Copy the private key.

> **NOTE** *Ensure that the private key is not seen by anyone, as a malicious party can load the key to another wallet and access the funds. My wallet used here is a dummy wallet established for the use of this book, so revealing it here is okay.*

12. Open your computer's terminal and type this:

```
cast wallet import ETHSepolia --interactive
```

Then, paste the private key, enter the password for the key, and when the keystore address is displayed, copy and paste it into a document (see Figure 7.48).

FIGURE 7.47: Private key

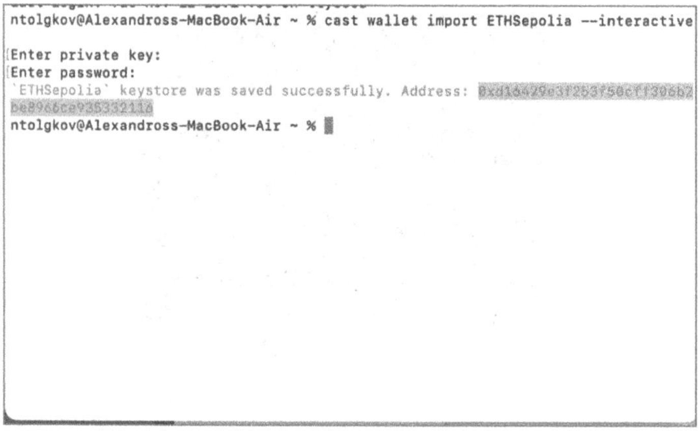

```
ntolgkov@Alexandross-MacBook-Air ~ % cast wallet import ETHSepolia --interactive
Enter private key:
Enter password:
`ETHSepolia` keystore was saved successfully. Address: 0xd16429e3f253f50cff306b2
be8966ce93533211d
ntolgkov@Alexandross-MacBook-Air ~ %
```

FIGURE 7.48: Storing MetaMask's private key

13. Go back to the VS studio terminal and deploy the contract to the Sepolia test network. Then type this:

```
forge script script/ZooManagement.s.sol --rpc-url
https://eth-sepolia.g.alchemy.com
/v2/etdMx3mb7nEzJ5n4dmwjUNEYFIkavK1j --account ETHSepolia -broadcast
```

14. The terminal will ask for the keystore password, as shown in Figure 7.49.

After adding the password, the contract is deployed on the Sepolia test network, as shown in Figure 7.50.

15. Copy the transaction hash used to deploy the contract (see Figure 7.51).

```
ntolgkov@Alexandross-MacBook-Air ZooManagement-Foundry % cast --to-dec 0x0000000000000000000000000000000000000000000000000000000000000313
787
ntolgkov@Alexandross-MacBook-Air ZooManagement-Foundry % forge script script/ZooManagement.s.sol --rpc-url https://eth-sepolia.g.alchemy.com/v2/etdMx3mb7nEzJ5n4dmwjUNEYFIka
vK1j --account ETHSepolia --broadcast
[*] Compiling...
No files changed, compilation skipped
Enter keystore password:
```

FIGURE 7.49: Keystore Password ETHSepolia

```
ntolgkov@Alexandross-MacBook-Air ZooManagement-Foundry % forge script script/ZooManagement.s.sol --rpc-url https://eth-sepolia.g.alchemy.com/v2/etdMx3mb7nEzJ5n4dmwjUNEYFIka
vK1j --account ETHSepolia --broadcast
[*] Compiling...
No files changed, compilation skipped
Enter keystore password:
Script ran successfully.

== Return ==
0: contract ZooManagement 0xa583f5741DF4463883CA27B5B0183cDcA35A9BD0

## Setting up 1 EVM.

==========================

Chain 11155111

Estimated gas price: 0.000014844 gwei

Estimated total gas used for script: 847041

Estimated amount required: 0.00067840771037660604 ETH

==========================

##### sepolia
✅  [Success]Hash: 0xb99cf54da54aa0e9d47ec8ccd7aa3c2d209c3dd28e5f6c29493f6d45a6236f3c
Contract Address: 0xa583f5741DF4463883CA27B5B0183cDcA35A9BD0
Block: 7070078
Paid: 0.000257602391192608 ETH (651728 gas * 0.395260586 gwei)

✅ Sequence #1 on sepolia | Total Paid: 0.000257602391192608 ETH (651728 gas * avg 0.395260586 gwei)

==========================

ONCHAIN EXECUTION COMPLETE & SUCCESSFUL.

Transactions saved to: /Users/beginning-solidity/ZooManagement-Foundry/broadcast/ZooManagement.s.sol/11155111/run-latest.json

Sensitive values saved to: /Users/beginning-solidity/ZooManagement-Foundry/cache/ZooManagement.s.sol/11155111/run-latest.json
```

FIGURE 7.50: Smart contract deployed on test network

```
##### sepolia
✅  [Success]Hash: 0xb99cf54da54aa0e9d47ec8ccd7aa3c2d209c3dd28e5f6c29493f6d45a6236f3c
```

FIGURE 7.51: Contract deployment transaction hash

16. Go to https://sepolia.etherscan.io, which is the block explorer of the Sepolia test network. Paste the transaction hash in the search pane, as shown in Figure 7.52, and press Enter.

FIGURE 7.52: Etherscan contract transaction hash pasted

You will see that the contract has been deployed on the SepoliaETH test network through the transaction, as shown in Figure 7.53.

FIGURE 7.53: Transaction of creation of the testnet smart contract

17. Click the To: address, as shown in Figure 7.54.

⑦ To:	[⊟ 0xa583f5741df4463883ca27b5bd183cdca35a98d0 **Created**] ⓒ ✅

FIGURE 7.54: To address

You will see the contract on Etherscan, as shown in Figure 7.55.

FIGURE 7.55: ZooManagement contract on Sepolia test network

CHAPTER 7 QUESTIONS

1. What is the purpose of the `foundry.toml` file, and how can it be customized for testing and deployment?

2. Explain the significance of the `forge-std` library in Foundry. Why is it beneficial for developers?

3. Describe the process of compiling a Solidity contract using Foundry. How can you identify and resolve compilation errors?

4. What is the role of the `forge build` and `forge compile` commands, and how do they differ in practice?

5. What is Anvil in Foundry, and how does it differ from other blockchain testing environments?

6. Walk through the process of adding the Anvil network to MetaMask, including setting up the RPC URL and Chain ID.

7. How do Anvil's mnemonic phrases and private keys work, and what security precautions should be taken when using them?

8. Describe the steps to deploy a contract locally using Foundry and Anvil. What are the key commands involved?

9. What is the purpose of deployment scripts in the `script` folder, and how is the `vm.start Broadcast` function utilized?

10. Explain the difference between deploying a contract with `forge create` versus using a deployment script. When would you use each?

11. Why is exposing a private key during deployment a critical security risk? How can this be avoided in real-world scenarios?

12. What are the best practices for securely managing private keys when deploying contracts on test or main networks?

13. How do you interact with a deployed contract using Foundry's `cast` tool? Provide an example using the `updateVisitorCount` function.

14. What is the difference between `cast send` and `cast call`? When would you use each?

15. Explain the process of deploying a smart contract to the Ethereum Sepolia test network using Alchemy. What role does the RPC URL play in this process?

Fundraising Contract

This chapter guides you through building a practical fundraising smart contract—a common real-world application that demonstrates several fundamental Solidity concepts and best practices. Through developing this contract, you'll learn how to handle cryptocurrency payments securely, integrate with external price feeds through Chainlink oracles, and implement proper access controls and security measures.

Consider a scenario where a charity wants to accept cryptocurrency donations but needs to ensure a minimum USD value for each contribution, regardless of ETH price fluctuations. This presents several challenges: How do you get reliable USD/ETH price data on-chain? How do you track donors and their contributions? How do you ensure only authorized parties can withdraw funds? The chapter walks through solving these real challenges step-by-step.

By the end of this chapter, you'll have built a production-ready fundraising contract that can serve as a template for similar financial applications. The concepts covered form the foundation for developing more complex DeFi protocols and financial smart contracts.

SETTING UP A FUNDRAISING CONTRACT

To start this project, you need to create a new Foundry project. To do so, follow these steps:

1. As always, type **ls** to see where you are located in the terminal. As shown in Figure 8.1, you are in the ZooManagement-Foundry folder.

FIGURE 8.1: The result of typing ls

2. To change folder locations, type **cd ...** Then type **ls** again to see where you are now located. In this example, as shown in Figure 8.2, you are located in the beginning-solidity folder, and various projects are included.

```
ntolgkov@Alexandross-MacBook-Air ZooManagement-Foundry % cd ..
ntolgkov@Alexandross-MacBook-Air beginning-solidity % ls
ZooManagement-Foundry              beginning-solidity-DAO              beginning-solidity-proxy-contracts    beginning-solidity-token
ntolgkov@Alexandross-MacBook-Air beginning-solidity %
```

FIGURE 8.2: The result of typing ls for the second time

3. To create a new project, type this:

```
mkdir Fundraising-contract
```

4. Type **ls** again to verify that the folder has been created successfully, as shown in Figure 8.3.

```
ntolgkov@Alexandross-MacBook-Air beginning-solidity % ls
Fundraising-contract              beginning-solidity-DAO              beginning-solidity-token
ZooManagement-Foundry             beginning-solidity-proxy-contracts
ntolgkov@Alexandross-MacBook-Air beginning-solidity %
```

FIGURE 8.3: The result of typing ls for a third time

5. The next step to get into the newly created folder is to type this:

```
cd Fundraising-contract
```

6. When inside Fundraising-contract, create a new project by typing **forge init (or forge init --force** if forge init does not work).

Figure 8.4 shows that the files for the new project have been installed.

```
ntolgkov@Alexandross-MacBook-Air Fundraising-contract % forge init
Initializing /Users/beginning-solidity/Fundraising-contract...
Installing forge-std in /Users/beginning-solidity/Fundraising-contract/lib/forge-std (url: Some("https://github.com/foundry-rs/forge-std"), tag: None)
Cloning into '/Users/beginning-solidity/Fundraising-contract/lib/forge-std'...
remote: Enumerating objects: 1935, done.
remote: Counting objects: 100% (1930/1930), done.
remote: Compressing objects: 100% (741/741), done.
remote: Total 1935 (delta 1290), reused 1729 (delta 1142), pack-reused 5 (from 1)
Receiving objects: 100% (1935/1935), 629.21 KiB | 494.00 KiB/s, done.
Resolving deltas: 100% (1290/1290), done.
    Installed forge-std v1.9.4
    Initialized forge project
ntolgkov@Alexandross-MacBook-Air Fundraising-contract %
```

FIGURE 8.4: Typing forge init to install a new Foundry project

7. Open the folder by selecting File ⇨ Open Folder ⇨ Fundraising-contract ⇨ Open.

If successful, a new instance or a new version of VS Code should open with a new project having the classic Counter.sol contracts in the script, src, and test folders, as shown in Figure 8.5.

8. Within the project, delete all three contracts, and then, in the src folder, create a Fundraising.sol contract, as shown in Figure 8.6.

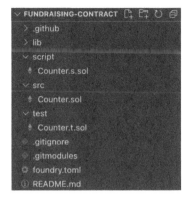

FIGURE 8.5: Fundraising-contract pane

FIGURE 8.6: Creating `Fundraising.sol`

Now you can start writing the contract in the `Fundraising` file. The following defines the license under which the contract will be released:

```
//SPDX-License-Identifier: MIT
```

The next line defines the Solidity version the contract will be using:

```
pragma solidity 0.8.27;
```

The next line defines the name of the contract:

```
contract Fundraising {
```

The `sendMoney` function in the following code is a public function (thus, it can be called both internally and externally) and is payable, meaning that this function enables the function to receive money in the form of ETH.

```
    function sendMoney() public payable {
        require(msg.value > 1e18, "Did not send enough money");

    }
}
```

Within the function, a `require` statement is used to ensure that specific criteria are met so the function executes successfully. In this case, the `require` statement requires that the `msg.value` variable is more than 1e18—that is, more than 1 ether. If the `require` statement does not meet that criteria, then it reverts the function. This means it rolls it back as if it never happened. You can attach a short message to the error when the function reverts.

The `msg.value` variable in Solidity stands for "message value." It represents the monetary value that is being sent. That economic value can be of any size—unless specified, as in this case. In traditional finance, `msg.value` straightforwardly represents the amount of money to be sent from one bank account to another. If a person were to send 100 USD from their bank account to a friend's bank account to pay for part of a meal they had together (assuming the other party paid for both of them), then the 100 USD is the `msg.value`, in this case, representing the amount of money being sent.

The difference with `msg.value` is that `msg.value` is calculated not in USD but in ETH. What is more, in wei, the smallest denomination of ETH, 1 ETH consists of 1,000,000,000,000,000,000 wei, which is 18 zeros. Hence, when the previous function is this:

```
require(msg.value > 1e18
```

it means making sure that the amount of money in ETH is more than 1e18 or 1 to the power of 18, which is 1,000,000,000,000,000,000 wei and hence 1 ETH. In Solidity, when you want to specify that a function should receive more than X amount of ETH, you have to think in wei. So instead of saying `require(msg.value > 1 ETH`, you have to say `require(msg.value > 1e18`. This is 1 + 18 zeros in terms of wei and, therefore, 1 ETH. If one were to specify 2 ETH, it would be 2e18. Alternatively, one can also use the ether keyword to specify one whole ETH. For example, it would be `require(msg.value > 1 ether`.

The message at the end of the preceding code block `"Did not send enough money"` is a short message to display when the requirement is not fulfilled. Hence, if one were to send 0.5 ETH to the contract, one would get that message as an error.

ORACLES

In a hypothetical scenario where you may want to send more than 10 USD to the `Fundraising` contract and not more than 1 ether, then changing the code in the previous section as follows would be necessary:

```
//SPDX-License-Identifier: MIT
pragma solidity 0.8.27;
contract Fundraising {
    uint256 public minimumAmountSent = 10;

    function sendMoney() public payable {
        require(msg.value > minimumAmountSent, "Did not send enough money");
    }
}
```

In the previous example, a public variable `minimumAmountSent` representing a hypothetical 10 USD is added, replacing the 1e18 number with the variable. The problem is that `msg.sender` is counted in ether, while `minimumAmountSent` is supposed to be in USD. A conversion needs to be made from the amount of ether to the price of USD. This can be done through *oracles*.

Blockchains are deterministic systems by nature, and therefore, without external assistance, they cannot interact with external data or events. Blockchains are not aware of the value of ether or any vital information. Besides doing their internal computations of smart contracts and reaching consensus, blockchains cannot perform any external computations.

This is solved by using what is called a *blockchain oracle*. Oracles can be thought of as devices that interact with the natural world or the off-chain world and provide external data that blockchains are not aware of to the blockchains. There are two main types of oracles:

➤ **Inbound Oracles:** Provide external data to a blockchain

➤ **Outbound Oracles:** Offer blockchain data to external systems

Chainlink is an oracle network that provides these decentralized oracles with data to work with their smart contracts and experiments. Chainlink's oracles are thus powerful tools that allow smart contracts to unlock countless use cases and features by requesting data through those oracles. The oracles perform an API call and fetch and feed the blockchain with the information. Application programming interfaces (APIs) can be seen as a list of rules utilized by programs created by developers to communicate and interact with one another and share information or data. In this case, the blockchain queries the Chainlink oracle for information, and the oracle performs an API call at the required location to fetch the data the blockchain needs.

Chainlink, as an oracle network, offers several services. However, this chapter will focus on Chainlink data feeds. Chainlink data feeds work through different data providers—usually companies—that run a Chainlink node similarly to an Ethereum node. Those data providers provide the data needed to an intermediary contract on-chain known as the *data contract*. Most of this data comes in the form of a price feed, which developers of DeFi smart contracts can use by importing it into the smart contracts they are working on.

To see an example of such a price feed, go to the `https://data.chain.link` website shown in Figure 8.7.

FIGURE 8.7: `https://data.chain.link` landing page

You will see two choices: Data Feeds and Data Streams. Click Data Feeds for this example and you will see the price feeds that exist as well as the networks for which the price feeds are provided, as shown in Figure 8.8.

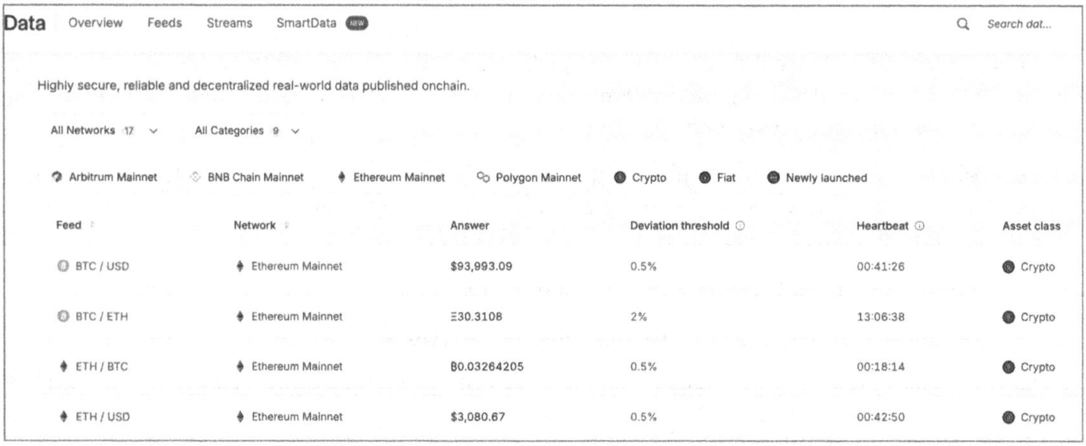

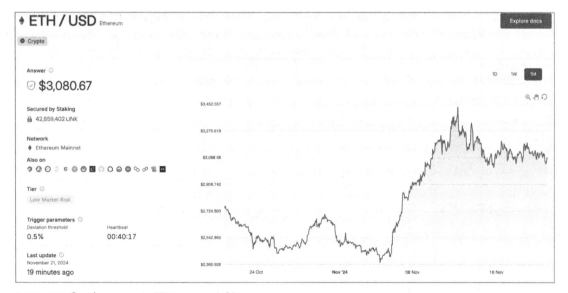

Data   Overview   Feeds   Streams   SmartData NEW   Q   Search dat…

Highly secure, reliable and decentralized real-world data published onchain.

All Networks 17 ∨   All Categories 9 ∨

? Arbitrum Mainnet   ◇ BNB Chain Mainnet   ♦ Ethereum Mainnet   ◌ Polygon Mainnet   ● Crypto   ● Fiat   ● Newly launched

Feed	Network	Answer	Deviation threshold ⓘ	Heartbeat ⓘ	Asset class
◎ BTC / USD	♦ Ethereum Mainnet	$93,993.09	0.5%	00:41:26	● Crypto
◎ BTC / ETH	♦ Ethereum Mainnet	Ξ30.3108	2%	13:06:38	● Crypto
♦ ETH / BTC	♦ Ethereum Mainnet	฿0.03264205	0.5%	00:18:14	● Crypto
♦ ETH / USD	♦ Ethereum Mainnet	$3,080.67	0.5%	00:42:50	● Crypto

FIGURE 8.8: Price feeds list

You can see the price feeds of, for example, BTC to USD, ETH to BTC, ETH to USD, and many more. If you click one of the feeds, for example, ETH to USD, you will see the price of Ethereum at that time, as shown in Figure 8.9.

FIGURE 8.9: Oracle answer in ETH price in USD

The information provided allows you to view the historical price of ETH over the past month and the number of LINK tokens staked to secure the price feed. Nodes stake LINK tokens in a manner similar to Ethereum. You can also check which other networks offer this price feed, as well as the potential percentage deviation in the price. In this case, the deviation is 0.5%, meaning the displayed price of

ETH could vary by up to 0.5% in either direction. For example, if the current price of ETH is shown as $3,080, the actual price could range from $3,064.60 to $3,095.40. If the price is above or below the deviation threshold of 0.5% or 60 minutes pass without the price moving above or below the deviation, a new answer or price is given. The last update shows how long the previous update to the price was.

If you scroll down, you will see the information shown in Figure 8.10.

Market statistics	Product information		Addresses
Market cap ⓘ $370,993,738,402	**Product type** ⓘ 🔵 Price	**Product sub-type** ⓘ 🔵 Reference	**Contract address** 0x5f4e...8419 ⃞
Circulating supply ⓘ 120,426,315 ETH	**Quote asset** ⓘ USD_FX		**ENS address** ⓘ eth-usd.data.eth
Volume (24hr) ⓘ $30,932,262,065			**Product name** ⓘ ETH/USD-RefPrice-DF-Ethereum-001

FIGURE 8.10: Market statistics, product information, and addresses

The information displayed includes market statistics, including the market capitalization in USD of the asset (in this case, ether), the circulating supply of ETH, and the trading volume of ETH in the last 24 hours. The production information section shows the type of product this feed is (price), the subtype of product (reference price), the currency in which the price of ETH is listed, the contract address of the price feed contract, the ENS address, and finally the product name in itself.

> **NOTE** ENS address is beyond the scope of this book, but I encourage you to do some research and find out what ENS and an ENS address is.

Scroll further down and you will see the list of companies running a node for this specific price feed, as shown in Figure 8.11.

Scroll even further down and you can see the nodes in detail, their latest answer, the date the answer was given, and details of the node on Etherscan through a link to Etherscan's website, as shown in Figure 8.12.

Similar to transaction gas, whenever a node operator delivers data to a smart contract, the Chainlink node operator is paid a small amount of Oracle gas in the Chainlink token.

The nodes shown in Figure 8.12 each run by the companies shown, reach out to get the information requested about the price of ETH in USD (but can be for any asset depending on the price feed contract), and then all individually sign the data in one transaction; one of the nodes will finally deliver the data to the data contract. If a node does not deliver the data to the data contract for one reason or another, another node from the group will attempt to do so until one of them succeeds. In the Oracle node system, reputation is of the utmost importance. Suppose one misses data updates or does not send transactions. In that case, one will quickly be marginalized and removed from the price feed network.

FIGURE 8.11: ETH/USD data feed Chainlink nodes

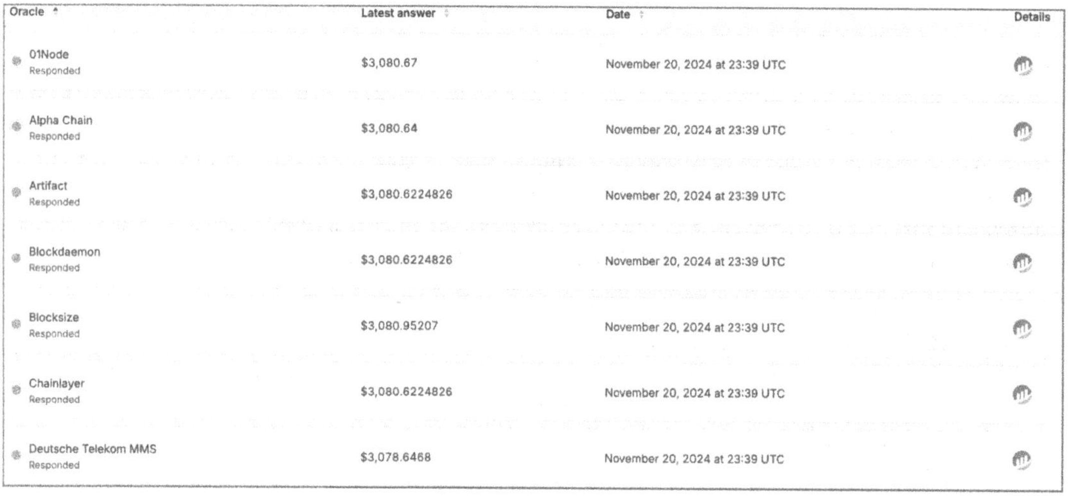

Oracle ▲	Latest answer ⇕	Date ⇕	Details
01Node Responded	$3,080.67	November 20, 2024 at 23:39 UTC	
Alpha Chain Responded	$3,080.64	November 20, 2024 at 23:39 UTC	
Artifact Responded	$3,080.6224826	November 20, 2024 at 23:39 UTC	
Blockdaemon Responded	$3,080.6224826	November 20, 2024 at 23:39 UTC	
Blocksize Responded	$3,080.95207	November 20, 2024 at 23:39 UTC	
Chainlayer Responded	$3,080.6224826	November 20, 2024 at 23:39 UTC	
Deutsche Telekom MMS Responded	$3,078.6468	November 20, 2024 at 23:39 UTC	

FIGURE 8.12: ETH/USD data feed Chainlink nodes list

To understand a data contract, visit the website `https://docs.chain.link`, as shown in Figure 8.13.

The landing page shows the documentation for the products that Chainlink offers. Click Data Feeds to be redirected to the data feeds documentation, which explains everything about data feeds in extreme detail. Then click Feed Addresses and then on Price Feed Addresses to see the page shown in Figure 8.14.

The Price Feed Addresses page will reveal different networks, as shown in Figure 8.15. Each network, including Ethereum's main network, has its price feed addresses.

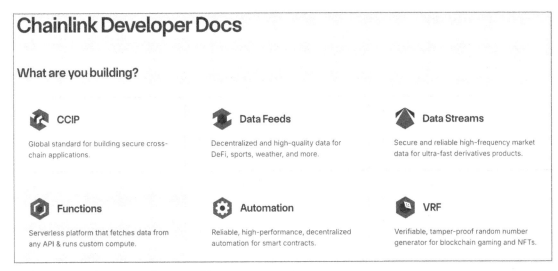

FIGURE 8.13: Landing page of `https://docs.chain.link`

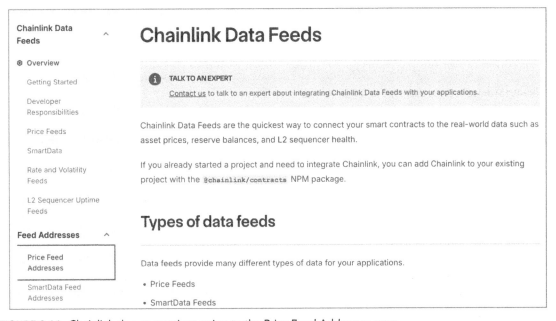

FIGURE 8.14: Chainlink documentation: going to the Price Feed Addresses page

We can see the price feed between the 1-inch token against the ether token and the 1-inch token against the USD. As shown in this chapter, the addresses can be copied and pasted on a smart contract and used to convert prices within the contract.

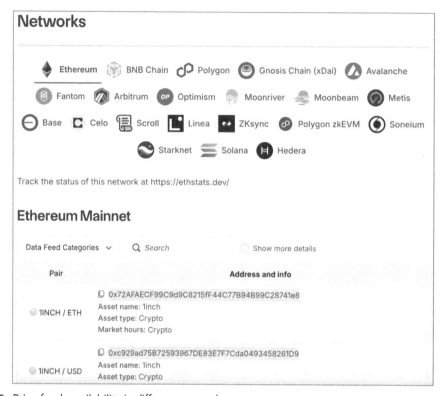

FIGURE 8.15: Price feeds availability in different networks

As shown in Figure 8.16, besides the strictly cryptocurrency-related price feeds, you can also find price feeds for fiat currencies against fiat currencies, such as the Australian dollar (AUD) against the US dollar's (USD) price or the Czech crown (CZK) against the US dollar's (USD) price. Price feeds include traditional financial assets such as EUTBL NAV, which refers to the Net Asset Value (NAV) of the European Union's T-bills money market fund (EUTBL).

Go back to the Data Feeds pane (see Figure 8.14) and click Getting Started below the Chainlink Data Feeds, as shown in Figure 8.17.

This opens the Consuming Data Feeds section of the documentation, as shown in Figure 8.18.

If you scroll down enough, you will come to the sample contract section, which can be opened in Remix (click Open in Remix for a closer inspection). The contract's code and explanation follows.

The following defines the license under which the contract will be released:

```
// SPDX-License-Identifier: MIT
```

The following defines the Solidity version to be used by the contract:

```
pragma solidity ^0.8.7;
```

FIGURE 8.16: List of price feeds on the Sepolia testnet

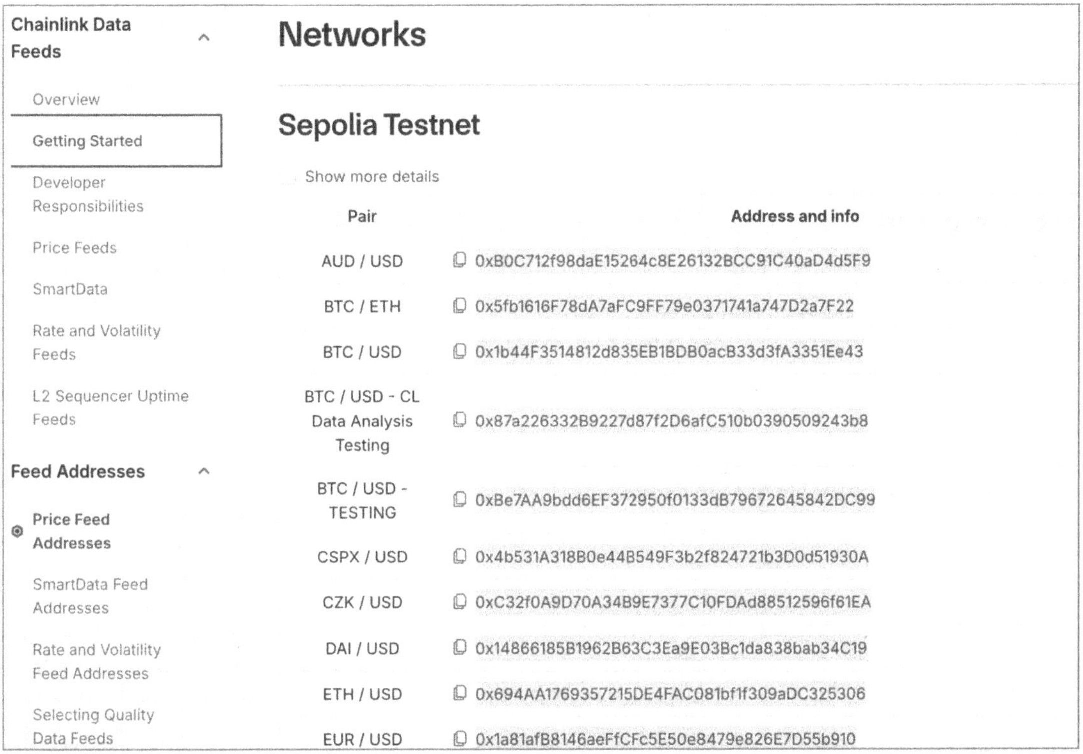

FIGURE 8.17: Chainlink documentation: going to the Getting Started page

Examine the sample contract

FIGURE 8.18: Sample contract example

The following imports the `AggregatorV3Interface` contract, which can be found on Chainlink's GitHub page. The contract provides functions for interacting with different price feeds.

```
import {AggregatorV3Interface} from
"@chainlink/contracts/src/v0.8/shared/interfaces/AggregatorV3Interface.sol";
```

The following defines the contract name:

```
contract DataConsumerV3 {
```

The following is a variable of type `AggregatorV3Interface`, which is the representation of a connection to a specific Chainlink price feed:

```
AggregatorV3Interface internal dataFeed;
```

The following is a constructor function. Constructors are special functions executed only once and automatically as the contract is deployed. They are not mandatory functions for each contract but are used quite often for different use cases and security considerations, such as setting the address that will own the contract to ensure that—for example—an owner can only call certain functions within the contract. If the contract does not have an owner, they will not be able to call the functions.

```
constructor() {
    dataFeed = AggregatorV3Interface(
        0x1b44F3514812d835EB1BDB0acB33d3fA3351Ee43
    );
}
```

The previous constructor sets the `dataFeed` variable to the `AggregatorV3Interface`, which represents the connection to the Ethereum address of `0x1b44F3514812d835EB1BDB0acB33d3fA3351Ee43`, which signifies the contract address of a specific Chainlink price feed that was shown previously on the list.

In this case, `0x1b44F3514812d835EB1BDB0acB33d3fA3351Ee43` is the Sepolia contract address for the pair of bitcoin (BTC) and US dollar (USD) as shown in earlier in Figure 8.17 and again in Figure 8.19.

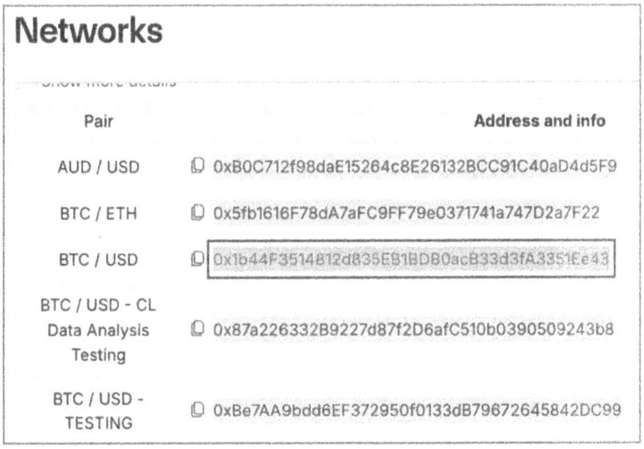

Networks

Pair	Address and info
AUD / USD	0xB0C712f98daE15264c8E26132BCC91C40aD4d5F9
BTC / ETH	0x5fb1616F78dA7aFC9FF79e0371741a747D2a7F22
BTC / USD	0x1b44F3514812d835EB1BDB0acB33d3fA3351Ee43
BTC / USD - CL Data Analysis Testing	0x87a226332B9227d87f2D6afC510b0390509243b8
BTC / USD - TESTING	0xBe7AA9bdd6EF372950f0133dB79672645842DC99

FIGURE 8.19: BTC/USD price feed

Without defining the `dataFeed` to the `AggregatorV3Interface`, the contract would not know how to locate and interact with the specific BTC/USD Chainlink price feed.

The following `getChainlinkDataFeedLatestAnswer` function is public, meaning it can be called by anyone internally or externally. It is a view function, meaning that it reads information from the blockchain but does not alter the blockchain's state, and it returns an integer.

```
function getChainlinkDataFeedLatestAnswer() public view returns (int) {
    (
        /* uint80 roundID */,
        int answer,
        /*uint startedAt*/,
        /*uint timeStamp*/,
        /*uint80 answeredInRound*/
    ) = dataFeed.latestRoundData();
    return answer;
}
}
```

Inside the contract, a tuple is used:

```
(
            /* uint80 roundID */,
            int answer,
            /*uint startedAt*/,
            /*uint timeStamp*/,
            /*uint80 answeredInRound*/
    )
```

Tuples in Solidity are a method to group different and multiple values together. They are not entirely unlike arrays. Arrays, however, save only those variables that are of the same type such as . If an array stores variables, it cannot store variables of a different type. Tuples, on the other hand, can.

Tuples always have a fixed size of variables. For example, once someone creates a tuple with a string, an address, and an int in terms of variables, this tuple now has a fixed size of four different variable types.

The tuple inside the contract has five variables:

1. `uint80 roundID`: the ID of the data.

    ➤   Oracle data is updated—as shown earlier with Heartbeat and Last update—in rounds, and each round represents different data communicated through the oracle at other times. The `roundID` helps identify the data for that round (see Figure 8.20).

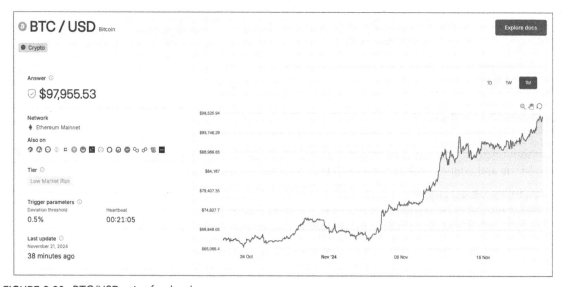

FIGURE 8.20: BTC/USD price feed web page

Previously, we saw the Heartbeat and Last update of the ETH/USD price feed pair. This price feed pair is the BTC/USD with the same information as the ETH/USD pair seen previously. In the BTC/USD example, the price is updated every 1 hour unless the price deviates more than 0.5% of the current price. Therefore, the RoundID would say that the price recorded from

10 a.m. to 11 a.m. has been identified with 1. The price recorded from 11 a.m. to 12 p.m. has the number 2. If the deviation changes at 12:36, number 3 will be from 12:36 to 13:36 or when the deviation changes again.

2. `int answer`: the latest price of BTC in USD

   ➤ This would be the latest price of BTC. In the image, it would be 97,955.53.

3. `uint startedAt`: The timestamp when the round started. A time mark as to when the price started.

4. `uint timeStamp`: Timestamp when the data was recorded. A time mark as to when the price was recorded.

5. `Uint80 answeredInRound`: The round in which the answer was computed. The answer computation or price can occur in the previous round just before starting the new round. Hence, the `answeredInRound` is a variable.

`latestRoundData` returns the tuple, which consists of the five previous variables, and hence, they are mentioned when calling the `dataFeed.latestRoundData`. After having called `latestRoundData` with its tuple and the variables it consists of, the return keyword is used to return one value from the tuple, which is the answer or price of the pair of BTC/USD or any price of a pair in other similar contracts.

DEPLOYING THE PRICE FEED CONTRACT THROUGH REMIX

Now that you know what the contract does, it is time to deploy it in Remix.

1. Open Remix and click Open in Remix to display the screen shown in Figure 8.21.

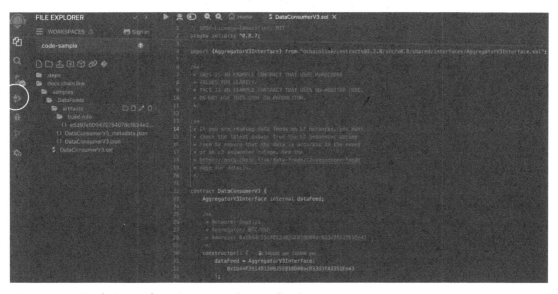

FIGURE 8.21: Deploying and running transactions on Remix

2. Compile the contract by pressing Command+S or Ctrl+S, depending on your operating system.

3. Click Deploy And Run Transactions using the circled icon at the left edge in Figure 8.21.

4. Once in the Deploy And Run Transactions section, click the environment's Remix VM (Cancun) and change it to Injected Provider MetaMask, as shown in Figure 8.22.

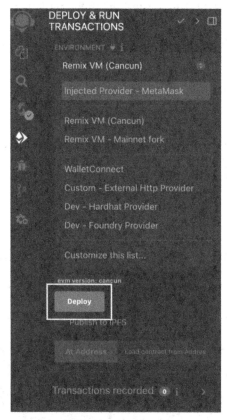

FIGURE 8.22: Changing environment and deploying the sample contract

5. After changing the environment to Injected Provider MetaMask, click the red Deploy button with the white letters shown in Figure 8.22. MetaMask will pop up, giving the network fee for the test network contract to be deployed and for the user of the MetaMask wallet to confirm the deployment.

6. Click Confirm, as shown in Figure 8.23.

Provided there is enough testnet ETH to confirm the transaction, after a wait of usually a few seconds, the contract should be deployed. You can see this at the bottom of the Deployed Contracts section, as shown in Figure 8.24.

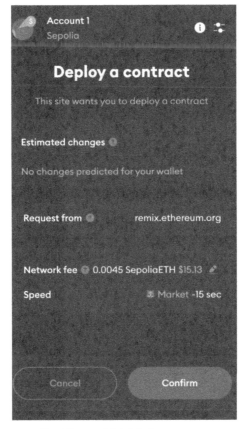

FIGURE 8.23: Contract deployment confirmation on MetaMask

FIGURE 8.24: The contract deployed

7. Click the arrow beside DATACONSUMERV3 to see the contract unfold with one single function called getChainlinkDataFeedLatestAnswer. Click the getChainlinkData FeedLatestAnswer function to display the price of BTC, as shown in Figure 8.25.

The price of BTC as per the function is 9808072634584. The number is significant because Chainlink reports prices of cryptocurrencies as precisely as possible. This means the oracle adds eight more decimal numbers to the price to ensure precision. Take the price—9808072634584—and count eight decimal numbers from right to left; then add a space to get 98080 72634584.

DATACONSUMERV3 AT 0XI
Balance: 0 ETH
getChainlink...
0: int256: 9808072634584

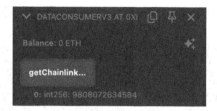

FIGURE 8.25: Price of BTC

For simplicity's sake, round 72634584 to 73. The price of bitcoin can be communicated easily as 98,080.73. Thus, 98,080.73 is the price of Bitcoin at the time of writing. The same procedure works for every cryptocurrency.

SOLIDITY INTERFACES

To ensure that the value of ether sent with the transaction is 10 or more USD, the ether needs to be converted to the value of USD. That requires getting the ETH/USD oracle price feed. To do that, follow these steps.

1. Go back to `https://docs.chain.link`, and go to the data feeds and then the price feed addresses. Scroll down to the Sepolia network, search for the ETH/USD pair, and copy it as shown in Figure 8.26.

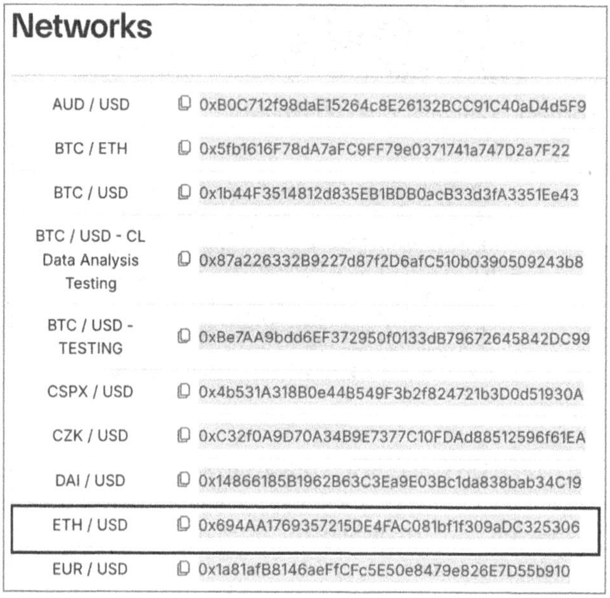

Networks
AUD / USD 0xB0C712f98daE15264c8E26132BCC91C40aD4d5F9
BTC / ETH 0x5fb1616F78dA7aFC9FF79e0371741a747D2a7F22
BTC / USD 0x1b44F3514812d835EB1BDB0acB33d3fA3351Ee43
BTC / USD - CL Data Analysis Testing 0x87a226332B9227d87f2D6afC510b0390509243b8
BTC / USD - TESTING 0xBe7AA9bdd6EF372950f0133dB79672645842DC99
CSPX / USD 0x4b531A318B0e44B549F3b2f824721b3D0d51930A
CZK / USD 0xC32f0A9D70A34B9E7377C10FDAd88512596f61EA
DAI / USD 0x14866185B1962B63C3Ea9E03Bc1da838bab34C19
ETH / USD 0x694AA1769357215DE4FAC081bf1f309aDC325306
EUR / USD 0x1a81afB8146aeFfCFc5E50e8479e826E7D55b910

FIGURE 8.26: ETH/USD price feed

2. Next, go to Chainlink's smart contract kit on GitHub (`https://github.com/smartcontractkit/chainlink`) and download the smart contracts locally using VS code and its terminal (see Figure 8.27).

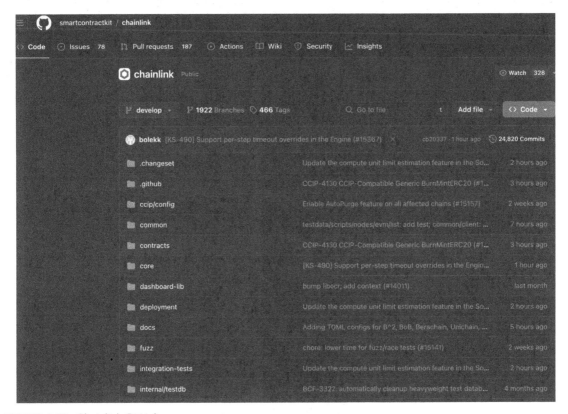

FIGURE 8.27: Chainlink GitHub

3. To do that, open VS Code and the terminal and type the following (see Figure 8.28):

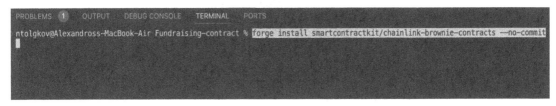

FIGURE 8.28: Downloading Chainlink brownie contracts

```
forge install smartcontractkit/chainlink-brownie-contracts –no-commit
```

4. Press the Enter key to start downloading the files, as shown in Figure 8.29.

FIGURE 8.29: Contracts being downloaded

If you run into any problems with this process, ask your favorite AI assistant. Write a prompt that includes the errors and ask how to mitigate them.

5. After the download finishes, import the `AggregatorV3Interface` contract as part of the contract kit that was just downloaded (see Figure 8.30).

FIGURE 8.30: Path of `AggregatorV3Interface`

6. The path to get to the AggregatorV3Interface is lib ⇨ chainlink-brownie-contracts ⇨ contracts ⇨ src/v0.8 ⇨ shared ⇨ interfaces. There you can see the `AggregatorV3Interface` .`sol` contract. Thus, when going back to the `Fundraising.sol` contract you have been working on in this chapter, you need to add the following import statement:

```
import {AggregatorV3Interface} from "lib/chainlink-brownie-
contracts/contracts/src/v0.8/shared/interfaces/AggregatorV3Interface.sol";
```

between the Solidity version and the definition of the name of the contract, as shown in Figure 8.31.

FIGURE 8.31: Import of `AggregatorV3Interface`

7. After this task is complete, you'll add two functions to the contract. First add the `sendMoney` function that was created previously (you add the second function in Step 8):

```
function priceOfOneETHInUSD() public view returns(uint256) {
```

The `priceOfOneETHInUSD` function is set to `public` and `view`, and returns an variable.

```
    AggregatorV3Interface priceFeed =
AggregatorV3Interface(0x694AA1769357215DE4FAC081bf1f309aDC325306);
```

The previous creates an instance of the `AggregatorV3Interface` contract called `priceFeed` and connects it to the 0x694AA1769357215DE4FAC081bf1f309aDC325306 price feed contract.

```
    (, int256 answer,,, ) = priceFeed.latestRoundData();
```

As shown earlier, `latestRoundData` comes with a tuple. However, explicitly mentioning the whole tuple is not necessary. You can use these formats:

➤ `uint80 roundId`.

➤ `int256 answer`:

➤ `startedAt`

➤ `updatedAt`

➤ `uint80 answeredInRound`

Each variable can be represented with a comma, and only the variable used in the function has to be mentioned. Hence, the `roundId`, `startedAt`, `updatedAt`, and `answeredInRound` parts are not mentioned in the function.

Then the `priceFeed.latestRoundData` retrieves the value of the int256 answer, which is the price of ETH.

```
    return uint256(answer * 1e10); }
```

Finally, the `return` converts the answer to a through typecasting, which requires typing the variable one wants to convert a value to and wrapping it in parentheses, as illustrated. This is done because `int` types can be negative, but the price of ether itself cannot be negative, and hence, converting the `int` answer type to an answer type is required.

Within the parentheses, the answer is multiplied by 1e10. As discussed in previous chapters, the smallest unit of ether is the wei, which, to be represented, must be reflected in ether's price. Thus, the multiplication takes the answer of the oracle, which would be 8 decimals, and increases it to 18 to ensure, just like with the earlier Bitcoin example, absolute precision in the price. This gives the price of 1 ether in USD terms.

```
}
```

The previous function only gets the price of ether in USD.

8. An additional function is needed to make the conversion itself:

```
function convertETHToUSD (uint256 amountOfETH) public view returns(uint256) {
```

The convertETHToUSD function has a local parameter of amountOfETH, which represents the amount of ETH you want to convert into USD in wei and is public and view and returns an variable at the end of the function.

```
    uint256 priceOfETH = priceOfOneETHInUSD();
```

The previous defines an priceOfETH and sets it to the function priceOfOneETHInUSD. Thus, priceOfETH is the price of 1 ETH in USD and has 18 decimals of precision as per the previous function.

```
    uint256 ethPriceInUSD = (priceOfETH *  amountOfETH) / 1e18;
```

The previous defines a ethPriceInUSD and sets it to the result of multiplying priceOfETH, which is the price of 1 ether in USD, by amountOfETH, which represents the amount of ETH in wei that you want to convert into USD, divided by 1e18.

The division by 1e18 happens because both priceOfETH and amountOfETH operate in 18 decimals for precision, the lowest amount of ETH. However, when two numbers with 18 decimals are multiplied, the result is not 18 decimals but 36.

For example, suppose the price of 1 ether is 1,000 USD and you want to convert 1 ether. In that case, 100000000000000 is multiplied by 100000000000000, which gives a result of 10000000000000000000000000000 and hence combines the decimals of both numbers. By dividing this number with 1e18, it scales the number back into 18 decimals, which is the precise number of decimals ether is using: 1000000000000000.

```
    return   ethPriceInUSD; }
```

Finally, the return keyword is used to return the ethPriceInUSD final amount.

```
}
```

9. After adding the two functions in steps 7 and 8, you need to edit the sendMoney function and the minimumAmountSent variable slightly:

```
uint256 public minimumAmountSent = 10e18;

address [] listOfSenders;
mapping (address sender => uint256 amountSent) public amountSentByAddress;

function sendMoney() public payable {
    require(convertETHToUSD(msg.value) >= minimumAmountSent, "Did not send
enough
```

```
money");
    listOfSenders.push(msg.sender);
    amountSentByAddress[msg.sender] = amountSentByAddress[msg.sender] +
msg.value;
```

This adds the `convertETHToUSD` function to the `require` function and wraps the `msg.value` in parentheses. This converts the ether sent, meaning the `msg.value` amount, into its equivalent in USD.

The `10e18` in the public `minimumAmountSent` variable converts the 10 USD into 18 decimals to match ether's 18 decimals.

To keep track of the addresses that sent money to the contract, an array has to be created with the address [] `listOfSenders`. In the `sendMoney` function, `listOfSenders.push(msg.sender)` is made to push the `msg.sender` address into the array and create a list of `msg.sender` addresses.

The `msg.sender` address is a variable of an address type that represents the address that is calling the `sendMoney` function. Thus, whenever an address calls the function, that address is defined as `msg` `.sender` and then added to the address [] `listOfSenders` list to keep track of who sent money to the contract.

However, `msg.sender` is a global variable. Although it is used with the `sendMoney` function, in this case it is not bound to be used only by this specific function; any function can use it. `msg.sender` is helpful for several use cases. Still, the most common is keeping track of addresses that interacted with a specific function, verifying ownership of cryptocurrencies, and controlling access to who could—or could not—call a particular function.

The `amountSentByAddress` mapping uses an address variable and links it to an `uint256` variable named `amountSent`. This variable tracks the total amount an address has sent to the contract at all times the address has interacted with the contract.

The `amountSentByAddress[msg.sender] = amountSentByAddress[msg.sender] + msg.value;` line updates the `amountSentByAddress` mapping to record the amount of ether sent by a specific address every time. For example, if an address sends 10 ether on Tuesday and decides to send 5 more ETH on Friday, this line of code will update the total amount sent to 10 + 5 = 15.

The `amountSentByAddress [msg.sender]` line queries the `amountSentByAddress` mapping for the value of `msg.sender`, the value of the address called the `sendMoney` function. Then, it sets the value of the address already sent plus the `msg.value`, which is the value of the new amount sent. In basic terms, this could also be written as `amountSentByAddress(0x address) = 5 ETH (sent previously) + 3 ETH (sent now) = 8 ETH` in total throughout the lifetime of this address interacting with the contract.

CREATING LIBRARIES

Code parts and functions being reused often can be converted into a library and used frequently without the need to code them from the start. In the code we have so far created, the following functions could be seen as reusable:

```
function priceOfOneETHInUSD() public view returns(uint256) {
    AggregatorV3Interface priceFeed =
```

```
AggregatorV3Interface(0x694AA1769357215DE4FAC081bf1f309aDC325306);
    (, int256 answer,,, ) = priceFeed.latestRoundData();
    return uint256(answer * 1e10);
}

function convertETHToUSD (uint256 amountOfETH) public view returns(uint256) {
    uint256 priceOfETH = priceOfOneETHInUSD();
    uint256 ethPriceInUSD = (priceOfETH * amountOfETH) / 1e18;
    return ethPriceInUSD;
}
```

This is because these functions get the price of 1 ETH in USD and then convert that price from the amount of ETH that wants to be converted to USD. These functions can be used in different contracts, not only for the fundraising contract being built.

A library in Solidity is a contract-like file that stores different highly reusable functions from other contracts. They help save time by not needing to retype those functions from scratch again. To create a library, one has to go back to VS Code and create a new file below the Fundraising.sol, as shown in Figure 8.32.

FIGURE 8.32: Library creation

To create this new library, follow these steps:

1. Within the new file shown in Figure 8.32, type this:

```
//SDPX-License-Identifier: MIT
pragma solidity ^0.8.28;
import {AggregatorV3Interface} from "lib/chainlink-brownie-
contracts/contracts/src/v0.8/shared/interfaces/AggregatorV3Interface.sol";

library ETHtoUSDConverter {

    function priceOfOneETHInUSD() public view returns(uint256) {
        AggregatorV3Interface priceFeed =
AggregatorV3Interface(0x694AA1769357215DE4FAC081bf1f309aDC325306);
        (, int256 answer,,, ) = priceFeed.latestRoundData();
```

```
        return uint256(answer * 1e10);
    }

    function convertETHtoUSD (uint256 amountOfETH) public view
returns(uint256) {
        uint256 priceOfETH = priceOfOneETHInUSD();
        uint256 ethPriceInUSD = (priceOfETH * amountOfETH) / 1e18;
        return ethPriceInUSD;
    }
}
```

This is the same as any contract, and the functions are already known. The only difference is that when defining the contract name, you have to use the keyword `library` instead of contract. The `AggregatorV3Interface` is also imported as it is required for the oracle's price feed.

2. In the fundraising smart contract, delete the `import from`:

```
import {AggregatorV3Interface} from "lib/chainlink-brownie-
contracts/contracts/src/v0.8/shared/interfaces/AggregatorV3Interface.sol";
```

And add this import instead:

```
import {ETHtoUSDConverter} from "./ETHtoUSDConverter.sol";
```

The change of imports is done because the `ETHtoUSDConverter` library is handling all the conversions now and has imported the `AggregatorV3Interface` contract. Hence, the `Fundraiser.sol` contract needs to import the `ETHtoUSDConverter` library instead to handle the conversions since the functions handling the conversion have been moved there, and the following functions need to be deleted from `Fundraiser.sol`:

```
function priceOfOneETHInUSD() public view returns(uint256) {
    AggregatorV3Interface priceFeed =
AggregatorV3Interface(0x694AA1769357215DE4FAC081bf1f309aDC325306);
        (, int256 answer,,, ) = priceFeed.latestRoundData();
        return uint256(answer * 1e10);
}

function convertETHtoUSD (uint256 amountOfETH) public view returns(uint256) {
    uint256 priceOfETH = priceOfOneETHInUSD();
    uint256 ethPriceInUSD = (priceOfETH * amountOfETH) / 1e18;
    return ethPriceInUSD;
}
```

3. Below the fundraising contract name, type this:

```
using ETHtoUSDConverter for uint256;
```

This is a directive that attaches the functions from the `ETHtoUSDConverter` library to all the `uint256` data types in the `Fundraiser.sol` contract. Through this attachment, every `uint256` value defined within the contract can use the library's functions, as shown next.

4. Add this in the `sendMoney` function:

```
function sendMoney() public payable {
    require(convertETHToUSD(msg.value) >= minimumAmountSent, "Did not send
enough
```

```
money");
    listOfSenders.push(msg.sender);
    amountSentByAddress[msg.sender] = amountSentByAddress[msg.sender] +
msg.value;
```

In the require line, change the convertETHToUSD(msg.value) part as it will not be recognized anymore, as the compiler will not know what convertETHToUSD is anymore.

Instead, change that line to this:

```
msg.value.convertETHToUSD()
```

And the whole line should look like this:

```
require(msg.value.convertETHToUSD() >= minimumAmountSent, "Did not send
enough money");
```

As mentioned, using ETHtoUSDConverter for the uint256 directive allows uint256 values to use the functions of the ETHtoUSDConverter library. Without updating the sendMoney function's require line, the compiler would not recognize the previous line as it is now part of the ETHtoUSDConverter library.

The Fundraiser.sol contract should now look like Figure 8.33.

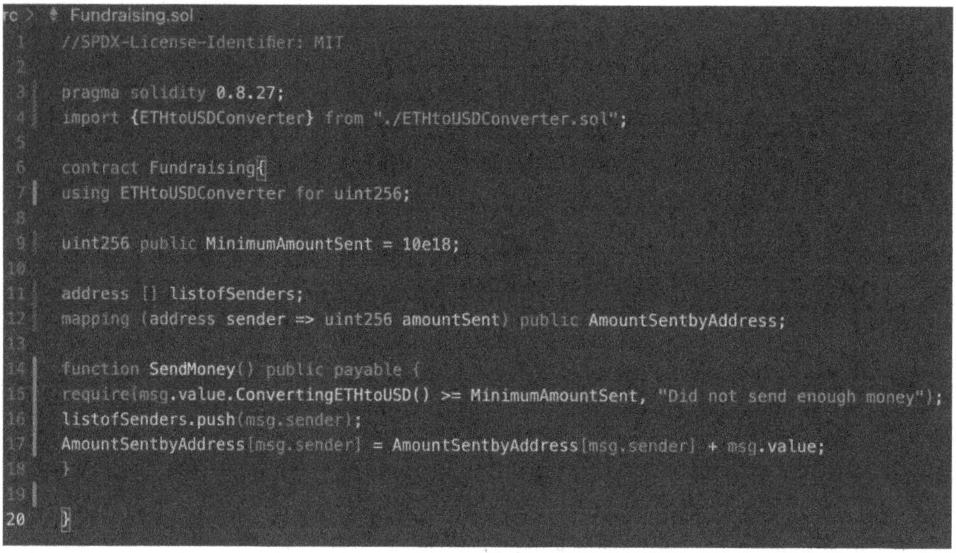

FIGURE 8.33: Fundraiser.sol contract status

The library should look like Figure 8.34

WITHDRAW FUNCTION

After creating the function to send money to the contract, collecting the addresses that send money to the contract, seeing how much money an address has sent throughout its lifetime, and converting

ETH to USD, it is time to build the `withdraw` function, which allows you to withdraw the money that the different addresses have sent.

```
ETHtoUSDConverter.sol
// SPDX-License-Identifier: MIT
pragma solidity 0.8.27;

import {AggregatorV3Interface} from "lib/chainlink-brownie-contracts/contracts/src/v0.8/shared/interfaces/AggregatorV3Interface.sol";

library ETHtoUSDConverter {

    function PriceofOneETHinUSD() internal view returns (uint256) {
        AggregatorV3Interface priceFeed = AggregatorV3Interface(0x694AA1769357215DE4FAC081bf1f309aDC325306);
        (, int256 answer, , , ) = priceFeed.latestRoundData();
        return uint256(answer * 1e10);
    }

    function ConvertingETHtoUSD(uint256 AmountofETH) internal view returns (uint256) {
        uint256 PriceofETH = PriceofOneETHinUSD();
        uint256 ETHPriceinUSD = (PriceofETH * AmountofETH) / 1e18;
        return ETHPriceinUSD;
    }
}
```

FIGURE 8.34: `Library.sol` library status

Resetting the Mappings

When withdrawing money, the first step is to reset all the mappings. This is done for security purposes and to prevent hacks or reentrancy attacks. If a contract allows withdrawals without resetting mappings and the `withdraw` function hasn't finished executing, a malicious actor could exploit this to drain funds. In that case, a malicious party can initiate the withdrawal function and drain the wallet first. This is called the Checks, Effects, Interactions (CEI) pattern. Checks is a reminder to check the conditions and requirements to meet such as resetting the mappings, updating balances, etc. Effects stands for the reminder of updating the state of the contract such as actually resetting the mappings and updating the balances. Interactions stands for the final step of performing the actual action, which is the withdrawal of the funds or the sending of the funds to another address.

To reset the mappings, you have to use the `for` loop. A `for` loop executes a particular piece of code repeatedly as long as a specified condition evaluates to be true. It is worth remembering that indexing in mappings, arrays, and any other data structure starts counting from 0. Thus, the first address saved will not be stored in number 1 but 0. The second address will be stored in number 1 and so forth. The index is written like this:

```
for(starting index, ending index, increment amount)
```

This uses the `for` keyword and then opens a parentheses pair, which uses a starting index as a basis for a statement to start as true.

For example, say Mike goes to the store and buys five apples. When he comes home, he eats all of them one after the other. If that were a `for` loop, it would look like this:

```
for(uint256 apple = 0; ./* remember the first apple starts counting at 0 */
apple
< 5;  apple++)
```

This loop starts counting from 0, the first apple Mike starts eating; hence, it is the starting index. The apple with index 4 is the fifth apple Mike will eat and, therefore, the last one and the ending index. The number of apples represents the increment, updated each time the loop runs.

In this case, it is apple++. The plus signs, ++, signify a shortcut you can use instead of writing apple = apple + 1, which would mean setting the number of apples to the variable apple plus one. If the number of apples is 0, it would become 1, then 2, then 3, and finally 4. The apples would have been exhausted, and the loop would have stopped.

Thus, instead of writing apple = apple + 1, you can substitute that with apple++, which means the same thing. This apple++ is not explicitly used only for the for loop. It can also be used in any other instance where you have to take an x variable and do x = x + 1.

When it comes to the Fundraiser.sol contract, the for loop should look like this:

```
function withdraw() public {
```

The function is called withdraw and is public, meaning it can be called both internally and externally.

```
for (uint256 senderIndex = 0; senderIndex < listOfSenders.length;
senderIndex++) {
```

The for keyword initializes the loop. Inside the parentheses, a uint256 variable named senderIndex is set to 0, representing the loop's starting index.

The condition senderIndex < listOfSenders.length determines when the loop will stop. The listOfSenders.length refers to the total number of elements currently in the listOfSenders array. For example, if the array contains five addresses, listOfSenders.length will return 5. Adding more addresses dynamically adjusts this value to match the array's size. The senderIndex++ increases the index by one every time the loop is successfully repeated.

```
address sender = listOfSenders[senderIndex];
```

Each repetition retrieves the address at the current index of that specific repetition number (senderIndex) from the listOfSenders array and stores it in the defined address that was defined and named as sender.

```
amountSentByAddress[sender] = 0;
} }
```

Finally, by using the sender address from the array, the previous resets the value in the amountSentByAddress mapping to 0.

Resetting the listOfSenders Array

The next step is to reset the listOfSenders array as well by typing the following:

```
listOfSenders = new address[](0);
```

This sets the `listOfSenders` array to a new array type of address `[]`, meaning that it still stores addresses and that the size of the array is set to zero. This, in effect, resets the previous array to zero.

Sending ETH from a Contract

After having reset both the mapping and the array, it is time to withdraw the funds from the contract. There are three different ways of withdrawing money from a contract: transfer, send, and call, each with its own advantages.

Transfer

The following withdrawal mechanism has a `msg.sender` address that is wrapped in the payable function:

```
payable(msg.sender).transfer(address(this).balance);
```

When a `msg.sender` address is wrapped in the `payable` keyword, it is converted into a payable address capable of receiving payments. The `.transfer` part is a function that sends money from a smart contract to another address. The `(address(this).balance` refers to the address of this contract being built now, and the balance refers to its monetary balance. The line of code transfers the balance of this smart contract's address to the `msg.sender` address, which signifies any address that will call the `withdraw` function of the contract as a whole.

There are several advantages and disadvantages of using this method to withdraw ether from the smart contract to another address:

Advantages

➤ It is a straightforward line of code to use.

➤ The transfer method has a gas limit of 2,300, enhancing security by preventing complex attacks that exceed this limit. Malicious attempts to exploit the withdraw function in combination with the transfer method will fail as they typically require more gas, causing the transfer to throw an error and revert.

Disadvantages

➤ The 2,300 gas cap and simplicity of the line of code have disadvantages, too, because when combined with a complex function, it would not be able to be reverted.

Send

The following method of sending money is the same as the transfer one, except for two differences. First, it replaces `.transfer` with `.send`, which, like `.transfer`, signifies the desire to send money from the contract to another address. The second difference is that unlike `.transfer`, it does not throw an error and revert but instead returns a Boolean value: `true` if the transfer succeeds, `false` if it fails.

```
bool sendSuccess = payable(msg.sender).send(address(this).balance);
require(sendSuccess, "Send failed");
```

The `require` statement in the end requires that the Boolean is positive and return `true`; if not, the `"Send failed"` message should be displayed.

The following are the advantages and disadvantages of using the send method:

Advantages

➤ It allows developers to handle failures in sending the funds programmatically, enabling them to display when the sending of funds fails.

➤ Similarly to the `transfer` method, the 2,300 gas still stands, protecting from various hacking attacks that may use import and inheritance, combining the function with other malicious functions to try and withdraw the funds.

Disadvantages

➤ Similarly, the 2,300 gas can be a disadvantage as the send does not offer the opportunity to be combined with more complex functions.

Call

```
(bool callSuccess,) = payable(msg.sender).call{value: address(this)
.balance}("");
require(callSuccess, "Call failed");
```

The following method of withdrawing Ether has several similarities to the previous ones:

```
(bool callSuccess,) = payable(msg.sender).call{value: address(this)
.balance}("");
require(callSuccess, "Call failed");
```

For one, it also uses an `msg.sender` address wrapped in `payable` to make the address capable of receiving funds, the `.call` similar to `.send` and `.transfer` signifies the desire to withdraw the funds from the contract and send it to the `msg.sender` address. Within the brackets there is a value, which means the value you may want to send in the withdrawal process. In this case, `address(this)` `.balance` signifies the withdrawal of all the funds within the contract. The `("")` part allows for the possibility to call another function in conjunction with transferring the funds, which is not possible in the two previous methods that were seen. Additionally, the Boolean in the `.call` method has an additional comma, unlike the Boolean of `.send`. This is because a variable called bytes memory `returnData` is being ignored. This variable is valid when a contract has been programmed to send data or a message with the withdrawal. By adding a comma in this case and not mentioning the bytes memory `returnData`, one lets the compiler know to ignore this part.

The advantages and disadvantages of using `.call` include the following:

Advantages

➤ No fixed gas limit allows transfers to recipients requiring more gas for execution.

➤ It can consist of additional data or specify gas limits if needed.

Disadvantages

➤ Forwarding all gas makes it more prone to hack attacks unless precautions are taken.

➤ It requires careful implementation to avoid bugs and vulnerabilities.

For the `Fundraiser.sol` contract, the `.call` function will be used. Thus, you should type this in your contract to withdraw ETH:

```
(bool callSuccess,) = payable(msg.sender).call{value: address(this).balance}
("");
require(callSuccess, "Call failed");
```

Generally, the different functions for withdrawing ETH are evaluated case by case, but the most used is the `.call` function.

Thus, the entire `withdraw` function should look like this:

```
function withdraw() public {
    for (uint256 senderIndex = 0; senderIndex < listOfSenders.length;
senderIndex++) {
        address sender = listOfSenders[senderIndex];
        amountSentByAddress[sender] = 0;
    }
    listOfSenders = new address[](0);

    (bool callSuccess,) = payable(msg.sender).call{value: address(this)
.balance}
("");
    require(callSuccess, "Call failed");
}
```

CONSTRUCTOR

One problem with the `withdraw` function created earlier in this chapter is that anyone can call the function and withdraw the money, which is impractical since the contract owner should be the only person who can withdraw the funds.

To make the contract owner the only address to withdraw the funds, you have to create a constructor—something that was briefly shown earlier in this chapter and that you will now see in more depth.

A constructor is a unique Solidity function executed only once. It is the first thing to be called and executed in a smart contract during deployment. In addition to setting the owner as the only person to withdraw the funds, constructors are usually used to define initial and crucial variables or execute logic that must happen once the contract is deployed. The constructor is always called and executed in the same transaction that deploys the contract. Hence, the caller of the constructor is always the address that deploys the whole contract.

Constructors do not use visibility levels, and the `function` keyword, like every other function in Solidity, does not define them.

To define a constructor, follow these steps:

1. Go to the `Fundraising.sol` contract and type the following:

    ```
    constructor () {
    }
    ```

    The `constructor` word tells the compiler that this is a constructor function. If necessary, local parameters can be defined within the parentheses, and the constructor's logic is included within the brackets.

2. To define the owner as the only address that can call the withdraw function, the first create an address variable that corresponds to the address of the owner:

    ```
    address public owner;
    ```

    This variable is a public address, meaning it can be called both internally and externally, and it is named `owner`.

3. After having defined the address, in the constructor:

    ```
    constructor () {
        owner = msg.sender;
    }
    ```

This declaration sets the owner address to the `msg.sender`. As previously mentioned, the constructor is called in the same transaction as when deploying a contract, and the `msg.sender` reflects the address that last interacted and is called a *function*. The `msg.sender` represents the contract's deployer. Within the constructor, the deployer as `msg.sender` is set as the owner.

The final result when it comes to the constructor in the `Fundraising` contract should look like Figure 8.35.

FIGURE 8.35: Defining a constructor

4. To complete the aim of having only the owner of the contract be able to call the `withdraw` function, a small addition has to be made to the `withdraw` function itself:

    ```
    function withdraw() public {
        require(msg.sender == owner, "Only the owner of the contract can
    withdraw");
        for (uint256 senderIndex = 0; senderIndex < listOfSenders.length;
    senderIndex++) {
            address sender = listOfSenders[senderIndex];
            amountSentByAddress[sender] = 0;
        }
        listOfSenders = new address[](0);
    ```

```
    (bool callSuccess,) = payable(msg.sender).call{value: address(this)
.balance}
("");
    require(callSuccess, "Call failed");
}
```

This addition includes the `require` statement inside the `withdraw` function. For an address to call the withdraw function, it is required to be equal to the `owner`. In Solidity, a single `"="` means "set to" as in `uint256 number = 1`; set the `uint256` called number to 1. The `"=="` means equal to; `msg.sender == owner` means the `msg.sender` address equals the address of the owner. Thus, the `require` statement becomes a requirement before being able to call the `withdraw` function in the first place.

MODIFIERS

While extremely useful, the problem with an access control mechanism like `require(msg .sender == owner, "Only the owner of the contract can withdraw")` is that if a contract has many access control mechanisms, then you have to copy and paste the same `require` statement to many functions. To avoid that, one can create what are known as *modifiers*.

Modifiers are blocks of code that can be reused to add functionality to a function. You can add the modifier to the function header beside the visibility levels of a function, such as `public`, `private`, `internal`, `view`, `returns`, etc.

To create a modifier, go to the bottom of the contract and type this:

```
modifier onlyTheOwnerCanExecute() {}
```

This is how a modifier is defined with the keyword `modifier`, parentheses, and brackets.

To create a modifier with `require(msg.sender == owner, "Only the owner of the contract can withdraw");`, move the statement from the `withdraw` function into the `onlyTheOwnerCan Execute` modifier and remove it from the function:

```
modifier onlyTheOwnerCanExecute() {
    require(msg.sender == owner, "Only the owner of the contract can
withdraw");
    _;
}
```

The `_;` of a modifier is a placeholder that tells the compiler where to insert and execute the code of the function that uses the modifier. Code before `_;` in the modifier runs *before the function*, and code after `_;` runs *after the function*, if present. This allows the modifier to control and extend the behavior of functions.

To add the modifier and thus the `require` statement into the `withdraw` function again, add the `onlyTheOwnerCanExecute` name onto the function header like this:

```
function withdraw() public onlyTheOwnerCanExecute {
    for (uint256 senderIndex = 0; senderIndex < listOfSenders.length;
senderIndex++) {
```

```
        address sender = listOfSenders[senderIndex];
        amountSentByAddress[sender] = 0;
    }
    listOfSenders = new address[](0);

    (bool callSuccess,) = payable(msg.sender).call{value: address(this)
.balance}
("");
    require(callSuccess, "Call failed");
}
```

TESTING THE CONTRACT BY DEPLOYING IT ON A TEST NETWORK

The contract so far should look like this:

```
//SPDX-License-Identifier: MIT

pragma solidity 0.8.27;
import {ETHtoUSDConverter} from "./ETHtoUSDConverter.sol";

contract Fundraising {
    using ETHtoUSDConverter for uint256;

    uint256 public minimumAmountSent = 10e18;

    address[] listOfSenders;
    mapping (address sender => uint256 amountSent) public amountSentByAddress;

    address public owner;

    constructor() {
        owner = msg.sender;
    }

    function sendMoney() public payable {
        require(msg.value.convertETHToUSD() >= minimumAmountSent, "Did not send
enough money");
        listOfSenders.push(msg.sender);
        amountSentByAddress[msg.sender] = amountSentByAddress[msg.sender] +
msg.value;
    }

    function withdraw() public onlyTheOwnerCanExecute {
        for (uint256 senderIndex = 0; senderIndex < listOfSenders.length;
senderIndex++) {
            address sender = listOfSenders[senderIndex];
            amountSentByAddress[sender] = 0;
        }
        listOfSenders = new address[](0);
```

```
        (bool callSuccess,) = payable(msg.sender).call{value: address(this)
.balance}("");
        require(callSuccess, "Call failed");
    }

    modifier onlyTheOwnerCanExecute() {
        require(msg.sender == owner, "Only owner can withdraw funds");
        _;
    }
}
```

To ensure that everything goes well, compile the contract by typing **forge build** in the terminal and pressing Enter. Figure 8.36 shows that the contract was compiled successfully.

```
ntolgkov@Alexandross-MacBook-Air Fundraising-contract % forge build
[⠿] Compiling...
[⠿] Compiling 1 files with Solc 0.8.27
[⠿] Solc 0.8.27 finished in 142.49ms
Compiler run successful!
ntolgkov@Alexandross-MacBook-Air Fundraising-contract % █
```

FIGURE 8.36: Compilation successful

> **NOTE** *If you have problems with the compilation, there are problems or errors in the code. Scan for mistakes and/or use an AI assistant by copying and pasting the contract code and the error message you get and ask the AI to see what problems there might be.*

After successfully compiling the contract, go to Remix to run it on the Sepolia Test Network to see how it works. This can be done through scripts as well, but Remix is an alternative that is used to quickly check if a contract works without the need to deploy scripts and go through the whole process.

1. On Remix, create the files for both the `Fundraiser.sol` contract as well as the `ETHtoUSDConverter.sol` library, as shown in Figure 8.37.

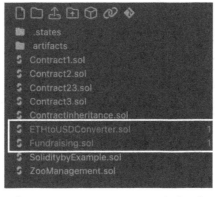

FIGURE 8.37: `Fundraising.sol` and `ETHtoUSDConverter.sol` in Remix

2. After creating the files, copy and paste the contract and the library into their respective files, as shown in Figures 8.38 and 8.39.

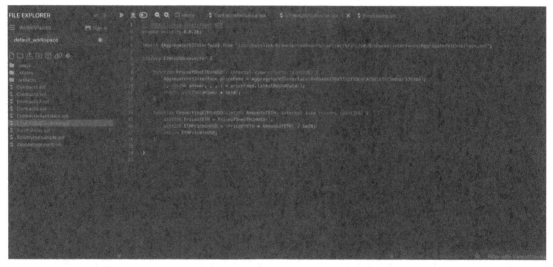

FIGURE 8.38: `ETHtoUSDConverter.sol` library

```
1    //SPDX-License-Identifier: MIT
2
3    pragma solidity 0.8.26;
4    import {ETHtoUSDConverter} from "./ETHtoUSDConverter.sol";
5
6    contract Fundraising {
7        using ETHtoUSDConverter for uint256;
8
9        uint256 public minimumAmountSent = 10e18;
10
11       address[] listOfSenders;
12       mapping (address sender => uint256 amountSent) public amountSentByAddress;
13
14       address public owner;
15
16       constructor() {
17           owner = msg.sender;
18       }
19
20       function sendMoney() public payable {
21           require(msg.value.convertETHtoUSD() >= minimumAmountSent, "Did not send enough money");
22           listOfSenders.push(msg.sender);
23           amountSentByAddress[msg.sender] = amountSentByAddress[msg.sender] + msg.value;
24       }
25
26       function withdraw() public onlyTheOwnerCanExecute {
27           for (uint256 senderIndex = 0; senderIndex < listOfSenders.length; senderIndex++) {
28               address sender = listOfSenders[senderIndex];
29               amountSentByAddress[sender] = 0;
30           }
31           listOfSenders = new address[](0);
32
33           (bool callSuccess,) = payable(msg.sender).call{value: address(this).balance}("");
```

FIGURE 8.39: `Fundraising.sol` contract

It is crucial to make two fundamental changes:

1. If required, change the solidity version to the one suggested by the compiler when the cursor is hovered over `//SPDX-License-Identifier: MIT`.

2. As shown in Figure 8.40, change the import path for the `chainlink-brownie-contracts` from `lib/chainlink-brownie-contracts/contracts/src/v0.8/shared/interfaces/AggregatorV3Interface.sol` to `@chainlink/contracts/src/v0.8/shared/interfaces/AggregatorV3Interface.sol`.

```
4    import {AggregatorV3Interface} from "@chainlink/contracts/src/v0.8/shared/interfaces/AggregatorV3Interface.sol";
```

FIGURE 8.40: Changed import path

3. Next, go to the Deploy & Run Transactions section. Once there, change the environment from its default position to Injected Provider MetaMask, ensure that the Contract to be deployed is the `Fundraising.sol`, and click Deploy (see Figure 8.41).

FIGURE 8.41: Demonstration of correct Environment and Deploy

4. As shown earlier in this chapter when deploying the `DataConsumerV3` contract, after clicking Deploy, the installed MetaMask extension will pop up asking for confirmation to deploy the contract. Ensure the contract is deployed on Sepolia; the test network gas fees the deployment of the contract will cost should pop up before the final confirmation button. After a few seconds, the contract should be automatically deployed.

Once the contract is deployed, you can see the functions that have been created and are available, as shown in Figure 8.42.

➤ `sendMoney`: To send money to the contract

➤ `withdraw`: To withdraw the funds from the contract

➤ `amountSentByAddress`: Asking for input on an address to see how much money the address has sent over its lifetime

➤ `minimumAmountSent`: The minimum amount you can send

➤ `owner`: The address of the owner of the contract

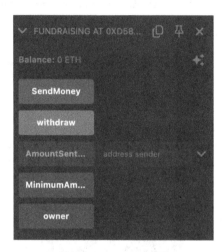

FIGURE 8.42: Contract functions

5. Go to the value section of the Deploy And Run Transactions pane and in the value section add 10000000000000000 (16 zeros) wei or 0.01 ETH. The result is shown in Figure 8.43.

FIGURE 8.43: Value: 10000000000000000 wei

6. Click the `sendMoney` function, and MetaMask will ask you to confirm the transaction, as shown in Figure 8.44.

7. Click the Confirm button and wait a few seconds for the transaction to be confirmed. When confirmed, you can see that the contract now has 0.01 ETH, as shown in Figure 8.45.

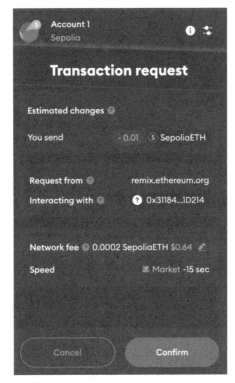

FIGURE 8.44: MetaMask confirmation

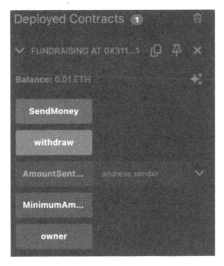

FIGURE 8.45: 0.01 ETH in the contract address

8. Go to the amountSentByAddress and copy your connected to Remix MetaMask address, as shown in Figure 8.46.

FIGURE 8.46: MetaMask address to be copied

9. Paste the MetaMask wallet's address in the blank "address sender" space and click the function amountSentByAddress. The amount that the address has sent in its lifetime will appear, as shown in Figure 8.47.

FIGURE 8.47: Lifetime wei sent by address

If another 0.01 ETH is to be sent to the address in the same way, then the same address will have double the money sent from what it has reflected now, as shown in Figure 8.48.

FIGURE 8.48: Lifetime wei sent by address doubled

You can now see that the balance is 0.02, and the amountSentByAddress is double what it was before.

Since the contract was deployed by the same address that sent the 0.02 ETH, the same address can withdraw the amount that it sent to the address by clicking Withdraw. In that case, MetaMask pops up again to confirm the transaction. However, before the confirmation, it is crucial to check the current balance of the address when it comes to SepoliaETH, as shown in Figure 8.49.

Then, the confirmation from MetaMask pops up for the confirmation of the transaction, as shown in Figure 8.50.

FIGURE 8.49: Sepolia address balance before withdrawal

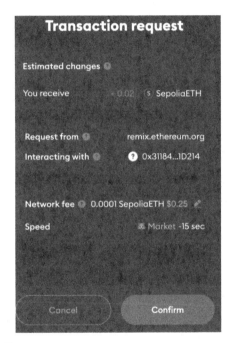

FIGURE 8.50: MetaMask confirmation

You can see that the MetaMask transaction request has in the "Estimated Changes" section that the address will receive 0.02 SepoliaETH. You can also see that the request comes from `https://remix.ethereum.org` (which makes sense since the wallet is connected to MetaMask), the address of the deployed contract that the wallet is interacting with, the network fee that will be paid for the transaction to take place, how much it is worth in USD (0.25), and the time that the transaction will take, which is 15 seconds.

After confirming the transaction and waiting for a few seconds, you can see that the balance of the contract has reverted to 0, as shown in Figure 8.51.

FIGURE 8.51: Contract balance and amount sent of address

As coded before in the contract, the amountSentByAddress has been reverted to 0. Meanwhile, the MetaMask address has gone to 0.0628 from 0.0429 before a 0.0199 increase in balance. It would be 0.02, but as per the message on MetaMask, there was a small gas fee to pay for the transaction. Hence, it is 0.0628 instead of 0.0629, as shown in Figure 8.52.

FIGURE 8.52: MetaMask address balance after withdrawal

In Remix's terminal, click View On Etherscan to view the latest transaction that occurred between the wallet address and the contract address, as shown in Figure 8.53.

Besides the 0.02 withdrawal, if you click the To address link you can see the contract address that was deployed and the various transactions that took place between MetaMask's externally owned account and the smart contract address, as shown in Figure 8.54.

IMMUTABILITY AND CONSTANTS

When you deploy the Fundraiser.sol contract again, this time not on the injected provider MetaMask but on the Remix VM (Cancun), as shown in Figure 8.55, go to the Remix terminal. You'll see a message of the successful deployment of the contract, as shown in Figure 8.56.

Click the message to display details of the transaction that it took to deploy the contract on the test network. Scroll down through the information, and you will eventually come across the gas costs for deploying the contract, as shown in Figure 8.57.

FIGURE 8.53: Transaction of the 0.02 ETH withdrawal

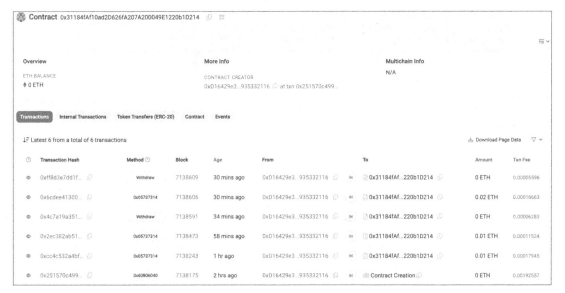

FIGURE 8.54: Smart contract address and transactions

The transaction cost of deploying the contract is 741,826 gas.

FIGURE 8.55: Remix VM Cancun

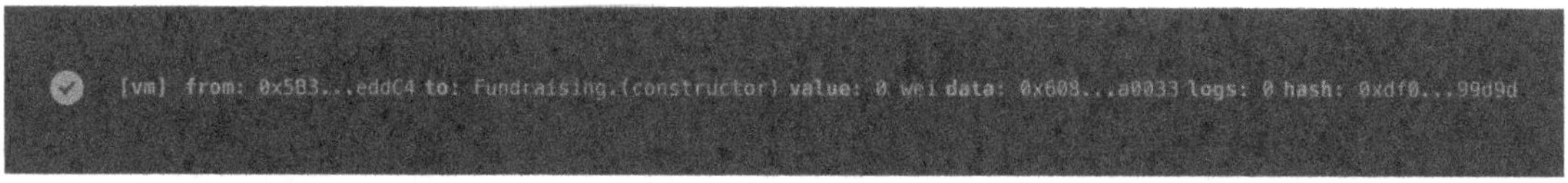

[vm] from: 0x5B3...eddC4 to: Fundraising.(constructor) value: 0 wei data: 0x608...a0033 logs: 0 hash: 0xdf0...99d9d

FIGURE 8.56: Successful deployment of contract message

gas	853100 gas
transaction cost	741826 gas
execution cost	642700 gas

FIGURE 8.57: Gas costs of deploying the contract in its current state

Solidity has a number of keywords that can be used with variables to lower gas costs when deploying a smart contract:

➤ **Constant:** This keyword is used, and the value is fixed at the compile time, which is when the compiler translates the code into bytecode for the EVM, and once a variable is declared constant, it cannot be altered anymore at all.

➤ **Immutable:** This keyword is used for values that are going to be used in the constructor of a contract and that will remain unchanged.

Let's look at the two variables in the `Fundraising.sol` contract:

```
uint256 public minimumAmountSent = 10e18;
```

Used in the `sendMoney` function, the `minimumAmountSent` variable needs to get the constant keyword in addition to the `public` keyword. Constant variables tend to be named with capital letters, so this line will change:

```
uint256 public constant MINIMUM_AMOUNT_SENT = 10e18;
```

If now the same contract were to be deployed with the only change being the `constant` keyword in the `minimumAmountSent` function, the gas costs would be reduced to 721,693 gas, as shown in Figure 8.58.

gas
829947 gas
transaction cost
721693 gas
execution cost
622595 gas

FIGURE 8.58: Gas costs with `constant` keyword

This is more than 20,000 gas that was saved with simply one additional keyword. If you go to Etherscan, you can see the current cost of gas in gwei (see Figure 8.59).

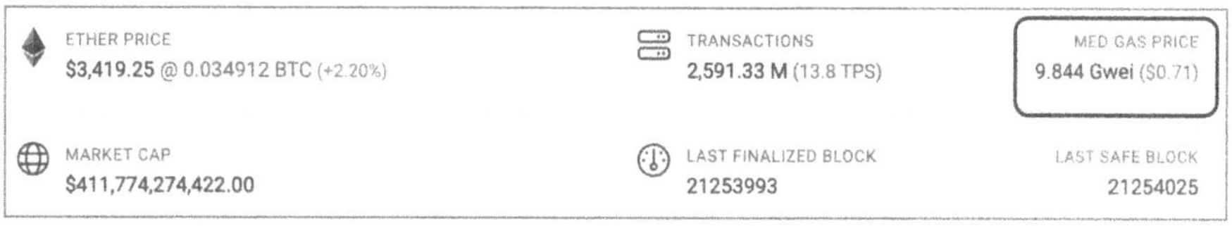
ETHER PRICE
$3,419.25 @ 0.034912 BTC (+2.20%)
TRANSACTIONS
2,591.33 M (13.8 TPS)
MED GAS PRICE
9.844 Gwei ($0.71)
MARKET CAP
$411,774,274,422.00
LAST FINALIZED BLOCK
21253993
LAST SAFE BLOCK
21254025

FIGURE 8.59: Current gas costs in Gwei via Etherscan

The gas price is 9.844 Gwei at the time of writing and 0.71 USD. Go to a gwei, ether, and wei converter (find these by searching online) and convert the 9.844 gwei into wei, as shown in Figure 8.60.

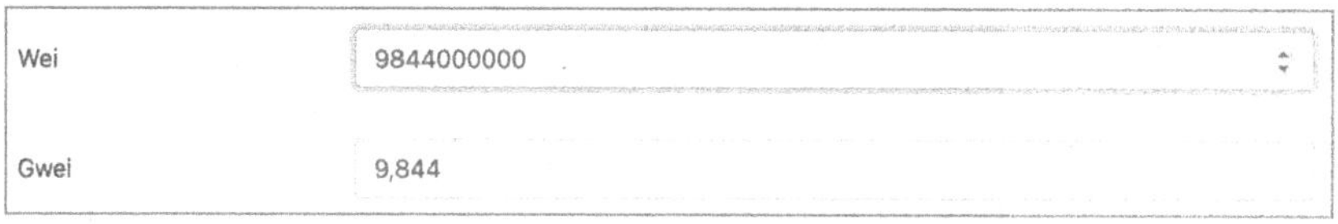
Wei
9844000000
Gwei
9,844

FIGURE 8.60: Gwei into wei conversion

Multiplying 741,826 (gas) * 9844000000 (wei) results in 7,302,535,144,000,000. Then go back to the gwei, ether, wei converter and paste the result in the wei box, as shown in Figure 8.61.

Thus, to execute the function without the `constant` keyword, one would at the time of writing, pay 24.94 USD.

If you were to use the constant keyword and have the gas costs be 721,693 instead, you can make the multiplication of 721,693 (gas) * 9844000000 (wei) which results in: 7,104,345,892,000,000. If you take that result to the wei, gwei, and ether calculator, you would discover that with the constant keyword being used you would pay 24.26 USD per transaction which is 68 cents less than you would otherwise pay (given in the conditions at the time of writing). See Figure 8.62.

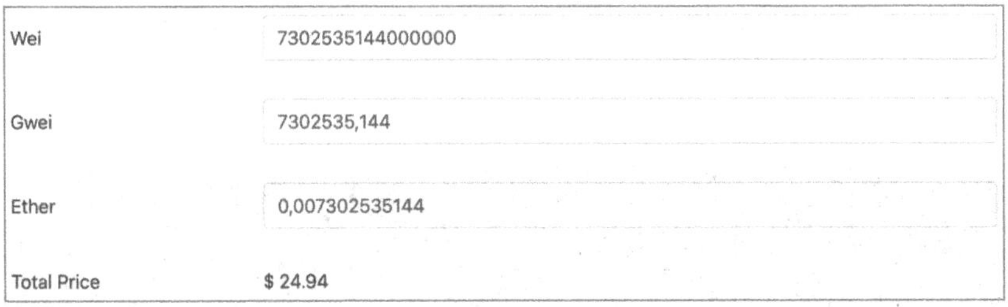

Wei	7302535144000000
Gwei	7302535,144
Ether	0,007302535144
Total Price	$ 24.94

FIGURE 8.61: Gas price without the `constant` keyword

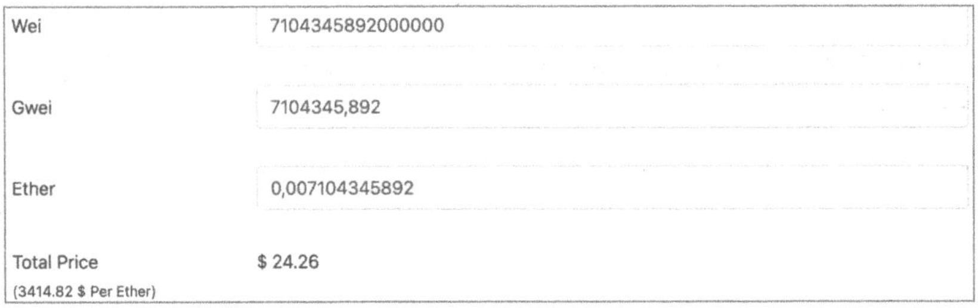

Wei	7104345892000000
Gwei	7104345,892
Ether	0,007104345892
Total Price (3414.82 $ Per Ether)	$ 24.26

FIGURE 8.62: Gas price with `constant` keyword

Okay, 68 cents might not look like much, but keep in mind two scenarios:

➤ **Scenario 1**: Say the same person is using the same function multiple times. Although possibly quite far-fetched with almost a 25 USD fee per transaction fee, a reduction fee of 68 cents per transaction is a significant amount.

➤ **Scenario 2**: Even if someone were to call the function once and pay 68 cents extra, if there were 10,000 people across the world that were to donate to the fundraiser contract, that would accumulate to 6,800 wasted USD in total.

Thus, with just one keyword a significant amount of money can be saved.

However, if you were to also add the `immutable` keyword to the owner address (see Figure 8.63), you can see that the gas costs fell even further to 698,522:

```
address public immutable i_owner;
```

gas	803301 gas
transaction cost	698522 gas
execution cost	600092 gas

FIGURE 8.63: Gas costs with immutable keyword

If you do the previous calculation with this gas price: 698,522 (gwei) * 9844000000 (wei) that would be: 6,876,250,568,000,000. When you use the result in the calculator, as shown in Figure 8.64, the transaction would be 23,53 USD which is saving 1,11 USD per transaction(s)

Wei	6876250568000000
Gwei	6876250,568
Ether	0,006876250568
Total Price	$ 23.53

FIGURE 8.64: Gas price with `constant` and `immutable` together

This illustrates the usefulness of these keywords. Use them to save gas wherever and whenever possible.

CUSTOM ERRORS

Another way to improve gas efficiency in the contract is through *custom errors*. Custom errors were introduced specifically to improve gas efficiency and serve as an alternative to the `require` statement.

You can implement custom errors using and defining the `error` keyword followed by a name.

To use a custom error, define a custom error at the very top of the file you are working on—even before the contract definition—by writing this:

```
error NotTheOwner();
```

Figure 8.65 shows what this looks like.

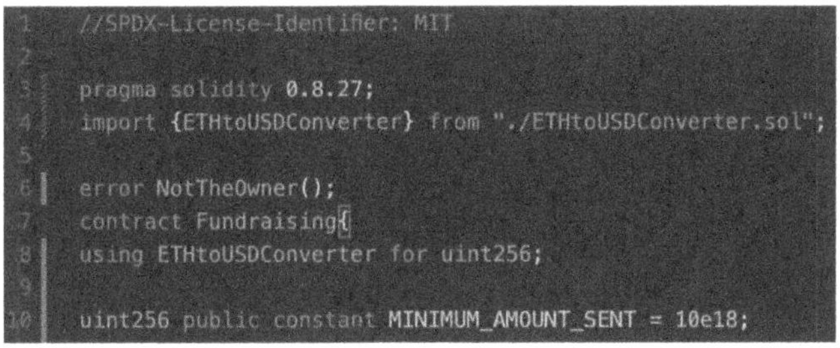

```
//SPDX-License-Identifier: MIT

pragma solidity 0.8.27;
import {ETHtoUSDConverter} from "./ETHtoUSDConverter.sol";

error NotTheOwner();
contract Fundraising{
using ETHtoUSDConverter for uint256;

uint256 public constant MINIMUM_AMOUNT_SENT = 10e18;
```

FIGURE 8.65: `error NotTheOwner();` example

If you examine the modifier created previously, you will see a problem that uses additional gas:

```
modifier onlyTheOwnerCanExecute() {
    require(msg.sender == owner, "Only owner can withdraw funds");
    _;
}
```

The problem with additional gas is the message `"Only owner can withdraw funds"`, as this requires extra storage in the block to be saved. Instead, you could replace the `require` statement within the modifier with an `if` statement and write this:

```
modifier  onlyTheOwnerCanExecute() {
    if(msg.sender != i_owner) {revert NotTheOwner();}
    _;
}
```

This defines the modifier with the same name, but within the modifier itself, the logic changes dramatically. Instead of a `require` statement as was created before, one uses an `if` conditionality statement, which says the following: "If the address message sender is not (the `!=` symbol means something is not equal) the owner, then revert the modifier, citing the error that was just defined." This problem solves the extra capacity messaging that letters can take.

RECEIVE AND FALLBACK FUNCTIONS

One common problem contracts that get money sent to them have is that people do not necessarily need to use the functions the smart contract has defined in order to send them money. A person can simply use the address of a smart contract and send them money without the need for a function. However, the problem with this method is that if someone sends money like this, the `sendMoney` function would not get triggered, and hence the owner of the function would not have the participant's information stored in the arrays and mappings that are probably predefined.

There are two functions in Solidity that have been designed for this exact purpose. When someone sends money to an address without using any functions, out of the blue, `receive` can be used to trigger and execute a certain function or custom-made code within the contract automatically such as, for example, `sendMoney` and store the address and the amount sent in the array and mappings that have been predefined.

The following shows how these two functions work and are created:

```
receive() external payable {
    sendMoney();
}

fallback() external payable {
    sendMoney();
}
```

`receive` will be triggered every time someone simply sends money with no messages and executes the logic within the `sendMoney` function. The `fallback` function is triggered when a transaction that is being sent has additional data such as a message attached to it.

The final project should look like this:

```
//SPDX-License-Identifier: MIT

pragma solidity 0.8.27;
import {ETHtoUSDConverter} from "./ETHtoUSDConverter.sol";

error NotTheOwner();
```

```
contract Fundraising{
    using ETHtoUSDConverter for uint256;

    uint256 public constant MINIMUM_AMOUNT_SENT = 10e18;

    address[] listOfSenders;
    mapping (address sender => uint256 amountSent) public amountSentByAddress;

    address public immutable i_owner;

    constructor() {
        i_owner = msg.sender;
    }

    function sendMoney() public payable {
        require(msg.value.convertETHToUSD() >= MINIMUM_AMOUNT_SENT,
"Did not send
enough money");
        listOfSenders.push(msg.sender);
        amountSentByAddress[msg.sender] = amountSentByAddress[msg.sender] +
msg.value;
    }

    function withdraw() public onlyTheOwnerCanExecute {
        for (uint256 senderIndex = 0; senderIndex < listOfSenders.length;
senderIndex++) {
            address sender = listOfSenders[senderIndex];
            amountSentByAddress[sender] = 0;
        }
        listOfSenders = new address[](0);

        (bool callSuccess,) = payable(msg.sender).call{value: address(this)
.balance}("");
        require(callSuccess, "Call failed");
    }

    modifier onlyTheOwnerCanExecute() {
        require(msg.sender == i_owner, "Only owner can withdraw funds");
        _;
    }
}
```

CHAPTER 8 QUESTIONS

1. Can you explain the purpose of Chainlink oracles in smart contracts and why they're necessary? Give a specific example of when you'd need one.

2. Walk me through the security considerations in implementing a withdrawal function in a smart contract. What pattern should you follow and why?

3. Compare and contrast the three methods of sending ETH from a smart contract (`.transfer`, `.send`, and `.call`). Which would you recommend in a modern contract and why?

4. Explain the importance of resetting mappings and arrays before performing withdrawals. What vulnerability does this prevent?

5. What's the purpose of the `using` directive in Solidity? Give an example of how you'd use it with a library.

6. How do Chainlink price feeds work? Explain the process from requesting data to receiving it in your smart contract.

7. Explain the difference between `constant` and `immutable` keywords in Solidity. How do they affect gas costs?

8. What's the purpose of a constructor in a smart contract, and how does it relate to setting contract ownership?

9. Can you explain the difference between `receive()` and `fallback()` functions? When would you use each?

10. How would you implement access control in a smart contract? Compare using require statements versus modifiers.

11. Explain how you would convert ETH to USD in a smart contract. What considerations do you need to keep in mind regarding decimals?

12. What's the purpose of the Checks-Effects-Interactions (CEI) pattern? Give an example of implementing it.

13. How do you handle decimal precision when working with price feeds in Solidity? Why is this important?

14. Explain the concept of custom errors in Solidity. How do they improve gas efficiency compared to require statements?

15. When implementing a fundraising contract, what mechanisms would you put in place to track donors and their contributions? Explain your data structure choices.

Building an ERC-20 Cryptocurrency

This chapter introduces you to one of the fundamental building blocks of the Ethereum ecosystem: the ERC-20 token standard. Through practical examples using both OpenZeppelin and manual implementation approaches, you'll learn how to create your own cryptocurrency token that adheres to the widely adopted ERC-20 standard.

Consider the challenge of creating a new digital currency: how do you ensure it can be traded on exchanges, stored in wallets, and interact seamlessly with other blockchain applications? The ERC-20 standard resolves these challenges by providing a standardized interface that enables interoperability across the Ethereum ecosystem. This chapter walks you through building both an OpenZeppelin-based implementation and a manual implementation to ensure you understand both the practical and theoretical aspects of token creation.

By working through this chapter's exercises, you'll gain the skills needed to create and deploy your own ERC-20 tokens, understanding both the convenience of using established libraries like OpenZeppelin and the underlying mechanics of the standard. These skills form the foundation for building more complex token-based applications and participating in the DeFi ecosystem.

INTRODUCTION TO ERC-20

There are two main types of blockchain tokens: ERC-20 tokens and ERC-721 tokens. (The next chapter will cover ERC-721 tokens.)

You can think of an ERC-20 contract as a digital database etched onto the Ethereum blockchain. That database has X number of tokens or data in it, defined by the developer creating the contract. The foremost thing it does is track who—of those who interact with the database—owns how many tokens or how many pieces of data. Thus, when one "sends" tokens from one address to another, all they technically do is interact with the smart contract to assign a certain amount of tokens to another address.

An Ethereum Request for Comment (ERC) is a token standard. Think of an ERC as a standard that all Ethereum community developers agree to use to standardize different processes. In the example of ERC-20, the token standardizes how fungible tokens are created in the Ethereum ecosystem. It thus helps different projects work together more efficiently, also called interoperability.

Fungible tokens are tokens that have the following characteristics:

➤ **Divisible:** Fungible tokens can be subdivided into smaller parts, in the same way that a 100 USD or 100 EUR bill can be divided into two notes of 50 USD/EUR, 5 notes of 20 USD/EUR, 10 notes of 10 USD/EUR, and so on. Similarly, a UNI token from the Uniswap protocol can be subdivided into 18 decimal places.

➤ **Interchangeable:** Each token or USD/EUR bill is of equal value and interchangeable. For example, if Alice has an undamaged 50 USD bill and Bill has another undamaged 50 USD bill, exchanging one for the other will not cause any difference. Even if done by a third party without Alice or Bill knowing, none of them would probably notice the change.

ERC-20 and similar standards provide developers, auditors, professionals, and others with a standard way of reading the code to understand and work with it.

In the context of languages such as English, French, Japanese, and others, you can think of ERC-20 as the grammatical and syntactical rules of Solidity that allow people to understand each other. In the same way, the ERC-20 standard standardizes the functions used to create a token. This is useful because if each developer used a different method to create a token, it would be complicated and time-consuming for others to understand what was being said.

In addition to the analogies of grammar and syntax of spoken language just mentioned, ERC-20 and similar standards define the vocabulary they use, especially words that can have a vague or double meaning that can cause confusion. If ERC-20 and similar standards did not exist, each developer would use their definitions or way of creating a token, confusing everyone else when working together, reading the code, or auditing it.

With an ERC-20 token, you can build various types of tokens, such as the following:

➤ **Governance tokens:** These tokens allow their owners to have a say in governing a specific protocol. They usually allow owners to propose changes to the protocol or vote on other changes. They also typically will enable them to delegate their voting power to someone else within their community to make decisions for them, re-delegate it back to themselves if they want, or delegate it again to another person to the previous one.

➤ **Security tokens:** These tokens allow owners to represent their ownership in certain traditional financial assets such as stocks, real estate, and more in parts or fractions. One token can, for example, represent one stock of a company. If a house is worth 100,000 USD, then one can create 100.000 tokens, and each token represents 1 USD of value of the house, allowing for fractional ownership and rent collection proportional to the % of the house owned, provided the house is being rented.

➤ **Centralized stablecoins:** These tokens have relatively stable values as they are usually pegged to a stable fiat currency such as the dollar, the euro, the Swiss franc, or another stable currency. They can also be pegged to a more stable commodity such as gold. They are centralized, meaning that a company most likely issues them, and that company can freeze the coins in someone's wallet if they want.

➤ **Decentralized stablecoins/algorithmic stablecoins:** These stablecoins try to remain stable in value through algorithmic mechanisms and strategies instead of being pegged to a real-world asset such as a fiat currency or a commodity. One example of an algorithmic strategy could be to automatically expand the total supply of tokens in circulation if there is high demand and shrink it automatically when there is low demand. No one can freeze decentralized stablecoins since no single party controls them. However, they are much less stable than centralized stablecoins, which can be frozen and are pegged to a traditional real-world asset.

➤ **Wrapped tokens:** These tokens represent other currencies and tokens, usually from different blockchains such as Wrapped Bitcoin (WBTC) on Ethereum.

THE PROCESS OF CREATING AN ETHEREUM IMPROVEMENT PROPOSAL

To create a new ERC standard, you must first create an Ethereum Improvement Proposal (EIP), a structured way of proposing a change for the better to Ethereum. This might be a proposal to change how the Ethereum protocol works, establish new best practices for developers and the whole community to adopt, or make any other form of improvement to Ethereum. All EIPs can be found on the website https://eips.ethereum.org. They include change proposals such as proposals to change the Ethereum core, changes in the network, changes in the interface when you download the Ethereum blockchain to your computer, ERC standards, and other change proposals.

To create an EIP proposal, you must develop an idea to improve Ethereum. Then, you prepare a draft of the proposal in the standard EIP format, which includes the following, in order:

1. The EIP number
2. Title of the EIP
3. Authors of the EIP
4. Date created
5. An abstract (a description of the problem in 200 words or less)
6. Motivation (short text describing why the existing solution, if any, is not enough to address the problem)
7. Specification (technical description of the syntax of any new proposal and its implementation)
8. Rationale (an explanation of the motivation that fueled the specific design and specification proposal implementation and why the proposer made those particular decisions in the technical description of the implementation in the way the proposer made them)

9. Security considerations (any security considerations that developers have to keep in mind if the EIP were to be implemented into the protocol)

10. Backward compatibility (a description of backward compatibilities, if any, and their consequences; backward compatibility is the ability of a software system to work with older versions of that software system)

11. Reference (an example of an implementation, if available and required)

12. Anything else an author might believe is crucial to add that the standard format does not include

Figures 9.1–9.3 show examples of an EIP proposal and of the ERC-20 EIP proposal specifically.

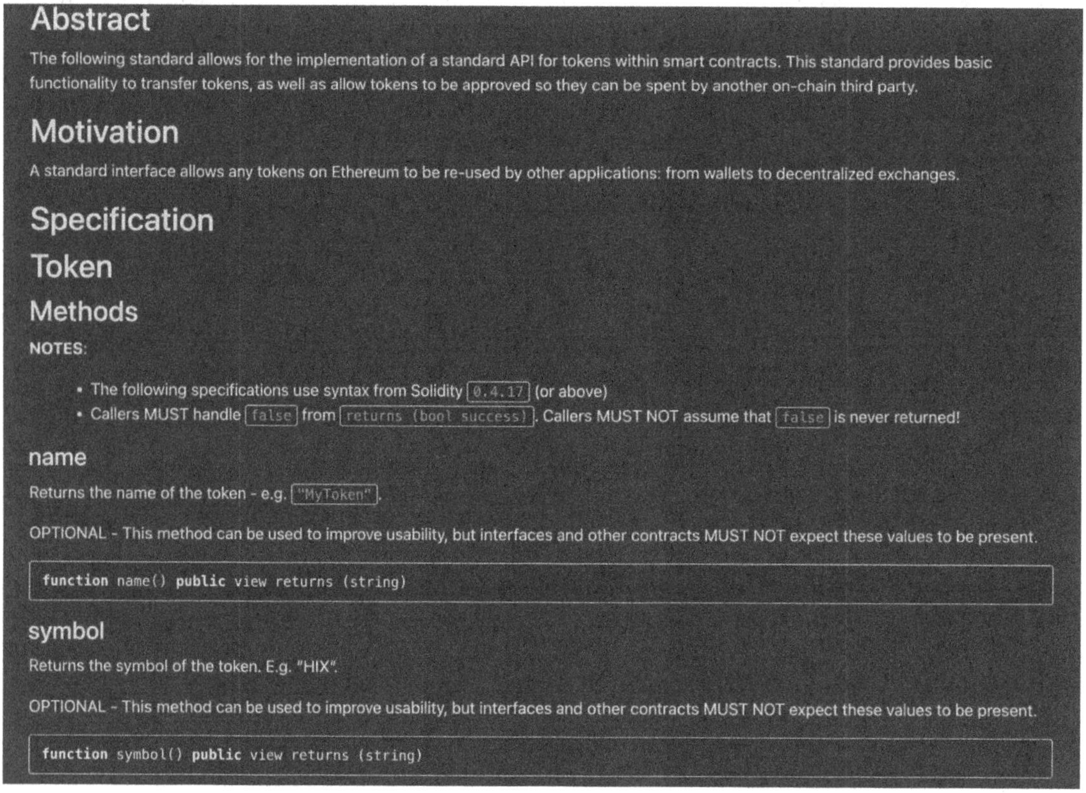

Abstract

The following standard allows for the implementation of a standard API for tokens within smart contracts. This standard provides basic functionality to transfer tokens, as well as allow tokens to be approved so they can be spent by another on-chain third party.

Motivation

A standard interface allows any tokens on Ethereum to be re-used by other applications: from wallets to decentralized exchanges.

Specification

Token

Methods

NOTES:

- The following specifications use syntax from Solidity `0.4.17` (or above)
- Callers MUST handle `false` from `returns (bool success)`. Callers MUST NOT assume that `false` is never returned!

name

Returns the name of the token - e.g. `"MyToken"`.

OPTIONAL - This method can be used to improve usability, but interfaces and other contracts MUST NOT expect these values to be present.

```
function name() public view returns (string)
```

symbol

Returns the symbol of the token. E.g. "HIX".

OPTIONAL - This method can be used to improve usability, but interfaces and other contracts MUST NOT expect these values to be present.

```
function symbol() public view returns (string)
```

FIGURE 9.1: ERC-20 EIP example #1

Building an ERC-20 Token with OpenZeppelin

OpenZeppelin is one of the most used tools in Ethereum development. It is a platform that has many reusable smart contracts available as libraries. The advantages of using reusable smart contracts from OpenZeppelin are primarily saving time and the fact that the smart contracts have been audited and are therefore secure.

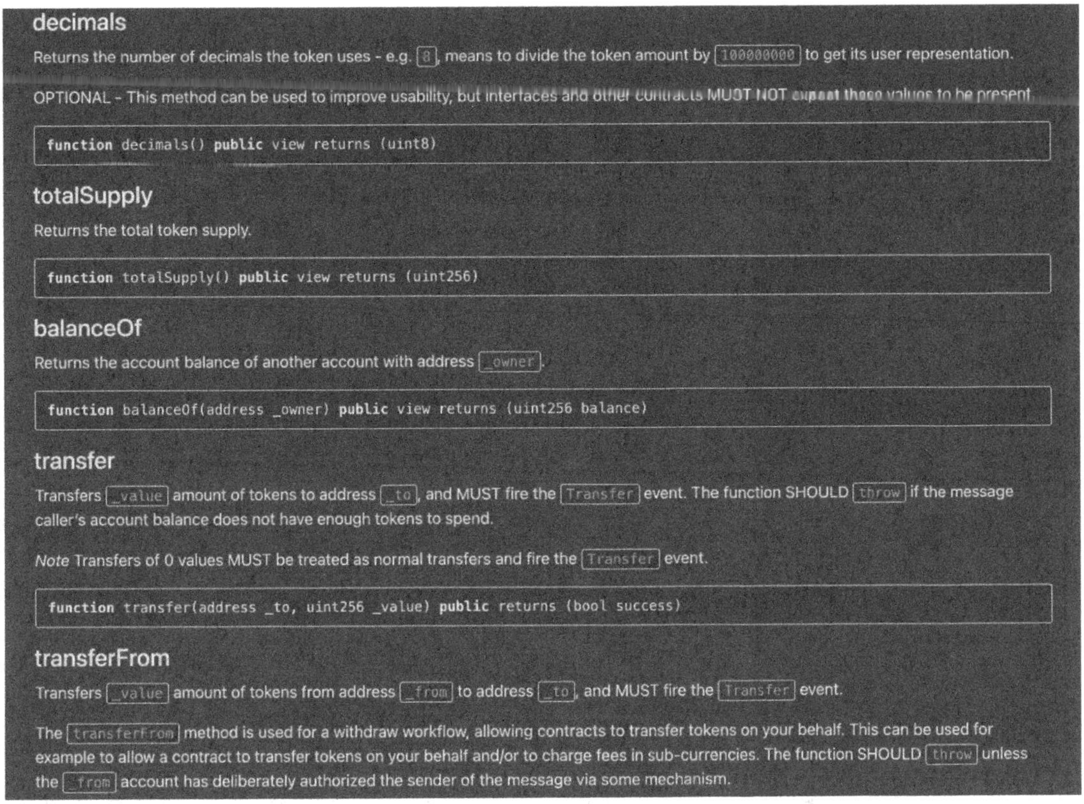

decimals

Returns the number of decimals the token uses - e.g. `8`, means to divide the token amount by `100000000` to get its user representation.

OPTIONAL - This method can be used to improve usability, but interfaces and other contracts MUST NOT expect these values to be present.

```
function decimals() public view returns (uint8)
```

totalSupply

Returns the total token supply.

```
function totalSupply() public view returns (uint256)
```

balanceOf

Returns the account balance of another account with address `_owner`.

```
function balanceOf(address _owner) public view returns (uint256 balance)
```

transfer

Transfers `_value` amount of tokens to address `_to`, and MUST fire the `Transfer` event. The function SHOULD `throw` if the message caller's account balance does not have enough tokens to spend.

Note Transfers of 0 values MUST be treated as normal transfers and fire the `Transfer` event.

```
function transfer(address _to, uint256 _value) public returns (bool success)
```

transferFrom

Transfers `_value` amount of tokens from address `_from` to address `_to`, and MUST fire the `Transfer` event.

The `transferFrom` method is used for a withdraw workflow, allowing contracts to transfer tokens on your behalf. This can be used for example to allow a contract to transfer tokens on your behalf and/or to charge fees in sub-currencies. The function SHOULD `throw` unless the `_from` account has deliberately authorized the sender of the message via some mechanism.

FIGURE 9.2: ERC-20 EIP example #2

To create an ERC-20 contract with OpenZeppelin, go to the `www.openzeppelin.com` landing page, as shown in Figure 9.4.

Hover over Products and select the Contracts Library option, as shown in Figure 9.5.

You are offered a choice between Solidity and Cairo as the programming language (see Figure 9.6). Solidity usually is selected by default; if not, select it and click Start Coding.

Then, the site will go to the OpenZeppelin documentation, where you find token standards and other information, as shown in Figure 9.7.

To create an ERC-20 token with OpenZeppelin, you have to create a new contract for Visual Studio Code. But first, you have to make a folder for that project through the terminal.

1. Open VS Code, display the terminal, type **`ls`**, and press the Enter key to see what's in the location where you currently are, as shown in Figure 9.8.

   You are currently in the `beginning-solidity` folder created a few chapters ago. There is currently only one other folder, `ZooManagement-Foundry`, in the current folder.

2. Create a new folder in the `beginning-solidity` folder. Type **`mkdir beginning-solidity-token`** and press the Enter key, as shown in Figure 9.9.

Note Transfers of 0 values MUST be treated as normal transfers and fire the `Transfer` event.

```
function transferFrom(address _from, address _to, uint256 _value) public returns (bool success)
```

approve

Allows `_spender` to withdraw from your account multiple times, up to the `_value` amount. If this function is called again it overwrites the current allowance with `_value`.

NOTE: To prevent attack vectors like the one described here and discussed here, clients SHOULD make sure to create user interfaces in such a way that they set the allowance first to `0` before setting it to another value for the same spender. THOUGH The contract itself shouldn't enforce it, to allow backwards compatibility with contracts deployed before

```
function approve(address _spender, uint256 _value) public returns (bool success)
```

allowance

Returns the amount which `_spender` is still allowed to withdraw from `_owner`.

```
function allowance(address _owner, address _spender) public view returns (uint256 remaining)
```

Events

Transfer

MUST trigger when tokens are transferred, including zero value transfers.

A token contract which creates new tokens SHOULD trigger a Transfer event with the `_from` address set to `0x0` when tokens are created.

```
event Transfer(address indexed _from, address indexed _to, uint256 _value)
```

Approval

MUST trigger on any successful call to `approve(address _spender, uint256 _value)`.

```
event Approval(address indexed _owner, address indexed _spender, uint256 _value)
```

FIGURE 9.3: ERC-20 EIP example #3

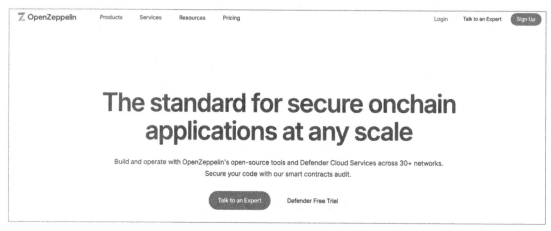

FIGURE 9.4: OpenZeppelin landing page

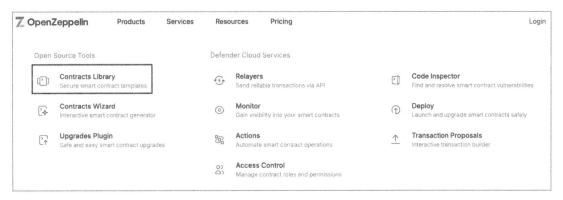

FIGURE 9.5: Contracts Library on OpenZeppelin

FIGURE 9.6: Choosing the programming language

3. Type **ls** again to see if the folder has been created, as shown in Figure 9.10.

   You can now see two folders where there was only one previously: ZooManagement-Foundry. Now there's the newly created beginning-solidity-token folder.

4. Go into the beginning-solidity-token folder by typing **cd beginning-solidity-token**, as shown in Figure 9.11.

   You can see that you are now in the beginning-solidity-token folder.

5. Type **forge init** to install a new project into the folder, as shown in Figure 9.12. If this does not work, try forge init –force.

   Here, you can see that the new project has been initialized.

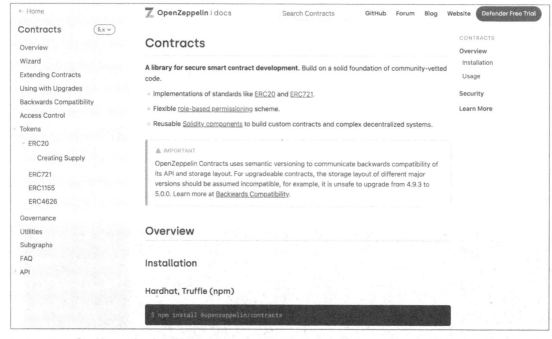

FIGURE 9.7: OpenZeppelin documentation

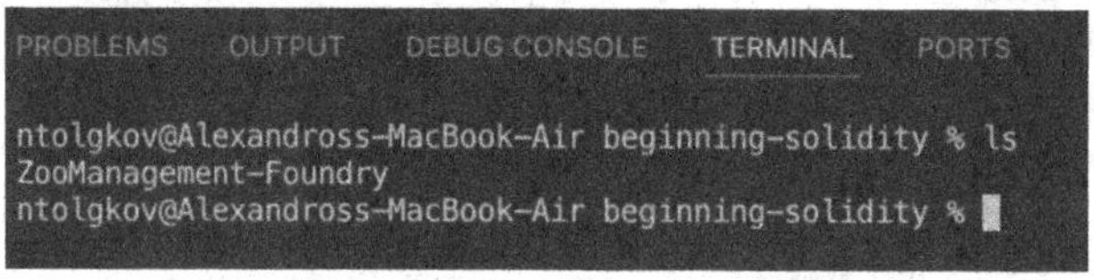

```
PROBLEMS    OUTPUT    DEBUG CONSOLE    TERMINAL    PORTS

ntolgkov@Alexandross-MacBook-Air beginning-solidity % ls
ZooManagement-Foundry
ntolgkov@Alexandross-MacBook-Air beginning-solidity %
```

FIGURE 9.8: Installing OpenZeppelin contracts: ls command

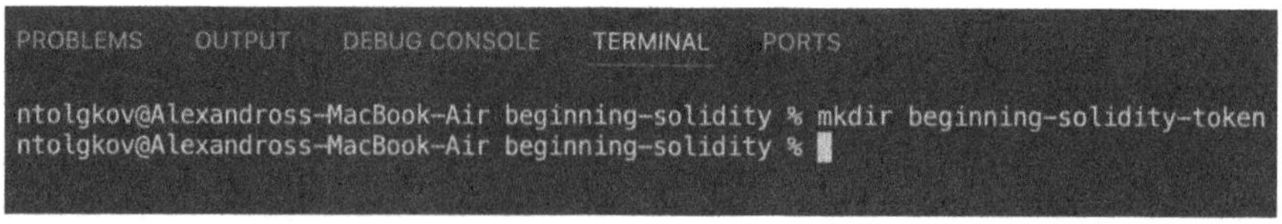

```
PROBLEMS    OUTPUT    DEBUG CONSOLE    TERMINAL    PORTS

ntolgkov@Alexandross-MacBook-Air beginning-solidity % mkdir beginning-solidity-token
ntolgkov@Alexandross-MacBook-Air beginning-solidity %
```

FIGURE 9.9: Installing OpenZeppelin contracts: mkdir beginning-solidity-token

```
PROBLEMS    OUTPUT    DEBUG CONSOLE    TERMINAL    PORTS

ntolgkov@Alexandross-MacBook-Air beginning-solidity % mkdir beginning-solidity-token
ntolgkov@Alexandross-MacBook-Air beginning-solidity % ls
ZooManagement-Foundry          beginning-solidity-token
ntolgkov@Alexandross-MacBook-Air beginning-solidity %
```

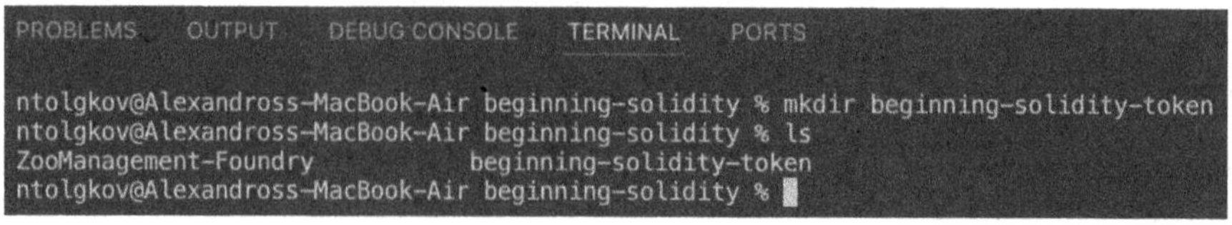

FIGURE 9.10: Installing OpenZeppelin contracts: second ls command

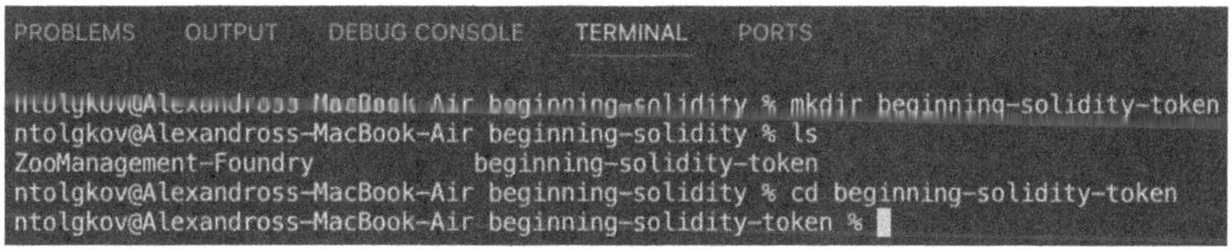

FIGURE 9.11: Installing OpenZeppelin contracts: `cd beginning-solidity-token`

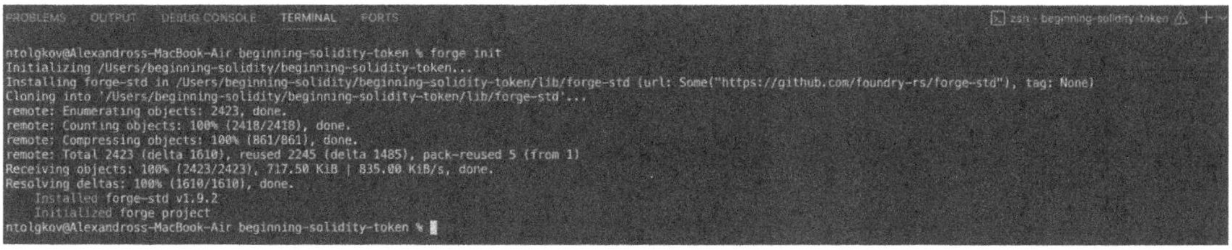

FIGURE 9.12: Installing OpenZeppelin contracts: `forge init` command

6. Open the folder by selecting File ➪ Open Folder, selecting `beginning-solidity-token`, and clicking Open to display the page shown in Figure 9.13.

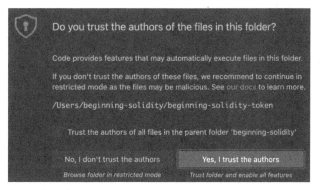

FIGURE 9.13: Opening the `beginning-solidity-token` folder

7. You are asked whether you trust the authors of the file you are opening. Since you are the author of the work you are opening, click "Yes, I trust the authors" (see Figure 9.14).

FIGURE 9.14: "Yes, I trust the authors" pop-up

8. Go to the Explorer pane and delete the `Counter.sol` contract inside the project and in the script, `src`, and `test` folders, as shown in Figure 9.15.

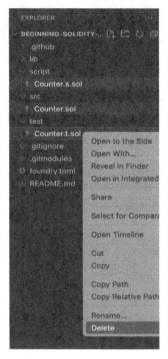

FIGURE 9.15: Deleting `Counter.s.sol`

9. Download the contract libraries from OpenZeppelin's GitHub (see Figure 9.16). Usually, Googling OpenZeppelin GitHub should be enough to give you the link result to click.

10. Get the URL link to the GitHub repository: `OpenZeppelin/open zeppelin-contracts` and download the smart contracts locally by typing **forge download** `OpenZeppelin/openzeppelin-contracts@5.0.2`.

    The `@5.0.2` signifies the latest version of the smart contract released at the time of writing this book. When you read this book, it might be a different version. To install this particular version of OpenZeppelin smart contract, type the following:

    ```
    forge install OpenZeppelin/openzeppelin-contracts --no-commit
    ```

11. Press the Enter key to start installing and downloading the OpenZeppelin contracts. Depending on your machine and the speed of your Internet connection, the contracts should be installed after a few seconds or minutes. Figure 9.17 shows the installed contracts.

12. To ensure everything is installed correctly, go to the Explorer pane and click the `lib` folder. Next, click the `openzeppelin-contracts` folder, then on the `contracts` folder, then on the `token` folder, and finally on the `ERC20` folder and the file `ERC20.sol` (see Figure 9.18).

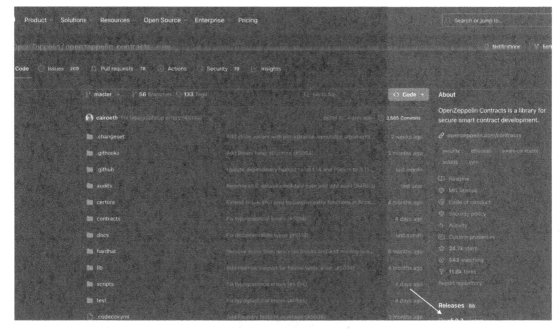

FIGURE 9.16: OpenZeppelin smart contracts version

FIGURE 9.17: OpenZeppelin smart contracts installed

When you click the `ERC20.sol` file, you see that the ERC-20 token contract has been implemented (see Figure 9.19).

13. Download the smart contract kit from OpenZeppelin; then create a new contract called `BeginingSolidityToken.sol`.

Create the contract interface and import and inherit the ERC-20 contract downloaded from OpenZeppelin to create a connection with the `BeginningSolidityToken.sol` contract, as shown in the following code:

```
//SPDX-License-Identifier: MIT

pragma solidity 0.8.27;

import {ERC20} from "../lib/openzeppelin-contracts/contracts/token/ERC20/
ERC20.sol";
contract BeginningSolidityToken.sol{
}
```

FIGURE 9.18: File path to `ERC20.sol`

Figure 9.20 shows the ERC-20 token that was downloaded.

Note that the ERC-20 token has a constructor. As you saw in previous chapters, when an inherited contract has a constructor, that constructor has to be included in the contract that inherits that constructor.

14. Add that constructor to the `BeginningSolidityToken` contract by typing the following code:

```
//SPDX-License-Identifier: MIT

pragma solidity 0.8.27;

import {ERC20} from "../lib/openzeppelin-contracts/contracts/token/ERC20/
ERC20.sol";

contract BeginningSolidityToken is ERC20 {
    constructor(uint256 initialSupply)
ERC20("BeginningSolidityToken", "BST") {
        _mint(msg.sender, initialSupply);
    }
}
```

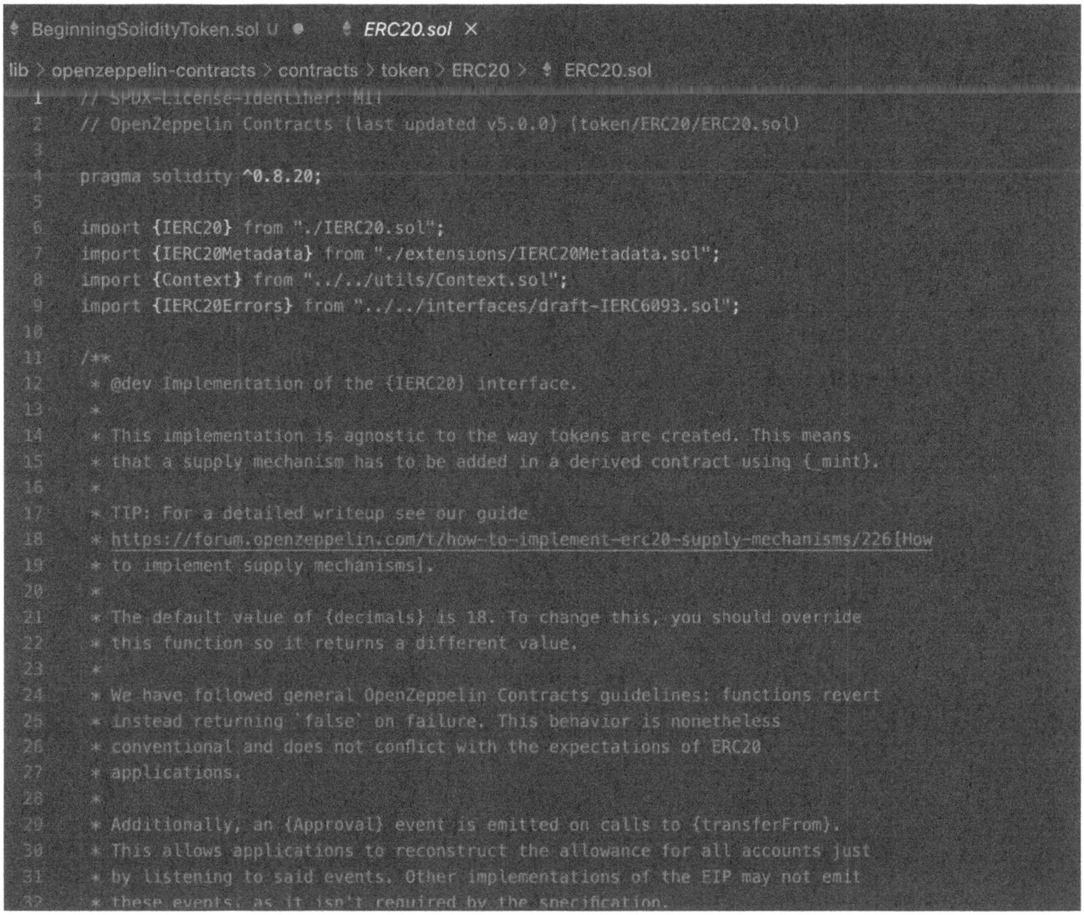

FIGURE 9.19: ERC20.sol

15. See if the contract compiles in the terminal by typing **forge build**, as shown in Figure 9.21.

After pressing the Enter key, you should get as a result a message saying that the contracts have been compiled successfully, as shown in Figure 9.22.

Building an ERC-20 Manually

Now that you know how to create an ERC-20 contract using OpenZeppelin, you should learn how to develop the ERC-20 token manually so you understand what each function of the contract (the ERC-20 token) does.

Go to the src folder and create another contract. In this example, the name of the contract is BeginningSolidityTokenManual.sol.

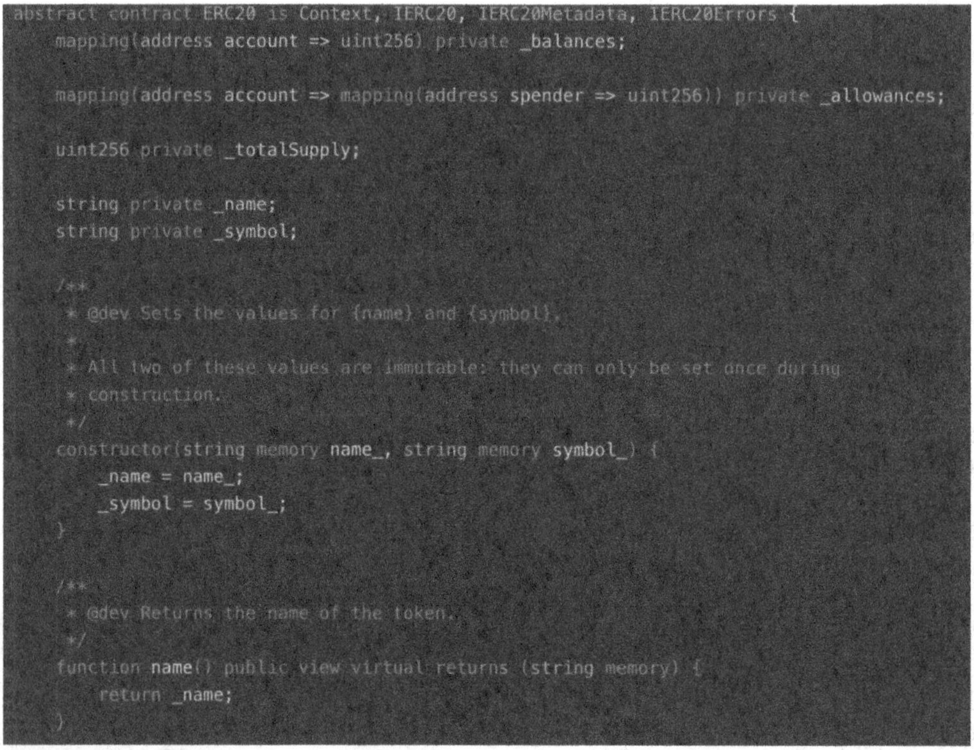

```
abstract contract ERC20 is Context, IERC20, IERC20Metadata, IERC20Errors {
    mapping(address account => uint256) private _balances;

    mapping(address account => mapping(address spender => uint256)) private _allowances;

    uint256 private _totalSupply;

    string private _name;
    string private _symbol;

    /**
     * @dev Sets the values for {name} and {symbol}.
     *
     * All two of these values are immutable: they can only be set once during
     * construction.
     */
    constructor(string memory name_, string memory symbol_) {
        _name = name_;
        _symbol = symbol_;
    }

    /**
     * @dev Returns the name of the token.
     */
    function name() public view virtual returns (string memory) {
        return _name;
    }
}
```

FIGURE 9.20: ERC-20 constructor

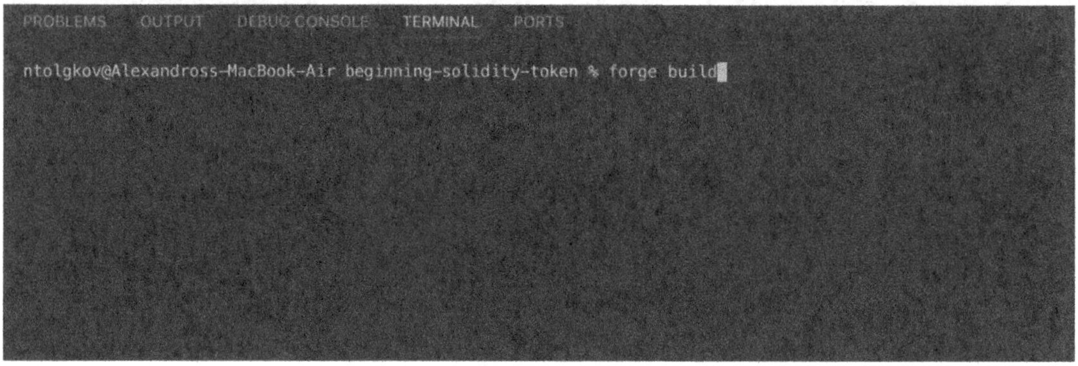

```
PROBLEMS    OUTPUT    DEBUG CONSOLE    TERMINAL    PORTS

ntolgkov@Alexandross-MacBook-Air beginning-solidity-token % forge build
```

FIGURE 9.21: `forge build` for contract

This line declares the license under which the contract will be available upon its release:

```
//SPDX-License-Identifier: MIT
```

This code declares the version of Solidity that will be used in the following contract:

```
pragma solidity 0.8.27;
```

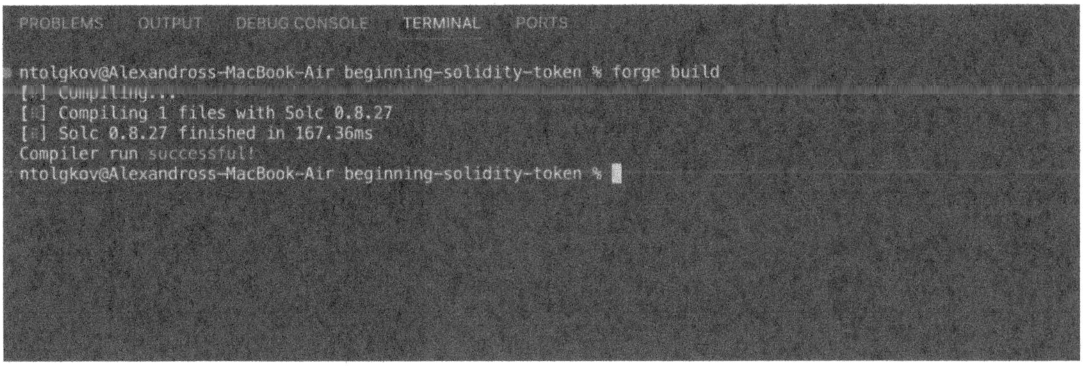

FIGURE 9.22: Contract compilation successful

The next code line states the contract's name and initializes it by opening a curly bracket:

```
.contract BeginningSolidityTokenManual {
```

The following variables are all `private`, meaning that they can be called only from within the contract. The first one declares a `string` _name, which is the name of the token to be deployed. If this was Bitcoin, the token's name would be Bitcoin. Technically, the name would be wrapped Bitcoin as the token would be pegged to the actual Bitcoin, but for simplicity's sake, let us say Bitcoin as an example.

```
string private _name;
string private _symbol;
uint8 private _decimals;
uint256 private _totalSupply;
```

The second variable, _symbol, declares a symbol, which is the token abbreviation to be used. Again, if this were Bitcoin, the acronym would be BTC.

The third variable, _decimals, declares the number of decimal places the token to be deployed will use. If the decimals are 18, then the token will be represented as 1000000000000000000 as shown in previous chapters; this helps with token fractionalization and enables people to own a fraction of a token instead of one whole token if they want to do so.

The fourth variable, _totalSupply, declares and keeps track of the total supply of the token to be deployed.

The following piece of the contract has two mappings. The first mapping, _balances, keeps track of token balances for each address that owns the tokens of this contract. This happens through each `address` variable, which displays its balance through the `uint256` variable. The mapping is private, meaning it can be called only within the contract.

```
mapping (address => uint256) private _balances;
mapping (address => mapping(address => uint256)) private _allowances;
```

The second mapping is a bit more complicated since it is a mapping inside a mapping. The first address of the mapping (`address => mapping`) is the token owner's address. In contrast, (address

=> uint256) is the address allowed by the owner address to spend a specific number of uint256 tokens. The mapping is private, meaning it can be called only within the same contract and is called _allowances.

The two declared events emit when different variables are executed successfully. The first event with the name Transfer has the following parameters: address indexed from, which represents the address that will send the tokens, and address indexed to, which represents the address that will receive the sent tokens by the previous address. As discussed in previous chapters, the indexed keyword makes the parameter a topic and makes it easier to be retrieved and filtered if required in the future, and the uint256 value represents the amount of tokens transferred from one address to the other.

```
event Transfer(address indexed from, address indexed to, uint256 value);

event Approval(address indexed owner, address indexed spender,
uint256 value);
```

The second event, Approval, also has three parameters: address indexed owner, which signifies the address of the owner who gives the approval to the next; address indexed spender to spend the tokens; and uint256 value, which, in this case, signifies the number of tokens that have been approved for spending.

In the following code, the declared function name is public, meaning it can be called both internally and externally. It is view, which means that it does not alter the state of the blockchain but only reads from it. The returns keyword returns a string variable stored in memory called _name.

```
function name() public view returns(string memory) {

    return _name;

}
```

The function symbol is the same as the name function. Still, instead of the _name variable, it returns the _symbol variable, which, in effect, returns the symbol, ticker, or abbreviation of the token to be created.

```
function symbol() public view returns (string memory) {
    return _symbol;
}
```

The decimals function is similar to the symbol and name functions. It returns an uint8, which represents the number of decimals used to create the token and its amount or total supply.

```
function decimals() public view returns(uint8) {
    return _decimals;
}
```

The `totalSupply` function is the same as the `symbol` and `name` functions, except it returns an `uint256` instead of a string, reflecting the token's total supply.

```
function totalSupply() public view returns (uint256) {
    return _totalSupply;
}
```

The `balanceOf` function declares a local address `_owner`. The visibility and `view` are the same as in the previous functions. The `balanceOf` function returns an `uint256`, which signifies the balance for the declared `_owner` address. The function uses the `_balances` mapping to return the value of the address `_owner`.

```
function balanceOf(address _owner) public view returns(uint256 balance) {
    return _balances[_owner];
}
```

The `transfer` function in the following code transfers tokens from one address (the sender of the tokens) to another (the receiver of the tokens). The function takes two parameters: the `address _to` and the `uint256 _value`. The transfer function is `public` but not a `view` function since it changes the state of the blockchain by sending tokens from one address to another. It returns a `boolean` to indicate whether the transfer of the tokens was successful.

```
function transfer(address _to, uint256 _value) public returns (bool success) {
```

As shown in the following code, the function uses the first `require` keyword to ensure that the recipient of the tokens is not a zero address (`!=`) or, as it is also called, a null address that no one uses. If it is, the `"ERC20: transfer to the zero address"` message will appear.

```
require(_to != address(0), "ERC20: transfer to the zero address");
```

The second `require` keyword ensures that the sender of the amount has enough tokens or `_value` in his `balance(s)` to send money. If not, the `"ERC20: transfer amount exceeds balance"` message will appear:

```
require(_balances[msg.sender] >= _value, "ERC20: transfer amount exceeds
balance");
```

The `_balances[msg.sender] -= _value` line, shown in the following code, subtracts the amount the sender wants to send. The line after this one, `_balances[_to] += _value`, takes the subtracted value of the earlier `msg.sender` and adds it to the address `_to`, which is the address to which `msg.sender` sends the money.

```
_balances[msg.sender] -= _value;

_balances[_to] += _value;
```

Finally, after the transfer of money is completed from the `msg.sender` address to the `_to` address, a Transfer event is emitted.

```
emit Transfer(msg.sender, _to, _value);
```

The `return true` of the `boolean` indicates that the transfer was completed successfully:

```
return true;

}
```

The following function ensures that a third party, `_from`, is allowed to spend tokens and send them to the address `_to` with a predetermined amount of tokens, `_value`:

```
function transferFrom(address _from, address _to, uint256 _value) public
returns(bool success) {
```

The function `transferFrom` has three parameters: `address _from`, `address _to`, and `uint256 _value`. It is a `public` function that can be called internally and externally. It `returns` a `boolean` `success`, which confirms that the transaction has been successful.

Like in the previous function, the first two `require` statements of the function try to ensure that neither `_from` address nor `_to` address is a zero address or null address.

```
require(_from != address(0), "ERC20: transfer from the zero address");

require(_to != address(0), "ERC20: transfer to the zero address");
```

The third `require` statement checks that the `_from` address has a sufficient balance when initiating a transfer of a certain amount:

```
require(_balances[_from] >= _value, "ERC20: transfer amount exceeds balance");
```

The fourth `require` statement, shown next, verifies that `msg.sender` has been allowed to transfer the specific `_value` or number of tokens from the owner address, which is the `_from` in this case. To simplify the fourth `require` statement, and the specific `_value` number of tokens, the statement is like saying "I allowed my friend Bob (`msg.sender`) to send a specific amount, 10 ether for example (`_value`), to Alice (`_to`)."

```
require(_allowances[_from][msg.sender] >= _value, "ERC20: transfer amount
exceeds
allowance");
```

The following code removes the tokens (`_value`) to be transferred from the `_from` address and adds the same amount of tokens to the `_to` address in the second line of the code:

```
_balances[_from] -= _value;

_balances[_to] += _value;
```

The following removes the specified amount that `msg.sender` has been allowed to spend from the amount that the address transferred:

```
_allowances[_from][msg.sender] -= _value;
```

The next code line emits an `event` that the `Transfer` has been completed:

```
emit Transfer( from,  to,  value);


return true;
```

The function returns `true` if the transaction was successful.

The `function approve` function has two parameters: an `address _spender` and an `uint256 _value`. It is `public` and returns a `boolean` as a success when a transaction is completed successfully.

```
}

function approve(address _spender, uint256 _value) public returns(bool
success) {
```

The next statement, is `require`, statement checks to see that the _spender address is not the zero or null address:

```
require(_spender != address(0), "ERC20: approve to the zero address");
```

The following line sets the allowance amount. The `msg.sender` sets the spending allowance by the spender address to the _value amount:

```
_allowances[msg.sender][_spender] = _value;
```

The following emits an event and logs the parameters of `msg.sender`, _spender, and _value:

```
emit Approval(msg.sender, _spender, _value);
```

This function returns `true` to ensure the action has been completed successfully:

```
return true;
```

The `allowance` function has two parameters: the _owner address and the _spender address. The function in `public` —which can be called both internally and externally—is `view` and does not alter the state of the blockchain as it only reads data from it and `returns` an `uint256  remaining`.

```
}

function allowance(address _owner, address _spender) public view
returns (uint256
remaining) {
```

The following returns the number of tokens that the _spender is still allowed to spend by the _owner after accessing the _allowances mapping:

```
return _allowances[_owner][_spender];
}
```

The contract should look like this:

```
//SPDX-License-Identifier: MIT

pragma solidity 0.8.27;

contract BeginningSolidityTokenManual {

    string private _name;
    string private _symbol;
    uint8 private _decimals;
    uint256 private _totalSupply;

    mapping (address => uint256) private _balances;
    mapping (address => mapping(address => uint256)) private _allowances;

    event Transfer(address indexed from, address indexed to, uint256 value);
    event Approval(address indexed owner, address indexed spender,
uint256 value);

    function name() public view returns(string memory) {
        return _name;
    }

    function symbol() public view returns (string memory) {
        return _symbol;
    }

    function decimals() public view returns(uint8) {
        return _decimals;
    }

    function totalSupply() public view returns (uint256) {
        return _totalSupply;
    }

    function balanceOf(address _owner) public view returns(uint256 balance) {
        return _balances[_owner];
    }

    function transfer(address _to, uint256 _value) public returns (bool
success) {
        require(_to != address(0), "ERC20: transfer to the zero address");
        require(_balances[msg.sender] >= _value, "ERC20: transfer
amount exceeds
balance");

        _balances[msg.sender] -= _value;
        _balances[_to] += _value;
        emit Transfer(msg.sender, _to, _value);
        return true;
    }
```

```
    function transferFrom(address _from, address _to, uint256 _value) public
returns(bool success) {
        require(_from != address(0), "ERC20: transfer from the zero address");
        require(_to != address(0), "ERC20: transfer to the zero address");
        require(_balances[_from] >= _value, "ERC20: transfer amount exceeds
balance");
        require(_allowances[_from][msg.sender] >= _value, "ERC20: transfer
amount
exceeds allowance");

        _balances[_from] -= _value;
        _balances[_to] += _value;
        _allowances[_from][msg.sender] -= _value;
        emit Transfer(_from, _to, _value);
        return true;
    }

    function approve(address _spender, uint256 _value) public returns
(bool success) {
        require(_spender != address(0), "ERC20: approve to the zero address");

        _allowances[msg.sender][_spender] = _value;
        emit Approval(msg.sender, _spender, _value);
        return true;
    }

    function allowance(address _owner, address _spender) public view returns
(uint256 remaining) {
        return _allowances[_owner][_spender];
    }
}
```

The preceding code demonstrates how to manually create an ERC-20 token and shows what each function of the ERC-20 standard does on its own. However, no one builds ERC-20 tokens manually anymore, as downloading and using OpenZeppelin is the standard and safest way to operate with ERC-20 contracts today.

DEPLOY YOUR ERC-20 CRYPTOCURRENCY

To deploy the ERC-20 contract created earlier in this chapter using the OpenZeppelin library, you need to write a script.

1. Go to the `script` folder and create a new contract (`DBeginningSolidityToken.s.sol`), as shown in Figure 9.23.

2. In that contract, type the following:

```
//SPDX-License-Identifier: MIT
import {BeginningSolidityToken} from "../src/BeginningSolidityToken.sol";
import {Script} from "forge-std/Script.sol";
pragma solidity 0.8.27;
```

```
contract DBeginningSolidityToken is Script  {

   function run() external {
       uint256 public constant INITIAL_SUPPLY = 100 ether;
       vm.startBroadcast();
       new BeginningSolidityToken(INITIAL_SUPPLY);
       vm.stopBroadcast();
   }
}
```

FIGURE 9.23: BeginningSolidityToken.s.sol

This contract states the license under which it will be released and imports two contracts, BeginningSolidityToken and Script, from their respective paths. For BeginningSolidityToken, the path is ../src/BeginningSolidityToken.sol. The two dots (..) signify leaving the current folder that the file is located in, in this case, the script folder. It then specifies the path to find the BeginningSolidityToken.sol file by selecting the folder the file is in, src, and then the name of the file itself. For the Script contract, the path is forge-std/Script.sol.

Next, the pragma solidity 0.8.27 line specifies the Solidity version. Then, the contract name, DBeginningSolidityToken, is specified, and the contract inherits the Script token.

Inside the contract, the classic run function is declared as external, meaning it can only be called externally. Within it, an uint256 constant public variable is declared with the name INITIAL_SUPPLY, and it is set to 100 ether. Finally, the vm.startBroadcast cheat code is used to signify broadcasting transactions. Within the vm.startBroadcast cheat code, a new instance of the BeginningSolidityToken contract is deployed and takes the INITIAL_SUPPLY variable as its supply of tokens, which as mentioned is 100 ether. To conclude the contract, the closing of the broadcast is declared with the VM.stopBroadcast cheat code.

To deploy the contract on Anvil to see if everything is okay, follow these steps:

1. Open the terminal and open Anvil by typing this:

   anvil

Anvil should start running (see Figure 9.24).

FIGURE 9.24: Anvil launched

2. Choose a random key from the list, click it, and copy it, as shown in Figure 9.25.

FIGURE 9.25: Anvil private keys

3. Encrypt it by typing this:

```
cast wallet import BeginningSolidityTokenKey --interactive
```

You can use a name other than `BeginningSolidityTokenKey` if you prefer.

4. Copy and paste the Anvil key you copied in step 2. The private key will be pasted into the terminal after you press Ctrl+V (or Command+V, depending on your operating system). However, it will not be visible to you for security purposes even if pasted. After pasting it, press the Enter key.

5. You will be asked for a password, as shown in Figure 9.26. Add one you can remember since every time you deploy a contract using this key, it will ask you for the password.

If this is done successfully, the following message should appear:

```
`BeginningSolidityTokenKey` keystore was saved successfully.
Address: 0x14dc79964da2c08b23698b3d3cc7ca32193d9955
```

FIGURE 9.26: Adding a password to protect private key

If you look at the whole terminal, you'll see what is shown in Figure 9.27.

FIGURE 9.27: Private key successfully stored

6. After having added the keystore, it is time to securely deploy the contract by typing this:

```
forge script script/DBeginningSolidityToken.s.sol:DBeginningSolidityToken
-rpc-url
http://localhost:8545 --account BeginningSolidityTokenKey
--sender 0x14dc79964da2c08b23698b3d3cc7ca32193d9955 -broadcast
```

7. Press Enter on your keyboard. The terminal will ask for the keystore password, as shown in Figure 9.28.

FIGURE 9.28: Keystore password before deployment

8. After you type the password, the contract will be successfully deployed, as shown in Figure 9.29.

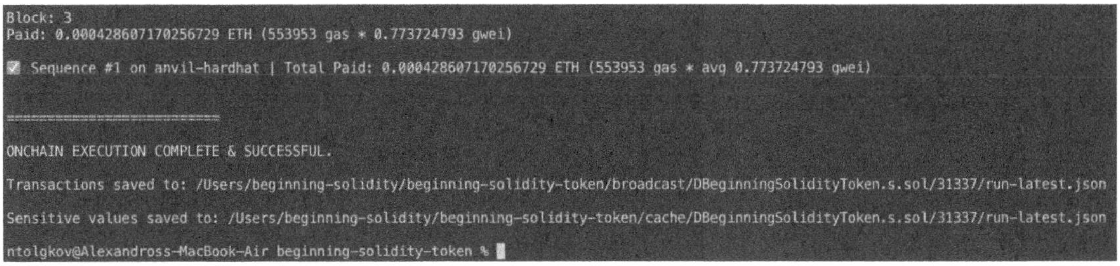

FIGURE 9.29: Contract deployment on Anvil successful

If something is going wrong, remember to use your AI companion. Copy and paste the error message, explain what you want to do, and ask the AI companion for advice.

CHAPTER 9 QUESTIONS

1. What makes a token fungible in the context of ERC-20? Explain the key characteristics.

2. What is the process of creating an Ethereum Improvement Proposal? What are the mandatory components?

3. Compare and contrast manual ERC-20 implementation versus using OpenZeppelin. What are the security implications?

4. Explain the purpose and implementation of the allowance and approve functions in an ERC-20 contract.

5. How do you handle decimals in ERC-20 tokens? Why is this important for token economics?

6. What's the difference between `transfer` and `transferFrom` in ERC-20? When would you use each?

7. Explain the role of events in ERC-20 contracts. Which events are mandatory, and why are they important?

8. How do you implement proper access control for an ERC-20 token? What security considerations should be kept in mind?

9. What's the significance of the double mapping used for allowances in ERC-20? Explain its structure and purpose.

10. How would you safely implement a token with an initial supply? Walk me through the constructor implementation.

11. What are the common vulnerabilities in ERC-20 implementations? How does OpenZeppelin help mitigate these?

12. Explain the role of the require statements in ERC-20's transfer functions. Why are they necessary?

13. How would you handle token decimals when displaying balances to users? What considerations should be made?

14. What's the purpose of the view functions in an ERC-20 contract? Which ones are required by the standard?

15. How would you deploy an ERC-20 token using Foundry? Walk me through the deployment script structure.

10

Borrowing and Lending Protocol

This chapter introduces you to stablecoins, an essential component of the decentralized finance (DeFi) ecosystem that bridges traditional finance with cryptocurrency by maintaining a stable value pegged to real-world assets. Through a detailed exploration and hands-on implementation, you'll learn how to create both a stablecoin token and its underlying protocol mechanism.

Consider the challenge of crypto's high volatility: how do you create a cryptocurrency that maintains a stable value for practical use in everyday transactions and financial services? This chapter tackles this challenge by demonstrating how stablecoins achieve price stability through various mechanisms including collateralization, algorithmic control, and hybrid approaches. You'll build a collateralized stablecoin system that handles deposits, minting, burning, liquidations, and health factor calculations.

By working through this chapter's implementation of a collateralized stablecoin protocol, you'll gain practical experience with the fundamental concepts of DeFi development. These skills form the foundation for building more complex financial applications on the blockchain, understanding risk management in DeFi, and working with real-world financial data through oracles.

WHAT IS A STABLECOIN?

There is no perfect form of money today, and cryptocurrencies are only sometimes suitable. As explained in Chapter 1, good money has three main characteristics:

> **Medium of exchange:** The intermediary commodity type of money that is widely acceptable in a particular region of the world. It enables the exchange of goods and services, eliminating the need for barter and solving the problem of the "double coincidence of wants" where people exchange goods with one another instead of using an intermediary tool to act as a medium of exchange. Traditional fiat currencies such as

the USD, EUR, Yuan, and Yen are—at least in the developed world—a reliable medium of exchange.

➤ **Unit of account:** Serves as a standard reference for valuing goods and services, helping with comparing prices and communicating how much one values a product or service—i.e., 4 USD for a kilo of apples—and is ready to pay for it. A type of money as a unit of account is active at least in a specific geographical location of the world, such as the United States for the USD, the European Union for the EUR, and so forth. Here, fiat currencies have the edge over cryptocurrencies as no cryptocurrency is used as a unit of account—at least for the moment—due to their volatility. In the future, as technology scales and more people and organizations buy Bitcoin and Ether, volatility will likely become less of a problem. But they are too volatile to be used as a unit of account for the moment.

➤ **Store of value:** Preserves one's purchasing power over time, either in the short or long term, encouraging saving and discouraging consumption. Currently, in the short term, fiat currencies are better stores of value than cryptocurrencies, as cryptocurrencies suffer from high volatility. However, in the long term, fiat currencies suffer significantly from inflation as it is possible to—in theory—create unlimited money through the Central Bank as long as it is paired with economic growth and a boost in productivity. Even like this, however, the annual inflation rate target is currently officially set at 2 percent, to encourage spending. In the long term, significant cryptocurrencies have a limited supply and preserve their value better if their demand stays the same or increases.

All types of cash fulfill the criteria following to be considered viable as money. Some forms of money do so better than others in one or another of these criteria:

➤ **Durability:** It cannot be damaged and is resistant to wear and tear.

➤ **Transportability:** It is easily and quickly transferrable across borders and physical (or digital) space.

➤ **Divisibility:** Fiat currencies have paper money and coins that can be split into smaller units for micro-transactions. Ether has ether, millimeter, micrometer, gwei, mwei, kwei, and wei and can be divided up to 18 decimals.

➤ **Fungibility:** Each unit is interchangeable with another without losing value. For example, 1 USD is interchangeable with another USD or 1 Ether for another.

➤ **Resistance to counterfeiting:** Avoid creating fake units of money.

Stablecoins are types of cryptocurrencies that try to merge the concept of fiat money with cryptocurrencies. They do so through different strategies, but most commonly through maintaining a stable peg to a significant fiat currency or commodity such as gold or a combination of various fiat currencies, different commodities other than gold, or a combination of fiat currencies and different commodities or other assets.

Most stablecoins are pegged to the USD because the USD is the most stable, used, and accepted currency in the world. Thus, it is a powerful monetary commodity or asset to use as an intermediary of exchange, a unit of account, and, in countries suffering from hyperinflation in the double or triple digits, as a short—and long-term—store of value.

As of writing this book, the market capitalization, that is, the worth of all fiat-pegged or backed stablecoins, was 176+ billion USD, with tether (USDT) having 75.2% of this market capitalization, sitting at almost 133 billion USD (see Figure 10.1).

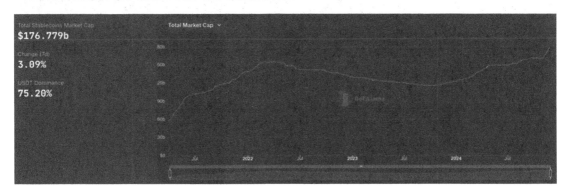

FIGURE 10.1 The combined value of all fiat-backed stablecoins worldwide

USDC, the second most significant player in USD-pegged stablecoins, has a market capitalization of almost 39 billion USD. The third player, FDUSD, has a market capitalization of nearly 1.822 billion USD. As shown in Figure 10.2, the margin between first, second, and third is quite large, and USDT is currently the most significant player in the market.

FIGURE 10.2 The three biggest USD-backed stablecoins—Tether (USDT), USD Coin (USDC), First Digital USD (FDUSD)—by market capitalization

When comparing the market dynamics between fiat-pegged stablecoins (see Figures 10.3 and 10.4), the USD is by far the most dominant to the point that other fiat-pegged stablecoins have almost no existence. Out of a total market capitalization or worth of almost 177 billion USD for all stablecoins, the USD stablecoin's market capitalization is 176.539 USD at the time of writing. In comparison, the combined value of all other fiat-pegged stablecoins was a mere 240 million USD, a more than 99% market dominance for the USD.

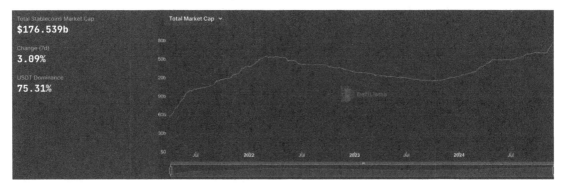

FIGURE 10.3 Market capitalization of only USD-pegged stablecoins

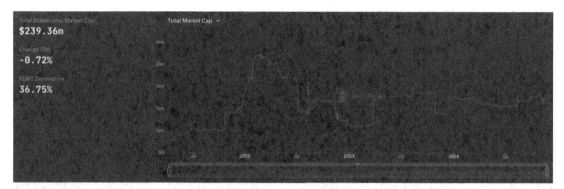

FIGURE 10.4 The combined value of all fiat-backed stablecoins worldwide minus the USD

TYPES OF STABLECOINS

Different stablecoins use different pegging strategies and technologies to maintain their peg to the asset they claim to be backed by. The following are two categories from which stablecoin taxonomy can start:

➤ **Centralized stablecoins:** Centralized stablecoins are managed by a centralized entity, similar to how a central authority manages the traditional fiat currencies, the central bank, or the Federal Reserve of their country. The biggest difference between these centralized stablecoins and their central bank counterpart is that private businesses manage them. In contrast, the original fiat currency is managed by a central bank or federal reserve, which can either be independent of the public and its own entity or part of a country's public institutions. Unlike Ether or bitcoin, these stablecoins are centralized and can even freeze the cryptocurrencies in their wallet address. Usually centralized stablecoins are the most stable category in terms of price provided the trust maintained to the entity does not get betrayed.

➤ **Decentralized stablecoins:** Decentralized stablecoins operate without a central authority, enhancing censorship resistance, openness, neutrality, transparency—as everything has to be done on-chain—immutability, and trustlessness. However, they face regulatory challenges and acceptance and can be more volatile than centralized stablecoins.

After those two broad categories, stablecoins branch out to specialized categories such as the price pegging mechanism and how each stablecoin maintains stability. A bit more specialized but still a bit general, there are four broad categories on how stablecoins maintain their price stability and peg:

➤ **Traditionally collaterallized stablecoins:** pegged to real-world assets such as fiat currencies and commodities. These types of collateral offer more stability, but the trade-off for stability is centralization.

➤ **Crypto collateralized stablecoins:** Pegged to different cryptocurrencies, crypto collateral is decentralized compared to traditional collateralized stablecoins but can face capital inefficiencies.

➤ **Algorithmic stablecoins:** Algorithmic stablecoins are not pegged to any currency, be that fiat currency, native cryptocurrency, or commodity. They rely on algorithms, which makes them capital efficient—as no entity needs to buy a currency or asset to peg and back the stablecoin with—and completely decentralized. However, they can pose stability risks and are generally more volatile than their counterparts.

➤ **Hybrid collateralized stablecoins:** Hybrid collateralized stablecoins can be as diverse as pegging the stablecoin to wrapped bitcoin with Ether and other decentralized native crypto-currencies, to having a stablecoin pegged to ether, USDC, and the price of electricity in a specific country, or, instead of electricity, an entirely physical asset such as real estate as well. Through diversifying collateral types, hybrid stablecoins can fight the risks and volatility that come with relying on a single asset—for example, a stablecoin that might be pegged to the price of electricity in Germany after the Russian invasion of Ukraine and subsequent closing off and blowing up of the Nord Stream pipeline—or a stablecoin pegged to the price of oil which tanked during the COVID-19 crisis due to the global lockdowns stopping global travel, industrial activity and operations besides the most essential ones. The complexity of hybrid collateralized stablecoins can pose challenges in understanding them for the average user; they also pose difficulties with transparency if some of the assets the stablecoin is pegged to are off-chain assets.

There are other more specialized but still general categories. Stablecoins can branch out to extremely deep specializations which makes it nearly impossible to go through them all in this book. The following gives an idea and a broad picture.

Off-chain collateralized stablecoins

➤ **Tether (USDT):** Tether maintains a 1 to 1 peg with the USD using a reserve system. For each USDT in circulation, Tether holds an equivalent of 1 USD in reserve. This is good for the USD as it generates additional demand for the fiat currency and improves its liquidity especially since some countries have started reducing the reserves they hold of the USD. This 1 to 1 peg helps in maintaining a relatively stable price as is evident in Figure 10.5.

How it works: Person A buys and deposits 1 USD into Tether's bank account. Tether mints and sends 1 USDT to Persons A's wallet address. Whenever Person A wants to, they can exchange the 1 USDT they got from Tether for 1 USD.

  ➤ **Main advantage:** Simple and straightforward method to maintain stability with the USD and the most stable price out of all methods described.

  ➤ **Main disadvantage:** Since Tether is a centralized entity, users have to trust that the company holds sufficient reserves and will fulfill the redemption requests in case people—and companies that may trust Tether—want to exchange their USDT back into USD.

  ➤ Stablecoins with identical or similar strategy include USD Coin (USDC), Binance USD (BUSD), Gemini Dollar (GUSD), TrueUSD (TUSD), and Pax Dollar (USDP). Figure 10.6 shows their logos.

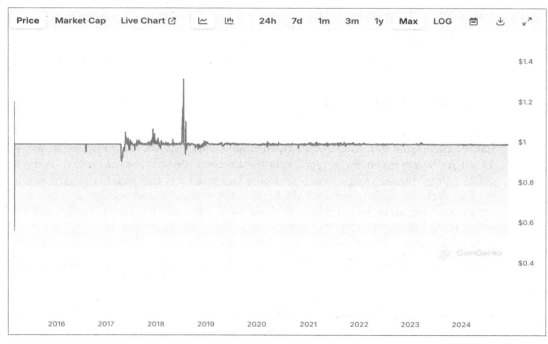

FIGURE 10.5 Price fluctuations of USDT when compared to the USD from 2015 to 2024

FIGURE 10.6 Stablecoin logos: USDT, USDC, BUSD, GUSD, TUSD, USDP

On-chain collateralized stablecoins

➤ **DAI:** DAI is pegged to the USD but backed by ether and other cryptocurrencies making it an on-chain crypto collateralized stablecoin as all the currencies it is pegged to are digital and on-chain. DAI is managed by MakerDAO (a decentralized autonomous organization), which oversees the issuance of DAI. On-chain collateralized stablecoins such as DAI use cryptocurrencies to back them. This bases DAI's value on the real-time intrinsic and perceived value of the cryptocurrencies that are backing DAI. The price of DAI is relatively stable, as shown in Figure 10.7.

➤ **How it works:** Person B deposits a higher-value quantity of ETH than the DAI one wants to borrow in exchange against the ETH deposited into MakerDAO's vault—MakerDAO's smart contract: 100 USD worth of ETH. Then, Person B can mint and borrow up to 50 USD worth of DAI—50 DAI. Person B can get their collateral back by repaying the 50 USD/DAI she borrowed at a later date. If the collateral's value drops below 100 USD but is still more than 50 USD, a portion of the ETH that Person B deposited is liquidated—meaning they lose part of their deposit. They can even lose their whole deposit when the price of ETH is about to fall below 50 USD.

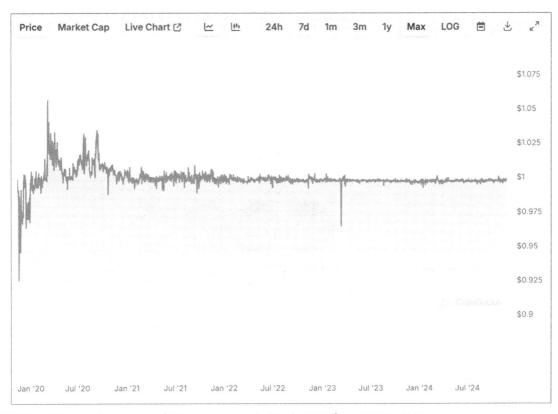

FIGURE 10.7 Price fluctuations of DAI when compared to the USD from 2020 to 2024

As mentioned, when you borrow DAI, you need to put up your ETH as collateral to secure the loan and ETH is volatile for the moment. The health factor is a metric that tells you how safe your loan is. If the value of your collateral is strong (close to or above the required amount), your health factor is high, and your loan is safe. If the value of your collateral drops too much, your health factor gets low, meaning your loan is at risk. If the collateral's value falls too far, the system steps in and liquidates it. This means someone else buys your collateral at a discounted price to pay off your debt. The buyer gets a bonus for doing this, while you, as the borrower, face a penalty for letting your loan become too risky.

➤ **Use cases:** DAI has several use cases since someone who borrows DAI gives more money as a guarantee than they receive. The primary use case is that if someone believes that the price of Ether will increase, they can lock up their ETH in MakerDAO's smart contract vault and get liquidity (cash) to use without selling their Ether. If their prediction was right, the price of Ether goes up, and they get their Ether back at its new higher value.

While having DAI on hand, you can use it for staking, trading, payments, lending, and using as a stable store of value if you are from a country whose fiat currency is highly volatile, such as Venezuela, Zimbabwe, and recently, as of 2024, Argentina. Another use case is cryptocurrency exchanges that borrow DAI to sell on their exchanges to traders and their customers, generating trading fees through that activity.

➤ Stablecoins with identical or similar mechanics: Liquity USD (LUSD), Synthetix USD (sUSD), GHO, Rai Reflex Index (RAI), and Magic Internet Money (MIM) (see Figure 10.8).

> **NOTE** Also, research the alternative stablecoins, and if they differ from the main mechanisms described here, understand how they do so.

FIGURE 10.8 Additional stablecoin logos: DAI, LUSD, sUSD, GHO, RAI, MIM

Algorithmic stablecoins

➤ **Ampleforth:** Ampleforth is an algorithmic stablecoin that uses what is known as the rebase model. It uses the USD as an example peg, and its algorithm works in the following way: If the stablecoin is equal to the price of 1 USD through an oracle, then it does nothing. If the value of the stablecoin is less than 1 USD, then the supply of the stablecoin will decrease through burning—destroying—a number of them. This is done to increase the price analogous to the coin's demand. On the other hand, if the price is more than 1 USD, then the algorithm mints new Ampleforth coins to bring the stablecoin price down. Ampleforth, although fully decentralized, suffers from price fluctuations as can be seen in Figure 10.9.

Figure 10.10 diagrams the relationship of decentralized and centralized stablecoins. The tree's main umbrellas are "Centralized," "Decentralized," and "Hybrid Collateralized." The "Hybrid Collateralized" can sometimes be highly centralized depending on the asset and strategy collateralization; it can be somewhere in the middle or highly decentralized. After a point, falling farther down the "centralized" or "decentralized" umbrella in the diagram does not imply further centralization or decentralization.

As an extra exercise, you can read the different types of stablecoins—both actual and hypothetical—mentioned in the diagram and use logic and what you have learned so far to decide to what degree the ones that appear to be somewhat in the middle are centralized and to what degree decentralized.

There is no best stablecoin; each has its trade-offs, risks, use cases, and benefits. Depending on what a user prefers, they use the stablecoin or stablecoins of their choice.

Now that you have a better understanding of stablecoins and the different types of stablecoins, the rest of this chapter guides you through creating a stablecoin and its skeleton or protocol so you can learn how it works.

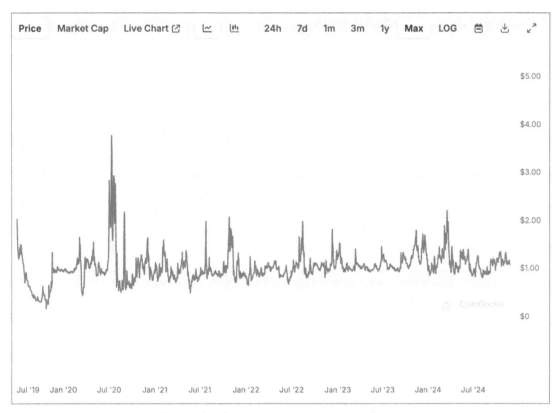

FIGURE 10.9 Price fluctuations of Ampleforth when compared to the USD from 2019 to 2024

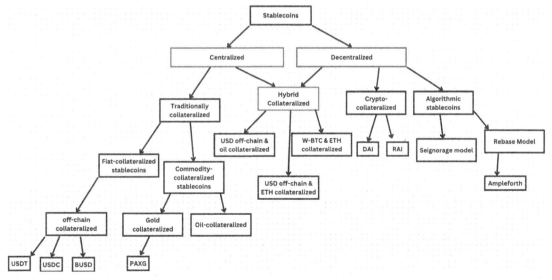

FIGURE 10.10 Stablecoin visualization

CREATING THE STABLECOIN

Follow these steps to create a stablecoin:

1. Type **ls** in the terminal to see where in your filesystem you are located (see Figure 10.11).

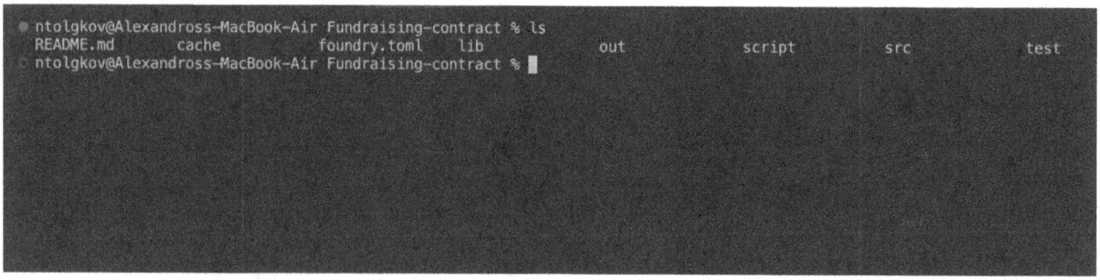

```
● ntolgkov@Alexandross-MacBook-Air Fundraising-contract % ls
  README.md        cache            foundry.toml    lib           out        script        src        test
○ ntolgkov@Alexandross-MacBook-Air Fundraising-contract % █
```

FIGURE 10.11 Fundraising contract directory

Figure 10.11 shows that you are in the directory of the fundraising contract.

2. To leave that folder, type **cd ..** Then type **ls** again to see where you are, as shown in Figure 10.12.

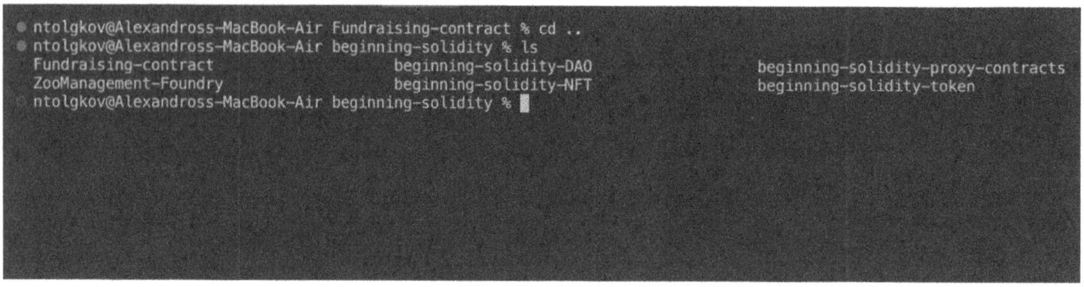

```
● ntolgkov@Alexandross-MacBook-Air Fundraising-contract % cd ..
● ntolgkov@Alexandross-MacBook-Air beginning-solidity % ls
  Fundraising-contract                beginning-solidity-DAO              beginning-solidity-proxy-contracts
  ZooManagement-Foundry               beginning-solidity-NFT             beginning-solidity-token
○ ntolgkov@Alexandross-MacBook-Air beginning-solidity % █
```

FIGURE 10.12 beginning-solidity directory

Now you are in the beginning-solidity directory.

3. Create a new folder or directory called beginning-solidity-stablecoin, and then press Enter:

   mkdir beginning-solidity-stablecoin

4. Type **ls** again to ensure the folder has been created. See Figure 10.13.

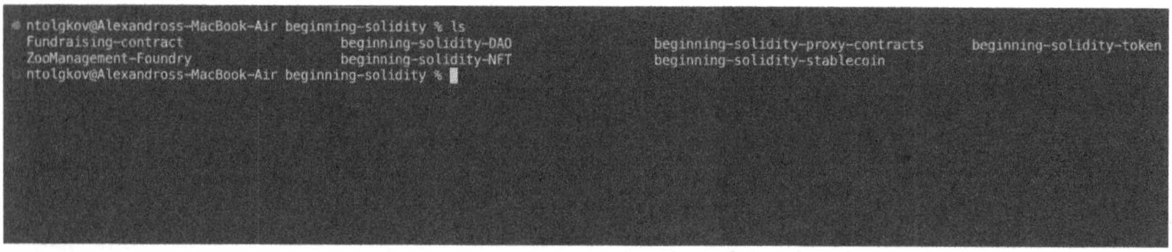

```
● ntolgkov@Alexandross-MacBook-Air beginning-solidity % ls
  Fundraising-contract                beginning-solidity-DAO              beginning-solidity-proxy-contracts    beginning-solidity-token
  ZooManagement-Foundry               beginning-solidity-NFT             beginning-solidity-stablecoin
○ ntolgkov@Alexandross-MacBook-Air beginning-solidity % █
```

FIGURE 10.13 ls after creating directory

5. Type **cd beginning-solidity-stablecoin** to get into the folder.

    Then, type **ls** again to ensure you are in the actual folder. If nothing shows up, then you are indeed in the folder.

6. Select File ⇨ Open Folder, as shown in Figure 10.14.

FIGURE 10.14 Opening a folder

On the files, choose the previously created beginning-solidity folder and then the beginning-solidity-stablecoin—or however you might have named the folder and click Open, as demonstrated in Figure 10.15.

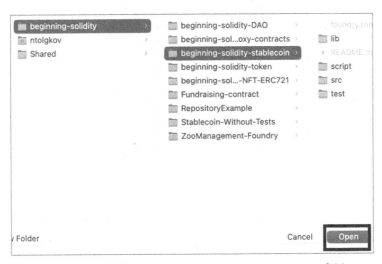

FIGURE 10.15 beginning-solidity and beginning-solidity-stablecoin folders

7. After having opened the beginning-solidity-stablecoin folder, a new Foundry project has to be created. To do so, in the terminal, type this:

    ```
    forge init --no-commit
    ```

8. After having installed the new project, type the following to install Chainlink's brownie contracts, as they will be useful:

    ```
    forge install https://github.com/smartcontractkit/chainlink-brownie-
    contracts
      --no-commit
    ```

You can also go to Chainlink's GitHub for the brownie contracts by searching with your browser and copy-pasting the URL during the writing of the `forge install` command as shown in this step.

9. After downloading the `brownie-smart-contracts`, you should download OpenZeppelin's contracts by typing this:

```
forge install https://github.com/OpenZeppelin/openzeppelin-contracts
--no-commit
```

10. After having installed the contracts, delete the `Counter.sol` contracts and create a `stablecoin.sol` file in the `src` folder, as shown in Figure 10.16.

> **NOTE** If you get any errors, use an AI assistant to get help. Copy-paste the errors and write a prompt that explains what you are trying to do. Ask for a solution and do what the AI suggests to solve the error.

FIGURE 10.16 `Stablecoin.sol`

Now that the `Stablecoin.sol` file has been created, it is time to start working on creating the stablecoin itself. To do that, type the code lines in the rest of this section.

```
//SPDX-License-Identifier: MIT
```

The previous defines the license under which the contract will be released.

```
pragma solidity 0.8.28;
```

The previous defines the Solidity version the contract is going to use.

```
import {ERC20Burnable, ERC20} from "../lib/openzeppelin-contracts/
contracts/token
/ERC20/extensions/ERC20burnable.sol";
```

The previous imports the ERC20Burnable and ERC20 contracts of the fungible tokens from the local library path that are available now that you have downloaded the OpenZeppelin contracts. The ERC20Burnable is an extension of the ERC20 contract that adds a burn functionality to the token, meaning it destroys a number of tokens.

```
import {Ownable} from "../lib/openzeppelin-contracts/contracts/access/
Ownable.sol";
```

Then, the Ownable contract is also imported from the local library path. The Ownable contract is usually used to give access control mechanisms to different functions, ensuring that only the contract owner can call certain functions.

```
contract Stablecoin is ERC20Burnable, Ownable {
```

The previous defines the name of the contract and inherits the ERC20Burnable and Ownable contracts.

```
error Stablecoin__MustBeMoreThanZero();
error Stablecoin__BurnMoreThanBalance();
error Stablecoin__NoMintingtoZeroAddress();
error Stablecoin__AmountMustBeMoreThanZero();
```

The previous are the various errors that are used with the `if` statements and when something needs to revert as they save gas.

```
constructor() ERC20("Stablecoin", "SBT") {}
```

The constructor previous calls the ERC20 of the parent contract and gives the token a name and a symbol. The name is Stablecoin, and the symbol is SBT.

```
function burn (uint256 _amount) public override onlyOwner {
```

The burn function takes a parameter `_amount` (`uint256`), is publicly accessible, and can only be called by the contract owner due to the `onlyOwner` modifier. It also overrides the parent contract's burn function.

```
uint256 balance = balanceOf(msg.sender);
```

The previous states a variable `balance`, which is then set to the balance of the `msg.sender`. Since the only person who can call this function is the contract owner, `msg.sender` signifies the contract owner.

```
if(_amount == 0) {
    revert Stablecoin__MustBeMoreThanZero();
}
```

The previous states that if the amount is equal to 0, then the function should revert to ensure that no one burns tokens when their balance is 0.

```
if (balance < _amount) {
    revert Stablecoin__BurnMoreThanBalance();
}
```

The previous states that if the amount being burnt is more than the balance, then the function should revert. Logically, the balance has to be more than the amount being burnt.

```
        super.burn(_amount);
    }
```

The previous calls the burn function of the parent contract, which is the ERC20Burnable, which has the function shown in Figure 10.17 within the contract.

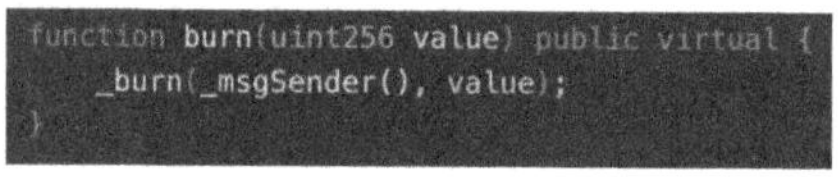

```
function burn(uint256 value) public virtual {
    _burn(_msgSender(), value);
}
```

FIGURE 10.17 Burn function of ERC20Burnable.sol

The burn function has a local parameter value of type uint256, which is public. It can be called internally and externally; virtual means the function can be overridden in a derived contract. Within the function itself, coins are burned through _burn. Within the parenthesis, it signifies that the tokens being burned are those of the function's caller. The value means the number of tokens to be burned.

```
        function mint(address _to, uint256 _amount) external onlyOwner
    returns(bool) {
```

The mint function previous takes two parameters: _to (the recipient's address) and _amount (the number of tokens to mint). It is external, meaning it can be called only outside the contract. It uses the onlyOwner modifier to restrict access to the contract owner. The function returns a Boolean to indicate success.

```
        if(_to == address(0)) {
            revert Stablecoin__NoMintingtoZeroAddress();
        }
```

The previous if statement states that if the _to address, which is the recipient of the mint function, is a zero or null address—the graveyard Ethereum address that no one uses—then the function should revert so that there is no possibility to mint tokens to the Zero address.

```
        if(_amount == 0) {
            revert Stablecoin__AmountMustBeMoreThanZero();
        }
```

The previous if statement states that if the _amount to be minted is equal to zero, then the function should revert.

```
        _mint(_to, _amount);
```

The previous _mint mints tokens. Within the parentheses, it has the address to which the tokens should be minted and the amount of tokens to be minted. The _mint is inherited by one of the parent contracts, ERC20.

```
        return true;
```

The previous at the end returns a `true` statement if the function is executed successfully.

```
    }
}
```

With that, the creation of the fungible Stablecoin is complete. It is now time to create the skeleton of the mechanism responsible for managing it.

THE STABLECOIN SKELETON

To work on creating the Skeleton of the Stablecoin, you need to create a new `StablecoinSkeleton.sol` file.

Within the newly created file, type the following:

```
//SPDX-License-Identifier: MIT
```

The previous defines the license under which the contract will be released.

```
pragma solidity 0.8.27;
```

The previous defines the Solidity version the contract will be using.

```
import {Stablecoin} from "./Stablecoin.sol";
```

The previous import imports the Stablecoin created earlier.

```
import {IERC20} from "@openzeppelin/contracts/token/ERC20/IERC20.sol";
```

The previous import imports the `IERC20.sol` contract, which ensures that the contract that imports it automatically meets all the requirements to comply with the ERC20 token standard.

```
import {ReentrancyGuard} from "@openzeppelin/contracts/utils/Reentrancy
Guard.sol";
```

The previous import imports the `ReentrancyGuard.sol` contract, which defends against reentrancy attacks, one of the most common attacks in the blockchain industry.

```
import {AggregatorV3Interface} from "@chainlink/contracts/shared/interfaces
/AggregatorV3Interface.sol";
```

The previous import imports the AggregatorV3Interface from Chainlink, enabling smart contracts to interact with and integrate price feeds of oracles that provide off-chain information such as the price of an asset, currency, etc.

```
contract StablecoinSkeleton is ReentrancyGuard {
```

The previous defines the contract and its name and inherits the `ReentrancyGuard` contract.

```
error StablecoinSkeleton__NeedsMoreThanZero();
```

The previous error is thrown when a wallet operation requires an amount greater than zero. Still, the wallet has zero tokens in the address.

```
error StablecoinSkeleton__TokenAddressAndPriceFeedAddressesMustHave
SameLength();
```

The previous error is thrown when the array of the token addresses array and the price feed addresses array do not match in the constructor. This is because there should be two token addresses for two price feeds. If more or fewer, there is a problem.

```
error StablecoinSkeleton__NotAllowedToken();
```

The previous is thrown when a user tries to interact with a token that is not allowed.

```
error StablecoinSkeleton__TransferFailed();
```

The previous is thrown when a transfer has failed.

```
error StablecoinSkeleton__BreaksHealthFactor(uint256 healthFactor);
```

The previous error indicates that a user's health factor has fallen following a critical threshold, which makes the system consider the user's position unsafe.

```
error StablecoinSkeleton__MintingFailed();
```

The previous is thrown when an attempt to mint stablecoins fails.

```
error StablecoinSkeleton__HealthFactorIsFine();
```

The previous is thrown when a liquidation attempt is attempted at a user whose financial health and health factor are previous 1 and thus previous the liquidation threshold.

```
uint256 constant LIQUIDITATION_THRESHOLD = 50;
```

The previous variable defines the liquidation threshold, which is 50% of the user's collateral that can be considered when calculating their health factor, as shown in Figure 10.18.

FIGURE 10.18 Health factor equation

The health factor is a crucial metric in decentralized finance and particularly collateralized lending protocols, as it is used to assess the financial safety of a user's position in the system by representing the ratio between the value of a user's collateral (adjusted for risk) and their debt (minted stablecoins in this context or the `totalSBTminted` function) when the two are divided between them and also taking the % of the liquidation threshold into account. In this case, the liquidation threshold is 50%. The health factor is typically expressed as greater than 1, with values following 1 indicating that the user's position is under-collateralized and at risk of liquidation.

For example, if someone's collateral value is 1,000 USD, and the liquidation threshold is 50%, then:

$$\text{Safe Debt Limit} = \text{Collateral Value} \times \text{Liquidation Threshold}$$

$$500 \text{ USD} = 1,000 \text{ USD} \times 50\%$$

The liquidation threshold is the line that, after crossing, the address gets liquidated. Liquidation is the process of selling collateral to repay debt when a loan is about to become under-collateralized. It is a mechanism automatically used and enforced by protocols to ensure stability and solvency.

```
mapping (address token => address priceFeed) s_priceFeed;
```

The previous private mapping s_priceFeed pairs the token address with the token's price feed to fetch the token's current price and thus calculate the collateral.

```
mapping (address user => mapping(address token => uint256 amount))
    s_collateralDeposit;
```

The previous private s_collateralDeposit mapping is a nested private mapping that tracks the amount of each token deposited as collateral by each user. It maps a user's address to another mapping of token addresses and the deposited amount.

```
mapping(address user => uint256 amountSBTminted) s_SBTminted;
```

The s_SBTminted mapping tracks the number of stablecoins minted by a user or address. It maps a user's address to the number of coins the user has minted.

```
address[] s_collateralTokens;
```

The s_collateralTokens array stores the list of token contract addresses that the protocol allows as collateral.

```
Stablecoin immutable i_stablecoin;
```

The previous private i_stablecoin variable is immutable, meaning it will be set in the constructor.

```
event CollateralDeposited(address indexed user, address indexed token,
    uint256 indexed amount);
```

The previous CollateralDeposited event is emitted whenever a user deposits collateral.

```
modifier collateralMoreThanZero(uint256 _amount) {
    if(_amount == 0) {
        revert StablecoinSkeleton__NeedsMoreThanZero();
    }
    _;
}
```

The previous `collateralMoreThanZero` modifier ensures that the `_amount` parameter is greater than zero. If the amount is zero, then the transaction reverts to the `StablecoinSkeleton__NeedsMoreThanZero` error shown previously.

```
modifier isAllowedToken(address token) {
    if(s_priceFeed[token] == address(0)) {
        revert StablecoinSkeleton__NotAllowedToken();
    }
    _;
}
```

The previous `isAllowedToken` modifier checks if a specific token address is of an allowed token. It does this by checking if a non-zero price feed address is associated with the token in the `s_priceFeed` mapping. If the token is not allowed, the transaction reverts to the `StablecoinSkeleton__NotAllowedToken`error.

```
constructor(address[] memory tokenAddresses, address[] memory
priceFeedAddress, address stablecoinAddress) {
```

The constructor previous sets up the `tokenAddresses` array, which contains the addresses of the tokens allowed as collateral. It also sets up the `priceFeedAddress` array, which holds the price feeds for those tokens.

```
if(tokenAddresses.length != priceFeedAddress.length) {
```

```
revert StablecoinSkeleton__TokenAddressAndPriceFeedAddressesMustHave
SameLength();
    }
```

The `if` statement verifies that the `tokenAddresses` and `priceFeedAddresses`arrays have the same length. If they do not match, it reverts the transaction with the error `StablecoinSkeleton__TokenAddressAndPriceFeedAddressesMustHaveSameLength`, which was seen before.

```
for (uint256 i = 0; i < tokenAddresses.length; i++) {
    s_priceFeed[tokenAddresses[i]] = priceFeedAddress[i];
    s_collateralTokens.push(tokenAddresses[i]);
}

i_stablecoin = Stablecoin(stablecoinAddress);
    }
```

The `for` loop iterates over the `tokenAddresses` array, mapping each token address to its corresponding price feed address in the `s_priceFeed` mapping and adding each token address to the `s_collateralTokens` array, which keeps a record of all allowed collateral tokens. This ensures that each allowed token has an associated price feed and is stored in a list for later reference. Finally, the `i_stablecoin` variable is set to point to the Stablecoin contract deployed at the provided stablecoin address.

```
function depositCollateralAndMintSBT(address tokenCollateralAddress,
uint256 amountCollateral, uint256 amountSBTtoMint) external {
```

The previous `depositCollateralAndMintSBT` function has two local parameters: an address `tokenCollateralAddress` and a uint256 that represents the SBT amount of stablecoins to be minted, `amountSBTtoMint`. The function is external, meaning it can only be called externally.

```
depositCollateral(tokenCollateralAddress, amountCollateral);
```

The line previous calls the `depositCollateral` function in this contract and deposits the predetermined collateral amount in the form of the token represented based on the `tokenCollateral Address` parameter.

```
mintSBT(amountSBTtoMint);
```

The function is the `mintSBT(amountSBTtoMint)` part of the code minus the specified number of stablecoins for the address.

```
    }

    function depositCollateral(address _tokenCollateralAddress,
uint256 _amountOfCollateral)
    public
    collateralMoreThanZero(_amountOfCollateral)
    isAllowedToken(_tokenCollateralAddress)
    nonReentrant
    {
```

The previous `depositCollateral` function has two local variables: an address `_tokenCollateral Address` and an uint256 `_amountOfCollateral`, representing the collateral's amount. It is a public function that can be called internally and externally. Then, it has a couple of modifiers—a particular block of code that runs before the function itself—the first modifier, `collateralMoreThanZero(_ amountOfCollateral)`, ensures that the `_amountOfCollateral` is greater than zero. If the amount is zero, the transaction is reverted. The second modifier, `isAllowedToken(_tokenCollateral Address)`, ensures that the address interacting and depositing collateral does so in the allowed token only and not in any token it may want to deposit otherwise. The `nonReentrant` modifier is a modifier that comes with the `ReentrancyGuard.sol` contract and prevents the function from being hacked with a reentrancy attack.

```
        s_collateralDeposit[msg.sender][_tokenCollateralAddress] +=
_amountOfCollateral;
```

The line previous interacts with the `s_collateralDeposit` mapping by referencing it and updating the user's address (`msg.sender`) who last interacted with the function. It additionally specifies the address of the token being deposited, enabling the contract to access the collateral balance for the specific token for the address that calls the `depositCollateral` function. Finally, the amount being deposited by the address is added to the total of collateral the address added throughout its lifetime into the protocol.

```
        emit CollateralDeposited(msg.sender, _tokenCollateralAddress,
_amountOfCollateral);
```

After the amount of collateral in the allowed token is deposited by the `msg.sender` address, the address that last interacted with the contract, the `CollateralDeposited` event is emitted to the blockchain nodes logs. All three values emitted are indexed, meaning they are easily recoverable if required from the logs. They represent the user (`msg.sender`), the token (`tokenCollateralAddress`—the token's address), and the amount deposited (`_amountOfCollateral`).

```
bool success = IERC20(_tokenCollateralAddress).transferFrom(
msg.sender,
address(this),
_amountOfCollateral
);
```

The IERC20 interface is used to interact with ERC-20 token contracts. Specifically, it allows the function to call the `transferFrom` function on the token contract at the address `_token CollateralAddress`. This facilitates transferring the specified `_amountOfCollateral` from the user (`msg.sender`) to the contract's address (`address(this)`). However, before this transfer can occur, the user must have already approved the contract to spend their tokens. The approve function, which the user needs to call separately, sets the maximum amount the contract can transfer on their behalf. With this prior approval, the `transferFrom` function will succeed.

```
if (!success) {
    revert StablecoinSkeleton__TransferFailed();
}
}
```

Finally, the previous `if` statement states that if the function is not successful (`!success`), it should revert using the `StablecoinSkeleton__TransferFailed` custom error.

```
function redeemCollateralForSBT(address tokenCollateralAddress, uint256
amountCollateral, uint256 amountSBTtoburn) external {
```

The `redeemCollateralForSBT` function has as a local parameter the address named `tokenCollateralAddress`, which represents the address of the token being redeemed as collateral, an `uint256 amountCollateral`, which refers to the amount of collateral the user wants to withdraw, and an `uint256 amountSBTtoburn`, which the user wants to burn—to destroy—to repay their debt.

```
burnSBT(amountSBTtoburn);
```

The previous calls the `burnSBT` to burn a specified amount of stablecoins from the user's balance. This reduces the debt in the function's caller's system since a specified amount of stablecoins that were minted are removed.

```
redeemCollateral(tokenCollateralAddress, amountCollateral);
```

This previous withdraws the specified amount of collateral with the token from the user's total collateral balance.

```
}
```

```
    function redeemCollateral(address tokenCollateralAddress, uint256
amountOfCollateral) public collateralMoreThanZero(amountOfCollateral)
nonReentrant {
```

The redeemCollateral function has a tokencollateralAddress variable of the address type, which represents the address of the token the user wants to redeem as collateral, and a uint256 variable called amountOfCollateral, which represents the amount of collateral the user wants to withdraw. The collateralMoreThanZero ensures that the collateral's value is more than zero, and the nonReentrant prevents reentrancy attacks.

```
        s_collateralDeposit[msg.sender][tokenCollateralAddress] -=
amountOfCollateral;
```

The user's deposited collateral is subtracted from the requested amount of the total amount deposited, which is currently in the smart contract.

```
        emit CollateralRedeemed(msg.sender, tokenCollateralAddress,
amountOfCollateral); [This event has not been declared. -TE]
```

An event of the redemption transaction is broadcasted and stored by the nodes in the EVM.

```
        bool success = IERC20(tokenCollateralAddress).transfer(msg.sender,
amountOfCollateral);
        if(!success) {
            revert StablecoinSkeleton__TransferFailed();
        }
    }
```

This is the token transfer using the .transfer method seen in previous chapters to transfer the amount to the function's caller. If the transfer is not successful, the function is reverted.

```
    function mintSBT(uint256 amountSBTToBeMinted) public
collateralMoreThanZero
(amountSBTToBeMinted) nonReentrant {
```

The mintSBT function has a local parameter, amountSBTToBeMinted, signifying the number of tokens a user wants to mint. The function is public, meaning it can only be called externally and internally. The collateralMoreThanZero modifier makes sure that the amountSBTToBeMinted is larger than 0 tokens. If not, the function will revert. The nonReentrant derives from ReentrancyGuard.sol and protects against reentrancy hacks.

```
        s_SBTminted[msg.sender] += amountSBTToBeMinted;
```

The previous updates the s_SBTminted mapping and the address of msg.sender—the last address to call the function—regarding the number of stablecoins minted by the address that called the function.

```
        revertIfHealthFactorDoesNotWork(msg.sender);
```

The previous line calls the revertIfHealthFactorDoesNotWork function and gives the address of the function's last caller—msg.sender—to ensure that the address passes the health factor. If not, the transaction is reverted.

```
        bool minted = i_stablecoin.mint(msg.sender, amountSBTToBeMinted);
```
The previous line of code calls the multifunction on the i_stablecoin contract, which is an instance of the Stablecoin contract initialized earlier in the constructor of this contract. The purpose of this function call is to mint a specified amount of stablecoins (amountSBTToBeMinted) for the caller of this function (msg.sender), who initiated the transaction.

The mint function in the Stablecoin contract returns a Boolean value (true or false), indicating whether the minting operation was successful. This return value is stored in the minted variable. It is critical because it determines the outcome of the subsequent error-handling logic. If the return value is false, the function execution reverts with the custom errorStablecoinSkeleton__MintingFailed(), ensuring that no unexpected or invalid state changes occur if minting fails.

```
        if(!minted) {
            revert StablecoinSkeleton__MintingFailed();
        }
```

The previous if statement states that if the tokens were not minted, the function should revert using the MintingFailed error.

```
    }

        function burnSBT(uint256 _amount) public collateralMoreThanZero(_amount) {
```

The burnSBT allows the function's caller to burn—to destroy—a specified number of tokens. This reduces the user's debt in the system. The function is public, which means it can be called both internally and externally, and the modifier collateralMoreThanZero ensures that the amount burned is more than zero tokens.

```
        s_SBTminted[msg.sender] -= _amount;
```
The user's minted stablecoins are decreased by the amount that will be burned or destroyed.

```
        bool success = i_stablecoin.transferFrom(msg.sender, address(this),
    _amount);
        if (!success) {
            revert StablecoinSkeleton__TransferFailed();
        }
```

The previous Boolean uses the transferFrom method—a method used in ERC20 token standards—to transfer a specified amount from the wallet address to the contract's address. If the transfer fails, the function reverts.

```
        i_stablecoin.burn(_amount);
```

Once the tokens are transferred, the contract calls the burn function of the ERC20Burnable contract to destroy the tokens.

```
        revertIfHealthFactorDoesNotWork(msg.sender);
    }
```

After burning the tokens, the function uses the `revertIfHealthFactorDoesNotWork` to ensure that the addresses' health factor remains valid.

```
    function liquidate(address _collateral, address _user, uint256
debtToCover)
external collateralMoreThanZero(debtToCover) {
```

The liquidate function has an address `_collateral`, which signifies the address of the collateral token that will be liquidated. The `_user` address is the user's address whose collateral is being liquidated. The `debtToCover` represents the amount of debt in USD the liquidator will repay on behalf of the user. The function is external, meaning it can only be called externally, and the modifier `collateralMoreThanZero` ensures that the `_debtToCover` is larger than 0.

```
    uint256 startingUserHealthFactor = healthFactor(_user);
```

The previous calculates the user's health factor by calling the function `Healthfactor`.

```
    if(startingUserHealthFactor >= 1e18) {
        revert StablecoinSkeleton__HealthFactorIsFine();
    }
```

The `if` statement checks if the health factor is at least one, meaning that the user is in a safe financial position. If yes, the function reverts.

```
    uint256 tokenAmountFromDebtCovered = getUSDValue(_collateral,
debtToCover);
```

The `getUSDValue` function converts the debt in USD into the equivalent quantity of the collateral token.

```
    uint256 bonusCollateral = (tokenAmountFromDebtCovered * 10) / 100;
```

The liquidator that liquidates the user is incentivized to do so by getting a 10% bonus. It is not always 10%; the bonus varies depending on the protocol, but in this specific case, the bonus has been defined as 10%.

```
    uint256 totalCollateralToRedeem = tokenAmountFromDebtCovered +
bonusCollateral;
    }
```

The previous adds the total collateral to be redeemed by the liquidator as the user's debt plus the bonus.

```
function _redeemCollateral(address AddressforTokenCollateral, uint256
amountofCollateral, address from, address to) private {

}
function getAccountInformation(address user) private view returns(uint256
totalSBTMinted, uint256 collateralValueInUSD) {
```

The getAccountInformation function has a local parameter user of address type. It is private, meaning that the function can only be called internally. It is a view function, meaning it does not alter the state of the blockchain but simply reads and retrieves information from it. It returns an uint256 totalSBTMinted, signifying the total number of stablecoins minted, and the uint256, which is the collateral's value in USD.

```
totalSBTMinted = s_SBTminted[user];
```

The previous line retrieves the total amount of stablecoins minted by the specified user address from the s_SBTminted mapping and assigns it to the totalSBTMinted variable.

```
collateralValueInUSD = getAccountCollateralValue(user);
```

The previous is called the getAccountCollateralValue function, which gives the user's address to calculate the total value of the user's collateral in USD. The result is assigned to the collateral ValueInUSD variable.

```
    }


function healthFactor(address _user) private view returns(uint256) {
```

The healthFactor function has a local address parameter called _user. It is private, meaning it can only be called internally. It is view, does not alter the state of the blockchain, only reads from it, and returns an uint256 variable at the end of the function.

```
    (uint256 totalSBTMinted, uint256 collateralValueInUSD) =
getAccountInformation(_user);
```

The previous line calls the getAccountInformation function and gives the user's address as the argument to retrieve two values: the total number of stablecoins the address has minted and the collateral it has deposited. This information can be used to assess the user's debt, financial position, and health.

```
    uint256 collateralAdjustedForThreshold = (collateralValueInUSD *
LIQUIDITATION_THRESHOLD) / 100;
```

The uint256 collateralAdjustedForThreshold represents the portion of the user's collateral in USD that is considered safe for minting stablecoins. It is calculated by multiplying the total collateral value (collateralValueInUSD) by the liquidation threshold (in this case, 50%) and dividing the result by 100 to convert the percentage into a fraction. This ensures that only a specific portion of the user's collateral can be safely used, reducing liquidation risk.

```
    return (collateralAdjustedForThreshold * 1e10) / totalSBTMinted;
    }
```

The return line calculates the health factor for a user, which was mentioned previously. The collateralAdjustedForThreshold represents the safe portion of the user's collateral in USD, which is adjusted by the liquidation threshold. This ensures that only a part of the whole collateral can be considered for minting stablecoins. The multiplication by 1e10 is for scaling purposes. As seen in previous chapters, Solidity does not work with fractions but with decimals, and this scaling effectively maintains integrity in the result for Solidity's purposes. Finally, the division by the `totalSBTMinted` determines the ration of safe collateral to be mint stablecoins. A higher result shows a safer position.

```
function revertIfHealthFactorDoesNotWork(address user) internal view {
```

The `revertIfHealthFactorDoesNotWork` function has a local parameter of type address and is named user. The function is internal, meaning that it can only be called internally. View means it does not change the state of the blockchain but only reads from it. The function aims to protect the system by ensuring a user's health factor is above the critical threshold. If the health factor is below the threshold, then the function reverts.

```
uint256 userHealthFactor = healthFactor(user);
```

The previous calls the `healthfactor` function, which calculates the user's health factor, and sets it to the uint256 variable of `userHealthFactor`.

```
if(userHealthFactor < 1) {

    revert StablecoinSkeleton__BreaksHealthFactor(userHealthFactor);
}
```

As mentioned previously, the health factor is usually represented by the digit 1. If the `userHealthFactor` is less than 1, the user's financial position is unsafe, and as a consequence, the transaction is reversed. The function, as a consequence, ensures that users with a low health factor cannot take actions that would further jeopardize their financial health.

```
}


    function getAccountCollateralValue(address user) public view returns
(uint256
totalCollateralValueInUSD) {
```

The `getAccountCollateralValue` function has a local parameter user of type address. It is public, meaning it can be called both internally and externally. It is a view function, meaning that it does not change the state of the blockchain but reads from it. At the end of the function, it returns a uint256 variable named `totalCollateralValueInUSD`.

```
for(uint256 i = 0; i < s_collateralTokens.length; i++) {
    address token = s_collateralTokens[i];
    uint256 amount = s_collateralDeposit[user][token];
    totalCollateralValueInUSD += getUSDValue(token, amount);
}
```

The `for` loop goes through all collateral tokens stored in the `s_collateralDeposit` mapping to calculate the total USD value of a user's collateral. The `for` loop starts with i set to zero and goes through the length of the whole `collateralTokens`. The address token = `s_collateralTokens[i]` gets the token address from index i in the `s_ collateralTokens` array. Then it assigns it to the token address variable. Then, the loop accesses `s_collateralDeposit` to get the token amount the user has deposited. Finally, the loop calls the `getUSDValue` function to calculate the USD value of the user's deposited token amount in the current token. The value is then added to the `totalCollateralValueInUSD`.

```
return totalCollateralValueInUSD;
```

At the end of the function, the `totalCollateralValueinUSD` is returned.

```
}

    function getUSDValue(address token, uint256 amount) public view
returns(uint256) {
```

The `getUSDValue` function has as local parameters an address called token and an uint256 amount. It is public, meaning it can be called both internally and externally. It is view, meaning it can only read from the blockchain and not change its state. At the end of the function, the function returns an `uint256`.

```
AggregatorV3Interface priceFeed =
AggregatorV3Interface(s_priceFeed[token]);
```

The `s_priceFeed` token retrieves the address of the price feed contract associated with the specified token from the `s_priceFeed` mapping. This connects each allowed token to its respective price feed.

The `AggregatorV3Interface(s_priceFeed[token])` creates a version of the AggregatorV3Interface contract at the price feed address.

```
(, int256 answer,,,) = priceFeed.latestRoundData();
```

The `priceFeed.latestRoundData` fetches the latest prices from the price feed through a tuple of which only the `int256 answer` variable is needed.

```
return((uint256(answer) * 1e10) * amount) / 1e18;
```

The line previous calculates the total USD value of a given token amount, accounting for the token's price in USD (from the price feed) and its decimal format. This ensures precision in the final USD value.

```
    }
}
```

CHAPTER 10 QUESTIONS

1. Explain the purpose of stablecoins in the cryptocurrency ecosystem and how they address the volatility of traditional cryptocurrencies.

2. What are the three main functions of "good money," and how do stablecoins aim to fulfill these functions compared to fiat currencies and cryptocurrencies?

3. Describe the differences between centralized and decentralized stablecoins. Provide examples of each and explain their trade-offs.

4. Outline the four broad categories of stablecoin collateralization (traditional, crypto, algorithmic, hybrid) and discuss their advantages and risks.

5. What is the health factor, and how does it contribute to the stability of a collateralized stablecoin system? What happens when a user's health factor falls below 1?

6. What is the role of the `ERC20Burnable` and `Ownable` contracts in the implementation of a stablecoin? Why are these contracts critical for functionality and security?

7. Why is it advantageous to use custom errors—for example, `Stablecoin__MustBeMore ThanZero`—in Solidity smart contracts instead of traditional revert statements?

8. Explain the logic behind the minting and burning functions in the stablecoin contract. How are security and integrity ensured during these operations?

9. What is the purpose of Chainlink price feeds in a stablecoin protocol, and how do they enhance system stability?

10. How does the `ReentrancyGuard` contract protect the stablecoin protocol from vulnerabilities? Provide an example of a reentrancy attack.

11. How does the `DepositCollateral` function update storage and ensure the security of user deposits?

12. Describe the liquidation process in a collateralized stablecoin system. How are liquidators incentivized, and how is the collateral-to-debt conversion handled?

13. What challenges do hybrid collateralized stablecoins face in ensuring transparency and user trust? Provide examples.

14. What happens if a user attempts to interact with a token not listed in the `s_PriceFeed` mapping? How does the contract prevent such interactions?

15. Why is it critical to verify a user's health factor before and after certain operations, such as minting or burning? How does the contract enforce this?

11

Building an ERC-721 Nonfungible Token

In this chapter, you'll learn how to create nonfungible tokens (NFTs) using Solidity and the ERC-721 standard. We'll explore everything from the fundamental concepts of NFTs to the practical implementation of smart contracts that power them. You'll discover how NFTs differ from fungible tokens, understand the role of metadata in NFT projects, and learn about the InterPlanetary File System (IPFS) for decentralized storage of NFT assets. Through hands-on coding exercises, you'll gain experience with OpenZeppelin's contracts and Foundry's development environment.

The chapter guides you through the complete process of building and deploying an NFT project on the Ethereum blockchain. You'll write and deploy smart contracts that handle NFT minting, transfers, and ownership management. You'll also learn how to integrate your NFTs with popular platforms like OpenSea and understand how to properly store and manage NFT metadata using IPFS. By the end of this chapter, you'll have the skills to create your own NFT collections and understand the best practices for NFT development, including security considerations and gas optimization techniques.

WHAT IS AN NFT?

The NFT abbreviation stands for nonfungible token. It refers to a unique item and is defined by the ERC-721 standard for nonfungible tokens. This standard is similar to the ERC-20 standard for fungible tokens that has been agreed upon by the Ethereum community.

The critical difference between an NFT and a fungible token is that fungible tokens are interchangeable amongst themselves, while nonfungible tokens are not. Think of the example in Chapter 9 of Alice and Bill exchanging undamaged 50 USD bills with each other. The $50 bills are fungible tokens because they have the same value and utility. Now consider Leonardo Da

Vinci's most famous painting, the *Mona Lisa*, and Vincent Van Gogh's *Starry Night*. Both have indisputable value: monetary, artistic, historical, and aesthetic. However, even if their economic value were fungible, like two undamaged $50 bills, their creative, historical, and aesthetic value is not. Each painting is unique, and personal preference plays a role in someone's choice of one over the other. The choice is subjective, and they would choose the one that aligns with their understanding of artistic, historical, and aesthetic value.

For those reasons, the two paintings can be seen as physical representations of NFTs. NFTs take the uniqueness of a unique physical item—whether tied to culture or anything else—and transfer it to the digital world, making that uniqueness verifiable on the blockchain. This process is called *tokenization of real-world assets* (tokenization of RWAs).

In addition to tokenizing real-world assets, NFT can create purely digital items without physical representation in the real world. The image the token is associated with is often not stored on the blockchain because storing pictures on the blockchain is too expensive due to gas fees. Instead, a pointer to the image—the Uniform Resource Identifier (URI)—is stored on the blockchain. In simpler terms, the URI acts like a link, like sharing a picture stored on Google Drive or Microsoft OneDrive. The image itself is stored in one of two ways. It can be stored on a centralized server, for example, Google Drive or Microsoft OneDrive. (However, if you want to stay true to the principles of decentralization, avoid this method at all costs.) The second way to store the image is called InterPlanetary File System (IPFS), which is a distributed and decentralized way of storing data off-chain. This is discussed in more detail later in this chapter.

That being said, the best way of storing pictures of NFTs—if one is to neglect the costs—is still on-chain. This is the best solution as it is the most trustless, tamper-proof, censorship-resistant, and transparent verifying method. As blockchain evolves throughout the years the high costs of storing small files on-chain might be mitigated somehow, but for the moment, it is extremely expensive to do so, despite the benefits.

An NFT at its most basic level is a unique numbered token within a collection. Think of it like a ticketing system: When a developer creates NFTs, they typically make a collection (let's say 100 tokens) and assign each one a unique number—Token 1, Token 2, Token 3, and so on. This is similar to standing in line and taking a numbered ticket from a machine while waiting your turn. The key difference is that NFTs exist digitally rather than physically.

Just as the person holding a numbered ticket in line is that ticket's owner, the person who possesses an NFT is its owner. NFTs are versatile, and thus they can represent a wide variety of use-cases:

➤ They can be linked to digital art.

➤ They can convey ownership rights to physical assets.

➤ They can even represent legal documents, such as property deeds.

For example, an NFT could be created that states: "The owner of this NFT is automatically the owner of X piece of land located in Y location around the world." This creates a digital representation of property ownership that can be transferred between parties.

SETTING UP THE NFT PROJECT

Before diving into the development of an NFT project, you need a well organized project structure and have all necessary tools and libraries in place. This section guides you through the foundational steps required to set up your project in Visual Studio Code (VS Code) and prepare your environment for building a nonfungible token (NFT) on the Ethereum blockchain using the ERC-721 standard.

The setup process involves the following:

1. Navigating the terminal in VS Code to identify and organize your working directory
2. Creating a new project folder to hold relevant files and dependencies
3. Initializing a Foundry project
4. Installing essential contract templates from OpenZeppelin

Let's begin by navigating your terminal, creating a project directory, and preparing the development environment for your NFT project.

1. As you've done in earlier chapters, use the `ls` command to see your current location, and if you are not in the folder you need to be in, type **cd** .. to navigate there.

2. To create a new directory or folder, type the following:

    ```
    cd beginning-solidity-NFT-ERC721
    ```

    If you are in the `beginning-solidity-NFT-ERC721` folder, you will see the folder's name at the top of the terminal, as shown in Figure 11.1.

```
ntolgkov@Alexandross-MacBook-Air ZooManagement-Foundry % mkdir beginning-solidity-NFT-ERC721
ntolgkov@Alexandross-MacBook-Air ZooManagement-Foundry % cd beginning-solidity-NFT-ERC721
ntolgkov@Alexandross-MacBook-Air beginning-solidity-NFT-ERC721 % []
```

FIGURE 11.1: `beginning-solidity-NFT-ERC721` folder created and entered

> **NOTE** *You may be in a completely different folder from what is shown in Figure 11.3. In that case, create a folder for all the project files and, after entering it, create a file for each project using the figures in this project as a guide, or using your own preferred project organization scheme. This demonstration only shows how to move, enter, and create folders using the terminal.*

3. Next, in VS Code, select File ➢ Open Folder, choose the correct folder to open (in this example, it is `beginning-solidity-NFT-ERC721`), and then click Open (see Figure 11.2).

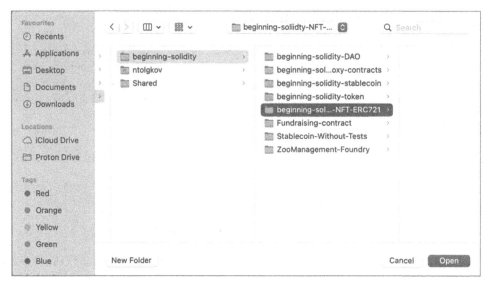

FIGURE 11.2: Opening the `beginning-solidity-NFT-ERC721` folder

4.   After opening the folder, the now classic question of whether one trusts the authors will appear. Click "**Yes, I trust the authors,**" as shown in Figure 11.3.

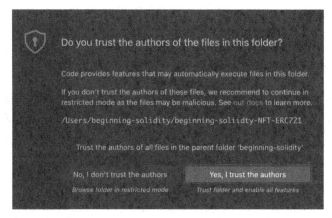

FIGURE 11.3: Yes, I trust the authors!

5.   In the project, type **forge init** to install a new Foundry project (see Figure 11.4).

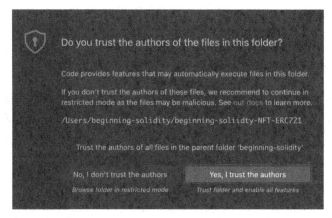

FIGURE 11.4: Foundry project installation pending

Upon installation, you should see the installed and initialized message shown in Figure 11.5.

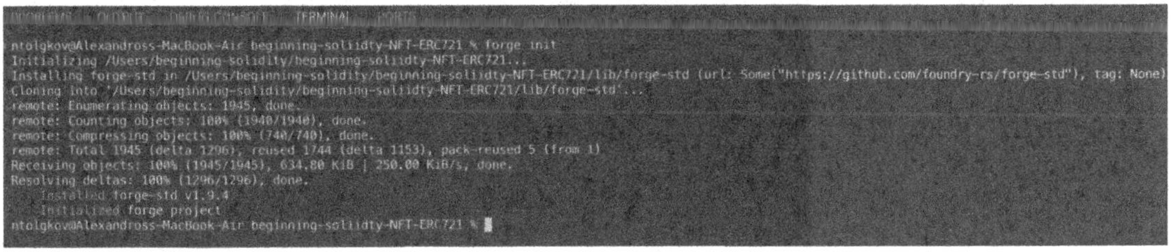

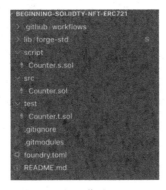

FIGURE 11.5: `foundry init` installed

You should also see the files shown in Figure 11.6 in the folders and files pane.

FIGURE 11.6: Files in the pane after `forge init` installation

6. As with ERC-20 (discussed in Chapter 9), the use of contract templates will be crucial, and hence, you should download the OpenZeppelin contracts in this project as well by typing this:

```
forge install https://github.com/OpenZeppelin/openzeppelin-contracts
--no-commit
```

The link can be found by searching online for "OpenZeppelin files GitHub"; the result should be one of the first. If you open the link in a browser, you will see what is shown in Figure 11.7.

After typing the link, the process of downloading the contracts should begin (see Figure 11.8).

Upon installing the contracts, you should see the message shown in Figure 11.9 in the terminal, confirming the installation.

The `openzeppelin-contracts` folder should appear in the `lib` directory, as shown in Figure 11.10.

If you click and go into the `openzeppelin-contracts` folder and, more specifically, the path lib → openzeppelin-contracts → contracts → token → ERC-721 → ERC721.sol (see Figure 11.11), you will find the `ERC721.sol` contract, which has the template of functions described in the following section.

FIGURE 11.7: GitHub OpenZeppelin

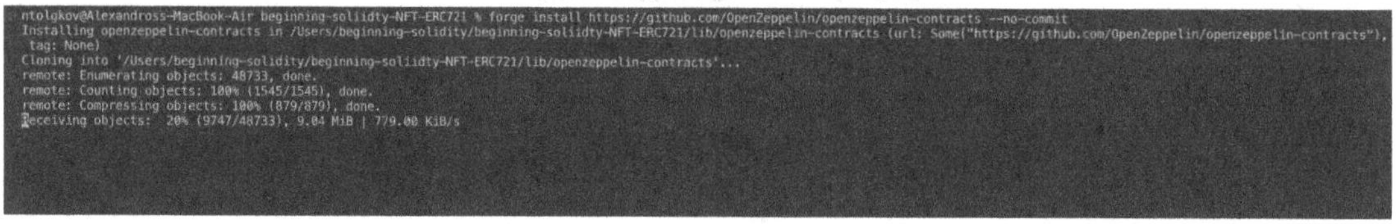

FIGURE 11.8: Downloading OpenZeppelin contracts from GitHub

FIGURE 11.9: Installed smart contracts

FIGURE 11.10: `lib` and `openzeppelin-contracts` folders

FIGURE 11.11: Path to `ERC721.sol`

ERC-721 CONTRACT BREAKDOWN

This section goes through the ERC-721 contract line by line.

The following states the license under which the contract will be released:

```
// SPDX-License-Identifier: MIT
```

The following states the Solidity version the contract will be using. In this case, it is 0.8.20, and the ^ helps make it compatible with any future versions of Solidity that will be released.

```
pragma solidity ^0.8.20;
```

The following imports the `ERC721.sol` contract. The `ERC721.sol` contract includes all the functions and events that an ERC-721 contract must consist of and implement to be considered an ERC-721 contract. This helps keep the different NFT projects that are created consistent and interoperable.

```
import {IERC721} from "./IERC721.sol";
```

The following imports the `IERC721Metadata.sol` contract. The `IERC721Metadata` contract improves the ERC-721 contract by having data related to the token's metadata. This allows NFTs to have names, symbols, and metadata describing unique token attributes, such as images, descriptions, and other properties. For example, if the NFT were a Pokémon card, the metadata would be the Pokémon's different statistics, such as strength, defense, etc. If it were a card of a football/soccer player such as Lionel Messi, Cristiano Ronaldo, Erling Haaland, Kylian Mbappe, and others, those would be speed, dribble, shot power, which foot the football player uses best, etc.

```
import {IERC721Metadata} from "./extensions/IERC721Metadata.sol";
```

The following imports the `ERC721Utils.sol` contract. The ERC721Utils contract is essential as, through its functions, it verifies if the recipient address can handle ERC-721 tokens. It handles two types of recipients: externally owned accounts or simple user addresses, and handles smart contract addresses. If this contract is not implemented, the NFT tokens being implemented could be lost forever because they are sent to an address that does not support ERC-721 tokens.

```
import {ERC721Utils} from "./utils/ERC721Utils.sol";
```

The following imports the `Context.sol` contract. The context contract provides information about the current transaction, such as its sender, value, or data. The context contract might be less necessary when using a single contract. Still, suppose there are imported contracts within a contract that have functions that execute transactions such as the transfer of funds. In that case, it is a crucial element to import as it helps avoid confusion in cases where a contract mistakenly executes a transaction and functions which are not native to the contract but imported.

```
import {Context} from "../../utils/Context.sol";
```

The following imports the `Strings.sol` library. The `Strings` library helps convert numbers to strings and hexadecimal strings when this is required. This is useful in cases where strings are used to communicate or generate token URIs (URLs), among other use cases. The library helps standardize and automate this process instead of having the developers write the functions of the library over and over again.

```
import {Strings} from "../../utils/Strings.sol";
```

The following imports the ERC165 standard and interface. This standard helps the smart contract declare the interfaces it supports, query other contracts, and understand what interfaces it supports. This helps with the detection, standardization, and interoperability of smart contracts on the Ethereum blockchain.

```
import {IERC165, ERC165} from "../../utils/introspection/ERC165.sol";
```

The following imports the `draft-IERC6093.sol` interface. The `draft-IERC6093.sol` interface sets several custom errors that replace the required function and make the contract more gas-efficient overall.

```
import {IERC721Errors} from "../../interfaces/draft-IERC6093.sol";
```

The following defines an `abstract` contract—a contract that cannot be deployed on its own but needs to be imported by another contract and inherited to be deployed as part of the contract. Abstract contracts are good for enforcing agreed-upon standards by the community, defining reusable functionality, and not having developers write the same functions all over again for every ERC-721 contract they deploy. Then, the contract gets a name and inherits a number of contracts: ERC165, IERC721, IERC721Metadata, and IERC721Errors. Within the contract the keyword using is used to attach the Strings to the `uint256` data types. This helps with conversions of integers to strings, which is useful for token IDs.

```
abstract contract ERC721 is Context, ERC165, IERC721, IERC721Metadata,
IERC721Errors {
    using Strings for uint256;
```

The following defines a `private` `string` variable, meaning it can be called only from within the contract with the name _name:

```
string private _name;
```

Similarly, the following defines another private string variable named _symbol:

```
string private _symbol;
```

The following mapping _owners tracks each token's owner (`address`). This happens through the `uint256 tokenId`, which, as mentioned at the beginning of the chapter, numbers the tokens created as if they were tickets with a number when waiting in a queue. The mapping is private, meaning it can be called only within the contract.

```
mapping(uint256 tokenId => address) private _owners;
```

In the following mapping, _balances track the number of NFTs owned by an address. The `uint256`, in this case, represents the count of tokens owned. Like _owners, this mapping is also private.

```
mapping(address owner => uint256) private _balances;
```

The _tokenApprovals mapping tracks which address has been approved to manage a specific token. The `tokenId` represents the token's number, which serves as an identifier, and the `address` is the address approved to operate the NFT. The _tokenApprovals mapping is also private.

```
mapping(uint256 tokenId => address) private _tokenApprovals;
```

The _operatorApprovals mapping is nested—a mapping within a mapping. It tracks the operator address—the address approved by the owner address—and which tokens have been approved by the owner address to be managed by the operator address. The Boolean, which returns a true or false value, shows whether the owner has approved the operator to manage a specific NFT. The _operatorApprovals mapping is private.

```
mapping(address owner => mapping(address operator => bool)) private
    _operatorApprovals;
```

The following `constructor`—the very first function called automatically upon contract deployment—gets a local variable string with the name_ and a string with the name symbol_. The _name global variable seen previously in the contract is set to the local variable name_ within the function. This allows the name of the token collection and its symbol to be set.

```
constructor(string memory name_, string memory symbol_) {
    _name = name_;
    _symbol = symbol_;
}
```

The following function `supportsInterface` has a unique local parameter called `bytes4`, and is named `interfaceId`. This parameter helps identify if the smart contract supports an interface. The function is `public`, meaning it can be called internally and externally within the contract. It is a `view` function, meaning that it does not change the state of the blockchain but only reads information from it; it is `virtual`, meaning that another contract that imports the contract and inherits it can override the function, and the function itself is overriding the same `supportsInterface` functions to be found in the imported and inherited contract (ERC165) and interface (IERC165). The function finally returns a Boolean function that shows something true or false.

Within the function itself, the line `interfaceId == type(IERC721).interfaceId` compares the `interfaceId` of the IERC721 contract (the NFT standard) to the interface ID of this contract. If the two contract interfaces match, the contract supports the ERC-721 standard.

The `interfaceId == type(IERC721Metadata).interfaceId` compares the `interfaceId` of the IERC721Metadata contract with the `interfaceId` of this contract. If they match, it means that the contract supports the additional metadata functionality.

If the `interfaceId` does not match with either contract, then the function delegates the check to the parent contract implementation of the `interfaceId` which is the ERC165 contract.

If the interfaces match, the Boolean returns true.

```
    function supportsInterface(bytes4 interfaceId) public view virtual
override(ERC165, IERC165) returns (bool) {
        return
        interfaceId == type(IERC721).interfaceId ||
        interfaceId == type(IERC721Metadata).interfaceId ||
        super.supportsInterface(interfaceId);
    }
```

The following `balanceOf` function has a local variable address named owner. It is `public`, `view`, and `virtual` and returns a `uint256` variable at the end of the function.

Within the function, an `if` statement occurs where the owner address equals Solidity's zero (`0`) address; then, the function will revert with a custom error called `ERC721InvalidOwner`. The `(address(0))`; part communicates that the custom error `revert` is due to the address being the zero address. If the `owner` address is not zero, then the function returns the `_balances` of the `owner` address. This means returning the token balance a specific address holds.

```
    function balanceOf(address owner) public view virtual returns (uint256) {
        if (owner == address(0)) {
            revert ERC721InvalidOwner(address(0));
        }
        return _balances[owner];
    }
```

The following `ownerOf` function has a local `uint256` parameter named `tokenId`. It is a `public view` function that returns the address of the current owner of a specific NFT, identified by its `tokenId`. It validates the token's existence by calling the internal `_requireOwned` function—seen a bit later in this contract—which ensures the token is valid and has not been burned. If the `tokenId` is valid, the function returns the associated `owner` address; otherwise, it reverts with an error.

```
    function ownerOf(uint256 tokenId) public view virtual returns (address) {
        return _requireOwned(tokenId);
    }
```

The following `name` function is `public`, `view`, `virtual`—meaning it can be overridden by a contract that imports this contract and inherits it—and it returns a string stored in memory. Within the function itself, it simply returns the variable `_name`, which is the name of the token collection.

```
function name() public view virtual returns (string memory) {
    return _name;
}
```

The following `symbol` function is `public`, `view`, and `virtual` and returns a string stored in `memory`. Within the function itself, it returns the symbol of the token collection.

```
function symbol() public view virtual returns (string memory) {
    return _symbol;
}
```

The following `tokenURI` function has a local `uint256` parameter called `tokenId`. It is `public`, `view`, and `virtual` and returns a string stored in `memory`. Within the function itself, the function ensures the token exists by delegating the check to the `_requireOwned` function, which will be seen in one of the functions later in this contract.

The function retrieves the URI for the token collections by calling the `_baseURI` function, another function defined later in the contract—similar to `_requireOwned`—and setting it to the defined `baseURI` string. The `baseURI` string acts as the starting point of the URL for the token collection. The function creates the entire URI by linking the base URI to the string representation of the `tokenId`. If the `baseURI` is empty, the function returns an empty string result.

```
    function tokenURI(uint256 tokenId) public view virtual returns
(string memory) {
        _requireOwned(tokenId);

        string memory baseURI = _baseURI();
        return bytes(baseURI).length > 0 ? string.concat(baseURI,
tokenId.toString()) : "";
    }
```

The following `_baseURI` function is `internal`. It can be called only from within the contract and contracts deriving from it, `view` and `virtual`—meaning it can be overridden by a contract that imports and inherits it—and returns a string stored in `memory`.

The `function` returns the base URI or original URI of the NFT collection provided it is overridden in the child contract.

```
function _baseURI() internal view virtual returns (string memory) {
    return "";
}
```

The following `approve` function has as local variables an `address to` and an `uint256 tokenId`. The function is `public` and `virtual`—overridable when imported and inherited.

Within the function itself, the function calls the `_approve` function, an `internal` function—shown later in the contract—to approve the management of a token (`tokenId`) by an approved address (`to`) by the approver and owner of the token `_msgSender`. Essentially, the function has the owner of an NFT approve another address to manage the token on their behalf.

```
function approve(address to, uint256 tokenId) public virtual {
    _approve(to, tokenId, _msgSender());
}
```

The getApproved function has a local variable of type uint256 named tokenId, it is public, view, virtual and returns an address at the end of the function. Within the function itself, the function calls the _requireOwned internal function, which checks if the token exists, has been minted, and has not been burned—destroyed. If it does not exist, then the function reverts. If the NFT exists, it returns the address which has been approved to manage a specific token (tokenId).

```
function getApproved(uint256 tokenId) public view virtual returns
(address) {
    _requireOwned(tokenId);

    return _getApproved(tokenId);
}
```

The setApprovalForAll function has local parameters, such as an address representing the operator and a Boolean indicating whether the operator will be approved or, if previously given approval, is being rejected. It is public and virtual. Within the setApprovalForAll function, the function is called an internal function _setApprovalForAll, which will be seen later in the contract. It enables the owner address of the NFTs (_msgSender()) to approve the operator address (operator) to manage all the NFTs the caller owns.

```
function setApprovalForAll(address operator, bool approved)
public virtual {
    _setApprovalForAll(_msgSender(), operator, approved);
}
```

The isApprovedForAll function has two function parameters, an address owner and an address operator. It is public, view, and virtual, and it returns a boolean at the end of it. Within the function, the function returns true if the owner address has approved the operator address to manage all assets of the owner address.

```
function isApprovedForAll(address owner, address operator) public
view virtual
returns (bool) {
    return _operatorApprovals[owner][operator];
}
```

The function transferFrom has three function parameters: an address from, an address to, and a uint256 tokenId. It is public and virtual. Within the function, an if statement checks that the to address does not equal the zero address of Ethereum—Ethereum's nonactive address. If the to address equals the zero address, the function reverts with the ERC721InvalidReceiver custom error.

The _update function updates the tokenId owner from the from address to the to address, which is the new owner of the NFT, while the previousOwner address is assigned the address of the previous owner of the NFT. At the end of the function, another if statement is declared, which ensures that if the previousOwner is not the from address—the previous owner of the NFT—the function should revert with the custom error ERC721IncorrectOwner.

```
    function transferFrom(address from, address to, uint256 tokenId) public
virtual {
        if (to == address(0)) {
            revert ERC721InvalidReceiver(address(0));
        }

        address previousOwner = _update(to, tokenId, _msgSender());
        if (previousOwner != from) {
            revert ERC721IncorrectOwner(from, tokenId, previousOwner);
        }
    }
```

The safeTransferFrom function is an overloaded function that has as local variables an address from and an address to an uint256 representing the tokenId. It is public, meaning it can be called both externally and internally.

Within the function itself, the function calls the other safeTransferFrom function, which has four parameters instead of three with the last one being ""*, a bytes data field allowing you to attach an extra data field to the transfer. The function transfers an NFT from the from address to the to address.

```
    function safeTransferFrom(address from, address to, uint256 tokenId)
public {
        safeTransferFrom(from, to, tokenId, "");
    }
```

The safeTransferFrom function has four parameters as shown in the previous function: an address from, an address to, an uint256 tokenId, and a bytes data type. The function is public and can be overridden due to the virtual keyword.

Within the function itself, it calls the transferFrom function with its variables of from, to, and tokenId. Then the function calls checkOnERC721Received to verify whether the to address is a smart contract. If it is, then it checks whether the to address implements the ERC721Receiver interface. If not, the transaction fails.

```
    function safeTransferFrom(address from, address to, uint256 tokenId, bytes
memory data) public virtual {
        transferFrom(from, to, tokenId);
        ERC721Utils.checkOnERC721Received(_msgSender(), from, to, tokenId,
data);
    }
```

The _ownerOf function has a local parameter uint256 tokenId, which is an internal function—meaning it can be called from within the contract and contracts deriving from it, meaning view and virtual. It returns an address. Within the function the function checks the _owners mapping, which contains the _owners of tokens to determine and return the address of the owner of a specific tokenId.

```
    function _ownerOf(uint256 tokenId) internal view virtual returns
(address) {
        return _owners[tokenId];
    }
```

The _getApproved function has a local parameter uint256 called tokenId. It is internal, view, virtual, and returns an address variable. Within the function, the mapping _tokenApprovals containing the addresses approved to manage tokens is checked, and it returns the address approved to manage a specific tokenId.

```
    function _getApproved(uint256 tokenId) internal view virtual
returns (address)
{
        return _tokenApprovals[tokenId];
    }
```

The _isAuthorized function has three local parameters: the address of the owner, the address of the spender, and an uint256 representing the unique identifier of the token, tokenId. The function is internal, view, and virtual and returns a boolean at the end of it. Within the function, the function returns true if the spender address does not equal the zero address and (the && means "and") owner address equals to spender or (the || can be interpreted as "or") the owner has given permission to the spender to become the operator and to manage all the tokens of the address or the owner has approved the spender and makes the spender address the operator to manage a specific token. If any of these combinations are correct, the Boolean returns true.

The function checks to see if the owner address has permitted the spender address to manage either a specific token or all of them.

```
    function _isAuthorized(address owner, address spender, uint256 tokenId)
internal view virtual returns (bool) {
        return
        spender != address(0) &&
        (owner == spender || isApprovedForAll(owner, spender) ||
_getApproved(tokenId) == spender);
    }
```

The _checkAuthorized function has three local parameters: the address of the owner, the address of the spender, and an uint256 that serves as the tokenId; the function is an internal view, and it is virtual. Within the function, there is an if statement calling the _isAuthorized function, which checks if the spender address has the right to manage the tokenId, and if not, then a second if statement takes place which checks if the owner's address equates to Ethereum's zero address. If it is, the function reverts using the ERC721NonexistentToken custom error. Suppose the owner's address does not equal the zero address of Ethereum. In that case, the function acts as if the token exists. Still, the spender address is not authorized to manage it and reverts with the custom error ERC721InsufficientApproval.

Keep in mind that the "!" in the !_isAuthorized(owner, spender, tokenId) part is called a *logical not operator*. It is used to invert the result of a Boolean. Thus, if the !_isAuthorized(owner, spender, tokenId) statement returns true, the ! will make it false, and if it is false, it will make it true. The logical not operator is used because the _checkAuthorized function is to check for unauthorized cases.

```
    function _checkAuthorized(address owner, address spender, uint256 tokenId)
internal view virtual {
        if (!_isAuthorized(owner, spender, tokenId)) {
            if (owner == address(0)) {
                revert ERC721NonexistentToken(tokenId);
            } else {
                revert ERC721InsufficientApproval(spender, tokenId);
            }
        }
    }
}
```

The following _increaseBalance function has two local parameters, an address representing an account and an uint128 representing value. The function is internal, virtual—meaning it can be overridden by a contract that has been imported and inherited. Within the function, the unchecked disables the overflow checks for arithmetic operations within the block of code. This helps save gas but the developer has to be aware to ensure that the value amount will not cause an overflow.

Consider the contract shown in Figure 11.12.

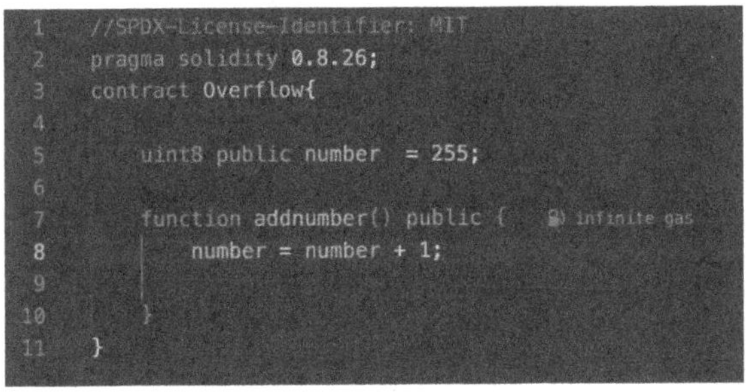

FIGURE 11.12: AddNumber contract

The contract has statements of its license, Solidity version, and contract name. It additionally declares a global uint8 public variable number set to 255. It is important to remember that uint8 as a variable has been designed so that the largest number it can contain is 255. It cannot go to 256. If you want to have a value equal to more than 255, another uint type should be used, such as uint16, 32, 256, etc.

If you deploy the contract and try to call the function addnumber, the function will revert as if there is a custom error. This is because the number cannot go to 256 by design (see Figure 11.13).

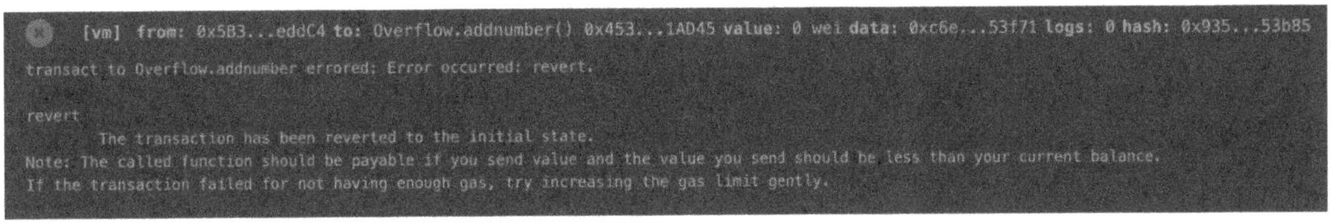

FIGURE 11.13: Function being reverted error message

However, if you use the `unchecked` keyword within the `addnumber` function, as shown in Figure 11.14, and then deploy the contract, as shown in Figure 11.15, you can see that the `uint8` is currently at 255.

FIGURE 11.14: `AddNumber` contract with unchecked keyword

FIGURE 11.15: uint8 at 255

If you click the `addnumber` function this time, however (see Figure 11.16), the number goes down to 0. If you click `addnumber` a few more times, say, five times, the value of the number will go from zero to five.

FIGURE 11.16: Clicking on unchecked addnumber will revert the 255 to 0

The `unchecked` keyword when used stops the automated check and `revert`, which has been embedded into the `uint8`—or any other variable and its arithmetic limit—allows for the value to go to 0.

The value going from 255 (its max value to 0) is called *overflow*. Hence, the `unchecked` keyword in a sense enables overflow. The `unchecked` keyword is useful when a developer knows that the result of a mathematical operation will never go above the maximum allowed for an `uint` type, causing an overflow. The `unchecked` keyword disables the extra computation required to prevent overflow making the contract more gas efficient. Hence, the usefulness, definition, and use case of the `unchecked` keyword shown in the following function.

Then, within the `unchecked` keyword, the `_balances` mapping is queried, and value is added to the balance of the account address. Thus, it adds a balance to an address.

```
    function _increaseBalance(address account, uint128 value)
internal virtual {
        unchecked {
            _balances[account] += value;
        }
    }
```

The following `_update` function has three local parameters: the address to, an `uint256` symbolizing the `tokenId`, and an address auth. It is an `internal`, `virtual` function that in the end returns an `address`. The function manages the transfer of ownership of a token. Within the function, an `address` variable with the name `from` is defined and is set to the current owner of the NFT with a specific `tokenId`.

Then, an `if` statement is declared to ensure that the authentication address (`auth`) is not set to Ethereum's address zero. If the auth address is not the zero address, a check is made to ensure that the `auth` address has the authority to perform the `tokenId` transfer operation.

Then, an `if` statement is used for the `from` address, which is the current owner of the NFT and, hence, a valid address. If the `if` statement holds, then any previous permissions by other addresses to that specific NFT are revoked, and the balance of the address is reduced by one—the NFT that is being transferred. If the address is Ethereum's zero address, then a minting operation would take place instead.

Then, an `if` statement is used for the `to` address to ensure that it is not Ethereum's zero address, and one token is added to its balance. If the address is zero, then it would burn the token.

Finally, the `_owners` mapping is updated to show the new owner address of the NFT. The `Transfer` event is emitted, signaling the transfer of the NFT token (`tokenId`) from the `from` address to the `to` address. In the end, the original `from` address is returned.

```
    function _update(address to, uint256 tokenId, address auth) internal
virtual
returns (address) {
        address from = _ownerOf(tokenId);

        if (auth != address(0)) {
            _checkAuthorized(from, auth, tokenId);
        }

        if (from != address(0)) {
            _approve(address(0), tokenId, address(0), false);

            unchecked {
                _balances[from] -= 1;
            }
        }
```

```
            if (to != address(0)) {
                unchecked {
                    _balances[to] += 1;
                }
            }

            _owners[tokenId] = to;

            emit Transfer(from, to, tokenId);

            return from;
        }
```

The following _mint function has an address to and an uint256 tokenId as local parameters and is internal. It is responsible for creating a new token and assigning ownership to the newly minted token. Within the function, an if statement checks that the to address does not equal Ethereum's zero address. Suppose the address does equal the zero address. In that case, the function reverts using the custom error ERC721InvalidReceiver, confirming that the address is a zero address (0), meaning you cannot mint to the zero address.

If the function does not revert, it declares a variable address named previousOwner and sets it to the value of the _update function, which is responsible for the transfer of tokens from one address to another and returning the previous owner of the token at the end of it. Then, an if statement is declared to ensure that the address to which the previousOwner address has been set is not Ethereum's zero address. If it is, then the function reverts using the custom error ERC721InvalidSender. That means you cannot mint a token that already has an owner.

```
        function _mint(address to, uint256 tokenId) internal {
            if (to == address(0)) {
                revert ERC721InvalidReceiver(address(0));
            }

            address previousOwner = _update(to, tokenId, address(0));
            if (previousOwner != address(0)) {
                revert ERC721InvalidSender(address(0));
            }
        }
```

The following _safeMint function creates a new token and assigns it to an address. It has two parameters/ address to is the address to which the token will be assigned, and the uint256 tokenId is the token to be minted. The function is internal. Within the function, the overloaded _safeMint function is called. An overloaded function has the same name as another function within the same contract. However, it has different parameters. Whenever a function is called (depending on the parameters stated), Solidity knows which one of the two functions to call. The to is the address which is the owner of the newly minted tokenId and the blank "" means there is no metadata for the specific token being minted.

```
        function _safeMint(address to, uint256 tokenId) internal {
            _safeMint(to, tokenId, "");
        }
```

The following _safeMint function is the overloaded function of the previous _safeMint function. It has three parameters: an address to, a uint256 tokenId, and bytes stored in memory named data. The function itself is internal and virtual. Within the function, the _mint function is called to mint a new token and then calls the checkOnERC721Received function from the ERC721Utils, which ensures that the to address can handle NFT or ERC721 tokens. This check checks only if smart contracts can handle the incoming NFTs to the address. For externally owned accounts (EOAs), the check can't verify if the account exists or is valid.

```
    function _safeMint(address to, uint256 tokenId, bytes memory
data) internal
virtual {
        _mint(to, tokenId);
        ERC721Utils.checkOnERC721Received(_msgSender(), address(0), to,
tokenId,
data);
    }
```

The following _burn function removes tokens from circulation by destroying them. It has a local parameter uint256 tokenId, an internal function. Within the function itself, an address previous Owner is stated. Then the _update function is called, which updates the token's location (tokenId) to the address zero, Ethereum's zero address, and sets the previousOwner address to the address of the previousOwner of the token before it got burned. Then, an if statement is declared, checking if the previousOwner equals Ethereum's zero address. If it does, the function reverts using the custom error ERC721NonexistentToken. It uses the tokenId parameter within it to indicate that the specified tokenId is invalid. This is done to ensure that only tokens that have an owner can be burned.

```
    function _burn(uint256 tokenId) internal {
        address previousOwner = _update(address(0), tokenId, address(0));
        if (previousOwner == address(0)) {
            revert ERC721NonexistentToken(tokenId);
        }
    }
```

The following _transfer function handles a token transfer from one address to another. The function is internal and has three local parameters: an address from, an address to, and a uint256 tokenId. Within the function, it begins with an if statement that ensures that the to address does not equal Ethereum's zero address. If it does, the function reverts using the custom error ERC721

After the if check, an address previousOwner is declared and set to the previous owner, returned by the update function. The update function is responsible for transferring one token from one address to another and, at the end of the function, returning the address of the previous owner of the NFT. Then, another if statement checks that the previousOwner address does not equal the zero address of Ethereum. If it does, the function reverts using the custom error ERC721IncorrectOwner. The custom error mentions the (tokenId) to showcase that the NFT is invalid as it is owned by the zero address—if the previousOwner address were indeed the zero address of Ethereum.

Finally, an `else if` statement is also declared, which checks if the `previousOwner` does not equal the `from` address returned at the end of the `_update` function. If it is not set to the `from` address, the function reverts using the custom error `ERC721IncorrectOwner`. This would mean that the address is trying to send the token owned by someone else.

```
function _transfer(address from, address to, uint256 tokenId) internal {
    if (to == address(0)) {
        revert ERC721InvalidReceiver(address(0));
    }
    address previousOwner = _update(to, tokenId, address(0));
    if (previousOwner == address(0)) {
        revert ERC721NonexistentToken(tokenId);
    } else if (previousOwner != from) {
        revert ERC721IncorrectOwner(from, tokenId, previousOwner);
    }
}
```

The following `_safeTransfer` function has parameters: an `address from`, an `address to`, and a `uint256 tokenId`. It is `internal`, and within the function itself, it calls the overloaded `_safeTransfer` function. This is called a wrapper function, which is created to call another—often more complicated—function to simplify the process.

```
function _safeTransfer(address from, address to, uint256 tokenId)
internal {
    _safeTransfer(from, to, tokenId, "");
}
```

The overloaded `_safeTransfer` function has four local parameters: an `address from`, an `address to`, a `uint256 tokenId`, and bytes stored in memory named `data`. The function is `internal` and `virtual`. Within the function, the `_transfer` function transfers the token ownership (`tokenId`) to the `to` address from the `from` address.

Then, the `checkOnERC721Received` function is called from the `ERC721Utils` contract to ensure that the new owner address, `to`, can handle ERC721 tokens.

```
function _safeTransfer(address from, address to, uint256 tokenId,
bytes memory
data) internal virtual {
    _transfer(from, to, tokenId);
    ERC721Utils.checkOnERC721Received(_msgSender(), from, to, tokenId,
data);
}
```

The `following _approve` wrapper function has three parameters: an `address to`, a `uint256` representing the `tokenId`, and an `address auth`. The function is `internal`. Within the function, the overloaded `_approve` function is called to begin the approval process of the ERC721 token.

```
function _approve(address to, uint256 tokenId, address auth) internal {
    _approve(to, tokenId, auth, true);
}
```

The following _approve function is the overloaded function that was called in the previous _approve function. It has four parameters: an address to, a uint256 tokenId, an address auth, and a Boolean emitEvent indicating whether an event needs to be emitted. The function is internal and virtual.

Within the function, an if statement is declared; if an event is emitted or if the auth address is not set to zero, then the newly declared owner address should be set to the returning address of the called _requireOwned function. Another if statement is stated, and if the auth address does not equal Ethereum's zero address and (&&) the owner address does not equal the auth address, then the function should revert. If the owner does not approve the auth address to manage all NFT tokens, then the function is reversed by the custom error ERC721InvalidApprover.

Another if statement is declared, and if an event is emitted, another event with the name Approval will also be emitted. Finally, the _tokenApprovals mapping is updated to add the address to the approved address for the specified NFT.

```
    function _approve(address to, uint256 tokenId, address auth, bool
emitEvent)
internal virtual {
        if (emitEvent || auth != address(0)) {
            address owner = _requireOwned(tokenId);

            if (auth != address(0) && owner != auth &&
!isApprovedForAll(owner,
auth)) {
                revert ERC721InvalidApprover(auth);
            }

            if (emitEvent) {
                emit Approval(owner, to, tokenId);
            }
        }

        _tokenApprovals[tokenId] = to;
    }
```

The following _setApprovalForAll function has three parameters, an address owner, an address operator, and a Boolean approved. The function is internal and virtual, and it is useful as it allows external systems to track the approved changes through the event emitted. Within the function, an if statement ensures that the operator address is not equal to the zero address of Ethereum. If it does equal the zero address of Ethereum, the function reverts with the custom error ERC721InvalidOperator.

Then, the function updates the _operatorApprovals nested mapping, which stores the owners' and the operators' addresses as approved or not through the Boolean. If approved, the operator address gets approval to manage the tokens of the owner address.

If this is successful, the function will emit the ApprovalForAll event.

```
    function _setApprovalForAll(address owner, address operator, bool
approved)
internal virtual {
```

```
                    if (operator == address(0)) {
                        revert ERC721InvalidOperator(operator);
                    }
                    _operatorApprovals[owner][operator] = approved;
                    emit ApprovalForAll(owner, operator, approved);
                }
```

The following _requireOwned function has one variable of type uint256 named tokenId. It is an internal view function that returns an address at the end of the function. It ensures that a specific token exists by returning the address of its owner. Within the function, an address owner is defined, and the function _ownerOf is called to set the address owner to the owner of a specific NFT.

Then, an if statement checks if the owner's address equals Ethereum's zero address. If so, the function reverts using the custom error ERC721NonexistentToken. At the end of the function, the owner address is returned.

```
            function _requireOwned(uint256 tokenId) internal view returns (address) {
                address owner = _ownerOf(tokenId);
                if (owner == address(0)) {
                    revert ERC721NonexistentToken(tokenId);
                }
                return owner;
            }
        }
```

INTRODUCTION TO IPFS

Before creating the NFT, you need to know what IPFS is and how it works. When you want to download a photograph from the Internet today, you communicate to the computer through clicks to download the desired picture. The laptop should access a specific domain name or IP address where the image is stored on a server taken care of by a company such as Google. This method of accessing a file is called *location-based addressing*. The computer receives an address such as an IP address or a domain name, which identifies the location of the desired file. It then "goes" to that IP address or the domain to access and download the file.

Suppose the server is experiencing problems, however, and is down. In that case, the computer will not be able to "go" to it; consequently, you will not be able to access and download the photograph. The photograph you cannot access due to the server being down has likely been downloaded by others worldwide. It is stored somewhere on their computer, a hard drive, or the storage server they use. Still, the computer could not communicate with the computers that previously downloaded that photograph. Hence, you can only access and download the picture when the company's server is back on.

The InterPlanetary File System (IPFS) was created to mitigate these problems. It is a decentralized, distributed file storage network—in some ways similar to a blockchain but not a blockchain—that allows a person to request data, in this case, the aforementioned photograph, in a peer-to-peer way from computers across the world that have downloaded the picture and store it for everyone else to access.

To accomplish that, every file that is stored on IPFS gets its hash—a "fingerprint," to put it simply. Whenever a computer wants to download a file—the photograph in this case—it asks IPFS's network of nodes. What node/computer has the file with this specific hash? The network then starts gossiping—that is, communicating—with one another until a computer is found that has the file with that particular hash. This allows the requesting computer to download the file using that hash.

The hash also helps with deduplication, which makes the IPFS storage system efficient and more ecologically friendly. This is because when a file with the same hash—and hence the same file—is published on IPFS twice, only one copy of it will be stored. This helps reduce digital waste that many centralized servers create, where a lot of data is stored and can be duplicated, eating away at storage.

The files on IPFS are stored in what are called *objects*. Each object can store up to 256 KB of data. A tiny file can be stored in one single IPFS object but if the file is bigger than 256 KB it is stored on multiple different objects each storing 256 KB worth of data of the bigger file. The IPFS system creates an object that links all these pieces of the file together, which one can access with ease to download the whole file in one go.

Like a blockchain, when data is added to IPFS, it becomes immutable and tamper-proof. Files stored are not updatable in themselves. That being said, however, if you want to make changes to the file that one has uploaded, then you need to upload the file on IPFS. IPFS creates a new object, and the previous link that would be directed to the last version of the file is replaced with a new one, which should be used to update the old link wherever it is referenced and mentioned. This way of updating and changing files can be repeated as often as required; similar to a blockchain, the entire file history is accessible to the other nodes on the network. This way of storing files is called *content-based addressing*.

IPFS is of the main strategies that developers use to store the pictures of NFTs as storing them on-chain is very expensive. While storing data on-chain is the best solution when feasible and affordable, IPFS is one of the leading decentralized and distributed alternatives that can be used to store data off-chain.

Downloading, Installing, and Using IPFS

This section covers downloading, installing, and using IPFS on the Windows and Mac operating systems. It also shows you how to integrate it with browsers via extensions and leverage its capabilities to manage and access files. Additionally, it explores how IPFS is used to store and retrieve NFT metadata and media files, linking them to blockchain-based platforms like OpenSea.

Downloading IPFS

Let's get started by downloading IPFS to your computer.

1. Go to the website `ipfs.tech`, shown in Figure 11.17.

2. On the website, scroll down to the "Get Started" section, as shown in Figure 11.18. Note that the website might look a bit different by the time you read this book.

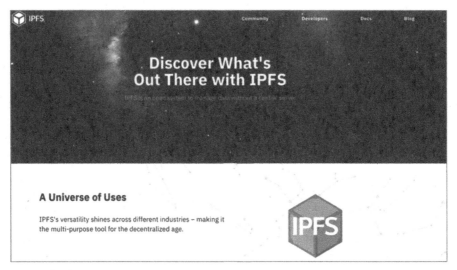

FIGURE 11.17: IPFS landing page

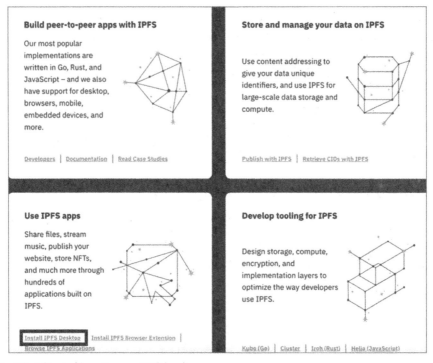

FIGURE 11.18: "Get Started" section on IPFS landing page

3. In the "Get Started" section, click the Install IPFS Desktop link in the lower left of Figure 11.18 to download the desktop version of IPFS. You will be redirected to a guide on installing the IPFS desktop application. And there are guides for Windows, macOS, and Ubuntu, as shown in Figure 11.19. We will cover only the Windows and macOS installations.

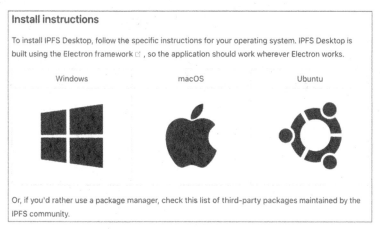

FIGURE 11.19: IPFS install guide

IPFS Windows Installation

1. Go to the IFPS Desktop downloads page, a clickable part of the text in the guide, as shown in Figure 11.20.

FIGURE 11.20: IPFS downloads page clickable text

The link will redirect you to IPFS's GitHub page, where if you scroll down, you will see several files.

2. Click the EXE file (see Figure 11.21), download it, and run it to install IPFS on a Windows machine.

macOS Installation

1. Go to the IPFS Desktop downloads page to get to IPFS' GitHub page and scroll down to the DMG file, as shown in Figure 11.22.

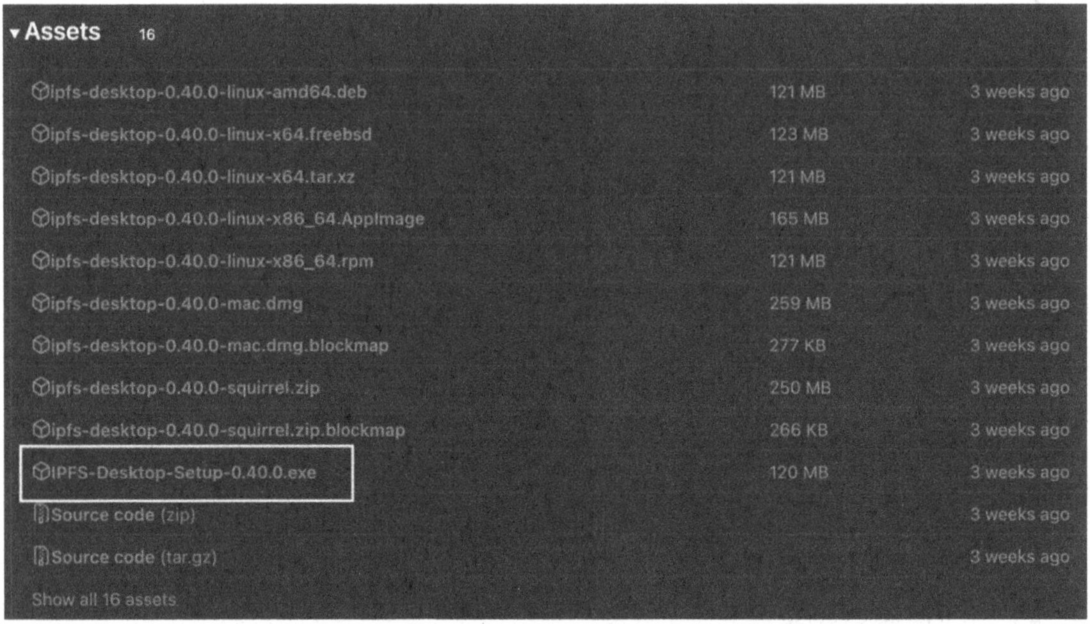

FIGURE 11.21: The EXE file one has to download and run to start downloading IPFS on Windows

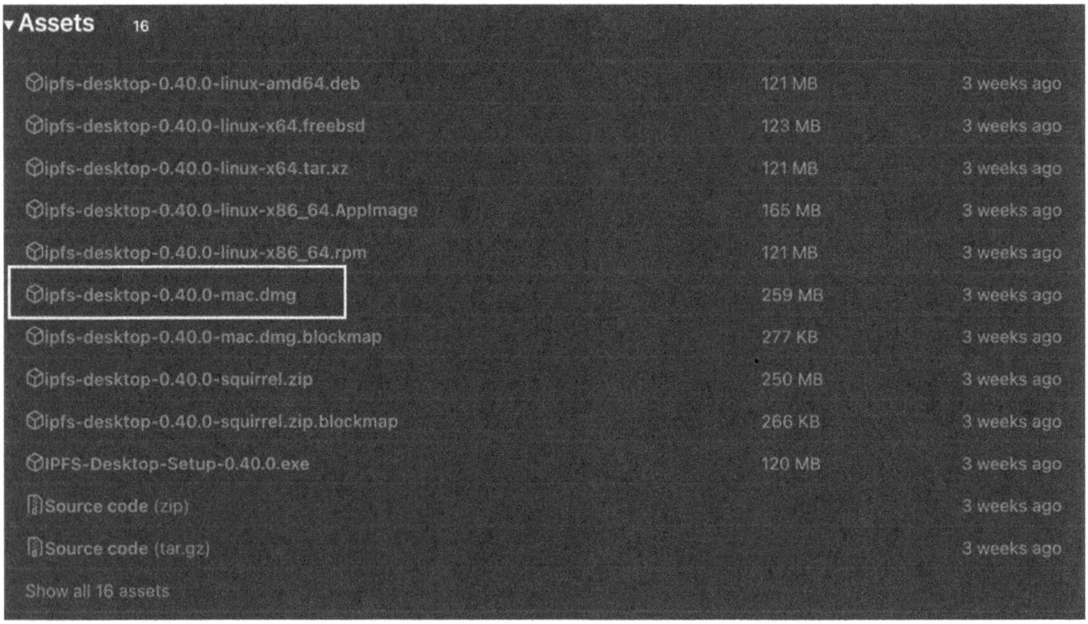

FIGURE 11.22: The DMG file has to download and run in order to start downloading IPFS on macOS

2. After downloading the DMG file, open and run it. The installation should complete automatically, and the IPFS client should pop up after the installation, as shown in Figure 11.23.

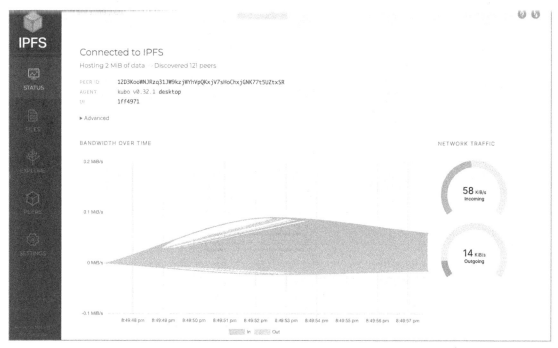

FIGURE 11.23: IPFS client

Upon closing the IPFS client, IPFS runs in the background on the top right of the screen on a Mac. On Windows, it will be on the bottom right. It's the "block" icon shown in Figure 11.24.

FIGURE 11.24: The block representing IPFS running in the background

Upon clicking the block, the choices shown in Figure 11.25 can pop up.

FIGURE 11.25: The choices available upon clicking the IPFS block

Installing the Browser Extension

IPFS also has a browser extension that is good to install as it makes it easier to access content through the browser.

1.   In the Get Started landing page of the IPFS website (refer to Figure 11.17), click Install IPFS Browser Extension, as shown in Figure 11.26.

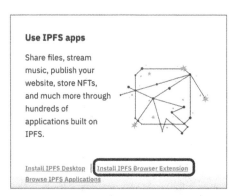

FIGURE 11.26: Install the IPFS browser extension

You are redirected to the page shown in Figure 11.27 with the browsers you can use to download the extension as well as the instructions for downloading it.

FIGURE 11.27: Availability of browsers to download IPFS browser extension

The Firefox Add-On extension landing page looks like Figure 11.28.

2.   To install the Firefox extension, click the Download Firefox And Get The Extension button.

3.   If you use a Chromium-based browser like Google Chrome or Brave Browser, click the Chrome Web Store instead to be redirected to its own IPFS extension download page, shown in Figure 11.29.

4.   To add the extension, click Add To Brave, Add To Chrome (or other Chromium browser you use).

5.   Depending on the browser you use, a small pop-up may appear asking for confirmation to add the extension to the browser. To do so, click Add Extension (see Figure 11.30).

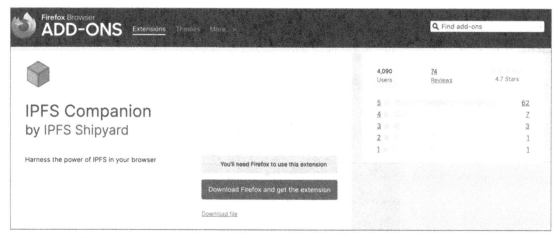

FIGURE 11.28: Firefox IPFS extension download landing page

FIGURE 11.29: Chrome Web Store IPFS Extension Download Landing page

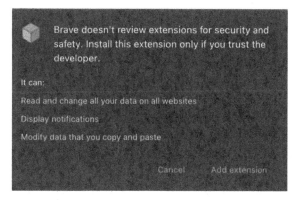

FIGURE 11.30: Potential pop-up warning

6. Click the extension in the puzzle icon of the browser on the top right just like you found MetaMask in Chapter 3 when installing it for the first time (see Figure 11.31).

FIGURE 11.31: Puzzle icon for extensions

7.   Pin the IPFS extension (see Figure 11.32) on the browser by clicking the pin icon so it is visible and easily accessible when you want to use the extension (see Figure 11.33).

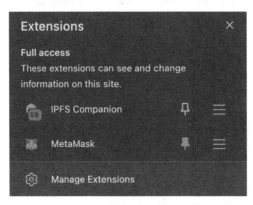

FIGURE 11.32: Pinning the IPFS extension

FIGURE 11.33: IPFS pinned

After pinning the extension and making it visible, when you click it, you will see a small pop-up like the one shown in Figure 11.34.

FIGURE 11.34: Browser Extension's pop-up

The peers in the pop-up refer to the nodes currently in the network to which your node—you own computer—is connected.

The gateway address allows you to access content through a browser, while the PRC has the same meaning as in Foundry. It allows for interaction with the node programmatically. Still, in this case, instead of calling functions of smart contracts, it will enable pinning files and retrieving files or generally managing the node through code. The http://127.0.0.1:5001 is used as an RPC-URL address, as shown before in Chapter 7, to send commands to your node.

Using IPFS

Now that you've learned how to download and install IPFS and the browser extension, let's turn to using it: uploading files, exploring content, understanding content identifiers (CIDs), and managing node settings. Additionally, you learn about pinning files for persistent storage, accessing data via gateways, and publishing content to the InterPlanetary Name System (IPNS).

On the topic of NFTs and blockchain integration, I demonstrate how IPFS interacts with popular platforms like OpenSea and tools such as Etherscan. I'll also provide instructions on retrieving metadata, exploring token attributes, and viewing content stored on IPFS.

Let's begin with uploading files.

1. There are two ways to upload a file on IPFS.

    a. Click Import in the extension to upload a file on IPFS (see Figures 11.35 and 11.36).

FIGURE 11.35: Importing a file

FIGURE 11.36: Importing a file (continued)

    You will have to either drop a file into the rectangular space or click Pick A file and pick a file from your computer to upload.

    b. If you click My Node instead, you will be redirected to the original IPFS landing page, as shown in Figure 11.38, which is beside the Import option in the extension.

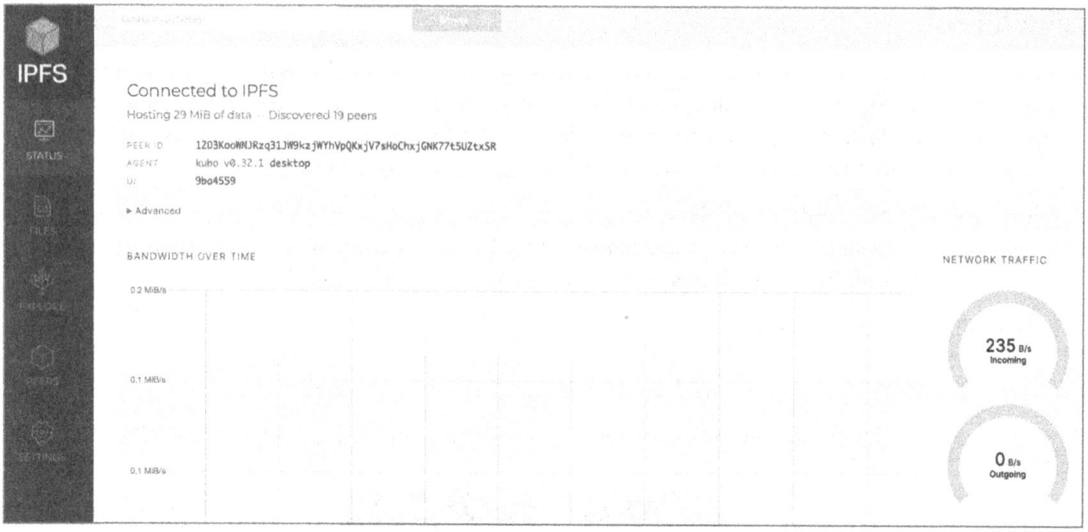

FIGURE 11.37: IPFS application landing page

The Files section allows you to upload files onto IPFS.

> **NOTE** On the IPFS application's landing page (see Figure 11.37), the Status section shows whether you are connected to IPFS, how much data is being hosted, how many peers are connected to the network, the peer ID (the unique identifier of the node/computer running IPFS, in this case, your computer), and the version of the IPFS application being used.
>
> The Explore section allows you to explore different content stored on IPFS provided you have the content identifier (CID) of the content you want to access—as the name suggests, the unique identifier for a specific piece of content. The Peers section shows the list of peer nodes connected to the IPFS decentralized and distributed network and some information about each node, such as the node's ID, latency, location, type of location, and more. The Settings section enables you to change specific options regarding the node one run, such as the storage, bandwidth, and additional ones.

When you want to upload a file on IPFS by clicking the Files section, a list of previously uploaded files will appear. If no files have been uploaded previously, the section will be blank, as shown in Figure 11.38.

2. Click Import to display the options shown in Figure 11.39. For this example, select a random file that you do not mind being public for everyone to see, such as a random picture on the Internet.

FIGURE 11.38: IPFS Files section

FIGURE 11.39: Import menu

These are the options for importing or uploading a file:

➤ **File** means a specific file from your computer.

➤ **Folder** means a particular folder from your computer.

➤ **From IPFS** imports a file on IPFS requiring the content identifier (CID) of the file—more on the CID later in this chapter.

➤ **New Folder** creates a new folder within the IPFS application.

3. For this exercise, the aim is to upload a simple random file found on the Internet, so click File to find the file you want to upload and upload it onto IPFS (see Figure 11.40).

FIGURE 11.40: File Girl.webp uploaded

Now that you have uploaded a file to IPFS, you can try accessing it.

1. After uploading a file, in this case, a file called `Girl.webp`, you can click the filename to see what the file consists of (see Figure 11.41).

FIGURE 11.41: File `Girl.webp` revealed

In this case, the file is simply a picture of a girl.

2. Click the More button on the top right in Figure 11.41 to display the list of options, as shown in Figure 11.42.

FIGURE 11.42: Table after clicking More

The small table of options that pops up has the following items:

➤ **Share link:** Creates a shareable link to the file stored on IPFS.

➤ **Copy CID:** Generates the link to the content ID. The difference between the share link and the copy CID is that the share link shares a web page link to view the file, while the CID only the hash that identifies the file.

➤ **Inspect:** Provides information on the file, such as its size, CID, and more.

➤ **Set pinning:** Allows other computers and nodes in the network to access the file, even if the only node hosting the file is your own as it allows for the file pinned to not be deleted.

➤ **Download:** Downloads the file to your computer.

➤ **Download as CAR:** Downloads the file in the Content addressable Archive (CAR) format, allowing it to be shared in offline environments such as LAN connections, Bluetooth, etc.

➤ **Rename:** Renames the file.

➤ **Remove:** Deletes the file from one's own IPFS node. However, if other nodes have stored the file, it does not disappear.

➤ **Publish to IPNS:** Publishes the file to the InterPlanetary Name System. IPNS allows a human-readable name to be assigned to specific content if needed.

3. Click Copy CID and paste the result in your browser, as shown in Figure 11.43.

FIGURE 11.43: CID pasted

4. Add the protocol name (`ipfs://`) at the beginning, as shown in Figure 11.44.

FIGURE 11.44: Protocol added

5. Presses Enter. A message will pop up asking whether you want to open an IPFS desktop (see Figure 11.45). Click Open IPFS Desktop.

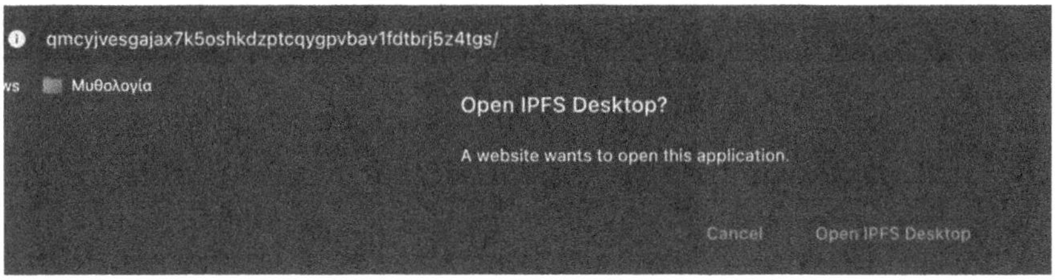

FIGURE 11.45: Opening the IPFS Desktop

The picture (or any other type of content stored on IPFS) will appear, as shown in Figure 11.46.

bafybeigs764lzfgydvmzsf6ndnzei5qvelmeaovlikw73jlijzuzmgjuva.ipfs.localhost:8080
Μυθολογία

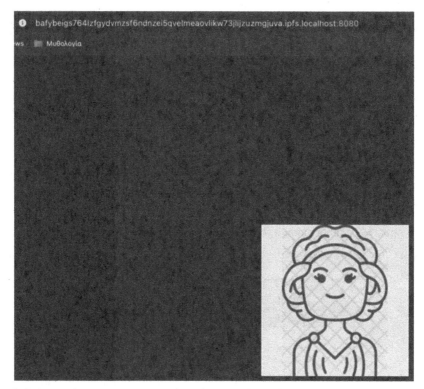

FIGURE 11.46: Girl picture demonstration appears on browser through IPFS

Suppose in the future there are problems accessing content in this way. In that case, a second way of accessing the content is through a gateway. This means another server, a centralized one, communicates with IPFS instead to fetch the content required. This is useful when you do not run an IPFS node or have access to IPFS for one reason or another.

To access the content in this way, go to the browser and type the following:

```
http://ipfs.io/ipfs/<CID>
```

Replace CID with the actual CID. Figure 11.47 shows the full entry for this example.

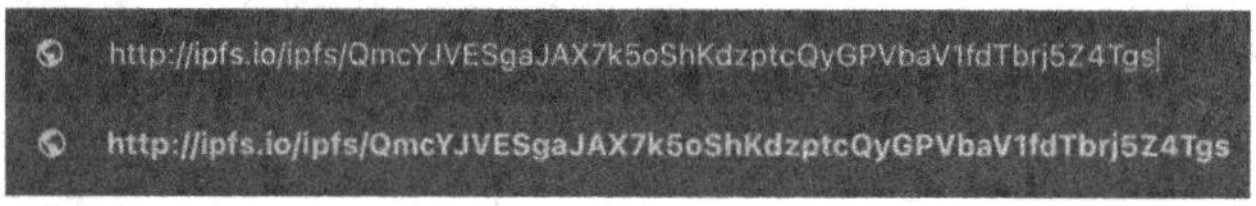

http://ipfs.io/ipfs/QmcYJVESgaJAX7k5oShKdzptcQyGPVbaV1fdTbrj5Z4Tgs
http://ipfs.io/ipfs/QmcYJVESgaJAX7k5oShKdzptcQyGPVbaV1fdTbrj5Z4Tgs

FIGURE 11.47: Using the browser to access an IPFS file through a gateway

Figure 11.48 shows the result.

FIGURE 11.48: Accessing the file through an IPFS gateway

NOTE *Always use an AI companion of your choice to ask questions or to have it expand on something you might not understand. This is simply an introduction to IPFS.*

OpenSea

OpenSea (`https://opensea.io`) is one of the biggest NFT marketplaces currently in existence. On their landing page (see Figure 11.49), you will see several different NFT collections. For this example, click Mutant Ape Yacht Club. You will be redirected to the MAYC collection landing page on OpenSea, as shown in Figure 11.50.

FIGURE 11.49: OpenSea landing page

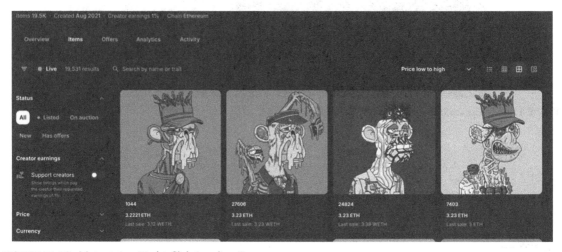

FIGURE 11.50: Mutant Ape Yacht Club Landing Page

If you click one of those apes, you will be redirected to its page. Upon scrolling down, you will see tabs such as Description, Traits, About Mutant Ape Yacht Club, and Details. If you click Details, you will see the contract address, the token's ID, the token standard used, the chain the token is available on when it was last updated, and the creator earnings (see Figure 11.51).

If you click the contract address 0x60e4. . .a7c6, you will be redirected to Etherscan, where you can see, among other things, the Transactions tab, showing all transactions taking place on that contract and its NFT collection (see Figure 11.52).

FIGURE 11.51: Token Details of one of the Apes on OpenSea

FIGURE 11.52: Mutant Ape Yacht Club contract on Etherscan

On the Contract tab (see Figure 11.53), you can see the code, read the contract, and write the contract.

As discussed in Chapter 3, a *read contract* is similar to the view keyword used in functions, which retrieves data from the blockchain when interacting with functions. At the same time, the *write contract* allows you to interact with the contract by changing the state of the blockchain, such as executing transactions and other similar functions. For this example, we'll look at the read contract (see Figure 11.54).

FIGURE 11.53: Contract tab

FIGURE 11.54: Read contract

On the Read Contract page, all the functions available in the ERC-721 contract deployed to create the Mutant Ape Yacht Club collection are shown. One of the functions is called `tokenURI` (see Figure 11.55).

If you click TokenURI, you will see a tokenId of type `uint256` that you can interact with. If you go back to the tab of the NFT on OpenSea, copy the token ID (see Figure 11.56), paste it into the `tokenId uint256` type, and click Query, a string will appear with a link (see Figure 11.57).

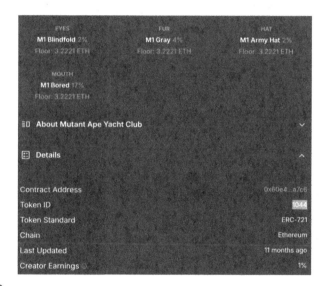

FIGURE 11.55: `tokenURI` function

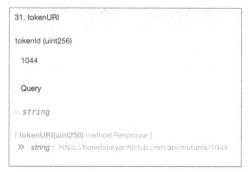

FIGURE 11.56: Token ID

FIGURE 11.57: String link to token information

The token information will appear, such as the NFT traits and the IPFS link to the token (see Figure 11.58). If you copy the link and paste it on yet another browser tab, you will see the ape picture being stored on IPFS (see Figure 11.59).

Pretty print
{"image":"ipfs://QmaQ9qRdPNPahHfaYY7n1x8CUoBisXizRx2XXFuy1sZTW2","attributes":[{"trait_type":"Background","value":"M1 Gray"},{"trait_type":"Fur","value":"M1 Gray"},{"trait_type":"Eyes","value":"M1 Blindfold"},
{"trait_type":"Clothes","value":"M1 Toga"},{"trait_type":"Hat","value":"M1 Army Hat"},{"trait_type":"Mouth","value":"M1 Bored"},{"trait_type":"Earring","value":"M1 Silver Hoop"}]}

FIGURE 11.58: Token information

FIGURE 11.59: Ape picture on IPFS

CREATING THE ERC-721 CONTRACT

Now that we know what an NFT is, what an ERC-721 contract looks like, and what IPFS is, it is time to create an ERC-721 contract and deploy it on IPFS.

Return to the VS Code and create a file called `NFT.sol` in the `src` folder (see Figure 11.60).

FIGURE 11.60: `NFT.sol` contract

Take a PNG icon from the web, create a folder within the current Foundry project, and add the PNG picture. For this example, the PNG picture of the girl shown previously will be used.

As you can see in Figure 11.61, a picture folder has been created, and the `girl.png` has been dragged into it to place it there. Do the same thing with your own PNG picture.

FIGURE 11.61: `Girl.png` in the picture folder

Within the `NFT.sol` document, type the following. I'll describe what each line does as we go.

The following defines the license under which the contract will be released:

```
///SPDX-License-Identifier: MIT
```

The following defines the Solidity version the contract will be using:

```
pragma solidity ^0.8.27;
```

The following imports the ERC721 token standard contract from the specified path it is located:

```
import {ERC721} from "../lib/openzeppelin-contracts/contracts/token/ERC721/
ERC721.sol";
```

The following defines the name of the contract and inherits the properties of the imported ERC721 contract:

```
contract NFT is ERC721 {
```

The following defines a private `uint256` variable with the name s_tokenCounter (the s_ signifies that this is a private variable).

```
        uint256 private s_tokenCounter;
```

The following mapping has keys of type `uint256` and its values are strings. It is private, and its name is s_tokenIDtoURI. When the token's ID is inserted, it returns the token's URL or URI.

```
        mapping(uint256 => string) private s_tokenIDtoURI;
```

The following constructor—the function executed automatically and first upon contract deployment—sets the name of the NFT collection to `NFTToken` and the symbol of the collection to `NFT`. In fungible tokens, the token's name could be ether, and the symbol ETH. The constructor also initializes the token counter variable—which counts the number of tokens—to 0.

```
constructor() ERC721("NFTToken", "NFT") {
    s_tokenCounter = 0;
}
```

The following `mintNFT` function has as a local parameter a string stored in memory named `tokenUri`, which represents the token URI of an NFT and is `public`. The function mints a new NFT.

Within the function, the mapping `s_tokenIDtoURI` is updated with the `tokenUri` to the respective token number through the `s_tokenCounter`. For example, if the `s_tokenCounter` is 0, meaning the first NFT, a `tokenUri` will be assigned to it. Then, the `_safeMint` function from the ERC721 contract is called. The `msg.sender` address is the address that called the function, and the `s_tokenCounter` is the number of the token being minted. Finally, the function adds the new NFT minted into the counter ensuring it has a new and unique number.

```
function mintNFT(string memory tokenUri) public {
    s_tokenIDtoURI[s_tokenCounter] = tokenUri;
    _safeMint(msg.sender, s_tokenCounter);
    s_tokenCounter++;
}
```

The following `tokenURI` function has as a local variable an `uint256 tokenId` representing the number of the NFT, the function is `public`, `view`, and it overrides the original `tokenURI` function to be found in the ERC721 contract and returns a string stored in memory.

Within the function, the function returns the token URI of a specific `tokenId` to be found in the mapping `s_tokenIDtoURI`.

```
function tokenURI(uint256 tokenId) public view override
returns(string memory)
{
    return s_tokenIDtoURI[tokenId];
}
}
```

WRITING A DEPLOYMENT SCRIPT AND DEPLOYING ON SEPOLIA

After writing the simple NFT contract, it is time to deploy it by writing a deployment script. To do so, one has to go to the project's script folder and create a new file called `NFT.s.sol` (see Figure 11.62). As shown in Chapter 8, the `.s` refers to the fact that the document is of a script type.

FIGURE 11.62: `NFT.s.sol` file creation

In the `NFT.s.sol` file, type the following. I'll describe each line as we go along.

The following defines the license under which the contract will be released:

```
//SPDX-License-Identifier: MIT
```

The following defines the solidity version the contract will be using:

```
pragma solidity ^0.8.27;
```

The following imports the `Script` contract from the specified path. The `Script` contract has different helper functions that help deploy contracts:

```
import {Script} from "forge-std/Script.sol";
```

The following imports the NFT contract written earlier from the specified path and the `src` folder:

```
import {NFT} from "../src/NFT.sol";
```

The following defines the name of the contract and inherits the `Script` contract:

```
contract DeployNFT is Script {
```

The `run` function is the standard function used when deploying a contract through scripting. It is an `external` function, meaning it can be called from outside the contract, and it returns an NFT contract type.

Within the function, the `vm.startBroadcast` cheat code broadcasts transactions onto the blockchain. Within the `vm.startBroadcast` cheat code, the `NFT nonfungibleToken = new NFT()` creates a new instance of the NFT contract and assigns it to the `nonfungibleToken` variable. The `vm.stopBroadcast` cheat code is then used to stop broadcasting transactions. Finally, at the end, it returns the `nonfungibleToken` contract, which was previously assigned the value of the newly deployed NFT contract and henceforth is the newly deployed NFT contract.

```
        function run() external returns(NFT) {
            vm.startBroadcast();
            NFT nonfungibleToken = new NFT();
            vm.stopBroadcast();
            return nonfungibleToken;
        }
    }
```

Before deploying the contract, you have to write another contract to interact with the deployed contract. This is preferable to using `cast` and is useful when repetitive tasks, such as minting NFTs, need to be taken care of. It also helps automate repetitive tasks. However, since it counts as deploying an extra smart contract, using the `cast` method shown in previous chapters is more convenient if the interaction occurs only once.

To write this contract more efficiently, you must download another repository from GitHub. The repository, Foundry DevOps, can be found at the following GitHub link: `https://github.com/Cyfrin/foundry-devops`.

To download the repository, you have to, as always, type the following:

```
    forge install  https://github.com/Cyfrin/foundry-devops --no-commit
```

When you press Enter, the files from the repository should have been downloaded, as shown in Figure 11.63.

FIGURE 11.63: Cyfrin DevOps installed

The file should be available in the library folder, as shown in Figure 11.64.

FIGURE 11.64: Foundry-DevOps in Library

After downloading the additional repository, it is time to create the new `ContractForInteractions.s.sol` file in the `script` folder (see Figure 11.65):

FIGURE 11.65: `ContractForInteractions.s.sol` file creation

Within the contract, type the following. As usual, I'll describe each line as we go along.

The following defines the license under which the contract will be released:

```
//SPDX-License-Identifier: MIT
```

The following defines the Solidity version the contract will be using:

```
pragma solidity ^0.8.27;
```

The following import imports the Script contract with different helper functions to help deploy a contract:

```
import {Script} from "forge-std/Script.sol";
```

The following imports the newly downloaded DevOpsTools contract from the specified location:

```
import {DevOpsTools} from "lib/foundry-devops/src/DevOpsTools.sol";
```

The following imports the NFT contract created previously from the `src` folder:

```
import {NFT} from "../src/NFT.sol";
contract InteractionsNFT is Script {
```

The following defines a public constant string. Its name is `Girl`, and it is set to the token URI of the NFT to be minted:

```
string public constant girl =
"ipfs://bafkreictv3p474nfilkyufpkeh2kqvll5kwxwobtupxpvesxpsufjc2xym";
```

The following external `run` function defines a local address with the name `mostRecentlyDeployed`. Then, using the DevOpsTools, it sets it to the most recently deployed NFT contract address on the blockchain through the `block.chained` keyword, which identifies the specific ID number of a blockchain and then calls the `mintNFTOnContract` function from the address.

```
function run() external {
    address mostRecentlyDeployed =
DevOpsTools.get_most_recent_deployment("NFT", block.chainid);
    mintNFTOnContract(mostRecentlyDeployed);
}
```

The following `mintNFTOnContract` function has as a local parameter, an address with the name `contractAddress`, and the function is `public`. Within the function itself, a `vm.startBroadcast` starts, which is a cheat code provided by the `Script` contract. It allows whatever transaction is after `vm.startBroadcast` to be broadcasted to the blockchain. When its counterpart, `vm.stopBroadcast`, is used, the broadcast of transactions to the blockchain ends.

Then the `vm.startBroadcast` the function calls the `mintNFT` function of the NFT contract in the specified address of the contract and mints the Girl NFT. Finally, the `vm.startBroadcast` is used at the end to stop broadcasting transactions to the blockchain.

```
function mintNFTOnContract(address contractAddress) public {
    vm.startBroadcast();
    NFT(contractAddress).mintNFT(girl);
    vm.stopBroadcast();
}
}
```

After creating the contract, you have to deploy the contract with the deploy script and then the contract with the interactions. To deploy the contract with the deploy script, you must create or use a new wallet, as in a previous chapter. This chapter will showcase this option within the VS Code terminal. However, the best practice is to use your own computer terminal in this case, as you will be using your private key to interact with the contracts; hence, the more steps are taken to secure the private key the fewer chances someone might get access to it and to one's funds.

Deploying the Contract

Follow these steps to deploy contract:

1. To begin, create the new wallet, replacing the italic text with the name you want for the wallet:

    ```
    cast wallet import <name of the new wallet you are creating > --interactive
    ```

For example:

```
cast wallet import MyWallet --interactive
```

2.   Press Enter. The terminal will ask for a private key, as shown in Figure 11.66.

FIGURE 11.66: Private key pasting

3.   Go to your MetaMask and click the arrow beside the account number, as shown in Figure 11.67.

FIGURE 11.67: MetaMask account arrow

4.   You will see the accounts you have. Click the three dots to the right of Account 1 (or any account you have if more than one). See Figure 11.68.

FIGURE 11.68: MetaMask account information

5.   After clicking the three dots, an option to click Account Details will appear (see Figure 11.69). Click it.

FIGURE 11.69: MetaMask account details

After clicking Account Details, you will be redirected to the wallet address and given the option to show your private key (see Figure 11.70).

FIGURE 11.70: MetaMask showing private key

6. The password to log in to the MetaMask wallet will be requested—not the seed phrase but the one entered when clicking the MetaMask logo on the browser (see Figure 11.71). Enter your password.

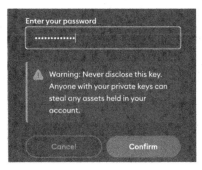

FIGURE 11.71: MetaMask entering your password

7. After typing the password and clicking Confirm, an option to hold to reveal the private key will appear. Click it and, as the message in Figure 11.72 says, hold until the private key is revealed.

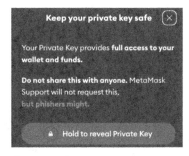

FIGURE 11.72: MetaMask Hold to reveal password

8. Once the private key is revealed (see Figure 11.73), copy it and return it to VS Code and Foundry.

FIGURE 11.73: MetaMask private key displayed

9. The copied private key should be pasted into the Enter Private Key space (see Figure 11.74). It will not be revealed, but upon pasting it, you should press Enter.

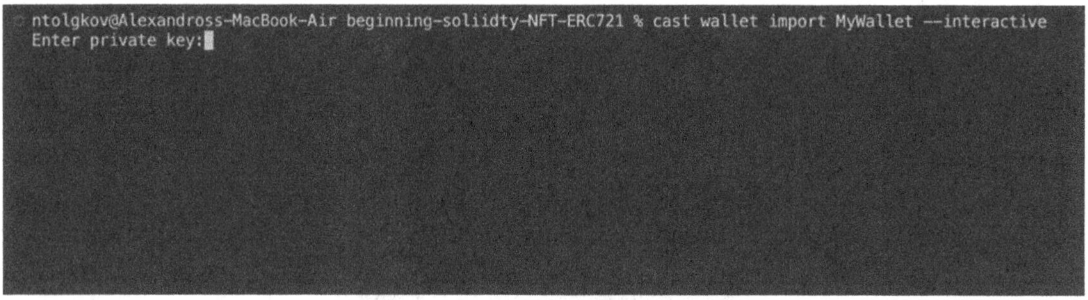

```
ntolgkov@Alexandross-MacBook-Air beginning-soliidty-NFT-ERC721 % cast wallet import MyWallet --interactive
Enter private key:
```

FIGURE 11.74: MetaMask entering private key

10. After pasting the private key, a password will be requested (see Figure 11.75). Remember this password as it will be requested whenever you want to deploy a contract. Enter your password.

```
ntolgkov@Alexandross-MacBook-Air beginning-soliidty-NFT-ERC721 % cast wallet import MyWallet --interactive
Enter private key:
Enter password:
```

FIGURE 11.75: MetaMask entering password

After typing the password and pressing Enter, a message saying that the Keystore was saved should appear. This message will give an address that must be copied and stored, as it will be required every time a smart contract is deployed (see Figure 11.76).

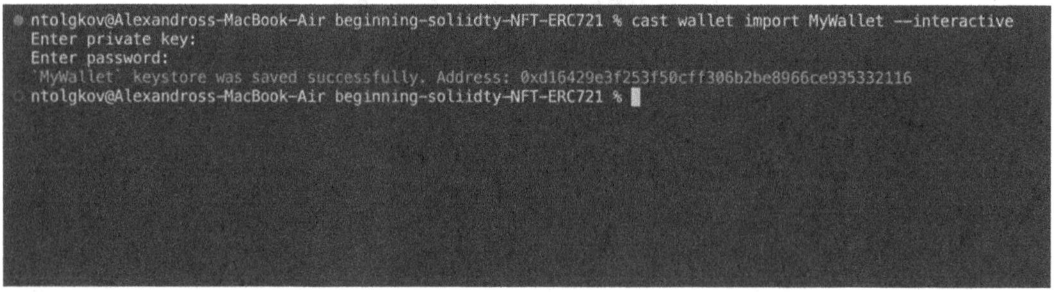

```
ntolgkov@Alexandross-MacBook-Air beginning-soliidty-NFT-ERC721 % cast wallet import MyWallet --interactive
Enter private key:
Enter password:
'MyWallet' keystore was saved successfully. Address: 0xd16429e3f253f50cff306b2be8966ce935332116
ntolgkov@Alexandross-MacBook-Air beginning-soliidty-NFT-ERC721 %
```

FIGURE 11.76: Keystore address

11. The next step is to deploy the two contracts starting from the NFT.s.sol. In the terminal, type the following:

```
forge script script/NFT.s.sol:DeployNFT --rpc-url https://eth-sepolia.g
.alchemy.com
/v2/etdMx3mb7nEzJ5n4dmwjUNEYFIkavK1j --account MyWallet --sender
0xd16429e3f253f50cff306b2be8966ce935332116 --etherscan-api-key
YRGWIRZAJ8TJPMEFDZZPYGFFUYNXF5II4S --broadcast
```

Keep in mind that the sender address will be different for you.

This script deploys the script of the `NFT.s.sol` file and the contract DeployNFT in particular. It gives the URL of an RPC, which is the one from Ethereum Sepolia, which you can find by going back to Alchemy's website. Then, the account is MyWallet, which has the private key created previously; the sender is the address of the Keystore that you have to save and use every time a smart contract is deployed. The `etherscan-api-key` is, as its name betrays, the API key that can be found on Etherscan.io upon registration. The `broadcast` is the keyword that broadcasts this command to the network.

12. After entering the command, you will be asked to add the password of the keystore that was added previously (see Figure 11.77).

FIGURE 11.77: Contract deployment keystore password request

Enter the password, press Enter, and wait a few seconds while the contract is successfully deployed on the Sepolia chain.

Upon deployment, a message will be displayed indicating a successful deployment (see Figure 11.78).

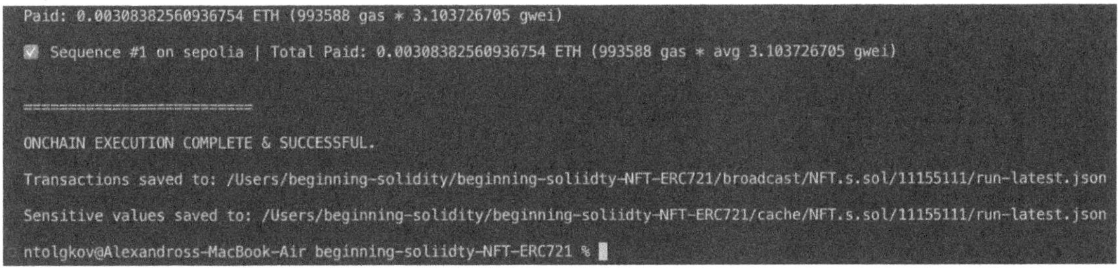

FIGURE 11.78: Contract successfully deployed

13. After the first contract is successfully deployed, the second contract, which will interact with the already deployed contract through minting NFTs, should also be deployed. To do this, type the following in the terminal:

```
forge script script/ContractForInteractions.s.sol:InteractionsNFT --rpc-url
https://eth-sepolia.g.alchemy.com/v2/etdMx3mb7nEzJ5n4dmwjUNEYFIkavK1j
--account
MyWallet --sender 0xd16429e3f253f50cff306b2be8966ce935332116 --etherscan-
api-key
YRGWIRZAJ8TJPMEFDZZPYGFFUYNXF5II4S  --broadcast
```

After pressing Enter in the terminal, the keystore password will be requested again. After filling it in and pressing Enter, you will have to wait a few seconds until the second contract is deployed, and a similar message indicating a successful deployment will be displayed (see Figure 11.79).

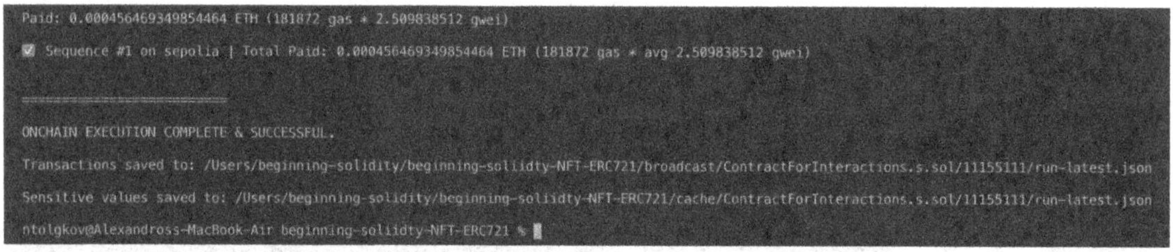

FIGURE 11.79: Interactions contract successfully deployed

If you scroll slightly up, you will see the transaction hash used to deploy the contract (see Figure 11.80).

FIGURE 11.80: Hash of contract deployment transaction

Copy the transaction hash, go to the Sepolia testnet Etherscan website (sepolia.etherscan.io), and paste the transaction hash into the explorer, where you can search addresses, transaction hashes, blocks, and tokens (see Figure 11.81).

FIGURE 11.81: Adding hash of transaction to Sepolia Etherscan

After pasting the transaction hash, click the blue magnifying glass button to see the results of the transaction hash (see Figure 11.82).

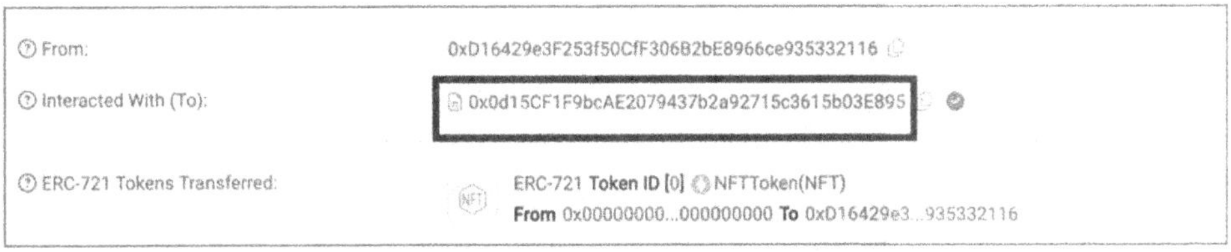
From:
0xD16429e3F253f50CfF306B2bE8966ce935332116
Interacted With (To):
0x0d15CF1F9bcAE2079437b2a92715c3615b03E895
ERC-721 Tokens Transferred:
ERC-721 Token ID [0] NFTToken(NFT)
From 0x00000000...000000000 To 0xD16429e3...935332116

FIGURE 11.82: Deployed contract address on Sepolia Etherscan

Click the blue contract address of Interacted With (To), which is the deployed contract (see Figure 11.83).

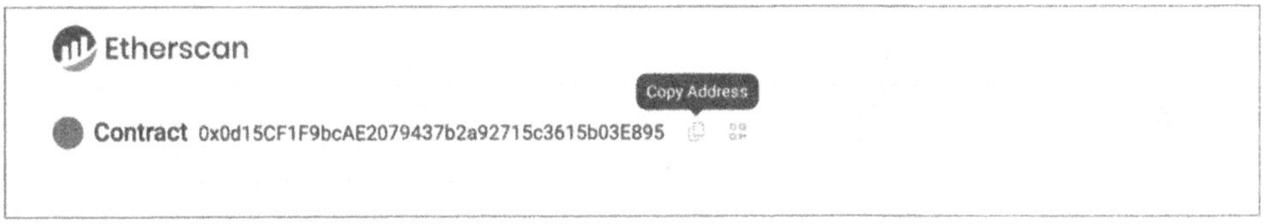
Etherscan
Copy Address
Contract 0x0d15CF1F9bcAE2079437b2a92715c3615b03E895

FIGURE 11.83: Copying address of deployed contract

There, you will see the contract address. Click the Copy Address button. After doing this, open your MetaMask wallet that can be found on your browser and click the NFTs tab, and if necessary scroll down a bit within the tab until the message "Import NFT" becomes visible (see Figure 11.84).

Tokens
NFTs
Activity
No NFTs yet
Learn more
+ Import NFT
MetaMask support

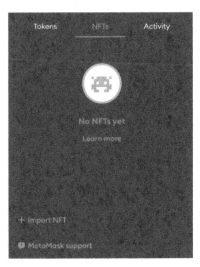

FIGURE 11.84: NFT section of MetaMask wallet

Click the Import NFT button (see Figure 11.85).

FIGURE 11.85: Importing NFT pane

Upon clicking Import NFT, a pane will appear. In the Address part, one should paste the copied smart contract address—the smart contract that mints and interacts with the `NFT.sol` contract. In the Token ID location, one should add 0, indicating the number of the NFT token that one wants to import. Since one token was minted through the deployment, 0 is the first. After that, one should click Import.

Upon clicking the Import button, the minted NFT and the picture of the girl can be displayed in one's MetaMask wallet (see Figure 11.86).

FIGURE 11.86: NFT imported

CHAPTER 11 QUESTIONS

1. Can you explain the differences between storing NFT data on-chain versus off-chain using IPFS? What are the trade-offs in terms of cost, decentralization, and security?

2. What is the purpose of the `_safeMint` function in an ERC-721 contract? How does it ensure secure minting compared to a regular `mint` function?

3. Describe the role of the `_isAuthorized` function. How does it verify token management permissions, and why is this critical for protecting ownership?

4. Given the immutability of IPFS, how would you handle a scenario where NFT metadata needs to be updated post-minting? Provide a solution that adheres to blockchain principles.

5. What is the role of the `tokenURI` function in an ERC-721 contract? How does it ensure the connection between an NFT and its off-chain metadata?

6. Explain the use of the logical NOT operator in the `_checkAuthorized` function. How does it contribute to gas efficiency in validation?

7. How does IPFS's content-based addressing overcome the limitations of traditional location-based addressing? Provide an example.

8. What is the difference between `_tokenApprovals` and `_operatorApprovals` in ERC-721 contracts? How do they manage permissions for individual tokens and collections?

9. Why is the `supportsInterface` function important in ERC-721 contracts? How does it ensure compatibility and interoperability?

10. How does IPFS store files larger than 256 KB? What implications does this have for NFT metadata storage and retrieval?

11. What is the purpose of the `_baseURI` function in an ERC-721 contract? How would you implement it for a cohesive NFT collection?

12. How does the `_transfer` function validate ownership and prevent edge cases like unauthorized transfers or transfers to invalid addresses?

13. Explain the use of the `unchecked` block in the `_increaseBalance` function. What are the benefits and potential risks associated with disabling overflow checks?

14. How would you design and implement a function for batch minting NFTs while maintaining correct token counting and URI assignment?

15. Describe the process of linking an NFT's on-chain data with its IPFS metadata. What steps would you take to validate the metadata's integrity and accessibility?

12

Upgradable Smart Contracts

This chapter explores the critical concept of upgradable smart contracts in Solidity, examining three main strategies: preset versatility, contract succession, and proxy-delegated upgrades. Through practical examples using a zoo contract system, you'll learn how to implement and manage upgradable contracts while carefully considering the tradeoffs between upgradeability, decentralization, and security.

Consider the real-world scenario of deploying a smart contract that later needs crucial updates—how do you maintain user trust and contract security while implementing necessary changes? This chapter addresses such challenges by demonstrating different upgrade patterns, their implementation details, and security considerations, using the progression from Zoo1 to Zoo2 contracts as a practical example.

By working through this chapter and its examples, you'll gain the knowledge needed to implement upgradeable contracts responsibly, understanding both the technical requirements and the broader implications for decentralization and security in blockchain applications. You'll learn to make informed decisions about when and how to implement contract upgradeability, while maintaining the trust and security expectations of your users.

INTRODUCING UPGRADABLE CONTRACTS

The state of smart contracts gets set upon deployment. The state changes when people stake their tokens, send money to pay for a service, delegate their voting power if they are part of a DAO (more on DAOs in Chapter 14), update their mappings and addresses that interact with them, update balances, and perform other similar actions. After deployment, no one can change the logic of the developer's contract, and it remains on-chain in that state forever. Smart contracts are immutable, and once deployed on the blockchain, no one can change the code that has been deployed; however, there are several strategies you can employ to update the contract in case a bug or other problem is discovered. The contracts that employ such strategies are called *upgradable smart contracts*. It is important to note that upgradable smart contracts carry the risk of losing the ethos and component of decentralization through repeatedly deploying smart contracts, which reintroduces a centralization component and which, in itself, carries the risk of adding functions to a newly deployed and upgradable contract that may scam the users of the smart contract. If you search online for the biggest crypto scams with smart contracts, many examples will surface where this was the case. Hence, when implementing upgradable smart contracts, think very carefully about the downside and possible consequences before implementing such strategies.

You could argue that if you can upgrade a smart contract, it is not entirely immutable. When implementing upgradeable smart contracts, one must carefully consider the core principles of immutability and decentralization. The chosen upgrade strategy should be evaluated for its implications on these principles, as different approaches can significantly impact the decentralized nature of the protocol. Each upgradeable smart contract strategy, as will be shown in this chapter, has advantages and disadvantages. Some disadvantages depend on the trade-offs expected. For developers, this includes developing and managing the contract, and the consequences to decentralization, (future) regulation, and immutability. From a user or community member's perspective, the dangers of interacting with the contract has implications such as potentially enabling a malicious actor to drain the contract's funds and disappear.

There are three significant strategies you can use to create upgradable contracts. Each will be explained in this chapter:

➤ Preset versatility upgrade

➤ Contract succession upgrade

➤ Proxy-delegated upgrade

Preset Versatility Upgrades

The preset versatility upgrade strategy requires foresight in terms of how the developer will write and design the contract that the developer will deploy. This strategy adds functions and parameters that allow for small changes within the contract upon deployment. With the preset versatility upgrade, a developer may *keep significant things* such as contract logic variables or add new storage to the contract, as any contract logic deployed will be on the blockchain forever. What a developer can change by using this upgrade strategy are the reward parameters they might have developed. For example, if a developer has set token rewards and these rewards are set initially to a 2% annual percentage yield, the reward could change to 4% or higher.

The advantage of preset versatility upgrades is that they are easy to implement as long as a developer has the foresight and vision to implement them. The disadvantage is that if they do not have the foresight to implement them, they would not have any other option but to switch to the contract succession upgrade (covered later in this chapter) to make any change they might have otherwise been able to plan had they had the foresight to do so before the original deployment.

Other variables are determining who has access to change the parameters mentioned. The fewer people who have access, the more centralized the protocol becomes, increasing the risk of errors or mismanagement. With greater centralization, a smaller group controls changes to the parameters, requiring the user community to place more trust in the contract's management. This increase in the required trust levels might not be a problem for people who do not care about decentralization, as banks are centralized, but people still use them. However, users for whom decentralization is of the utmost importance and those who especially know how to read code will stay as far away as they can from the protocol and will not use it.

Introduction to CertiK

People who do not know how to read code but still care about decentralization might trust external auditing companies such as CertiK. CertiK has developed a system to rate every blockchain, Web3, and cryptocurrency project, and the ratings and information are publicly available.

After accessing the CertiK website at www.certik.com, you can search for a project by name or token. As shown in Figure 12.1, this example uses Uniswap.

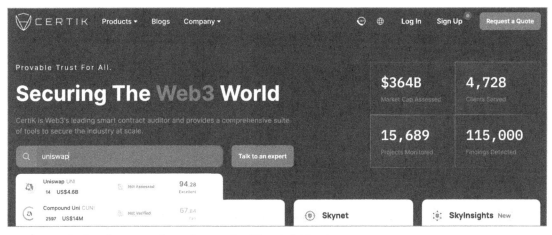

FIGURE 12.1: Typing the name of a project on CertiK and clicking it

After you click the project name with the logo and the score, a general security score will pop up, as shown in Figure 12.2.

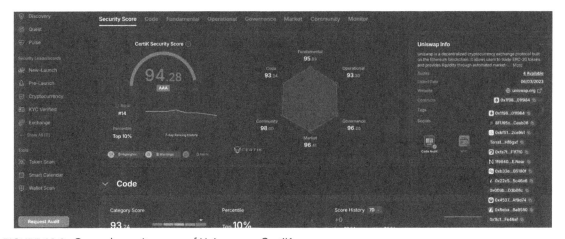

FIGURE 12.2: General security score of Uniswap on CertiK

The general security score comprises—at the time of writing—a general security score (94.28), a ranking (#14), a percentile in terms of quality (top 10%), the seven-day ranking history of the project, and a project rating on different domains such as code, fundamental, operational, market, community and governance.

Additionally, you can find general information about the following:

- What the project is
- How many audits are available on the project
- The date listed of the project
- The website of the project
- The various contract addresses on the different blockchains the project operates on
- Links to Coinmarketcap and Coin Gecko, two websites that list more economic data on the project selected
- The X account of the project
- The Discord server link of the project
- The GitHub link of the project
- If the project has been audited
- If it has implemented know your customer (KYC)
- If the project has a bug bounty

    A bug bounty is a contest between good-intentioned hackers (known as *white hats*) where the hackers try to find vulnerabilities in the code of a project. If they find hacks, they report them to get fixed and collect a reward.

In the next category of the report, called Code, shown in Figure 12.3, you can see the following:

- The category score
- The top percentile in which the protocol falls
- Whether CertiK made the audit or another auditing firm (third-party audit)
- How many users approve of the protocol and the number of audits the protocol underwent
- The date the audit took place, the name of the auditing firm, and a link to the PDF of the audit

If you click one of the reports and scroll down, a table of the issues detected in the code and each issue's severity will be reported, as shown in Figure 12.4. You can see what the problems with the code are even if you are not technical enough to read the code yourself, minimizing the risk—for those who know how to do their research—of being scammed.

FIGURE 12.3: CertiK code overview

Another category in the report is that of project fundamentals (see Figure 12.5), where you can see the following:

➤ The category score

➤ The percentile of the project in the category of fundamentals

➤ Whether the project has undergone a know your customer (KYC) procedure

➤ Which centralized exchanges (CEX) have the token available

➤ The project maturity metrics including how mature the project is, how old the project is, how many years ago the UNI token in itself was launched, a maturity timeline, active users in the last seven days, total transactions that took place with the token in the previous seven days, and a geographic divide of where the users of the last seven days are located

The operational category (see Figure 12.6) consists of the following:

➤ A category score for Uniswap

➤ The top percentile comparison to other projects in this category

➤ Whether a bug bounty program is available through CertiK or another party

➤ A website scan to evaluate network security, application security, and DNS health, and whether subcategories in these security domains have problems.

The next category of Uniswap is governance, shown in Figure 12.7, where the category score is displayed as well as the top percentage to determine where Uniswap stands in terms of quality when compared to other projects within the governance category; you can see the centralization scanning subcategory, which displays different tests and whether a contract has a specific function such as *self-destruct*, which allows for the contract to self-destruct; *mint*, which helps to mint more coins infinitely; whether the code is open source; if there are proxy contracts; and more.

Issues Found

Critical Risk	0
High Risk	0
Medium Risk	6
Low Risk	5
Informational	7
Gas Optimizations	3
Total Issues	21

Summary of Findings

[M-1] Calls to `LimitOrderRegistry::newOrder` might revert due to overflow	Resolved
[M-2] New orders on a given pool in the opposite direction, separated by zero/one tick space, are not possible until previous `BatchOrder` is removed from the order book	Resolved
[M-3] Calls to `LimitOrderRegistry::cancelOrder` might revert due to overflow	Resolved
[M-4] A malicious user can cancel an ITM order at a given target tick by calling `LimitOrderRegistry::cancelOrder` with the opposite direction, separated by one tick space	Resolved
[M-5] Malicious validators can prevent orders from being created or cancelled	Resolved
[M-6] Gas griefing denial-of-service on `performUpkeep`	Resolved
[L-1] Perform additional validation on Chainlink fast gas feed	Acknowledged
[L-2] Withdrawing native assets may revert if wrapped native balance is zero	Resolved
[L-3] `call()` should be used instead of `transfer()` on address payable	Resolved
[L-4] Fee-on-transfer/deflationary tokens will not be supported	Acknowledged
[L-5] Fulfillable ITM orders may not always be fulfilled	Acknowledged
[I-1] Spelling errors and incorrect NatSpec	Resolved
[I-2] Avoid hardcoding addresses when contract is intended to be deployed to multiple chains	Resolved
[I-3] Validate inputs to `onlyOwner` functions	Acknowledged
[I-4] Limit orders can be frozen for one side of a Uniswap v3 pool if `minimumAssets` has not been set for one of the tokens	Acknowledged
[I-5] Improvements to use of ternary operator	Resolved
[I-6] Move shared logic to internal functions called within a modifier	Acknowledged
[I-7] Re-entrancy in `LimitOrderRegistry::newOrder` means tokens with transfer hooks could take over execution to manipulate price to be immediately ITM, bypassing validation	Resolved
[G-1] Use stack variables rather than making repeated external calls	Resolved

FIGURE 12.4: Issues in code report by Cyfrin

The market category shown in Figure 12.8 demonstrates the market analytics for a token, such as the following:

➤ The token price

➤ The volume traded within 24 hours

➤ Market capitalization

➤ How many centralized exchanges have the token listed

➤ The market capitalization held by each exchange

➤ The exchange's token holdings and the supply each exchange holds

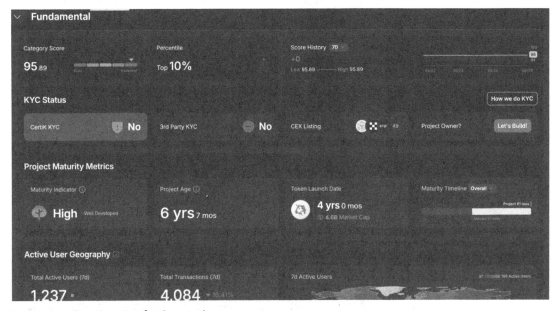

FIGURE 12.5: CertiK project fundamentals

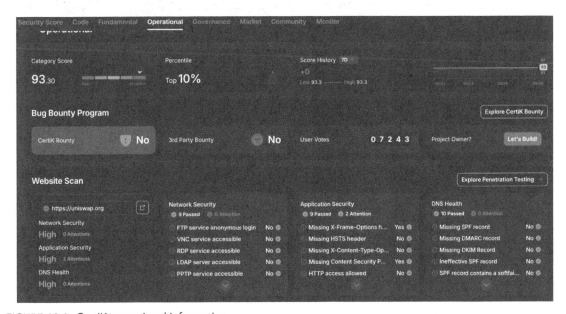

FIGURE 12.6: CertiK operational information

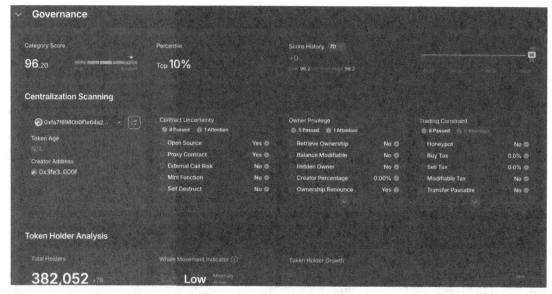

FIGURE 12.7: CertiK governance information

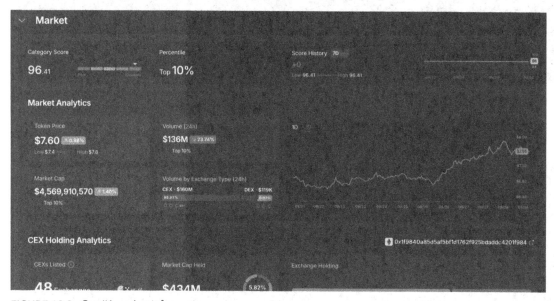

FIGURE 12.8: CertiK market information

Finally, the community category (see Figure 12.9) demonstrates the social media following, mainly the activity on one of the leading platforms for blockchain and Web3: Twitter/X.

As you can see, people who may not know how to read code properly but know how to do research can use external auditing firms to avoid being manipulated or fooled.

FIGURE 12.9: CertiK community overview

Contract Succession Upgrade

One criticism of the preset versatility upgrade and the proxy-delegated upgrade is that preplanning or having the ability to upgrade your contract completely cancels out the smart contract's decentralization and immutability. To maintain both decentralization and immutability, a smart contract needs to be deployed once and not have any preset possibilities of change through the preset versatility upgrade strategy or proxies. Communities that espouse the philosophy of decentralization to the core might use the contract succession upgrade strategy instead.

In the contract succession method, the development team deploys an initial contract, designs and develops a new smart contract when changes are needed, deploys it, and then communicates to their community to migrate from the old contract to the new one. This method maintains blockchain's ethos and ethics of immutability and decentralization by requiring developers to deploy entirely new contracts for changes. Users choose to migrate and begin using the new contract on their terms. Smart contract auditors benefit from the contract succession upgrade approach. The method makes contracts easier to audit since developers don't implement special state-changing functions. Auditors can read the contract without needing to analyze additional functionality.

As true to the ethics and ethos of decentralization as the contract succession method might be, it has its downsides. For one, it requires a lot of ongoing communication efforts and work to not only migrate the current community to the new contract but also spread the word about the new contract to potential new users, contacting centralized cryptocurrency exchanges and asking them to change the old token address to the new one so people can interact with the smart contract. Additionally, as the community migrates to a new contract, this may introduce problems with contract verification becoming a requirement before the community starts interacting with the new contract itself, where nefarious parties may try to create a malicious smart contract to deplete the balance of some users from within the community who might fall prey to scams. Finally, suppose these smart contract successions become frequent. In that case, the community might lose trust or motivation and leave the project altogether due to the frequent changes required.

Proxy Delegated Upgrade

The final way of upgrading contracts discussed in this chapter is the proxy-delegated upgrade method. Proxy-delegated upgrades take place through proxy contracts, which can refer to a function in the original contract and apply changes to the function. When a user calls a function, they call it in the original contract, but the code logic of the proxy contract gets executed instead. Proxy-delegated upgrades are ideal when you want to maintain the current smart contract address and update parts of the logic in the smart contract.

The primary benefit of using proxy-delegated upgrades is that the community of users does not notice any changes since they keep interacting in their experience with the same contract address. In the backend or background, changes occur through proxy contracts. The major downside of using proxy contracts is that it becomes complex to implement such changes, especially if you have a very lengthy original contract with many functions. Due to the complexity, these changes may introduce unintentional vulnerabilities in the smart contract.

One of the main functions that proxy contracts use is the delegate. This low-level function enables delegation to a logic contract. Delegation to a logic contract means that if there are two contracts, contract A and contract B, contract A can re-route the call of a function to another contract, in this case, to contract B. Contract B executes its code through the re-routing process. Delegation and re-routing work well because users continue to interact with the same contract address (Contract A), even though Contract B executes the functions. Developers must consider several variables when they design and implement proxy-delegated upgrades:

➤ **The user:** The user is the person who interacts with the contract, calling functions to stake his cryptocurrencies, sending them to another address, sending them to a friend or anyone else, and generally calling functions and using a smart contract.

➤ **The proxy contract:** Users and the community interact with the proxy contract (the front-end contract) when they connect their wallets and click buttons to execute transactions and functions. The proxy contract re-routes function calls to the logic contract based on which function the user calls. The logic contract then executes new or upgraded functions that differ from the original functionality. The proxy contract maintains the storage capacity for each function.

➤ **The logic contract(s):** The logic contract(s) contains the (upgraded) functions and logic for the entire decentralized application. Developers can change the logic contract by deploying a new one and configuring the proxy contract to re-route user calls to the new logic contract. Unlike imported contracts, the logic contract does not require a constructor function. The logic contract operates independently of the proxy contract, as delegation, rather than importing, handles the re-routing.

Figure 12.10 illustrates the proxy and logic contract relationship.

➤ Developers can break up a single logic contract into different logic contracts—sometimes called *facets*—based on individual functions. This approach implements a diamond pattern for proxy delegated upgradability (see Figures 12.11, 12.12, and 12.13). Splitting a logic contract into multiple contracts offers several advantages:

Proxy and logic contract example:

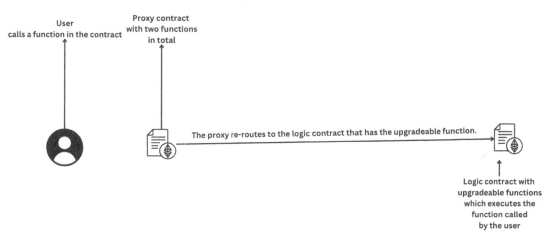

FIGURE 12.10: Proxy and logic contract example

Proxy and Logic contracts diamond implementation example 1:

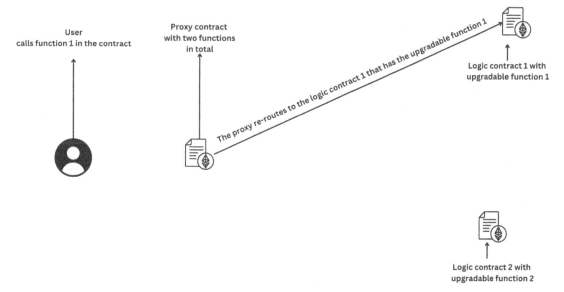

FIGURE 12.11: Proxy and logic contracts diamond implementation example 1

➤ Teams can upgrade individual functions without impacting other functions within the same contract. The modular design allows for deploying updates to specific functions instead of replacing the entire contract. This architectural approach is called *modularity*.

Proxy and Logic contracts diamond implementation example 2:

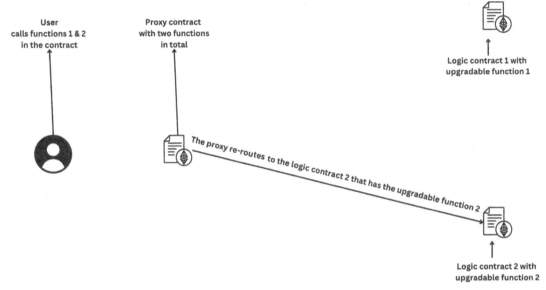

FIGURE 12.12: Proxy and logic contracts diamond implementation example 2

Proxy and Logic contracts diamond implementation example 3:

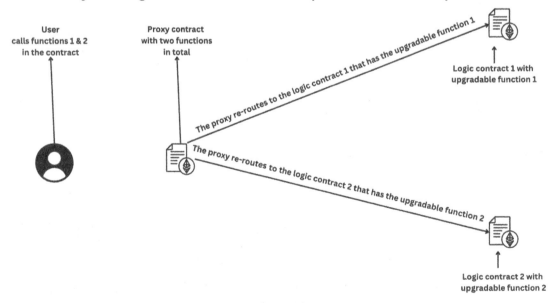

FIGURE 12.13: Proxy and logic contracts diamond implementation example 3

> ➤ Splitting a contract enables adding, replacing, or removing functions over time, in addition to updating specific functions. This is known as *flexibility*.

> ➤ It overcomes contract limitations. In some instances, a smart contract might reach its limit similarly to X/Twitter, which currently has a typing limit of 280 characters in the free version of the social media application. Breaking the contract into facets solves this limitation.

➤ **The administrator(s):** An administrator or group decides when, which, and how to upgrade a smart contract, and determines what smart contract re-routing should occur. The administrator concept creates a problem by introducing centralized parties, which creates a central point of failure since administrators can control smart contract upgrades, contradicting the technology's intended purpose. While on-chain governance can mitigate centralization, having a single person, entity, or small group serve as administrator still centralizes control.

Using proxy contracts has several downsides and challenges as well, such as the following:

➤ **Storage clashes:** As discussed in the previous chapters, Solidity has 32-byte storage slots, which start from 0, as counting in computer science begins from 0. Both the proxy contract and the logic contract have separate storage layouts. When the proxy contract delegates a function call to the logic contract, it uses its own storage. Suppose the storage layouts of both contracts do not precisely match. In that case, variables may end in the wrong slots, causing errors in behavior and data corruption.

➤ **Function selector clashes:** When proxy contracts delegate a call to one of the logic contracts, the proxy contracts use a function selector to find a function. A function selector is the first 4 bytes of the keccak256 hash of the function's signature (name and parameter types). When a proxy contract delegates calls to a logic contract, it uses these function selectors to determine which function to execute. Function selector clashes occur when two different functions end up having the same 4-byte selector, which can lead to unexpected and potentially dangerous behavior. For example, if someone uses a function to withdraw their tokens, a function that destroys the contract may be triggered, assuming such a function exists and has the same function selector as the withdraw function.

To counter possible function selector clashes, there are a couple of strategies you can implement when using proxy contracts.

The first strategy is called the *transparent proxy pattern*. In this implementation strategy of a proxy contract, owners or administrators can call only administrator or owner functions and can't call any functions in the implementation contract that are being used by users. This minimizes the risk of having function selectors clash with one another.

In the following example, you can see such a transparent proxy pattern implementation:

```
contract TransparentProxy {

    address public admin;
    address public implementation;

    modifier ifAdmin() {
```

```
            if (msg.sender == admin) {
                _;
            } else {
                _fallback();
            }
        }
```

The `modifier` ensures that only the administrator can call a function.

In the following function, a require statement ensures that the administrator cannot call the `_fallback` function:

```
        function _fallback() internal {
            require(msg.sender != admin, "Admin can not call function");
            (bool success,) = implementation.delegatecall(msg.data);
            require(success);
        }
```

In the following function the `ifAdmin` modifier ensures that only the administrator can call the `upgradeTo` function:

```
        function upgradeTo(address newImplementation) external ifAdmin {
            implementation = newImplementation;
        }
    }
```

The second proxy strategy is called *universal upgradable proxy* (UUPS). UUPS adds the logic of upgrading into the implementation itself. Through this, the Solidity compiler will display a message saying that two functions have the same selector. This strategy saves gas.

USING DELEGATECALL

To build the proxy and upgradeable smart contracts, you have to learn about the `delegatecall` function. The `delegatecall` function allows a contract to—in theory—borrow the function of another contract and execute it, as demonstrated here:

```
    // SPDX-License-Identifier: MIT
```

The preceding states the license under which the developers will release the contract.

This code states the Solidity version of the contract:

```
    pragma solidity ^0.8.26;
```

This states the name of the contract:

```
    contract B {
```

These three lines create three variables: an `uint256` that is public (meaning it can be called both internally and externally) called `num`, a `public address sender`, and a `public uint256 value`.

```
        uint256 public num;
        address public sender;
        uint256 public value;
```

The `public` and `payable` `setVars` function accepts an `uint256` parameter called `_num` and can receive ETH if needed. The function sets the `uint256` `num` to `_num`, assigns the `msg.sender` to the address `sender`, and stores `msg.value` in `uint256`

```
function setVars(uint256 _num) public payable {
    num = _num;
    sender = msg.sender;
    value = msg.value;
    }
}
```

Here, a second contract in the same file is defined:.

```
contract A {
```

Identically, the following three lines create three variables: an `uint256` that is `public` (meaning it can be called both internally and externally) called `num`, an `address` `sender` that is `public`, and an `uint256` `value` that is `public` as well:

```
uint256 public num;
address public sender;
uint256 public value;
```

The following `setVars` function has parameters for the address `_contract` and the `uint256` `_num`, which is `public` and `payable`. A `delegatecall` function uses the `address` `_contract` to call and execute the `setVars` function from contract B. It is imperative to understand that `delegatecall`, in this case, does not simply call the `setVars` `function`, it is as if it is copy-pasting it and has its code literally in contract B and then calls it. The `boolean` `(bool)` success signals true if the `delegatecall` function executes successfully while the `bytes` variable returns the `data` of the call—in this case returns nothing. The `abi.encodeWithSignature("setVars(uint256)", _num)` part creates the data necessary for calling the `setVars` `function`. Its parameter `_num` is an `uint256` specified in the code line.

```
function setVars(address _contract, uint256 _num) public payable {
    (bool success, bytes memory data) = _contract.delegatecall(
        abi.encodeWithSignature("setVars(uint256)", _num)
    );
```

As shown in Figure 12.14, you can use Remix to see what the code does.

FIGURE 12.14: `SoliditybyExample.sol`

The first step is to create a Solidity file for the contract. I used `SoliditybyExample` because the code used in this chapter can be found on the website: `https://solidity-by-example.org/delegatecall`.

```solidity
// SPDX-License-Identifier: MIT
pragma solidity ^0.8.26;

contract B {
    uint256 public num;
    address public sender;
    uint256 public value;

    function setVars(uint256 _num) public payable {      // 68898 gas
        num = _num;
        sender = msg.sender;
        value = msg.value;
    }
}

contract A {
    uint256 public num;
    address public sender;
    uint256 public value;

    function setVars(address _contract, uint256 _num) public payable {    // infinite gas
        (bool success, bytes memory data) = _contract.delegatecall(
            abi.encodeWithSignature("setVars(uint256)", _num)
        );
    }
}
```

FIGURE 12.15: Copy-pasting the code of `solidity-by-example.org`

The second step, shown in Figure 12.15, is to copy-paste the code into Remix.

The squiggly lines should not be of concern as the errors are—or should be if there are no changes to the code—due to unused variables, and the code should still be able to be deployed.

The next step is to compile the contracts through Command+S or Ctrl+S or by going to the Solidity compiler icon, clicking Compile SoliditybyExample, and deploying Contract B first, as shown in Figure 12.16.

To deploy contract B, go into the Contract section of the Deploy & Run Transactions pane and click the contract you want to deploy. In this case, it is Contract B; thus, clicking B – SoliditybyExample.sol is the right choice. Afterward, click Deploy for the contract to be deployed, scroll down on the pane to the deployed contract, and click the contract to expand, as shown in Figure 12.17.

As you can see, the `uint256 num` value, the `address sender` value, and the `uint256 value` are all currently 0. As shown in Figure 12.18, if we call the `setVars function` and add 255 there, the num value becomes 255.

FIGURE 12.16: Deploying Contract B

FIGURE 12.17: `setVars` to 255 in contract B

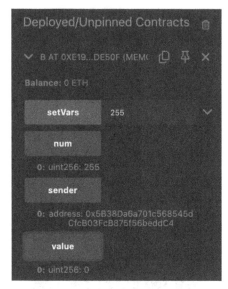

FIGURE 12.18: Result of setting `setVars` in contract B to 255

The sender's address is the address of the pseudo-wallet used by Remix (see Figure 12.19).

FIGURE 12.19: Remix's pseudo-wallet address

The `uint256 value` will be 0 as no ETH is being sent.

Now, to demonstrate how the proxy contract works, Contract A will be deployed in the same way that Contract B was deployed (see Figure 12.20).

FIGURE 12.20: Calling `setVars` from contract A by referencing contract B's address

To reference the previous contract and call the `setVars` function through contract A as if it was copy-pasted and running through contract A and not contract B, copy the contract address of contract B as shown in Figure 12.21, paste it into contract A's `setVars`, add a comma, and after the comma the number you want to add. In this case, 121.

FIGURE 12.21: Copying the contract address of contract B

After adding 0xE645D1e7bDA5Ef4932cDAA11394fA984dd4F2fb9,121 to contract B's `setVars` function, you should see the value reflected in the `num` variable and the `address sender`, as shown in Figure 12.22.

FIGURE 12.22: Result of calling `setVars` from contract A by referencing the address of contract B

Note what happens under the hood regarding storage with the different variables of contracts A and B. The names of variables are not important, especially in contract A. One could rename them. How proxy contracts enumeration works is through storage enumeration. For example:

```solidity
// SPDX-License-Identifier: MIT
pragma solidity ^0.8.26;

contract B {
    uint256 public num;
    address public sender;
    uint256 public value;
```

```
        function setVars(uint256 _num) public payable {
            num = _num;
            sender = msg.sender;
            value = msg.value;
        }
}

contract A {
    uint256 public num;
    address public sender;
    uint256 public value;

    function setVars(address _contract, uint256 _num) public payable {
        (bool success, bytes memory data) = _contract.delegatecall(
        abi.encodeWithSignature("setVars(uint256)", _num)
        );
        }
}
```

In contract B, there are these variables:

```
num = _num;
sender = msg.sender;
value = msg.value;
```

And in contract A, the same variables appear:

```
uint256 public num;
address public sender;
uint256 public value;
```

However, it is crucial to understand that if in contract A, you were to change the names of the variables, for example:

```
uint256 public variable1;
address public variable2;
uint256 public variable3;
```

This would not impact the end result that was shown previously because the variables in delegatecall are based on the storage factor. The storage in the background stores the variables in this logic:

```
Storage Slot 0: = _num
variable1 = _num;

Storage slot 1:  = msg.sender
variable2 = msg.sender

Storage slot 2: = msg.value
variable3 = msg.value
```

Thus, the variables of both contracts correspond to each other in the background through this storage method.

Coming back to the Storage clashes problem seen earlier, suppose you want to add additional storage slots to ensure no incompatibility errors. In that case, you have to use the following variable:

```
Uint256[50] private __gap;
```

This creates a specified empty reserved space of slots for future upgradable versions to add new variables if required. This is usually added at the end of each logic contract.

OpenZeppelin UUPS PROXIES

If you want to understand upgradable contracts in depth, then technical practice is paramount, so building an upgradable contract from scratch is crucial. To start building a contract, it's a best practice to create a folder or directory for the proxy contract to keep each project in order.

1. To make a directory, first type **ls** to see in what folder or directory you are currently in, as shown in Figure 12.23.

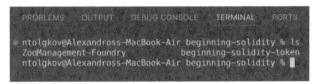

FIGURE 12.23: List (`ls`) command #1

In this example, there are two folders: `ZooManagement-Foundry` and `beginning-solidity-token`. Both directories are in the `beginning-solidity` folder you created at the beginning of this book. If you are in another folder, typing **cd ..** will take you to the parent folder. The ideal location for creating new folders is the `beginning-solidity` folder as it gives an overview of all the other available projects and keeps everything in order, allowing both the developer of the files to access them quickly and enabling someone who has not worked with these files before to find, open, and work on them without confusion.

2. After you're in the desired folder, next create a new folder by typing this:

```
mkdir beginning-solidity-proxy-contracts
```

Then type **ls** again to see if the folder has been created is a good practice. Figure 12.24 shows that the `beginning-solidity-proxy-contracts` folder has been created.

FIGURE 12.24: List (`ls`) command #2

3. Type **`cd beginning-solidity-proxy-contracts`** to move to that folder.
4. Next type **`forge init`** (or `forge init --force` if the additional `--force` is required) to create a new project. After entering the newly created `beginning-solidity-proxy-contracts` folder and typing `forge init`, the terminal messages in Figure 12.25 show that the new project files have been installed in them.

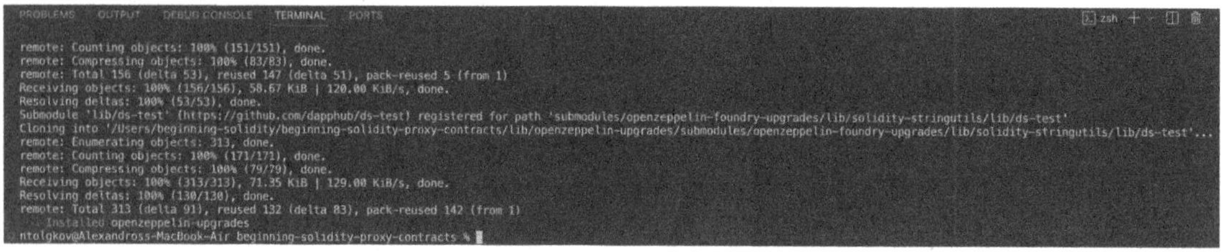

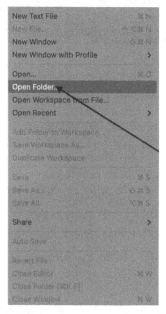

PROBLEMS OUTPUT DEBUG CONSOLE TERMINAL PORTS
zsh
remote: Counting objects: 100% (151/151), done.
remote: Compressing objects: 100% (83/83), done.
remote: Total 156 (delta 53), reused 147 (delta 51), pack-reused 5 (from 1)
Receiving objects: 100% (156/156), 58.67 KiB | 120.00 KiB/s, done.
Resolving deltas: 100% (53/53), done.
Submodule 'lib/ds-test' (https://github.com/dapphub/ds-test) registered for path 'submodules/openzeppelin-foundry-upgrades/lib/solidity-stringutils/lib/ds-test'
Cloning into '/Users/beginning-solidity/beginning-solidity-proxy-contracts/lib/openzeppelin-upgrades/submodules/openzeppelin-foundry-upgrades/lib/solidity-stringutils/lib/ds-test'...
remote: Enumerating objects: 313, done.
remote: Counting objects: 100% (171/171), done.
remote: Compressing objects: 100% (79/79), done.
Receiving objects: 100% (313/313), 71.35 KiB | 129.00 KiB/s, done.
Resolving deltas: 100% (130/130), done.
remote: Total 313 (delta 91), reused 132 (delta 83), pack-reused 142 (from 1)
Installed openzeppelin-upgrades
ntolgkov@Alexandross-MacBook-Air beginning-solidity-proxy-contracts %

FIGURE 12.25: `forge init`

5. Open the folder in a new VS Code instance. To open a file, click File at the top left of the screen (not shown) and then Open Folder, as shown in Figure 12.26.

New Text File
New File...
New Window
New Window with Profile
Open...
Open Folder...
Open Workspace from File...
Open Recent
Add Folder to Workspace...
Save Workspace As...
Duplicate Workspace
Save
Save As...
Save All
Share
Auto Save
Revert File
Close Editor
Close Folder [⌘K F]
Close Window

FIGURE 12.26: Opening `beginning-solidity-proxy-contracts` #1

6. The window shown in Figure 12.27 will open. Click the folder you want to open and then click the blue Open button to open the folder.
7. After opening the folder, delete all the `Counter.sol` files in the script, `src`, and test folders and create two files, `Zoo1.sol` and `Zoo2.sol`, in the `src` folder, as shown in Figure 12.28.

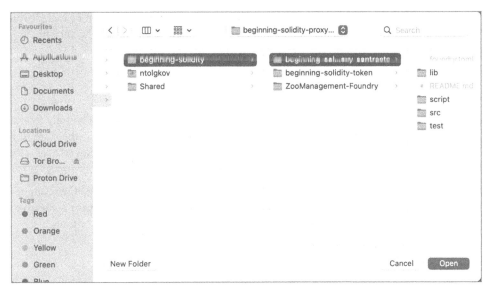

FIGURE 12.27: Opening `beginning-solidity-proxy-contracts` #2

FIGURE 12.28: Zoo1 and Zoo2

8. In the `Zoo1.sol` contract, type the following code lines:

    `//SPDX-License-Identifier: MIT`

    This specifies the license under which the contract will be released:

    `pragma solidity 0.8.27;`

    This specifies the solidity version to be used in this contract:

    `contract Zoo1 {`

    This defines a contract name and starts a new contract:

    `    uint256 internal numberOfVisitors;`

This defines a variable of type uint256 that is internal, meaning it can be called from within this contract itself and contracts that derive from it and the name of the variable is numberOfVisitors:

```
function getNumberOfVisitors() external view returns(uint256){
    return numberOfVisitors;
}
```

The getNumberOfVisitors function is external meaning it can be called only from outside of the contract. Due to the view keyword, the function does not change the state of the blockchain; it only reads and retrieves information from it. The function returns a variable of type uint256, and it is the numberofVisitors defined earlier.

The following version function is external, is pure, meaning that it neither changes the state of the blockchain nor does it retrieve any information from it and returns a variable of type uint256 which in this case is 1, which gives away the version of the contract.

```
function version() external pure returns(uint256){
    return 1;
}
}
```

9. The second contract Zoo2.sol should look like this:

```
//SPDX-License-Identifier: MIT

pragma solidity 0.8.27;
contract Zoo2 {

    uint256 internal numberOfVisitors;

    function setNumberOfVisitors  (uint256 _number) external {}
```

This defines a variable of type uint256 that is internal, meaning it can be called from within this contract itself and contracts that derive from it and that the name of the variable is numberofVisitors.

The getNumberofVisitors function is external meaning it can only be called from outside of the contract. Due to the view keyword the function does not change the state of the blockchain, only reads and retrieves information from it, the function returns a variable of type uint256 and it is the numberofVisitors defined earlier.

```
function getNumberOfVisitors() external view returns(uint256){
    return numberOfVisitors;
}
```

The following version function is external and pure, meaning that it neither changes the state of the blockchain nor does it retrieve any information from it and returns a variable of type uint256 , which in this case is 2, which gives away the version of the contract.

```
function version() external pure returns(uint256){
    return 2;
}
```

After creating the two zoo contracts, Zoo1 and Zoo2, the next step is to work on upgrading Zoo1 to Zoo2.

Follow these steps to do this:

1. Download a package of smart contracts on GitHub by going to OpenZeppelin's GitHub repository with the link to access OpenZeppelin upgrade contracts:

   `https://github.com/OpenZeppelin/openzeppelin-contracts-upgradeable`

   Another way of accessing the contract would be to type **Open-zeppelin-contracts-upgradeable github** on Google, and the GitHub repository should be among the first results that will be displayed, as shown in Figure 12.29.

FIGURE 12.29: GitHub `OpenZeppelin-contracts-upgradable`

2. Copy the URL link of the repository, go on VS Code, and install the contracts by typing **forge install OpenZeppelin/openzeppelin-contracts-upgradeable -no-commit** and pressing Enter (see Figure 12.30).

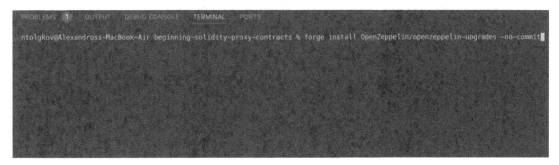

FIGURE 12.30: Script to download OpenZeppelin GitHub contracts

Upon successful completion of the downloading process, you should see Figure 12.31.

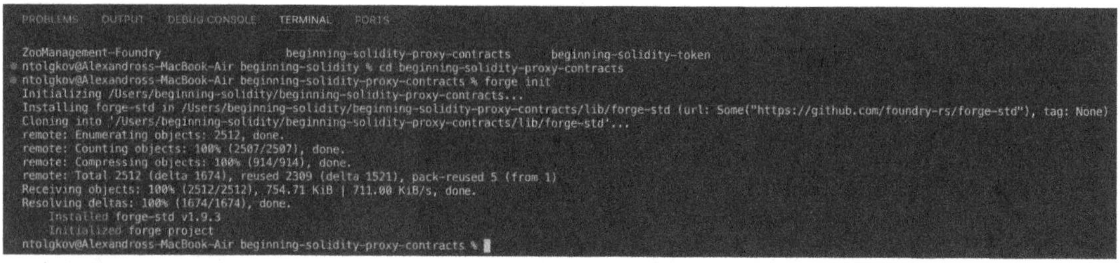

FIGURE 12.31: Message upon successful completion of downloading the GitHub `OpenZeppelin-contracts-upgraeable`

Importing UUPSUpgradeable.sol

Continue building the upgradable contract by importing several different contracts to `Zoo1`. The first of those contracts is the `UUPSUgradeable.sol` contract. (Importing `Initializable.sol` is covered in the next section.)

ABSTRACT CONTRACTS

The `UUPSUpgradeable.sol` contract is an abstract contract. An abstract contract becomes abstract through the `abstract` keyword, which comes before the name of the contract at the beginning of the smart contract and is defined after the pragma and the version of Solidity being used and defined in the contract (see Figure 12.32).

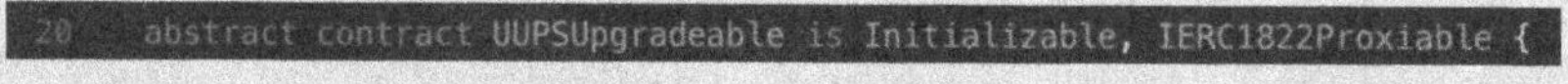

FIGURE 12.32: Abstract keyword

Abstract contracts consist of both defined and undefined functions; defined functions have already been implemented. When importing the contract, you can simply call them from the contract that does the import. Undefined functions are not yet implemented. The contract "expects" the contract that does the import to implement those functions instead.

The following is an example of a defined function:

```
function _checkNotDelegated() internal view virtual {
    if (address(this) != __self) {
        revert UUPSUnauthorizedCallContext();
    }
}
```

This function is called `_checkNotDelegated` and is internal, meaning that it can be called only from the same contract or from contracts that derive from it. It is `view`, reading information from the blockchain instead of changing its state. It is `virtual` and thus overridable if needed, and it checks through conditionality (`if`) whether the address of the contract is the `__self` address. If not, then it reverts.

The following is an example of an undefined function:

```
function __UUPSUpgradeable_init() internal onlyInitializing {
}
```

This function is called `__UPSUpgradeable_init()`, is `internal`, and has the `onlyInitializing` modifier, which comes from a contract that the `UUPSUpgradeable.sol` contract inherits from, which is called `Initializable.sol`.

Abstract contracts have several advantages. For example, they help define and standardize specific functions that can be reused multiple times without the author or developer repeating snippets of code multiple times, avoiding repetition and making the contract more compact and readable. Through unimplemented functions, abstract contracts help strike a balance between standardization, freedom, and flexibility, where developers can implement the function as they see fit to the needs of the contract they are creating.

Figure 12.33 shows the path to the `UUPSUpgradeable` contract that will be used to upgrade version 1 of the zoo contract to version 2 of the zoo contract. It starts with `lib` to openzeppelin-contracts-upgradeable, then to `proxy`, and then to `utils`, and then finally the `UUPSUpgradeable.sol` contract is displayed.

FIGURE 12.33: `UUPSUpgradeable.sol` path

When clicking the `UUPSUpgradeable.sol` contract (refer to Figure 12.33), the contract will pop up, as shown in Figure 12.34. When you scroll down, you will find the function shown in Figure 12.35.

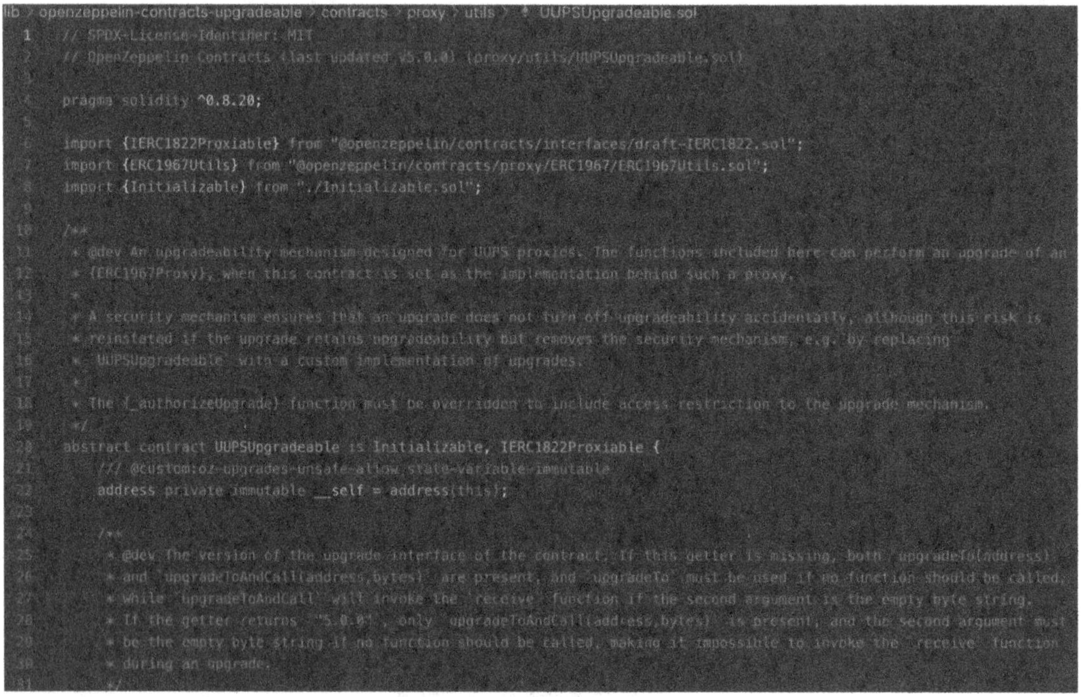

FIGURE 12.34: `UUPSUpgradeable.sol` contract

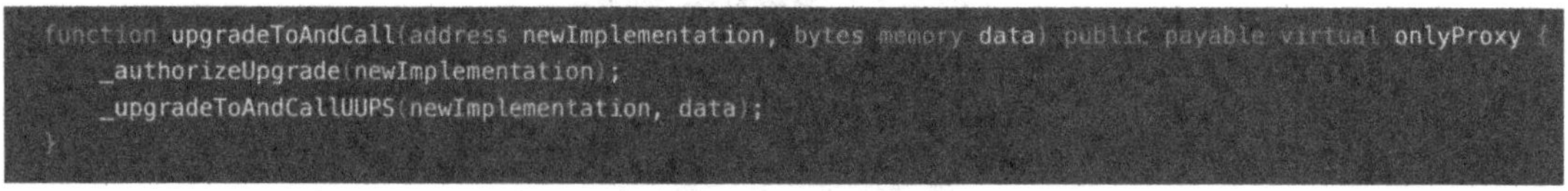

FIGURE 13.35: `upgradeToAndCall` function for `UUPSUpgradeable.sol`

THE UPGRADETOANDCALL FUNCTION

As new versions of the upgradeable contracts are released and downloaded, the upgradeToAndCall function might look slightly different from what it looks like in Figure 12.35. To help you understand what the function does, here's a line-by-line breakdown with explanations.

The upgradeToAndCall function is public, meaning that it can be called both internally and externally. It is also payable, which means it can receive ETH if needed. This function can be overridden by another function in a contract that inherits the `UUPSUpgradeable.sol` contract. Additionally, it uses the `onlyProxy` keyword which ensures that the function can only be called by a proxy contract.

```
function upgradeToAndCall(address newImplementation, bytes memory
data) public payable virtual onlyProxy {
```

The function also has two local parameters: an address, `newImplementation`, that denotes the address of the logic contract that needs to be upgraded, and the `bytes` data that refers to additional data that may need to be passed to the contract optionally.

The following part of the function is the "access control" part and has to be included by the contracts that inherit from `UUPSUpgradeable`. The function checks if the authorized party initiates the contract upgrade.

```
_authorizeUpgrade(newImplementation);
```

The following part of the code performs the actual upgrade:

```
_upgradeToAndCallUUPS(newImplementation, data);
}
```

Thus, in short, the function upgrades the logic contract.

When it comes to the contract itself, you have to import `UUPSUpgradeable.sol` to `Zoo1.sol`:

```
//SPDX-License-Identifier: MIT
pragma solidity 0.8.27;
import {UUPSUpgradeable} from "../lib/openzeppelin-contracts-upgradeable/
contracts/
proxy/utils/UUPSUpgradeable.sol";
contract Zoo1 is UUPSUpgradeable {

    uint256 internal numberOfVisitors;

    function getNumberOfVisitors() external view returns(uint256){
        return numberOfVisitors;
    }

    function version() external pure returns(uint256){
        return 1;
    }
}
```

The next step is to add the `_authorizeUpgrade` function from the `UUPSUpgradeable.sol` contract into the `Zoo1` contract, as shown in Figure 12.36.

```
function _authorizeUpgrade(address newImplementation) internal override {}
```

```
function _authorizeUpgrade(address newImplementation) internal virtual;
```

FIGURE 12.36: `_authorizeUpgrade` function

This is an undefined function whose primary purpose is to give access to the wallet address with the authority to perform the upgrade. If you leave it blank, then anyone will be able to upgrade it. A particular address has to be defined to authorize the upgrade. If the caller is not the address defined, the function should revert:

```
function _authorizeUpgrade(address newImplementation) internal override {
    if (msg.sender != owner){
        revert;
    }
}
```

The contract with the _authorizeUpgrade function should look like this:

```
//SPDX-License-Identifier: MIT
pragma solidity 0.8.27;

import {UUPSUpgradeable} from "../lib/openzeppelin-contracts-upgradeable/
contracts/
proxy/utils/UUPSUpgradeable.sol";
contract Zoo1 is UUPSUpgradeable {

    uint256 internal numberOfVisitors;

    function getNumberOfVisitors() external view returns(uint256){
        return numberOfVisitors;
    }

    function version() external pure returns(uint256){
        return 1;
    }

    function _authorizeUpgrade(address newImplementation) internal override {}

}
```

INITIALIZER

Proxied contracts do not use a constructor. This is because storage is stored in the proxy contract, not the logic contract. Suppose a constructor is set in the logic contract and takes a hypothetical variable uint256 and sets it from 0 to 10 upon deployment of the contract. In that case, the proxy will have the same uint256 in storage set to 0, creating an incompatibility.

Even so, there is a way to use a constructor's logic through a second external function, which is usually called an *initializer*. Like every other function, it is called through the proxy contract and is executed by the logic contract. When deploying an initializer, for the function to mimic the constructor and be called only once, additional precautions must be added to ensure the function will only be called once as intended.

The process is as follows:

1. Deploy the proxy contract.

2. Deploy the logic contract.

3. Call initializer function through the deployed proxy contract to be executed by the logic contract.

One usual way of using the initializer function is first to call the _disableInitializers function in the constructor function, in this case, Zoo1.sol. To find the _disableInitializers function, one has to import an additional contract called Initializable.sol that has been downloaded from the OpenZeppelin contract's upgradeable GitHub page together with the UUPSUpgradeable.sol.

Similar to the UUPSUpgradeable.sol contract, it has the same file path; only the name of the imported contract changes at the end of the import, as shown in Figure 12.37.

FIGURE 12.37: Initializable.sol file path

Upon clicking Initializable.sol, the contract should pop up (see Figure 12.38).

Scroll down, or press Command+F or Ctrl+F, and type **_disableInitializers** to find the function within the contract, as shown in Figure 12.39.

The _disableInitializers function is internal, meaning that it can be called from within the contract and contracts deriving from it; it is virtual, meaning it can be overridden. The following line of code is referenced from the InititializableStorage struct defined at the beginning of the Initializable contract. The $ in the code is a variable name that may be marked as invalid because its name does not consist of letters, which is why the // solhint-disable-next-line var-name-mixedcase is used.

The first if command ensures that the contract is not currently being initialized. If the contract is being initialized as per the _initializing function, then the function reverts. The second checks if the _initialized variable—from the InitializableStorage struct—is set to the maximum value of type `uint64`. If the `_initialized` is not set to the maximum value, then the function sets the `_initialized` variable to the maximum value and emits an event to propagate that the contract is locked. This is done to ensure no new initializer with a later version can be called.

```
// SPDX-License-Identifier: MIT
// OpenZeppelin Contracts (last updated v5.0.0) (proxy/utils/Initializable.sol)

pragma solidity ^0.8.20;

/**
 * @dev This is a base contract to aid in writing upgradeable contracts, or any kind of contract that will be deployed
 * behind a proxy. Since proxied contracts do not make use of a constructor, it's common to move constructor logic to an
 * external initializer function, usually called `initialize`. It then becomes necessary to protect this initializer
 * function so it can only be called once. The {initializer} modifier provided by this contract will have this effect.
 *
 * The initialization functions use a version number. Once a version number is used, it is consumed and cannot be
 * reused. This mechanism prevents re-execution of each "step" but allows the creation of new initialization steps in
 * case an upgrade adds a module that needs to be initialized.
 *
 * For example:
 *
 * [.hljs-theme-light.nopadding]
 * ```solidity
 * contract MyToken is ERC20Upgradeable {
 *     function initialize() initializer public {
 *         __ERC20_init("MyToken", "MTK");
 *     }
 * }
 *
 * contract MyTokenV2 is MyToken, ERC20PermitUpgradeable {
 *     function initializeV2() reinitializer(2) public {
 *         __ERC20Permit_init("MyToken");
 *     }
 * }
```

FIGURE 12.38: `Initializable.sol` contract

```
    function _disableInitializers() internal virtual {
        // solhint-disable-next-line var-name-mixedcase
        InitializableStorage storage $ = _getInitializableStorage();

        if ($._initializing) {
            revert InvalidInitialization();
        }
        if ($._initialized != type(uint64).max) {
            $._initialized = type(uint64).max;
            emit Initialized(type(uint64).max);
        }
    }
```

FIGURE 12.39: `_disableInitializers` function

When it comes to the initialization of contracts, the `_disableInitializers` function helps with the security of the smart contract as it stops any potential malicious new initialization of the contract, which is useful when it comes to constructors whose function is executed only once upon deployment and never again.

> **NOTE** *If something is not entirely clear to you now in this function, don't worry;*
> *those parts will be shown and elaborated on in the coming chapters.*

Go back to Zoo1 and do the following:

1. Import the `Initializable.sol` contract by going below the `UUPSUpgradeable` contract import and provided that this is also the path of the reader's computer, if not, change it to the correct path, typing: `import {Initializable} from "../lib/openzeppelin-contracts-upgradeable/contracts/proxy/utils/Initializable.sol";`

2. Create a constructor function in Zoo1 that calls the `_disableInitializers` function like this: `constructor() {_disableInitializers(); }`.

3. Create an initialize function in the Zoo1 contract: `function initialize () public initializer { __Ownable_init();}`.

   ➤ This is the same thing as writing `owner = msg.sender` and setting the address to the owner, ensuring it is the owner of the address.

4. Import the `OwnableUpgradeable.sol` contract by typing **import {OwnableUpgradeable} from "../lib/openzeppelin-contracts-upgradeable/contracts/access/OwnableUpgradeable.sol";**.

   ➤ This contract allows—among other things—the owner to change the address of the contract owner and enables an owner of a contract to relinquish.

5. In case of errors, change the order of the imported contracts to `contract Zoo1 is Initializable, OwnableUpgradeable, UUPSUpgradeable`.

6. Change the access control `_authorizeUpgrade` to `onlyOwner` so that only the owner could change it if it were to be called: `function _authorizeUpgrade(address newImplementation) internal override onlyOwner {}`.

In the end, the final Zoo1 contract looks like this:

```
//SPDX-License-Identifier: MIT
pragma solidity 0.8.27;
import {UUPSUpgradeable} from "../lib/openzeppelin-contracts-upgradeable/
contracts
/proxy/utils/UUPSUpgradeable.sol";
import {Initializable} from "../lib/openzeppelin-contracts-upgradeable/
contracts
/proxy/utils/Initializable.sol";
import {OwnableUpgradeable} from "../lib/openzeppelin-contracts-upgradeable
/contracts/access/OwnableUpgradeable.sol";
contract Zoo1 is Initializable, OwnableUpgradeable, UUPSUpgradeable {

    uint256 internal numberOfVisitors;
```

```
    constructor() {
        _disableInitializers();
    }

    function initialize () public initializer {
        __Ownable_init(msg.sender);
    }

    function getNumberOfVisitors() external view returns(uint256){
        return numberOfVisitors;
    }

    function version() external pure returns(uint256){
        return 1;
    }

    function _authorizeUpgrade(address newImplementation) internal view
override
onlyOwner {
        require(newImplementation != address(0), "Invalid implementation
address");
    }

}
```

The Zoo2 contract, to be interoperable, should look like this:

```
//SPDX-License-Identifier: MIT

pragma solidity 0.8.27;
import {UUPSUpgradeable} from "../lib/openzeppelin-contracts-upgradeable/
contracts
/proxy/utils/UUPSUpgradeable.sol";
import {Initializable} from "../lib/openzeppelin-contracts-upgradeable/
contracts
/proxy/utils/Initializable.sol";
import {OwnableUpgradeable} from "../lib/openzeppelin-contracts-upgradeable
/contracts/access/OwnableUpgradeable.sol";

contract Zoo2 is Initializable, OwnableUpgradeable, UUPSUpgradeable {

    uint256 internal numberOfVisitors;

    constructor() {
        _disableInitializers();
    }

    function initialize() public initializer {
        __Ownable_init(msg.sender);
    }

    function setNumberOfVisitors (uint256 _number) external {}

    function getNumberOfVisitors() external view returns(uint256){
        return numberOfVisitors;
```

```
    }

    function version() external pure returns(uint256){
        return 2;
    }

    function _authorizeUpgrade(address newImplementation) internal
view override
onlyOwner {
        require(newImplementation != address(0), "Invalid implementation
address");
    }
}
```

DEPLOYING THE PROXY CONTRACT

After creating the contracts as shown in the previous sections, the next step is to deploy them. To do so, go to the script folder and create a file. The contract Zoo1 will be the one to be scripted for deployment. The file to be created is DeployZoo.s.sol.

In the DeployZoo.s.sol contract, type the following lines.

This specifies the license under which the contract will be released:

```
//SPDX-License-Identifier: MIT
```

This specifies the version of Solidity used in the contract:

```
pragma solidity 0.8.27;
```

This specifies the contracts to be imported and the contracts path, which directory or folder they can be found in to be imported:

```
import {Script} from "forge-std/Script.sol";
import {Zoo1} from "../src/Zoo1.sol";
```

This defines the name of the contract and inherits the Script contract that was deployed earlier:

```
contract DeployZoo is Script {
```

The run function is essential for every deployable contract in the script folder. It is external and returns an address.

```
    function run() external returns(address) {
```

The following calls the deployZoo function, which stores its address in the proxy variable. The second line of code returns the proxy variable.

```
        address proxy = deployZoo();
        return proxy;
    }
```

The following `deployZoo` function is public and returns an address. Within the function, the first line creates a new instance of the `Zoo1` contract through the `new` keyword. The new `Zoo1` contract is stored in the zoo instance.

```
function deployZoo() public returns(address){
    Zoo1 zoo = new Zoo1();
    }
}
```

This is the logic part of the contract, and a proxy will be used to point to a delegate call. For that to happen, you need to use a proxy. The proxy used in this example is `ERC1967Proxy` and can be found in the OpenZeppelin GitHub repository (see Figure 12.40). To implement this, download the `ERC1967Proxy` contract and import it into the `DeployZoo.s.sol` contract. To download the contract, use this command:

```
forge install Openzeppelin/openzeppelin-contracts  --no-commit:
```

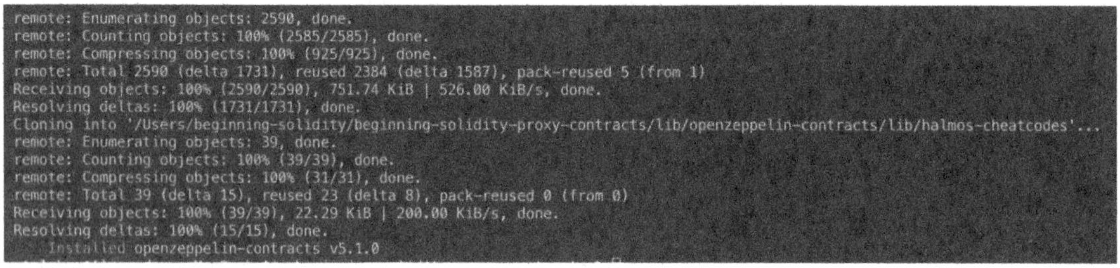

FIGURE 12.40: Successfully installed package with `ERC1967Proxy` contract

After the contracts have been installed, you should import the contract into the `DeployZoo.s.sol` contract:

```
//SPDX-License-Identifier: MIT

pragma solidity 0.8.27;

import {Script} from "forge-std/Script.sol";
import {Zoo1} from "../src/Zoo1.sol";
import {ERC1967Proxy} from "../lib/openzeppelin-contracts/contracts/
proxy/ERC1967
/ERC1967Proxy.sol";
```

The following just imports the additional `ERC1967Proxy` contract that was downloaded earlier:

```
contract DeployZoo is Script {

    function run() external returns(address) {
        address proxy = deployZoo();
        return proxy;
    }

    function deployZoo() public returns(address) {
        Zoo1 zoo = new Zoo1();
```

```
                ERC1967Proxy proxy = new ERC1967Proxy(address(zoo), "");
                return address(proxy);
        }
    }
```

Like before, the deployZoo function is public and returns an address. Within the function, the first line creates a new instance of the Zoo1 contract through the new keyword. The new Zoo1 contract is stored in the zoo instance.

However, this time, the addition of the new line creates a new ERC1967Proxy contract, which is initialized by the zoo's address in the same function with no initialization data. Finally, the function returns the proxy's address, enabling users to interact with the proxy contract.

The ERC1967Proxy contract's constructor provides and utilizes both the address zoo and initialization data, as shown in Figure 12.41.

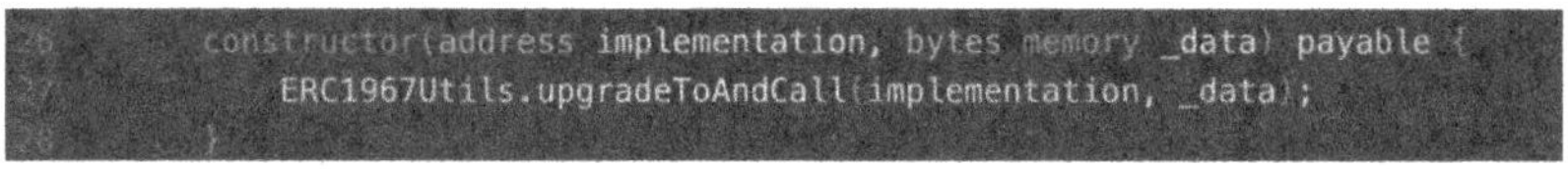

FIGURE 12.41: ERC1967Proxy contract constructor

After completing the deployable contract successfully, to ensure everything went fine, open your terminal and type **forge build**, and press the Enter key. If all went well, you should see the message in Figure 12.42.

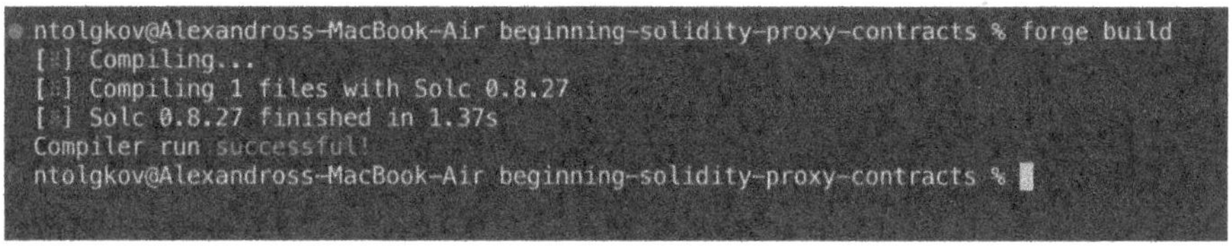

FIGURE 12.42: forge build successful

CHAPTER 12 QUESTIONS

1. What are the three main strategies for upgrading smart contracts, and what are the key trade-offs between them in terms of decentralization and complexity?

2. When implementing storage slots in upgradeable contracts, why do we need to use a gap variable like uint256[50] private __gap;? What problem does this solve?

3. Explain the difference between using a constructor versus an initializer in upgradeable contracts. Why can't we use constructors in proxy patterns?

4. Walk me through how delegatecall works in proxy patterns. How does storage slot mapping work between the proxy and implementation contracts?

5. What are storage clashes in proxy patterns? How can they occur and what are the best practices to prevent them?

6. Explain the difference between the Transparent Proxy Pattern and the Universal Upgradeable Proxy Standard. What are the gas implications of each?

7. In the context of proxy patterns, what are function selector clashes, and how can they lead to security vulnerabilities?

8. When implementing the `_authorizeUpgrade` function in a UUPS pattern, what security considerations should be taken into account?

9. Why is the order of inheritance important when implementing upgradeable contracts with multiple inherited contracts like `Initializable`, `OwnableUpgradeable`, and `UUPSUpgradeable`?

10. What's the purpose of `_disableInitializers()` in upgradeable contracts, and when should it be called?

11. How does `ERC1967Proxy` work, and what are its key components? Walk me through the deployment process of an upgradeable contract using `ERC1967Proxy`.

12. What security risks are introduced by making a contract upgradeable? How can these risks be mitigated?

13. In the diamond pattern for proxy contracts, what are facets, and what problems do they solve?

14. Can you explain how `msg.sender` and `msg.value` are handled in proxy patterns using `delegatecall`? What are the implications for contract security?

15. What role do external auditing tools like CertiK play in validating upgradeable contracts? What key metrics should developers look for in audit reports?

13

Decentralized Autonomous Organizations

Decentralized autonomous organizations (DAOs) represent a groundbreaking evolution in the way organizations operate. At their core, DAOs are communities or entities governed by rules encoded in smart contracts rather than traditional hierarchical structures. By leveraging blockchain technology, DAOs ensure transparency, automation, and a level of decentralization that conventional organizations often struggle to achieve. Decisions are made collectively, with governance power distributed among token holders, allowing for a more democratic and inclusive approach to managing resources and pursuing shared goals. This chapter delves into the foundational concepts of DAOs, their governance mechanisms, and practical steps to create and interact with them, blending theory with hands-on programming to provide a comprehensive understanding of this transformative concept.

WHAT IS A DAO?

When looking at traditional organizations or corporations, you will see, besides people contributing to the organization to extract profit or to achieve a purpose, that the organization has a set of rules and procedures that regulate the conduct of participants. These regulations range from simple things such as the dress code to protocols for what happens when a specific event occurs such as a fire, at lunchtime, how people work and how, or who makes the decisions and governs the organization. Together these protocols define the organization's governance.

Governance in and of itself is usually associated with politics, but that is not the only use case of governance. Governance can be applied to for-profit, nongovernmental organizations, and any human organization. Even a family has a governance structure where the adult has the final say or decision about how someone who is not an adult, their child, conducts themselves in various events and ways. All governance systems are top-down, meaning that someone at the top gives the final decision or order for something to take place, be it the president or prime minister of a country, and although those are, most of the time, elected democratically, that does not mean their governance approach is not top-down.

A public company's CEO is appointed by its board of directors who, in turn, are elected by the company's shareholders. Shareholders hold voting power within the company proportional to the percentage of shares they own and can elect the board of directors to whom a CEO answers.

Public companies have, in theory, a more "decentralized" governance due to having diverse shareholders compared to private companies (see Figure 13.1) where usually one person or family is the sole business owner. In practice, however, few, if any, companies have decentralized governance as most of the shares are usually concentrated in the hands of a few people, such as the founders, early investors, and possibly early employees. As will be explained, decentralized autonomous organizations have varying degrees of decentralization in their governance.

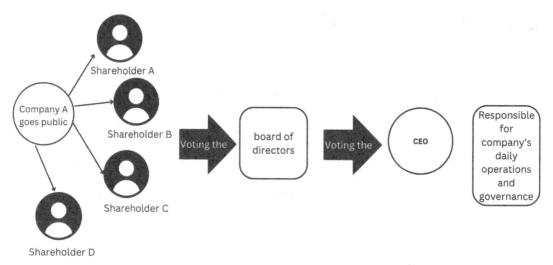

FIGURE 13.1 Approximate representation of the governance of a traditional public company

Decentralized autonomous organizations are leaderless organizations governed by a transparent set of rules encoded in smart contracts deployed on the blockchain. Their governance and daily operations are entirely transparent and on-chain. DAOs are entirely digital entities created and deployed on the blockchain. Their transactions and operations are propagated and maintained by the blockchain network nodes they are deployed on. DAOs are indifferent about who interacts with them; they simply receive information in the form of votes and execute functions, orders, or requests—depending on the definition of these terms you want to use—based on the governance rules encoded in their smart contracts.

DAOs are organizations or communities whose members come together to achieve a common goal or cause. Their operation is deterministic because they have been coded in a specific way. Hence, their rules cannot change—unless they deploy an upgradable contract.

In DAOs, governance takes place through tokens whose owners are usually distributed across the globe. These tokens can be ERC-20 tokens or ERC-721 tokens, and they aim to decentralize the governance of a protocol that has been created. These governance tokens, besides giving governance rights to holders, may also provide rights to profit sharing through fees that the protocol accumulates. These tokens can be earned in different ways:

➤ By participating and working for the DAO and contributing to activities the smart contract itself cannot automate

➤ Through minting early tokens to protocol creators and early investors

➤ By being gifted to addresses or people that fulfill specific criteria in a process called an *airdrop*

➤ By being bought on decentralized or centralized exchanges like any other token

Token holders can perform several activities, including submitting governance proposals. The DAO sees these proposals as executable code and not directions for a human team to implement. Voting on such proposals also depends on each DAO's rules. The other members of the DAO vote upon the proposals, and upon reaching a certain threshold of quorum or consensus, such as more than 50%, the proposal is accepted and autonomously implemented by the DAO.

In theory, DAOs do not need a central management team to make operational decisions. However, today, as people experiment with decentralized autonomous organizations and their potential, most DAOs do have some form of management team, especially in the beginning. This is because every DAO starts centralized, often with just one member or a few members. As more members join, it gradually becomes decentralized through changes to its governance structure and smart contract logic.

The following are some examples of DAO governance in practice:

➤ **Uniswap:** Governance token holders can vote on proposals and delegate their tokens. To submit a proposal, a token holder should hold at least 1,000 UNI tokens; 2.5 million UNI tokens are required to proceed to the final on-chain voting stage.

➤ **Compound:** Token holders must delegate their tokens to others not required to hold the COMP token for voting. Holders must stake 1% of tokens to submit a proposal, with a 3-day window to be voted upon. When most token holders vote in favor of a proposal, it is put on the list for implementation after 2 days.

➤ **Curve:** CRV holders lock up their tokens and get other veCRV tokens with which they can vote and make proposals. A user has to have at least 2,500 veCRV tokens to create a proposal, but there is no minimum on voting.

➤ **Synthetix:** The organization has five different DAOs and no governance token. Anyone can propose improvements. However, the Spartan Council initiates the approval of the proposals: eight annually elected individuals review the proposals, interview the proposals' authors, and, if successful, implement the changes to the protocol. In the case of Synthetix, the proposals are entirely decentralized. Still, the approval is not decentralized but rather is similar to a board of directors in traditional corporate governance schemes.

DAOs have several different levels of decentralization that you can measure:

➤ **Level 1, token holders:** How sparsely are governance tokens distributed and held by the token holders? Suppose there is a supply of 1 million governance tokens and only a few addresses hold 80–90% of them. In that case, this is a point of centralization for the DAO. One way of seeing the token distribution is the website `coincarp.com`, which shows the rich list of every token listed. You can see, for example, the distribution of Uniswap's UNI token in Figure 13.2.

#	Address		Quantity	Percentage	7d Change
1	0x1a9c8182c09f50c8318d769245bea52c32be35bc		382,798,855	38.28%	-130,330
2	0xf977814e90da44bfa03b6295a0616a897441acec	Binance	31,896,706	3.19%	6,814,552
3	0x47173b170c64d16393a52e6c480b3ad8c302ba1e		23,047,481	2.30%	--
4	0x3d30b1ab88d487b0f3061f40de76845bec3f1e94		16,776,072	1.68%	--
5	0xbdf7347e4164ee0796d9b4f0a5f2dce9b77756b7		13,254,690	1.33%	--
6	0x090d4613473dee047c3f2706764f49e0821d256e		12,944,473	1.29%	-16,028
7	0x0ec9e8aa56e0425b60dee347c8efbad959579d0f		12,611,331	1.26%	--
8	0x878f0822a9e77c1dd7883e543747147be8d63c3b		10,713,376	1.07%	--
9	0x6cc5f688a315f3dc28a7781717a9a798a59fda7b	OKX	10,659,140	1.07%	-142,872
10	0xa29b574fea8d85b6c2a1b7071e6160212cf94097		9,000,000	0.90%	--

Top 100 Richest Uniswap Addresses Ethereum

FIGURE 13.2 CoinCarp UNI token distribution

You can see that some addresses have tags such as OKX or Binance, signifying that these wallets belong to centralized exchanges. This is another point of contention. While the primary reason a centralized exchange holds tokens is to sell them, the centralized exchanges still technically own the tokens in their wallets; even if someone buys the token off of the exchange, as long as the token stays on the exchange, it technically remains in one of the wallets of the exchange. The exchange can potentially use the tokens to vote. Considering the policy of a centralized exchange regarding voting, if you care about governance, it is always good.

➤ **Level 2, delegates:** One possible avenue a token holder can take is to delegate their vote to another address or person if they do not have the time to vote. This delegation can be revoked by the owner of the tokens at any point, and the owner can choose to either vote themselves or redelegate their vote to someone else. The delegates can become dangerously centralized.

Suppose that a DAO has 1,000 token holders. Half of those token holders, 500 of them, delegate their tokens to the remaining 500 token holders, which is a potential, although unlikely, scenario used for illustrative purposes. Suddenly, there is a situation where the voters have been halved from 1,000 to 500. Thus, the decentralization of the voting has been halved as well. In practice, this scenario is even worse as people usually tend to delegate their voting power to a much smaller number of delegates, thereby centralizing the voting even more.

➤ **Level 3, proposals:** There are several things to consider in proposals:

  ➤ Who can make the proposals, and how many tokens does one have to own to propose?

  ➤ Who can vote? How many tokens does one have to own to vote?

  ➤ What addresses make the most proposals? If it is always the same addresses making new proposals and the same addresses voting again and again, then this denotes centralization.

  ➤ If the proposals of the same addresses get accepted time and time again and not those of other addresses, it is possible that the proposals of these other addresses are terrible, and the proposals of the addresses that get accepted are excellent. However, it can also be possible that this is another form of centralization and possibly corruption where only a few addresses have a say in changes to the protocol.

➤ **Level 4, smart contract:** Upgradable contracts, while offering flexibility, can introduce centralization risks to a DAO, particularly if access control mechanisms allow specific individuals to call critical functions within the contract. This centralization can lead to vulnerabilities, including the possibility of a *rug pull*. A rug pull is a type of scam in the cryptocurrency space where the contract owner—often a single individual or a small group—exploits their access privileges to withdraw funds deposited by thousands of users, subsequently disappearing with the stolen money. Scammers often invoke "privacy concerns" to justify their anonymity, presenting fake names, stories, and backgrounds—similar to the pseudonymous approach of Satoshi Nakamoto. This anonymity enables them to execute the withdrawal function and vanish without accountability.

EXPLORING THE AAVE PROTOCOL

Now that you know what a decentralized autonomous organization is in theory, it is time to see a practical DAO to learn how token holders vote on and submit their proposals.

In this section, you will explore the Aave protocol, a decentralized platform that is also a DAO that allows users to lend, borrow, and earn interest on their cryptocurrencies. You will be guided through the process of interacting with Aave's governance features, from connecting a wallet to engaging with DAO proposals.

You will learn about the following:

➤ Aave's decentralized application (DApp)

➤ How to connect a MetaMask wallet

➤ Aave's Ethereum Market

➤ How to access and interact with Aave's governance proposals

➤ Snapshot, a tool used to gauge community sentiment about specific proposals

The Aave protocol is accessible at `aave.com`, shown in Figure 13.3.

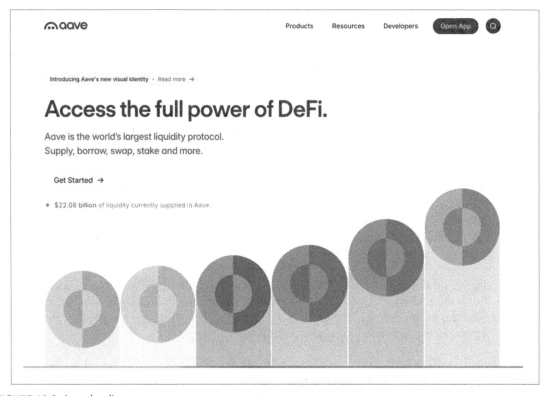

FIGURE 13.3 Aave landing page

The Aave protocol allows users to lend, borrow, and earn interest on their cryptocurrencies. Follow these steps to learn how to interact with the Aave protocol:

1. Click the Open App button at the top right of the website. You will be redirected to the decentralized application dashboard of Aave, shown in Figure 13.4.

2. Click Connect Wallet (at the top right in Figure 13.4) to connect the MetaMask wallet you installed in Chapter 12.

FIGURE 13.4 Aave Ethereum Market landing page

3. A pop-up will appear asking what kind of wallet you want to connect with (see Figure 13.5). Since in Chapter 12 you installed MetaMask as a browser wallet, if you log in through a browser, you must click the Browser Wallet option to connect.

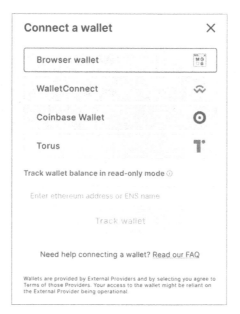

FIGURE 13.5 Connecting MetaMask to Aave

After having connected, you should see Aave's Ethereum Market, shown in Figure 13.6.

FIGURE 13.6 Aave Ethereum Market landing page with wallet connected

4. On the top left of the screen next to the Aave logo, there are several buttons: Dashboard, Markets, Stake, Governance, and More. Click Governance.

You will be redirected to Aave's Governance page and will be able to see the voting proposals of the DAO currently in the voting period and those that have completed their voting period (see Figure 13.7).

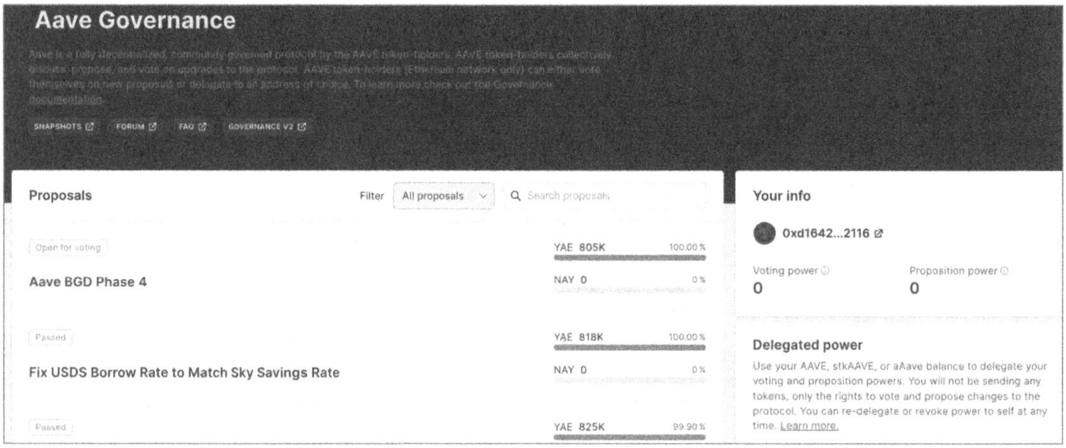

FIGURE 13.7 Aave Governance forum

5. Click the first proposal, in this case Aave BGD Phase 4. You will see the proposal overview and the specific proposal on the left. The example in Figure 13.8 shows a simple summary, motivation, and specification in this case. On the right side, you can see how much voting power you have (in terms of tokens being held by the address of the wallet one connects with), the voting results, (in this case an overwhelming yes with 805k and 100% of the results voting yes), the top 10 addresses, and what they voted for.

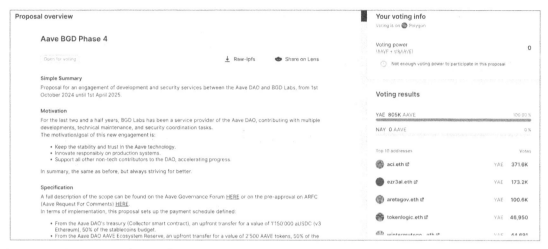

FIGURE 13.8 Aave proposal example

Scroll down and you will see the proposal details on the right: creation date, open for voting, voting closed, and payloads executed, as shown in Figure 13.9.

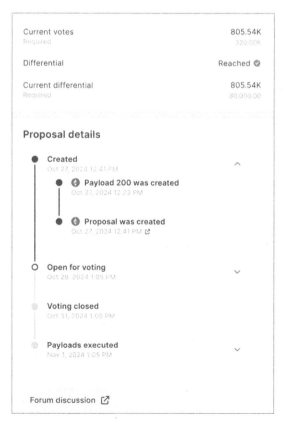

FIGURE 13.9 Aave proposal lifecycle

To create a proposal, a specific address has to initiate the process. A short time after the proposal has been created, the proposal is open for voting by other token holders and addresses. The voting process has a closing date, at which point voting ends. If the proposal is successful, it is executed. The submission of a proposal is recorded as a transaction and stored on the chain.

6. At the bottom of the proposal details and lifecycle is a Forum Discussion button. Click it to be redirected to the Aave forum, shown in Figure 13.10.

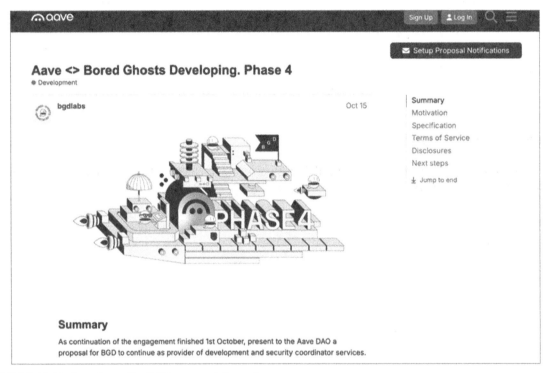

FIGURE 13.10 Aave forum for DAO proposal discussion

You want to go here because, before submitting a proposal for voting, you have to create a thread on Aave's forum to discuss the proposal and receive feedback from the community on their idea (see Figure 13.11). In other words, submitting a proposal for voting is not enough and is not the first step in submitting a proposal for a DAO.

Snapshot

Another tool often used to gauge a community's sentiment about a proposal is Snapshot, a decentralized governance tool that allows DAOs to create and vote on proposals for their protocols. One of Snapshot's features is that it allows you to create a mock proposal and have the community vote on it without the proposal being executed, just to see what would likely happen if the vote were, in fact, a reality. After that, the actual proposal could be submitted for voting.

FIGURE 13.11 Example of discussions on Aave's forum

To access Snapshot, go to `snapshot.org`. Figure 13.12 shows Snapshot's landing page with the main DAOs displayed. Aave, in this case, is the first result.

FIGURE 13.12 Snapshot landing page

If you click Aave's Join button, it will ask to connect a wallet. As shown in Figure 13.13, this example uses MetaMask for the same reason that wallet was used earlier in this chapter.

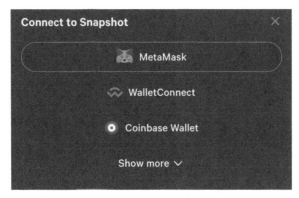

FIGURE 13.13 Connecting to Snapshot through MetaMask

Upon connecting to the MetaMask wallet, you will be directed to a somewhat familiar screen with proposals (see Figure 13.14).

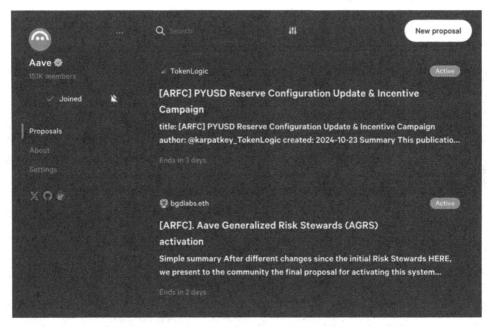

FIGURE 13.14 Aave Snapshot mock proposal landing page

If you click the first proposal, you will see a similar structure to the previous proposal on Aave's website. However, this one measures sentiment instead of executing the proposal (see Figure 13.15).

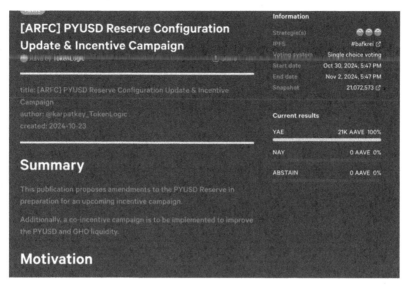

FIGURE 13.15 Aave mock proposal example

POTENTIAL VOTING ARCHITECTURES FOR A DAO

Several architectural designs and tools are available for building a DAO. Among these, the voting mechanism used by the DAO is one of its most crucial elements as that is how the community of the organization, most of the time, engages with the organization itself and participates.

One of the most used, standard, and straightforward ways of helping a DAO make decisions is to create an ERC-20 or an NFT token and use the token's ownership proportionality to reflect each member's voting and proposal power.

This approach, however, can have its downsides as the person with the most wealth (tokens) has more decision-making power and will use it to benefit themselves than someone who may not be able to afford the same or higher number of tokens. Additionally, if one is wealthy enough, it is possible to purchase tokens to be malicious in one's voting patterns or to prevent a decision from being taken and then sell the tokens after accomplishing that, as nothing prevents one from doing so.

One potential solution to this is the skin-in-the-game method. The skin-in-the-game method is when one votes for a decision, and their vote is recorded. Suppose that a vote leads to a bad outcome. In that case, their tokens are forfeited, enabling a sort of punishment for those with malicious intent and accountability on what one votes for. However, the problem with this method is determining and defining what a bad outcome is; what is considered bad enough to punish people? Was the intent of the voter malicious or simply naive? If naive, should they still be punished for it?

Another potential solution to this problem—and the most difficult one—is proof of humanity. Proof of humanity is when the users of a protocol get just one vote for simply being users of the protocol. Thus, one person equals one vote. The problem with this solution here is Sybil's resistance: How can the protocol developers be sure that one person equals one vote? Not one person having 1,000 votes if they were to create 1,000 different addresses and use them all to vote and thus hack the odds in their favor? This problem has not yet been solved—maybe the readers of this book will be able to solve the problem? Proof of humanity can be seen as analogous to showing identification in elections—but in a decentralized way—and ensuring that you are one person voting once and do not come to vote multiple times and cheat the system.

A problem with on-chain voting seen earlier such as in Figure 13.7 and onward is that any other transaction costs gas fees. If a DAO has 1,000 people and it costs 50 USD per vote, your community just spent 50,000 USD for a single vote, which is not economically sustainable in the long term. The advantage of this is that everything is on-chain, transparent, and will stay on the blockchain forever. The disadvantage, of course, is the high cost incurred by the voters. An alternative to on-chain voting is off-chain voting while remaining entirely decentralized. Using IPFS, explained in Chapter 10, it is possible to sign a voting transaction without sending it to the blockchain, skipping paying gas. By sending the voting transaction to IPFS' decentralized database, you can use an oracle to propagate it.

THE DAO TOOLKIT

Using coding or coding tools is not always necessary when you want to build a DAO. You can search online for and use tools such as Aragon and Colony to create DAOs without needing to code at all. However, the "drag and drop" method of creating DAOs has limitations as it is a standard way of creating DAOs and thus entails minimized flexibility, limiting what you can do if you want to be more creative in the DAO rules and what the DAO can do.

Snapshot, mentioned earlier in this chapter, is an additional tool for measuring the sentiment of a specific DAO proposal without the proposal being executed automatically if it passes the vote. Users can—as demonstrated earlier—connect their wallets on Snapshot and vote with the tokens they own. Snapshot transactions are stored on IPFS and, hence, are gasless.

Another tool is Gnosis Safe, a multisignature wallet that can be used as the DAO's treasury. Gnosis can be useful at the very beginning of DAO formation when the DAO is still centralized to some extent. Finally, Zodiac, which comes along with Gnosis Safe as an add-on, is a suite of DAO tools ranging from cross-chain governance to time locks and other features that are worth exploring.

SETTING UP THE DAO PROJECT

After having seen how DAOs work in a nontechnical way, it is time to build your own DAO to see how they work in a technical way, so you'll have the full picture of how a DAO works.

1. In Visual Studio Code, type **ls** to see where VS Code is located, as shown in Figure 13.16.

   In this example, the terminal shows that VS Code is located in the `beginning-solidity` directory where you can see other directories such as `ZooManagement`, `Solidity-proxy-contracts`, and the `erc-20` token.

2. Create a new directory for the DAO project by typing this:

   ```
   mkdir beginning-solidity-DAO
   ```

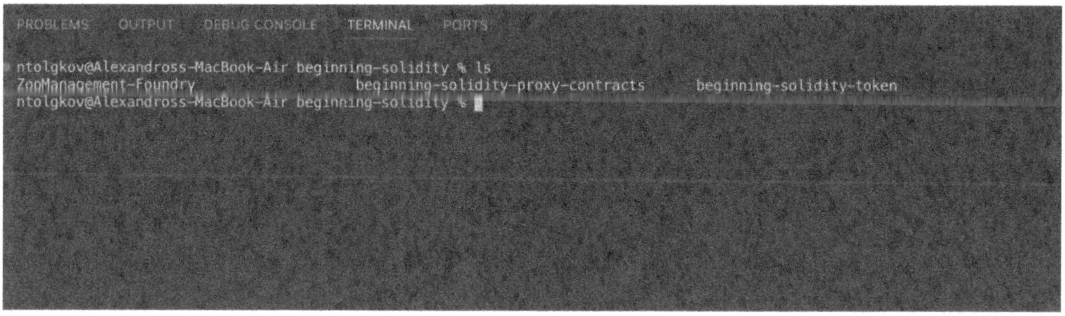

FIGURE 13.16 Directory location

This will create a new directory named `beginning-solidity-DAO`. To ensure that it has been created, type **ls** again and see if the folder can be seen (see Figure 13.17).

FIGURE 13.17 `beginning-solidity-DAO` **directory creation**

3. The folder is in the `beginning-solidity` directory, so type the following to enter the folder:

    `cd beginning-solidity-DAO`

4. Type **ls** again to enter the DAO folder (see Figure 13.18).

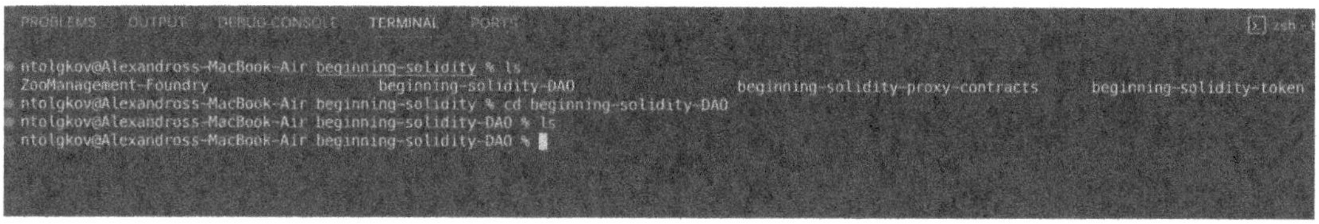

FIGURE 13.18 Migrating to the DAO folder created

5. On the File tab at the top of the VS Code screen, click Open Folder (see Figure 13.19).

6. After clicking Open Folder, click the DAO folder you want to open and then click the blue Open button (see Figure 13.20).

7. Now, in VS Code's terminal, type this:

    `forge init`

or, if that does not work, type this:

```
forge init --force
```

This will install the whole package you need to start working on a new Solidity project (see Figure 13.21).

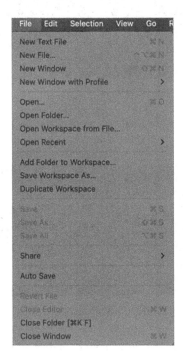

FIGURE 13.19 File options

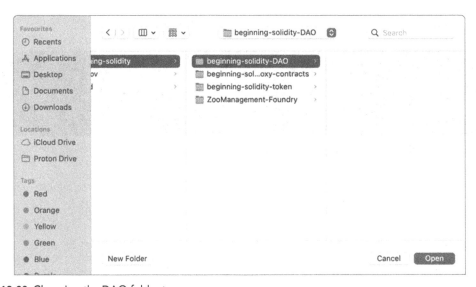

FIGURE 13.20 Choosing the DAO folder to open

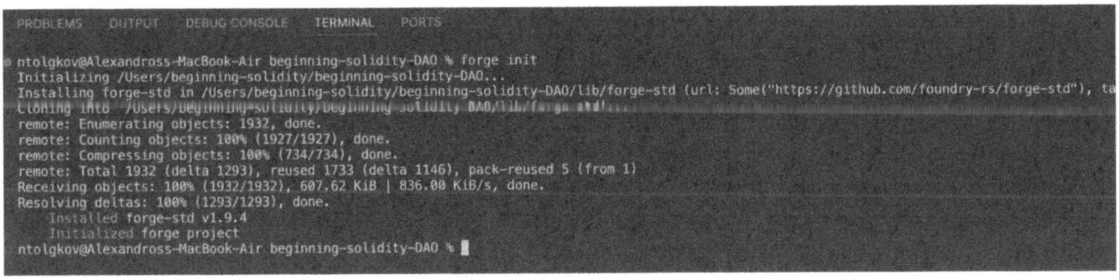

FIGURE 13.21 Installing a new project

ADDING THE RETRIEVABLENUMBER.SOL CONTRACT

The purpose of the `RetrievableNumber.sol` contract you create in this section is to demonstrate how to implement access control through OpenZeppelin's available downloadable contracts. Access control enables a specific address to be the only address that can call a specific function. This is useful to know in order to implement the standard access control method currently used in the industry.

1. In the left pane of VS Code, you will see the `Counter.sol` file in the `script`, `src`, and `test` folders (see Figure 13.22). Delete those.

FIGURE 13.22 Deleting pre-installed contracts

2. Next, add a Solidity file called `RetrievableNumber.sol` to the `src` folder (see Figure 13.23).

3. Within the contract, type the following to define the license under which the contract will be released, the Solidity version, and the contract name:

```
//SPDX-License-Identifier: MIT
pragma solidity 0.8.27;
contract RetrievableNumber {
}
```

FIGURE 13.23 Creation of `RetrievableNumber.sol`

4. After that, go to OpenZeppelin's OpenZeppelin-contracts GitHub and copy and paste the URL of the website, as shown in Figure 13.24.

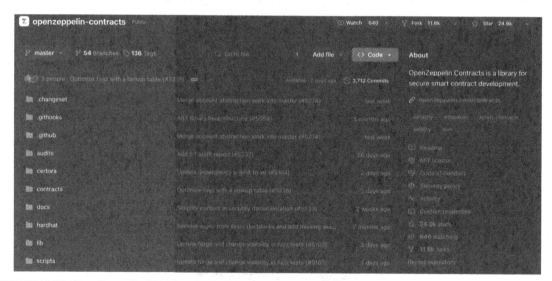

FIGURE 13.24 OpenZeppelin GitHub contracts

and type the following in the terminal:

```
forge install <paste the link here> --no-commit
```

Then wait for the contract package to be installed (see Figure 13.25).

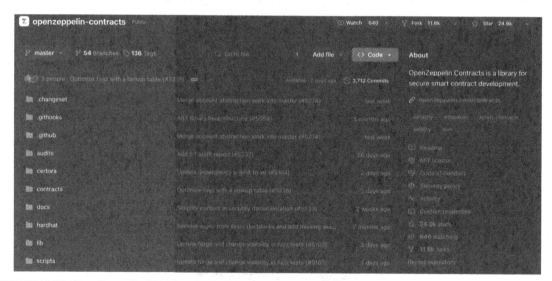

FIGURE 13.25 Contract package being installed

Figure 13.26 shows the terminal after the package has been installed.

FIGURE 13.26 Contract package installed

5. Import the `Ownable.sol` contract into the `Retrievable.sol` contract. The `Ownable.sol` contract (see Figure 13.27) implements an access control function that allows only a specific address to have access and call a function.

FIGURE 13.27 `Ownable.sol` path

6. Now you need to import the Ownable contract. The path to the `Ownable.sol` contract that has been downloaded with the OpenZeppelin package is lib ⇨ openzeppelin-contracts ⇨ contracts ⇨ access ⇨ Ownable.sol.

To import the contract, write the following in the `RetrievableNumber.sol` contract:

```
//SPDX-License-Identifier: MIT

pragma solidity 0.8.27;
import {Ownable} from "../lib/openzeppelin-contracts/contracts/access/
Ownable.sol"
```

The `..` serves as returning to the parent folder, in this case, the `src` folder. Thus, the `..` can be interpreted as "leaving the `src` folder" and then going inside the `lib` folder.

```
contract RetrievableNumber is Ownable {
```

The contract with the name `RetrievableNumber` inherits from the `Ownable` contract.

7. Next, to finish this contract, type the following:

```
uint256 private s_number;
```

This creates a private `uint256` variable s_number, which can be called only from within the contract.

The following creates an event that needs to be emitted. The name suggests that it should be emitted when a number is changed.

```
 event NumberChanged(uint256 number);
```

The following store function creates a `uint256 newNumber` parameter. It is `public`, meaning it can be called both internally and externally. However, it can be called only by the contract owner—that will be the DAO. Within the function itself, the s_number is set to the `newNumber` parameter, and after that, an event is emitted that the number changed to `newNumber`.

```
    function store (uint256 newNumber) public onlyOwner {
        s_number = newNumber
        emit NumberChanged(newNumber);
    }
```

The following `retrieveNumber` function is `external`, meaning that it can be called externally only. It is also a `view` function, meaning that it can only read information from the blockchain and not change its state. Finally, it returns an `uint256` variable.

```
function retrieveNumber() external view returns(uint256) {
        return s_number;
    }
```

Within the function itself, the s_number variable is returned.

```
    }
```

The previous is a pretty basic contract, but for our purposes in this chapter, it will do the job.

VOTING TOKEN CONTRACT

After the `RetrievableNumber.sol` contract, you have to create the Voting Token contract, a classic ERC-20 token with a few minor changes.

First, you have to create a new file called `VotingToken.sol` in the `src` folder (see Figure 13.28).

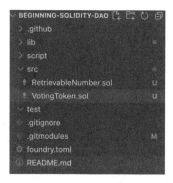

FIGURE 13.28 VotingToken file creation

Instead of implementing the ERC-20 contract from scratch, OpenZeppelin has a tool that is called Contracts Wizard, which can be found on OpenZeppelin's website for documentation (see Figure 13.29) at https://docs.openzeppelin.com/contracts/5.x/wizard.

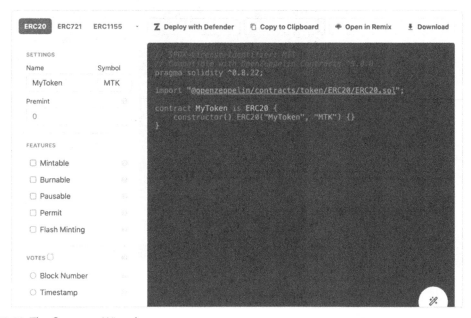

FIGURE 13.29 The Contracts Wizard

The Contracts Wizard is a web-based tool that generates standard and secure smart contracts based on the needs of a developer. For the needs of the DAO that is being created and for the voting token, select the following to develop the contract required for this occasion (see Figure 13.30):

➤ Votes

➤ Block Number

The contract that shows up should be copied and pasted to the VS Code. I'll walk you through it line by line.

The following defines the license under which the contract will be released:

```
// SPDX-License-Identifier: MIT
```

The following defines the Solidity version of the contract:

```
pragma solidity ^0.8.22;
```

The following imports the ERC20.sol contract, which is the standard implementation of an ERC-20 contract:

```
import "@openzeppelin/contracts/token/ERC20/ERC20.sol";
```

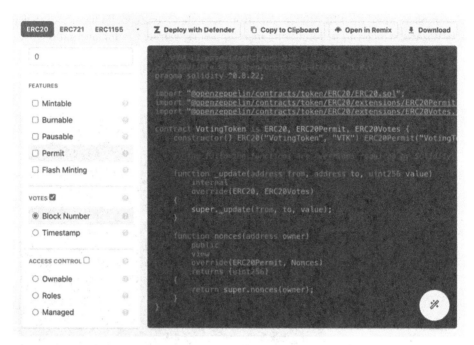

FIGURE 13.30 Ticker example

The following imports the ERC20Permit.sol contract, which adds token approval functionality that saves gas:

```
import @openzeppelin/contracts/token/ERC20/extensions/ERC20Permit.sol";
```

The following imports the Imports ERC20Votes contract, which adds voting powers to the token:

```
import "@openzeppelin/contracts/token/ERC20/extensions/ERC20Votes.sol";
```

The following defines a VotingToken contract and inherits the ERC20, ERC20Permit, and ERC20Votes contract properties:

```
contract VotingToken is ERC20, ERC20Permit, ERC20Votes {
    constructor() ERC20("VotingToken", "VTK") ERC20Permit("VotingToken") {}
```

The constructor sets up the token's name, VotingToken, and its abbreviation, VTK. The constructor also initiates the permit functionality.

The _update function sets three parameters: an address from, an address to, and a uint256 value. It is an internal function, meaning it can be called internally or through contracts deriving from it. It overrides the ERC20 and ERC20Votes implementations.

```
function _update(address from, address to, uint256 value)
    internal
    override(ERC20, ERC20Votes)
    {
```

```
        super._update(from, to, value);
    }
```

The `super._update(from, to, value)` calls the `_update` function's parent implementation and tracks the votes.

The `super` keyword is used to call an original function defined in the parent contract of a child contract.

```
    function nonces(address owner)
    public
    view
    override(ERC20Permit, Nonces)
    returns (uint256)
    {
        return super.nonces(owner);
    }
}
```

The `nonces` function defines an address parameter named `owner`. It is `public`, meaning it can be called both internally and externally. It is a `view` function, which means it does not change the state of the blockchain but rather only reads from it. It overrides the ERC20Permit and Nonces and returns an `uint256` variable.

The function returns the number of transactions the owner executes within the contract.

This completes the voting token contract. The next step in building the DAO is to create the governance contract.

OPENZEPPELIN'S CONTRACTS WIZARD

OpenZeppelin's Contracts Wizard can also make governance contracts in addition to the ERC-20 and ERC-721 contracts.

Figure 13.31 shows OpenZeppelin's Governance contract generator.

On the left of the code are the settings you can configure (see Figures 13.31 and 13.32):

➤ **Name:** This is the name of the contract to be created.

➤ **Voting Delay:** How many days before the proposal is submitted before the voting starts?

➤ **Voting Period:** How long does the voting period take to be completed upon commencement?

➤ **Proposal Threshold:** This is the minimum number of votes an address has to have to submit a proposal.

➤ **Quorum:** What is the % of votes required to pass a vote?

➤ **Token Decimals:** How many decimals should the token have?

➤ **Votes:** This is whether an ERC-20 token or an ERC-721 token carries out the votes.

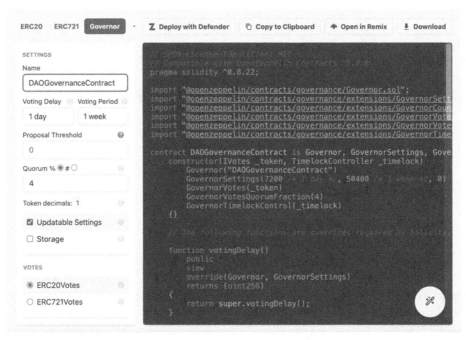

FIGURE 13.31 OpenZeppelin's Governance contract generator settings

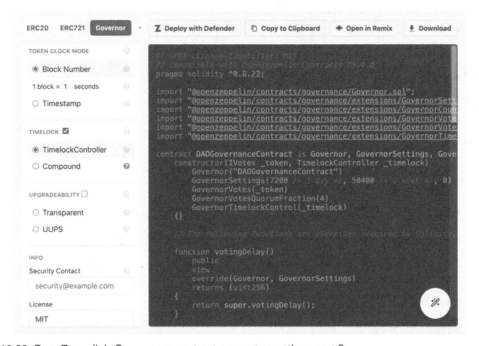

FIGURE 13.32 OpenZeppelin's Governance contract generator settings part 2

➤ **Token Clock Mode**: This determines how time is measured in the contract. There are two options: by the number of the block—depending on the block production time per blockchain, this can change—and by the timestamp.

➤ **Timelock**: This security measure establishes a timeline for when proposals have been positively voted upon and when the proposals are executed. Within the timelock function, there are two options:

  ➤ **TimelockController**: Uses a model developed by OpenZeppelin for access control—the addresses with permission to execute certain functions. Within that model, there are several roles:

    ➤ **Proposer**: The proposer has the distinct permission to schedule transactions if required.
    ➤ **Executor**: The executor can execute transactions after the predetermined delay.
    ➤ **Canceller**: The canceller can cancel planned or scheduled transactions
    ➤ **Admin**: The admin can grant or revoke the above roles from the addresses to which they have been assigned.

  To maintain decentralization, the admin function can be assigned to the governance contract, and the token holders can vote on the proposer, executor, and canceller roles. There are several advantages and disadvantages when using OpenZeppelin's TimelockController.

  Advantages

  ➤ Allows for a certain flexibility in terms of roles when it comes to governance.
  ➤ Allows to schedule multiple transactions at the same time.
  ➤ Through the built-in role management, one can change the addresses of the roles if required.

  Disadvantages

  ➤ **Gas costs**: Adding these functions to the contract increases its complexity, and when a smart contract's complexity increases, the gas costs for executing it rise as well, making the smart contract more expensive to run.
  ➤ **Limits emergency responses**: Through the execution delay of the timelock, the response to emergencies can be limited depending on how long the timelock is and how urgent the response is. The timelock does not significantly limit the emergency response if the urgency is not high. However, this is generally a tricky part since even a delay of just one day could potentially present an emergency that needs to be acted upon within hours or, even worse, minutes, limiting the general security of the system but giving more flexibility to respond to emergencies.
  ➤ Suppose there are plans to upgrade the contract in the future. In that case, TimelockController introduces additional **complexity** to the **upgradability** of the contract. Additionally, the complexity adds problems to the user experience as users must understand the additional role system and how the DAO system works. Some people who are into intellectual challenges might enjoy it. People who want simplicity to be maximized might not find the feature attractive.
  ➤ Complicates the auditing process. One of the main security processes all smart contracts should undergo is being audited by third parties, ideally multiple times by different auditing firms. Adding the Timelock Controller into the system complicates the auditing process. It will increase the time an auditor has to spend on the contract.

➤ **Compound:** The compound timelock has several advantages and disadvantages when compared to the TimelockController as it is a simpler model:

  ➤ It has only one admin address for everything that can be assigned to the smart contract DAO address, and it is fixed.

  ➤ Less flexible in terms of permission structures.

  Advantages

  ➤ It is much less complex for users to understand as it is much less complex and is easier to upgrade.

  ➤ Fewer gas costs.

  Disadvantages

  ➤ Limited flexibility if one requires it in the future.

  ➤ It allows for less complex DAO structures if one needs to add complexity, such as the Synthetix structure, which supports five DAOs. Note that Synthetix has no governance token, but some DAOs are similar in complexity to Synthetix but do have governance tokens.

  ➤ Ironically enough, a TimelockController might be easier to scale due to its flexibility and complexity. Simple systems can only get one so far in terms of scalability. However, one can always opt for a Compound model and later upgrade it to a TimelockController. The problem with this would be educating the existing community about the complexity added after the upgrade.

➤ **Upgradability:** The upgradability feature is about what kind of proxy contract strategy one would use to upgrade their contract later if required:

  ➤ **UUPS:** This book uses the UUPS strategy, which is cheaper to deploy and has lower transaction costs than the transparent strategy because it requires less gas.

  ➤ **Transparent:** It usually works with a proxy contract that holds the delegate calls an implementation contract that has the logic, and an admin who can upgrade the implementation. It allows for a much more precise separation of functions that can be called by an admin and functions that users can call, and it is much simpler to implement and understand. However, it generally has higher gas costs compared to UUPS.

➤ **License:** The familiar //SPDX-License-Identifier and the license under which the contract will be available upon deployment and release.

THE GOVERNANCE CONTRACT

Now you need to create the governance contract for the DAO.

1. Set the following options. All of the choices might be different in a real-world setting. This is simply an example to show how it works:

  ➤ **Name:** DAOGovernanceContract

  ➤ **Voting Delay:** 1 day

- ➤ **Voting Period:** 1 week
- ➤ **Proposal Threshold:** 0
- ➤ **Quorum:** 4%
- ➤ **Token Decimals:** 18 and Updatable Settings
- ➤ **Votes:** ERC20Votes
- ➤ **Token Clock:** Block Number 1 block = 12 seconds
- ➤ **Timelock:** on and TimelockController
- ➤ **Upgradability:** Turned off

2. Copy the result from top to bottom, as shown in Figure 13.33.

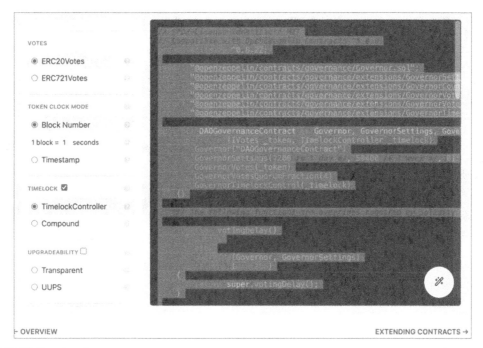

FIGURE 13.33 Copying the DAOGovernanceContract

3. Create a Solidity file in the src folder called DAOGovernanceContract.sol, as shown in Figure 13.34.

4. Paste the copied contract into the DAOGovernanceContract.sol file and press Command+S or Ctrl+S to save (see Figure 13.35).

   With that, the DAO is almost completed. However, to understand what this contract is doing, it is crucial to go line by line and explain each function.

FIGURE 13.34 Creating a DAOGovernanceContract.sol in VS Code

FIGURE 13.35 Copied DAOGovernanceContract into the DAOGovernanceContract.sol

The abovefollowing declares the license under which the contract will be released:

```
// SPDX-License-Identifier: MIT
```

The following above declares the Solidity version used in this contract:

```
pragma solidity ^0.8.22;
```

The following imports contacts:

```
import "@openzeppelin/contracts/governance/Governor.sol";
import "@openzeppelin/contracts/governance/extensions/GovernorSettings.sol";
import "@openzeppelin/contracts/governance/extensions/GovernorCountingSimple
.sol";
import "@openzeppelin/contracts/governance/extensions/GovernorVotes.sol";
import "@openzeppelin/contracts/governance/extensions/
GovernorVotesQuorumFraction.sol";
import "@openzeppelin/contracts/governance/extensions/GovernorTimelockControl
.sol";
```

The contracts are as follows:

➤ `Governor.sol`: This is the base governance contract. It creates and manages the proposals submitted, implements the voting mechanisms, executes successful voting proposals, and tracks the addresses of the proposals and their history.

➤ `GovernorSettings.sol`: This is the contract that manages the time between the creation of the proposal and when voting begins, sets the duration of the voting window in terms of blocks, and adds the proposal threshold in terms of how many tokens one has to have at minimum to propose a proposal—if applicable.

➤ `GovernorCountingSimple.sol`: This counts the votes received

➤ `GovernorVotes.sol`: This adds voting possibility through an ERC-20 token.

➤ `GovernorVotesQuorumFraction.sol`: This adds quorum or majority needed calculations

➤ `GovernorTimelockControl.sol`: This adds the timelock functionality for proposals to be executed.

The abovefollowing defines the contract, its name, and its inheriting properties of contracts:

```
contract DAOGovernanceContract is Governor, GovernorSettings,
GovernorCountingSimple, GovernorVotes, GovernorVotesQuorumFraction,
GovernorTimelockControl {
```

➤ `Governor`

➤ `GovernorSettings`

➤ `GovernorCountingSimple`

➤ `GovernorVotes`

➤ `GovernorVotesQuorumFraction`

➤ `GovernorTimelockControl`

The constructor is the first function to be executed upon deployment of the contract:

```
constructor(IVotes _token, TimelockController _timelock)
Governor("DAOGovernanceContract")
GovernorSettings(7200, 50400, 0)
GovernorVotes(_token)
GovernorVotesQuorumFraction(4)
GovernorTimelockControl(_timelock)
{}
```

The constructor does the following:

➤ Adds a name to the contract as `DAOGovernanceContract`.

➤ Adds a voting delay—the time upon which the voting can start after a proposal has been submitted—of 7200 blocks, which translates to one human day in the real world. In addition, the voting period is 50400 blocks or one human week, and finally, the threshold to create a proposal, as assigned in the OpenZeppelin Contracts Wizard, is 0 tokens.

➤ Adds the voting token address of the ERC20 token that enables the voting process in the first place.

➤ Adds the quorum which was defined as 4% in the OpenZeppelin Contracts Wizard.

➤ Adds the timelock controller address, which sets the delay between a successful proposal being passed and its execution.

The votingDelay function is public, meaning it can be called both internally and externally. It is also a view function, meaning it does not alter the state of the blockchain but merely reads data from it. This function overrides the same function in the contracts Governor and GovernorSettings and returns an uint256 variable.

```
function votingDelay()
    public
    view
    override(Governor, GovernorSettings)
    returns (uint256)
    {
        return super.votingDelay();
    }
```

Inside the function itself, the votingDelay function returns the parent contract's version of the votingDelay function through the super keyword used to call the original function from the parent contract. This original function stems from the GovernorSettings contract.

One question you might have when reading this is: Why override the votingDelay function in the GovernorSettings contract and then call it again with the super keyword within the function itself?

The answer is that Solidity has a problem called Diamond Problem Resolution. When a contract inherits from multiple contracts and two or more of those contracts have a function with the same name, you must override both and then communicate to the compiler within the contract that you want to call the original function within the parent contract.

```
function votingPeriod()
public
view
override(Governor, GovernorSettings)
returns (uint256)
{
    return super.votingPeriod();
}
```

The votingPeriod function is almost identical to the votingDelay function. The only crucial difference is that it handles the period of the voting process itself, and the super keyword, in this case, calls the GovernorSettings version of the votingPeriod function.

```
function quorum(uint256 blockNumber)
public
view
override(Governor, GovernorVotesQuorumFraction)
```

```
returns (uint256)
{
    return super.quorum(blockNumber);
}
```

The quorum function is similar to the votingDelay and votingPeriod functions in that it is public, is view, and overrides the Governor contract's version of the same function. In this case, the GovernorVotesQuorumFraction contract's version of the same function.

Within the function, it also uses the super keyword to call the quorum function of the parent contract, which in this case is the GovernorVotesQuorumFraction contract. The essential difference is the uint256 blockNumber parameter, which allows checking the quorum requirement at different points in time.

This is useful because when someone designs the token economics scheme of a specific token, they may add a vesting schedule during which the supply of the token increases over time as more tokens are released into the economy. In the short term, this causes the token to inflate and a short-term reduction in price, given that the demand for the token stays the same or is reduced.

For example, say Token X has a total supply of 1 million tokens. Of these tokens, the initial supply that the economy and community participants can buy is only 250,000. The other 750,000 can be scheduled to be released over X years. For example, in 20 years, if a linear release schedule is applied, 750,000 / 20 = 37,500 tokens are released yearly into the economy.

If we multiply the initial supply of 250,000 tokens by 0.04 – 4, which is the 4% quorum given to OpenZeppelin's Contracts Wizard—that would be 10,000 tokens for a total 4% quorum.

Next year, with 37,500 more tokens the circulating supply is raised to 287,500. If 287,500 is multiplied by 4%, the quorum changes to 11,500. With 37,500 more tokens being released the following year, the total quorum will also change. This will continue until the total supply is released to the circulating supply.

Similarly, tokens can be burned or destroyed by sending them to the null address. The null address is not associated with anyone. It is usually used to burn or destroy tokens by sending tokens to that address. As someone destroys X amount of a token, the token's price increases provided that the demand stays the same or increases because you now have fewer tokens in supply—aka selling fewer cakes when the demand for the cakes is the same or increases. The less something there is, and the more people want to buy it, the more the price increases.

Thus, by adding more tokens to the economy, the uint256 blockNumber can track and calculate the number of tokens in circulation and adjust the quorum accordingly. The calculation happens with each new block generated.

```
function state(uint256 proposalId)
public
view
override(Governor, GovernorTimelockControl)
returns (ProposalState)
{
    return super.state(proposalId);
}
```

The state function has an uint256 proposalId parameter, is public, view, overrides the Governor and GovernorTimelockControl contracts, and returns the ProposalState enum and within the functions returns the original state function of GovernorTimelockControl and the proposalId number.

In Solidity, an enum is a predefined data type. It serves to create custom types with a predetermined set of possible values. In the case of the ProposalState these values are as follows:

➤ Pending

➤ Active

➤ Canceled

➤ Defeated

➤ Succeeded

➤ Queued

➤ Expired

➤ Executed

Essentially, the function checks and returns the state of a proposal in the DAO governance. It tracks the proposal lifecycle and determines what actions can be taken. For security purposes, it goes hand in hand with the TimelockController.

```
function proposalNeedsQueuing(uint256 proposalId)
public
view
override(Governor, GovernorTimelockControl)
returns (bool)
{
    return super.proposalNeedsQueuing(proposalId);
}
```

The function proposalNeedsQueuing has a parameter uint256 called proposalId, is public, view, and overrides the contracts Governor and GovernorTimeControl and returns a Boolean.

Within the function itself, it calls the original proposalNeedsQueuing function from the GovernorTimelockControl contract and adds the proposalId.

The proposalNeedsQueuing function checks if a proposal needs to be put in a queue before execution as part of the timelock mechanism. For example, if two proposals are passed more or less at the same time, the earlier one has to be queued first, and the later one comes as a second to keep an order of preference.

```
function proposalThreshold()
public
view
override(Governor, GovernorSettings)
returns (uint256)
```

```
    {
        return super.proposalThreshold();
    }
```

The proposalThreshold is public; view overrides the Governor and GovernorSettings contract and returns an uint256 variable.

It calls the original proposalThreshold function from the GovernorSettings contract within the function.

The proposalThreshold function returns the number of tokens a user needs to create a proposal.

```
    function _queueOperations(uint256 proposalId, address[] memory targets,
    uint256[] memory values, bytes[] memory calldatas, bytes32 descriptionHash)
        internal
        override(Governor, GovernorTimelockControl)
        returns (uint48)
    {
        return super._queueOperations(proposalId, targets, values, calldatas,
    descriptionHash);
    }
```

The _queueOperations function takes as parameters uint256 proposalId, address[] memory targets, uint256[] memory values, bytes[] memory calldatas, and bytes32 descriptionHash.

Each parameter has its purpose:

➤ proposalId: ID of the proposal

➤ address [] memory targets: Contract addresses to call

➤ uint256 [] memory values: ETH amounts to send

➤ bytes [] memory calldatas: Function calls with parameters

➤ bytes32 descriptionHash: Hash of proposal description

The function is internal, meaning it can be called from within the contract and contracts that derive from it. It overrides the Governor and GovernorTimelockControl contracts and returns a uint48.

The original _queueOperations function from the GovernorTimelockControl contract is returned within the contract.

In essence, the function handles the queuing of the proposal in the timelock controller after it has passed and is awaiting the delayed period to be executed.

The process flow of this function goes like this: Proposal passes ⇨ _queueOperations called ⇨ Proposal stored in Timelock ⇨ Wait required delay period ⇨ Can execute after delay.

The _executeOperations function has the following parameters: uint256 proposalId, address[] memory targets, uint256[] memory values, bytes[] memory calldatas, bytes32 descriptionHash:

```
function _executeOperations(uint256 proposalId, address[] memory targets,
uint256[] memory values, bytes[] memory calldatas, bytes32 descriptionHash)
    internal
    override(Governor, GovernorTimelockControl)
    {
        super._executeOperations(proposalId, targets, values, calldatas,
descriptionHash);
    }
```

The parameters are the same as those used in the _queueOperations function.

The function is internal; it overrides the Governor and GovernorTimelockControl contracts and, within the contract, calls the original _executeOperations function from the GovernorTimelockControl contract.

In essence, it takes care of executing a proposal's operations after the proposal has passed and the timelock delay period has expired.

```
function _cancel(address[] memory targets, uint256[] memory values, bytes[]
memory calldatas, bytes32 descriptionHash)
    internal
    override(Governor, GovernorTimelockControl)
    returns (uint256)
    {
        return super._cancel(targets, values, calldatas, descriptionHash);
    }
```

The _cancel function has as parameters: address[] memory targets, uint256[] memory values, bytes[] memory calldatas, bytes32 descriptionHash.

Each parameter has its use:

➤   address[] memory targets: The contract addresses to call.

➤   uint256[] memory values: ETH amounts that would have been sent.

➤   bytes[] calldatas: Function calls with parameters.

➤   bytes32 descriptionHash: Hash of proposal description.

The process flow goes like this: Proposal Active ⇨ Cancel called ⇨ Proposal State canceled ⇨ Will not be executed.

The function cancels a DAO governance system proposal before it gets executed.

```
function _executor()
internal
view
override(Governor, GovernorTimelockControl)
returns (address)
{
    return super._executor();
}
}
```

The _executor function is an internal view function that overrides the Governor and

GovernorTimelockControl contracts and returns an address. In the function itself, the original
_executor function is called the contract GovernorTimeControl. It returns the address of the
timelock controller to ensure that only authorized users can execute.

TIMELOCK CONTRACT

The last component that needs to be built for our DAO is the Timelock contract. You need to create a
new file in the src folder called TimelockContract.sol (see Figure 13.36).

FIGURE 13.36 TimelockContract.sol contract created

The next step is to write the contract. This is the license under which the contract will be released:

```
//SPDX-License-Identifier: MIT
```

Then, this is the Solidity version the contract will have to use:

```
pragma solidity 0.8.28;
```

This imports the TimelockController.sol contract from the project's library:.

```
Import {TimelockController} from "../lib/openzeppelin-contracts/contracts/
governance/TimeLockController.sol";
```

This defines a contract named TimeLockContract and inherits the contract TimelockController
from it.

```
contract TimeLockContract is TimelockController {
```

The constructor defines the minDelay, which is the minimum time in seconds that must pass between
an operation proposal and when it can be executed; the proposers, the addresses that can initiate new
proposals; the executors, the addresses that can execute the operations after the timelock period; and
finally, msg.sender, which is the deployer's address, which is passed as the administrator address.

```
constructor(uint256 minDelay, address[] memory proposers, address[] memory
```

```
executors)
    TimelockController(minDelay, proposers, executors, msg.sender)
    {}
}
```

After adding this contract and running **forge build** to ensure everything is compiling, the DAO is ready and complete.

CHAPTER 13 QUESTIONS

1. What are the key differences between traditional organizational governance and DAO governance?

2. Explain the four levels of decentralization in DAOs and the challenges associated with each.

3. How does token-weighted voting potentially lead to plutocracy, and what are some solutions to mitigate this?

4. Describe the role of Snapshot in DAO governance and its integration with on-chain systems.

5. Explain the functionality and importance of the `Ownable.sol` contract in DAO governance systems.

6. Walk through the lifecycle of a DAO proposal, from forum discussion to execution.

7. What are the main differences between on-chain and off-chain voting mechanisms, and when would you use each?

8. Explain the "skin-in-the-game" voting mechanism and its advantages and challenges.

9. What is proof of humanity in DAO governance, and how can Sybil resistance be ensured?

10. Describe the technical implementation of the `RetrievableNumber.sol` contract, focusing on its access control and event system.

11. What specific functionalities do `ERC20Votes` and `ERC20Permit` add to a DAO's voting token?

12. Compare the TimelockController and Compound timelock models. What factors influence choosing one over the other?

13. How would you implement dynamic quorum requirements to handle token supply changes over time?

14. What are the security implications of the timelock mechanism, and how do they impact emergency response capabilities?

15. Explain the significance of OpenZeppelin's `Governor` contracts and how each contributes to DAO governance.

14

Introduction to Smart Contract Security

In this chapter, you are introduced to smart contract security and auditing, which is crucial knowledge for any Solidity developer who wants to minimize the chances of their smart contract being hacked. The chapter will go through what a smart contract auditing process consists of and how long the process usually should take.

Additionally, the chapter goes through a number of smart contract security techniques such as manual code review, static analysis, fuzz testing, and formal verification. Finally, the chapter provides a few tips on how to prepare your code for auditing when delivering it to an auditing firm or freelancer.

THE IMPORTANCE OF SMART CONTRACT SECURITY

This chapter is a simple introduction to a complex and lengthy topic that would require its whole book to go through in-depth: smart contract security. It provides a foundational overview of smart contract security, helping developers understand what a smart contract auditor does and how they think. It covers the high-level processes and approach of smart contract auditing without diving deeply into technical details.

The Chainalysis chart in Figure 14.1 shows the scale of cryptocurrency hacks between 2016 and 2023, measured in billions of USD. The increase from 0.2 billion in 2016 to almost 4 billion in 2022 demonstrates the importance of security in the cryptocurrency industry and how crucial it is for developers to adopt a security-focused mindset and to gain a basic understanding of what and how a smart contract auditor thinks and operates.

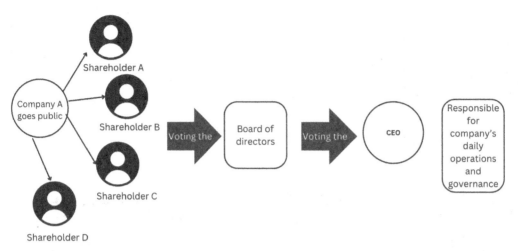

FIGURE 14.1: Total value in hacks

SMART CONTRACT AUDITING AND SECURITY BEST PRACTICES

When considering Solidity and security, what should come immediately to mind is smart contract auditing. A smart contract audit is a time-restricted review of the contract from a security perspective. Its goal is to minimize the likelihood that a smart contract will be hacked. A smart contract auditor aims to find as many vulnerabilities as possible within a predefined period and inform and educate the protocol's developers on security best practices moving forward. Smart contract auditors use several techniques and tools to find smart contract vulnerabilities, which they then report to the protocol's team.

Developers need to have their smart contracts audited to reduce the risk that their smart contracts will be hacked and drained of the money deposited by users. It is worth remembering that a smart contract, after deployment, is immutable and operates in a permissionless environment where its code is visible to both users and developers. That can attract malicious users and developers who would do anything possible to drain a protocol that might have the slightest vulnerability. Thus, anything that can be done to minimize the probability of a smart contract being hacked has to be done before deployment, and that includes smart contract audits.

Unless the smart contract to be deployed is straightforward, one smart contract audit is often insufficient to satisfy the security needs of minimizing hacking attacks. Upon being coded, a protocol usually embarks on a multistage security journey involving many kinds of audits through different services and techniques, from formal verification to competitive audits and bug bounty programs.

There are many companies and individuals offering auditing services. These are some of the most well-known brands of smart contract auditing:

➤ Trail of Bits

➤ OpenZeppelin

➤ MixBytes

➤ Cyfrin Audits

➤ Sigma Prime

A protocol team that desires to have its protocol audited usually has to make the first contact with an independent auditor. If the protocol is still under development, the auditor has some lead time to add the team to the auditor's schedule instead of doing things hastily or waiting for an extended period after the protocol has been developed.

The time needed to audit the code is primarily based on several parameters, such as smart contract complexity, scope, and lines of code. If you were to give an approximate estimate, however, based on the lines of code and assuming average auditing complexity, the duration might look something like this:

LINES OF CODE:	DURATION:
100	3 days
1,000	1–5 weeks
2,500	2–5 weeks
5,000	4–4.5 weeks

This is simply an approximate picture of how much an audit might usually take. However, auditing times can vary depending on the parameters of code complexity, lines of code, and scope. Thus, 100 lines of code might take anywhere from two to five days to complete, depending on complexity. The initial conversation usually is to get an approximate price range for the audit, the time of start and end, and possibly a downpayment—in case an auditor asks for one after having assigned you a spot in their schedule.

Unless a potential extension has been discussed, after the initial period ends, the auditor will deliver a report to the protocol team with all the bug and problem discoveries ranked by severity and importance. They are usually ranked high, medium, or low in importance and criticality. Some of the suggestions might be about improving gas efficiency, code structure, and refactoring improvements, as well as suggestions for best practices. Not everything will necessarily be as critical as a bug that could drain your protocol of all its money—although that may be part of it if such a bug has been discovered—but some suggestions will simply be improving the code in various ways.

Chapter 12 gave you a glimpse of an auditing report through CertiK.com, as shown in Figure 14.2.

Figures 14.3–14.5 show a typical audit report. While the content may vary slightly depending on the auditing firm, as each has its own methodology, the contents of each firm's report would be similar to what's shown. Differences may include variations in presentation and the inclusion of additional details.

Once the auditor or the auditing firm has presented the protocol's team with the report, the team has to implement the changes. After the changes have been implemented, the auditor will make a final audit and provide a report about the issues that have been fixed. If by fixing those issues, the

Uniswap V3 Limit Orders Audit Report

Prepared by Cyfrin
Version 2.0

Lead Auditors
Giovanni Di Siena
Hans

Assisting Auditors
Alex Roan

FIGURE 14.2: Cover of Uniswap V3 audit report by Cyfrin

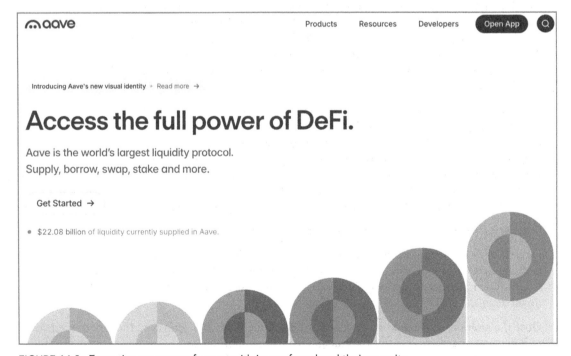

FIGURE 14.3: Executive summary of report with issues found and their severity

FIGURE 14.4: Each issue found reported in detail and its status

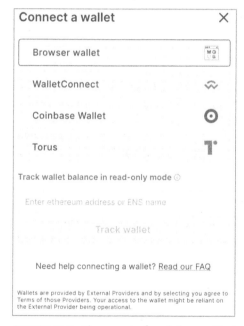

FIGURE 14.5: The report of each issue with description of the issue, the impact the issue has on the protocol, and a recommended mitigation

development team has not introduced new ones, the changes will be documented, and a report will be provided to both the team and the public. That report will specify which initial bug fixes were implemented, ensuring that, at the very least, the issues with the biggest severities have been fixed. If they have not been fixed, the final audit report will mention that too.

The development team can do the following to make the auditor's life easier, help the auditing process go smoothly, and ensure that the auditors do not have a hard time understanding the code—which can in itself minimize any possible errors the auditors might have done otherwise:

➤ Be sure there is clearly written documentation. The code should have comments, especially in places where it might not be clear or is complex about what it might do and especially why the team decided to write the code in the way it did, thus explaining the thought process behind the code.

➤ Test the code with the unit, fuzz, and invariant testing, among other methods.

➤ Establish communication channels between the auditing and development teams in case the auditing team has questions while going through the code.

➤ Create a detailed walk-through video of the code and deliver it to the auditors before the auditing process starts.

After auditing, the protocol development team should take the recommendations seriously to ensure their protocol is not hacked or drained by a malicious party. It is worth keeping in mind that after the auditing process has been completed, any additional code, either on top of the existing code or that is added to mitigate the errors noted by the auditors, is new and unaudited. There have been instances where, after the auditing process was completed, the development team decided to add a small piece of code to the protocol, and that small piece of code was the reason the protocol was hacked.

A final thing worth keeping in mind is that one audit is often not enough—unless the codebase of a protocol is basic. Multiple audits help by having numerous eyes and people with varying expertise and experience look at the code, which minimizes the chance of critical vulnerabilities going unnoticed. Suppose your protocol and its smart contracts have—or will have—100 million or 200 million USD of user's funds locked into it. In that case, it is worth adding a little bit of extra budget to do multiple audits, as no matter how many audits one does, the auditing firms are not going to ask for 100 or 200 million USD. That's how much money the users of a protocol and the protocol may lose if a critical vulnerability is discovered and exploited by a malicious party.

All that said, remember that having your code audited does not 100% guarantee that the code is entirely bug-free. If that were the case, everyone would get their protocol audited, and there would never be any hacks. Besides the fact that there might be new vulnerabilities no one is aware of—as the security and auditing field is constantly evolving in the same way Solidity as a language is growing— the auditing process should be looked at as a joint venture journey between the protocol's development team and the auditing firm or independent auditors. The auditors find as many bugs as possible within an agreed upon time frame—for example, 2 weeks—and teach the protocol developers different strategies to ensure future security of the protocol, especially in cases of updating the protocol in the future.

Another strategy to minimize the damage a potential hack might do to a protocol is purchasing insurance. These are several insurance dealers to protect the smart contract from being hacked:

➤ Nexus Mutual (https://nexusmutual.io)

➤ Insurance (https://insurace.io)

➤ ease (`https://ease.org`)

➤ Neptune Mutual (`https://neptunemutual.com`)

➤ Defi protection (`https://defiprotection.com`)

Finally, to ensure that the protocol or smart contracts you want to audit are ready to be audited, it would be good meet the following criteria:

➤ Use the latest major version of Solidity—unless there is a reason to use an older version.

➤ Use known/established libraries where possible. OpenZeppelin contracts are preferred because they prioritize security above all else, and most auditors are already familiar with them. Solmate contracts can be a good alternative for functions where gas optimization is paramount.

➤ Have tests for "happy path" user stories and tests that expect reverts for actions that are supposed to fail. All tests should be passing.

➤ Incorporate fuzz tests. Fuzzing has proven to be highly effective in uncovering bugs. Tools like Foundry and Echidna allow both stateless and stateful fuzzing. The Foundry Invariants reference guide provides an overview of how to set up your contract invariants for fuzzing. If you're using Hardhat, it is worthwhile to also include one of the above tools to enhance your testing capabilities.

➤ Run a static analysis tool (Slither preferred, MythX is an alternative) on your code and consider what it tells you. They often raise flags for nonissues, but they can sometimes catch low-hanging fruit, so it's worth doing.

➤ Prepare the deploy script and mock upgrade scripts (if applicable) and include them as part of audit scope. Deployments and upgrades are as important as runtime code and require the same amount of security attention.

➤ Document all functions. Use the NatSpec documentation for `public`/`external` functions. Consider this part of the public interface of the contract.

➤ Make sure contracts compile without any errors or warnings from the compiler.

➤ Run the code through a spellchecker.

➤ Avoid using assembly as much as possible. Use of assembly increases audit times because it throws away Solidity's guardrails and must be checked much more carefully.

➤ Document the use of `unchecked`. Concretely describe why it is safe to not perform arithmetic checks on each code block. Do this preferably for each operation.

➤ Any `public` function that can be made `external` should be made `external`. This is not just a gas consideration, but it also reduces the cognitive overhead for auditors because it reduces the number of possible contexts in which the function can be called.

➤ Have at least one trusted Solidity dev or security person outside your organization sanity check your contracts. If your code is a tire fire and in need of major changes, you want to hear about that early and from a trusted friend (for free) rather than after an expensive audit.

SECURITY TECHNIQUES USED FOR AUDITING

Protocol developers must know, at least on a fundamental level, the tools smart contract auditors use. This is not only to ensure that the auditor one deals with knows what they are doing but also because it is the protocol developer in the end who is responsible for the protocol and not the auditor, who can be seen as an employee of the developer hired to go through the code and give a professional expert opinion on vulnerabilities. If something goes wrong with the code, the final blame is on the protocol creator and not the auditor who was hired. Consequently, a developer should have security in their mind from the beginning of developing the protocol while working on it and not as something done in the end. This helps design and create secure protocols from day 1. There is no well-established standard in the audit process, but in a typical audit review, the smart contracts or contracts to be audited go through manual review.

Manual review is the process by which a smart contract auditor goes through the documentation of the code line by line to ensure that the code is doing what it is designed to do according to the documentation. Thus, the first step should be to read the documentation and understand what the team of developers tried to accomplish and what the code is supposed to do. Then, ensure that each line of code does just that. Many of the bugs people find are logic errors. The best way to understand if the logic of a function or any piece of code is wrong is to understand what the protocol does by reading the documentation. This is why, from the perspective of a development team, preparing detailed, clean, straightforward, and easy-to-read documentation is crucial so the smart contract auditor can do their job without any complications or misunderstandings. Suppose a smart contract auditor misunderstands the documentation due to poor quality. In that case, the smart contract auditor may falsely think that a function does what it is supposed to do when, in actuality, it does not. Worse yet, they might be unable to detect any crucial vulnerabilities they otherwise might have detected.

When doing manual reviews, one thing the auditor has to do is to set time limit on themselves. One can look at a specific code and work on it forever, proposing solutions, testing for countless possible attacks, trying to find ways to improve it, and detecting bugs. The key is to say, "I am going to spend X amount of total hours" reviewing this code the best way I can and will note down the vulnerabilities I find and communicate to the protocol's development team." After reviewing the code for vulnerabilities, the final step is for the auditor to deliver a readable and clear report to the development team.

Another crucial security tactic is *test suites* and the different kinds of tests one performs in the test folder of a Solidity project. Testing your smart contracts is crucial and is why pages were spent in previous chapters of this book explaining testing, how to perform testing, and how to think about the different kinds of testing.

Another tool in the toolbox of a smart contract auditor is what is called *static analysis*. Static analysis uses automated tools to read the code and look for keywords that detect that vulnerabilities might be present. One prominent tool for static analysis is AI tools such as ChatGPT and other language models, which allow users to paste their code and ask for feedback. Remember that AIs are not fault-free and might make mistakes, especially the earlier versions.

Fuzz testing is another security technique. Fuzz testing involves continuously generating and providing random data to the functions of the smart contract, undergoing fuzz testing to ensure that there are no potential vulnerabilities in the code.

Differential testing means writing the same code in different ways and then comparing each function's code version to one another.

Formal verification is another tool and method of securely testing smart contracts. In theory, it converts the smart contract into a mathematical version and checks to see if the functions and code hold true. A simple example is that 100 + 100 equals 200. This will always hold true.

Taking the previous human language analogies used in this book, while spoken languages are dynamic and constantly evolving, mathematics is unchanging and precise. For example, in the simple calculation of 100 + 100 = 200, altering the numbers changes the result, but the process itself remains accurate and consistent. This is analogous to formal verification in smart contracts, where the code is translated into mathematical representations. The process verifies whether the expected outcomes of the code hold true, helping to identify potential vulnerabilities. Formal verification, therefore, ensures mathematical precision and reliability in smart contract functionality.

Formal verification has several techniques that can be employed, each with its advantages—although this chapter, simply an introduction, will not cover all of them. One of those techniques is called *symbolic execution*. Symbolic execution converts the code into a symbolical, mathematical expression and then compares the result to see if it holds. Symbolic execution is one of the most time-intensive methods to employ when it comes to smart contract auditing. A lot of auditing firms do not use it to its full extent because of that and because as helpful as it may be—especially if a computationally heavy process is involved—even symbolic execution is not a silver bullet that ensures that the code has no bugs.

HAVING HIGH CONFIDENCE AND ASSURANCE THAT YOUR SMART CONTRACT IS SAFE

As mentioned in this chapter, you cannot be sure if your smart contract is 100% bug-free. The only assurance you can have is that the code becomes safer through different processes. The following are the various levels of assurance and safety to implement to have a safer smart contract based on industry standards:

➤ **Level 1: Unit testing:** The absolute minimum one can do to ensure their code is safe is to perform a unit test for each function that they write and ensure that the test code coverage is, if not entirely at 100%, at least high enough for the crucial parts of the code.

➤ **Level 2: Fuzz test:** Fuzz testing feeds random data into your smart contract functions to uncover vulnerabilities. Fuzz testing is crucial for developers in their elemental security journey as it can discover edge cases that other methods could have missed.

➤ **Level 3: Static analysis:** After unit testing and fuzz testing, which are dynamic ways of testing smart contracts—meaning that you actually have to execute the code that you have written—static analysis auditors simply read the code to uncover potential vulnerabilities.

➤ **Level 4: Formal verification:** Formal verification is the technique of using a mathematical model and conversion to ensure that the smart contract system works properly without bugs.

CHAPTER 14 QUESTIONS

1. Define a smart contract audit, and explain why it is essential in the context of Solidity development.

2. Describe the key phases of a smart contract audit from initial contact to final verification.

3. What are the four primary levels of security assurance for smart contracts, and how do they differ?

4. Why is multiple auditing often necessary for complex protocols? Provide examples of scenarios where one audit might be insufficient.

5. Explain the differences between unit testing, fuzz testing, and static analysis in smart contract security.

6. What is formal verification, and how does it compare to other testing approaches in terms of thoroughness and complexity?

7. Why should documentation quality be a priority during smart contract development and auditing?

8. Explain the role and limitations of AI tools in the static analysis of smart contracts.

9. A protocol has added a small code change after completing an audit. What risks does this introduce, and what actions should the team take?

10. What are the typical severity levels in audit reports, and what types of issues fall under each level?

11. Why is it recommended to make public functions external where possible? Discuss both gas optimization and security implications.

12. What security measures can a protocol take in addition to audits to protect against potential hacks?

13. How does code complexity affect the duration and depth of a smart contract audit?

14. What is symbolic execution, and why is it considered a time-intensive method in auditing?

15. Why is it critical to prepare deployment and upgrade scripts before an audit, and how do they impact the audit process?

15

The First (or One of the First) Stepping Stones

In this book, you have learned what money is, including its history, its importance, and how it relates to cryptocurrencies (Ethereum specifically), and you've learned about Solidity programming. You have learned about block explorers, MetaMask, essential Solidity and programming concepts, NFTs, fungible cryptocurrencies, DAOs, crowdsourcing contracts, a DeFi protocol, smart contracts, gas optimization techniques, and basic familiarity with security and auditing. But even with all this work, the book is but an introduction to all the concepts in Solidity and serves as one of the first steps you will take to start your Solidity journey. If you have studied the book thoroughly, you should have an intermediate level of Solidity development knowledge.

Throughout this book, we also went through several GitHub repositories: Cyfrin, OpenZeppelin, and Chainlink. GitHub is a platform that enables developers to upload the code they have been working on throughout their careers, provided that the code is open-source—open for everyone to see and use—and not closed-source and proprietary in various ways. A good way to prove that you have experience with Solidity—or any other language you may want to learn after Solidity—is to upload to GitHub the projects they have been working on.

UPLOADING PROJECTS TO GitHub

Using the NFT contract that you worked on in this book as an example, the process of uploading the project to GitHub is as follows:

1. Go to GitHub's website, and sign up for an account if you do not have one already. To do so, provide an email address, create a username and password, and confirm your password. Then check your email to verify your new account.

2. Log onto GitHub's landing page. On the top right is a user profile. Click it to display several choices. One of them will be Your Profile (see Figure 15.1).

AlexNtolgkov
Alexandros Ntolgkov
Set status
Your profile

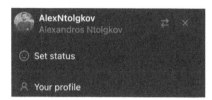

FIGURE 15.1: GitHub profile

3. Click Your Profile and then Repositories at the top left (see Figure 15.2).

Overview
Repositories 8

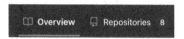

FIGURE 15.2: GitHub overview

4. On the repositories page, click New (see Figure 15.3).

Language
Sort
New

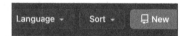

FIGURE 15.3: New GitHub page

5. Next, add a name to the repository that is being created (see Figure 15.4).

Repository name *

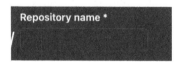

FIGURE 15.4: Naming the repository

6. Now click Create Repository on the same page (see Figure 15.5).

Create repository

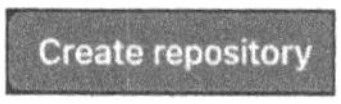

FIGURE 15.5: Creating a repository

7. On the newly created repository's page, you will see the instructions for adding the NFT project to the repository (see Figure 15.6).

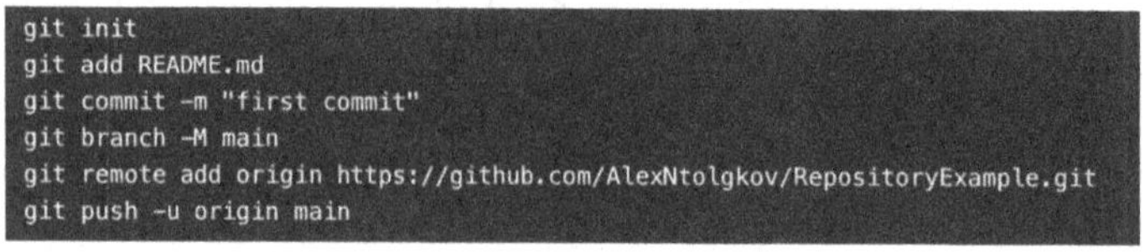

git init
git add README.md
git commit -m "first commit"
git branch -M main
git remote add origin https://github.com/AlexNtolgkov/RepositoryExample.git
git push -u origin main

FIGURE 15.6: Instructions to add the project to the GitHub repository

Follow the instructions and add each Git line one after the other. After pressing Enter, you should be able to push the work to your GitHub repository. This should be repeated for every project in this book, with each project having its own repository to be pushed onto.

After the project has been pushed onto GitHub successfully, the final result should look like Figure 15.7.

6.1 Medium Risk

6.1.1 Calls to `LimitOrderRegistry::newOrder` might revert due to overflow

Description: Reasonable input could cause an arithmetic overflow when opening new orders because large multiplications are performed on variables defined as `uint128` instead of `uint256`. Specifically, in `LimitOrder-Registry::_mintPosition` and `LimitOrderRegistry::_addToPosition` the following lines (which appear in both functions) are problematic:

```
uint128 amount0Min = amount0 == 0 ? 0 : (amount0 * 0.9999e18) / 1e18;
uint128 amount1Min = amount1 == 0 ? 0 : (amount1 * 0.9999e18) / 1e18;
```

Impact: It is not possible for users to create new orders with deposit amounts in excess of `341e18`, limiting the protocol to working with comparatively small orders.

Proof of Concept: Paste this test into `test/LimitOrderRegistry.t.sol`:

```
function test_OverflowingNewOrder() public {
    uint96 amount = 340_316_398_560_794_542_918;
    address msgSender = 0xE0b906ae06BfB1b54fad61E222b2E324D51e1da6;
    deal(address(USDC), msgSender, amount);
    vm.startPrank(msgSender);
    USDC.approve(address(registry), amount);

    registry.newOrder(USDC_WETH_05_POOL, 204900, amount, true, 0);
}
```

Recommended Mitigation: Cast the `uint128` value to `uint256` prior to performing the multiplication:

```
uint128 amount0Min = amount0 == 0 ? 0 : uint128((uint256(amount0) * 0.9999e18) / 1e18);
uint128 amount1Min = amount1 == 0 ? 0 : uint128((uint256(amount1) * 0.9999e18) / 1e18);
```

GFX Labs: Fixed by changing multipliers from 18 decimals to 4 decimals in commits f9934fe and c731cd4.

Cyfrin: Acknowledged.

6.1.2 New orders on a given pool in the opposite direction, separated by zero/one tick space, are not possible until previous `BatchOrder` is removed from the order book

Description: New order creation will revert with `LimitOrderRegistry__DirectionMisMatch()` if the direction opposes any existing orders at the current tick price. Due to the calculation of lower/upper ticks, this also applies to orders separated by one tick space. In the event price deviation causes existing orders to become ITM, it is not possible to place new orders in the opposing direction until upkeep has been performed for the existing orders, fully removing them from the order book.

Impact: This edge case is only an issue in the following circumstance:

- Any number of users place an order at a given tick price.
- Price deviates, causing this `BatchOrder` (and potentially others) to become ITM.
- If upkeep has not yet been performed, either through DoS, oracle downtime, or exceeding the maximum number of orders per upkeep (in the case of very large price deviations), the original `BatchOrder` remains on the order book (represented by a doubly linked list).
- So long as the original order remains in the list, new orders on a given pool in the opposite direction, separated by zero/one tick space, cannot be placed.

FIGURE 15.7: Project added to the GitHub repository

FINDING A JOB IN THE CRYPTO INDUSTRY

As an intermediate-level Solidity developer, you could apply and possibly be hired for junior roles. On your résumé, you can now add the following skills:

- ➤ Solidity
- ➤ Remix
- ➤ VS Code
- ➤ IPFS
- ➤ Alchemy
- ➤ Foundry
- ➤ On-chain analysis

Another addition to your CV is the newly acquired GitHub personality repository, which potential employers can access to see your skill level in Solidity. Several websites that may help you to find a job as a Solidity developer are LinkedIn, Indeed.com, and the websites Crypto Jobs list, Cryptocurrency Jobs, and Web3 Jobs. Another strategy is to find crypto recruiters on LinkedIn, connect with them, send them your résumé, and ask for a short meeting to explain what you are looking for so they can help you find a Solidity developer job. Additionally, going to hackathons—events where people use their skills and thoughts to create new blockchain solutions—is a good way to expand your network, participate in challenges, improve skills, and potentially meet new employers.

The average salary you can currently expect is $150,000 USD, with a range of between 60,000 USD and 285,000 USD, as per Web3.career. That said, although not as volatile as cryptocurrencies, salary can fluctuate with demand. During cryptocurrency bull markets where the demand for Solidity developer peaks, the salary can be higher, while during bear markets it is on average lower.

To prepare for interviews, you can use an AI companion by explaining that you are looking for a Solidity developer role—junior or otherwise—and the AI should provide thorough interview questions that a recruiter would ask. Upon getting the questions, you feed the answers into the same chat session with the AI companion to ask for feedback.

CONTINUING WITH SOLIDITY EDUCATION

If you want to expand and practice your Solidity skills, online games and challenges have been created for free so aspiring developers can learn and practice them:

- ➤ **Speedrun Ethereum:** This platform creates ever-increasing challenges for aspiring blockchain developers to complete through instructions that one can follow and learn.
- ➤ **Crypto Zombies:** In this video game, the player codes in Solidity to solve challenges and continue further in the game.
- ➤ **Solidity by Example:** This website has Solidity code examples and explanations that allow aspiring developers to enhance their skills.

Now that you've reached the conclusion of this book, remember that the knowledge and skills you've gained are only the beginning of your journey as a Solidity developer. Every step you take from here—applying for your first role, participating in hackathons, or tackling new challenges—will bring you closer to mastering this transformative technology. The blockchain industry is dynamic and full of opportunities for those willing to learn and innovate. So, go out there, put your knowledge into practice, and take pride in contributing to the future of decentralized technology. Your journey has just begun, and the possibilities are limitless.

Answers to Chapter Questions

CHAPTER 1 WHAT IS MONEY AND A BRIEF HISTORY OF IT?

1. **Q1:** Explain Bitcoin's fixed supply model and its halving schedule. How does this differ from traditional monetary policies?

   A1: Bitcoin's fixed supply model limits the total number of bitcoins to 21 million. This scarcity is achieved through a predictable issuance schedule embedded in its protocol. New bitcoins are released to the network as rewards for miners who validate transactions, but this issuance rate decreases over time. Approximately every four years, the reward is halved in an event known as the *halving*. Currently, 3.125 bitcoins are mined every 10 minutes.

   This predictable and deflationary approach sharply contrasts with traditional monetary policies managed by central banks, which have the authority to increase the money supply through mechanisms like quantitative easing. Fiat currencies, in contrast to Bitcoin, are often inflationary, with new money printed as needed to stimulate economies or address debt. While Bitcoin's model ensures scarcity and predictability, traditional systems offer flexibility but are susceptible to inflation and human intervention.

2. **Q2:** Define smart contracts, and explain how they differ from traditional contracts. What are their key advantages?

   A2: Smart contracts are self-executing agreements where the terms of the contract are directly written into lines of code. These digital agreements operate on blockchain networks like Ethereum, automatically executing actions when specific conditions are met. Unlike traditional contracts, which often rely on intermediaries such as lawyers or financial institutions to enforce terms, smart contracts function autonomously and without human involvement.

The advantages of smart contracts lie in their efficiency and trustlessness. They remove intermediaries, reducing costs and the risk of human error. Moreover, their transparency allows anyone to verify the terms of the contract on the blockchain. Immutable and tamper-proof, they offer a higher level of security compared to traditional paper contracts. This makes them particularly suitable for decentralized applications where trust is distributed among many participants.

3. Q3: What are the three main properties of money? For each property, explain how Bitcoin and Ethereum fulfill or fail to fulfill them.

A3: Money is defined by three core properties: medium of exchange, store of value, and unit of account. As a medium of exchange, bitcoin and ether both excel in durability and transportability, with their networks running globally across thousands of computers. Bitcoin's transaction time of approximately 10 minutes is slower than ether's 12 seconds, though Ethereum's high gas fees often hinder its usability.

When it comes to store of value, bitcoin is frequently compared to digital gold due to its fixed supply and deflationary nature. Although highly volatile in the short term, its long-term value has trended upward. Ethereum, on the other hand, lacks a capped supply, which weakens its appeal as a store of value.

Finally, as a unit of account, both cryptocurrencies face challenges. The price of bitcoin is still primarily quoted in fiat currencies, while ether has made strides within specific contexts, such as the pricing of NFTs. However, neither is widely stable enough to replace fiat currencies in this role.

4. Q4: Describe how asset tokenization works in real estate. What are the key benefits and challenges?

A4: Asset tokenization in real estate involves creating digital representations of property ownership using blockchain technology. A house, for example, can be tokenized into either fungible tokens, where fractional ownership is distributed among many tokens, or as a nonfungible token (NFT) representing the entire property. These tokens can then be traded on blockchain platforms, facilitating a more liquid and accessible market.

The key benefits of this process include increased liquidity, as property ownership can be bought or sold globally without the need for lengthy legal procedures. Tokenization also enhances transparency, as blockchain records are immutable and easily verifiable. However, challenges remain in integrating tokenized real estate into traditional legal frameworks, as well as ensuring security against potential exploits in smart contract systems. The adoption of this technology also depends on market and regulatory acceptance.

5. Q5: What is a DAO? Explain its governance structure, and provide an example of a real-world DAO.

A5: A decentralized autonomous organization (DAO) is a blockchain-based entity that operates through predefined smart contracts. Governance in a DAO is decentralized, with token holders having the right to propose and vote on changes. Decision-making power is distributed among the participants rather than centralized in a single authority.

An example of a real-world DAO is VitaDAO, which funds research on human longevity. Token holders in VitaDAO vote on research proposals and negotiate ownership of intellectual property resulting from the funded projects. This decentralized approach enables collective decision-making while ensuring that all stakeholders have a say in the organization's direction.

6. Q6: Compare and contrast centralized exchanges (CEXs) with decentralized exchanges (DEXs). What are the key technological limitations of DEXs?

    A6: Centralized exchanges like Coinbase and Binance operate as traditional financial platforms, where users trust the exchange to manage their funds. These exchanges offer high liquidity, user-friendly interfaces, and a familiar experience for those accustomed to traditional finance.

    Decentralized exchanges, such as Uniswap, operate through smart contracts, allowing users to trade directly without intermediaries. While DEXs offer greater transparency and censorship resistance, they face technological limitations such as lower transaction throughput, high gas fees on networks like Ethereum, and the inability to support cross-chain asset exchanges without additional infrastructure.

7. Q7: How do primitive forms of money like whale teeth and shells compare to modern cryptocurrencies in terms of the properties of money?

    A7: Primitive forms of money like whale teeth and shells served as mediums of exchange within specific cultural contexts. These items were durable, transportable, and fungible for their time. Cryptocurrencies, however, vastly surpass these primitive forms in transportability and durability due to their digital nature, allowing global, instant transactions without physical limitations. Both forms reflect the societal values of their respective eras, demonstrating how money evolves with technology.

8. Q8: Explain how the Bretton Woods system worked and how its collapse led to the current fiat system.

    A8: The Bretton Woods system, established in 1944, pegged major currencies to the US dollar, which itself was backed by gold at a fixed rate of $35 per ounce. This system facilitated global trade by providing a stable reference for international currency exchange. However, growing economic pressures, particularly the United States' inability to maintain sufficient gold reserves, led to the system's collapse in 1971. This marked the transition to fiat currencies, which are not backed by physical assets but rely on trust in government-issued money.

9. Q9: What are the security features of Bitcoin and Ethereum networks? How do they maintain network integrity?

    A9: Bitcoin secures its network through a proof-of-work consensus mechanism, where miners validate transactions by solving complex mathematical problems. As long as 50% or more of the network's miners remain honest, the blockchain is resistant to attacks.

    Ethereum, having transitioned to proof-of-stake, relies on validators who stake ether to secure the network. Both networks ensure integrity through decentralization, with transaction histories replicated across thousands of nodes. This makes them highly resilient to tampering and censorship.

10. Q10: Describe how fractional reserve banking emerged historically and its relationship to modern banking.

    A10: Fractional reserve banking originated when early banks began issuing receipts for coin deposits. These receipts served as money, and banks soon realized they could lend out a portion of the deposited funds while keeping only a fraction in reserve. This system allowed banks to create money through loans, a practice still central to modern banking. While it enables economic growth, it also introduces risks, as banks must manage liquidity to meet withdrawal demands.

11. Q11: What role do NFTs play in digital identity and customer loyalty programs? Provide specific examples.

    A11: NFTs are increasingly used to establish digital identities and enhance customer loyalty. For example, NFTs can securely represent an individual's personal data, granting control over its sharing and monetization. In customer loyalty programs, Le Bristol hotel in France launched an NFT collection offering exclusive perks like private pool access and culinary experiences, fostering deeper engagement with loyal customers.

12. Q12: How does Aave's peer-to-peer lending system work, and how does it differ from traditional banking?

    A12: Aave is a decentralized lending platform where users deposit cryptocurrencies into liquidity pools. Borrowers can access these funds by providing collateral, and smart contracts handle the lending and repayment process. Unlike traditional banks, Aave operates without intermediaries, offering global access and eliminating credit checks. Its decentralized nature contrasts sharply with the centralized oversight of conventional banking systems.

13. Q13: Explain the concept of fungibility in both traditional and crypto contexts. How do fungible and nonfungible tokens differ?

    A13: Fungibility refers to the interchangeability of an asset. In traditional contexts, money is fungible because one $10 bill is identical to another. Cryptocurrencies like Bitcoin and Ethereum are also fungible. However, nonfungible tokens (NFTs) are unique and cannot be exchanged on a one-to-one basis. While fungible tokens represent uniform value (e.g., currency), NFTs represent unique assets such as digital art or property deeds.

14. Q14: What were the limitations of the barter system, and how did they lead to the development of primitive money?

    A14: The barter system required a double coincidence of wants, meaning each party needed to want what the other offered. This inefficiency, along with the difficulty of dividing goods or storing value, led to the development of primitive money. Items like shells and grain, with their inherent value and acceptability, became early solutions to these problems, facilitating trade in more complex economies.

15. Q15: How have cultural and societal values historically influenced the acceptance and evolution of different forms of money? Provide examples from the text.

A15: Cultural and societal values have always shaped money's evolution. For example, whale teeth symbolized wealth and status in Pacific Island societies, while shells held monetary and spiritual significance in Africa and Asia. Modern money continues this tradition, with national currencies often decorated to reflect historical figures, architecture, and cultural achievements, reinforcing collective identity and pride.

CHAPTER 2 AN INTRODUCTION TO ETHEREUM'S ARCHITECTURE

1. Q1: Explain how Ethereum's proof-of-stake consensus mechanism works and what role validators play in block creation.

   A1: Ethereum's proof-of-stake (PoS) mechanism relies on validators who commit a certain amount of ether (32 ETH minimum) as collateral to ensure their honesty. Validators are randomly chosen to propose and validate new blocks of transactions. Once a block is created, it is broadcast to the network. Other validators verify the block's correctness through a process called *gossiping*, ensuring consensus. Validators are rewarded with transaction fees and block rewards. If a validator attempts dishonest behavior, their staked ether can be slashed or forfeited.

2. Q2: What is the blockchain trilemma, and how does it currently affect Ethereum?

   A2: The blockchain trilemma states that a blockchain can excel in only two of the three attributes: scalability, security, and decentralization. Ethereum prioritizes security and decentralization but struggles with scalability, currently supporting only about 20 transactions per second. This limitation leads to high gas fees and slower transaction processing during times of high demand.

3. Q3: Compare and contrast optimistic rollups versus zero-knowledge rollups as Layer 2 scaling solutions.

   A3: Optimistic Rollups assume all transactions are valid by default and compute proofs only when disputes arise. They rely on fraud proofs to detect and correct errors. Optimistic rollups are compatible with the Ethereum Virtual Machine (EVM) and are slower than zero-knowledge rollups because of dispute resolution timeframes.

   Zero-knowledge rollups (ZK-Rollups) process transactions off-chain and submit cryptographic proofs (zero-knowledge proofs) to Ethereum. These proofs validate all transactions without revealing additional data, enhancing privacy. ZK-Rollups are faster and more efficient than optimistic rollups but require advanced cryptographic techniques.

4. Q4: Describe how gas fees are calculated in Ethereum. What components make up the total gas fee?

   A4: Gas fees are calculated using this formula:

   Gas Used × (Base Fee + Priority Fee)

   Base Fee: Automatically set by the network, reflecting the minimum cost to include a transaction in a block.

Priority Fee: An additional fee set by the user to incentivize validators to prioritize their transaction.

5. Q5: What key limitations of Bitcoin did Ethereum aim to address according to Vitalik Buterin's whitepaper?

A5: The limitations of Bitcoin that Ethereum set out to mitigate are as follows:

Lack of Turing Completeness: Bitcoin's scripting language is too limited to support complex applications.

Value Blindness: Bitcoin cannot natively compare or evaluate transaction values.

Statelessness: Bitcoin cannot remember the state of past transactions, making it unsuitable for complex applications.

Blockchain Blindness: Bitcoin cannot interact with blockchain data beyond simple transactions.

6. Q6: Explain the concept of smart contracts and their four key properties.

A6: Smart contracts are—as their name implies—digital agreements written in code between two or more parties. Their characteristics are as follows:

Immutable: Once deployed, their code cannot be altered.

Deterministic: They execute the same way every time under the same conditions.

Self-Executing: They automatically perform predefined actions when conditions are met.

EVM-Based: They operate within the Ethereum Virtual Machine when it comes to Ethereum specifically, which isolates them from external systems.

7. Q7: What is Danksharding, and how does it differ from traditional sharding?

A7: Danksharding splits Ethereum's Layer 1 into smaller shards for efficient transaction processing but focuses on data blobs—large, temporary data segments attached to blocks. Unlike traditional sharding, which divides both transaction and data layers, Danksharding prioritizes scaling data availability to enhance Layer 2 solutions like rollups. These data blobs are deleted after two weeks, optimizing storage.

8. Q8: Describe the different types of Ethereum nodes and their roles in the network.

A8: The different types of Ethereum nodes are as follows:

Full Nodes: Store the entire blockchain history and validate all transactions and blocks.

Archive Nodes: Retain all historical data from the genesis block.

Standard Full Nodes: Store only recent blocks (e.g., the latest 128), fetching older data as needed.

Light Nodes: Store only the headers of recent blocks and rely on full nodes for detailed data.

9. Q9: How do Validiums work as a Layer 2 scaling solution, and what are their main advantages?

A9: Validiums process transactions off-chain, storing data off-chain while submitting validity proofs on-chain. This reduces the computational burden on Ethereum's main chain. Their advantages include the following:

High Scalability: Allows for more transactions.

Privacy: Keeps sensitive data off-chain.

Efficiency: Reduces gas fees by minimizing on-chain computation.

10. Q10: Explain the remaining stages in Ethereum's development roadmap (Surge, Scourge, Verge, Purge, Splurge).

A10:

Surge: Has already been implemented.

Scourge: Addresses decentralization concerns and prevents Miner Extractable Value (MEV).

Verge: Improves data organization and retrieval to enhance efficiency.

Purge: Reduces node storage requirements by eliminating redundant data.

Splurge: Introduces account abstraction and final optimizations for usability and efficiency.

11. Q11: What is the relationship between wei and ether? Name three denominations of ether and their values.

A11:

1 ether (ETH) equals to 1,000,000,000,000,000,000 wei (10^{18} wei), which is the smallest unit of ether, just as 1 cent is the smallest denomination of a dollar or a euro.

Denominations:

Gwei: 1 billion wei (10^9 wei).

Mwei (Lovelace): 1 million wei (10^6 wei).

Kwei (Babbage): 1,000 wei (10^3 wei).

12. Q12: How does Ethereum achieve finality in its block confirmation process?

A12: Finality is achieved when a block becomes irreversible, typically after multiple subsequent blocks are added. Validators verify the block's correctness, and once consensus is reached, it becomes final. This process usually takes around 12 minutes on Ethereum.

13. Q13: What are the essential characteristics that define a decentralized application (DApp)?

A13: A DApp must be open-source and autonomous, store data publicly on a blockchain, and (optionally) use tokens to maintain security and incentivize network participation.

14. Q14: Explain how side-chains work with Ethereum and provide two examples.

A14: Side-chains are independent blockchains that operate in parallel with Ethereum. Assets are transferred via locking them in a smart contract on Ethereum and minting equivalents on the side-chain. Side-chains reduce the load on Ethereum's main chain. Examples include Polygon, a Layer 2 side-chain for scaling Ethereum, and Ronin, which is used primarily for gaming applications.

15. Q15: What roles do the base fee and priority fee play in transaction processing on Ethereum?

A15:

The Base Fee: The minimum cost required to include a transaction in a block, dynamically adjusted by network demand.

The Priority Fee: An optional tip paid by the user to prioritize their transaction over others.

CHAPTER 3 WALLETS, METAMASK, AND BLOCK EXPLORERS

1. Q1: Explain the key differences between hosted wallets, browser wallets, and hardware wallets, including their respective advantages and disadvantages.

A1: Hosted wallets, browser wallets, and hardware wallets differ significantly in functionality, security, and convenience.

Hosted wallets are managed by third parties, often cryptocurrency exchanges, where the private keys are not controlled by the user. While they offer unparalleled convenience and require no specialized hardware or software knowledge, they come with significant drawbacks. Users must trust the hosting provider, which poses risks such as exchange hacks, mismanagement, or even government intervention.

Browser wallets, on the other hand, integrate directly with web browsers, providing a lightweight solution ideal for frequent, small-value transactions. They are quick to set up and easy to use but are particularly susceptible to phishing attacks and malicious websites. This vulnerability arises because browser wallets interact with the internet directly, making them less secure than offline alternatives.

Hardware wallets are often considered the most secure option, as they store private keys offline. These devices provide robust security against online threats and are generally resistant to malware. However, they are less convenient for daily use and come with a financial cost, as they must be purchased separately. Additionally, there is a potential risk of supply chain attacks if the device is tampered with before it reaches the user.

2. Q2: What are the risks associated with hosted wallets, and how can users mitigate these risks effectively?

A2: Hosted wallets, while user-friendly, introduce substantial risks. The primary concern lies in the user relinquishing control of their private keys to a third party, which could lead to catastrophic consequences if the hosting exchange is compromised. High-profile examples, such as the collapses of Mt. Gox and QuadrigaCX, illustrate how customers can lose access to their funds due to mismanagement, fraud, or insolvency. Furthermore, authoritarian governments could seize funds stored on centralized exchanges.

To mitigate these risks, users should employ strategies such as diversifying their holdings across multiple reputable exchanges to avoid "putting all their eggs in one basket." It is also wise to transfer funds to personal wallets whenever possible, reducing dependency on third-party custodians. Researching the security track record of exchanges and avoiding lesser-known platforms is another vital step in safeguarding assets.

3. Q3: Describe how to set up and use a homemade hardware wallet using an old smartphone. What are the trade-offs compared to commercially available hardware wallets?

A3: Transforming an old smartphone into a hardware wallet is a practical way to secure cryptocurrency holdings without purchasing a dedicated device. The process involves resetting the device, removing SIM and SD cards, and installing a secure app like Airgap Vault. Once installed, the phone should be permanently disconnected from the Internet by enabling airplane mode. Users can then create or import a seed phrase and sync the wallet with an app on their everyday phone for convenience.

This DIY approach offers benefits such as cost savings, resistance to supply chain attacks, and enhanced privacy since no third-party vendor is involved. However, it also has limitations. Unlike commercially available hardware wallets, repurposed smartphones lack advanced security features like fire or water resistance and biometric encryption. While they can provide adequate security for less critical funds, they are not ideal for long-term or large-scale holdings.

4. Q4: How can malicious websites exploit users by mimicking legitimate URLs? Provide examples and strategies for mitigating this risk.

A4: Malicious websites often exploit users by creating URLs that closely resemble legitimate ones. For instance, a phishing site might replace a character in `binance.com` with a visually similar one, such as the Greek letter α, making `binαnce.com` look deceptively genuine. Another example is swapping a lowercase *l* for an uppercase *I* in `acala.network`, creating the fake URL `acaIa.network`.

These tactics aim to deceive users into entering sensitive information or connecting their wallets, leading to loss of funds. To mitigate such risks, users should bookmark frequently visited websites and access them exclusively via these bookmarks. Double-checking URLs and avoiding clicking links from untrusted sources, such as unsolicited emails or messages, further reduces vulnerability to phishing attacks.

5. Q5: Describe a sophisticated job search scam involving browser wallets. What steps can individuals take to avoid falling victim to such schemes?

A5: Job search scams targeting browser wallet users often rely on social engineering and trust-building. Scammers posing as recruiters might request the public address of the applicant's wallet to verify their Web3 experience. Over time, they conduct what appears to be a legitimate interview process, even assigning tasks to create a sense of authenticity. In the final stage, they ask the victim to connect their wallet to a supposed company portal to test a feature. Once the wallet is connected, the scammers drain the funds.

To avoid falling victim to such schemes, job seekers should exercise caution when sharing wallet details. Verifying the legitimacy of recruiters and the platforms they represent is crucial.

Additionally, users should refrain from connecting wallets to unfamiliar or unverified websites, regardless of the context.

6. Q6: Explain the concept of SIM swap attacks, and provide an example of how even high-profile individuals, such as Vitalik Buterin, have been affected. What steps can users take to protect themselves?

    A6: A SIM swap attack occurs when an attacker convinces a telecom provider to transfer a victim's phone number to a new SIM card, granting them access to SMS-based two-factor authentication (2FA). A notable example is Vitalik Buterin, the co-founder of Ethereum, who fell victim to a SIM swap that compromised his Twitter account. The attacker used the access to post malicious links, causing followers to lose a combined $700,000.

    To protect against such attacks, users should avoid SMS-based 2FA and instead use app-based authentication like Google Authenticator. Adding a PIN to their SIM card and requesting enhanced security protocols from their telecom provider also reduces the likelihood of falling prey to this exploit.

7. Q7: What is a multisignature wallet, and how does it enhance security? Provide an example of its use in both individual and organizational contexts.

    A7: A multisignature wallet requires multiple approvals to authorize transactions, enhancing security by reducing the risk of unauthorized access. For individuals, a wallet could be set up to require signatures from two out of three devices. This ensures that even if one device is compromised, the funds remain secure.

    In organizational settings, such as a decentralized autonomous organization (DAO), a multisignature wallet can be configured to require approval from several team members. This prevents unilateral decision-making and adds an additional layer of accountability. However, it's important to craft the multisignature scheme carefully to avoid scenarios where malicious actors could collude.

8. Q8: What are HD wallets, and how do they simplify managing multisignature setups? What is a potential vulnerability associated with HD wallets?

    A8: Hierarchical deterministic (HD) wallets generate a master private key from which multiple child keys can be derived. This feature simplifies managing multisignature setups by allowing users to control multiple addresses using a single root key. For instance, in a multisignature wallet requiring three keys, an HD wallet can generate all necessary keys without creating separate wallets.

    However, the centralization of the master key creates a vulnerability. If the master key is compromised, all associated child keys—and the funds they control—are at risk.

9. Q9: Describe the process of installing MetaMask, creating a new wallet, and importing an existing wallet using a seed phrase. What security precautions should users take during these steps?

A9: Installing MetaMask begins by downloading the browser extension from the official website. Users can then create a new wallet by setting a password and securing the generated seed phrase. To import an existing wallet, they select the import option, enter the seed phrase, and set a new password.

Security precautions are essential throughout this process. The seed phrase must be stored securely and offline, as anyone with access to it can control the wallet. Users should verify that they are downloading MetaMask from the official website and avoid entering their seed phrase on any untrusted platform.

10. **Q10:** What are Ethereum testnets, and why are they essential for developers? Provide examples of testnets and their primary use cases.

    A10: Ethereum testnets are networks that simulate the Ethereum blockchain, allowing developers to experiment without spending real ether. These networks are crucial for testing smart contracts and decentralized applications (DApps) before deploying them on the mainnet.

    Examples include Sepolia, designed for efficient contract testing, and Holesky, used for staking and infrastructure testing.

11. **Q11:** Explain how to connect MetaMask to a decentralized application (DApp) like Uniswap and perform a token swap. What precautions should users take during this process to avoid phishing attacks?

    A11: To connect MetaMask to a DApp like Uniswap, users visit the application's official website, launch the app, and connect their wallet. They can then select tokens, specify the amount to swap, and confirm the transaction in their wallet.

    To avoid phishing attacks, users must ensure they are on the correct website by double-checking the URL and bookmarking trusted sites. Reviewing transaction details before confirming also helps prevent unauthorized transfers.

12. **Q12:** What are proxy contracts, and how do they allow for upgradability in smart contract logic? How can users interact with proxy contracts using Etherscan?

    A12: Proxy contracts separate a contract's logic from its storage, enabling updates to the logic without altering stored data. This feature allows developers to introduce new functionalities or fix issues in deployed contracts.

    On Etherscan, users can interact with proxy contracts by selecting Read As Proxy or Write As Proxy to engage with the contract through its proxy interface.

13. **Q13:** What information can be obtained from block explorers like Etherscan? Explain the anatomy of a transaction, address, and block using specific attributes provided by a block explorer.

    A13: Block explorers like Etherscan provide insights into transactions, addresses, and blocks. A transaction entry reveals details such as the sender, receiver, amount, gas fees, and status. Address pages display balances, token holdings, and transaction histories, while block summaries include the block height, timestamp, validator information, and gas usage.

14. **Q14:** How can block explorers be used to identify scam tokens or NFTs in a wallet? What should users do if they find suspicious tokens in their wallets?

    A14: Block explorers can help identify scam tokens or NFTs by highlighting suspicious activity or tokens flagged as malicious. Users should avoid interacting with or importing these tokens into their wallets, as doing so may expose them to hacks or scams. Instead, they should leave such tokens untouched and refrain from engaging with the associated smart contracts.

15. **Q15:** In 2021, Vitalik Buterin, the founder of Ethereum, burned or removed from circulation 6 billion USD in Shiba Inu tokens, half of the supply of the meme token sent to his wallet for free by the founders of the meme token project. Vitalik used a null address to burn the tokens.

    Go to one of the block explorers and take a look at the address to which Vitalik sent the burned tokens. The burned tokens are still there, of course, since no one uses the address or has the keys to it:

    Address: 0xdEAD000000000000000042069420694206942069

    Based on what you learned, use your new skills to detect how many Shiba Inu tokens the address has. What else, if anything, can you see the address containing it?

    This is the transaction hash of Vitalik's transaction to burn the Shiba Inu tokens:

    `0x125714bb4db48757007fff2671b37637bbfd6d47b3a4757ebbd0c5222984f905`

    Go on a block explorer and take a look at it. What is the block height within which the transaction is? How many block confirmations have occurred since the transaction and block were confirmed? How many Shiba Inu tokens did Vitalik send to the zero address? What is the difference in numbers between the current Shiba Inu tokens in the address and the amount Vitalik sent?

    Since block confirmations happen approximately every 12 seconds and are updated in real time on a block explorer, how long ago was the burning of half of the Shiba Inu token supplied by Vitalik? Use the number of block confirmations you observed when you first accessed the transaction to calculate your hours, days, weeks, months, and years.

    A15: The address at the time of writing this answer has 410,429,485,075,252 Shiba Inu tokens, which amount to 8,861,172,582.77 USD at the time of writing.

> TOKEN HOLDINGS
>
> \>$9,715,222,414.34 (>371 Tokens) ⓘ   ∨   🗔
>
> Search for Token Name
>
> ERC-20 Tokens (>200)   ⇳
>
> 🦊 SHIBA INU (SHIB) $8,861,172,582.77
> 410,429,485,075,252 SHIB   @0.00

FIGURE A.1 Shiba Inu token holdings at the zero address and their value in USD

Vitalik sent 410,241,996,771,871 Shiba Inu tokens to the zero address. This amount minus 410,241,996,771,871 equals 187,488,303,381 tokens, which is the difference between the Shiba Inu currently in the address and the amount sent by Vi-talik.

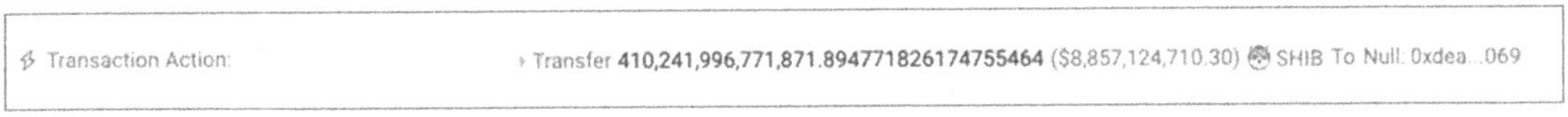

Transaction Action: › Transfer **410,241,996,771,871**.8947718261747554644 ($8,857,124,710.30) SHIB To Null: 0xdea...069

FIGURE A.2 Number of tokens Vitalik sent (and their value in USD, at the time of writing)

Block: ✔ 12448006 **9131474 Block Confirmations**

FIGURE A.3 Block height and block confirmations, at the time of writing

The block height is 12448006, and the number of confirmations at the time of writing this answer is 9131474.

CHAPTER 4 REMIX, DATA TYPES, VISIBILITY, AND HELLOWORLD

1. **Q1:** How does learning Solidity compare to learning a human language in terms of syntax, vocabulary, and grammar? Provide examples to illustrate these similarities and differences.

   A1: Learning Solidity is like learning a human language because both have rules (syntax and grammar) and specific ways of expressing ideas. For instance, just as English uses punctuation and grammar rules to form sentences, Solidity uses semicolons (;) to end statements and follows strict rules for defining data types and functions. Similarly, just as you'd learn vocabulary in a human language, in Solidity, you learn specific keywords like `pragma`, `uint`, `string`, and `address`. However, unlike human languages, Solidity communicates with computers and is case-sensitive, meaning `number` and `Number` are distinct.

2. **Q2:** Explain the role of the Remix IDE in developing, testing, and deploying Solidity contracts. How do its features support smart contract development?

   A2: The Remix IDE is a browser-based development environment that simplifies the process of writing, testing, and deploying Solidity contracts. It provides features like a code editor, compiler, and debugger, which allow developers to catch errors, test smart contracts in a virtual environment, and interact with them before deployment. For example, you can write a `HelloWorld` contract, deploy it within Remix, and instantly see its output by interacting with its functions.

3. **Q3:** What is the purpose of the `SPDX-License-Identifier`, and why should every Solidity file begin with it?

   A3: The `SPDX-License-Identifier` specifies the license under which the code is distributed. It is encouraged to ensure legal clarity and compliance, especially in open-source projects. For instance, `// SPDX-License-Identifier: MIT` declares the code is licensed under the MIT license. Without this line, the compiler will throw a warning.

4. **Q4:** What does the `pragma` directive communicate to the compiler, and how does specifying a Solidity version enhance compatibility and security?

A4: The `pragma` directive specifies the version of Solidity the contract is written for, such as `pragma solidity 0.8.25`. This ensures the contract will compile only with compatible versions of the Solidity compiler. By restricting the compiler version, developers can avoid unexpected behavior caused by syntax changes or bugs introduced in newer versions.

5. Q5: Describe the difference between signed (`int`) and unsigned (`uint`) integers in Solidity. How would you declare and initialize each?

A5: A signed integer (`int`) can hold both positive and negative values, while an unsigned integer (`uint`) can hold only non-negative values.

```
int number = -5;
```

```
uint unsignedNumber = 35;
```

6. Q6: How are string and address data types declared in Solidity? Provide examples of their use in smart contracts.

A6: Strings are used to store text, and addresses represent Ethereum addresses.

```
string name = "Alexandros";
```

```
address myAddress = 0xd0A7f0e336af86aCC72d85af1EDf25790bAd76a4;
```

7. Q7: What are Booleans and bytes in Solidity, and how are they declared? Discuss how bytes can optimize gas usage.

A7: Booleans store true or false values, and bytes store binary data and are gas-efficient because they allow direct manipulation of binary data, reducing computational overhead compared to strings.

```
bool isTrue = true;
```

```
bytes myBytes = "Alexandros";
```

8. Q8: What are the key components of declaring a variable in Solidity, and why is proper initialization critical?

A8: When declaring a variable in Solidity, you specify the data type, a variable name, and (optionally) an initial value.

```
int myNumber = 10;
```

Proper initialization is critical because of the following criteria in Solidity:

Type Safety: Solidity is a statically typed language, meaning variables must contain values that match their declared type to prevent runtime errors.

Gas Efficiency: Proper initialization helps optimize gas usage, particularly when using appropriate data types like bytes instead of string for certain operations.

Contract Security: Well-initialized variables help prevent unexpected behavior and potential vulnerabilities in the smart contract.

Memory Management: Proper initialization ensures efficient use of blockchain storage and memory resources.

9. **Q9:** Discuss the four function visibility levels in Solidity: `public`, `private`, `external`, and `internal`. When would you use each?

    A9:

    Public: Accessible by anyone, both externally and internally. Use this for functions meant to be called by users or other contracts.

    Private: Accessible only within the contract where it is defined. Use for internal logic that shouldn't be exposed.

    External: Accessible only from outside the contract. Use for API-like functions.

    Internal: Accessible only within the contract and its derived contracts. Use for shared logic in inheritance hierarchies.

10. **Q10:** Differentiate between `view` and `pure` functions in Solidity. Provide examples of when each might be used and their impact on gas usage.

    A10: View functions are designed to operate without changing the state of the blockchain. They simply retrieve and show data from the blockchain, which does not require gas. However, there is an important caveat: if a view function is called within another function that costs gas, that call will contribute to the gas cost. We can see this in practice with a simple HelloWorld contract example:

    View: Reads blockchain state but does not modify it. For example:

    ```
    function getBalance() public view returns (uint) {
        return address(this).balance;
    }
    ```

    Pure functions are more restrictive than view functions: they neither read nor modify the blockchain state at all. Instead, these functions depend entirely on the parameters defined within the function itself. Pure functions offer two main benefits:

    1. They can improve gas efficiency when needed

    2. They improve safety by proactively helping to avoid bugs or other unforeseen issues

    Pure: Does not read or modify the blockchain state. For example:

    ```
    function add(uint a, uint b) public pure returns (uint) {
        return a + b;
    }
    ```

11. **Q11:** Explain the structure of the `HelloWorld` contract as described in the text. How does it demonstrate the basics of Solidity?

    A11: The `HelloWorld` contract demonstrates Solidity fundamentals such as SPDX licensing, specifying a Solidity version, defining a contract, and creating variables and functions.

12. Q12: Why is gas optimization important in Solidity, and how do smaller data types like `uint8` and bytes contribute to efficiency?

     A12: Gas optimization reduces transaction costs and improves efficiency on the Ethereum network. Using smaller data types like `uint8` or converting strings to bytes minimizes memory usage and computational overhead, resulting in lower gas fees.

13. Q13: How does case sensitivity in Solidity help prevent errors? Provide examples where incorrect capitalization might lead to a compiler error.

     A13: Solidity treats `variable` and `Variable` as different identifiers. For example:

     ```
     uint myNumber = 10;
     ```

     ```
     Uint mynumber = 20;
     ```

     The `Uint mynumber = 20;` will throw an error because `Uint` is undefined.

14. Q14: Outline the steps to deploy a Solidity contract in Remix IDE and interact with it. What common mistakes might occur during deployment?

     A14:

     1. Open Remix IDE and create a new `.sol` file.

     2. Write the contract code, starting with `SPDX-License-Identifier` and `pragma` statements.

     3. Compile the contract to check for errors.

     4. Go to the Deploy & Run Transactions tab, select the environment, and click Deploy.

     5. Interact with the deployed contract by calling its functions.

     Common mistakes include omitting the `pragma` statement, using incompatible compiler versions, or failing to fund the deployment account with enough ETH.

15. Q15: If a Solidity contract fails due to a type mismatch or incorrect visibility, how would you identify and resolve the issue using Remix IDE tools?

     A15: To identify and resolve the issue, review the error messages in the compiler tab. For type mismatches, ensure data types are compatible with their usage. For visibility issues, verify the intended scope of the function or variable. Debug the code using Remix's debugger, step through the contract, and modify the affected lines to resolve the issue.

CHAPTER 5 ZOOMANAGEMENT

1. Q1: What is the main difference between dynamic arrays and fixed-size arrays in Solidity, and how does this affect gas efficiency?

     A1:

     Dynamic arrays can grow or shrink in size, allowing for flexible storage of data. However, they are less gas-efficient since dynamic arrays can grow indefinitely and can consume significant gas.

Fixed-size arrays have a predefined length, which limits the number of elements but improves gas efficiency because their size does not change, eliminating the problem with the higher gas costs.

2.   Q2: When implementing a require statement in a Solidity function, why is it important to place it at the beginning of the function?

A2: The `require` statement should be placed at the beginning of a function to validate inputs or conditions before executing the function's logic. This prevents unnecessary gas expenditure on operations that would ultimately fail due to invalid input or conditions.

3.   Q3: How does the mapping data structure in Solidity differ from arrays, and what advantage does it offer when looking up values?

A3:

Mappings store key-value pairs, enabling efficient data lookup by key. Unlike arrays, mappings do not have indices and cannot be iterated directly.

Advantage: Mappings provide constant-time complexity for lookups, making them more gas-efficient and practical for scenarios where direct access by a unique key is needed.

4.   Q4: Explain the relationship between the virtual and override keywords in Solidity inheritance. When are they required?

A4:

The `virtual` keyword marks a function in a parent contract as overridable by a child contract.

The `override` keyword in the child contract indicates that it is replacing the parent contract's implementation.

5.   Q5: In Solidity, what is the purpose of memory keyword when working with string parameters in functions?

A5: The `memory` keyword specifies that a variable—for example, a string—exists temporarily during the function execution. It avoids the need for storing the data permanently in the blockchain, which saves gas and reduces storage costs.

6.   Q6: How do you properly import a contract that is located two folders above the current contract's location in Solidity?

A6: Use the `../` syntax to move up one folder. For two folders above, the path would be:

```
import "../../Contract.sol";
```

7.   Q7: What happens when you try to add more elements than specified to a fixed-size array in Solidity?

A7: Solidity will throw an error if you try to add more elements than the fixed size of the array. For example, attempting to add a fourth element to an array declared as `Animal[3]` will fail.

8. Q8: What are the key differences between single inheritance and multilevel inheritance in Solidity?

   A8:

   Single Inheritance: A child contract inherits from one parent contract.

   Multilevel Inheritance: A child contract inherits from a parent contract, which itself inherits from another (grandparent) contract.

9. Q9: When creating a struct in Solidity, what types of data can be stored within it and how is it typically used?

   A9: Structs can store various data types such as `string`, `uint`, `address`, etc. They group related data, making it easier to manage and organize. For example, an `Animal` struct may contain fields for `species`, `name`, and `age`.

10. Q10: What is the significance of case sensitivity in Solidity, particularly when working with contract names and variables?

    A10: Solidity distinguishes between uppercase and lowercase letters. For instance, `Animal` and `animal` are treated as distinct identifiers. Carelessness in capitalization can lead to compilation errors.

11. Q11: How does the `new` keyword function in Solidity when deploying contracts, and what does it return?

    A11: The `new` keyword is used to deploy a new instance of a contract. It returns the address of the newly deployed contract, which can be used to interact with it.

12. Q12: Why might a developer choose to use an older version of the Solidity compiler instead of the latest version?

    A12:

    Stability: Older versions are less likely to have undiscovered bugs.

    Compatibility: Existing code or libraries may not work with newer versions.

    Audit Confidence: Audited code often targets specific versions for assurance.

13. Q13: In the context of the `ZooManagement` contract, how does the `push()` function work with dynamic arrays?

    A13: The `push()` function adds a new element to the end of a dynamic array. For example, in the `ZooManagement` contract, `listofAnimals.push()` adds a new animal to the array.

14. Q14: What is the purpose of a factory contract in Solidity, and what advantages does it offer?

    A14: Factory contracts automate the deployment of multiple instances of a contract. They provide tracking of deployed contracts through arrays or mappings, ensuring easier management and interaction with multiple instances.

15. Q15: How are mappings used to track multiple variables in a contract? (Use the `ZooManagement` example's animal tracking system.)

    A15: Mappings store relationships between keys and values. In the `ZooManagement` contract, mappings like `nameToAge` or `speciesToName` associate animal attributes (e.g., name, species, age), allowing efficient lookups without iterating through arrays.

CHAPTER 6 INSTALLING MICROSOFT VISUAL STUDIO CODE AND FOUNDRY

1. Q1: What are three key advantages of VS Code over the Remix IDE for professional Solidity development?

   A1: Visual Studio Code (VS Code) offers several distinct advantages over Remix, making it the preferred choice for professional Solidity development. First, its multilanguage support allows developers to work with various programming languages such as JavaScript, Python, and Solidity within a single environment. This versatility is essential for projects that integrate multiple technologies. Second, VS Code operates offline, providing a robust and reliable development experience even without Internet access. In contrast, Remix is web-based and requires connectivity, which can be a limitation in certain scenarios. Lastly, VS Code's advanced features, such as integrated debugging, extension support, and split-screen functionality, empower developers to manage large-scale and complex projects efficiently, which goes beyond the capabilities of Remix.

2. Q2: Describe the process of configuring multiple synchronized terminals in VS Code, and explain why this might be useful during blockchain development.

   A2: To configure multiple synchronized terminals in VS Code, open the terminal by pressing Ctrl+J (Windows) or Cmd+J (Mac). Once the terminal is visible, click the "split terminal" icon to create additional terminal instances. Each terminal instance can be used independently for different tasks, such as running a blockchain node, deploying contracts, or executing tests. This setup is particularly useful during blockchain development because it enables parallel task execution. For example, a developer might run a local blockchain in one terminal, observe logs in another, and execute commands or scripts in a third, all within the same workspace.

3. Q3: Compare and contrast the five terminal types available in VS Code (Bash, Zsh, JavaScript Debug Terminal, PowerShell, Cmd). When would you use each?

   A3: Bash, commonly used on Linux and macOS, is ideal for file manipulation, scripting, and automating tasks. Z shell (Zsh), an enhanced version of Bash, offers additional features like autocomplete and plugins, making it a user-friendly choice for developers. The JavaScript Debug Terminal is specialized for debugging JavaScript-based applications, which may include front-end blockchain interfaces. On Windows, PowerShell serves as a powerful terminal for scripting and managing the system, while Cmd is a simpler alternative for basic tasks. Depending on your operating system and development needs, you can choose the terminal type that best suits your workflow.

4. Q4: Walk through the complete process of installing Foundry, including handling potential dependency issues with libusb. What troubleshooting steps would you take if installation fails?

A4: The process of installing Foundry begins by visiting `getfoundry.sh` and running the command `curl -L https://foundry.paradigm.xyz | bash` in your terminal. If a dependency like `libusb` is missing, as indicated by an error message, you must install it. For macOS and Linux, install Homebrew by copying the script from the Homebrew website and pasting it into the terminal. After Homebrew is installed, use `brew install libusb` to resolve the dependency issue. Once all dependencies are addressed, run `foundryup` to complete the Foundry installation. If any step fails, consult the error messages and troubleshoot accordingly, possibly using an AI assistant for guidance.

5. **Q5:** How would you utilize VS Code's split screen functionality to effectively monitor smart contract tests, deployment scripts, and contract code simultaneously?

A5: VS Code's split-screen functionality allows developers to monitor smart contract tests, deployment scripts, and contract code simultaneously. Open multiple files, and then drag and position them side by side or stacked vertically within the workspace. For instance, you could have your main contract open on the left, deployment scripts in the middle, and test files on the right. This arrangement facilitates seamless cross-referencing, enabling you to make changes in one file while observing its effects in others.

6. **Q6:** Explain how you would configure essential Solidity extensions in VS Code, specifically Juan Blanco's Solidity extension and Even Better TOML. What functionality do they provide?

A6: Two critical extensions for Solidity development in VS Code are Juan Blanco's Solidity extension and Even Better TOML. Juan Blanco's extension enhances the development experience by providing syntax highlighting, code completion, and detailed hover information for Solidity code. Even Better TOML complements this by adding syntax highlighting for TOML files, which are often used for Foundry configuration. Installing these extensions from the Extensions pane is straightforward and ensures an efficient and streamlined development process.

7. **Q7:** What security considerations should be taken when installing VS Code extensions, particularly for blockchain development?

A7: When installing extensions in VS Code, especially for blockchain development, security should be a top priority. Extensions are not always verified by Microsoft, so install only those from trusted developers or widely recognized sources. Be cautious of extensions requiring excessive permissions, and regularly review your installed extensions to ensure they are up-to-date and free from vulnerabilities. Avoid installing unnecessary extensions to minimize the risk of introducing security loopholes.

8. **Q8:** Outline the step-by-step process of initializing a new Foundry project and handling common permission-related errors.

A8: To initialize a new Foundry project, start by opening the terminal (Ctrl+J or Cmd+J) and navigating to your desired directory using the `cd` command. Create a new directory with `mkdir <project-name>` and navigate into it. Run `forge init` to initialize the project. If you encounter errors, such as permission issues, prepend commands with `sudo`, or you can also run `forge init --force` or consult an AI assistant to troubleshoot. Once initialized, the project structure will include essential files and folders like `contracts`, `test`, and `lib`, providing a foundation for further development.

9. Q9: How would you use VS Code's search functionality to find specific function definitions across multiple smart contract files?

    A9: VS Code's search functionality, accessible via Ctrl+Shift+F or Cmd+Shift+F, enables developers to locate specific function definitions across multiple files. Enter the function name in the search bar, and VS Code will display all occurrences within the project. Use the Files To Include and Files To Exclude options to refine your search, making it easier to pinpoint the exact function you need.

10. Q10: Describe how to effectively use VS Code's minimap feature when navigating large smart contract codebases.

    A10: The minimap in VS Code provides a visual representation of the entire file, appearing alongside the scrollbar. When working on large smart contract codebases, the minimap allows you to quickly scroll through the file and identify significant sections of code. Clicking and dragging within the minimap provides a faster way to navigate than scrolling line by line, saving time and effort.

11. Q11: What's the difference between VS Code's stable and insider editions? When would you recommend using each for blockchain development?

    A11: The stable edition of VS Code is the officially released version, offering a reliable and bug-free experience, making it ideal for production environments. The Insider edition, a beta version, provides early access to new features but may include bugs or unstable functionality. For blockchain development, the stable edition is recommended unless you need to experiment with the latest features.

12. Q12: Explain how to configure the Cloak extension to protect sensitive contract deployment information when coding in public spaces.

    A12: Cloak is a valuable extension for protecting sensitive information like private keys when working in public spaces or streaming code. Install it from the Extensions pane and configure it to obscure sensitive parts of your code. Cloak ensures that private data remains hidden, reducing the risk of accidental exposure.

13. Q13: Detail the process of syncing VS Code settings across multiple development machines for consistent blockchain development environments.

    A13: To maintain a consistent development environment across multiple machines, enable VS Code's Settings Sync feature. Log in using your GitHub or Microsoft account, and your extensions, themes, and configurations will be synchronized automatically. This is especially useful for developers working on multiple devices.

14. Q14: How would you utilize keyboard shortcuts to optimize your smart contract development workflow in VS Code?

A14: Keyboard shortcuts significantly enhance productivity in VS Code. Common shortcuts include saving files (Ctrl+S or Cmd+S), opening the terminal (Ctrl+J or Cmd+J), and switching between files (Ctrl+Tab). Developers can customize these shortcuts via the Keyboard Shortcuts menu to align with their personal workflow, reducing repetitive actions and saving time.

15. Q15: Describe how to effectively use VS Code's Explorer pane for managing multiple smart contract projects and their dependencies.

A15: The Explorer pane in VS Code is central to managing multiple projects and their dependencies. It allows developers to open folders, view file structures, and navigate between files easily. Use the Open Folder or Clone Repository options to bring projects into the workspace. The pane's intuitive interface simplifies project organization, making it easier to manage dependencies and related files.

CHAPTER 7 FOUNDRY ZOOMANAGEMENT

1. Q1: What is the purpose of the `foundry.toml` file, and how can it be customized for testing and deployment?

A1: The `foundry.toml` file is a configuration file in Foundry that allows developers to customize the behavior of various tools, such as testing, deployment, and contract compilation. Customization can include specifying the Solidity compiler version, setting default networks for deployment, configuring gas limits, or defining the location of libraries and dependencies. It acts as a central point for managing project-specific settings.

2. Q2: Explain the significance of the forge-std library in Foundry. Why is it beneficial for developers?

A2: The `forge-std` library is a standard library in Foundry that provides pretested contracts, tools, and utility functions to streamline development and testing processes. It saves developers time by offering reusable components, ensures reliability due to widespread adoption, and reduces the risk of errors by standardizing common operations. Examples include utilities for testing, logging, and cheat codes like `vm.startBroadcast`.

3. Q3: Describe the process of compiling a Solidity contract using Foundry. How can you identify and resolve compilation errors?

A3:

Process: Open a terminal and navigate to the project directory. Use the commands `forge build` or `forge compile` to compile the contracts. The terminal will display messages indicating the success or failure of the compilation.

Identifying Errors: Compilation errors are displayed in the terminal, often pointing to the file and line where the issue occurs.

Resolving Errors: Review the error messages, fix issues (e.g., syntax errors or missing braces), save the file, and recompile.

4. Q4: What is the role of the `forge build` and `forge compile` commands, and how do they differ in practice?

   A4:

   `forge build`: Compiles the project and generates build artifacts such as ABI and bytecode. It processes all files in the project.

   `forge compile`: Similar to `forge build` but primarily focuses on checking and compiling contracts without generating complete build artifacts. In practice, they are used interchangeably for contract compilation.

5. Q5: What is Anvil in Foundry, and how does it differ from other blockchain testing environments?

   A5: Anvil is Foundry's built-in testing environment, simulating an Ethereum blockchain locally. It provides prefunded test accounts, private keys, and fast execution. Unlike public testnets, Anvil operates entirely on your local machine, ensuring faster testing and better control over the blockchain state.

6. Q6: Walk through the process of adding the Anvil network to MetaMask, including setting up the RPC URL and Chain ID.

   A6: Open MetaMask and click on the network selector dropdown.

   Select Add A Custom Network.

   Fill in the details:

   Network Name: Anvil (or any custom name).

   RPC URL: `http://127.0.0.1:8545`.

   Chain ID: `31337`.

   Currency Symbol: ETH (or a custom name).

   Save the configuration and select the new Anvil network in MetaMask.

7. Q7: How do Anvil's mnemonic phrases and private keys work, and what security precautions should be taken when using them?

   A7: Anvil generates a mnemonic phrase and private keys for test accounts. The mnemonic phrase is human-readable and can derive multiple accounts. Security precautions include using these keys only in local or test environments and ensuring they are not shared or used in production.

8. Q8: Describe the steps to deploy a contract locally using Foundry and Anvil. What are the key commands involved?

   A8: Start Anvil by typing **anvil** in the terminal.

   Open a new terminal and deploy using the following command:

   ```
   forge create <ContractName> --rpc-url http://127.0.0.1:8545 --interactive.
   ```

Enter a private key from Anvil when prompted.

The contract address and transaction details will be displayed upon successful deployment.

9. **Q9:** What is the purpose of deployment scripts in the script folder, and how is the `vm` `.startBroadcast` function utilized?

   A9: Deployment scripts in the `script` folder automate the contract deployment process. The `vm.startBroadcast` function marks the beginning of transactions that interact with the blockchain, ensuring that subsequent operations are executed as transactions.

10. **Q10:** Explain the difference between deploying a contract with `forge create` versus using a deployment script. When would you use each?

    A10: `forge create`: Manually deploys a contract, requiring the user to input private keys and parameters.

    Deployment Script: Automates deployment, supports more complex logic, and is reusable.

    Use Case: Use `forge create` for simple contracts or quick tests, and deployment scripts for production or complex deployments.

11. **Q11:** Why is exposing a private key during deployment a critical security risk? How can this be avoided in real-world scenarios?

    A11: Exposing a private key allows attackers to access funds and interact with the blockchain on behalf of the key owner. To avoid this, use environment variables, hardware wallets, or secure key management tools.

12. **Q12:** What are the best practices for securely managing private keys when deploying contracts on test or main networks?

    A12: Store keys in secure environments (e.g., using `cast wallet` or hardware wallets).

    Use encrypted keystore files.

    Avoid hard-coding keys in scripts or exposing them in logs.

    Use tools like `cast wallet` for interactive and secure key storage.

13. **Q13:** How do you interact with a deployed contract using Foundry's cast tool? Provide an example using the `updateVisitorCount` function.

    A13:

    ```
    cast send <contract-address> "updateVisitorCount(uint256)" <value> --rpc-url
    <rpc-url> --account <account>
    cast send 0x31A65C6d4EB07ad51E7afc890aC3b7bE84dF2Ead "updateVisitorCount
    (uint256)"
    21 --rpc-url http://127.0.0.1:8545 --account wallet1
    ```

14. **Q14:** What is the difference between `cast send` and `cast call`? When would you use each?

    A14:

    `cast send`: Executes a state-changing function (e.g., updating variables).

    `cast call`: Queries state without modifying it (e.g., retrieving values).

    Use `cast send` for transactions and `cast call` for data retrieval.

15. **Q15:** Explain the process of deploying a smart contract to the Ethereum Sepolia test network using Alchemy. What role does the RPC URL play in this process?

    A15:

    Create an Alchemy account and generate a new app for Sepolia.

    Copy the Sepolia RPC URL.

    Import your MetaMask private key using `cast wallet`.

    Deploy the contract with this:

    ```
    forge script script/<script-name>.s.sol --rpc-url <alchemy-rpc-url> --account
    <account> --broadcast
    ```

    The RPC URL connects the deployment script to the Sepolia network, enabling communication with Ethereum nodes.

CHAPTER 8 FUNDRAISING CONTRACT

1. **Q1:** Can you explain the purpose of Chainlink oracles in smart contracts and why they're necessary? Give a specific example of when you'd need one.

    A1: Chainlink oracles provide smart contracts with access to external data, enabling blockchain systems to interact with off-chain environments. Smart contracts, by nature, cannot directly access data such as real-world prices, weather conditions, or stock information. Chainlink bridges this gap, fetching external data and delivering it to the blockchain in a tamper-proof manner.

    Example: A fundraising smart contract might require a minimum donation of $10, regardless of ETH's fluctuating price. A Chainlink ETH/USD price feed oracle can fetch the latest conversion rate, allowing the contract to calculate if the donated ETH value meets the $10 threshold.

2. **Q2:** Walk me through the security considerations in implementing a withdrawal function in a smart contract. What pattern should you follow and why?

    A2: Implementing a withdrawal function requires ensuring secure state management to prevent vulnerabilities like reentrancy attacks.

Follow the CEI Pattern:

Checks: Verify conditions (e.g., only the owner can withdraw).

Effects: Update the contract state (e.g., reset mappings/arrays).

Interactions: Transfer funds as the final step to minimize external calls' risk.

Why? The CEI pattern ensures attackers cannot reenter the contract during an uncompleted withdrawal process, thus securing funds.

3. Q3: Compare and contrast the three methods of sending ETH from a smart contract (`.transfer`, `.send`, and `.call`). Which would you recommend in a modern contract, and why?

A3:

`.transfer`:

Sends 2300 gas, reverting on failure.

Advantages: Simple and secure.

Disadvantages: Limited gas may fail with advanced recipient logic.

`.send`:

Sends 2300 gas, returning a Boolean on success/failure.

Advantages: Allows programmatic handling of failure.

Disadvantages: Still limited by 2300 gas.

`.call`:

Flexible gas and capability to call external functions.

Advantages: Suitable for complex interactions.

Disadvantages: Riskier, prone to reentrancy if mishandled.

4. Q4: Explain the importance of resetting mappings and arrays before performing withdrawals. What vulnerability does this prevent?

A4: Resetting mappings and arrays prevents reentrancy attacks, where a malicious actor exploits an uncompleted transaction to repeatedly withdraw funds. By resetting the state before transferring funds, the contract ensures no exploitable data remains accessible during the transaction.

5. Q5: What's the purpose of the `using` directive in Solidity? Give an example of how you'd use it with a library.

A5: The `using` directive allows attaching library functions to a specific data type, enhancing code readability and reuse.

Example:

```
using ETHtoUSDConverter for uint256;
uint256 amount = 1 ether;
uint256 usdValue = amount.convertETHToUSD();
```

Here, `convertETHToUSD` from the `ETHtoUSDConverter` library is applied to any `uint256`.

6.   **Q6:** How do Chainlink price feeds work? Explain the process from requesting data to receiving it in your smart contract.

A6:

Requesting Data: A smart contract uses the `AggregatorV3Interface` to query Chainlink's on-chain price feed contract.

Oracle Nodes: Multiple independent nodes fetch data from trusted off-chain APIs.

Aggregation: Nodes report data to an aggregator contract, which calculates the median value and updates the price feed.

```
function getLatestPrice() public view returns (int) {
    (, int price,,,) = priceFeed.latestRoundData();
    return price;
}
```

7.   **Q7:** Explain the difference between the `constant` and `immutable` keywords in Solidity. How do they affect gas costs?

A7:

`constant`: Fixed at compile time and never changes.

`immutable`: Set once during construction and cannot be modified afterward.

Gas Impact: Both reduce storage costs, with `constant` offering the most savings.

8.   **Q8:** What's the purpose of a constructor in a smart contract, and how does it relate to setting contract ownership?

A8: Constructors initialize key variables and logic during contract deployment. For instance, setting the contract owner ensures only the deployer has administrative rights, enabling controlled access to sensitive functions like `withdraw`.

9.   **Q9:** Can you explain the difference between the `receive()` and `fallback()` functions? When would you use each?

A9:

`receive()`: Handles plain ETH transfers without data.

`fallback()`: Handles ETH transfers with attached data or when no `receive()` is defined.

Use: Implement `receive()` for direct ETH donations and `fallback()` for broader compatibility.

10.   **Q10:** How would you implement access control in a smart contract? Compare using `require` statements versus modifiers.

A10:

Require Statements: Explicitly check access control conditions within each function.

Modifiers: Encapsulate access control logic, reducing redundancy and improving readability.

```
modifier onlyOwner() {
    require(msg.sender == owner, "Not the owner");
    _;
}
```

11. **Q11:** Explain how you would convert ETH to USD in a smart contract. What considerations do you need to keep in mind regarding decimals?

A11: To convert ETH to USD, use a Chainlink price feed for accurate conversion rates. Handle decimals carefully, as ETH and USD values operate with different decimal precisions.

Considerations:

ETH: 18 decimals.

Price feed: 8 decimals (e.g., multiply by `1e10` for uniformity).

12. **Q12:** What's the purpose of the Checks-Effects-Interactions (CEI) pattern? Give an example of implementing it.

A12: The CEI pattern minimizes risks like reentrancy by ensuring the following:

Checks: Verify the sender is authorized.

Effects: Update state variables.

Interactions: Transfer funds as the last step.

Example:

```
function withdraw() public {
    require(msg.sender == owner, "Not owner");
    uint balance = address(this).balance;
    owner = address(0); // Update state
    payable(msg.sender).transfer(balance); // Interact
}
```

13. **Q13:** How do you handle decimal precision when working with price feeds in Solidity? Why is this important?

A13: Price feeds typically have fewer decimals than ETH. Adjust the scale by multiplying or dividing as needed. Misaligned decimals can cause significant calculation errors, making adjustments crucial for accuracy.

14. **Q14:** Explain the concept of custom errors in Solidity. How do they improve gas efficiency compared to require statements?

A14: Custom errors reduce gas costs by replacing verbose `require` strings with compact error definitions.

```
error NotOwner();
modifier onlyOwner() {
```

```
        if (msg.sender != owner) revert NotOwner();
        _;
}
```

15. **Q15:** When implementing a fundraising contract, what mechanisms would you put in place to track donors and their contributions? Explain your data structure choices.

A15:

Data Structures:

Mapping: Store contributions per address.

```
  mapping(address => uint256) public contributions;
```

Array: Track all donor addresses.

```
  address[] public donors;
```

Mechanism: Update both on each contribution for complete tracking:

```
function contribute() public payable {
    donors.push(msg.sender);
    contributions[msg.sender] += msg.value;
}
```

CHAPTER 9 BUILDING AN ERC-20 CRYPTOCURRENCY

1. **Q1:** What makes a token "fungible" in the context of ERC-20? Explain the key characteristics.

A1:

Divisibility: ERC-20 tokens can be subdivided into smaller units defined by their `decimals` parameter (e.g., up to 18 decimal places).

Interchangeability: Each token is of equal value and interchangeable.

Standardized Interface: The ERC-20 standard ensures consistent functionality and interoperability across Ethereum projects.

2. **Q2:** What is the process of creating an Ethereum Improvement Proposal (EIP)? What are the mandatory components?

A2:

Steps:

1. Develop an idea for improving Ethereum.

2. Draft the proposal in the EIP standard format.

3. Submit it for discussion and potential inclusion.

Mandatory Components:

EIP number, title, author(s), creation date.

Abstract (problem description).

Motivation (why existing solutions are insufficient).

Specification (technical details).

Rationale (justification for design decisions).

Security considerations.

Backward compatibility.

Reference implementation (if applicable).

3.   Q3: Compare and contrast manual ERC-20 implementation versus using OpenZeppelin. What are the security implications?

A3:

Manual Implementation:

Requires a deep understanding of the ERC-20 standard.

Greater risk of introducing bugs or security vulnerabilities.

OpenZeppelin:

Provides audited, reusable libraries.

Reduces time and ensures robust, battle-tested implementations.

Security Implications:

OpenZeppelin mitigates vulnerabilities such as reentrancy and overflows.

Manual implementation demands rigorous testing to avoid similar issues.

4.   Q4: Explain the purpose and implementation of the allowance and approve functions in an ERC-20 contract.

A4:

Purpose: Facilitate delegated transfers.

`approve`: Authorizes a third party (spender) to spend a specific amount on the user's behalf.

`allowance`: Checks the remaining amount the spender is authorized to spend.

Implementation:

`approve`: Sets the `_allowances` mapping with the spender and value.

`allowance`: Reads the `_allowances` mapping for the given owner and spender.

5.   Q5: How do you handle decimals in ERC-20 tokens? Why is this important for token economics?

A5:

Handling:

Define decimals (e.g., `18`) during token creation.

Balances and transfers are stored and calculated in smallest units.

Importance:

Facilitates fractional ownership and transactions.

Aligns token economics with real-world usability.

6.   Q6: What's the difference between `transfer` and `transferFrom` in ERC-20? When would you use each?

A6:

`transfer`: Transfers tokens directly from the sender to another address.

`transferFrom`: Allows a spender to transfer tokens on behalf of an owner, provided prior approval.

Usage:

Use `transfer` for personal transfers.

Use `transferFrom` for delegated transfers.

7.   Q7: Explain the role of events in ERC-20 contracts. Which events are mandatory, and why are they important?

A7:

Role: Log state changes for transparency and off-chain processing.

Mandatory Events:

`Transfer`: Logs token transfers.

`Approval`: Logs approvals for delegated spending.

Importance: Enables seamless integration with wallets and DApps.

8.   Q8: How do you implement proper access control for an ERC-20 token? What security considerations should be kept in mind?

A8:

Implementation: Use modifiers like `onlyOwner` for privileged functions (e.g., minting).

Security Considerations:

Avoid hard-coded addresses.

Implement thorough testing.

9.   Q9: What's the significance of the double mapping used for allowances in ERC-20? Explain its structure and purpose.

A9:

Structure:

_allowances[owner][spender] stores the amount the spender is allowed to spend on the owner's behalf.

Purpose: Facilitates secure and efficient delegated transfers.

10.   Q10: How would you safely implement a token with an initial supply? Walk me through the constructor implementation.

A10:

Constructor Implementation:

```
constructor(uint256 initialSupply) ERC20("TokenName", "SYM") {
    _mint(msg.sender, initialSupply);
}
```

Steps:

Set the name and symbol.

Use _mint to allocate the initial supply to the creator's address.

11.   Q11: What are the common vulnerabilities in ERC-20 implementations? How does OpenZeppelin help mitigate these?

A11:

Vulnerabilities:

Reentrancy attacks.

Overflow/underflow.

Invalid approvals.

Mitigation:

OpenZeppelin uses safe math and audited libraries.

12.   Q12: Explain the role of the require statements in ERC-20's transfer functions. Why are they necessary?

A12:

Role: Enforce conditions like sufficient balance and valid addresses.

Necessity: Prevents invalid transactions and potential exploits.

13. **Q13:** How would you handle token decimals when displaying balances to users? What considerations should be made?

    A13:

    Handling: Convert balances using `decimals` (e.g., `balance / (10**decimals)`).

    Considerations: Ensure accurate rounding and user-friendly display formats.

14. **Q14:** What's the purpose of the view functions in an ERC-20 contract? Which ones are required by the standard?

    A14:

    Purpose: Provide state information without modifying it.

    Required Functions:

    `name, symbol, decimals, totalSupply, balanceOf, allowance`

15. **Q15:** How would you deploy an ERC-20 token using Foundry? Walk me through the deployment script structure.

    A15:

    Steps:

    1. Write a deployment script importing the ERC-20 contract and `forge-std/Script.sol`.

    2. Use `vm.startBroadcast()` and `vm.stopBroadcast()`, and deploy the contract in between them.

    3. Deploy the contract with the desired initial supply.

    4. Run the script with `forge script`.

CHAPTER 10 BORROWING AND LENDING PROTOCOL

1. **Q1:** Explain the purpose of stablecoins in the cryptocurrency ecosystem and how they address the volatility of traditional cryptocurrencies.

    A1: Stablecoins minimize cryptocurrency volatility by pegging their value to stable assets such as fiat currencies or commodities. This stability makes them more suitable as a medium of exchange, a unit of account, and a store of value, addressing the high volatility that makes cryptocurrencies unsuitable for these functions.

2. **Q2:** What are the three main functions of "good money," and how do stablecoins aim to fulfill these functions compared to fiat currencies and cryptocurrencies?

    A2:

    Medium of Exchange: Stablecoins provide a reliable medium of exchange by maintaining a stable value, unlike volatile cryptocurrencies.

Unit of Account: Stablecoins are pegged to fiat currencies like the USD, making them more suitable for pricing and valuation.

Store of Value: Stablecoins mitigate short-term volatility and provide a more reliable store of value compared to cryptocurrencies.

3. Q3: Describe the differences between centralized and decentralized stablecoins. Provide examples of each and explain their trade-offs.

A3:

Centralized stablecoins (e.g., USDT, USDC) are issued and managed by private entities with reserves backing their value. They offer stability but require user trust in the issuer.

Decentralized stablecoins (e.g., DAI) operate without central control, relying on smart contracts and collateral. They provide censorship resistance and transparency but may face higher volatility and regulatory challenges.

4. Q4: Outline the four broad categories of stablecoin collateralization (traditional, crypto, algorithmic, hybrid) and discuss their advantages and risks.

A4:

Traditional: Backed by fiat or real-world assets (e.g., USDT). Stable but centralized and trust-dependent.

Crypto: Backed by cryptocurrencies (e.g., DAI). Decentralized but capital inefficient and volatile.

Algorithmic: Maintain value through supply adjustments (e.g., Ampleforth). Decentralized and efficient but riskier.

Hybrid: Use a mix of collateral types. More resilient but complex and harder to understand.

5. Q5: What is the health factor, and how does it contribute to the stability of a collateralized stablecoin system? What happens when a user's health factor falls below 1?

A5: The health factor measures the ratio of a user's collateral (adjusted for risk) to their debt. A health factor below 1 indicates under-collateralization, triggering liquidation to stabilize the system.

6. Q6: What is the role of the `ERC20Burnable` and `Ownable` contracts in the implementation of a stablecoin? Why are these contracts critical for functionality and security?

A6: `ERC20Burnable` allows tokens to be destroyed, supporting supply adjustments. `Ownable` restricts sensitive operations like minting and burning to the contract owner, ensuring controlled access.

7. Q7: Why is it advantageous to use custom errors—for example, `Stablecoin__MustBeMore ThanZero`—in Solidity smart contracts instead of traditional revert statements?

A7: Custom errors save gas by providing specific error messages without the overhead of longer revert strings, improving efficiency and debugging clarity.

8   Q8: Explain the logic behind the minting and burning functions in the stablecoin contract. How are security and integrity ensured during these operations?

A8:

Minting: Verifies that the recipient is valid and the amount is positive before minting tokens.

Burning: Ensures the amount is positive and the caller has sufficient balance. Both functions use access controls (`onlyOwner`) and error handling to maintain integrity.

9. **Q9:** What is the purpose of Chainlink price feeds in a stablecoin protocol, and how do they enhance system stability?

A9: Chainlink price feeds provide reliable, real-time asset valuations, enabling accurate collateral calculations and reducing systemic risks from incorrect price data.

10. **Q10:** How does the `ReentrancyGuard` contract protect the stablecoin protocol from vulnerabilities? Provide an example of a reentrancy attack.

A10: `ReentrancyGuard` prevents reentrant calls by locking functions during execution. Without it, an attacker could exploit a vulnerable function (e.g., `withdraw`) to repeatedly call and drain funds before the balance updates.

11. **Q11:** How does the `DepositCollateral` function update storage and ensure the security of user deposits?

A11: It validates the collateral amount and token, updates the `s_collateralDeposit` mapping, emits an event for transparency, and uses `transferFrom` to securely move tokens to the contract.

12. **Q12:** Describe the liquidation process in a collateralized stablecoin system. How are liquidators incentivized, and how is the collateral-to-debt conversion handled?

A12: If a user's health factor falls below 1, their collateral is liquidated to repay their debt. Liquidators receive a bonus (e.g., 10%) of the collateral to incentivize participation.

13. **Q13:** What challenges do hybrid collateralized stablecoins face in ensuring transparency and user trust? Provide examples.

A13: Complexity and off-chain assets make hybrid stablecoins less transparent. For instance, if a stablecoin uses diverse assets like real estate, verifying reserves becomes difficult for users.

14. **Q14:** What happens if a user attempts to interact with a token not listed in the `s_PriceFeed` mapping? How does the contract prevent such interactions?

A14: The `isAllowedToken` modifier checks if a token has a corresponding price feed. If not, the transaction reverts with a custom error, ensuring only approved tokens are used.

15.   **Q15:** Why is it critical to verify a user's health factor before and after certain operations, such as minting or burning? How does the contract enforce this?

A15: Ensuring the health factor remains above 1 prevents under-collateralization and system instability. The `revertifHealthFactordoesNotWork` function enforces this by reverting transactions that lower the health factor below 1.

CHAPTER 11 BUILDING AN ERC-721 NONFUNGIBLE TOKEN

1.   **Q1:** Can you explain the differences between storing NFT data on-chain versus off-chain using IPFS? What are the trade-offs in terms of cost, decentralization, and security?

A1: On-chain storage embeds the NFT data directly within the blockchain, ensuring immutability, transparency, and trustlessness. However, this approach is extremely expensive due to high gas fees, especially for large files. Off-chain storage using IPFS is cost-effective and decentralized. IPFS stores data in a peer-to-peer network and retrieves it using content-based addressing. The trade-off is trust: IPFS depends on nodes pinning the data to ensure its availability, which may introduce risks of data unavailability if nodes fail to retain it.

2.   **Q2:** What is the purpose of the `_safeMint` function in an ERC-721 contract? How does it ensure secure minting compared to a regular `mint` function?

A2: The `_safeMint` function ensures that the recipient address can handle ERC-721 tokens by calling `onERC721Received` on the recipient if it is a contract. This prevents tokens from being sent to contracts that cannot handle them, avoiding token loss. In contrast, a regular `mint` function does not include this safety check.

3.   **Q3:** Describe the role of the `_isAuthorized` function. How does it verify token management permissions, and why is this critical for protecting ownership?

A3: The `_isAuthorized` function verifies if a spender has the right to manage a specific token by checking if they are the owner, have been approved for the token, or are an operator with overall approval. This ensures unauthorized parties cannot transfer or manage tokens, maintaining the integrity of token ownership.

4.   **Q4:** Given the immutability of IPFS, how would you handle a scenario where NFT metadata needs to be updated post-minting? Provide a solution that adheres to blockchain principles.

A4: To update metadata, upload the new file to IPFS, which generates a new CID. Then, update the token's `tokenURI` mapping in the contract to point to the new CID. This preserves the immutability of the original file while allowing the updated metadata to be associated with the NFT.

5.   **Q5:** What is the role of the `tokenURI` function in an ERC-721 contract? How does it ensure the connection between an NFT and its off-chain metadata?

A5: The `tokenURI` function returns the metadata URI associated with a specific token ID. This URI acts as a pointer to off-chain metadata, typically stored on IPFS. It ensures the metadata can be retrieved and verified, linking the token to its description, images, and attributes.

6. **Q6:** Explain the use of the logical NOT operator in the `_checkAuthorized` function. How does it contribute to gas efficiency in validation?

   A6: The logical NOT operator (`!`) in `_checkAuthorized` simplifies validation by quickly determining if a spender is unauthorized. If the spender is not authorized, the function immediately reverts, avoiding additional unnecessary checks.

7. **Q7:** How does IPFS's content-based addressing overcome the limitations of traditional location-based addressing? Provide an example.

   A7: Content-based addressing in IPFS retrieves files based on their unique hash (CID), not their location. This ensures that the file can be accessed from any node storing it, even if the original server is down. For example, a digital artwork stored on IPFS can be accessed as long as at least one node retains its CID.

8. **Q8:** What is the difference between `_tokenApprovals` and `_operatorApprovals` in ERC-721 contracts? How do they manage permissions for individual tokens and collections?

   A8:

   `_tokenApprovals`: Manages approvals for specific tokens, allowing an address to manage only one token.

   `_operatorApprovals`: Grants blanket approval to an operator, enabling them to manage all tokens owned by a specific address. This is more efficient for bulk operations.

9. **Q9:** Why is the `supportsInterface` function important in ERC-721 contracts? How does it ensure compatibility and interoperability?

   A9: The `supportsInterface` function declares the interfaces a contract supports, such as `IERC721` or `IERC721Metadata`. This allows other contracts and systems to query compatibility, ensuring that the contract adheres to the ERC-721 standard and interoperates seamlessly with wallets and marketplaces.

10. **Q10:** How does IPFS store files larger than 256 kb? What implications does this have for NFT metadata storage and retrieval?

    A10: IPFS splits files larger than 256 kb into multiple objects, each storing 256 kb, and creates a linking object to reassemble them. This approach allows efficient storage and retrieval but requires all parts to be accessible, emphasizing the need for reliable pinning by nodes.

11. **Q11:** What is the purpose of the `_baseURI` function in an ERC-721 contract? How would you implement it for a cohesive NFT collection?

A11: The `_baseURI` function defines the common prefix for token URIs in a collection. It simplifies URI generation by appending the token ID to the base URI. For example, if `_baseURI` returns `ipfs://CID/`, the `tokenURI` function can concatenate it with the token ID.

12. **Q12:** How does the `_transfer` function validate ownership and prevent edge cases like unauthorized transfers or transfers to invalid addresses?

    A12: The `_transfer` function checks if the sender is authorized, the token exists, and the recipient is valid (not the zero address). It reverts on failure, preventing unauthorized transfers, token burns without explicit intent, or transfers to invalid addresses.

13. **Q13:** Explain the use of the `unchecked` block in the `_increaseBalance` function. What are the benefits and potential risks associated with disabling overflow checks?

    A13: The `unchecked` block disables Solidity's default overflow checks, reducing gas costs. This is safe if the developer ensures values will not exceed limits. However, improper use can lead to overflows, causing unintended behaviors like resetting balances to zero.

14. **Q14:** How would you design and implement a function for batch minting NFTs while maintaining correct token counting and URI assignment?

    A14: Implement a `batchMint` function that takes an array of URIs. Loop through the array, mint each token using `_safeMint`, increment the token counter, and assign each URI to the corresponding token ID in the mapping. Validate input length to avoid exceeding gas limits.

15. **Q15:** Describe the process of linking an NFT's on-chain data with its IPFS metadata. What steps would you take to validate the metadata's integrity and accessibility?

    A15: Upload the metadata to IPFS and obtain the CID. Store the CID in the contract's `tokenURI` mapping for the corresponding token ID. Validate the CID's format during assignment and ensure accessibility by pinning the file on reliable IPFS nodes or using a pinning service.

CHAPTER 12 UPGRADABLE SMART CONTRACTS

1. **Q1:** What are the three main strategies for upgrading smart contracts, and what are the key trade-offs between them in terms of decentralization and complexity?

    A1:

    Preset Versatility Upgrades:

    Tradeoffs: Easy to implement but require foresight. Limited flexibility for changes, and more centralized control for managing parameters may deter users valuing decentralization.

    Contract Succession Upgrade:

    Tradeoffs: Maintains decentralization and immutability but is cumbersome, requiring community migration and frequent communication. Can erode user trust with repeated migrations.

Proxy Delegated Upgrade:

Tradeoffs: Maintains the same address, simplifying user experience but introduces complexity, potential storage clashes, and centralization risks.

2. Q2: When implementing storage slots in upgradeable contracts, why do we need to use a gap variable like `uint256[50] private __gap;`? What problem does this solve?

A2:

Purpose: The `uint256[50] private __gap;` reserves extra storage slots for future versions of the contract.

Problem Solved: Prevents storage clashes when new variables are added in later upgrades.

3. Q3: Explain the difference between using a constructor versus an initializer in upgradeable contracts. Why can't we use constructors in proxy patterns?

A3:

Constructors: Initialize contracts during deployment. Not used in proxies because storage resides in the proxy, not the logic contract.

Initializers: Mimic constructor logic but are called explicitly through the proxy, ensuring the logic is executed only once.

4. Q4: Walk me through how `delegatecall` works in proxy patterns. How does storage slot mapping work between the proxy and implementation contracts?

A4:

Mechanism: Executes a function in the logic contract but uses the proxy contract's storage.

Storage Mapping: Variables are mapped to the proxy's storage layout. Matching storage layout between proxy and logic contracts is critical.

5. Q5: What are storage clashes in proxy patterns? How can they occur, and what are the best practices to prevent them?

A5:

Occurrence: They happen when storage layouts of proxy and logic contracts differ.

Prevention:

Use the __gap variable for reserved storage.

Strictly align storage layouts in proxy and logic contracts.

6. Q6: Explain the difference between the Transparent Proxy Pattern and Universal Upgradeable Proxy Standard (UUPS). What are the gas implications of each?

A6: Transparent Proxy:

Admin functions are separate from user-accessible ones.

Gas Implication: Higher due to additional checks.

UUPS (Universal Upgradeable Proxy Standard):

Upgrade logic is in the implementation.

Gas Implication: More gas-efficient but riskier if not properly secured.

7. Q7: In the context of proxy patterns, what are function selector clashes, and how can they lead to security vulnerabilities?

A7: Risk: When two functions have identical 4-byte selectors, unintended behavior or vulnerabilities may occur.

Prevention: Use patterns like Transparent Proxy or ensure unique function selectors.

8. Q8: When implementing the `_authorizeUpgrade` function in a UUPS pattern, what security considerations should be taken into account?

A8: Ensure Access Control: Restrict upgrades to authorized addresses.

Verification: Check the new implementation address for correctness and security.

9. Q9: Why is the order of inheritance important when implementing upgradeable contracts with multiple inherited contracts like `Initializable`, `OwnableUpgradeable`, and `UUPSUpgradeable`?

A9: Importance: Determines how storage and initialization functions are inherited and executed.

Best Practice: `Initializable`, `OwnableUpgradeable`, `UUPSUpgradeable`

10. Q10: What's the purpose of `_disableInitializers()` in upgradeable contracts, and when should it be called?

A10: Purpose: Prevents further initialization of the contract.

When Called: In the constructor of the logic contract to secure against reinitialization attacks.

11. Q11: How does ERC1967Proxy work, and what are its key components? Walk me through the deployment process of an upgradeable contract using ERC1967Proxy.

A11:

Key Components:

Storage slot for implementation address.

Logic for delegating calls to the implementation.

Deployment Process:

1. Deploy logic contract.

2. Deploy proxy with logic contract address.

3. Initialize the proxy.

12. **Q12:** What security risks are introduced by making a contract upgradeable? How can these risks be mitigated?

    A12:

    Risks:

    Centralization in upgrade authority.

    Storage clashes.

    Vulnerable upgrades introducing bugs or exploits.

    Mitigation:

    Strong access control mechanisms.

    Proper auditing.

    Reserved storage slots.

13. **Q13:** In the diamond pattern for proxy contracts, what are facets, and what problems do they solve?

    A13:

    Definition: Modular logic contracts that can be upgraded independently.

    Problem Solved: Avoids monolithic designs and function limits, increasing flexibility.

14. **Q14:** Can you explain how `msg.sender` and `msg.value` are handled in proxy patterns using `delegatecall`? What are the implications for contract security?

    A14:

    Behavior: The proxy retains the original `msg.sender` and `msg.value`, passing them to the logic contract.

    Security Implications: Ensures the original context is preserved but requires careful validation in the logic contract to prevent abuse.

15. **Q15:** What role do external auditing tools like CertiK play in validating upgradeable contracts? What key metrics should developers look for in audit reports?

    A15:

    Role: Validate smart contract security and highlight vulnerabilities.

    Key Metrics:

    Security scores.

    Code issues and their severity.

    Governance and operational risks.

    Audit completeness.

CHAPTER 13 DECENTRALIZED AUTONOMOUS ORGANIZATIONS

1. Q1: What are the key differences between traditional organizational governance and DAO governance?

    A1: Traditional organizations rely on top-down governance structures where decisions are made by a central authority, such as a CEO or board of directors.

    DAOs operate on decentralized, transparent, and on-chain governance through smart contracts, enabling global token holders to vote and make decisions collectively without centralized leadership.

2. Q2: Explain the four levels of decentralization in DAOs and the challenges associated with each.

    A2:

    Token Holders: Decentralization depends on how governance tokens are distributed. Concentration of tokens in a few wallets leads to centralization.

    Delegates: Delegation can centralize voting power if many token holders delegate to a small group of individuals.

    Proposals: Centralization occurs if only a few addresses consistently create proposals or if their proposals are exclusively accepted.

    Smart Contracts: Upgradable contracts and access control mechanisms can introduce centralization or security risks (e.g., rug pulls).

3. Q3: How does token-weighted voting potentially lead to plutocracy, and what are some solutions to mitigate this?

    A3:

    Plutocracy Risk: Wealthier individuals or entities can acquire more tokens, giving them disproportionate voting power to influence decisions for personal benefit.

    Solutions:

    Skin-in-the-Game: Penalize malicious or poor voting decisions by forfeiting tokens.

    Proof of Humanity: Assign one vote per verified individual to ensure equality (though Sybil resistance remains a challenge).

4. Q4: Describe the role of Snapshot in DAO governance and its integration with on-chain systems.

    A4: Snapshot enables off-chain voting by allowing users to sign votes without incurring gas costs. Votes are stored on IPFS and can be integrated with on-chain governance systems using oracles.

5. Q5: Explain the functionality and importance of the `Ownable.sol` contract in DAO governance systems.

    A5: `Ownable.sol` provides access control by defining an owner with exclusive rights to call specific functions. This ensures critical operations can only be performed by authorized entities, enhancing security.

6. Q6: Walk through the lifecycle of a DAO proposal, from forum discussion to execution.

    A6:

    Forum Discussion: Proposal ideas are shared and discussed on platforms like forums.

    Snapshot Voting: Mock votes gauge community sentiment.

    Proposal Submission: Formal submission on-chain, meeting any thresholds.

    Voting: Token holders vote on the proposal during the voting period.

    Timelock: Approved proposals are queued for a delay before execution.

    Execution: The proposal is executed on-chain after the timelock period.

7. Q7: What are the main differences between on-chain and off-chain voting mechanisms, and when would you use each?

    A7:

    On-Chain: Transparent and immutable but incurs high gas costs. Suitable for critical decisions.

    Off-Chain: Gasless and efficient but requires integration with oracles for execution. Ideal for sentiment gauging or less critical decisions.

8. Q8: Explain the "skin-in-the-game" voting mechanism and its advantages and challenges.

    A8:

    Advantages: Ensures accountability by penalizing voters for poor or malicious decisions.

    Challenges: Defining what constitutes a "bad outcome" and determining whether malicious or naive intent caused it.

9. Q9: What is proof of humanity in DAO governance, and how can Sybil resistance be ensured?

    A9:

    Proof of humanity assigns one vote per verified individual, promoting equality.

    Sybil Resistance Challenges: Preventing users from creating multiple wallets for extra votes. Current solutions include identity verification mechanisms, but no perfect solution exists yet.

10. Q10: Describe the technical implementation of the `RetrievableNumber.sol` contract, focusing on its access control and event system.

A10:

Access Control: Uses the `onlyOwner` modifier to restrict the `store` function to the owner.

Event System: Emits the `NumberChanged` event when the stored number is updated, enabling transparency and tracking.

11. **Q11:** What specific functionalities do `ERC20Votes` and `ERC20Permit` add to a DAO's voting token?

   A11:

   ERC20Votes: Adds governance voting capabilities to the token.

   ERC20Permit: Introduces gas-efficient token approvals using signatures.

12. **Q12:** Compare the TimelockController and Compound Timelock models. What factors influence choosing one over the other?

   A12:

   TimelockController:

   Flexible role-based permissions.

   Suitable for complex governance structures.

   Higher gas costs and reduced emergency response times.

   Compound Timelock:

   Simple structure with a single admin.

   Lower gas costs and easier to implement.

   Limited flexibility for future changes.

13. **Q13:** How would you implement dynamic quorum requirements to handle token supply changes over time?

   A13:

   Use the `quorum` function with a `blockNumber` parameter to calculate quorum dynamically based on the token supply at a specific block. For example, if the total supply increases due to vesting, the quorum adjusts proportionally.

14. **Q14:** What are the security implications of the timelock mechanism, and how do they impact emergency response capabilities?

   A14:

   Security Benefits: Prevents impulsive or malicious execution by enforcing a delay between proposal approval and execution.

   Tradeoffs: Limits the DAO's ability to respond quickly to emergencies, potentially leaving vulnerabilities unaddressed during the delay.

15. Q15: Explain the significance of OpenZeppelin's Governor contracts and how each contributes to DAO governance.

    A15:

    Governor: Manages proposals, voting, and execution.

    GovernorSettings: Configures voting delays, periods, and thresholds.

    GovernorCountingSimple: Counts votes.

    GovernorVotes: Enables voting with ERC-20 tokens.

    GovernorVotesQuorumFraction: Calculates the quorum needed for proposals.

    GovernorTimelockControl: Adds timelock functionality for secure execution.

CHAPTER 14 INTRODUCTION TO SMART CONTRACT SECURITY

1. Q1: Define a smart contract audit, and explain why it is essential in the context of Solidity development.

    A1: A smart contract audit is a time-restricted code review focused on identifying security vulnerabilities. It is essential because deployed smart contracts are immutable and operate in a permissionless environment, making them highly susceptible to hacks. Audits help minimize the likelihood of vulnerabilities being exploited.

2. Q2: Describe the key phases of a smart contract audit from initial contact to final verification.

    A2:

    Initial Contact: The development team reaches out to the auditor with the finalized code or near-completion code.

    Code Review: The auditor performs a manual and/or automated review of the code.

    Report Delivery: The auditor provides a report detailing vulnerabilities ranked by severity (high, medium, low).

    Fix Implementation: The development team implements the recommended changes.

    Final Verification: The auditor verifies that fixes were applied correctly and no new vulnerabilities were introduced.

3. Q3: What are the four primary levels of security assurance for smart contracts, and how do they differ?

    A3:

    Unit Testing: Ensures individual functions work as intended.

    Fuzz Testing: Tests functions with random inputs to uncover edge cases.

Static Analysis: Uses tools to review code for vulnerabilities without executing it.

Formal Verification: Converts code into mathematical models to prove correctness rigorously.

4. Q4: Why is multiple auditing often necessary for complex protocols? Provide examples of scenarios where one audit might be insufficient.

A4:

No single audit can guarantee 100% security. Multiple audits ensure broader coverage and catch vulnerabilities that one team might overlook. For instance, a protocol with $200 million TVL should undergo multiple audits due to the high stakes involved.

5. Q5: Explain the differences between unit testing, fuzz testing, and static analysis in smart contract security.

A5:

Unit Testing: Tests specific functions to ensure they perform as expected.

Fuzz Testing: Feeds random inputs to identify unexpected behavior or edge cases.

Static Analysis: Analyzes code without execution to detect common vulnerabilities.

6. Q6: What is formal verification, and how does it compare to other testing approaches in terms of thoroughness and complexity?

A6:

Formal verification uses mathematical models to prove a smart contract's correctness. It is more rigorous than other methods, such as unit or fuzz testing, but is time-intensive and not commonly used due to its complexity.

7. Q7: Why should documentation quality be a priority during smart contract development and auditing?

A7:

Clear and thorough documentation helps auditors understand the intended functionality of the code, reducing misunderstandings and the risk of missed vulnerabilities.

8. Q8: Explain the role and limitations of AI tools in the static analysis of smart contracts.

A8:

AI tools can assist in identifying potential vulnerabilities by analyzing code. However, they are not fault-free and may produce false positives or miss context-specific issues. Developers should use AI as a supplementary tool alongside other security measures.

9. Q9: A protocol has added a small code change after completing an audit. What risks does this introduce, and what actions should the team take?

A9:

The change introduces unaudited code, potentially opening new vulnerabilities. The team should re-audit the updated code to ensure security.

10. **Q10:** What are the typical severity levels in audit reports, and what types of issues fall under each level?

A10:

High Severity: Critical vulnerabilities, such as potential fund loss.

Medium Severity: Issues that could affect functionality but are not critical.

Low Severity: Minor improvements, such as gas optimization or code readability.

11. **Q11:** Why is it recommended to make public functions external where possible? Discuss both gas optimization and security implications.

A11:

Gas Optimization: External functions are cheaper to call than public functions.

Security: Reducing contexts in which a function can be called minimizes potential misuse.

12. **Q12:** What security measures can a protocol take in addition to audits to protect against potential hacks?

A12:

Use insurance (e.g., Nexus Mutual, Neptune Mutual).

Employ multiple audits from different firms.

Conduct comprehensive pre-audit preparations, including rigorous testing.

13. **Q13:** How does code complexity affect the duration and depth of a smart contract audit?

A13:

More complex code takes longer to audit due to the increased scope and potential vulnerabilities. For example, 100 lines of code may take 3–5 days, whereas 5,000 lines could take up to 4.5 weeks.

14. **Q14:** What is symbolic execution, and why is it considered a time-intensive method in auditing?

A14:

Symbolic execution converts code into mathematical expressions and tests them rigorously. It is time-intensive due to the computational resources required and the complexity of ensuring correctness.

15. **Q15:** Why is it critical to prepare deployment and upgrade scripts before an audit, and how do they impact the audit process?

    A15:

    Deployment and upgrade scripts are critical parts of the protocol and must be secure. Including them in the audit scope ensures they are reviewed with the same rigor as runtime code, reducing risks during deployment.

INDEX

Z